The Member States of the European Union

The New European Union Series

Series Editors: John Peterson and Helen Wallace

The European Union is both the most successful experiment in modern international cooperation and a daunting analytical challenge to students of politics, economics, history, law, and the social sciences. The EU of the twenty-first century will be fundamentally different from its earlier permutations, as monetary union, enlargement, a new defence role, and globalization all create pressures for a more complex, differentiated, and truly new European Union.

The New European Union series brings together the expertise of leading scholars writing on major aspects of EU politics for an international readership.

The series offers lively, accessible, reader-friendly, research-based textbooks on:

Policy-Making in the European Union

The Institutions of the European Union

The History of European Integration

Theorizing Europe

The Member States of the European Union

The International Relations of the European Union

The European Union: How Does it Work?

The Member States of the European Union

Edited by

Simon Bulmer

and

Christian Lequesne

OXFORD
UNIVERSITY PRESS

Great Clarendon Street, Oxford OX2 6DP

Oxford University Press is a department of the University of Oxford.
It furthers the University's objective of excellence in research, scholarship,
and education by publishing worldwide in

Oxford New York

Auckland Cape Town Dar es Salaam Hong Kong Karachi
Kuala Lumpur Madrid Melbourne Mexico City Nairobi
New Delhi Shanghai Taipei Toronto

With offices in

Argentina Austria Brazil Chile Czech Republic France Greece
Guatemala Hungary Italy Japan Poland Portugal Singapore
South Korea Switzerland Thailand Turkey Ukraine Vietnam

Oxford is a registered trade mark of Oxford University Press
in the UK and in certain other countries

Published in the United States
by Oxford University Press Inc., New York

British Library Cataloguing in Publication Data

Data available

Library of Congress Cataloging in Publication Data

Data available

Typeset by Newgen Imaging Systems (P) Ltd., Chennai, India
Printed in Great Britain
on acid-free paper by
Ashford Colour Press Limited, Gosport, Hampshire

ISBN 0–19–925281–5   978–0–19–925281–7

3 5 7 9 10 8 6 4 2

Outline contents

Detailed contents

Preface

When this project was conceived it was in the context of a European Union with fifteen member states. It is now published in an EU with twenty-five member states. The EU's Constitutional Treaty was signed in October 2004, indicating how the dynamic of integration continues. However, our authors' submission deadlines did not allow us to incorporate the latter development, and the whole ratification process may well be quite protracted. Like editors of similar volumes before us, therefore, we have had to balance the need for measured analysis against an ever-changing set of circumstances in the EU.

In developing the thinking behind the volume we have sought to offer something different from the existing books on member state–EU relations. We have, in consequence, gone beyond accounts of the EU policy-making procedures of the individual member states. The book thus comprises three parts. The first explores the key analytical issues associated with relations between the member states and the EU. The second puts the member states under the spotlight. Instead of having individual chapters on each state—something which would be a huge task with twenty-five member states—we have included some comparative chapters. The ten new member states acceded just before the manuscript was finalized. In consequence, the chapter on those states is more about the challenges they faced than about their post-accession experience. Member state–EU relations are, of course, bi-directional. Hence the volume also incorporates a section devoted to 'Europeanization', the term that is used for capturing the impact of European integration upon the member states, and key thematic areas associated with its effects.

We owe a huge debt to our colleagues from Oxford University Press for helping us to realize the project. We thank Angela Griffin, Sue Dempsey and, in particular, Ruth Anderson, who saw the project through its final stages. Thanks are also due to the production team of Nicola Bateman, Mick Belson, and Margaret Shade.

Our authors have worked with high professionalism, accepting to rewrite parts of the manuscript in short periods of time. We are very grateful to each of them for their contribution to make the book—we hope—a success. Helen Wallace and John Peterson, as series editors, have offered us strong support during the gestation period. We thank them for their confidence, help, and patience.

Meetings both in Paris and Prague have been possible through the financial support associated with Simon Bulmer's Jean Monnet Chair.

Our final expression of thanks goes to our families—Helen Bulmer in Manchester, Monique, Matthieu, and Juliette Lequesne in Paris and now Prague.

Manchester-Paris/Prague, October 2004

List of Boxes

List of Figures

List of Tables

List of Abbreviations and Acronyms

AER	Assembly of European Regions
CAP	Common Agricultural Policy
CCRLA	Consultative Council of Regional and Local Authorities
CERES	Centre d'Etudes de Recherches et d'Education Socialiste
CEMR	Council for European Municipalities and Regions (originally the Council of European Municipalities)
CFDT	Confédération Française Démocratique du Travail
CGT	Confédération Générale du Travail
CFSP	Common Foreign and Security Policy
CLRAE	Standing Conference of Local and Regional Authorities of Europe
COR	Committee of the Regions
COREPER	Committee of Permanent Representatives
CSFP	Common Foreign and Security Policy
DEFRA	Department for the Environment, Food and Rural Affairs
DC	Christian Democrats
DG	Directorate General
DGEC	Directorate General of European Countries
DGEI	Directorate General of European Integration
DIDAYEP	Board of the Management of Agricultural Markets
DTI	Department of Trade and Industry
EACs	European Affairs Committees
EAGGF	European Agricultural Guidance and Guarantee Fund
ECSC	European Coal and Steel Community
EDC	European Defence Community
EEC	European Economic Community
EFTA	European Free Trade Association
EMS	European Monetary System
EMU	Economic and Monetary Union
EP	European Parliament
EPC	European Political Cooperation
ERP	European Recovery Program
ESDP	European Security and Defence Policy
ETUC	European Trades Union Confederation
EU	European Union
FCO	Foreign and Commonwealth Office
FDI	Foreign Direct Investment
FNSEA	Fédération Nationale des Syndicats d'Exploitants Agricoles
FO	Force Ouvriére
FPÖ	Freedom Party
GDP	Gross Domestic Product
GPPA	Gabinete de Planeamento e Política Agro-Alimentar

IFADAP	National Institute for the Support of Agricultural Fishing
IGC	Intergovernmental Conference
INGA	Instituto Nacional de Intervenção e Garantia Agricola
IPSA	Instrument for Structural Policies for Pre-Accession
IULA	International Union of Local Authorities
JHA	Justice and Home Affairs
MAE	Ministero degli Affari Esteri
MEDEF	Mouvement des Entreprises de France
NATO	North Atlantic Treaty Organization
OECD	Organization for Economic Cooperation and Development
OEEC	Organization for European Economic Cooperation
ÖGB	Austrian Trade Union Conference
OMC	Open Method of Coordination
ÖVP	Christian Democrats
OPEKEPE	Organization for the Distribution of European Agricultural subsidies
PASOK	Panellinio Socialistiko Kinima
PC	Parti Communiste
PCI	Partito Communista Italiano
PHARE	Poland and Hungary: Aid for the Restructuring of Economies
PP	Partido Popular
PRAKO	Conference of Presidents of the Chambers of Agriculture
PS	Parti Socialiste
PSI	Parti Socialista Italiano
PSOE	Partido Socialista Obrero Español
QMV	Qualified Majority Voting
Recite	Regions and Cities of Europe
RPR	Rassemblement pour la République
RRF	Rapid Reaction Force
SAPARD	Special Accession Programme for Agricultural and Rural Development
SEA	Single European Act
SGP	Stability and Growth Pact
SGCI	General Secretariat of the Interministerial Committee in France
SIGMA	Support for Improvement in Governance and Management in Central and Eastern European Countries
SMP	Single Market Programme
SOG	senior officials group
SPÖ	Sozialdemokratische Partei Österreichs
SSEU	State Secretary for the European Union
TEU	Treaty on European Union
TINA	There is no alternative
UDF	Union pour la Démocratie Française
UKREP	UK Permanent Representation to the European Union
UMP	Union pour un Mouvement Populaire
UNICE	Union of Industries of the European Community
VÖI	Vereinigung der Österreichischen Industrie
WEU	Western European Union

List of Contributors

DAVID ALLEN, Loughborough University
JEFFREY J. ANDERSON, Georgetown University
RICHARD BALME, Sciences Po Paris and Hong Kong Baptist University
FEDERIGA BINDI, University of Rome Tor Vergata
TANJA A. BÖRZEL, Free University of Berlin
SIMON J. BULMER, University of Manchester
MANUELA CISCI, ECOTER S.r.l.—Istituto di Ricerca e Progettazione
  Economica e Territoriale, Rome
MORTEN EGEBERG, University of Oslo
GERDA FALKNER, Institute of Advanced Studies, Vienna
KLAUS GOETZ, London School of Economics and Political Science
BÉATRICE HIBOU, CNRS-CERI, Paris
ERIK JONES, Bologna Center of the Johns Hopkins University
HUSSEIN KASSIM, Birkbeck College, University of London
ROBERT LADRECH, Keele University
BRIGID LAFFAN, University College Dublin
CHRISTIAN LEQUESNE, CERI-Sciences Po, Paris and CEFRES, Prague
CLAUDIO M. RADAELLI, University of Exeter
VIVIEN A. SCHMIDT, Boston University
HELEN WALLACE, European University Institute, Florence
CORNELIA WOLL, Max Planck Institute for the Study of Societies, Cologne

Chapter 1

The European Union and its Member States: An Overview

Simon Bulmer and Christian Lequesne

Contents

Summary

The European Union (EU), like other international institutions, is composed of a set of member states. They are key actors in making EU policy, and their role in this process is central to understanding the integration process and policy-making. At the same time, European integration has had an important impact upon the member states: the phenomenon that has come to be termed 'Europeanization'. In this chapter we review, first of all, why the member states matter in the EU. We then review the analytical issues raised and the theoretical perspectives deployed in exploring the impact of member states on the EU and the Europeanization of the member states. Finally, we explain the logic and structure of this volume: how the relationship between the member states will be portrayed in the chapters and parts of the book that follow.

Introduction: why member states matter

The European Union is built upon foundations made up of its member states. However, the early years of studying European integration were characterized by a pre-occupation with supranational institutions and with theories of integration that made little effort to make connections between developments *within* member states and those at EU level. From the 1990s onwards the tide turned somewhat. From different disciplinary perspectives Alan Milward, an economic historian, and Andrew Moravcsik, a political scientist, explored the relationships between the member states and the EU through detailed empirical and/or theoretical analyses (Milward 1995; Moravcsik 1993; 1998). Both these analysts took the member state as the unit of analysis. The member state—and specifically its national government—was seen as a gatekeeper aggregating national interests before representing them in EU-level debates. The centrality of the nation state in this interpretation prompted others to offer a more multi-layered approach that also identified connections between regional and other actors within states and the dynamics of the European Union (Marks, Hooghe and Blank 1996; Kohler-Koch 1996). The impact of member states on the EU thus became intertwined with mainstream debates in international relations and political science concerning the role of interests, institutions and identity. The state itself became problematized, as commentators argued that traditional notions of statehood were weakening. For many international relations analysts developments such as globalization and European integration are seen as heralding the end of the traditional, all-powerful, 'Westphalian' state. The recent challenges posed by groups such as Al Qaeda have highlighted additional threats to a model of international relations based around the nation state. For analysts working within comparative politics frameworks this broad phenomenon is characterized as the 'hollowing out of the state'—from above and below—as international and subnational pressures simultaneously reduce the autonomy of the nation state.

The emergence of Europeanization as a concern in the literature re-examines many of these themes, except viewed from the other end of the telescope, as it were. This literature has wide concerns: with the impact of the EU on state institutions, on public policy, on political forces, and so on. In the Europeanization literature national governments have never been regarded as gatekeepers, controlling the effects of integration within the member state. Nevertheless, different analytical approaches have been developed, as we shall see.

Before exploring these issues we need to clarify some preliminary questions.

- What exactly is meant by the term 'member state'?
- How and why do member states matter to understanding the European Union?

Here we use the term 'member states' as shorthand to comprise *all* political actors and institutions within a member state. We are not using it as a synonym for national governments. The latter usage, prominent in early intergovernmentalist accounts of the EU, brings with it a number of problems. First of all, such accounts understood the EU as the interplay of national governments and ignored the process of preference formation beneath the governments. Secondly, another legacy of cruder variants of intergovernmentalism is that member governments were seen as unitary actors. This assumption, we believe, is a matter for empirical exploration and not a prior assumption. Thirdly, and also a legacy of early intergovernmentalist thinking, was the understanding of national governments as the 'gatekeepers' of integration. In other words, as gatekeepers they were presumed to have a monopoly of contacts between national actors and the EU political system. In the heavily populated EU policy-making arena of the contemporary era this assumption looks highly problematic. This is why we have used a definition that is more neutral as regards the different theoretical approaches to understanding the EU.

Member states matter as key actors in EU decision-making, whether in the decisions of the European Council or Inter-governmental Conferences (IGCs) on the 'architecture' of the EU, on the one hand, or in the more routine policy decisions of the Council and its supporting committee structure, on the other. They are also key actors in the implementation of European policy: in providing the administrative sub-structure on which the EU depends in most areas, if its policies are to achieve their goals. Helen Wallace summarizes the situation thus:

Most of the policy-makers who devise and operate EU rules and legislation are from the member states themselves. They are people who spend the majority of their time as national policy-makers, for whom the European dimension is an extended policy arena, not a separate activity. Indeed much of EU policy is prepared and carried out by national policy-makers and agents who do not spend much, if any, time in Brussels (H. Wallace 2000: 7).

As indicated already, member states also matter in the theoretical and analytical debates concerning integration and governance. They are attributed varying levels of importance by different approaches. But how do member states matter in the real world of the EU?

First, the 'state of the European Union' at any one time is reflective of a balance of unifying (EU) and territorial forces/institutions. This balance represents the interplay of national and integrationist forces. They are not diametrically opposed forces in a zero-sum game but interact, for example to find creative policy solutions. Thus, the EU of today is different from that prior to eastern enlargement; the balance of interests is different. As and when ratified, the EU will change after ratification of the Constitutional Treaty because it will recalibrate the institutional and organizational framework within which the member states interact.

Second, territoriality matters in the EU: it is the main organizing principle. Identity, democracy and legitimacy tend to be located predominantly at the member state level (albeit often with a layering of these within the state concerned). Similarly, the predominant form of institutional organization within the EU is along national lines: whether, most obviously, in the Council hierarchy or in the distribution of commissioners or MEPs. The territoriality principle predominates in the institutions of policy-making, policy-implementation, and of the judicial system.

However, European integration has made the territoriality of politics more permeable, as have forces in the global economy, patterns of technological change and so on. Thus, the importance of territoriality does not mean that the era of the Westphalian state has been 'frozen' into the EU. On the contrary, European integration has gone hand-in-hand with a number of transformative changes to the state system: the erosion of national boundaries; some hollowing-out from below as a result of internal regionalism; the emergence of new forms of governance which have altered traditional boundaries between the public and private spheres (for instance, so-called networked governance); and the growth of para-public agencies, that is, bodies that have autonomy from government, and are responsible for regulatory governance (for instance, the European Central Bank). European integration has not been the sole cause of these developments; indeed, in some cases it may not have been the cause at all. But the key point here is that changes in patterns of governance within member states are closely inter-linked with the development of the EU. In many cases the EU is simply regarded by national governments as an additional resource to address global policy challenges.

Third, member states (that is not just governments) are key players in the politics of the European Union. Territorial-based interests are articulated *upwards* into EU arenas. Empirical and analytical study of this process of upward articulation may be concerned with the role of actors, institutions and the attempt to project national policy preferences into the EU arena.

Fourth, at the same time, the EU is an important factor in member state politics. Its activities impinge upon political actors, institutions, policies, and identities at this level. This *downwards* direction of flow—often termed 'Europeanization'—may be studied in isolation or as part of an iterative (that is repeated) and interactive process. Iteration and interaction mean that the upwards and downwards flows between the two levels of governance are related to one another. This relationship is explored in particular by Tanja Börzel in Chapter 3.

The dynamic interaction of member states and the EU is important in a number of specific ways.

- National governments and other actors must devise ways of making effective inputs into the political process at the supranational level.

- National governments and other actors must devise ways of incorporating EU business into their organization of business at the national level.

- For all actors within a member state—whether governmental, institutional, parties, interest groups or less formal parts of civil society—the EU creates a changing opportunity structure. New tactical and strategic opportunities are opened up in terms of 'projection' for all these types of political actor.

- However, these new opportunities do not come without cost, for all these types of political actor are also subject to new constraints: policy commitments, legal obligations and so on.

- This interaction raises questions of logics: should the 'logic' of political action in Brussels prevail or that of political action in the member state concerned? Does the EU act as a centripetal force, causing convergence in member states' patterns of governance and policies? Or is it compatible with distinctive national patterns? Do distinctive patterns remain?

- The types of actors confronted with these issues in their interaction with the EU are national governments (ministers and officials), para-public agencies (for instance, national competition agencies), national parliaments, subnational government, political parties, interest groups and civil society. Also affected, albeit in a slightly different way, are national courts, through the judicial process, and, in a more diffuse sense, public opinion and conceptions of identity.

- Finally, are the EU institutions the agents of national governments? Or are national government institutions becoming administrative arms of the EU's institutions, for instance as a growing number of monetary policy decisions are taken at supranational level? Similar questions may be asked of transnational political parties or transnational interest groups: do they remain the agents of their national constituent member organisations?

These are amongst the key questions with which the theoretical and empirical literatures on the relationship between the member states and the EU are concerned. Of course, there are other perspectives on the European Union apart from the territorial focus of EU–member state relations. However, many contemporary issues in the EU benefit from a territorial analysis, not least because national governments retain important powers in the EU institutional system. In the next section we explore the different ways in which the member states' role in the EU system can be understood in theoretical terms.

Analysing the role of member states in the EU

The early theoretical debates about European integration, starting in the 1950s, were initially a quasi-monopoly of international relations theorists. The principal debate was between neo-functionalists and intergovernmentalists (for instance, see Rosamond 2000: chapters 3 and 6). Neo-functionalists looked at the dynamics behind the accumulation of powers at supranational level. The main weakness of this theory proved to be its assumption that national governments would readily give up their authority to the EU. In 1965 a dispute between the French President, Charles de Gaulle, and the European Commission as well as other national governments made plain that this assumption was seriously flawed. Whilst it has enjoyed a small revival from the late-1980s, neo-functionalism does not really have much to offer on EU–member state relations. In reviewing other theoretical approaches, we consider intergovernmentalism, which placed the member state at the centre of bargaining; as well as more recent theoretical including institutionalism and new governance approaches.

Intergovernmentalism: the member state at the centre of EU bargaining

For many years the principal representative of intergovernmentalism was Stanley Hoffmann. The main foundations of his approach were set out in a string of publications, re-stated in a collection (Hoffmann 1995).

- The EU is seen first of all as a venture in cooperation amongst states, which are rational actors and whose domestic functioning is governed by principles of authority and hierarchy.
- In a context of generalized economic interdependence, the EU constitutes a more profound form of 'international regime'—defined as a set of common norms, institutions and policies allowing those states to manage more efficiently specific

issue areas such as trade, agriculture or the environment (Hoffmann 1982; Levy, Young, and Zürn 1995).

- The resulting 'pooled sovereignty' does not lead to a diminution of the role of the states, but on the contrary to a strengthening of that role, encouraging their adaptation to constraints imposed by the international environment.

- The creation of one regime does not necessarily lead to the creation of others by an automatic spill-over effect, as supposed by neo-functionalists.

In terms of international relations (IR) theory Hoffmann was never a 'pure realist' asserting, like Kenneth Waltz for instance (Waltz 1979), that a state's national interest derives solely from its position in the international system. Rather, he worked on the basis that member states—and specifically national governments—jealously guarded their power for sound domestic reasons. This concern to take account of the domestic–foreign relationship was also found in the 'domestic politics approach', which sought to investigate the domestic context within states in order to understand the political processes at the EU level (Bulmer 1983).

While variants of intergovernmentalism were above all the work of an American IR theorist, their spread in Europe was later facilitated by work on the economic history of integration. Alan Milward considered that the heavy interdependence of markets in coal, agriculture, and trade left European welfare states after 1945 with hardly any alternative to organizing themselves collectively in order to bestow welfare policies on their citizens (Milward 1995). Refuting the thesis that states renounced part of their sovereignty in creating common EU institutions, Milward asserted, on the contrary, that this was a means for each of them to recover individually.

The revival of intergovernmentalist approaches also came about through the theory of rational choice, which gained substantial ground in American political science from the 1980s. Starting from the hypothesis that states desire to cut transaction costs in an open economy, rational choice theorists consider European integration above all as a collective action whose aim, for each state, is to optimize gains. Geoffrey Garrett's work on the establishment of the single market is a good example (Garrett 1992). Member states' political preferences were accorded importance, although in practical terms this meant central governments' preferences, since he did not explore their origins in the societies composing them.

It was out of concern to restore the relationship between state and society that Andrew Moravcsik devised in the early 1990s another approach: 'liberal intergovernmentalism'. This has become an established reference in the literature and cannot be ignored by anyone interested in European integration (Moravcsik 1993; 1998). In pursuit of the ambitious project of building a theory of European integration, Moravcsik starts from three research postulates:

- The state is a rational actor in Europe.
- Power in the EU is the result of bargaining amongst states.
- Liberal theory is needed to explain the formation of national preferences within the state.

The first two hypotheses are quite similar to assumptions made by Stanley Hoffmann, although Moravcsik's work has also entailed extensive empirical illustration (see Moravcsik 1998). The formation of national preferences constitutes liberal intergovernmentalism's (LI) most original contribution. While LI sees bargaining among states as a confrontation of national interests, it also sees in those interests demands addressed by domestic societal actors to 'their' national government. In developing this model Moravcsik was influenced by Robert Putnam's two-level game approach: an analytical framework which has its own independent value for understanding the role of member governments in EU negotiations (Putnam 1988). Putnam's two-level game approach drew on the bargaining literature from industrial relations to highlight the different dynamics that exist in upper tier negotiations (international organizations or the EU) and the interplay with the domestic politics of the participating states.

LI is insightful into EU–member state relations even though Moravcsik is using them to explain European integration rather than looking at those relations in their own right. However, LI is not without its critics and rivals. Here we mention four, which are particularly relevant to the concerns of this book. First, in seeing the EU member states through the prism of central governments alone, Moravcsik neglects their internal diversity (multi-party coalitions, relations between central executives and regional authorities, rivalry amongst agencies and bureaucracies, presidential versus parliamentary systems, and so on). As Part 2 of this book shows, this diversity between member states is great. That diversity is indispensable for understanding their different positions within the EU. Next, in assuming that the EU is an arena where *large* member states exercise power, Moravcsik simplifies the decision-making games considerably. Let's take a concrete example. It is not at all certain that the convergence of domestic policy preferences in Germany, France, and the UK on the single market carried more weight in the adoption of the Single European Act than the doubling of structural funds desired by the Mediterranean States and Ireland and institutional reforms to which the Benelux countries were very attached (Moravcsik 1998). Third, Moravcsik sees in EU institutions only agencies created by the member states with the purpose of increasing the initiative and influence of national governments, although they are also organizations which develop their own ideas and interests in relation to the states that have set them up. Lastly, as regards preference-formation within states, there is a strong assumption that interests can only be advanced via national governments rather than via other routes, such as direct lobbying in Brussels.

Criticisms of this nature led to the emergence of alternative approaches to understanding European integration and EU governance. We concentrate on two such alternatives—institutionalism and new governance approaches—and the insights offered by them into the study of member state–EU relations.

Institutionalism and member state–EU relations

As the momentum of integration developed from the mid-1980s, so neo-functionalism enjoyed some revival amongst analysts. Although they took care to distinguish their analysis from that of Ernst Haas and Leon Lindberg as leading original exponents of neo-functionalism, Wayne Sandholtz and John Zysman (Sandholtz and Zysman 1988), or Wayne Sandholtz and Alec Stone Sweet (Sandholtz and Stone Sweet 1998) argued that a series of transnational alliances between economic actors, conscious of the changes imposed by globalization, could explain the development of the EU's supranational institutions. These authors did not deny at all the importance of convergence between governments as a condition for institutionalization but this was not the area they emphasized. Whilst they did not take forward the understanding of relations between member states and the EU, Mark Pollack sought to do so by making explicit the institutional links between the national governments and the supranational institutions. Focusing his work on the question of delegation of authority, from a rationalist perspective Pollack considered supranational institutions to be 'agents' created by 'principals' (the member states) to reduce the transaction costs in the functioning (or governance) of the EU (Pollack 1997).

The development of so-called new institutionalism emerged in political science during the 1980s and was based on two simple assertions (March and Olsen 1995).

- Institutions are more than the reflections of underlying social forces.

- Institutions do more than produce a neutral arena for political interaction.

Although more a catalogue of research hypotheses than a coherent theory, new institutionalism gave birth to several variants (see Schneider and Aspinwall 2001 for an overview). Arguably the most prominent of these was historical institutionalism (Steinmo, Thelen, and Longstreth 1992), which was quickly taken up by some analysts of European integration. Pierson (1996) explained that the EU can only be analysed in relation to institutions, which are the contemporary receptacles of a historical process. They give institutions quite a broad meaning including formal structures, norms, and policies, as well as informal ones. From this approach, aiming to rehabilitate the effects of structure, two methodological implications emerged for the study of the EU.

- Politics at the EU level is no longer seen as a series of strategic decisions made by national governments but as a 'path dependent' process with a series of critical situations and unforeseen consequences.

- Institutions at supranational and national levels should no longer be regarded only as instruments in the service of outside pressures but as structures capable of integrating experiences and norms over the course of time.

Although these observations are targeted at the EU as a whole, it is not difficult to see how they can be applied to relations between member states and the EU by taking the level of analysis downwards. For instance, it is possible to see how different historical and institutional legacies have impacted on how member states conduct their European policy (see Bulmer and Burch 2001 for a comparison of Britain and Germany). So, just as institutionalists argued that European integration and policy decisions were not just the product of member state preferences, so national European policy could be interpreted as not just the product of the interplay of domestic preferences.

The return of federalist studies is another institutionalist development which contributed to the rehabilitation of the member state in the analysis of European integration. Alberta Sbragia restored credit to federalist analysis of the EU in the 1990s (Sbragia 1993). Amongst the factors making comparative federalism relevant, Sbragia mentioned the fact that within the EU the continuing problem of balance between territorial interests and functional interests is at issue. This view offers useful trails for researchers who wish to conceptualize the two dynamics—at Community and inter-state levels—which have presided over the formation of the EU since its beginning (Quermonne 2001). Similarly it makes it possible to develop theories about the dialectical relationship between a de-territorialized political project and interests that remain firmly rooted in member states' territories, as one can see empirically in studying EU policies and politics (Lequesne 2004).

The fact that federal political systems have tended in recent decades to develop from their original dualist form towards an ever-increasing overlap between the levels of government ('cooperative federalism') is also a pertinent element for analysing the ongoing obligation to find consensus between the different member states' institutions at one level, and the EU institutions at the other level (Scharpf 1988; Croisat and Quermonne 1999). Cooperative federalism also makes it possible to reflect on the exercise of democracy in political systems which tend to attach importance to interaction among executive authorities (ministers, specialized committees of civil servants) at the expense of control by parliaments and societies. Works inspired by federalism have the advantage of studying not only EU member state relations as a process but also as a 'political order'.

New governance approaches and member state–EU relations

From the 1990s there has been quite a strong convergence between IR and comparative politics theorists in moving from the idea of nation states being powerful in both the international and domestic spheres. Instead governing has been presented as the interaction of a large number of actors: public and private (Leca 1996). Authors adopting this standpoint have often resorted to the notion of *governance*. While this notion was quickly taken up by the EU institutions themselves (European Commission 2001) to push for the pluralist engagement of civil society in the running of politics, its primary sense is analytical. James Rosenau, for instance, resorts to governance to describe how international politics concerns not only the activities of states but also of informal, non-governmental mechanisms whereby those persons and organizations move ahead, satisfy their needs and pursue their wants (Rosenau 1992). Similarly, Renate Mayntz uses the concept of governance to stress that the dynamics of Western societies tend to give ever greater autonomy to social groups, and that analysis of the state therefore implies identifying modes of horizontal coordination among sub-systems rather than traditional patterns of hierarchical authority and vertical administration (Mayntz 1993).

Given the absence of a single 'ruler' and of a clear divide between 'public' and 'private' actors in the EU, it is quite understandable that some researchers, wanting to distance themselves from state-centric thinking, should have chosen to analyse the EU as a governance model (Hooghe 1996; Marks *et al.* 1996; Armstrong and Bulmer 1998; Kohler-Koch 1996). In these works, the member state is no longer in a situation of monopoly or of hierarchical superiority. EU politics and policies are the results of interactions between the Commission, the member states, regions and interest groups. Understanding the EU in terms of governance raises questions about the conditions for the emergence of the political agenda. On the one hand, in an ever increasing number of fields the process of problem-definition has been transferred away from national governments to the European level (Muller 1996). On the other hand, at the member state level, policy-making has become more technocratic such that specialized experts (civil servants of national ministries, interest group representatives) exercise more power than in the 'traditional' European state. Conflicts therefore centre less on problems of representation than around control of expertise (Radaelli 1999).

A further contribution made by the new governance approach to the EU is to explore policy networks: pluralist networks as configurations of actors (including national officials, Commission officials, representatives of interest groups, etc.) which do not conform to a single institutional model but, on the contrary, tend to become differentiated through the gradual emergence of internal rules of the game in each sector. Reproducing the type-casting used for the study of policy making in the UK (Marsh and Rhodes 1992), writers distinguished different types of policy networks at the EU level according to their stability and the elements underlying transactions by their members (Richardson 1996; Peterson 2004; Peterson and Bomberg 1999). Member state actors are not excluded from the policy networks. They share the trans-actions with other member state actors and with supranational actors. Moreover, policy networks make negotiation the dominant mode of political transaction at the European level. This permanence of negotiation is strengthened by the fact that the main EU policies are regulatory ones (Majone 1996). Regulatory policies encourage actors subjected to them (especially national administrations and interest groups) to negotiate with the EU Commission the precise obligations involved.

The new governance approach has shed light on a wide array of issues in European integration. For example, it has made it possible to redefine the relationships between European integration and democracy. Through the diffuse nature of the EU polity comes the question of democratic accountability. 'Who is accountable for what?' is a frequent question in the national debates on the EU (Jachtenfuchs and Kohler-Koch 1996; 2004). In the debate about the EU's constitution this theme emerged as consid-eration of whether there should be a listing of the EU's competences. The principal draw-back of the governance approach has been that the 'shedding of light' has not entailed the creation of any *theory* of member state–EU relations providing the clear reference-points, however criticized they may be, of liberal intergovernmentalism.

The overall picture in respect of conceptualizing member state–EU relations is that there has been no major effort to theorize them as a subject matter in its own right. However, a number of theories and frameworks focusing primarily on EU-level phenomena have shed light on member state–EU relations as a secondary effect. As the EU has become a more extensive level of governance over the last two decades, so momentum developed for trying to understand the opposite direction of influence, namely the EU's impact on member states. Which brings us to *Europeanization*.

Analysing Europeanization

Exploring the impact of integration upon the member states (and sometimes upon applicants or near-neighbours of the EU) is generally termed 'Europeanization'. However, there are three other developments in the literature which deserve prior exploration because they provide an important context for the Europeanization literature. They relate to three propositions:

- that integration strengthens the state;
- that integration creates a new multi-level politics thereby recalibrating how domestic actors respond to integration; and
- that the EU has transformed governance.

In a 1994 paper Andrew Moravcsik developed the first of these arguments, namely that the European Community strengthens the nation state (Moravcsik 1994). This argument chimed with his own 'bottom-up' liberal intergovernmentalist analysis of integration; the link being provided by the centrality of 'the state'. Little further exploration of this argument has been undertaken. But just as Moravcsik's theoretical interpretation of integration was contested, so too was this paper.

One of his 'adversaries' on integration theory, Wayne Sandholtz, argued for an alternative interpretation of the impact of integration upon member states (Sandholtz 1996). He suggested that integration could create new 'options for domestic actors in their choice of allies and arenas' (multi-level politics), and induce changes in domestic institutions and policies. What Sandholtz was making clear by 'multi-level politics' was much the same point as made by Gary Marks and his collaborators (for example Marks, Hooghe, and Blank 1996), namely that national governments neither represent the sole objects of integration nor the exclusive link between national politics and the EU (Sandholtz 1996: 412). Essentially he was arguing that domestic actors—governmental or societal—recalibrate their goals as a result of EU membership. His concern was not with domestic change per se but with reinforcing a non state-centred understanding of integration. However, he went further and argued that domestic actors could exploit the supranational situation to secure domestic change. Predating more recent analyses he pointed to the French and Italian governments exploiting the requirements of the European Monetary System and European Monetary Union respectively to secure domestic policy reform (Sandholtz 1996: 423–6).

The 'transformation of governance' argument is especially associated with Beate Kohler-Koch and her collaborators. Her argument is that integration has not only shifted the distribution of power between multiple levels of authority but has also shifted the boundary between the public and private spheres (Kohler-Koch 1996: 360). The character of the state—its institutional structures and political processes—is transformed as part of this process (also see Jachtenfuchs and Kohler-Koch 1996: 22–3; Kohler-Koch and Eising 2000): quite the reverse of Moravcsik's argument.

The three propositions outlined above may be seen as precursors to the literature explicitly termed 'Europeanization'. This literature is at a relatively early stage of conceptual development. The current 'state of the art' in the literature is proceeding cautiously from using Europeanization as a loose background concept to one which is more systematized in nature (see Featherstone and Radaelli 2003 and Radaelli 2003 for discussion). However, we can at least identify a number of common points of departure which have arisen since Robert Ladrech's early exploration of Europeanization in France (Ladrech 1994).

First, there is no 'theory' of Europeanization. Second, Europeanization is normally used to look at the impact of the EU on member states: something which might better be termed 'EU-ization', were it not for this being a dreadful word. However, with the

EU's growing importance as a facilitating arena for the exchange of policy ideas and practice, such as through the Lisbon process in the employment arena, the exact role of the EU—as source or facilitator of change—is being placed in question. Third, there seems little point using Europeanization as a synonym for European integration, although the term is sometimes deployed in this casual manner. The distinction is this: where European integration is concerned with political and policy development at the supranational level, Europeanization is concerned with the consequences of this process for (chiefly) the member states and politics within them. Fourth, unless the actors within member states are entirely passive in their response to Europeanization, they are likely to respond through making inputs into the integration or policy-making processes. Hence, there is a clear link between the literatures discussed in the two parts of this chapter. However, each literature tends to concentrate on a different direction of flow in the EU policy 'cycle': bottom-up or top-down.

Beyond these observations a broad aspiration in the development of Europeanization as a concept should be to ensure precision of use, whilst not pre-empting empirical findings. Box 1.1 highlights five different definitions. The first two—those by Ladrech

---

Box 1.1 Alternative definitions of Europeanization

Ladrech (1994: 17): 'Europeanization is an incremental process reorienting the direction and shape of politics to the degree that EC political and economic dynamics become part of the organizational logic of national politics and policy-making'.

   This definition was made in the context of empirical examination of constitutional change within France.

Börzel (1999: 574): 'a process by which domestic policy areas become increasingly subject to European policy-making'.

   This definition was made in connection with a study of sub-national policy responses within Spain and Germany.

Risse, Cowles, and Caporaso (2001: 3): '*the emergence and development at the European level of distinct structures of governance*, that is, of political, legal and social institutions associated with political problem solving that formalizes interactions among the actors, and of policy networks specializing in the creation of authoritative European rules' [italics in original].

   This definition was made in connection with a project exploring change in domestic institutional and policy structures.

Héritier (2001): 'the process of influence deriving from European decisions and impacting member states' policies and political and administrative structures. It comprises the following elements: the European decisions, the processes triggered by these decisions as well as the impacts of these processes on national policies, decision processes and institutional structures'.

   This definition was given in connection with a cross-national study of putting EU transport policy into operation.

Radaelli (2003: 30): Europeanization refers to: 'Processes of (a) construction (b) diffusion and (c) institutionalisation of formal and informal rules, procedures, policy paradigms, styles, 'ways of doing things' and shared beliefs and norms which are first defined and consolidated in the making of EU decisions and then incorporated in the logic of domestic discourse, identities, political structures and public policies'.

   This definition arises from an encompassing survey of the majority of relevant literature on Europeanization.

and Börzel—are tailored rather to the specific empirical field of enquiry of their respective studies. However, they are notable also because Robert Ladrech was one of the first scholars to shine a light on Europeanization, and because Tanja Börzel's definition here has the real advantage of concision. The remaining ones attempt a more encompassing definition. It is striking that the one used by Risse, Cowles, and Caporaso comes close to overlapping with European integration. However, the concern of their project with domestic change brings their interest into line with other scholars of Europeanization.

Johan Olsen has also sought to map the definitions of Europeanization and arrived at five different usages of the term (2002: 923–4).

First, Europeanization arising from '*changes in external boundaries*'. The most obvious example is the extension of the policies, rules, institutional requirements and values in the new member states which acceded in 2004.

Secondly, he identifies Europeanization as '*developing institutions at the European level*'. This definition is concerned with the development of a central governance capacity in the EU, with its implications of constraints and opportunities for political actors at the domestic level.

Thirdly, he sees the classic definition of Europeanization as the '*central penetration of national systems of governance*'. This is arguably the core definition of Europeanization (see above) and covers adjustment processes in respect of institutional structure, policy, patterns of political behaviour and so on at lower levels of the mutli-levelled European political system.

A fourth definition is to identify Europeanization as '*exporting forms of political organization*'. Here the term is deployed where the EU seeks to export its values, such as through the Lomé/Cotonou Conventions or through its foreign policy to states or regions that can quite well be beyond Europe itself.

A final variant is Europeanization as '*a political unification project*'. Like the earlier second definition, this one is about the development of capacity at the EU level. The distinction here is that it is interpreted more widely in this definition, namely in terms of political integration. [emphasis in original]

Our own preference is for the first, third and fourth of these definitions but we agree with Johan Olsen's argument that the key issue is that the term is clearly defined when it is applied.

How may these different understandings of Europeanization be compared and contrasted? Kevin Featherstone has undertaken a useful review that plots the origins of the literature and its coverage (Featherstone 2003). Employing a review of publications utilizing the term in the period up to 2001, he draws up a fivefold classification of the areas covered: historical processes, cultural diffusion, institutional adaptation and policy (or policy process) adaptation. Vivien Schmidt (2002) has suggested a different categorization, distinguishing between economic, institutional, and ideational adaptation. We prefer using the relatively straightforward classification of the impact of Europeanization, namely upon policy, polity (that is institutions and patterns of government) and politics (including political parties and interest groups). This framework is also utilized by Börzel and Risse, who elaborate on it further (see 2003: 60).

Three features are prominent in the Europeanization literature:

- the concern with adjustment processes is ever-present;
- how to measure the impact of Europeanization;
- and institutionalist analysis is very prominent.

The first of these arises from a core concern of Europeanization, namely identifying the 'missing link' (Goetz 2000: 222) between EU pressure for change and domestic adaptation. The second arises from the predominance of institutionalist analysis in explaining the mechanisms of change, that is the 'missing link'. Risse, Cowles, and Caporaso, for instance, see Europeanization explicitly in terms of 'political institutionalization' (2001: 3). However, this institutionalist perspective is pervasive and can also be seen in the work of Christoph Knill (2001; also Knill and Lehmkuhl 1999), Tanja Börzel (1999; also Börzel and Risse 2003), Vivien Schmidt (2002), Johan Olsen (1996); Adrienne Héritier *et al.* (2001); and Claudio Radaelli (2003). Johan Olsen has offered a clear statement expounding why the institutionalist account of adjustment is so prominent:

The most standard institutional response to novelty is to find a routine in the existing repertoire of routines that can be used. . . . External changes are interpreted and responded to through existing institutional frameworks, including existing causal and normative beliefs about legitimate institutions and the appropriate distribution, exercise and control of power (Olsen 2002: 933).

As Olsen demonstrates through his choice of terminology, historical legacies—that is existing institutional frameworks—and the normative dimension are key to adjustment processes, thus bringing together analysts working from the perspectives of historical and sociological institutionalism.[1]

The initial concern of the Europeanization literature was with domestic adaptation being driven by the need to achieve 'goodness of fit' with EU arrangements. This perspective was prominent in Cowles, Caporaso, and Risse's edited collection (2001). However, as Knill and Lehmkuhl (1999) argued—see also Bulmer and Radaelli in this volume—'goodness of fit' implies the existence of a clear EU model or policy template. However, in other cases—for instance, where a very loose policy framework exists—this pattern of adjustment seems inappropriate. It seems similarly inappropriate where the Open Method of Co-ordination prevails and member states are looking at each other's practice to see what they may learn but without a clear coercion to make any policy adjustment at all.

The measurement of Europeanization effects is very important. There is the very clear risk that Europeanization studies may attribute all empirical findings of adjustment to EU-effects. However, this danger, which we may illustrate by reference to the Europeanization of policy, may attribute to Europeanization changes that have in fact been brought about by other developments. Changes in member states' telecommunications policies, for example, may indeed have come about because of Europeanization, but they may also have pre-dated Europeanization, such as early reforms in the United Kingdom, or they may be attributable to globalization. It is also worth pointing out that politicians may invoke the need to comply with EU rules as a discipline that actually facilitates fitting in with global pressures (Hay and Rosamond 2002). The discourse of Europeanization—that is the terms in which the phenomenon is presented by political actors—may screen out other forces which are, in fact, at work. To conclude, quantitative

---

[1] See Aspinwall and Schneider (2001) for a review of the different variants of institutionalism used in EU studies, or Hall and Taylor (1996) for the wider social science context.

measurement may prove elusive but it is important to ask the 'measurement' question in order to be sure that the cause of change does, in fact, lie with Europeanization.

An interactive approach to constructivism

The distance between the Europeanization literature and a constructivist approach to understanding EU–member state relations is not great. Some of the Europeanization literature tends to emphasize the interactive nature of the relationship, for instance in Tanja Börzel's understanding of the process as consisting of member states seeking to 'upload' policy to the EU level as well as having to adjust domestically to the EU as part of 'downloading' (see Chapter 3). The constructivist turn in international relations embraced an explicitly interactive approach to understanding a range of empirical questions. What, then, are the key insights that constructivism can add to the study of the relationship?

First, it can reveal that interests are socially constructed as well as (or even instead of) the product of material interests. This position is clearly at odds with a liberal intergovernmentalist view of member state–EU relations. It can explore whether national participants in the EU policy process are socialized into different values and behaviour that might impact upon their presentation of national policy. Social learning by national policy-makers is brought into the picture (see Checkel 1999).

Second, it also regards political space and territorial units as socially constructed. Hence it can capture the greater fluidity of European governance associated with multi-level governance, whereby the nation state is no longer automatically the gatekeeper between the EU and subnational government (Christiansen 1997). From this perspective the nation state concept is put under the microscope.

Third, the empirical concern of constructivism shifts towards the more cultural end of an institutionalist spectrum: to norms, values, and identities. Norms and values may be uploaded or downloaded as much as more concrete policy preferences or institutional models. Moreover, national identity may be understood to be constructed in interaction with the EU, thereby breaking another of the traditional tenets of international relations (see, for instance, Marcussen *et al.* 1999; Risse 2001).

Fourth, it opens up new research approaches: ones which may include the role of discourse as a means of understanding member states' diplomacy in the EU, whether generally or on a specific issue (Diez 1999; Parsons 2000). Although some applications of discourse analysis are quite rarefied, others insert it alongside more institutionally grounded understandings of Europeanization, such as in the work of Vivien Schmidt (2001).

These constructivist insights do come at some cost. Identifying cause and effect becomes more complex. And for the more casual student of EU–member state relations this development may mean a loss of trusted reference points.

Previewing the book

The themes identified here all feature in the chapters and parts that follow. We restrict ourselves here to explaining the three parts of the book that follow.

In Part 1 we focus on analytical understandings of the relationship between the member states and the EU, with contributions that explore matters from both ends of the telescope. From a bottom-up perspective: How is member state power to be understood in the EU? At the same time Europeanization is discussed in greater depth.

In Part 2 the perspective shifts to a geographical focus. It is becoming increasingly difficult to cover all states in a single volume, following the 2004 enlargement to twenty-five members. Nevertheless, we asked our contributors to write in a manner such as to achieve this end. This part of the book gives most of the large member states a free-standing chapter. Other states are treated by groupings or by pairings. Some of the latter are perhaps less than immediately obvious, such as the chapter by Gerda Falkner and Brigid Laffan on Austria and Ireland. However, an exercise such as this is a useful corrective to a tendency to regard one's member state as unique, requiring instead a grounding in the techniques of comparative politics. We have chosen to treat all the new member states in a single chapter. This measure is practicable in these early days of their membership. They face common challenges. Moreover, the literature on the diplomacy of individual states, and their experiences of Europeanization, is still in its early stages. In all the chapters, except for the new member states owing to their recent accession, the contributors seek to look both at the impact of their state/s on the EU and at Europeanization-effects.

In Part 3, the focus is on Europeanization, with the chapters adopting a thematic approach. The themes addressed are the impact of Europeanization on governance structures, political forces, public policy, and the European political economy. Through these four themes our aim has been to cover the key issues as well as to give illustrative applications of the Europeanization literature.

The volume aims to present a comprehensive approach to the relationships between member states and the EU. It cannot be exhaustive. For instance, some may criticize it for not having a chapter on the Europeanization of sub-national government. Nevertheless, our approach is distinctive from existing studies, which *either* adopt a geographical approach (for instance, Wessels, Maurer, and Mittag 2003; Kassim, Peters, and Wright 2000) *or* a thematic one (for instance, Cowles, Caporaso, and Risse 2001; Featherstone and Radaelli 2003) rather than bringing both together. Finally, we have sought to contextualize the three parts of the book, including through giving a brief guide to existing literature, and pull things together by providing editorial commentary. We hope that the resulting volume makes EU–member state relations accessible to a wider range of students than heretofore. Interest has grown significantly since the days when we wrote our theses on this subject matter (Simon Bulmer on Germany and Christian Lequesne on France).[2] But, we believe, it is only in recent years that this area of EU studies has been receiving the attention it deserves.

[2] Both theses were subsequently published, see Bulmer (1986) and Lequesne (1993).

Further reading

A good overview of the analytical and theoretical literature on European integration is offered by Rosamond (2000). For major treatments of European integration 'from below' that take a nation state-centred, or intergovernmentalist, perspective, see Hoffmann (1982), Moravcsik (1998) and Milward (1995). For important critiques of the intergovernmental interpretation, see Marks, Hooghe, and Blank (1996), Pierson (1996). Good starting-points for exploring the Europeanization literature are: Olsen (2002), Cowles, Caporaso, and Risse (2001) and Featherstone and Radaelli (2003). Further guidance on this literature is available at the end of subsequent chapters.

Weblinks

General websites on EU–member state relations scarcely exist, although later chapters identify more specific sites for individual countries or themes. However, a good source of scholarship, that brings together several series of working papers, including specifically on Europeanization is available at <http://eiop.or.at/erpa/>. The ARENA series and the Queen's Papers on Europeanization, accessed via this site, are particularly valuable but relevant papers can be found in the others as well. The EU's own website is also a huge resource <http://europa.eu.int>.

References

Armstrong, K., and Bulmer, S. (1998), *The Governance of the Single European Market*, (Manchester: Manchester University Press).

Aspinwall, M., and Schneider, G. (2001), 'Institutional research on the European Union: mapping the field' in Schneider and Aspinwall, 1–18.

Börzel, T. (1999), 'Towards Convergence in Europe? Institutional Adaptation to Europeanization in Germany and Spain', *Journal of Common Market Studies*, 39: 4, 573–96.

Börzel, T., and Risse, T. (2003), 'Conceptualizing the Domestic Impact of Europe', in Featherstone and Radaelli, 57–80.

Bulmer, S. (1983), 'Domestic politics and EC policy-making', *Journal of Common Market Studies*, 21: 4, 261–80.

Bulmer, S. (1986), *The Domestic Structure of European Community Policy-Making in West Germany* (New York: Garland Inc.).

Bulmer, S., and Burch, M. (2001), 'The "Europeanisation" of Central Government: the UK and Germany in historical institutionalist perspective', in G. Schneider and M. Aspinwall, 73–96.

Checkel, J. (1999), 'Social Construction and Integration', *Journal of European Public Policy*, 6: 4, 545–60.

Christiansen, T. (1997), 'Reconstructing European Space: From Territorial Space to Multilevel Governance', in K. E. Jørgensen (ed.), *Reflective Approaches to European Governance* (Basingstoke: Macmillan), 51–68.

Cowles, M. G., Caporaso, J., and Risse, T. (eds) (2001), *Transforming Europe: Europeanization and Domestic Change* (Ithaca, NY: Cornell University Press).

Croisat, M., and Quermonne, J-L. (1999), *L'Europe et le fédéralisme* (Paris: Montchrestien).

Diez, T. (1999), 'Speaking "Europe": The Politics of Integration Discourse', *Journal of European Public Policy*, 6: 4, 598–613.

European Commission (2001), *White Paper on European Governance* (Brussels: OOPEC).

Featherstone, K. (2003), 'Introduction: In the Name of "Europe" ', in Featherstone and Radaelli, 3–26.

Featherstone, K., and Radaelli, C. (eds) (2003), *The Politics of Europeanization* (Oxford: Oxford University Press).

Garrett, G. (1992), 'International cooperation and international choice: The European Community's internal market', *International Organization* 46/2 (Spring, 1992): 533–60.

Goetz, K. H. (2000), 'European integration and national executives: a cause in search of an effect', *West European Politics*, 23: 4, 211–31.

Hall, P., and Taylor, C. R. (1996), 'Political Science and the Three New Institutionalisms', *Political Studies*, 44: 5, 936–57.

Hay, C., and Rosamond, B. (2002), 'Globalisation, European integration and the discursive construction of economic imperatives', *Journal of European Public Policy* 9/2: 147–67.

Héritier, A. *et al.* (2001), *Differential Europe. The European Union Impact on National Policymaking* (Lanham, MD: Rowman & Littlefield).

Hoffmann, S. (1982), 'Reflection on the nation-state in Western Europe today', *Journal of Common Market Studies*, 21, 21–37.

Hoffmann, S. (1995), *The European Sisyphus. Essays on Europe, 1964–1994*, (Boulder, CO, Westview Press).

Hooghe, L. (ed.) (1996), *Cohesion Policy and European Integration* (Oxford: Oxford University Press).

Jachtenfuchs, M., and Kohler-Koch, B. (1996), 'Regieren im dynamischen Mehrebenensystem', in M. Jachtenfuchs and B. Kohler-Koch (eds), *Europäische Integration* (Opladen: Leske and Budrich), 15–44.

Jachtenfuchs, M., and Kohler-Koch, B. (2004), 'Governance and Institutional Development', in A. Wiener and T. Diez (eds), *European Integration Theory* (Oxford: Oxford University Press), 97–115.

Kassim, H., Peters G.B., and Wright, V. (eds) (2000), *The National Co-ordination of EU Policy. The Domestic Level* (Oxford: Oxford University Press).

Knill, C. (2001), *The Europeanisation of National Administrations Patterns of Institutional Change and Persistence* (Cambridge: Cambridge University Press).

Knill, C., and Lehmkuhl, D. (1999), 'How Europe Matters. Different Mechanisms of Europeani zation', European Integration online Papers (EIoP) 3: 7 <http://eiop.or.at/eiop/texte/1999-007a.htm>.

Kohler-Koch, B. (1996), 'Catching up with Change: the transformation of governance in the European Union', *Journal of European Public Policy*, 3: 3, 359–80.

Kohler-Koch, B., and Eising, R. (eds) (2000), *The Transformation of Governance* (London: Routledge).

Ladrech, R. (1994), 'Europeanization of Domestic Politics and Institutions: The Case of France', *Journal of Common Market Studies*, 32: 1, 69–88.

Leca, J. (1996), 'La gouvernance de l'Union européenne sous la Ve République. Une perspective de sociologie comparative', in F. d'Arcy and L. Rouban (eds), *De la Ve République à l'Europe. Hommage à Jean-Louis Quermonne* (Paris: Presses de Sciences Po).

Lequesne, C. (1993), *Paris–Bruxelles. Comment se fait la politique européenne de la France* (Paris: Presses de Sciences Po).

Lequesne, C. (2004), *The Politics of Fisheries in the European Union* (Manchester: Manchester University Press).

Levy, M., Young, O., and Zürn, M. (1995), 'The study of international regimes', *European Journal of International Relations*, 1, 267–330.

Majone, G. (1996), *La Communauté européenne: un Etat régulateur* (Paris: Montchrestien).

March, J., and Olsen, James (1995), *Rediscovering Institutions: The Organisational Basis of Politics* (New York: Free Press).

Marcussen, M. *et al.* (1999), 'Constructing Europe: The Evolution of French, British, and German Nation-State Identities', *Journal of European Public Policy*, 6: 4, 614–33.

Marsh, D., and Rhodes, R. A. W. (eds) (1992), *Policy Networks in British Government* (Oxford: Clarendon Press).

Marks, G., Hooghe, L., and Blank, K. (1996), 'European Integration from the 1980s', *Journal of Common Market Studies*, 34: 3, 341–78.

Marks, G. *et al.* (1996), *Governance in the European Union* (London: Sage).

Mayntz, R. (1993), 'Governing failures and the problem of governability: some comments on a theoretical paradigm', in J. Kooiman (ed.), *Modern Governance* (London: Sage).

Milward, A. (1995), *The European Rescue of the Nation–State* (London: Routledge; Berkeley: University of California Press).

Moravcsik, A. (1993), 'Preferences and Power in the European Community: A Liberal Intergovernmentalist Approach', *Journal of Common Market Studies*, 31: 4, 473–524.

Moravcsik, A. (1994), 'Why the European Community Strengthens the State: Domestic Politics and International Co-operation', Working Paper No. 52 (Harvard University: Center for European Studies).

Moravcsik, A. (1998), *The Choice for Europe: Social Purpose and State Power from Messina to Maastricht* (Ithaca, NY: Cornell University Press).

Muller, P. (1996), 'Un espace européen de politiques publiques', in Y. Mény, P. Muller, and J. L. Quermonne (eds), *Politiques publiques en Europe* (Paris: L'Harmattan), 11–24.

Olsen, J. (1996), 'Europeanization and Nation State Dynamics', in S. Gustavsson and L. Lewin (eds), *The Future of the Nation State* (Stockholm: Nerenius and Santerus), 245–85.

Olsen, J. (2002), 'The Many Faces of Europeanization', *Journal of Common Market Studies*, 40: 5, 921–52.

Parsons, C. A. (2000), 'Domestic interests, ideas and integration: the French case', *Journal of Common Market Studies*, 38: 1, 45–70.

Peterson, J. (2004) 'Policy Networks', in A. Wiener and T. Diez (eds), *European Integration Theory* (Oxford: Oxford University Press), 117–35.

Peterson, J., and Bomberg, E. (1999), *Decision-Making in the European Union* (Basingstoke: Palgrave).

Pierson, P. (1996), 'The path to European integration. A historical institutionalist analysis', *Comparative Political Studies*, 29: 2, 123–63.

Pollack, Mark A. (1997), 'Delegation, agency and agenda setting in the European Community', *International Organization*, 51: 1, 99–135.

Putnam R. (1988), 'Diplomacy and Domestic Politics: The Logic of Two-Level Games', *International Organization*, 42, 427–60.

Quermonne, J-L. (2001), *Le système politique de l'Union européenne* (Paris: Montchrestien).

Radaelli, C. (1999), *Technocracy in the European Union* (London: Longman).

Radaelli, C. (2003), 'The Europeanization of Public Policy', in Featherstone and Radelli (2003), 27–56.

Richardson, J. (1996), 'Actor-based models of national and EU policy-making', in H. Kassim and A. Menon (eds), *The European Union and National Industrial Policy* (London: Routledge), 26–51.

Risse, T. (2001), 'A European Identity? Europeanization and the Evolution of Nation-State Identities', in Cowles, Caporaso, and Risse, 198–216.

Risse, T., Cowles, M. G., and Caporaso, J. (2001), 'Europeanization and Domestic Change: Introduction', in Cowles, Caporaso, and Risse, 1–20.

Rosamond, B. (2000), *Theories of European Integration* (Basingstoke: Macmillan Press Ltd).

Rosenau, J. (1992), 'Governance, order and change in world politics', in J. Rosenau and E-O. Czempiel (eds), *Governance without Government. Order and Change in World Politics* (Cambridge: Cambridge University Press).

Sandholtz, W. (1996), 'Membership Matters: Limits of the Functional Approach to European Institutions', *Journal of Common Market Studies*, 34: 3, 403–29.

Sandholtz, W., and Stone Sweet (eds) (1998), *European Integration and Supranational Governance* (Oxford: Oxford University Press).

Sandholtz, W., and Zysman, J. (1998), 'Recasting the European bargain', *World Politics*, 42, 95–128.

Sbragia, A. (1993), 'The European Community: A Balancing Act', *Publius: The Journal of Federalism*, 23, 23–38.

Scharpf, F. (1988), 'The joint decision trap: lessons from German federalism and European integration', *Public Administration*, 66, 95–128.

Schmidt, V. (2001), 'The politics of economic adjustment: when does discourse matter?', *Journal of European Public Policy*, 8: 2, 247–64.

Schmidt, V. (2002), 'Europeanization and the Dynamics and Mechanics of Economic Policy Adjustment', *Journal of European Public Policy*, 9: 6, 894–912.

Schneider, G., and Aspinwall, M. (eds) (2001), *The Rules of Integration: Institutionalist Approaches to the Study of Europe* (Manchester: Manchester University Press).

Steinmo, S., Thelen, K., and Longstreth, F. (eds) (1992), *Structuring Politics: Historical Instititutionalism in Comparative Analysis* (Cambridge: Cambridge University Press).

Wallace, H. (2000), 'The institutional setting', in Wallace and Wallace, 3–37.

Wallace, H., and Wallace W. (eds.) (2000), *Policy-Making in the European Union*, 4th edn. (Oxford: Oxford University Press).

Waltz, K. (1979), *Theory of International Politics* (New York: McGraw Hill).

Wessels, W., Maurer, A., and Mittag, J. (eds) (2003), *Fifteen into One? The European Union and its Member States* (Manchester: Manchester University Press).

Part I

Analytical Approaches

Introduction

In setting up the empirical chapters of this volume it is important to have some analytical reference points for understanding what follows. In view of our twofold concerns in the volume, namely with how the member states impact upon the EU, and how the EU impacts on them (Europeanization), the two chapters that follow take the analytical issues associated with each concern.

Power and influence is central to the study of politics. However, it is curiously under-studied in explicit terms in EU studies. There are, it is true, analyses of the power balance between the intergovernmental and supranational institutions of the Union. Examination of member state power is, however, very limited. Existing comparative studies of the member states in the EU normally focus on institutional adjustment and thus set up the empirical studies with organizational issues: whether member states are converging (Rometsch and Wessels 1996); issues of effectiveness of organization (Wessels, Maurer, and Mittag 2003); or both of these (Kassim, Peters, and Wright 2000; Kassim, Menon, Peters, and Wright 2001). Helen Wallace takes a different approach in Chapter 2 by exploring how member states input into the EU policy process, and what resources they have at their disposal. It provides a useful reminder as to what national *governments* are seeking to achieve in their European diplomacy, whether singly or in bilateral relationships of which that between France and Germany is the most developed. It also provides a useful corrective to studies of member state EU policy-making that can become overly focused on procedures and process without assessing whether these are effective in Brussels policy-making arenas.

In Chapter 2, Tanja Börzel shifts attention to Europeanization. Her chapter examines the state of debates on domestic adjustment to the challenges of the EU. In line with most analysts she employs an institutionalist perspective in reviewing the existing literature. However, she makes important distinctions between the rational-actor approach used by analysts deploying rationalist institutionalism and the norm-following approach deployed by sociological institutionalists. In the former approach political actors are seen to act in a strategic manner, exploiting political opportunity structures. In the latter rational action is modified by the need to conform to group values on 'appropriate' behaviour. These two patterns of action are then deployed as offering different insights into key questions in Europeanization studies. She maps the different dimensions of member state polities that are open to Europeanization; how domestic political resources and norms/values may be modified; how institutional adaptation comes about; and offers categorizations of the extent of adjustment. Building upon her own research, she then connects the subject matter of these two chapters by presenting Europeanization not only as top-down (or 'down-loading') but also bottom-up (or 'up-loading').

EU–member state relations are a two-way process, analytically and empirically. The two chapters capture this situation in analytical terms and are designed to set the scene for the empirical chapters in Parts 2 and 3.

References

Kassim, H., Peters, G. B., and Wright, V. (eds) (2000), *The National Co-ordination of EU Policy. The Domestic Level* (Oxford: Oxford University Press).

Kassim, H., Menon, A., Peters G. B., and Wright, V. (eds) (2001), *The National Co-ordination of EU Policy: The European Level* (Oxford: Oxford University Press).

Rometsch, D., and Wessels, W. (eds) (1996), *The European Union and Member States* (Manchester: Manchester University Press).

Wessels, W., Maurer, A., and Mittag, J. (eds) (2003), *Fifteen into One? The European Union and its Member States* (Manchester: Manchester University Press).

Chapter 2

Exercising Power and Influence in the European Union: The Roles of Member States

Helen Wallace

Contents

Summary

The European Union is characterized by a shifting balance between the member states and the supranational institutions. There is also a shifting balance between the member states in terms of their power and influence within the Union. Developments such as the May 2004 enlargement and the Constitutional Treaty act as a spur for the shifting balance. Against this backdrop the chapter focuses on how member states—here principally understood as member governments—influence the European Union. It then explores the resources that individual member governments can call upon to try and increase their imprint upon the European Union's work. The chapter offers benchmarks for analysing the roles of the states, as considered in Part 2 of the volume.

Introduction

The European Union (EU) operates through an evolving political process which engages its member states in a system of shared governance. The member states are not external to the EU system, but integral parts of it. Indeed in a sense one can describe the EU as the collective property of the participating member states. These, in various guises and through a multiplicity of channels, shape the EU, both enabling the EU institutions to act and constraining when, where and how they act. This system of shared governance has not resolved itself into a clearly defined form that structures all the interactions of the member states with the EU institutions. Instead we find many different kinds of interaction, which make simple generalization misleading, all the more so since there is a continuing debate about how to specify the relative roles and powers of the member states within the EU system (Kohler-Koch 2003).

This system has several features which need to be borne in mind in assessing how the member states fit into it. First, there is no clear hierarchy which makes the EU either superior to or subordinate to its member states. In some policy fields the EU level of action predominates, while in others the member state level of action predominates. And very often policy powers are shared between the two levels of governance. To put this another way, in some policy fields the member states as 'principals' have delegated a policy competence more or less completely to the EU system, while in others there is only partial delegation (Pollack 2003). However, this can change, and even in fields of extensive delegation it is conceivable for a policy power to be retracted by the member states from the EU, as is under discussion, for example, in the case of the common agricultural policy or to be decentralized, as in the field of competition policy.

Second, the EU system is in a kind of constant flux, in that practice, experience, and experiments over time alter the ways in which the member states are involved in the EU system. Indeed in recent years there has been a proliferation of new modes of governance emerging within the EU, sometimes as new ways of dealing with old shared policies, and sometimes as a way of engaging collectively with policies previously outside the terrain of the EU. Typically the newer modes of governance that are emerging involve complex sharing of policy responsibilities between the EU and the member state levels of governance, and often they involve the use of 'soft' methods of policy development rather than 'hard' rules and powers (Wallace 2001).

Third, periodically efforts are made explicitly to redesign the EU system in a formal way, traditionally through Intergovernmental Conferences (IGCs), and recently with the additional experiment of the European Convention. Formal redesign can of course alter significantly the relationships—and the 'balance'—between the member states and the EU institutions. However, there is not a consistent pattern of development towards an ever clearer division of powers between the EU and the member states. On the contrary, the underlying trend is for policies to be developed by a sharing of responsibilities between EU and national levels of governance.

Fourth, the membership of the EU is not stable, but alters periodically with successive enlargements. Thus, on the one hand, the core characteristics of member states as such differ over time, altering the range of policy needs and objectives, and, on the other hand, the relationships among member states alter, changing coalition politics and patterns of influence within the EU. Moreover, national policies and cultures also vary over time and between countries, with the consequence that individual member states differ considerably in the ways that they approach their involvement in the EU system. As a result it is important to look at the differences among member states in their ways of engaging with the EU process and at the variations in their experiences of Europeanization (Héritier *et al.* 2001).

For all of these reasons understanding the EU system represents a continuing challenge not only to the analyst but to the practitioner. The ways in which member states behave within the system affect the character of the system itself. In observing how member states behave we can also therefore gain insights into the nature of the overall political process within the EU. Some kinds of behaviour are conducive to the deepening of political integration and to a strengthening of the political autonomy of the EU, while others tend to weaken or to dilute integration. The supranational explanation of the EU presumes that there is an autonomous source of European political authority separate from the political authority of member governments, and that member states are loose aggregates. The intergovernmental explanation insists that the crucial interactions are those which take place among the governments of the member states, governments with the capacity to act coherently and strategically. Evidence has to be collected about the behaviour of member states in order to judge which of these explanations is more persuasive.

The member states are present in one form or another in all of the institutional processes of the EU (Wessels *et al.* 2003). Thus, most obviously, the Council and the European Council are the places in which the member states are most explicitly present and 'represented' in the EU institutional system. In some instances the member states behave in a rather collegiate fashion within the Council, while in other instances they operate much more separately and competitively. In contrast it might be supposed that the European Commission would and should behave rather independently of the member states. Yet in practice the Commission is involved in continuous dialogue with the member states—and needs to be in order to exercise its delegated powers. Sometimes, however, individual member states seek to influence the internal deliberations of the Commission through 'their nationals' in the college or in the services of the Commission. Even within the rather autonomous legal system of the EU and its independent courts one can find traces of influence from the member states, either in terms of the impact of their legal cultures or in terms of interventions by the member states in individual legal cases.

We need therefore to clarify the definition of 'member states'. At first glance this looks simple. The EU treaties are signed by the 'member states' under international law. The EU institutions are peopled sometimes by representatives *of* the member states, as in the Council and the European Council, and sometimes by appropriately chosen persons *from* the member states, as in the other EU institutions—the Commission, the Parliament, the Courts, and so forth. Reality is, as usually, rather more complex. The Council and the European Council are the key institutions in which the member states are represented, and here it is the member 'governments' which are present. The treaties dignify these representatives through the language of states, but those involved are actually serving politicians, and their officials, from currently incumbent governments. They thus have political agendas and preferences as successful parties and politicians in office, which may—or may not—be representative more broadly of the concerns of the states which they represent.

To distinguish between member states and member governments is not just a matter of splitting hairs. The term 'member states' works more easily in classical international organizations than it does in the case of the EU, which through its multi-dimensional institutional processes allows a variety of actors from the member states to play a part. Member governments are gatekeepers between the state polities and the EU system only up to a point. Member governments are subject to influences from other political actors from their own states which use the EU arena sometimes for other and different purposes. Governments are not monoliths, but comprise a variety of functional and political preferences. Similarly people other than those from incumbent governments speak for opinion in the member states in the variety of EU institutional fora. Thus parliamentarians, subnational authorities, national agencies, social partners, pressure groups, non-governmental organizations, and so forth from the member states are present in the EU political process, as well as member governments. Any of these may claim a voice on behalf of the member states in policy debates. The more decentralized or devolved a member state is the more scope for actors other than central governments to play an important role also as regards the EU.

Most of what follows in this chapter concerns the roles of *member governments* in the EU system. Much of the focus is on the Council and the European Council, including national preparations for Council negotiations, and on the ways in which member governments seek to influence what happens in other EU institutions, for example, by efforts to influence the work of the Commission, or of members of the European Parliament.

Member governments do not, however, impact on the EU system only by their explicit actions within the EU institutions. They also shape the impacts of the EU within the polities of the member states. And they use other channels to influence each other and the politics of European policy inside other member states. As member governments adopt and adapt their domestic procedures for establishing domestic preferences on EU issues and for articulating these preferences in EU fora, so they condition and shape the domestic debate in their own countries (Featherstone and Radaelli 2003). These domestic processes are important influences on how the parameters are set for transmitting each member state's concerns into the EU process.

One other important feature of the behaviour of member governments within the EU system broadly defined is the interaction which takes place among member governments away from 'Brussels' and rather in each other's capitals, through diplomatic and other exchanges, or in other domestic fora. The point here is that there are many horizontal interactions among governments, not only through formal intergovernmental exchanges, but also through party linkages (note here the apparent increase in salience of meetings of party leaders in advance of European Council meetings), and through many informal mechanisms for influencing opinion-formation in other member states. There is thus a pronounced dimension of 'multiple bilateralism' in the EU system. The Franco-German version of this is the best documented and according to most observers the most influential, but this special bilateral relationship is only part of a wider pattern of interactions and a wider range of bilateral relationships between member countries, at both governmental and non-governmental levels. Indeed there is something of a trend towards more activism on the part of pairs or groups of member states seeking to project particular policy or political preferences within the EU system. The combined efforts of the Polish and Spanish governments in the 2003 IGC to retain the provisions of the Treaty of Nice on voting weights is an apt example.

This chapter provides, first, an overview of the points of access for member governments to the EU institutional process. Secondly, it identifies some headings under which we might assess the exercise of power and influence in the EU by member states, and especially the governments of those member states. Thirdly, it comments on ways of comparing the performance of different member governments in the EU system.

Points of access in the EU system for the member governments

Member governments have points of access in the EU system at all phases of its policy and political processes, namely the successive phases of policy design, policy negotiation, policy legitimation, and policy implementation.

Policy design

In the traditional areas of EU policy, subject to traditional Community methods, the formal right of policy initiative and policy design rests with the Commission. However, the Commission does not invent policy proposals in a vacuum; its officials draw on a wide variety of sources in developing policy ideas and crafting policy proposals. Indeed, according to its own assessments, the majority of Commission initiatives derive from a suggestion put forward at some stage by one or other government, flanked by ideas emanating through other channels within the system. The Commission operates a system of advisory committees and expert groups through which it gathers opinions on possible policy initiatives and promotes processes of deliberation (Joerges and Dehousse 2002). Many of these involve 'experts' from the member states precisely in order to ensure that the policy experiences and preferences of the member states are fed into the deliberative process. In addition the Commission services include officials who are seconded national experts from the member states again, precisely to ensure that relevant knowledge and experience is incorporated into policy design.

A distinction should be drawn here between 'expertise' and formally represented views from member states, although in practice the line cannot always be drawn clearly. This channel of expertise provides opportunities for member governments to feed their preferences into the process in an activist way, if they so choose. After all one of the skills of successful negotiation is the ability to shape the foundations of the proposal on the table. Activist governments can and do try to be 'pacesetters' in exporting their ideas to the Commission, in the hope that a proposal, formally articulated by the Commission, can incorporate their preferences clothed in the garb of the collective interest. Reactivist governments play less of a role in the phase of policy design, either sitting on the fence until proposals become fully articulated or listing problems rather than solutions (Jordan 2002). The example of environmental policy is particularly apt. Here we can see a recurrent pattern in which the 'greener' member states, typically the more prosperous, have been very active as 'leaders' in exporting their preferences for stronger environmental controls to the Union. In contrast, the 'less green', often the less prosperous, member states, have been 'laggards', finding themselves pushed into importing such environmental controls and finding that they cramp their economic development. Note also, however, that member states may switch sides, as the British did in 1997 to become 'greener' after the election of the Labour Government, and as the Danish did to become 'less green' after the election in 2002.

Detailed case studies across the range of Community policies reveal the imprints of governmental successes in setting the agenda for discussion. These successes depend crucially on how far governments, or parts of governments, exploit their points of access to the formative phases of policy development. These include the channels to particular parts of the Commission—an individual Commissioner and her/his *cabinet*, a particular directorate-general, or a specialized service. Here we can observe considerable variations of practice between governments and between issue areas in how these opportunities are exploited. There is a risk that the Commission could find itself captured by the pressures emanating from the member states and lose its independence. The formal rule is that Commissioners on taking office have to swear an oath of independence and not to take instructions from the governments of the countries from which they come, and the same principle applies to officials in the services of the Commission. However, this intended neutrality came under challenge in the Constitutional Convention discussion about how the composition of the college should be determined. The insistence by some governments on having one Commissioner 'from' each member state suggested that the college should have a representative character, and that Commissioners might be expected to act on behalf of the countries from which they come. Propositions designed to reduce the size of the college to somewhat fewer than the number of member states were designed to counteract this notion of incorporating national representation within the Commission. The October 2004 agreement on the Constitutional Treaty sought a balance between these approaches, with a commitment to retaining the current system of one Commissioner per member state until 2014.

In some areas of EU policy development governments play a more explicit role in framing policy proposals, especially in those fields of policy often styled as 'intergovernmental'. In the Common Foreign and Security Policy (CFSP), or the further steps towards creating an EU defence capability, it is from member governments rather than the Commission that the main framing proposals have emerged. The St Malo declaration by the French and British governments in 1998 was a key example (Forster and Wallace 2000). Interestingly the Swedish and Finnish governments played an important role in defining what became the 'Petersberg tasks' for action under CFSP. In the field of justice and home affairs, where the Commission enjoys a parallel (rather than sole) right of initiative, member governments are often in practice active policy initiators. More recently, in December 2003 the British, French, and German governments reached agreement on new steps to develop a collective European defence capability.

The Lisbon Strategy provides an interesting contrast. The Strategy was agreed by the European Council in March 2000 as a means of promoting economic and socio-economic policy reforms in fields relevant to generating growth and innovation where the EU lacked many specific policy powers. To this end it was agreed to use different policy techniques, in particular the open method of coordination. This involves forms of soft policy cooperation and a process of cross-country evaluation, comparison, and benchmarking. This deliberately builds in a more explicit role for member governments in developing policy propositions, policy designs and in anchoring national policy objectives and reforms to European targets and objectives. Here it could be argued that the EU role is more that of a catalyst or facilitator than that of an architect or designer (Sapir Report 2004). The jury remains out on the success of this approach. A high-level expert group, chaired by the former Dutch prime minister, Wim Kok, was due to report on the Lisbon Strategy in November 2004.

Policy negotiation

The phase of policy negotiation is crucially important for the exercise of power and influence by member governments within the EU. It is around this phase, mostly played out through the Council and the European Council, including in the many preparatory working groups and high level groups of national officials, that member governments make their most explicit investment of effort to influence the outcomes (Hayes-Renshaw and Wallace 1997). It is towards this phase of policy negotiation that the national coordinating procedures of governments are mainly directed (Kassim *et al.* 2000 and 2001).

The ministerial sessions of the Council constitute the phase of the EU process which is most actively covered by the media and it is here that the nationality labels are placed most explicitly on the policy-influencing and power-projection activities of the member states. However, the many meetings of working groups and committees that prepare the ministerial level of the Council provide the fora for most of the negotiations among officials from member governments on EU policies (Lewis 2002). This indeed constitutes the most active and intensive interface for member governments with the EU system, and it is here that a very large proportion of business is transacted in more or less final form on EU legislation, policy coordination, and funding programmes.

The Council as the regular forum of the member governments can be viewed through different lenses (Wallace 2002). It has different facets or images in different areas of EU policy: (a) as a tandem partnership with the Commission, notably in areas where EU powers are well developed; (b) as a collusive 'club' of governments facing especially new challenges; (c) as a location for persistent competition among member governments; (d) as an arena for 'networked governance'; and (e) as a forum for developing policies through 'intensive transgovernmentalism' in fields where explicit EU powers are not yet developed and hence where the role of the Commission remains modest. The important point to note here is that the Council has multiple roles and multiple personalities, which imply different kinds of behaviour by member governments, a mixture of symbiosis and of tensions. Many would add a sixth image of the Council as a European 'legislature', since it provides, alongside the European Parliament, one of the two main institutional channels for developing EU legislation.

One strand in the reform debate is the call for the Council to be made explicitly and predominantly into a legislative chamber.

Currently the Council is something of a 'black box', since it still meets mostly in secret. This makes it difficult to track in detail the behaviour of member governments and to document how the Council operates as a negotiating forum. Some steps are under way to make the Council more 'transparent', both as regards the release of internal documents and for it to 'meet in public' when operating in 'legislative' mode. Among practitioners within the Council the trend towards greater acceptance for more transparency is quite marked. Let us note, however, that this trend has two different logics. One is the logic of advocating that the Council at ministerial level should be made into something more like a parliamentary chamber for the 'member states'. The other—and quite opposite logic—rests on the view that the formal sessions of the Council are decreasingly the venue for the critical bargains to be struck, since (especially in an enlarging EU) smaller, more intimate and less formal negotiating venues are already being developed, a trend which some practitioners expect to be reinforced.

This latter point reflects another element in the reform debate, namely the charge that the Council has become in many ways an inefficient institution (Wallace and Hayes-Renshaw 2003). The Council suffers from coordination problems and from the segmentation of its work across many different formations of specialist ministers from the member governments. The General Affairs Council, composed traditionally of foreign ministers, was intended to do two different jobs: on the one hand, to develop the external policies of the EU; and, on the other hand, to manage cross-sectoral coordination. It became less and less effective as a coordination body, a development which probably reflects the declining influence of foreign ministers and ministries in national capitals vis-à-vis their colleagues responsible for EU 'domestic' business. Conversely the weight of the Ecofin Council of economics and finance ministers has increased in recent years, partly reinforced by the arrival of economic and monetary union (EMU), but also a reflection of the generally heavy weight of finance ministers within most national governments. The sectoral formations of the Council have different characteristics partly depending on how extensively developed EU powers are in any given policy field. Thus in fields such as agricultural policy the relevant national ministers and officials from the member governments operate as a relatively tight knit club, brought together by their shared functional concerns, although competing with each other for advantage and resources.

The uneven performance of the Council is something of a puzzle. On the one hand it reflects the differing degrees of engagement of national ministers in the EU process, as well as some differences among policy domains. On the other hand, it is a product of the diffuseness of the EU process which has now spread across so many areas of public policy that it is hard for overall control or coordination to be exercised either at the EU level or in national policy coordination in the capitals of the member states. Reform of the Council has become a subject of active discussion, in terms of both formal treaty changes and 'non-treaty' reforms of procedures and practices. Both discussions are ostensibly pushing in the same direction, namely to reduce the number of formations of the Council, to streamline its procedures, to tighten up coordination, and to make it more effective as regards producing outputs. The implication is that a smaller number of leading national ministries from the member governments should filter and focus the inputs from member governments into the phase of EU policy negotiation and decision. Thus, for reforms in this direction to be effective presupposes that member governments should operate more cohesively and strategically in defining and defending their policy preferences on EU issues.

As noted above, the system used to rest on the assumption that foreign ministries would be able to provide the filtering and focusing mechanisms in the member states, and then transmit the resulting national preferences through the General Affairs Council. Latterly this proposition has been viewed as somewhat unrealistic and instead attention has shifted rather towards heads of government. Broadly at the EU level the European Council has emerged as the forum through which strategic choices are made and highly political bargains are struck (de Schoutheete and Wallace 2002). Specialist groups of ministers in the regular Council sessions are often not able to reach solid agreements without reference to heads of government. In some fields, notably the pursuit of the Lisbon Strategy, a direct policy development role has been assigned to the European Council in its spring meetings. Thus, each 'spring Council' reviews the targets for making Europe the 'most dynamic knowledge-based economy in the world' by 2010. Heads of state or government meet to assess in a form of mutual peer review the progress being made in each member state to embrace structural reforms and to promote innovation, using a range of comparative indicators and test practice. The intention is that good practice should be spread across the Union. This reliance on more intervention from the European Council, a body which meets some four or five times a year, does not provide a consistent and continuous locus of negotiation and decision capacity for the EU. In the discussions of Council reform it is frequently argued that coordination and responsibility for the follow through need to be assigned to 'European' ministers from member governments who are located close to the heart of their governments, perhaps as 'deputy prime ministers'. This again begs questions about the ways in which member governments organize their conduct of EU business.

Policy legitimation

Once policies are negotiated and agreed in the Council of the EU, they have to be made legitimate and thereby 'ratified' within the member states in order to take effect. This may seem a puzzling comment given the legal autonomy of the EU and given that many decisions are either directly applicable (under the original treaty terminology 'regulations' and certain kinds of 'decisions') or are able in certain conditions to be made directly effective (typically 'directives', occasionally treaty articles as such). However, these formal rules for incorporating EU decisions into the operating practices of the member states tell only part of the story. For EU policies to bite and to be followed through requires that they are 'owned' by the member states, where the relevant actions are needed and that they are legitimated in the domestic systems of the member states. Thus they need to be actively endorsed by member governments and absorbed into the 'normal' procedures and mindsets of domestic policy-making.

There are significant variations in the way member governments address this task, both procedurally and behaviourally. In some member states there is a kind of contract between the national government and the national political class that EU policy positions should be explicitly negotiated and ratified through a formal political process in some way. Thus, as is well known, Danish ministers negotiate with Danish parliamentarians through both ex ante and ex post consultations. The implication is that the domestic political class has to give active political assent to what its ministers are doing on its behalf in 'Brussels'. Versions of this occur in other member states, and thus in Finland and Sweden similar parliamentary processes take place around the main policy issues under negotiation in Brussels. Sometimes the consultative net is systematically spread further. In Austria, for example, there are often more broadly based consultations, even negotiations, with a range of domestic societal and economic, as well as political, actors on EU issues. Typically in member states with a federal or devolved system of government regional authorities often are engaged in consultations and sometimes negotiations with their central governments over the development of EU policies. In other cases, however, the management and incorporation of EU decisions into the domestic process rests rather in the hands of the European specialists, consulting as and when appropriate with specialised interests, and often with very little regular engagement of national parliaments.

The issue of political legitimation has become a key one for the EU and an interesting facet of the reform debate, particularly against the background of survey evidence of public opinion which suggests that ordinary citizens find the EU process remote and difficult to comprehend. Given the considerable variations among member states of political culture, political practice and constitutional organisation, it is hard to envisage EU-wide mechanisms for policy legitimation. On the contrary, what seem to be needed are national mechanisms and processes that would be more predictable and reliable in providing endorsement for EU policies and policy objectives. This is a concern not only as regards the macro and strategic decisions on major EU policies such as the adoption of the euro or the big budgetary bargains based on periodic negotiations of the 'financial perspectives'. Given that so many policy areas are shared between EU and member states—the development of the Lisbon Strategy is a salient example—it seems important that member states should develop stronger means to legitimate this partnership in shared governance (Sapir Report 2004).

How to do this is not entirely obvious. Observing the ways in which individual member states address this challenge is set to be one of the more interesting windows on the development of the EU over coming years. It was striking that in the aftermath of the negotiation of the Nice Treaty the Laeken Declaration reiterated the call for a greater role for national parliamentarians in the EU process. It is also striking that the European Convention in 2003 failed to find a convincing way of responding to this call, although the summoning of the Convention, with members drawn from national parliaments, was in itself intended as a partial response. More broadly, those who have examined the issues of how to audit the democratic performance of the EU indicate that legitimation of EU policy-making requires a variety of processes within the member states in order to nest the EU process within the domestic policies of its member states (Lord 2004).

Policy implementation

It has always been the case that the bulk of EU policy decisions are implemented through agencies of one kind or another in the member states. Although the Commission has responsibilities for executing Council decisions, in only a few fields does this involve direct administration by the Commission services or its own sub-contracted agencies. Much more commonly, there is either some form of partnership between the Commission and relevant national agencies or the national agencies themselves put EU policies into practice. Occasionally, these latter act only to implement EU policies, as is the case of the intervention agencies for applying the market support arrangements for the common agricultural policy. More commonly national and sometimes subnational agencies absorb the EU dimension of policy into their normal domestic work. It is important to recognize therefore that much of the implementation of EU policy is framed by the regular contours of domestic policy regimes, with variations as a consequence among member states of style and to some extent of substance. Chapter 3 deals with this process in more detail.

Several factors are at work which are altering the ways in which EU policies are implemented within the member states. One of these is the recognition that the central administrative resources of the EU, and especially the Commission, are simply too overstretched to be able to deliver policies directly, especially in an enlarged Union. Thus, notably in the field of competition policy, a shift is under way from direct administration of the EU rules of competition by DG Competition of the Commission to a decentralised form of 'steered network', which involves a division of labour with the national competition authorities.

A second trend is towards forms of contracting out the delivery of public policy, both regulatory and allocative (for some funded programmes) to quasi-autonomous agencies. This trend can be observed both in the member states and in the EU system, as for example in the establishment of food standards agencies for dealing with both standards and risk assessment, or the presence of independent agencies to allocate funding in fields such as research and innovation, or new operating agencies such as Europol and Eurojust. Indeed it is becoming something of a trend in public policy management across Europe for central government machinery to be reduced and for new kinds of agencies to emerge. Thus there is an emerging debate in the EU about how to find the most appropriate mechanisms for delivering public policies (Sapir Report 2003). In some cases both national and EU systems are beginning to acknowledge forms of self-regulation in especially fast-changing areas of market regulation such as financial services.

A third factor at work is the trend, accelerated by the development of the Lisbon Strategy, towards comparison and benchmarking for good and best practices in the delivery of both national and EU policies. The emergence of these techniques, imported from the business community, recognizes the relevance of fitting delivery mechanisms to varied contexts and conditions and the value of some experimentation to achieve good results. Thus, rather than a uniform policy template, a deliberate variety of methods is encouraged.

A fourth factor which is shifting more of the policy implementation away from the Commission is the disturbing evidence of the weaknesses and sometimes abject failings of the Commission as a policy delivery institution. The criticisms of the Santer Commission that erupted in 1998, compounded by the allegation of maladministration by Eurostat in 2003, have eroded confidence in the managerial capacities of the Commission. Such doubts make it even more likely that EU policy implementation is likely to be handled in the future more by decentralized than by centralized mechanisms.

For all of these reasons we are likely to see EU policy implementation more and more explicitly recognized as the responsibility of the member states. Moreover, the new emphasis on benchmarking and so forth implies a recognition of difference in delivery techniques as virtuous, provided the outcome is appropriate. In addition reliance on forms of contracting out to autonomous agencies diffuses responsibilities in such a way that member governments will in some cases (in the regulatory arena, for example) not be able to speak directly for—or instruct—those who implement some EU rules and policies in their countries. The assessment of changing patterns of policy implementation is thus set to become a field that will benefit from careful cross-country comparative research.

Power and influence in the EU system

It is a core objective of all member governments to exercise influence in support of their preferences within the EU system, and in each member state assessments are made about what are judged to be the most appropriate and effective ways of influencing the outcomes. There are, however, no agreed definitions of the forms of influence—or power—available within the EU and the ways that these are exercised, nor of how to measure their impacts. As has already been indicated, the many points of access for member governments to the EU system provide a range of opportunities for attempts to influence what happens. This section identifies a variety of kinds of influence and influencing techniques that are available. These range from softer techniques of persuasion to harder techniques of coercion. By and large the EU system is characterized more by softer techniques than by the exercise of hard power, a reflection of the character of the EU as a sophisticated form of cooperative multilateral and negotiated governance.

Some rational choice studies of the EU focus on the exercise of member governments' power within the Council of the EU, drawing on various power indices and resting on the assumption that power is expressed through the voting weights, rules, and practices of the Council. Such studies are valuable in drawing our attention to the strategic behaviour of governments, both in building coalitions and sometimes in exercising veto power. Studies of this kind would be more persuasive if the Council routinely took most of its decisions by formal voting. The difficulty is that explicit voting is not the predominant mode of decision. For decisions subject to unanimity voting rules, we can perhaps get a handle on when and how veto power is exercised by individual member governments. Otherwise mostly the voting weights and rules impact indirectly, through implicit voting and apparently consensual methods, on decisions technically eligible for qualified majority voting (QMV). Consequently, we have to find ways of assessing the implicit exercise of power, a much more difficult task.

Many studies analyse the EU in terms of principal/agent relationships. Generally such studies define the member states or governments as the principals, which choose—or sometimes refuse—to delegate tasks to the EU system, with the other actors in the system, usually but not always the Commission, acting as agents of the member states or governments (Pollack 2003). The underlying argument is that member governments retain the power to choose when and whether to delegate tasks to EU agents, either partially or completely. The freedom to make this choice may, however, be understood differently in different member states. The notion of a go-it-alone alternative may look more plausible for some member states than for others, given that interdependencies are not symmetrical within the EU. Oddly at the extremes both little Luxembourg and large Germany seem locked in to the process of delegation, although for differing reasons. Geographic encirclement does not guarantee acceptance of a compulsion to delegate to the EU—take the example of Switzerland, still self-excluded from the EU—although geographical peripherality may increase the propensity to resist delegation. Britain, Denmark, Greece, and Sweden provide relevant illustrations of this.

One important factor here seems to be how the EU agents are viewed in terms of their trustworthiness by member government principals. Majone (2000; 2001) has written on the relevance of understanding willingness to delegate to the EU collective agents as closely connected to trust. Where the member governments have a high level of confidence in the collective system, they go beyond treating it as an agent and regard it as a repository of trust (a fiduciary). Here we might contrast the fiduciary character—that is to say, the trust dimension—of delegation in some areas of EU policy thus broadly, for example, in the sphere of economic regulation or in the establishment of the euro, with the unwillingness to delegate more than partially in other policy domains.

Monetary policy is an interesting example of contrasting patterns of delegation within the same domain. Monetary policy in the narrow sense of currency management has been pretty much entirely delegated to the European Central Bank, working closely with national central banks, which in turn have been required to become independent of national government controls within their national settings. However, the associated issues of fiscal and budgetary policies have not been delegated to a collective agency. Indeed the Stability and Growth Pact (SGP), intended as a bridge to introduce collective disciplines over national policies, was grievously challenged in November 2003, when member states that were breaching the SGP rules, notably France and Germany, were able to resist the sanctions that the Commission wished to apply.

A further form of power projection by member governments might be by the use of threats and coercion, including, for example, the threat of defection rather than cooperation. Extreme threats of defection are very rare in the history of the EU: only the Gaullist 'empty chair' policy in 1965 and the British 'non-cooperation' policy in 1996 seem to fit into this category. More frequently attempts at coercion are made through assertive issue-linkage, a common negotiating strategy in the Council, that is a government will not agree to **X**, unless **Y** is also agreed.

An alternative way of exercising negative power is by the use of the veto on issues that are subject to unanimity rules (that is where 'no-saying' is entirely legitimate under the Council decision rules). Again this is common behaviour, although more frequently used by some governments than others. Interestingly, appeal to the 'Luxembourg compromise' (that is attempts to veto on issues that would otherwise be decided by QMV), is an extremely rare practice, so rare that some commentators—and indeed some practitioners—regard the Luxembourg compromise as a dead letter (Teasdale 1993). The Treaty of Amsterdam introduced the procedure (slightly modified in the Treaty of Nice) known informally as the 'emergency brake' as a last resort for an isolated member state. As yet we have no working experience of this procedure.

All in all therefore the EU system is relatively free of explicit threats and explicit vetoes other than those legitimately available under unanimity voting rules. What is slightly less clear is why this should be so. One answer is that there is a strong procedural norm of consensus-building, and therefore cooperative games are the typical procedure. Another answer is that member governments exercise influence in more indirect ways which make extreme behaviour mostly redundant. Nonetheless many insiders now argue that the Union system is becoming more vulnerable to explicit threats or vetoes from 'powerful' member governments.

One complicating factor is that the EU rests on a mix of both symmetrical and asymmetrical allocations of formal and informal power to the separate member states. To the extent that the EU operates like either a classical international organization or a formal confederation each member state operates within the EU system on a basis of parity. Thus each member state counts as one when the EU Council reaches decision by either unanimity or simple majority. But for many purposes, notably the weighted voting rule and—until November 2004—the allocation of Commissioners to particular nationalities, power is allocated according to criteria of relative size, population, or, under the rules of the European Coal and Steel Community, relative economic stake. These asymmetries have become harder to handle in an enlarging EU in which (especially among the new members) there is a proliferation of smaller countries among the member states. These latter include states a good deal smaller than many Länder or provinces/regions (even cities) in larger member states. The acrimony of the negotiations over treaty changes at the European Council in Nice in December 2000 already suggested that these asymmetries are set to be an increasingly important source of friction within the EU. The breakdown of the IGC in December 2003 on the issue of voting weights was further evidence of this friction, although later resolved in 2004. The pressures from the German Länder, and equivalents in some other member states, are another sign of this concern.

Political weight

Member governments have differing endowments of political weight within the negotiating processes of the EU. Factors that are relevant include: 'objective' factors, such as size, population, or geopolitical position; but also more 'subjective' factors, to do with, for example, historical position, including date of accession to the EU (founders versus late entrants); or centrality to the issues under negotiation (thus militarily engaged countries, such as France or the UK, carry more weight on European defence questions than neutral and non-aligned countries).

Political practice

How a government behaves as a member of the EU also has an impact. Governments that pursue accommodating and consensus-seeking policies, for example, acquire a kind of peer respect within the system. This is a resource on which governments can call in seeking understanding for their concerns. A capacity for coalition-building with other 'like-minded' governments is often a valuable tool for reinforcing influence. Conversely governments that operate in a more singular way may extract advantage under unanimity rules, although suffer under QMV if they are outside the coalition system. Member states that pursue tough bargaining strategies may be very effective in conditioning the negotiating environment.

A different aspect of political practice has to do with the 'fit' between domestic political practice and the procedural norms of the EU system. To take an obvious example the Federal Republic of Germany has a polycentric system of government (that is, it has no single centre of power due to a federal system of government and the presence of coalition administrations at both levels) which sits more easily with the EU system than do the political practices of the historically monocentric and single party-dominant governmental system of a country like the UK. German politicians can more easily draw on the experience of cognate domestic political practice in devising ways of influencing the EU process than can their British counterparts. This observation begs the prior question of how far the EU system bears the imprints of the political practices of its member states. Some member states have been more effective than others in 'exporting' their political and policy practices to the EU level. In such cases the process of 'Europeanization' is much more straightforward than for those member states which recurrently find themselves under pressure from the EU system to 'import' new policies and practices. Here we should note that Europeanization needs to be understood not only as a 'top-down' process, whereby European influences are transmitted from the EU level into the domestic political processes of the member states. Europeanization is also a 'bottom up' process, whereby domestic factors condition and shape the opportunities for and the character of European policy regimes (see also Chapter 3).

Economic weight

Economic weight also affects the influence that a member government can wield in the development of EU policies. Here again Germany provides the key illustration. In overall terms Germany has been by a margin (and was even before unification) the largest national economy within the EU, a factor which gives added pertinence to the German voice or voices in EU negotiations. Both on issues affecting the development of macro-economic or monetary policies and on topics relating to particular economic sectors, German concerns compel attention. It is not only that in broad terms Germany is the largest economy, but also that Germany is the first trade partner of every other EU member state (to the extent that national economies are a meaningful concept in today's interdependent world). Similarly for a variety of reasons Germany is by far the largest net contributor to the EU collective budget,[1] and hence German opinions on EU expenditure issues tend to be taken very seriously in EU decision-making. In the fierce argument about the economic Stability and Growth Pact the combined economic and political weight of Germany and France led in November 2003 to a suspension of the sanctions that should have been imposed.

[1] The Netherlands has, however, become the largest 'contributor' to the EU budget in terms of amounts per capita of the population.

Social and economic practice

Influence through example is one of the assets on which a member government may be able to draw in developing an argument within the EU. Thus—to take two recent examples—Irish ministers are able to point to the apparent success of the Irish social partnership model as one of the contributory causes of Ireland's recent economic performance. Similarly, Finnish ministers are well placed to argue convincingly from their experience of technological innovation. The ability to deploy arguments grounded in observable practice within a particular member state has always conferred advantage. In a period where cross-country comparisons have become an explicit policy tool for the EU the weight of reported practice has become much more important.

Persuasive ideas

Ideas count as well as practice—and the ability to turn practice into a framing concept can be particularly valuable. The rectitude of 'sound money', derived from West German monetary policy, became the persuasive idea in the development of the case for EMU. Some years earlier it had been the British government's ideas about market liberalization that had framed what became the single European market. The notion that broader international trade liberalization was virtuous as a governing idea had been rooted even earlier from the persuasive arguments of the more liberally minded among the EU governments. The flanking of the single market by elements of redistribution or 'cohesion' policies gained credence from the persuasive ideas of some governments, which set the frame for policy development. In none of these cases were the persuasive ideas solely sourced from the arguments or the experience of individual governments. But the advocates of each of these policies, often in the Commission or in other institutions, were able to draw persuasive ideas out of the arguments of individual governments in order to give more impetus to policy proposals. Many of the principles of EU jurisprudence were borrowings from the experience of one or other member state.

Compelling demands

A different kind of impetus for EU policy development has come from compelling demands from one or another member government, sometimes more, sometimes less harshly stated. The term 'demandeur' is a frequent epithet used in descriptions of bargaining, especially on distributional issues. The British were 'demandeurs' of budgetary equity, as the French had been of 'financial solidarity' (that is common financing) for the common agricultural policy. These are both examples of strong demands on critical issues of huge importance for the development of EU regimes. At a more micro level member governments may be able to argue that something is an essential requirement to address a specific domestic concern or external requirement. Take the history of the EU banana regime as an example of a series of compelling needs from several member governments producing in this case an awkward and costly collective policy (Stevens 2000). In addition the ability to project specific national concerns as compellingly important (domestic elections are often an irresistible pretext) is part of what produces a pattern of Council negotiations with a log-rolling character.

Credibility and consistency

The various bases for influence from which member governments can argue their cases illustrate a mixture of shorter and longer term considerations. By and large a member government's scope for influencing EU policy and political outcomes is cumulative over time, although governments can be extractive on individual issues depending on the contingency of the moment. More importantly factors of influence developed and deployed iteratively over time make a difference to the credibility of a government's overall policy stance and political approach to the EU. A degree of predictability makes a government a more credible interlocutor—both for good and for ill. Governments acquire reputations as more or less consensus-minded in general, or as, for example, more or less liberal or protection-minded on issues of regulation and trade, and similarly advocates of one or other position on recurrent generic issues.

How consistent or predictable a government is depends on both its behaviour within the relevant EU fora and on how domestic policy-making operates on EU issues. Here we should note that there are considerable variations in the ways that individual governments coordinate national European policies, with many different factors both of domestic practice and of European policy preferences impinging on the domestic process (see also Chapter 12). As a general observation we can note that these domestic patterns become deeply embedded over time, creating national path dependencies of policy development and of negotiating styles. To take a current example—the British Labour Government elected in 1997 developed some very different European policy aims from those of its predecessors. It has, however, proved difficult in practice to move away from deeply ingrained habits of policy management and policy projection.

Britain presents a particularly sharp example because so much of a premium has been put in the British system on attempting to craft and to sustain an overall interdepartmental and nationally unified policy. In some other member states policy is defined more permissively, allowing more room for individual branches of government to pursue their more specialized policy preferences. Thus by and large the credibility and predictability of British policy has historically been judged both in the UK and elsewhere in the EU on the assumption that there was a more or less monolithic British approach. Germany offers a clear contrast, with its much more decentralized policy process, both in [Bonn] Berlin and between Bund and Länder. This more decentralized process, however, has made individual German policy positions harder for other partners to predict. There is a danger here that national policies become vulnerable to caricature. Thus to revert briefly to the British case— actually British European policy has become more polycentric, both because of territorial devolution and because there have been changes in the balance of influence between British ministries, as well as differences in the influence of particular British ministries on EU policy developments.

We should note here that the segmentation of work in EU institutional practice (both Commission and Council) lends itself to a fragmentation of policy inputs from individual member governments. It provides opportunity structures for individual ministers and groups of ministers to develop their own EU clubs, as in the case of agriculture or the environment. The sectorialization of the process aggravates coordination problems at both EU and member state levels. As was noted earlier attempts are being made to reform the Council in order to counteract this sectorialization. On the other hand the trend towards greater decentralization of policy delivery may tend to retain the forces of fragmentation within the EU system.

Drawing comparative conclusions

First and foremost, it is a rational and logical objective for all member governments to maximize their influence on the shaping of Union policies and on the way in which agreed policies are applied within their countries. Governments are often all responsible to their domestic electorates for their performance in office. However, some governments define their objectives in a singular way, that is taking a narrow and focused view of their interests, while others situate their particular objectives within a range of more collective interests.

Second, there are clear differences across countries and over time among member governments in the extent to which they influence the outcomes of EU bargaining. Here we need constantly to bear in mind that these differences may be of two quite different kinds. One relates to the strategies, tactics and skills which individual governments are able to deploy in pursuing their objectives—some are more effective, others less so, in persuading the Commission or partner governments to accept their arguments. However, the other source of differences has to do with the substance of the issues being negotiated. Thus of course governments seek to tailor Union policies in order to achieve a good fit with their domestic economic characteristics or with deeply embedded societal or political circumstances.

Third, the Union system provides multiple and iterative opportunities for each member government to exercise its voice—or voices—in shaping Union policies. These opportunities are continuously proliferating, as the agenda of Union policy-making extends, and as new fora are added for developing dialogue and bargaining among member governments and within the EU institutions. This proliferation of fora has made it harder and harder for gatekeepers in individual governments to act as filters or to provide authoritative coordination. Thus the Union's system risks becoming increasingly fragmented and individual governments find themselves increasingly challenged by the range of Union processes. We can observe large contrasts between member states in the ways in which their governments respond, as subsequent chapters in this volume reveal.

Fourth, however, the Union is in some senses not a stable system. Changes in membership, not least with the enlargement of 2004, necessarily provoke changes in the practices of the Union. These efforts at reform are in turn a matter of contestation, as was clear in late 2003 when the IGC negotiating the proposed constitutional treaty failed to reach agreement on key proposals. Thus in examining the workings of the Union and the behaviour of member governments we need to keep open minds on the patterns of evolution. There are cross-cutting tensions between, on the one hand, pressures to simplify and to consolidate the way the Union works, and, on the other hand, persisting differences among the member states in their preferences as to the design of the Union.

Further reading

Useful context to understanding EU–member state relations is provided by exploring the EU from other perspectives, including its policy process (Wallace and Wallace 2000; Wallace, Wallace and Pollack 2005 edition forthcoming) and its institutions (Peterson and Shackleton 2002). The Council is the institution to which member government's efforts at power and influence are directed (see, for instance, Hayes-Renshaw and Wallace 1997; new edition forthcoming). Comparative studies of how member states interact with the EU are offered by Kassim *et al.* (2000; 2001) and Wessels, Maurer, and Mittag (2003).

Weblinks

There are few if any websites dealing directly with the analytical concerns of this chapter. However, since member governments' access to the EU is predominantly through the Council, a familiarity with its site is worthwhile <**http://www.ue.eu.int**>. Many suppliers of commentary on developments in Brussels offer websites that require subscription or some form of registration, so are not listed here. One site that is on open access at the time of writing is EurActiv.com <**http://www.euractiv.com**>, which has a useful set of links on governance.

References

Featherstone, K., and Radaelli, C. M. (eds) (2003), *The Politics of Europeanisation* (Oxford: Oxford University Press).

Forster, A., and Wallace, W. (2000), 'Common Foreign and Security Policy', in H. Wallace and W. Wallace, W. (eds), *Policy-Making in the European Union* (Oxford: Oxford University Press), 461–91.

Hayes-Renshaw, F., and Wallace, H. (1997), *The Council of Ministers of the European Union* (London: Macmillan).

Héritier, A., Kerwer, D., Knill, C., Lehmkuhl, D., Teutsch, M., Dovillet, A-C. (2001), *Differential Europe—New Opportunities and Restrictions for Policy-Making in Member States* (Lanham, MD: Rowman and Littlefield).

Joerges, C., and Dehousse, R. (eds) (2002), *Good Governance in Europe's Integrated Market* (Oxford: Oxford University Press).

Jordan, A. (2002), *The Europeanisation of British Environmental Policy* (London: Palgrave).

Kassim, H., Menon, A., Peters B. G., and Wright, V. (eds) (2000), *The National Coordination of EU Policy: The Domestic Level* (Oxford: Oxford University Press).

Kassim, H., Menon, A., Peters, B. G., and Wright, V. (eds) (2001), *The National Coordination of EU Policy: The European Level* (Oxford: Oxford University Press).

Kohler-Koch, B. (ed.) (2003), *Linking EU and National Governance* (Oxford: Oxford University Press).

Lewis, J. (2002), 'National Interests: Coreper', in J. Peterson, and M. Shackleton, (eds) *The Institutions of the European Union*, 277–98.

Lord, C. (2004), *A Democratic Audit of the European Union* (London: Palgrave).

Majone, G. (2000), 'The Credibility Crisis of Community Regulation', *Journal of Common Market Studies*, 38/2 273–302.

Majone, G. (2001), 'Two Logics of Delegation; Agency and Fiduciary Relations in EU Governance', *European Union Politics*, 2/1 103–21.

Peterson, J., and Shackleton, M. (2002), *The Institutions of the European Union* (Oxford University Press).

Pollack, M. (2003), *The Engines of European Integration: Delegation, Agency and Agenda Setting in the EU* (Oxford: Oxford University Press).

Sapir Report (2004), *An Agenda for a Growing Europe: Making the EU Economic System Deliver* (Oxford: Oxford University Press).

de Schoutheete, P., and Wallace, H. (2002), *The European Council* (Paris: Notre Europe).

Stevens, C. (2000), 'Trade with Developing Countries: Banana Skins and Turf Wars', in H. Wallace and W. Wallace (eds), *Policy-Making in the European Union* (Oxford: Oxford Univeristy Press), 401–26.

Teasdale, A. (1993), 'The Life and Death of the Luxembourg Compromise', *Journal of Common Market Studies*, 31/4 567–79.

Wallace, H. (ed.) (2001), 'The Changing Politics of the European Union', special issue of *Journal of Common Market Studies*, 39/4.

Wallace, H. (2002), 'The Council: an Institutional Chameleon', *Governance*, 15/3 325–44.

Wallace, H., and Hayes-Renshaw, F. (2003), *Reforming the Council: A Work in Progress* (Stockholm: Swedish Institute for European Policy Studies).

Wallace, H., and Wallace, W. (eds) (2000), *Policy-Making in the European Union*, 4th edn. (Oxford: Oxford University Press).

Wallace, H., Wallace, W., and Pollack, M. (2005), *Policy-Making in the European Union*, 5th edn. (Oxford: Oxford University Press).

Wessels, W., Maurer, A., and Mittag, J. (eds) (2003), *Fifteen into one? The European Union and its Member States* (Manchester: Manchester University Press).

Chapter 3

Europeanization: How the European Union Interacts with its Member States

Tanja A. Börzel

Contents

Summary

The chapter reviews the 'state of the art' of the Europeanization debate. It explores three key aspects of Europeanization: the dimensions, mechanisms, and outcomes of domestic impact. While by now most students of the European Union agree that the effect of Europeanization on the member states is not uniform but differential, there is still little consensus on how to account for variation in the processes, degrees and the outcomes of domestic change. Nor has much attention been paid to how the member states have responded to the increasing effect of the European Union on their domestic institutions, policies and political processes. The chapter concludes with some considerations on how to conceptualize the feedback loops between 'top-down' and 'bottom-up' dynamics in the relationship between the EU and its member states.

Introduction

This chapter seeks to identify concepts and theories to analyse and explain the relationship between the member states and the European Union. The empirical studies in Parts 2 and 3 of this volume provide ample illustration of how member states try to shape European institutions and policies and how European processes and outcomes feed back on the domestic institutions, policies, and political processes of the member states. While acknowledging that the relationship between the member states and the European Union is an interactive one, most attention is focused on one side of the equation. European level processes are 'bracketed', (that is taken as fixed, to analyse their effects at the member-state level or vice versa).

For a long time, European studies have been mostly concerned with the 'bottom-up' dimension of the EU–member state relationship exploring the role of the member states in the European institution-building process. In recent years, however, there has been a growing body of 'top-down' analysis of the effect of the evolving European system of governance on the member states (Marks, Hooghe, and Blank 1996; Cowles, Caporaso, and Risse 2001; Goetz and Hix 2000).[1] A comprehensive understanding of the relationship between the member states and the European Union requires the systematic integration of the two dimensions. Nevertheless, this chapter will mainly adopt a top-down perspective looking at how the European Union has affected the member states and to what extent it has changed their domestic institutions,

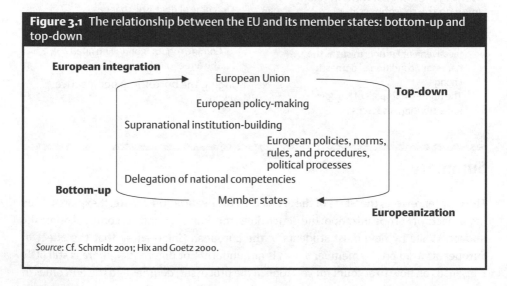

Figure 3.1 The relationship between the EU and its member states: bottom-up and top-down

Source: Cf. Schmidt 2001; Hix and Goetz 2000.

[1] Part of the literature refers to the effect of the European Union on the member states as 'Europeanization' (Ladrech 1994; Radaelli 2000). Others reserve the term Europeanization for the 'emergence and the development at the European level of distinct structures of governance' (Risse, Cowles, and Caporaso 2001: 1). On the various concepts of Europeanization see Börzel and Risse (2001); Olsen (2002).

policies and political processes. More specifically, three questions will be addressed:

(1) Where does the European Union affect the member states (*dimensions of domestic change*)?

(2) How does the European Union affect the member states (*mechanisms of domestic change*)?

(3) What is the effect of the European Union on the member states (*outcome of domestic change*)?

The chapter will review existing analyses and their different insights into each of the three questions. The chapter will conclude with reflections on how to conceptualize the feedback loops between 'top-down' and 'bottom-up' dynamics in the relationship between the EU and its member states.

From bottom-up to top-down

For decades, research in the field of European Studies adopted a 'bottom-up' perspective in analysing the relationship between the European Union and its member states (see also Bulmer and Lequesne in this volume). The literature was mainly concerned with how to conceptualize and explain processes and outcomes of European integration. Theoretical debates were dominated by two competing paradigms of European integration that significantly disagree on the role that member states play at the European level (for the intellectual history of the debate see, for example, Caporaso and Keeler 1993). Intergovernmentalist approaches take the member states and their governments as the main agents driving European integration and policy-making to protect the geopolitical interests and the economic concerns of their constituencies (Hoffmann 1982; Taylor 1991; Moravcsik 1991; 1998). Neofunctionalism and multi-level governance approaches, by contrast, privilege domestic interests (such as business associations, trade unions, and regions) that press for further integration to promote their economic or political interests, as well as supranational actors (particularly the European Commission and the European Court of Justice) that seek to increase the power of European institutions over the member states (Haas 1958; Sandholtz and Stone Sweet 1998; Hooghe and Marks 2001).

In the 1990s students of European integration became increasingly interested in the impact of European processes and institutions on the member states (see also Bulmer and Lequesne in this volume). The first studies focused on the consequences of European integration for the autonomy and authority of the member states. In order to theorize the domestic impact of Europe, the explanatory logics of the two major paradigms of European integration were essentially turned around. If intergovernmentalist approaches were correct in assuming that member-state governments controlled European integration while supranational institutions themselves exercised little independent effect, the power of the member states would not be challenged. Rather, European integration should enhance the control of national governments over domestic affairs since it removed issues from domestic controversy into the arena of executive control at the European level (Milward 1992; Moravcsik 1994).

Proponents of neofunctionalist or supranationalist approaches suggested exactly the opposite, namely that the European Union provided domestic actors, such as regions and interest groups, with independent channels of political access and influence at the European level enabling them to circumvent or bypass their member states in the European policy process (Marks 1993; Marks, Hooghe, and Blank 1996; Sandholtz 1996). Between the two competing paradigms, a third group of scholars emerged that rejected the zero-sum game conception of the relationship between the EU and its member states, in which one level was to be empowered at the expense of the other. They argued that the different levels of government would become increasingly dependent on each other in European policy-making. As a result, European integration would neither strengthen nor weaken but transform the member states by fostering the emergence of cooperative relationships between state and non-state actors at the various levels of government (Kohler-Koch 1996; Rhodes 1997; Kohler-Koch and Eising 1999).

Despite a general disagreement on the concrete impact of European integration, most of the earlier studies expected to see some kind of convergence among the member states either leading to more centralization, decentralization, or cooperation in the national political systems. Such convergence was to result from a redistribution of power resources among national governments, and domestic actors, with some gaining new opportunities to pursue their interests and others being constrained in their action capacities (Börzel 2002b: 18–22). Yet, empirical studies on the domestic impact of Europe found little evidence for convergence. Moreover, they identified alternative mechanisms of domestic change that worked through the internalization of new norms, rules, and shared practices rather than changes in political opportunity structures (Mény, Muller, and Quermonne 1996; Cowles, Caporaso, and Risse 2001).

Integration theories are inadequate to account for the differential impact of Europe on the member states. Their major concern has been to explain the dynamics and outcomes of the European integration process rather than its domestic effects, which appear to fall more into the realm of comparative politics and public policy. The European Union was traditionally seen as the preserve of international relations. But with the establishment of the Single Market and the European Monetary Union propelling the delegation of domestic competencies to the European level, the disciplinary boundary became increasingly porous (Risse-Kappen 1996; Hix 1999). Comparativists could no longer ignore the effects of the European Union on the domestic institutions, policies, and political processes of the member states. As we will see in the following sections, comparative politics and public policy offer a more fine-grained analytical toolkit for the task in hand. Unlike international relations theory, these branches of political science are better suited to trace processes and outcomes of domestic change as a consequence of European integration and EU policy-making.

Studying the effect of the European Union on the member states

Dimensions of domestic change

The analytical tool box of comparative politics and public policy provides three main categories, which allow to analyse the effect of the European Union on its member states and to trace processes of domestic change: polity, policy, and politics (see Bulmer and Lequesne in this volume).

While it is useful to analytically distinguish between the three dimensions of domestic change, reality is more complex. European policies, processes, and institutions tend to affect not only one but two or all three dimensions. Domestic policy changes, for instance, often have broader repercussions since problem-solving approaches and policy instruments are closely linked to legal and administrative structures and patterns of interest intermediation (Héritier *et al.* 2001; Knill 2001).

Mechanisms of domestic change

The literature has identified several mechanisms through which Europe can affect the member states. Christoph Knill and Dirk Lehmkuhl distinguish between *institutional compliance*, where the EU prescribes a particular model which is 'imposed' on the member states, *changing domestic opportunity structures*, which leads to a redistribution of resources between domestic actors, and *policy framing*, which alters the beliefs of domestic actors (Knill and Lehnkuhl 1999; Knill 2001; on framing see also Radaelli 2000; Kohler-Koch 1996). Others emphasize *judicial review* (that is the right of any affected party to challenge deficient implementation of Community Law before national courts) (Weiler 1991; Conant 2001). A more indirect mechanism of domestic change is *regulatory competition*, triggered by the dismantling of trade barriers, which

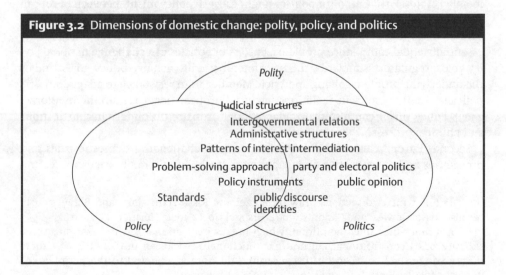

Figure 3.2 Dimensions of domestic change: polity, policy, and politics

Polity

Judicial structures
Intergovernmental relations
Administrative structures
Patterns of interest intermediation

Problem-solving approach   party and electoral politics
Policy instruments   public opinion
Standards   public discourse
identities

Policy   Politics

provides firms with exit options from national jurisdictions (Sun and Pelkmans 1995; Kerwer and Teutsch 2001).

The different causal mechanisms of domestic change can be grouped around two theoretical approaches that draw on different strands of neo-institutionalist reasoning: rationalist institutionalism and sociological institutionalism. There is a third body of literature that has been referred to as 'organizational ecology'. While it will be discussed separately, I will argue that the theoretical arguments can be largely subsumed under the other two approaches. The three approaches pose different propositions on when and how Europe affects the member states and what the consequences are (see Figure 3.7).[2] Yet, they share two major assumptions:

1. The impact of Europe on the member states is differential (i.e. varies across member states and policy areas).

2. The differential impact of Europe is explained by the 'goodness of fit' between European and national policies, institutions, and processes, on the one hand, and the existence of 'mediating factors' or intervening variables that filter the domestic impact of Europe, on the other hand.

Inconvenient Europe: misfit as the necessary condition of domestic change

Irrespective of the theoretical approach chosen, most studies find that there must be some 'misfit' (Börzel 1999; Duina 1999) or 'mismatch' (Héritier 1996) between European and domestic policies, processes, and institutions. The 'goodness of fit' (Risse, Cowles, and Caporaso 2001) or congruence between the European and the domestic level determines the degree of pressure for adaptation generated by Europeanization on the member states. Only if European policies, institutions, and/or processes differ significantly from those found at the domestic level, do member states feel the need to change. *The lower the compatibility between European and domestic processes, policies, and institutions, the higher is the adaptational pressure Europe exerts on the member states.*

There are two types of misfits by which Europe exerts adaptational pressure on the member states. First, European policies might cause a 'policy misfit' between European rules and regulations, on the one hand, and domestic policies, on the other (cf. Héritier, Knill, and Mingers 1996; Schmidt 2001; Börzel 2003). Here, policy misfits essentially equal compliance problems. European policies can challenge national policy goals, regulatory standards, the instruments used to achieve policy goals, and/or the underlying problem-solving approach. Member state resistance to adapt domestic policies usually results in violations against European legal requirements (Börzel 2003). Policy misfit can also exert adaptational pressure on underlying institutions and political processes.

Second, Europe can cause 'institutional misfit' challenging domestic rules and procedures and the collective understandings attached to them.[3] European rules and

---

[2] The following two sections draw on Börzel and Risse 2001, 2003, and Börzel 2002b; see also Risse, Cowles, and Caporaso 2001; Hix and Goetz 2000; Héritier *et al.* 2001.

[3] For a more fine-tuned definition, which breaks institutional misfit down into three sub-categories (constitutional, cultural, and functional) see Hansen and Scholl 2002. Others have distinguished between misfit concerning the core as opposed to the periphery of domestic institutions (Knill and Lenschow 2001a; Knill 2001).

procedures, which give national governments privileged decision powers vis-à-vis other domestic actors, conflict with the territorial institutions of highly decentralized member states which grant their regions autonomous decision powers (Börzel 2002b). The accessibility of the European Commission for societal interests challenges the statist business–government relations in France and the corporatist system of interest mediation in Germany (Cowles 2001). Europe might even threaten deeply collective understandings of national identity as it touches upon constitutional principles such as state sovereignty (Risse 2001; Checkel 2001). The degree of institutional fit has also implications for the 'bottom-up' dimension of the EU–member state relations. Thus, Bulmer and Katzenstein argue that the congruence in 'constitutional order', 'norms and conventions', and patterns of sectoral (or 'meso-level') governance between Germany and the EU has allowed Germany to play a leading role in shaping supranational institution-building and the making of European policies (Bulmer 1997; Katzenstein 1997). This, they have argued, has in turn reduced adaptational pressures on its domestic institutions, processes and policies, creating a kind of virtuous circle. While these findings have been contested (Risse, Cowles, and Caporaso 2001; Héritier *et al.* 2001; Börzel 2003), they point to an important feedback loop between top-down and the bottom-up processes to which I will return in the concluding section.

Some studies have questioned the explanatory power of the goodness of fit. First, Knill and Lehmkuhl argue that the relevance of misfit is limited to the EU's market-correcting policies, such as environmental regulations, which positively prescribe or impose a concrete model for domestic compliance. Market-making policies, by contrast (for example transport liberalization) would leave the member states too much flexibility and discretion in order to exert pressure for adaptation; instead they would provide domestic actors with new opportunities for achieving domestic reforms (Knill and Lehnkuhl 1999; Schmidt 2001). Yet, a European policy can only empower domestic actors *if* there is a certain misfit with domestic regulations. Accordingly, it is not only 'integration through law' that can produce misfit at the domestic level. Softer forms of integration in the 'shadow of law' or 'without law', such as the Open Method of Coordination (OMC) (Héritier 2002), may equally challenge domestic institutions, policies, and processes inducing processes of social learning (Dyson 2003), or empowering domestic reform coalitions (Anderson, K. 2002).

Secondly, Héritier *et al.* criticize the static perspective, which ignores that the goal-posts of goodness of fit may change over time depending on the stage of the national policy process. Even if European policies initially fit domestic regulations, they may empower domestic actors to introduce changes that go against European requirements resulting in 'ex-post' misfit. For instance, France had already deregulated its transport sector when it met the EU demands for liberalization. But the latter strengthened those domestic actors that pushed for re-regulating the impact of liberalization in order to safeguard public interest goals (Héritier *et'al.* 2001). The French case may indeed call for a more dynamic perspective that looks at the relation between the EU and its member states over time rather than taking a snapshot picture at a given point of time (Goetz 2000; Risse, Cowles, and Caporaso 2001). Such a dynamic perspective would also allow to account for the recursive dimension of the domestic impact of Europe, where member states respond to European pressures by trying to (re)shape European policies and institutions in order to reduce the misfit (see below).

A third criticism, finally, focuses on the fragility of domestic institutions. If they are in a performance crisis or in endogenous transition, domestic institutions may not be sufficiently robust in order to be challenged by European policies, processes, and institutions (Morlino 1999; Knill and Lenschow 2001a). This applies, in particular, to the Southern European member states and the Central and Eastern European accession countries, where EU membership has been associated with institution-building rather than institutional change. Nevertheless, domestic actors are socialized into new norms and values redefining their identities. Similarly, EU accession may provide new resources (money, expertise, ideas, legitimacy) that empower domestic actors to overcome crisis and shape the transition process, respectively (Grabbe 2003).

Most studies take misfit only as a necessary condition of domestic change. They identify intervening variables that mediate between European pressures for adaptation and member state responses. Depending on the theoretical approach chosen, however, the literature emphasizes different 'mediating factors'.

The domestic impact of Europe: redistributing resources

Resource-dependency approaches are usually based on some sort of rationalist institutionalism, which assumes that actors are rational, goal-oriented, and purposeful (cf. Hall and Taylor 1996). Rational actors follow a 'logic of consequentialism' (March and Olsen 1989; 1998) in the sense that they have a fixed and ordered set of preferences and they act instrumentally in order to maximize their expected utilities by deploying the resources at their disposal. As any individual or corporate actor is dependent on others to achieve his or her goals, actors have to exchange their resources to produce desired outcomes. The resource exchange is based on the mutual assessment of resources, strategies, and interests. Actors will engage in strategic interaction using their resources to maximize influence over outcomes, while trying to become as little dependent as possible on the others with whom they interact. The strategy by which actors seek to maximize their utilities, (that is the decision with which actors they exchange what kind of resources), depends on the availability and relative value of their own resources, as well as the estimated value of the resources and the anticipated exchange behaviour (interests and strategies) of others.

Rationalist institutionalism views social institutions, including the EU, as external constraints on the behaviour of actors with given identities and preferences. From this perspective, Europe is largely conceived as an emerging political opportunity structure which offers some actors additional legal and political resources to exert influence, while severely constraining the ability of others to pursue their goals (Héritier *et al.* 2001; Hix and Goetz 2000; Kohler-Koch and Eising 1999). Such changes in the political opportunities and constraints for domestic actors can result in a redistribution of resources among them, empowering some over others. The 'differential empowerment' may not only alter domestic institutions but also change domestic policies and political processes.

While earlier works suggested that European integration favours particular groups of domestic actors (e.g. governments) over others (e.g. regions and interest groups), or vice versa (see above), empirical evidence clearly shows that the effect of the European political opportunity structure varies significantly. For instance, while French firms gained more autonomy vis-à-vis their national government by circumventing them in the European policy process (Schmidt 1996), Spanish firms did not (Aguilar Fernandez 1993). The Italian regions have been far less able to ascertain their domestic power vis-à-vis the central state than their Austrian or British counterparts (Jeffery 1997).

The European political opportunity structure only leads to a redistribution of resources and differential empowerment at the domestic level if, first, there is considerable misfit, which provides actors with new opportunities and constraints. And second, the literature has identified two mediating factors that influence the capacities of domestic actors to exploit new opportunities and avoid constraints with opposite effects: *multiple veto players* and *facilitating formal institutions*.

Despite the pressure to adapt 'misfitting' domestic institutions and policies to European requirements, the existence of *multiple veto points* can empower domestic actors with diverse interests to avoid constraints and, thus, effectively inhibit domestic adaptation (Tsebelis 1995; Haverland 2000; Héritier *et al*. 2001). The more power is dispersed across the political system and the more actors have a say in political decision-making, the more difficult it is to foster the domestic 'winning coalition' necessary to introduce changes in response to Europeanization pressures. A large number of institutional or factual veto players thus impinges on the capacity of domestic actors to achieve policy changes and qualifies their empowerment. The European liberalization of the transport sector, for example, empowered societal and political actors in highly regulated member states, which had been unsuccessfully pushing for privatization and deregulation. But while the German reform coalition was able to exploit European policies to overcome domestic opposition to liberalization, Italian trade unions, and sectoral associations successfully blocked any reform attempt (Héritier *et al*. 2001).

Existing *facilitating formal institutions* can provide actors with the resources necessary to exploit European opportunities and thus promote domestic adaptation (Risse, Cowles, and Caporaso 2001). These resources may be material, such as utilzing European funding to facilitate change, or ideational, such as importing ideas prevalent in the EU to the same end. The European political opportunity structure may thus offer domestic actors additional resources. But they are not able to deploy them when they lack the necessary action capacity. Direct relations with European decision-makers provide regions with the opportunity to circumvent their central government in European policy-making. But many regions do not have sufficient resources (manpower, money, expertise) to be permanently present at the European level and, thus, to exploit the new opportunities. In the UK, public agencies and related complementary institutions helped women's organizations with the means to use EU equal pay

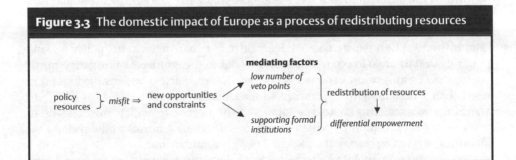

Figure 3.3 The domestic impact of Europe as a process of redistributing resources

and equal treatment directives in furthering gender equality. In the absence of such a formal institution, French women were not able to overcome domestic resistance to implement the EU equal pay and equal treatment policies (Caporaso and Jupille 2001; Tesoka 1999).

A low number of veto points and the existence of facilitating formal institutions determine whether policy and institutional misfit lead to a redistribution of resources and the differential empowerment of domestic actors as a result of which domestic processes, policies, and institutions get changed.

The domestic impact of Europe as a process of socialization

Socialization approaches draw on the sociological strand of neo-institutionalism, which contrast the rationalist 'logic of consequentialism' with a constructivist 'logic of appropriateness' (March and Olsen 1989; 1998). According to this logic, actors are guided by collectively shared understandings of what constitutes proper (i.e. socially accepted) behaviour in a given rule structure. Such collective understandings and intersubjective meaning structures strongly influence the way actors define their goals and what they perceive as rational action. Rather than maximizing their subjective desires, actors seek to 'do the right thing' (that is, to fulfil social expectations in a given situation). For example, it would be rational for a commuter who is exhausted after a long working day to keep his or her seat on the train ride home. However, most people probably yield their seat to elderly or pregnant women because this is what 'good citizens' are expected to do.

For sociological institutionalism, institutions do not simply regulate actors' behaviour by providing opportunities and constraints. They constitute actors by giving them a fundamental understanding of what their interests are and what the appropriate means may be to pursue these interests. Actors do not adhere to institutional norms and rules as a matter of choice but internalize them, take them for granted and follow them out of habit. From this perspective, European institutions are more than a political opportunity structure. They entail new rules, norms, practices, and structures of meaning, which the member states have to incorporate. Domestic actors are socialized into European norms and rules of appropriateness through processes of persuasion and social learning and redefine their interests and identities accordingly (cf. Checkel 1999a). This perspective generates expectations about the differential impact of Europeanization, since 'misfit' constitutes the starting condition of a socialization process. The more European norms, ideas, structures of meaning, or practices resonate (fit) with those at the domestic level, the more likely will they be incorporated into existing domestic institutions (Olsen 1996: 272) and the less likely they are to produce domestic change. The idea of cooperative governance emulated by the European Commission fits German cooperative federalism but challenges statist policy-making practices in Italy and Greece (Kohler-Koch 1998a). Yet, cognitive or normative misfit does not necessarily result in domestic change. Domestic actors and institutions often resist change despite significant pressure for adaptation.

Again, two mediating factors account for the degree to which misfit leads to processes of socialization by which actors internalize new norms and develop new identities: *norm entrepreneurs* and *cooperative informal institutions*.

Norm entrepreneurs mobilize at the domestic level to persuade actors to redefine their interests and identities in light of the new norms and rules by engaging them in processes of social learning. There are two types of norm- and idea-promoting agents. *Epistemic communities* are networks of actors with an authoritative claim to knowledge and a normative agenda (Haas 1992). They legitimate new norms and ideas by providing scientific knowledge about cause-and-effect relationships. In case of the single currency, the coalition of central bankers and national technocrats successfully advocated a monetarist approach which produced dramatic changes in domestic monetary policy, even in countries such as Italy and Greece which had to undergo painful adaptation (Dyson and Featherstone 1999; Radaelli 1998). *Advocacy* or *principled issue networks* are bound together by shared beliefs and values rather than by consensual knowledge (Keck and Sikkink 1998). They appeal to collectively shared norms and identities in order to persuade other actors to reconsider their goals and preferences. Such processes of complex or 'double-loop' learning (Agyris and Schön 1980), in which actors change their interests and identities as opposed to merely adjusting their means and strategies, occur rather rarely. While persuasion and social learning are mostly identified with processes of policy change, they can also have an effect on domestic institutions. As Checkel argues, Germany underwent a profound and constitutive change of its citizenship norms resulting from a learning process instigated by an advocacy network (Checkel 2001). And Kohler-Koch shows how the European Commission as an 'ideational entrepreneur' seeks to socialize domestic actors into new practices of cooperative governance by involving them in the formulation and implementation of European policies through transnational networks (Kohler-Koch 1999; Kohler-Koch *et al.* 1998b).

A cooperative political culture and other *cooperative informal institutions* are conducive to consensus-building and burden-sharing. Informal institutions entail collective understandings of appropriate behaviour that strongly influence the ways in which domestic actors respond to Europeanization pressures. First, a consensus-oriented or cooperative decision-making culture helps to overcome multiple veto points by rendering their use for actors inappropriate. Cooperative federalism prevented the German *Länder* from vetoing any of the European Treaty revisions, which deprived them of core decision powers (Börzel 2002b). Likewise, the litigational culture of Germany encouraged its citizens to appeal to national courts for the deficient application of Community Law, while such a culture was absent in France where litigation is much lower (Conant 2001). Secondly, a consensus-oriented political culture allows for a sharing of adaptational costs, which facilitates the accommodation of pressure for adaptation. Rather than shifting adaptational costs upon a social or political minority, the 'winners' of domestic change compensate the 'losers'. The consensual corporatist decision-making culture in the Netherlands and Germany facilitated the liberalization of the transport sector by offering compensation to the employees as the potential losers of the domestic changes (Héritier *et al.* 2001). Likewise, Vivien Schmidt shows that a particular discourse may also enhance the capacity of domestic actors to impose or negotiate adaptations to European requirements (Schmidt 2000). Cognitive arguments about the logic and necessity of new policies and institutional change serve relevant actors to legitimate costly adaptations and increase their acceptance. While an 'ideational discourse' facilitates the adoption of reform decisions, 'interactive discourse' helps to communicate these decisions to the general public.

A recent study looking at the domestic impact of Europe on the German parliament argues, however, that cooperative informal institutions may impair rather than

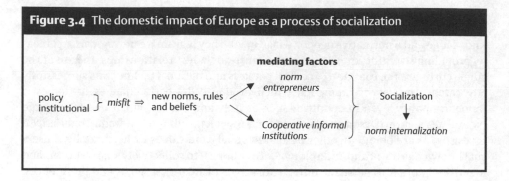

Figure 3.4 The domestic impact of Europe as a process of socialization

facilitate domestic change. The 'permissive consensus', which has existed in the Federal Republic of Germany since the late 1950s, when all major parties had coalesced around both the economic and political dimension of the European integration project, has prevented the German parliament from adapting its scrutiny procedures to the requirements of European policy-making and from making effective use of their participatory rights (Hansen and Scholl 2002). While the argument is plausible, it refers to a *substantive* pro-integrationist consensus among German elites rather than collectively shared understandings and beliefs (informal institutions) about cooperation and consensus-seeking as appropriate behaviour in public policy-making.

The existence of norm entrepreneurs and cooperative informal institutions affects whether European ideas, norms and the collective understandings, which do not resonate with those at the domestic level, are internalized by domestic actors giving rise to domestic change.

The domestic impact of Europe as a process of institutional adaptation

Institutional adaptation draws on organizational theory. It refers to the 'long-term substitution of existing practices and structures with new ones' (Olsen 1997: 159). Organizational theory identifies different causal mechanisms through which institutional adaptation can evolve. Like socialization approaches, institutional adaptation adopts a sociological institutionalist understanding of actors' behaviour and the nature of institutions (Powell and DiMaggio 1991). But its explanations follow a more structuralist reasoning emphasizing processes of institutional isomorphism. Institutions that frequently interact, are exposed to each other or are located in a similar environment develop similarities over time in formal organizational structures, principles of resource allocation, practices, meaning structures, and reform patterns (DiMaggio and Powell 1991; Meyer and Rowan 1991). This poses serious problems in explaining variation in institutional adaptation to a similar environment.

Some sociological institutionalists have addressed this problem by pointing at the 'inefficiency of history' in matching institutional practices and structures to environments and reforms (March and Olsen 1989: 54–6, March and Olsen 1995: 40–4). Institutions develop robustness towards changes in their functional and normative environments. First, institutional adaptation is path dependent. Existing institutions are not simply to be replaced or harmonized with new rules, norms, and practices. Profound and abrupt transformation, with a sudden elimination and replacement of established practices, meanings, and resource allocations, should be only expected under special circumstances (Olsen 1997: 162). Second, the more new institutional rules, norms, and practices are institutionalized, and the more they 'match' the constituting principles of already existing institutions (goodness of fit), the more likely are institutions to incorporate these new rules, norms, and practices (Olsen 1997: 161). Variation in institutional adaptation is explained by the different degrees to which new and existing institutions match each other. If institutional isomorphism is to evolve, it is the result of a long-term process in which some institutions have to undergo deeper change than others do.

Institutional adaptation approaches also view European institutions as new norms, rules, practices, and structures of meaning, which are diffused to the member states. Institutional isomorphism points to four diffusion mechanisms, which can result in domestic change (Olsen 2002; Knill and Lehnkuhl 1999; Radaelli 2000):

- *Coercion*: The EU positively prescribes or imposes a model with which the member states have to comply, (for example European monetary integration that requires the member states to meet certain macro-economic targets related to public deficits, debt, and inflation rates and make their central banks independent) (Dyson 2000).

- *Imitation and normative pressure*: Member states emulate a model recommended by the EU to avoid uncertainty (*imitation*) or that has been successfully implemented by other states (*normative pressure*) as occurred in the liberalization of the telecommunication sector, where member states have introduced independent regulatory agencies that monitor, license, and regulate (Schneider 2001).

- *Competitive selection* (regulatory competition): while the EU neither imposes nor recommends a model, member states compete for the most efficient domestic arrangements in order to avoid comparative disadvantages. Transport liberalization policies, for instance, by which the EU demands the member states to open their market to non-resident competitors, do not say how a liberalized market is to be governed. But EU liberalization puts pressure on member states to change their market regulations in order to avoid regulatory burdens restricting the competitiveness of their domestic industry (Kerwer and Teutsch 2001).

- *Framing*: European actors can behave as 'ideational entrepreneurs', trying to alter the beliefs and expectations of domestic actors by disseminating new ideas and concepts, such as the principle of cooperative governance, which the Commission propagated in order to improve European regional development (Kohler-Koch 2002).

Figure 3.5 The domestic impact of Europe as a process of institutional adaptation

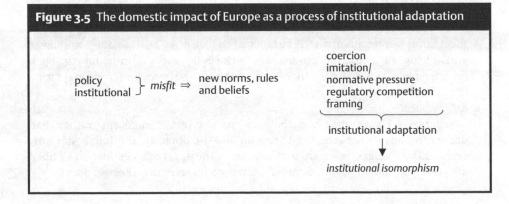

Each of the four diffusion mechanisms is captured by either resource-dependency or socialization approaches. The coercion into a European model that does not fit domestic policies, institutions, and processes can empower domestic reform coalitions and/or socialize them into new norms and beliefs. Likewise, regulatory competition as a result of market-making policies induces domestic change through limiting the opportunities of states to protect their markets while creating new opportunities for customers to buy goods and services from foreign providers. Moreover, EU demands for market liberalizing may empower domestic actors by providing them with political legitimacy to push for deregulation and privatisation (Héritier *et al.* 2001: 257). Mimetic imitation, normative pressure and framing work through processes of social learning, often induced by norm or ideational entrepreneurs, which seek to persuade domestic actors to alter their beliefs and interests in response to European requirements.

Subsuming institutional adaptation under the other two approaches also allows to account for variation beyond the 'goodness of fit' since the isomorphism literature has failed to specify mediating factors that help explain why domestic institutions facing similar degrees of misfit still vary with regard to the outcome of domestic change. This is all the more true since the different processes or mechanisms of domestic change are complementary rather than mutually exclusive. Mediating factors often occur simultaneously reinforcing their effects but at times also pulling in different directions (Hansen and Scholl 2002). Or they characterize different phases in processes of change. Future research has to figure out how the causal mechanisms relate to each other (Börzel and Risse 2003; Olsen 2002).

Outcome of domestic change

While we have rather specific ideas about when and how Europe affects the member states, we know less about outcomes, that is, the scope and direction of domestic change.

Deep impact? The scope of domestic change

The literature broadly distinguishes between five different outcomes regarding the scope or degree of change (Héritier *et al.* 2001; Radaelli 2000; Cowles, Caporaso, and Risse 2001).

- *Inertia*
  Inertia refers to the absence of change. This is not the result of a fit between European and domestic policies, institutions, and processes that may reaffirm existing arrangements. Rather, member states resist the adaptations necessary to meet European requirements. Resistance to change often leads to non-compliance with European legislation against which the European Commission can open infringement proceedings, thereby increasing the pressure for adaptation (Börzel 2001).
- *Retrenchment*
  Resistance to change may have the paradoxical effect of increasing rather than decreasing misfits between the European and the domestic level. Italy not only resisted the changes necessary to liberalize its transport market. Instead of liberalization, the Italian government has increased intervention (Kerwer 2001).

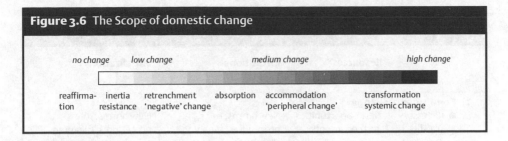

Figure 3.6 The Scope of domestic change

- *Absorption*
  Member states incorporate European requirements into their domestic institutions and policies without substantial modifications of existing structures and the logic of political behaviour. The degree of change is low.
- *Accommodation*
  Member states accommodate European pressure by adapting existing processes, policies and institutions in their periphery without changing core features and the underlying collective understandings attached to them (Knill 2001). One way of doing this is by 'patching up' new policies and institutions onto existing ones without changing the latter (Héritier 2001). The degree of domestic change is modest.
- *Transformation*
  Member states replace existing policies, processes, and institutions by new, substantially different ones, or alter existing ones to the extent that their core features and/or the underlying collective understandings are fundamentally changed. The degree of domestic change is high affecting the core of system-wide political, economic and social structures (Risse, Cowles, and Caporaso 2001: 15), such as the constitutional balance of power between domestic institutions, the political culture of a country or macroeconomic policies and the currencies of the member states.

The different theoretical approaches generate different propositions about the scope of domestic change (see Figure 3.7). They all take misfit as the necessary condition of domestic change and converge around the expectation that the lower the misfit, the smaller the pressure for adaptation and thus the lower the degree of domestic change. But the three approaches depart on the effect of high misfit. For resource dependency, the higher the misfit, the more likely domestic reform coalitions will be empowered. Whether high misfit results in transformation or only accommodation depends on the number of veto points and the existence of supporting institutions. Institutional adaptation and socialization, by contrast, would expect high misfit challenging core features of domestic policies and institutions to result in inertia since domestic actors will refuse to simply replace norms, rules, and practices by new ones (Knill 2001). Actors are more open to learning and persuasion if new norms, rules, and practices resonate with the ones they are familiar with (Checkel 1999b). Transformation should only occur under exceptional circumstances, such as performance crises (Olsen 1996) or powerful norm entrepreneurs supported by some coercive pressures in the form of sanctions (Risse, Ropp, and Sikkink 1999).

Figure 3.7 Approaches to the domestic impact of Europe in comparison

	Resource dependency	Institutional adaptation	Socialization
1) Conditions of change			
■ necessary (misfit)	New opportunities and constraints	New norms, rules, procedures, meaning structures	New norms, rules, procedures, meaning structures
■ sufficient (mediating factors)	Low number of veto points formal supporting institutions		Norm entrepreneurs informal cooperative institutions
2) Process of Change			
	Redistribution of resources resulting in differential empowerment	Institutional Adaptation through coercion, mimetic imitation, normative pressure, regulatory competition, and framing resulting in isomorphism	Socialization through persuasion and social learning resulting from norm internalization
3) Outcome of Change			
■ scope of change	*Increases* with the degree of misfit, the declining number of veto points and/or the presence of formal institutions	Low misfit: *low* (absorption) Medium misfit: *medium* (accommodation) High misfit: *low* (inertia; retrenchment) *high* (transformation) under conditions of crisis	Low misfit: *low* (absorption) Medium misfit: *Medium* (accommodation) if presence of norm entrepreneurs and/or cooperative institutions; High misfit: *low* (inertia, retrenchment) in the absence of norm entrepreneurs and cooperative institutions; *medium* (accommodation) in the presence of norm entrepreneurs and cooperative institutions; *high* (transformation) if exceptionally powerful norm entrepreneurs or under conditions of crisis
direction of change	differential impact, 'clustered convergence'	Convergence over time as result of isomorphism	Differential impact, 'clustered convergence'

Coming together or driving apart? The direction of domestic change

Is Europe making the member states more similar? The literature has found little evidence for a homogenization or *convergence* of domestic institutions, policies, and processes toward common models and approaches (Cowles, Caporaso, and Risse 2001; Héritier *et al.* 2001; Anderson 2002). This does not mean that Europe has no effect on the member states. Its domestic impact is not the same as convergence. Europe may cause convergence (Schneider 2001; Harcourt 2003) but in most cases it rather does not. This is not too surprising if we accept that the effect of European policies, institutions, and processes is filtered through existing domestic institutions, policies, and interests. The number of veto points, supporting formal institutions, norm entrepreneurs, and cooperative informal institutions mediate between European pressures for adaptation and the outcome of domestic change. We should expect at best some 'clustered convergence' among member states facing similar pressures for adaptation because similar actors are empowered and are likely to learn from each other in searching effective ways of responding to European pressures (Börzel 1999). Institutional adaptation approaches appear to lean more towards convergence since they draw on arguments about institutional isomorphism (see Figure 3.7). Institutions that frequently interact are expected to become more alike. Yet, institutional isomorphism only evolves over time and is mediated through institutional path dependencies, even though the concept is not clearly specified (e.g. by identifying mediating factors (see above)).

Despite its differential impact, however, Europe has not caused *divergence* among the member states either, driving them further apart. There are no indications that member state variation in their domestic institutions and policies has increased.[4] The dominant finding is persistence and diversity that needs to be explained. Consequently, measuring convergence and divergence may be of limited use in analysing the domestic impact of Europe, particularly since answers vary according to the level at which one looks for convergence or divergence (Knill and Lenschow 2001b).

Finally, the convergence we observe does not necessarily originate at the European level (Schneider 2001; Schmidt 2001). This also applies to domestic change in general. Europe is not always the driving force but complements and enhances trends that were already affecting the member states. We have to employ counterfactuals and test for alternative explanations (Schmitter 1999: 296–7; Goetz 2000: 225–8). Globalization appears to be the major rival for Europeanization in driving domestic change. While some studies have attempted to separate effects of Europeanization and globalization (Verdier and Breen 2001; Schneider 2001), it is often difficult to isolate the 'net effect' of Europe and to disentangle it from other sources of domestic change not only at the global, but also at the national and local level (Anderson, J. 2003).

Tracing the causes, processes, and outcomes of domestic change becomes even more 'muddled' if we seek to account for the interactive and recursive nature of the relationship between the EU and its member states.

---

[4] Convergence in general is defined by a decreasing variation in the relevant indicators (Martin and Simmons 1998; cf. Unger and van Waarden 1995).

Bringing the bottom-up perspective back in

The relationship between the EU and its member states is not a one-way street. Member states are not merely passive receivers of European demands for domestic change. They may proactively shape European policies, institutions, and processes to which they have to adapt later (Bomberg and Peterson 2000; see already Wallace 1971 and Héritier *et al.* 1994). Moreover, the need to adapt domestically to European pressures may have significant return effects at the European level, where member states seek to reduce the misfit between European and domestic arrangements (Dyson 2003; Jeffery 2003).

One way of linking the bottom-up and top-down dimension in the relationship between the EU and its member states is to focus on the role of national governments in the ascending (policy formulation decision-making) and descending (implementation) stage of the European policy process. This is not to say that supranational actors, such as the European Commission or the European Parliament, are irrelevant to European policy-making. Nor do member state governments necessarily 'gate-keep' the access of domestic interests to the European policy arena. Nevertheless, national executives hold a key position in both the decision-making and the implementation of European policies and thus influence the way in which member states shape European policies and institutions and adapt to them (see Bulmer and Lequesne in this volume).

The European policy process can be conceptualized as a 'reciprocal relationship' (Andersen and Liefferink 1997: 10; 1998) between political negotiations at the domestic and the European level. At the domestic level, actors pressure their national executives to pursue policies at the European level that are favourable to their interests. At the European level, the member state governments push for European policies that satisfy domestic pressures, while minimizing their adverse consequences at the domestic level (Putnam 1988: 434). Two-level game approaches establish a systematic relationship between domestic and European politics, with the national governments functioning as the core intermediators between the two. Furthermore, two-level game approaches provide a link between the ascending (decision-making) and the descending (implementation) stage of the European policy process (see also Helen Wallace's Chapter 2). Except for treaty revisions, European decisions are legally binding for the member states and, hence, do not require ratification at the domestic level. Yet, while regulations are directly applicable, national parliaments must transpose directives into national law. Moreover, both regulations and transposed directives have to be practically applied and enforced by national administrations. Compliance problems with European policies often arise when public administrators, economic and societal actors are not willing to bear the implementation burden (Börzel 2000; 2003). They usually blame their national governments for the costs, which European policies place on them. At the same time, member state governments are held responsible by the Commission and the European Court of Justice, if European policies are not properly implemented and complied with. Consequently, member state governments tend to be rather cost sensitive in European policy-making.

An effective strategy of maximizing the benefits and minimizing the costs of European policies is to 'up-load' or export national policies to the European level. First, 'up-loading' reduces the need for legal and administrative adaptation in 'down-loading' (that is incorporating European policies into national policy structures). The more a European policy fits the domestic context, the lower the costs of adaptation in the implementation process. In the absence of an elaborate policy structure, misfitting European policies may still inflict significant costs since these structures have to be built-up in the first place. Second, 'up-loading' prevents competitive disadvantages for domestic industry. Imposing strict standards on lower-regulating member states maintains the competitive situation of the industry in higher-regulating countries. Likewise, European liberalization and deregulation policies open new markets for industries from low-regulating countries that benefit from lower production costs. Finally, 'up-loading' may enable national governments to address problems, which pre-occupy their constituencies but cannot be effectively dealt with at the domestic level anymore (for example organized crime, environmental pollution, immigration).

Member states share a general incentive to up-load their policy arrangements to the European level. But since they have distinct social, political, and economic institutions, they often compete for policies that conform to the preferences of their constituencies (Héritier 1996). Thus, the British government, which runs a country with a rather open economy, may push for liberalization and deregulation in a policy sector. The French government, by contrast, wishes to defend its traditional approach of protecting certain industries from external competition (Ambler and Reichert 2001). Likewise, high-regulating countries seek to harmonize their strict social or environmental standards at the European level where they may meet the vigorous opposition of industrial latecomers, which want to avoid competitive disadvantages for their industry. But not only do member state governments pursue diverging and often competing policy preferences. They also differ in their capacity to successfully engage in the European policy contest.

In environmental policy, the Northern European 'first-comers' (Denmark, Netherlands, Germany, Sweden, Finland, Austria) not only have a strong incentive to harmonize their strict environmental standards at the European level to avoid competitive disadvantages for their industries and avoid adaptations in their regulatory structures. They also have the action capacity (resources) to actively shape European policies according to their environmental concerns and economic interests. The Southern European 'late-comers' (Greece, Spain, Portugal, Italy) lack both the policies and the action capacity (money, staff power, expertise, administrative coordination) to up-load them to the European level (cf. Börzel 2002a; 2003). Since they are policy takers rather than policy makers, the Southern member states are far more likely to run into serious policy misfit than the Northern pace-setters. The result is a somewhat paradoxical situation where those member states with the most limited policy-making capacities bear the highest implementation costs since they have to adapt their domestic policies and institutions much more than their Northern counterparts.

The regulatory contest in European (environmental) policy-making illustrates the interactive and recursive nature of the relationship between the EU and its member states, where bottom-up dynamics in the EU policy process have serious implications for explaining the domestic impact of European policies on the member states.

Others have made similar arguments about a 'competition among different national modes of governance', where 'Member States aim to reduce their adaptation costs by transferring their national modes of governance to the European level' (Eising and Kohler-Koch 1999: 271; cf. Bulmer 1997; Bulmer, Jeffery, and Paterson 2000). Future research should systematically explore the links and feedback loops between the bottom-up and top-down dimension of the relationship between the EU and its member states.

Further reading

Goetz and Hix (2000) as well as Featherstone and Radaelli (2003) offer good surveys of the intellectual puzzles posed by Europeanization as well as exploring the tool kit for addressing them. Cowles, Caporaso, and Risse (2001) and Héritier *et al.* (2001), offer pioneering book-length Europeanization studies that follow particular, yet different, analytical approaches and test conceptual hypotheses.

Web links

The most relevant website to issues relating to Europeanization is offered by the webportal that brings together various online papers on EU studies <**http://eiop.or.at/erpa/**>. Several of the published chapters and articles on Europeanization were first available at this site, notably on the European Integration online papers series. There are also specific paper series, also accessible via this portal, that are dedicated to Europeanization.

References

Aguilar Fernandez, S. (1993), 'Corporatist and Statist Design in Environmental Policy: The Contrasting Roles of Germany and Spain in the European Community Scenario', *Environmental Politics* 2/2, 223–47.

Agyris, C., and Schöq, D. (1980), *Organizational Learning* (Reading, MA: Addison-Wesley).

Ambler, J., and Reichert, M. S. (2001), 'France: Europeanism, Nationalism, and the Planned Economy', in E. E. Zeff and E. B. Pirro (eds), *The European Union and the Member States. Cooperation, Coordination, and*

Compromise (Boulder, CO: Lynne Rienner), 29–57.

Andersen, M. S., and Liefferink, D. (1997), 'Introduction: The Impact of the Pioneers on EU Environmental Policy', in M. S. Andersen and D. Liefferink (eds), *European Environmental Policy. The Pioneers* (Manchester: Manchester University Press), 1–39.

Anderson, J. (2002), 'Europeanization and the Transformation of the Democratic Polity', *Journal of Common Market Studies* 40/5, 793–822.

Anderson, J. (2003), 'Europeanization in Context: Concept and Theory', in K. Dyson and K. H. Goetz (eds), *Germany and Europe: A 'Europeanised' Germany?* (Oxford: Oxford University Press), 37–53.

Anderson, K. (2002), 'The Europeanization of Pension Arrangements: Convergence or Divergence?', in C. De la Porte and P. Pochet (eds), *Building Social Europe through the Open Method of Co-ordination* (Brussels: Peter Lang), 251–83.

Bomberg, E., and Peterson, J. (2000), 'Policy Transfer and Europeanization: Passing the Heineken Test?' *Queen's Paper on Europeanization* (2/2000) <http://ideas.uqam.ca/ideas/data/erpqueens.html>.

Börzel, T. (1999), 'Towards Convergence in Europe? Institutional Adaptation to Europeanisation in Germany and Spain', *Journal of Common Market Studies* 37/4, 573–96.

Börzel, T. (2000), 'Why there is no Southern Problem. On Environmental Leader and Laggards in the EU', *Journal of European Public Policy* 7/1, 141–62.

Börzel, T. (2001), 'Non-Compliance in the European Union. Pathology or Statistical Artefact?', *Journal of European Public Policy* 8/5, 803–24.

Börzel, T. (2002a), 'Pace-Setting, Foot-Dragging, and Fence-Sitting: Member State Responses to Europeanization', *Journal of Common Market Studies* 40/2, 193–214.

Börzel, T. (2002b), *States and Regions in the European Union. Institutional Adaptation in Germany and Spain* (Cambridge: Cambridge Univeristy Press).

Börzel, T. (2003), *Environmental Leaders and Laggards in the European Union. Why There is (Not) a Southern Problem* (London: Ashgate).

Börzel, T., and Risse, T. (2000), 'When Europe Hits Home: Europeanization and Domestic Change', *European Integration on-line Papers* 4/15 <http://eiop.or.at/eiop/texte/2000-015a.htm>.

Börzel, T., and Risse, T. (2003), 'Conceptualising the Domestic Impact of Europe', in K. Featherstone and C. Radaelli (eds), *The Politics of Europeanisation* (Oxford: Oxford University Press).

Bulmer, S. (1997), 'Shaping the Rules? The Constitutive Politics of the European Union and German Power', in P. J. Katzenstein (ed.), *Tamed Power: Germany in Europe* (Ithaca, NY: Cornell University Press), 49–79.

Bulmer, S., Jeffery, C., and Paterson, W. (2000), *Germany's European Diplomacy. Shaping the Regional Milieu* (Manchester: Manchester University Press).

Caporaso, J., and Jupille, J. (2001), 'The Europeanization of Gender Equality Policy and Domestic Structural Change', in M. G. Cowles, J. A. Caporaso, and T. Risse (eds), *Transforming Europe. Europeanization and Domestic Change* (Ithaca, NY: Cornell University Press), 21–43.

Caporaso, J., and Keeler, J. (1993), 'The European Community and Regional Integration Theory', in A. Cafruny and G. Rosenthal (eds), *The State of the European Community II: The Maastricht Debate and Beyond* (Boulder, CO: Lynne Rienner).

Checkel, J. (1999a), 'International Institutions and Socialization'. *ARENA Working Paper* (5).

Checkel, J. (1999b), 'Norms, Institutions, and National Identity in Contemporary Europe', *International Studies Quarterly* 43/1, 83–114.

Checkel, J. (2001), 'The Europeanization of Citizenship?' in M. G. Cowles, J. A. Caporaso, and T. Risse (eds), *Transforming Europe. Europeanization and Domestic Change* (Ithaca, NY: Cornell University Press), 180–97.

Conant, L. (2001), 'Europeanization and the Courts: Variable Patterns of Adaptation among National Judiciaries', in M. G. Cowles, J. A. Caporaso, and T. Risse (eds), *Transforming Europe. Europeanization and Domestic Change* (Ithaca, NY: Cornell University Press), 97–115.

Cowles, M. G. (2001), 'The TABD and Domestic Business-Government Relations', in M. G. Cowles, J. A. Caporaso, and T. Risse (eds), *Europeanization and Domestic Political Change* (Ithaca, NY: Cornell University Press), 159–79.

Cowles, M. G., Caporaso, J., and Risse, T. (eds) (2001), *Transforming Europe. Europeanization and Domestic Change* (Ithaca, NY: Cornell University Press).

DiMaggio, P., and Powell, W. (1991), 'The Iron Cage Revisited: Institutional Isomorphism and Collective Rationality in Organizational Fields', in W. W. Powell and P. J. DiMaggio (eds), *The New Institutionalism in Organizational Analysis* (Chicago, London: University of Chicago Press), 63–82.

Duina, F. (1999), *Harmonizing Europe. Nation-States within the Common Market*. (New York: State University of New York Press).

Dyson, K. (2000), 'EMU as Europeanization: Convergence, Diversity and Contingency', *Journal of Common Market Studies* 38/4, 645–66.

Dyson, K. (2003), 'Economic Policies: From Pace-Setter to Beleaguered Model', in K. Dyson and K. H. Goetz (eds), *Germany and Europe: A Europeanized Germany* (Oxford: Oxford University Press), 201–29.

Dyson, K., and Featherstone, K. (1999), *The Road to Maastricht* (Oxford: Oxford University Press).

Eising, R., and Kohler-Koch, B. (1999), 'Governance in the European Union. A Comparative Assessment', in B. Kohler-Koch and R. Eising (eds), *The Transformation of Governance in the European Union* (London: Routledge), 267–85.

Featherstone, K., and Radaelli, C. (2003) (eds), *The Politics of Europeanization* (Oxford: Oxford University Press).

Goetz, K. (2000), 'European Integration and National Executives: A Cause in Search of an Effect?', *West European Politics, Special Issue* 23/4, 211–31.

Goetz, K., and Hix, S. (eds) (2000), *Europeanised Politics? European Integration and National Political Systems* (London: Frank Cass).

Grabbe, H. (2003), 'Europeanisation Goes East. Power and Uncertainty in the EU Accession Process', in K. Featherstone and C. Radaelli (eds), *The Politics of Europeanisation* (Oxford: Oxford University Press).

Haas, E. (1958), *The Uniting of Europe: Political, Social, and Economic Forces, 1950–1957* (Stanford, CA: Stanford University Press).

Haas, P. (1992), 'Introduction: Epistemic Communities and International Policy Coordination', *International Organization* 46/1, 1–36.

Hall, P., and Taylor, R. (1996), 'Political Science and the Three New Institutionalisms', *Political Studies* XLIV/5, 936–57.

Hansen, T., and Scholl, B. (2002), 'Europeanization and Domestic Parliamentary Adaptation. A Comparative Analysis of the Bundestag and the House of Commons', *European Integration online Papers* 6 (15): http://eiop.or.at/eiop/texte/2002-015a.htm.

Harcourt, A. (2003), 'Europeanization as Convergence: The Regulation of Media Markets in the European Union' in K. Featherstone and C. Radaelli (eds), *The Politics of Europeanisation* (Oxford: Oxford University Press), 179–202.

Haverland, M. (2000), 'National Adaptation to European Integration: The Importance of Institutional Veto Points', *Journal of Public Policy* 20/1, 83–103.

Héritier, A. (1996), 'The Accommodation of Diversity in European policy-making and Its Outcomes: Regulatory Policy as a Patchwork', *Journal of European Public Policy* 3/2, 149–76.

Héritier, A. (2001), 'Differential Europe: National Administrative Responses to Community Policy', in M. G. Cowles, J. A. Caporaso, and T. Risse (eds), *Transforming Europe. Europeanization and Domestic Change* (Ithaca, NY: Cornell University Press), 44–59.

Héritier, A. (2002), 'New Modes of Governance in Europe: Policy-Making without Legislating?', in A. Héritier (ed.), *Common Goods. Reinventing European and International Governance* (Langham, MD: Rowman & Littlefield), 185–206.

Héritier, A., Kerwer, D., Knill, C., Lehmkuh D., Teutsch, M., and Douillet, A.-C. (2001), *Differential Europe. The European Union Impact on National Policymaking* (Lanham, MD: Rowman & Littlefield).

Héritier, A., Knill, C., and Mingers, S. (1996), *Ringing the Changes in Europe. Regulatory Competition and the Redefinition of the State: Britain, France, Germany* (Berlin, New York: De Gruyter).

Héritier, A., Knill, C., Mingers, S., and Becka, M. (1994), *Die Veränderung von Staatlichkeit in Europa. Ein regulativer Wettbewerb*.

Deutschland, Großbritannien, Frankreich.
(Opladen: Leske and Budrich).

Hix, S., (1999), *The Political System of the European Union* (London: Macmillan).

Hix, S., and Goetz, K. (2000), 'Introduction: European Integration and National Political Systems', *West European Politics, Special Issue* 23/4, 1–26.

Hoffmann, S. (1982), 'Reflections on the Nation-State in Western Europe Today', *Journal of Common Market Studies* 20/1–2, 29–37.

Hooghe, L., and Marks, G. (2001), *Multi-Level Governance and European Integration* (Lanham: Rowman & Littlefield).

Jeffery, C. (ed.) (1997), *The Regional Dimension of the European Union. Towards a Third Level in Europe?* (London: Frank Cass).

Jeffery, C. (2003), 'The German Länder and Europe: From Milieu-Shaping to Territorial Politics', in K. Dyson and K. H. Goetz (eds), *Germany and Europe: A Europeanized Germany?* (Oxford: Oxford University Press), 97–108.

Katzenstein, P. (1997), 'United Germany in an Integrating Europe', in P. J. Katzenstein (ed.), *Shaping the Rules? The Constitutive Politics of the European Union and German Power* (Ithaca, NY: Cornell University Press), 1–48.

Keck, M., and Sikkink, K. (1998), *Activists Beyond Borders: Advocacy Networks in International Politics* (Ithaca, NY: Cornell University Press).

Kerwer, D. (2001), *Regulatory Reforms in Italy. A Case Study in Europeanisation* (Aldershot: Ashgate).

Kerwer, D., and Teutsch, M. (2001), 'Elusive Europeanisation. Liberalising Road Haulage in the European Union', *Journal of European Public Policy* 8/1, 124–43.

Knill, C. (2001), *The Transformation of National Administrations in Europe. Patterns of Change and Persistence* (Cambridge: Cambridge University Press).

Knill, C. and Lehmkuhl, D. (1999), 'How Europe Matters. Different Mechanisms of Europeanization', *European Integration on-line Papers* 3/7 <http://eiop.or.at/eiop/texte/1999-007a.htm>.

Knill, C., and Lenschow, A. (2001a), 'Adjusting to EU Environmental Policy: Change and Persistence of Domestic Administrations', in M. G. Cowles, J. A. Caporaso, and T. Risse (eds), *Transforming Europe. Europeanization and Domestic Change* (Ithaca, NY: Cornell University Press), 116–36.

Knill, C., and Lenschow, A. (2001b), ' "Seek and Ye Shall Find": Linking Different Perspectives on Institutional Change', *Comparative Political Studies* 34, 187–215.

Kohler-Koch, B. (1996), 'The Strength of Weakness. The Transformation of Governance in the EU', in S. Gustavsson and L. Lewin (eds), *The Future of the Nation State. Essays on Cultural Pluralism and Political Integration* (Stockholm: Nerenius & Santerus), 169–210.

Kohler-Koch, B. (1998a), 'Europäisierung der Regionen: Institutioneller Wandel als sozialer Prozeß', in B. Kohler-Koch (ed.), *Interaktive Politik in Europa. Regionen im Netzwerk der Integration* (Opladen: Leske and Budrich), 13–31.

Kohler-Koch, B. (1999), 'The Evolution and Transformation of European Governance', in B. Kohler-Koch and R. Eising (eds), *The Transformation of Governance in the European Union* (London: Routledge), 14–35.

Kohler-Koch, B. (2002), 'European Networks and Ideas: Changing National Policies?', *European Integration on-line Papers* 6 (6): <http://eiop.or.at/eiop/texte/2002-006a.htm>.

Kohler-Koch, B., and Eising, R. (eds) (1999), *The Transformation of Governance in Europe* (London: Routledge).

Kohler-Koch, B. *et al.* (1998b), *Interaktive Politik in Europa. Regionen im Netzwerk der Integration* (Opladen: Leske and Budrich).

Ladrech, R. (1994), 'Europeanization of Domestic Politics and Institutions: The Case of France', *Journal of Common Market Studies* 32/1, 69–88.

Liefferink, D., and Andersen, M. S. (1998), 'Strategies of the "Green" Member States in EU Environmental Policy-making', *Journal of European Public Policy* 5/2, 254–70.

March, J., and Olsen, J. (1989), *Rediscovering Institutions* (New York: The Free Press).

March, J., and Olsen, J. (1995), *Democratic Governance.* (New York: The Free Press).

68 TANJA A. BÖRZEL

March, J., and Olsen, J. (1998), 'The Institutional Dynamics of International Political Orders', *International Organization* 52/4, 943–69.

Marks, G. (1993), 'Structural Policy and Multilevel Governance in the European Community', in A. Cafruny and G. Rosenthal (eds), *The State of the European Community II: Maastricht Debates and Beyond* (Boulder: Lynne Riener), 391–410.

Marks, G., Hooghe, L., and Blank, K. (1996), 'European Integration from the 1980s: State-centric v. Multi-level Governance', *Journal of Common Market Studies* 34/3, 341–78.

Martin, L., and Simmons, B. (1998), 'Theories and Empirical Studies of International Institutions', *International Organization* 52/4, 729–57.

Mény, Y., Muller, P., and Quermonne, J.-L. (eds) (1996), *Adjusting to Europe: The Impact of the European Union on National Institutions and Policies* (London: Routledge).

Meyer, J., and Rowan, B. (1991), 'Institutional Organizations: Formal Structure as Myth and Ceremony', in W. W. Powell and P. J. DiMaggio (eds), *The New Institutionalism in Organizational Analysis* (Chicago and London: University of Chicago Press), 41–62.

Milward, A. (1992), *The European Rescue of the Nation-State* (Berkeley, CA.: University of California Press).

Moravcsik, A. (1991), 'Negotiating the Single European Act: National Interests and Conventional Statecraft in the European Community', *International Organization* 45(1), 19–56.

Moravcsik, A. (1994), *Why the European Community Strengthens the State: Domestic Politics and International Cooperation*. Working Paper, 52. (Cambridge, MA.: Harvard University).

Moravcsik, A. (1998), *The Choice for Europe: Social Purpose and State Power From Rome to Maastricht* (Ithaca, NY: Cornell University Press).

Morlino, L. (1999), 'Europeanization and Representation in Two Europes: Local Institutions and National Parties'. Paper presented at the conference 'Multi-Party Systems: Europeanization and the Reshaping of National Political Representation', European University Institute, Florence, 16–18 December 1999.

Olsen, J. (1996), 'Europeanization and Nation-State Dynamics', in S. Gustavsson and L. Lewin (eds), *The Future of the Nation-State* (London: Routledge), 245–85.

Olsen, J. (1997), 'European Challenges to the Nation State', in B. Steunenberg and F. v. Vught (eds), *Political Institutions and Public Policy* (The Hague et al.: Kluver Academic Publishers), 157–88.

Olsen, J. (2002), 'The Many Faces of Europeanization', *Journal of Common Market Studies* 40/5, 921–50.

Powell, W., and DiMaggio, P. (eds) (1991), *The New Institutionalism in Organizational Analysis* (Chicago and London: University of Chicago Press).

Putnam, R. (1988), 'Diplomacy and Domestic Politics. The Logic of Two-Level Games', *International Organization* 42/2, 427–60.

Radaelli, C. (1998), 'Networks of Expertise and Policy Change in Italy', *South European Society and Politics* 3/2, 1–22.

Radaelli, C. (2000), 'Whither Europeanization? Concept Stretching and Substantive Change', *European Integration on-line Papers* 4 (8): <http://eiop.or.at/eiop/texte/2000-008a.htm>.

Rhodes, R. A. W. (1997), *Understanding Governance. Policy Networks, Governance, Reflexivity and Accountability* (Buckingham and Philadelphia: Open University Press).

Risse, T. (2001), 'A European Identity? Europeanization and the Evolution of Nation-State Identities', in M. G. Cowles, J. A. Caporaso, and T. Risse (eds), *Transforming Europe. Europeanization and Domestic Change* (Ithaca, NY: Cornell University Press), 198–216.

Risse, T., Cowles, M. G., and Caporaso, J. A. (2001), 'Europeanization and Domestic Change: Introduction', in M. G. Cowles, J. A. Caporaso, and T. Risse (eds), *Transforming Europe. Europeanization and Domestic Change* (Ithaca, NY: Cornell University Press), 1–20.

Risse, T., Ropp, S., and Sikkink, K. (eds) (1999), *The Power of Human Rights. International Norms and Domestic Change* (Cambridge: Cambridge University Press).

Risse-Kappen, T. (1996), 'Exploring the Nature of the Beast: International Relations Theory and Comparative Policy Analysis Meet the European Union', *Journal of Common Market Studies* 34/1, 53–80.

Sandholtz, W. (1996), 'Membership Matters: Limits of the Functional Approach to European Institutions', *Journal of Common Market Studies* 34/3, 403–29.

Sandholtz, W., and Stone Sweet, A. (eds) (1998), *European Integration and Supranational Governance* (Oxford: Oxford University Press).

Schmidt, V. (1996), *From State to Market? The Transformation of French Business and Government.* (Cambridge: Cambridge University Press).

Schmidt, V. (2000), 'Democracy and Discourse in an Integrating Europe and a Globalizing World', *European Law Journal* 6/3, 277–300.

Schmidt, V. (2001), Europeanization and the Mechanisms of Economic Policy Adjustments', *European Integration on-line Papers* 5/6 <http://eiop.or.at/eiop/texte/2001-006a.htm>.

Schmitter, P. (1999), 'Reflections on the Impact of the European Union upon "Domestic" Democracy in its Member States', in M. Egeberg and P. Lægreid (eds), *Organizing Political Institutions. Essays for Johan P. Olsen* (Oslo: Scandinavian University Press), 289–98.

Schneider, V. (2001), 'Institutional Reform in Telecommunications: The European Union in Transnational Policy Diffusion', in

M. G. Cowles, J. A. Caporaso, and T. Risse (eds), *Transforming Europe. Europeanization and Domestic Change* (Ithaca, NY: Cornell University Press), 60–78.

Sun, J-M., and Pelkmans, J. (1995), 'Regulatory Competition in the Single Market', *Journal of Common Market Studies* 33/1, 67–89.

Taylor, P. (1991), 'The European Community and the State: Assumptions, Theories and Propositions', *Review of International Studies* 17/1, 109–25.

Tesoka, S. (1999), *Judicial Politics in the European Union: Its Impact on National Opportunity Structures for Gender Equality.* MPIfG Discussion Paper, 99/2. (Köln: Max-Planck-Institut für Gesellschaftsforschung).

Tsebelis, G. (1995), 'Decision Making in Political Systems. Veto Players in Presidentialism, Parliamentarism, Multicameralism and Multipartism', *British Journal of Political Science* 25/3, 289–325.

Unger, B., and van Waarden, F. (1995), 'Introduction: An Interdisciplinary Approach to Convergence', in B. Unger and F. van Waarden. (eds), *Convergence or Diversity? Internationalization and Economic Policy Response* (Avebury: Aldershot), 1–35.

Verdier, D., and Breen, R. (2001), 'Europeanization and Globalization. Politics against Markets in the European Union', *Comparative Political Studies* 34/1, 227–62.

Wallace, H. (1971), 'The Impact of the European Communities on National Policy-Making', *Government and Opposition* 6/4, 520–38.

Weiler, J. (1991), 'The Transformation of Europe', *Yale Law Journal* 108/8, 2403–83.

Part II

The Member States

Introduction

This Part of the book is organized by member state. It does not take the conventional approach of having one chapter for each member state. With twenty-five members, that kind of format would dictate a large book and exclude other perspectives on the relationship between the EU and its states. In consequence, we devote some chapters to individual states; we treat others in groupings, including those which acceded in May 2004; and finally we offer some comparative chapters. We have both participated in EU–member state projects where authors have advanced the case for the 'exceptionalism' of 'their' state. Yet, comparison is part of the interest in such studies, so we have sought to promote this approach explicitly.

The common themes which we asked the authors to address were the history and politics of the European issue in the member state concerned; its European diplomacy; institutional adaptation; and policy adaptation. This was a wide remit and could best be accommodated in the single-country chapters. The comparative and grouping chapters have, for obvious reasons, had to be more selective. As noted in the Preface, our contributors had no opportunity to consider the agreement in June 2004 on a Constitutional Treaty. There remains a series of steps as to when or, indeed, whether the Treaty will be approved. By contrast, we have included all twenty-five member states in our coverage, even though accession was recent.

The prevailing literature on EU–member state relations is quite developed. We leave aside here the studies of individual countries, since we are interested in identifying themes that have arisen in the main comparative studies. Several edited collections have addressed all, or nearly all, of the EU member states (Rideau 1997; Rometsch and Wessels 1996; Wessels, Maurer, and Mittag 2003; Manners and Whitman 2000; Zeff and Pirro 2001). Other comparative studies have had a slightly narrower research agenda, such as EU policy coordination in the national capitals (Kassim, Peters, and Wright 2000); member state coordination in Brussels (Kassim, Menon, Peters, and Wright 2001); the role of member state parliaments in EU policy-making (Norton 1996; Maurer and Wessels 2001); the role of sub-national regions (Jeffery 1997; Jones and Keating 1995). One other comparative study that deserves mentioning has addressed the role of small states in the European Union (Hanf and Soetendorp 1998).

A theme that emerges from virtually all these studies is that there is considerable divergence in the practices within member states: in their executives, parliaments, and regions. The requirements of engagement with the European Union have been translated into prevailing domestic patterns rather than resulting in some 'identikit' form of adaptation. To take an illustration of this discussion, Wolfgang Wessels suggested that member states would react and adapt in three steps (Wessels 1996: 35–6).

- Europeanization would be the first step. A growing number of national actors would respond to the impact of the EU by seeking 'voice': an improved means of participation. National actors would be affected in a similar way, but Europeanization was seen as only the first of three steps.

- 'Fusion' would represent the second step. Fusion was understood to mean that national and EU structures would become organically connected. National processes of interaction would be increasingly influenced by the EU, with a 'change of policy styles' as the potential outcome (Wessels 1996: 36).
- 'Convergence' was presented as the third step, where 'we expect that the constitutional and institutional set-up of member states will converge towards one common model, which is not yet achieved but which is . . . "in the making" ' (Wessels 1996: 36). Thus 'the pre-existing differences among member states will slowly, and partly unnoticed, disappear'.

Although writing in the context of one of the first comparative studies (Rometsch and Wessels 1996), this conclusion is fairly representative, although others would doubtless disagree about the exact categories of adaptation advanced by Wessels. The findings of that study are echoed in a follow-up volume (Mittag and Wessels 2003).

A further theme from the literature relates to whether efficiency at coordinating European policy translates into effectiveness in the EU (Wright 1996: 165). Hussein Kassim has argued that the member governments have different coordination ambitions (2000: 243). The classic contrast is perhaps between the high coordination aspirations of the UK and the more modest ones in Germany, where ministerial autonomy is greater, coalition politics prevail and a federal system places constraints on what can be achieved in Berlin alone. And yet there is little doubt that Germany's imprint upon the EU is greater than the UK's. This situation alerts us to the diverse range of factors that bear upon member states' power and influence in the EU (see Helen Wallace's chapter in this volume). Effectiveness at coordination is only one of them!

A further theme that has emerged from the literature is that national governments have strengthened their domestic position at the expense of national parliaments because they have better access to EU policy-making than the latter do. Parliaments have been playing 'catch-up' in the adaptation game, with the possible exception of the Danish Folketing. However, if twenty-five member states adopted its method of mandating ministers, the EU would arguably grind to a complete halt, since negotiating mandates would be too rigid to achieve any agreements in Brussels.

The contributors to Part 2 are not testing a specific hypothesis, unlike some of these earlier studies. That is not the nature of our enterprise. However, it is important to be aware of these debates in what follows. It is also important to be aware of the great diversity of member states in the EU of twenty-five. From micro-states such as Malta and Luxembourg to the largest, namely Germany, at the other end of the spectrum. Following eastern enlargement, levels of economic development are also diverse. In addition, 'playing the EU game' inevitably entails a learning process. There have now been five enlargements in the period since 1973, so that process is at different stages for the different states. Finally, there is considerable variation in the weight of the individual states, as measured in the number of votes they have in the Council of the EU or in the number of Members of the European Parliament that they elect. This information is summarized in Table Part II.1.

Table Part II.1 Member state indicators in the EU of 25

Member state	Accession date[1]	Population (million)	Votes in Council[2]	MEPs 2004–7
Austria	1995	8.14	10	18
Belgium	1952	10.31	12	24
Czech Republic	2004	10.27	12	24
Cyprus	2004	0.76	4	6
Denmark	1973	5.37	7	14
Estonia	2004	1.37	4	6
Finland	1995	5.20	7	14
France	1952	59.34	29	78
Germany	1952	82.43	29	99
Greece	1981	10.60	12	24
Hungary	2004	10.01	12	24
Ireland	1973	3.88	7	13
Italy	1952	58.02	29	78
Latvia	2004	2.37	4	9
Lithuania	2004	3.69	7	13
Luxembourg	1952	0.45	4	6
Malta	2004	0.39	3	5
Netherlands	1952	16.10	13	27
Poland	2004	38.64	27	54
Portugal	1986	10.34	12	24
Slovakia	2004	5.40	7	14
Slovenia	2004	1.99	4	7
Sweden	1995	8.91	10	19
Spain	1986	40.41	27	54
United Kingdom	1973	60.11	29	78

[1] Accession to the EC/EU or, for founder-members, to the European Coal and Steel Community.
[2] From 1 November 2004, a qualified majority is reached:

■ if a majority of member states (in some cases a two-thirds majority) approve AND
■ if a minimum of votes is cast in favour—which is 72.3% of the total.

In addition, a member state may ask for confirmation that the votes in favour represent at least 62% of the total population of the Union. If this is found not to be the case, the decision will not be adopted. It must be recalled, of course, that not all decision-making is undertaken by qualified majority vote.

Source: Eurostat data <http://europa.int.eu> webpages.

References

Hanf, K., and Soetendorp, B. (eds) (1998), *Adapting to European Integration: Small States and the European Union* (Harlow: Addison Wesley Longman).

Jeffery, C. (ed.) (1997), *The Regional Dimension of the European Union: Towards a Third Level?* (London: Frank Cass).

Jones, B., Keating, M. (eds) (1995), *The European Union and the Regions* (Oxford: Oxford University Press).

Kassim, H. (2000), 'Conclusion—The National Co-ordination of EU Policy: Confronting the Challenge', in Kassim, Peters, and Wright, 235–64.

Kassim, H., Peters, G. B., and Wright, V. (eds) (2000), *The National co-ordination of EU Policy. The Domestic Level* (Oxford: Oxford University Press).

Kassim, H., Menon, A., Peters, G. B., and Wright, V. (eds) (2001), *The National Co-ordination of EU Policy: The European Level* (Oxford: Oxford University Press).

Manners, I., and Whitman, R. (eds) (2000), *The Foreign Policies of European Union Member States* (Manchester: Manchester University Press).

Maurer, A., and Wessels, W. (eds) (2001), *National Parliaments on their way to Europe: losers or latecomers?* (Schriften des Zentrum für Europäische Integrationsforschung (ZEI), Baden-Baden: Nomos Verlagsgesellschaft).

Mittag, J., and Wessels, W. (2003), 'The "One" and the "Fifteen"? The Member States between procedural adaptation and structural revolution', in Wessels, Maurer, and Mittag, 413–54.

Norton, P. (eds) (1996), *National Parliaments and the European Union* (London: Frank Cass).

Rideau, J. (ed.) (1997), *Les Etats membres de l'Union européenne. Adaptations, mutations, résistances* (Paris: LGDJ).

Rometsch, D., and Wessels, W. (eds) (1996), *The European Union and Member States* (Manchester: Manchester University Press).

Wessels, W. (1996), 'Institutions of the EU System: models of explanation', in Rometsch and Wessels, 20–36.

Wessels, W., Maurer, A., and Mittag, J. (eds) (2003), *Fifteen into One? The European Union and its Member States* (Manchester: Manchester University Press).

Wright, V. (1996), 'The National Coordination of European Policy-Making: Negotiating the Quagmire', in J. Richardson (ed.), *European Union: Power and Policy-Making* (London: Routledge).

Zeff, E., and Pirro, E. (2001), *The European Union and the Member States: Cooperation, Coordination and Compromise* (Boulder, CO: Lynne Rienner).

Chapter 4
Germany and Europe: Centrality in the EU

Jeffrey J. Anderson

Contents

Summary

Germany's relationship to Europe since the end of the Second World War has been one of change within a broader mosaic of continuity. In the 1950s, as the European project began to take formal shape, the Federal Republic emerged as the eastern outpost of Western Europe, which shaped profoundly not just its security policies, but its larger diplomatic and foreign economic objectives. With the end of the Cold War and the gradual expansion of the EU, Germany's geographical position in Europe has shifted toward the centre, which brings with it a host of interesting implications. Throughout, however, Germany's relationship to Europe has been unique among the member states. Its size and wealth puts it in the same class as heavyweights like France and the United Kingdom. Yet the openness of German elites to the upward transfer of national sovereignty to Brussels, the high level of public support for the basic principle of integration, and the relative ease of coordination between national and supranational policymaking communities are far more reminiscent of the small member states. Since unification, new policy accents and a new-found assertiveness characterize the German approach to Europe. All things considered, then, the German case takes on great significance in the study of integration and its impact on the member states, both for historical reasons and because of the analytical puzzles it raises.

Introduction

Of the fifteen EU member states, Germany's place in Europe has changed most dramatically over the years, in both literal and figurative terms. In the 1950s, as the European integration process gathered momentum, the Federal Republic took up a position as the eastern outpost of Western Europe. With the end of the Cold War and the gradual expansion of the EU, Germany's geographical position in Europe has shifted toward the centre—*das Land in der Mitte*—and the possible ramifications are the subject of much speculation in the press and academe. In a more abstract sense, Germany has gone from object to subject of the integration process. Much like NATO, the European Economic Community was conceived as a way of taming or domesticating German economic and political might, and Bonn's European policies bore these birthmarks well into the postwar period. As democracy consolidated and capitalism flourished in the Federal Republic, German elites grew more self-confident, and began to actively shape the course of integration, a process that has intensified since unification.

In short, Germany's journeys on the continent over the past half-century are unrivalled. Its relationship to Europe is similarly unique. Size and economic clout put it at the top of the class of larger member states, alongside France and the United Kingdom, whose relations with Brussels have often been fraught. Yet the openness of German elites to the upward transfer of national sovereignty to Brussels, the high level of public support for the basic principle of integration, and the relative ease of coordination between national and supranational policymaking communities are far more reminiscent of the small member states. As such, the German case takes on great significance in the study of integration and its impact on the member states.

In the following pages, I will explore the case of 'Germany and Europe'. The first section provides a brief overview of the history and politics of the European issue in the Federal Republic of Germany, from the early postwar years on up through the current period framed by the looming EU objectives of enlargement and internal reform. The analysis then moves to the European diplomacy pursued by Germany over the years, with emphasis on the special relationship with France, as well as the indirect impact of Germany's close ties with the United States. The chapter concludes with two sections that take up the extent of 'Europeanization' in Germany, defined here as sets of structures, cognitive frameworks, and processes operating at or below the level of the member states in the overlapping realms of polity, economy, and society that derive, either directly or indirectly, from European integration (Anderson 2002: 796).

History and politics of the European issue in Germany

The trademark characteristics of German foreign policy in the postwar period consisted of 'reflexive support for an exaggerated multilateralism' (Anderson 1997: 85), a relatively relaxed, perhaps even post-modern, approach to national sovereignty, and a deep-seated pacifism (Markovits and Reich 1997; Duffield 1998; Berger 1998; Banchoff 1999). These principles received perhaps their fullest expression in Germany's approach to European integration. Based on hard-nosed instrumental calculations and a transformed collective identity, German elites embraced the European project as a means of achieving an 'equality of rights' with their European neighbours, which was seen as essential to the realization of a litany of postwar foreign policy objectives: the rehabilitation of Germany's international credentials; the political priority of reunification; and economic reconstruction and recovery (Bulmer and Paterson 1987: 5–6; Milward 1992: 197–8; Berger 1996; Markovits and Reich 1997). Over the course of several decades, European integration became an important element in the national matrix of economic and political values. Political elites and average citizens increasingly viewed the Community not just as a reliable source of economic and political benefits, but as a core component of the national model of political economy and even the German sense of self. In short, Germany experienced a 'Europeanization of state identity' (Katzenstein 1997: 29).

Bonn's European policies sought to create supranational policy and governance frameworks that would support the Federal Republic's successful domestic economic formula. European struts for the German social market economy took many forms. The federal government consistently pushed its European partners to consider economic and monetary cooperation and strict competition policy, so as to create a level playing field for its firms and to limit negative externalities arising from other countries' fiscal policy decisions. The social dimension found expression and support in EC environmental policy, the Common Agricultural Policy (CAP), and regional and industrial assistance programmes. At the broadest level, the common market itself as well as the EC's generally liberal orientation to trade with third countries were crucial prerequisites for Germany's 'apolitical "politics of productivity" ' (Gowa 1989: 34).

By the end of the 1980s, the Federal Republic and the European Community shared many similarities, leading scholars to speak in terms of broad-based congruence (Bulmer 1997; Katzenstein 1997). This national-supranational congruence resulted from reciprocal influence and adjustment, and not from the forceful projection of Germany's model onto the rest of Europe. Nevertheless, whenever and wherever possible, Bonn sought to extend the multilateralism on which the European project rested. The result was a splendid irony: German political elites initially embraced the Community as a means of levelling the diplomatic playing field in Europe, but then used membership to encourage the spread of a markedly different conception of those rights among their European partners (Bulmer and Paterson 1987: 9–11).

Some but not all of this would change with the fall of the Berlin Wall in November 1989 (Bulmer and Paterson 1996). The German government adopted a policy of rapid unification based on the principle of institutional transfer—namely, the straightforward extension of the 'West Germany in Europe' model to eastern Germany. There was no evidence of official stocktaking exercises among mainstream political elites, suggesting that German support for multilateralism had become embedded in the definition of national interest and national identity. The challenge facing the government was how to reconcile unification to the standing requirements and obligations of membership in the dense web of international organizations. The drive for continuity did not imply a rigid defence of the status quo, however; German elites tackled the issue of how to adjust or modify international institutions such as NATO and the European Community to cope with the changed realities in a post-Cold War Europe; for example, German leaders attached the highest priority to EC enlargement to the east.

Despite—and according to many observers, precisely because of—the course charted by the federal government, tremendous social and economic problems quickly erupted in the new Länder and spilled over into the rest of Germany. In the process, cherished axioms of postwar political economy in West Germany were called into question. A decade and a half after unification, this has produced an intriguing pattern of change and continuity in Germany's policies toward Europe.

As a later section will document, there have been tangible changes in various EU policy areas, although even here the outlines of West German approaches are recognizable. Regarding larger integration objectives, the German position since unification reveals a blend of old and new. Berlin remains an ardent proponent of the Community method and of the long-term goals of widening and deepening. A major reference point for German policy makers continues to be the perceptions and concerns of their neighbours. Chancellor Kohl repeatedly declared that integration was irreversible, and rejected accusations that Germany was trying to dominate Europe. The government's foreign policy approach remained multilateralist. The Maastricht Treaty, formulated in part to further embed the Federal Republic in the west, represented at least on paper a significant deepening of political and especially economic integration for the twelve member countries.

The Bonn government expressed continuing support for EMU, a strengthened European Parliament, greater use of qualified majority voting in the Council, closer cooperation in the fields of foreign policy and internal security, and enlargement. With France, Germany also began to explore 'flexibility' options designed to allow subsets of EU members to push ahead more rapidly with integration in certain areas, and succeeded in inserting favorable language into the Treaty of Amsterdam signed in October 1997 (Petite 1998; Bulmer, Jeffery, and Paterson 2000).

Amidst the overall impression of continuity, however, new accents have emerged. Since unification, issues connected to European integration are more likely to be the stuff of domestic political conflict than they were in the past. Berlin's augmented fiscal conservatism in Europe is a direct reflection of intensified fiscal conservatism at home, in no small part due to the debt overhang associated with unification and the budgetary stringencies of participation in the single currency. In response to domestic criticism and to genuine concerns about glaring loopholes in the TEU, the federal government, in conjunction with the Bundesbank, held to a strict interpretation of the admission criteria, and eventually succeeded in pushing the 'Stability and Growth Pact for Europe' through the Council in 1997. The purpose of this resolution was to ensure that EMU members continued to pursue fiscal policies consistent with the convergence criteria after the introduction of the single currency. The German political leadership, starting under Helmut Kohl and carrying over into the present Schröder government, displayed a more cautious attitude to eastern enlargement, borne of a greater awareness of and sensitivity to the financial costs of admitting populous, poor members from Central and Eastern Europe. More broadly, elites and the mass public in unified Germany now convey a keener sense of the limits of political integration. For several years now, there has been no more expansive talk in official circles of a 'United States of Europe'.

The Nice summit, held in December 2000, showcased this new German blend of EU policy continuity and change. Nice represented the conclusion of an intergovernmental conference (IGC) designed to prepare the EU institutionally for enlargement. Members were faced with a contentious agenda; discussion points included a firm date for enlargement; the size and composition of the European Commission as well as the voting weights assigned to members in the Council of Ministers; the extension of qualified majority voting (QMV) to new areas in Council proceedings; the size and composition of the European Parliament; enhanced cooperation; and a new IGC to determine the division of responsibilities between European, national, and subnational authorities.

At Nice, the Berlin government was intent on preserving the country's traditional commitments and objectives within the larger integration framework. Chancellor Gerhard Schröder deferred to French demands, including continued parity in Council voting weights for France and Germany, out of respect for the Franco-German partnership, thereby helping to avert a failed summit, which would have dealt a blow to the momentum behind the European project. Berlin also succeeded in holding the door open to eastern enlargement. In these and other senses, the 'old' Germany was clearly visible. By the same token, however, Berlin sought a privileged institutional position, along with the other large member states, in an enlarged Union. Schröder declined to insist on the 'double majority' formula for taking Council decisions (binding decisions result from a majority of member states representing a majority of the EU population), a proposal backed by the European Commission and the smaller member governments and one that had drawn German support prior to the summit. Instead, Schröder insisted on the option of a 62 per cent threshold for Council decisions (Council majorities representing less than 62 per cent of the EU population will not prevail), which puts Germany in an advantageous veto position. Berlin also demanded a follow-up summit to Nice, to establish a clear division of responsibilities among the various levels of governance in the EU. This was the 'new' Germany in action; in this sense, Berlin had displaced Bonn.

The German government's post-Nice pronouncements on Europe have strengthened the impression of movement within continuity. A few days after the conclusion of the Nice summit, Chancellor Schröder called for a seven-year moratorium on the free circulation of laborers from Central and Eastern European applicants as a condition for entry into the European Union. Joined by Austria, the Germans justified this demand in terms of reducing the inevitable economic and social strains of enlargement. The German position generated consternation in applicant countries like Poland and the Czech Republic. In November 2001 Schröder delivered an address at the SPD's annual party conference in which he laid out, in very general language, the government's vision of a constitution for Europe. Surface appearances gave the impression of a very radical proposal—strengthening the European Parliament, turning the Council of Ministers into an upper legislative chamber of states (*Staatenkammer*), transforming the Commission into a directly elected and therefore accountable political executive. In a word, Berlin looked to be up to its old game: federalization, with the final goal a United States of Europe modelled closely along German constitutional lines.

Reading carefully between the lines, the German vision is far more conservative. Responsibility for the European Union's agricultural and structural/cohesion policies, which together constitute nearly three-quarters of the annual EU budget expenditures, are to be returned to the member states. Decision-making in remaining areas of EU competence, including the common foreign and security policy, is to be fully democratized. Unified Germany is in no way turning its back on integration; rather, it is seeking to establish clear and final parameters that will secure the place of national, regional, and local authorities. The government's blueprint is far more sober and far less quixotic than the versions bandied about in German elite circles even a decade ago. How this blueprint shapes up in practice will depend on how the EU assimilates its new members and is further conditioned by putting the 2004 Constitutional Treaty into practice.

European diplomacy

As outlined above, Germany threw itself into the uniting of Europe after 1949; Hanrieder has described this early postwar period alternately as one in which 'necessity overwhelmed choice' and 'choice coincided with necessity' (Hanrieder 1989: 2 and 7). There is truth in both formulations, especially if one takes a somewhat longer term view of things. German policymakers initially were motivated primarily by instrumental calculations, but in a short matter of time, 'Germany in Europe' became an established norm of foreign policymaking. To be sure, Bonn elites viewed Europe as a vehicle for achieving a litany of concrete policy objectives: reunification, reconstruction and recovery, security, democratic consolidation, and macroeconomic performance. Alongside these goals, however, the Germans sought through Europe to rehabilitate themselves on the international stage, and to reassure neighbours and distant allies of the profundity of the internal political transformation that had resulted from total defeat.

Achieving these myriad and complex objectives in the face of enduring scepticism and mistrust across the European continent called forth a particular art of diplomacy. The contrasting templates of French grandeur and British aloofness, both of which nonetheless placed a clear sense of national purpose and interest at the forefront of policy, were ruled out virtually by definition; no one would sit for such brazenness from the Germans, and those in power in Bonn knew this full well. Wearing national interests on their diplomatic sleeve would have guaranteed failure. Instead, the Germans adopted an approach to European diplomacy that took its lead from the smaller European democracies, which were quite adept at the politics of demure consensualism.

During the postwar period, up through 1989, it was quite common to see Germany described as an economic giant and a political dwarf. There is certainly a kernel of truth in this formulation; at no point during this forty-year period did the Federal Republic's political gravitas and style match its economic prowess and capabilities, in the manner of a France or Britain. The dwarf–giant antinomy, however, obscures far more than it illuminates. Germany was by no means a weak or minor participant in the European integration project. In fact, as discussed above, the Europe that had emerged by the end of the 1980s shared several striking elements with the German national model, an outcome that can hardly have happened by accident. Germany's effective yet—at least for a large state—unique European diplomacy is best described, with apologies to Theodore Roosevelt, as 'Speak softly and carry a big checkbook'.

Speaking softly meant, for the most part, avoiding the lead position on major issues, whether specific to a policy area (for example the Common Agricultural Policy) or relating to general integration goals (enlargement, institutional reform, etc.). Leadership was exercised behind the scenes and, whenever possible, in transparent alliance with other member governments. The centrality of the Franco-German partnership must be seen in this light (Kocs 1995; Baun 1996; Bulmer, Jeffery, and Paterson 2000). For the Germans, standing shoulder to shoulder with or, as was often the case, slightly astern of the French meant compromising on otherwise strongly held preferences; external trade and competition policies provide numerous examples. The benefits, consisting of decisive political weight attended by comfortable diplomatic cover in the corridors of power in Brussels, far outweighed the costs. The original decisions to proceed with the uniting of Europe in the 1950s, as well as subsequent initiatives like the Werner Plan for Economic and Monetary Union in the late 1960s, the single market initiative in the 1980s, and even the single currency initiative, which bore fruit after German unification, owe their realization in large part to the Franco-German tandem. As Bulmer, Jeffery, and Paterson point out, Germany in the 1980s began to diversify its approach to strategic partnerships within the EC, seeking out partners like the United Kingdom and some of the smaller members on a variety of issues. Yet the 'privileged partnership' with France remained central to Bonn's European diplomacy (Bulmer, Jeffery, and Paterson 2000: 53).

Achieving goals, particularly the much desired contextual or 'milieu' goals so central to the smooth functioning of the German social market economy, often came at a specific price. Bonn's 'chequebook diplomacy' in fact underpinned most if not all of the major advances in integration up through the 1980s. As the largest net contributor to the EC budget, Germany always stood to pay a larger proportion of the costs of any new programmes or initiatives. As a case in point, during interstate bargaining over the Single European Act in the mid-1980s, the poorer member countries voiced mounting concerns about the economic and social implications of a barrier-free market for their underdeveloped regions, which could not be expected to compete for mobile investment and jobs at a level commensurate with the more dynamic, prosperous areas of the Community. Since each of these poorer member countries—Spain, Portugal, Greece, and Ireland—had the power to scuttle agreement on the key reform provisions of the 1992 package, their demands for some form of compensation carried a great deal of weight. The doubling of the structural funds in 1988 represented a side payment from the wealthier to the poorer member states designed to assure final agreement on the SEA; Germany underwrote this substantial budgetary commitment (Marks 1992: 202–4).

The collapse of the Berlin Wall and the instantaneous reframing of the unification question confronted Germany's European diplomacy with a host of challenges, the most urgent of which, at least initially, was unification. Although Moscow held the key to unification, Europe was far from irrelevant (Pond 1993; Zelikow and Rice 1995). The Bonn government faced two tasks stemming from EC membership: first, to calm its EC partners about the implications of unification for stability in Europe; and secondly, to bring about EC accession for the eastern region in a timely and mutually acceptable manner.

It soon became painfully apparent that most of Germany's neighbours did not share its elation about the prospect of unification. British Prime Minister Margaret Thatcher warned against a 'rash' resolution of the German Question, while French President François Mitterrand described German unification as 'a legal and political impossibility' (Görtemaker 1994: 155). These and other expressions of doubt and concern, which continued into 1990, were received with anger and consternation in Bonn. To cope with the ghosts of Germany's past, political elites both in and outside of the Federal Republic sought refuge in European integration.

Bonn's insistence that any political formula for unification must embody an explicit European dimension resonated with the architectural designs of Jacques Delors, President of the EC Commission, and key members like France, which were eager to secure an irreversible affirmation of integration from Germany. In March 1990, Kohl announced his government's unwavering support for the goal of economic and monetary union, and one month later, he and the French president called for the convening of an intergovernmental conference on political union to run parallel to formal discussions over EMU, which would chart a course toward a stronger, more democratic Community and a common foreign and security policy. The result, of course, was the Treaty on European Union, negotiated at Maastricht in December 1991 and signed by the leaders of the twelve member governments in early February 1992 (Baun 1996; Sandholtz 1993). In many ways, the resulting Treaty on European Union, agreed at Maastricht, can be seen as the supranational price tag for national unification. For the second time in forty years, Bonn requested 'the golden handcuffs' offered by its European partners (Garton Ash 1993: 358).

Unification opened up institutional questions—voting weights in the Council; number of Commissioners appointed by Germany; size of the German delegation in the European Parliament—that threatened to upset the delicate balance established for the twelve members by the existing treaty framework. To the relief of its partners and of the Commission, Bonn declined to press any issues pertaining to the Council and Commission, although it did request an increase in the size of the German EP delegation by eighteen members, a matter that was ultimately resolved at Maastricht. Regarding the Community's secondary legislation, Bonn eschewed a Mediterranean strategy of long transition periods and significant derogations for the acceding region, which went a long way toward allaying concerns among its fellow EC members. Instead, Bonn sought a rapid convergence to EC standards, with few exceptions.

The hope and expectation of European neighbours that the unified Germany would continue to speak softly and carry a big chequebook were soon dashed. As unification was becoming a legal reality over the course of 1990, the Yugoslavian crisis erupted at the southern doorstep of the Community, providing an occasion for the unified Germans to unveil a new voice on regional security issues. The European Community's attempt to present a united front faltered in mid-July 1991, when the German government announced that the Community would have to consider accepting the independence of Slovenia and Croatia if the strife worsened and mediation efforts faltered. Although this represented a clear break with the EC's declared position, the Germans reiterated their pledge to continue working with other Community members to find a solution to the crisis. Yet on the eve of the Maastricht summit, Bonn announced that it would formally recognize Slovenia and Croatia by the end of the year, even if this meant breaking ranks with the UN, the US, and a majority of its EC partners. Ultimately, this display of foreign policy muscle pulled the EC in its wake; however, the appearance of unity in Brussels was purchased at a high price, as Bonn's 'solo' left a bitter aftertaste in the mouths of many Community members. While Germany's decision did not violate the text produced at Maastricht, it was interpreted by many in and outside of Germany as violating the spirit of the accords. It also failed abjectly in its objectives, as the conflict continued to rage in Croatia, and soon engulfed Bosnia-Herzegovina.

Starting in the 1990s, Germany also began to seek a less confining grasp within the Franco-German partnership, so much so that by the time of the Nice Summit in December 2000 (see above), clear differences—admittedly papered over at the summit—were becoming highly visible. On issues ranging from constitutional reform to enlargement to reform of the Common Agricultural Programme, the gap between the French and German positions, accompanied by a certain coolness in personal relations between President Chirac and Chancellor Schröder, grew more concrete and, for many, more worrisome. Efforts to rejuvenate the Franco-German partnership in early 2003, on the occasion of the fortieth anniversary of the Elysée Treaty, revolved around a renewed push on EU institutional reform, with special attention to securing the influence of the larger member governments, and open opposition to US foreign policy on Iraq. The initiative met with open scepticism and unease from smaller EU members, as well as from the candidate member countries in Central and Eastern Europe.

On budgetary matters, the domestic financial drain of unification led slowly but inexorably to a much more sceptical approach on the part of the Germans to big ticket items and initiatives. Although it is certainly indisputable that Germany consented to a second major increase in the structural funds in the context of negotiations over the EMU provisions of the Maastricht Treaty in 1991—another side payment to the poorer EU members—thereafter the Bonn government maintained an increasingly tighter grip on the purse strings, and made Germany's 'net contributor' status a political issue in relations with the Commission and its EU partners. In recent years, Germany's share of overall EU budget contributions has eased somewhat, as has its deficit on the operational budget balance, but the issue remains a sensitive one nevertheless (see Table 4.1).

Table 4.1 Germany and the EU Budget, 1995–2001

	Contributions to the EU budget (% total)	Total Receipts from the EU Budget (% total)	Operational Budget Balance (Mio. ECUs)
1995	31.4	12.1	−11092
1996	29.2	13.3	−10406
1997	28.2	12.8	−10553
1998	25.1	12.9	−8044
1999	25.5	12.4	−8494
2000	24.8	12.5	−8280
2001	24.4	12.9	−6953

Source: European Commission, 'Allocation of 2001 EU Operating Expenditure by Member State', September 2002 <http://Europa.eu.int/comm./budget/agenda2000/reports.en.htm>.

Overall, Germany's European diplomacy in recent years has grown more assertive and less idealistic. Many signature characteristics of the West German approach Europe, such as a basically pro-integration orientation and a clear preference for collective approaches to problem solving, remain in place. However, with the costly addition of the poorer regions of eastern Germany and mounting public concern over who will foot the bill for Europe's grand plans, there is newfound sobriety in the 'new' Germany about the future trajectory of the integration process, as well as a new assertiveness in defending national interests—some of which have changed appreciably with unification. In the past, West Germany consistently evaluated Community decisions in terms of the integrity of existing rule frameworks or 'milieu', rather than who got what (Anderson 1999; Bulmer, Jeffery, and Paterson 2000). This was less true after the mid-1990s; increasingly, Berlin is paying attention to the bottom line in Brussels. Unification reshuffled the cards inside Germany, transforming the domestic context in which European policy is made, and making it impossible for the German government to satisfy domestic constituencies with its traditional policy priorities at home and in Brussels. The sum total of the mix of continuity and change is a new German diplomacy in Europe, one that looks more normal but remains distinctive among the large member states.

Integration and institutional adaptation in Germany

According to Bulmer, Germany and the European Union shared a marked level of congruence that embraced policy objectives, norms and doctrines, and institutions of governance (Bulmer 1997). Institutionally, the most striking similarities involved the vertical distribution of authority and the horizontal organization of the policy process. Regarding the former, both employed versions of cooperative federalism, in which executive authority and competencies were distributed across multiple levels of the polity (Scharpf 1988; Sbragia 1992). As for the latter, each manifested a highly sectorized policy process (Bulmer and Paterson 1987). There is a strong element of coincidence in these patterns of congruence—neither Europe nor Germany recast the other in its image over the course of nearly a half decade of integration. Beneath these broad structural similarities, a duet of mutual adaptation between Germany and the emerging European unfolded over the years. There were and are two sides to this coin; in this section, the focus is on institutional adaptation at the national level. What are the most salient examples of the Europeanization of German institutions?

Obvious and unsurprising evidence of Europeanization is omnipresent throughout the German federal bureaucracy. The Chancellery and the federal ministries have all created European units and in some instances entire departments devoted to the evaluation, monitoring, coordination, and implementation of European issues and policies. For some, like the Foreign Ministry and the Ministry of Economics, this has been so since the beginning. For others, like Interior and Justice, the emergence of an institutionalized European policy dimension is far more recent, and parallels the expansion of competencies and responsibilities that has taken place at the European level. The growing domestic political salience of the European policy dimension was showcased in 1998, when the incoming Social Democratic Minister of Finances, Oskar Lafontaine, succeeded in wresting responsibility for European policy coordination from the Ministry of Economics, which significantly enhanced the power of his ministry.

The lower house of the German parliament, the Bundestag, has also adapted institutionally to the growing salience of the European level of policymaking. In 1992 the Bundestag for the first time appointed a Standing Committee on European Union Affairs to handle the growing volume of legislative output from Brussels; up until that time, EC matters had been dealt with in traditional departmental standing committees. Although this institutional adaptation, which finds an anchor in the Basic Law, has improved the capacity of the lower house to monitor EU developments, the Bundestag continues to face substantial obstacles to effective and timely participation in the complex EU policymaking process, a situation that differs imperceptibly from those confronting other national legislatures.

Perhaps the most far-reaching effects of Europeanization are to be found in the German federal system. As the European Community's capacity and willingness to act in ways that impinged on federal intergovernmental relations began to blossom in the 1980s, the Länder began to take account of the European dimension. Much has been written about the speed with which the federal states began to establish representations, or quasi-embassies, in Brussels so as to monitor and where possible influence the policy process in areas of great significance, such as regional and competition policies as well as agriculture (Hooghe and Marks 1996; Marks *et al.* 1996). Parallel to the administrative innovations taking place at the federal level, outlined above, Land ministries began to install European units and divisions; in several instances, Land governments took the step of creating Europe ministries to oversee formulation and coordination of European policies at the state level.

In addition to these adaptations on the ground, so to speak, European integration has prompted reform at the level of the national constitution. The process began in earnest with the ratification of the Single European Act in 1986–7; as Jeffery points out,

the Act was greeted in principle with outright enthusiasm by the Länder. The problem lay in the scale and scope of the transfers of (Länder) competence envisaged for the Single Market process. This had an energizing effect . . . on the Länder. There followed a concerted campaign to gain adequate access to Europeanizing/-ized decision-making processes (Jeffery 2003, 100).

The galvanization of Länder interest and concern culminated in the aftermath of unification, during debates surrounding the ratification of the Maastricht Treaty. The treaty sparked a wide-ranging constitutional debate among the federal government and the Länder, which was eventually resolved in the form of a new Article 23 that provides for a significant reordering of the formal relationships between the political executive and the legislature, notably the Bundesrat. The Länder, which participate in the federal legislative process via the Bundesrat, argued that EC matters could no longer be considered foreign affairs but were in fact a form of 'European domestic policy' and as such, the Länder were entitled to represent the interests of Germany in Brussels on EC affairs that impinged on their powers and competencies. Since formal ratification of the treaty required Bundesrat approval, the demands of the Länder carried decisive weight in discussions with a sceptical coalition government and deeply concerned civil servants (Ress 1994; Jeffery 1999). Although the dire forecast of a complete loss of federal control on European issues has yet to be proved correct, the fact remains that the Länder now enjoy increased influence over some aspects of the integration process (Hüttmann and Knodt 2000). Schröder's successful demand that the EU should deal with the vertical distribution of competences in the constitutional debate originated in a consensus among the Länder that a firewall against EU encroachment has to be erected at the regional level.

Looking beyond the confines of formal government structures to civil society, evidence of Europeanization is also apparent. German interest groups have responded to the growing scope and importance of European policymaking with an organizational push that has given many a physical presence in Brussels, often matched by a significant capacity to influence the EU policy process. These trends are especially salient among business interest associations, but also apply to environmental groups, farmers' organizations, and to a lesser extent labour. German interest associations have also adapted to integration internally; the days when EC/EU matters could be handled within established bureaucratic channels designed to address federal and state policy questions are long gone. Nevertheless, there has been no general exodus of organized interests as yet from Berlin to Brussels; nor has there been a sweeping transformation of the political agenda for interest groups. These actors in Germany (and elsewhere) remain firmly embedded in national policy networks, view their interests and objectives using primarily national frames of reference, and often make primary use of their national policy networks in shaping and coping with EU policy initiatives.

Much the same can be said for political parties in Germany. To be sure, one can readily identify organizational adaptation by the parties that is consistent with an increasingly significant EU policy process. Moreover, as suggested above, European issues in recent years have thrust their way onto the national political agenda, in a manner that has no real precedent in postwar German history. That said, German political parties remain inherently national actors, whose orientation and nesting is firmly anchored in the domestic context. And, despite the politicization of Europe in intra- and inter-organizational discourse, party dynamics in this area remain decidedly pro-European; the all party consensus, although perhaps more sober-minded than in years past, remains intact.

Integration and policy adaptation in Germany

After a half century in the midst of an ever closer union, it would be startling if Germany's public policies did not reveal a European imprint. As outlined above, by the 1970s Germany had achieved a comfortable fit with the European Community; congruence extended from institutional and normative elements to the specific content and structure of public policies. Unification disrupted these various policy equilibriums, resulting in an interesting mix of continuity and change by the first few years of the new millennium. What follows is a brief analysis of the extent of adaptation in several key areas of German public policy.

Official government support for economic and monetary union has been a constant since Maastricht, although the German public retained deep reservations about the

Table 4.2 2002 Broad Economic Policy Guidelines (BEPGs) Recommendations to Germany on Budgetary Policy

'[. . .] considering that Germany is a member of the euro area, budgetary policy should aim to:

i.   ensure that the 3 per cent of GDP reference value for the general government deficit will not be breached. Use any potential growth dividend to reduce the 2002 deficit below the 2.5 per cent of GDP targeted in the last updated stability programme;

ii.   aim at a sufficient decline of the 2003 deficit to ensure that a close-to-balance position in 2004 can be achieved. To this end, continue expenditure restraint and ensure that any budgetary room for manoeuvre be used to reduce the deficit;

iii.   implement the necessary reform of the healthcare system in order to reduce expenditure pressures and to contribute to improving the quality and economic efficiency of medical care; and

iv.   adopt in the current parliamentary term the agreed changes to the Haushalfsgrundsätzegesetz and enable an effective control of the agreements reached in the special session of the Finanzplanungsrat of 21 March 2002.

Source: European Commission (2002), 172.

single currency right up to the date of its unveiling on 1 January 2002. Since taking power in 1998, Chancellor Schröder has clashed repeatedly with the Commission over the Germany's budgetary performance and the Stability and Growth Pact criteria. In 2003 Germany exceeded the 3 per cent ceiling for national budgetary deficits, as set down in the Pact (European Commission 2003). Berlin was thus called on the carpet a number of times by the Commission and the Council. Its 2003 and 2004 overshoots occurred despite the latter having issued a set of strong recommendations, entailing far-reaching domestic reforms, in June 2002 (see Table 4.2). In light of the fact that Germany pushed most aggressively for the adoption of a stringent version of the Stability Pact criteria, the current situation is full of irony.

Tensions have also emerged over interest and exchange rates stemming from the newly Europeanized realm of monetary policy. Schröder has made numerous public statements calling on the European Central Bank to adopt a looser grip on the monetary reins in the interests of economic growth and job creation. The soaring value of the Euro in the first half of 2003 has also generated concerns in business and government circles, since it poses thorny problems for German exporters and complicates the task of engineering economic recovery.

A less conflictual story emerges in the trade policy area. For obvious reasons, the Federal Republic maintained a strong free-trade orientation, linked intimately to the national objective of export-led growth, which presumed an expanding, barrier-free European market. The EC also helped the German economy by creating a zone of monetary stability and contributing to open international trade, and the multilateral framework created by the EC strengthened Germany's hand in dealing with international trade matters and bilateral trade relations with third countries. The importance of the Franco-German partnership on occasion led Germany to trim its sails on trade matters, but for the most part its strong preference for a liberal trade policy was reflected in the Community's approach to international trade rounds.

Germany's liberal trade orientation came through the unification process unscathed. Political elites and representatives of business and labour agreed on the need to maintain a free-trade orientation, since the mounting costs of unification could only be financed through increased exports, which presupposed international trade liberalization. This manifested itself in strong, public support for a successful conclusion to the Uruguay Round of the General Agreement on Tariffs and Trade (GATT), and in opposition to attempts by the European Commission to expand its competencies in the trade field, which the German government suspected would benefit protectionist member states.

The same priorities that characterized German trade policy applied to the internal market, leading national policymakers and producer groups to support the dismantling of potential and actual market barriers to internal trade in the EC, with the exception of areas it considered economically or politically sensitive, like telecommunications, financial services, and insurance. Germany's liberal orientation to internal market policy can be seen clearly in its role in discussions over the single market initiative. Although the impetus for the SEA originated elsewhere, the Kohl government provided crucial weight behind the act's two main components, teaming with Britain to strengthen the case for the completion of the internal market and with France to push through a key package of procedural reforms (Sandholtz and Zysman 1989; Moravcsik 1991; Cameron 1992). German support for the completion of the internal market did not diminish after or because of unification.

Policy continuities are less apparent in other areas, such as the environment. Among EC member governments, Germany along with Denmark staked out a position as an ardent advocate of strict and comprehensive environmental regulation at the supranational level. On issues ranging from auto emissions standards to the protection of the ozone layer, Germany repeatedly adopted a hard line, insisting on ambitious and exacting targets supported by policy instruments with teeth (Jachtenfus 1990; Weizsäcker 1990). Frequently, the West Germans resorted to threats of unilateral action to force their EC partners to adopt a stricter approach, as in the case of auto emission standards in the 1980s. Bonn also strongly advocated insertion of the environmental passages into the SEA, in particular the opt-out clause, of which it made frequent use—German environmental standards were often more demanding than their EC regulatory counterparts.

Germany's self-appointed role as the EC's environmental 'golden boy' (*Musterknabe*) stemmed from two sources. First, environmental issues were especially salient in domestic politics, owing to the rise of the Green Party (*Die Grünen*), which entered the Bundestag in the 1983 federal elections, and the role of natural disasters like the dying of the forests (*Waldsterben*) as well as the Chernobyl nuclear accident and Sandoz chemical spill on the Rhine, both of which occurred in 1986. Second, the export orientation of the German economy, coupled with the country's wealth, enabled political elites to marry a stringent, supranational environmentalism to economic growth and competitiveness, on the logic that German firms were best positioned to compete and to succeed in an EC characterized by the most stringent environmental standards possible.

Unification's impact on German EC/EU environmental policy was generally confined to the issue of derogations for old eastern German industry and local authorities. Germany remained a force for strengthening European-level competencies and policies in this area. Where differences arose between Bonn and Brussels, they involved areas such as energy, climate, and waste disposal policies in which the objectives of the Commission were not sufficiently ambitious for the German side. Germany maintained its pre-unification support for the need to harmonize 'upwards' in the EC/EU. In some instances where Bonn was unable to prevail with its stringent line, such as the setting of minimum standards for refuse dumps and the recycling and packaging directive, it insisted on the right to retain its more exacting national regimes, even at the cost of Commission legal challenges. In other areas like the energy tax, however, the government ultimately declined to go it alone, citing the limited benefits such a move would bring and the negative consequences for industrial competitiveness in Germany. The federal government set its sights instead on collective action in Brussels and voluntary targets for reduced CO_2 emissions by German industry. The sources of Germany's greater reluctance to engage in national policy 'solos' resides in the changed domestic politics of the environment after 1990. Thus, overall, the impact of unification on German environmental policy is subtle yet undeniable.

In the realm of competition policy as applied to state aid, one can find evidence of more marked departures from the government's standard line. Germany was an ardent proponent of a strict application of the rules derived from Articles 92–94 of the Rome Treaty, which prohibit state subsidies that distort intra-Community trade. In practice, officials regarded state aids as a necessary evil, distinguishing between assistance to cushion the social upheaval caused by the structural decline of an industry and aid intended merely to prop up inefficient producers. Germany was not averse to the former type of aid, consistent as it was with the basic tenets of the social market economy, but regarded the latter with deep scepticism. In Brussels, Bonn found a supportive regulatory environment, and sought to keep the level of state aid across the Community as low as possible, believing that German firms would thrive in a relatively subsidy-free environment. At the same time, it worked to ensure that German firms and regions retained access to state aids, whether provided by Brussels or Bonn, so long as the Community permitted some form of sectoral and regional aid.

Right after unification, Germany maintained its traditional approach as the Commission came under growing pressure from France, Spain, and other member governments to soften its approach with an eye to serving the competitive needs of European industry. Commission pledges to scrutinize the subsidy practices of the wealthier member governments with greater intensity met with Bonn's approval, and in private German officials welcomed the prospect of supranational support for their own efforts to contain subsidy practices in the western Länder. However, the mounting economic dislocation, and attendant political pressures, in eastern Germany soon forced changes in practice, if not in public principle. Beneath the appearance of continuity, there lurked a growing interventionism in the restructuring of the eastern German economy, particularly in sensitive sectors like shipbuilding and steel, that was both framed and instigated by the challenges of privatization. Central to Bonn's slide into a policy of 'state interventionism with a bad conscience' (Lehmbruch 1991: 597) were the eastern Länder, which utilized their legislative prerogatives and institutionalized access to the privatization process to push the federal government into actions that diverged increasingly from its competition rhetoric and from EU guidelines. In the absence of strong German support, the EU's state aid regime weakened over the course of the 1990s. Tensions between Berlin and Brussels over the administration of EU competition policy have continued into the new millennium, and have even moved from disagreements over individual aid cases to institutionalized features of the German political economy model (for example the *Landesbanken*).

Outright policy reversals surface in two other areas. Prior to unification, federal regional policy existed in uneasy tension with its EC counterpart, the structural funds. Between 1979 and 1989, the Federal Republic received modest amounts from the structural funds. Over this same period of time, Germany became the target of sustained and largely successful efforts by the European Commission to limit the area coverage of federal and state regional programmes as well as their assistance rates. Federal officials bridled at the Commission's interventions, arguing that they interfered with constitutional obligation under Article 72 of the Basic Law to secure an equality of living standards within Germany. They also criticized the EC competition authorities for subverting the fragile political compromises reached among the Länder and the federal government.

In the aftermath of unification, Germany's position vis-à-vis the structural funds changed from reluctant supplier of regional benefits to adamant demandeur. The eastern German region quickly materialized as the poorest in all of Europe, with a mix of sectoral and labour market problems that were unprecedented in postwar West European history. As a result, the German approach to EU regional policy shifted dramatically in response to the novel problems in the eastern region. Germany quickly moved from disinterested yet austere paymaster of EU regional policy to ardent supplicant, concerned with getting a fair share of Brussels resources to cope with the difficult economic situation in the eastern German region. The price was a 'Europeanization' of the domestic regional policy framework; the inclusion of the eastern region into the EU's regional policy framework was attended by the importation of the European Commission's Southern development model, which emphasized basic infrastructure development. This occurred in spite of the express opposition of the Federal Ministry of Economics.

West German agricultural policy, both at home and in Europe, was tailored to the relative structural homogeneity of the domestic farming sector (Hendriks 1991). German governments pursued a consistent CAP policy that centered around the maintenance of high prices for its farmers and a structural policy supportive of small-scale farming. The introduction of Europe's agri-monetary system after the collapse of Bretton Woods, based on so-called green exchange rates, offered Bonn the opportunity to shield German farmers from the agricultural price reductions otherwise demanded by the appreciation of the Deutsche Mark. When CAP reform took centre stage in Brussels in the 1980s (Moyer and Josling 1990), Germany shunned any proposed solutions that entailed price reductions. Instead, Germany sought to address the problem of overproduction and runaway costs through set-asides and co-payment procedures when and if guaranteed production thresholds were exceeded.

After unification, Germany's objectives for the Common Agricultural Policy increasingly acknowledged the needs of larger, competitive farming units—a clear departure from pre-unification days. This policy shift resulted from the addition of the vastly larger farms of the former German Democratic Republic in 1990, and has had the effect of moving the German government somewhat closer to the efficiency-oriented agricultural camp in the EU (for example the Netherlands, UK), which seeks to reform the CAP by, among other things, eliminating expensive price support programmes, thereby favouring larger, more competitive farms. The German shift on agriculture comes at a time when the CAP framework is undergoing intense review in the context of eastern enlargement, and at a minimum opens up additional options for market-oriented reform proposals down the road. Although still innately cautious on the larger issue of CAP reform, particularly where price support mechanisms are concerned, the Germans are now adamant about reducing their financial obligations as the policy framework is extended eastward; this has put them in direct conflict with the French, who have resisted any redistribution of the burdens of carrying the CAP.

Conclusions

It has become commonplace to argue that Europe is an increasingly important and in some ways determining factor for national politicians, bureaucrats, interest groups, and even mass publics. Since the mid-1980s, when integration regained forward momentum with the launching of the single market initiative, the reach of Europe has extended outward and downward, in a dizzying mix of mundane and profound ways. Yet in the case of Germany, this characterization is misleading; from the very beginning, Europe has mattered decisively. It was central to the rehabilitation of the new Germany's international credentials, in a purely practical or instrumental sense, and it was central to a refounding of the country's political identity. Even among the smaller member countries, which are said to be much more open to the contextual effects of Europe, there is no parallel to the course charted by the Federal Republic since 1949.

Germany's relationship to Europe has been a portrait of motion within stability. The paradox has become more vivid since 1990; although unification failed to launch a sweeping reassessment of Germany's place in Europe, one would be well advised to refrain from utilizing terms like 'seamless continuity' or 'status quo'. Something has changed in the last decade or so; unification reshuffled the domestic political and economic deck, transforming the context in which European policy is made, and making it impossible for the German government to satisfy domestic constituencies with its traditional policy priorities at home and in Brussels. The sum total of the mix of policy shifts and policy continuity constitutes a new Germany in Europe, one that is normalizing, yet still distinctive among the large member states, and one that remains of central importance.

Clear implications for 'Germany in Europe' have yet to take shape. The enlarged European Union has arrived, a Constitutional Treaty awaits ratification and the EU's finances are again under review. Germany's weakening inclination to underwrite expensive initiatives, coupled with a less starry-eyed approach to Europe and a willingness to speak loudly and clearly when its interests are at stake, has added a novel element to interstate bargaining over integration. This will almost certainly slow the pace of integration and raise the level of public discord among the member states over long-terms goals and short term solutions. It may well temper the cumulative ambitions of Europe's would-be state-builders. It will not mean the end of the European project.

Further reading

Banchoff, T. (1999), *The German Problem Transformed: Institutions, Politics, and Foreign Policy, 1945–1995* (Ann Arbor: University of Michigan Press).

Berger, T. (1998), *Cultures of Antimilitarism: National Security in Germany and Japan* (Baltimore, MD: Johns Hopkins University Press).

Bulmer, S., Jeffery, C., and Paterson, W. (2000), *Germany's European Diplomacy: Shaping the Regional Milieu* (Manchester: Manchester University Press).

Duffield, J. (1998), *World Power Forsaken: Political Culture, International Institutions, and German Security Policy after Unification* (Stanford, CA: Stanford University Press).

Dyson, K., and Goetz, K. (2003), *Germany, Europe and the Politics of Constraint* (Oxford: Oxford University Press).

Katzenstein, P. (ed.) (1997), *Tamed Power: Germany in Europe* (Ithaca, NY: Cornell University Press).

Markovits, A., and Reich, S. (1997), *The German Predicament: Memory and Power in the New Europe* (Ithaca, NY: Cornell University Press).

Weblinks

The federal government's website is an important source of official information <**http://www.bundeszentrale.de**>, with foreign policy accessible at <**http://www.deutsche-aussenpolitik.de**>. For analysis there are several German and internationally based sites: the American Institute for Contemporary German Studies <**http://www.aicgs.org**>; the Aspen Institute <**http://www.aspenberlin.org**>; the Deutsche Gesellschaft für Auswärtige Politik <**http://www.dgap.org**>; the Institut für Europäische Poltik (IEP) <**http://www.iep-berlin.de**> and, especially for economic issues, the Zentrum für Europäische Wirtschaftsforschung <**http://www.zei.de**>.

References

Anderson, J. (1997), 'Hard Interests, Soft Power, and Germany's Changing Role in Europe', in P. Katzenstein, 80–107.

Anderson, J. (1999), *German Unification and the Union of Europe* (New York: Cambridge University Press).

Anderson, J. (2002), 'Europeanization and the Transformation of the Democratic Polity, 1945–2000', *Journal of Common Market Studies* 40/5, 793–822.

Banchoff, T. (1999), *The German Problem Transformed: Institutions, Politics, and Foreign Policy, 1945–1995* (Ann Arbor: University of Michigan Press).

Baun, M. (1996), *An Imperfect Union* (Boulder, CO: Westview).

Baun, M. (1996), 'The Maastricht Treaty as High Politics: Germany, France, and European Integration', *Political Science Quarterly* 110/4, 605–24.

Berger, T. (1998), *Cultures of Antimilitarism: National Security in Germany and Japan* (Baltimore, MD: Johns Hopkins University Press).

Berger, T. (1996), 'Norms, Identity, and National Security in Germany and Japan', in P. Katzenstein (ed.), *The Culture of National Security: Norms and Identity in World Politics* (New York: Columbia University Press), 317–56.

Bulmer, S. (1997), 'Shaping the Rules? The Constitutive Politics of the European Union and German Power', in Katzenstein, 49–79.

Bulmer, S., and Paterson, W. (1987), *The Federal Republic of Germany and the European Community* (London: Allen & Unwin).

Bulmer, S., and Paterson, W. (1996), 'Germany in the European Union: Gentle Giant or Emergent Leader', *International Affairs*, 72, 9–32.

Bulmer, S., Jeffery, C., and Paterson, W. (2000), *Germany's European Diplomacy: Shaping the Regional Milieu* (Manchester: Manchester University Press).

Cameron, D. (1992), 'The 1992 Initiative: Causes and Consequences', in Sbragia, 23–74.

Duffield, J. (1998), *World Power Forsaken: Political Culture, International Institutions, and German Security Policy after Unification* (Stanford, CA: Stanford University Press).

European Commission (2003), 'Communication from the Commission to the Council and the European Parliament: Public Finances in EMU—2003', SEC (2003) 571, accessed at <http://europa.eu.int/eur-lex/en/com/cnc/2003/com2003_0283en01.pdf>.

Garton Ash, T. (1993), *In Europe's Name* (New York: Random House).

Görtemaker, M. (1994), *Unifying Germany, 1989–90* (New York: St Martin's Press).

Gowa, J. (1989), 'Bipolarity and the Postwar International Economic Order', in Katzenstein, 33–50.

Hanrieder, W. (1989), *Germany, America, Europe* (New Haven, CT: Yale University Press).

Hendriks, G. (1991), *Germany and European Integration: The Common Agricultural Policy: An Area of Conflict* (New York: St Martin's Press).

Hooghe, L., and Marks, G. (1996), 'Europe With the Regions: Channels of Subnational Representation in the European Union', *Publius*, 26/1, 73–92.

Hüttmann, M., and Knodt, M. (2000), 'Die Europäisierung des deutschen Föderalismus', *Aus Politik und Zeitgeschichte*, 52–3, 31–8.

Jachtenfuchs, M. (1990), 'The European Community and the Protection of the Ozone Layer', *Journal of Common Market Studies*, 28, 261–77.

Jeffery, C. (1999), *Recasting German Federalism: The Legacies of Unification* (London: Cassell).

Jeffery, C. (2003), 'The German Länder and Europe: From Milieu-Shaping to Territorial Politics', in *Germany and Europe: A Europeanized Germany?*, K. Dyson and K. H. Goetz (eds) (Oxford: Oxford University Press), 97–108.

Katzenstein, P. (1989), *Industry and Politics in West Germany* (Ithaca, NY: Cornell University Press).

Katzenstein, P. (1997), 'United Germany in an Integrating Europe', in Katzenstein, 1–48.

Katzenstein, P. (ed.) (1997), *Tamed Power: Germany in Europe* (Ithaca, NY: Cornell University Press).

Kocs, S. (1995), *The Franco-German Relationship and Europe's Strategic Choices, 1955–1995* (Westport, CT: Praeger).

Lehmbruch, G. (1991), 'Die deutsche Vereinigung: Strukturen und Strategien', *Politische Vierteljahresschrift*, 32, 585–604.

Markovits, A., and Reich, S. (1997), *The German Predicament: Memory and Power in the New Europe* (Ithaca, NY: Cornell University Press).

Marks, G. (1992), 'Structural Policy in the European Community', in Sbragia, 202–4.

Marks, G., Nielson, F., Salk, J., and Ray, L. (1996), 'Competencies, Cracks, and Conflicts: Regional Mobilization in the European Union', *Comparative Political Studies*, 29(2), 164–93.

Milward, A. (1992), *The European Rescue of the Nation-State* (Berkeley: University of California Press).

Moravcsik, A. (1991), 'Negotiating the Single European Act: National Interests and Conventional Statecraft in the European Community', *International Organization*, 45, 651–88.

Moyer, H., and Josling, T. (1990), *Agricultural Policy Reform: Politics and Process in the EC and the USA* (Ames, IA: Iowa State University Press).

Petite, M. (1998), 'The Treaty of Amsterdam', Harvard Jean Monnet Chair Working Paper Series No. 2/98.

Pond, E. (1993), *Beyond the Wall: Germany's Road to Unification* (Washington, DC: Brookings Institution).

Ress, G. (1994), 'The Constitution and the Maastricht Treaty: Between Cooperation and Conflict', *German Politics*, 3, 48–74.

Sandholtz, W. (1993), 'Choosing Union: Monetary Politics and Maastricht', *International Organization*, 47, 1–39.

Sandholtz, W., and Zysman, J. (1989), '1992: Recasting the European Bargain', *World Politics*, 42, 95–128.

Sbragia, A. (1992), 'Thinking about the European Future', in Sbragia, *Euro-Politics*, 257–91.

Sbragia, A. (ed.) (1992), *Euro-Politics* (Washington, DC: Brookings Institution Press).

Scharpf, F. (1988), 'The Joint-Decision Trap; Lessons from German Federalism and European Integration', *Public Administration*, 66, 239–78.

Weizsäcker, E. (1990), 'Environmental Policy', in C. Schweitzer and D. Karsten (eds), *The Federal Republic of Germany and EC Membership Evaluated* (London: Pinter Publishers), 49–50.

Zelikow P., and Rice, C. (1995), *Germany Unified and Europe Transformed: A Study in Statecraft* (Cambridge, MA: Harvard University Press).

Chapter 5

France: Between Integration and National Sovereignty

Richard Balme and Cornelia Woll

Contents

Summary

This chapter explores France's relationship with the EU in terms of a long-standing ambiguity: between support for integration, on the one hand, and the wish to preserve national sovereignty, on the other. The first part of the chapter explores this tension in terms of the history of France's role and diplomacy in the European integration project. The tension is clear, given that European integration derived from the ideas of French founding fathers Jean Monnet and Robert Schuman but ran into its first major challenge from a French President, Charles de Gaulle. In the second part, attention shifts to the impact of Europeanization. We explore its impact on legal and institutional arrangements in France; on French public policy; and on public opinion, political cleavages and interest groups.

Introduction

The most constant element of the discussion on European integration in France is the persistent disagreement between pro-Europeanists and national sovereignists (Dyson and Featherstone 1999). Even though both camps agree on the fundamental importance of Europe for France, developments in French diplomacy have to be understood as the balancing out of these contradictory ambitions.

As adamant as the French might have been about wanting to preserve national sovereignty, European integration has had a profound effect on the French political system. Through direct institutional transformation, changing policy-making opportunities for both policy-makers and citizens and a shift in political ideas, political activity in France has adapted to the EU. This chapter traces these transformations. We highlight that public policies and policy paradigms changed more than domestic actors, even though cleavage lines have been affected by the integration process.

French diplomacy for Europe—history and politics

France's initial interest in European integration was part of power politics in the restructuring of the post-Second World War order. Confronted with American hegemony after the Second World War, France called upon European cooperation to regain a status of world power. General Charles de Gaulle expressed this most clearly.

What is the purpose of Europe? It should be to allow us to escape the domination of the Americans and the Russians. The six of us ought to be able to do just as well as either of the superpowers. [. . .] Europe is a means for France to regain the stature she has lacked since Waterloo, as the first among the world's nations (Peyrefitte 1994: 159).

It is true that European integration aimed at containing Germany. However, France also needed Europe in order to support her own position and influence towards the new world powers. Consequentially, one cannot find a unique French vision of European integration but rather a spectrum between two poles: wanting integration and wanting to preserve national sovereignty. Keeping in mind these contradictory goals is the key to understanding the logic behind the French initiatives for integration and the reservations France had throughout the process.

The following section is structured around this contradiction. First, it presents the designs that aimed at making European integration an extension of French influence in world politics. It then turns towards the more ambitious designs for further European integration. A last part examines how the tensions have become more and more problematic over time.

Extending French influence through European integration

French efforts for European cooperation immediately after the Second World War as well as the establishment of a European Defence Community were motivated by the sovereignist logic. It is true that French pro-Europeanists helped these projects to take shape, but the drive and the political will came from power politics most clearly identifiable in the stance of the first President of the Fifth Republic, Charles de Gaulle, who coined the term '*Europe des patries*'.

The Birth of Europe

The Schuman Plan of 9 May 1950, proposing the European Coal and Steel Community (ECSC), is generally considered the birth of European integration. Educated in pre-First World War Germany, French foreign minister Robert Schuman, aimed at proposing an alternative to the Anglo-American idea of leaving the strategically vital Ruhr mines to the control of the new German government. Instead, he suggested putting German and French coal and steel industries under joint management.

The person behind Robert Schuman was Jean Monnet, who some even consider the real author of the Schuman Plan (Gillingham 1991). Jean Monnet was a brandy indus-try businessman who had become the head of the *Commissariat au Plan de Modernisation et d'Equipement*—a governmental body for the planning and modernization of the economy. His close connections to the US, where he had worked for over two decades and befriended important statesmen such as Dean Acheson or John Foster Dulles, were crucial for the international success of the ambitious continental European plans, but also earned him the mistrust of important French leaders (Dûchene 1994). When the ECSC began operating in 1952, Monnet was the President of its 'govern-ment', the ECSC High Authority, where he was one of the co-authors of the European Atomic Energy Community (EURATOM). Together with the European Economic Community (EEC), the two communities were brought about by the Treaty of Rome, signed on 25 March 1957.

The beginnings of the European Communities (EC) were marked by disputes within France over the shape of the new construction. Jean Monnet came to personify a supra-nationalist version of Europe. While his style was compatible with the pro-European socialist government of Guy Mollet (1956–7), it was much less so with the government of Charles de Gaulle, who returned to power in June 1958, and who conceived of Europe as an alliance against the growing economic and strategic hegemony of the US.

De Gaulle's vision was decisive in early EC history and led to two historical stand-stills. First, de Gaulle's mistrust of close British–American connections led to his resolute opposition to British membership throughout the 1960s. Second, in an effort to block an increase in Community capacities, de Gaulle pulled France's representat-ives out of the Council and its preparatory body, the Committee of Permanent Representatives (COREPER), in 1965. The crisis, known as the Empty Chair Crisis, ended some six months later, in January 1966, with the Luxembourg Compromise. Nonetheless, European integration advanced more smoothly only after the resignation of President de Gaulle in April 1969, when the examination of membership applications of Britain, Ireland, and Denmark was resumed.

European defence

Another French design for Europe was the European Defence Community (EDC) proposed in October 1950. Only five years after the Second World War, with the devel-opment of the Cold War, the question of national defence capacities and especially of the rearmament of Germany arose. Modelled after the earlier Schuman Plan, French Prime Minister René Pleven suggested a fusion of European forces and equipment under a European political authority. Again, the proposal was made in opposition to the Anglo-Saxon solution of German rearmament independent of French control.

Despite strong opposition in France and throughout Europe against both a fusion of forces and the mere idea of German rearmament, the treaty was signed after a long series of torrid discussions on 27 May 1952, by the six members of the ECSC. Within France, however, unease continued as many issues concerning Germany, the new EDC capabilities and the extent of the remaining national forces remained unresolved. France, in the middle of a process of de-colonization, considered its own forces vital for its national interest, especially after a decisive defeat at Dien Bien Phu in May 1954. Ratification of the treaty became increasingly unlikely. Even though similar discussions were engaged in all member countries, it was the vote of the National Assembly on 30 August 1954, which decided the fate of the EDC. 319 votes, coming from the unlikely partners of the Communists and the Gaullists, opposed it, 264 votes, mainly from the *Movement Républicain Populaire*, supported it, twelve abstained and thirty-one took no part in the vote (Daniel and Aron 1956).

The EDC had been both conceived and defeated by France (Fursdon 1980) and with it fell the hopes for a political community within Europe. Early plans for a federal structure had to be abandoned and the EC followed the path of a market community. The fundamental question of German rearmament was eventually solved by a British solution: through the Paris agreements of October 1954, Italy and Germany joined the Western European Union (WEU), which was integrated militarily into the NATO framework. At the same time, a sovereign Germany joined NATO, since the control of German rearmament was assured under the WEU.

Nonetheless, France continued to look for a higher degree of European coordination independently of NATO. In 1961, it was de Gaulle who wanted to bring about a 'union of states' with the Fouchet Plan proposing a coordinated foreign and defence policy. Apart from Konrad Adenauer, the European partners were unenthusiastic about the plan which distanced Europe from the US and assigned a dominant role to French leadership. The Benelux countries especially rejected the project, and the Fouchet Plan eventually collapsed after a series of unproductive meetings in the beginning of 1962.

De Gaulle's vision for Europe has been called that of a 'French Europe' (Sotou 1996). Europe remained a means of opposing the Anglo-Saxons under the NATO regime. Having gained nuclear capability in the 1960s, France grew increasingly discontented with US control within NATO. The tensions climaxed in 1966, when General de Gaulle withdrew France from NATO's integrated military command.[1]

Deepening European integration

Attempts to form a political and defence union failed because of French aversion to supranational decision-making and the other member states' distrust of European integration under French control and conditions. As the European member countries grew closer, France therefore relied more and more on bilateral or trilateral diplomacy to advance her ideas, most notably with Germany, enabling France to act on a 'continental' European consensus. The Elysée Treaty of Friendship and Reconciliation

---

[1] Nonetheless, France continued to participate in other alliance activities within NATO.

signed by Charles de Gaulle and German Chancellor Konrad Adenauer in January 1963 laid the foundations for this cooperation. The Franco-German axis developed through the meetings between French President Georges Pompidou and German Chancellor Willy Brandt, but especially through the work of Valéry Giscard d'Estaing and Helmut Schmidt, who spoke at least weekly on the telephone and met regularly to discuss their political aims.

Even after the accession of the United Kingdom to the EC, the Franco–German axis stayed crucial as the motor of European integration, laying the foundations for several essential projects of deeper integration. Three projects are presented in detail below: the French initiative for increased political union, the construction of a social Europe and the Economic and Monetary Union (EMU).

Political union

In March 1985, the Commission—by then headed by Jacques Delors, the former French finance minister—issued a White Paper containing some 300 proposals that would eliminate existing barriers to the single internal market. The recommendations of the Dooge Report released during the same month suggested an IGC, which was to take place under the Italian presidency, on the preparation of a 'European Union'. While the British, along with the Danish and to a lesser degree the Dutch, were opposed to a new institutional edifice, the Germans and the French seemed willing to rethink the Treaty of Rome. After difficult negotiations and a divided vote, the Milan Council agreed to the Single European Act (SEA) during the Luxembourg summit in December 1985. At home, François Mitterrand tried to rally public support for the seemingly abstract enterprise in Brussels, declaring, 'France is our country, Europe our future'.

The efforts of the French government were crucial for making European affairs an acceptable political ambition in France, but it was Jacques Delors who gave Brussels' 'bureaucracy' a new image, both at an organizational and a symbolic level. His first step in doing so was to 'presidentialize' his power as the head of the Commission. With the help of political advisers brought in from France, Delors transformed a horizontal power structure into a vertical one—more informal, quicker and efficient than the previous multinational bureaucracy. Conscious of images, Delors had a gigantic clock installed in the Commission building in Brussels, counting down to the end of 1992, the year of the completion of the single market. Moreover, Delors succeeded in giving the government of the European Communities a state-like appearance. In 1985, he chose the blue flag with a circle of yellow stars of the Council of Europe for the European Commission. Without consulting any of the member governments, he decided to adopt it as the flag for the EC shortly after. In June 1986, at the great surprise of the European heads of state present, the star-circle flag flew at the G7 meeting in Tokyo (Grant 1994: 8). Two years later, it widely was used in Europe and throughout the world to represent the EC.

Negotiations between governments towards political union advanced in the late 1980s. However, some of the most fundamental questions concerning the architecture of the new union had remained unresolved in 1991. Helmut Kohl supported Jacques Delors's vision of a reinforced supranational structure, considering it similar to the ideas of German federalism. In the traditional French manner, François Mitterrand, on the other hand, was not ready to give up some of France's sovereign powers to the hands of European bureaucrats and deputies and prepared a counter-proposition to the supranational tree-like structure. They suggested Europe be constructed on three pillars, all under roof of the Council of Ministers. The French structure ultimately imposed itself in the Treaty on European Union after the federal structure had been rejected by ten of the twelve member states on 30 September 1991.

Social Europe

For the socialist government, the SEA was a market agreement and therefore constituted only 'the vital minimum for Europe' (Mitterrand 1986). François Mitterrand, the first socialist President of the Fifth Republic, was somewhat considered 'an ugly socialist duckling among a group of white capitalist geese' (Favier and Martin-Roland 1990: 362). His European partners were suspicious of the new member who had declared during his Presidential campaign 'Europe will be socialist, or it won't happen'. During his first appearance at the European Council Mitterrand proposed fiscal stimulation through consumer spending, a European social dimension, state aid for industrial development. For most European partners, and especially the British, the proposals were unacceptable. Between the French and the British governments, there was little common ground: while Margaret Thatcher undertook a turn towards privatization in her home country, Mitterrand followed the road of nationalization.

Led by Jacques Delors, the Commission's work programme helped to solidify some French demands. Based on contributions from the European Parliament and the Economic and Social Committee, the Council of Ministers published a draft Charter of Fundamental Rights for Workers in October 1989. At the same time, a document called 'The Social Dimension of 1992' was adopted, posing the question of a social dialogue at the European level.

The inclusion of the new social provisions in the Treaty of the European Union (TEU), however, threatened to foreclose a general agreement at Maastricht. With France refusing to modify the text and Britain insisting on less commitments, the final compromise was to agree to disagree. The EU adopted the social provisions attached to the Treaty, while the UK formally 'opted out'.[2]

Economic and monetary union

The most impressive instance of Franco-German cooperation is the case of EMU. France's initial interest in monetary integration grew during the 1960s, largely in response to the increasing instability of the world system and the perceived need to separate Europe from the influence of the US dollar. As was the case with respect to defence, it was mostly the French who were sensitive to this issue, whereas the other Europeans were not enthusiastic about a confrontation with the US. Early discussions thus advanced slowly or not at all. Throughout the 1970s and 1980s, the German Deutschmark dominated the first attempts at a linked exchange rate system, first the 'snake'[3] and then the European Monetary System (EMS) after 1979, created again by

---

[2] The British later accepted the Social Protocol and the Agreement at Amsterdam in 1997 under Tony Blair.

[3] The snake, in force between 1972 and 1979, was a linked exchange rate mechanism within Europe, floating as a bloc against the US dollar. France entered the snake in 1974, exited in 1975, and re-entered in 1976.

a Franco-German initiative between German Chancellor Helmut Schmidt and French President Valéry Giscard d'Estaing.

The EMS succeeded in assuring increasing monetary stability for the period between 1979 and 1992, a period where international exchange markets were severely shaken. Unfortunately, this stability was accompanied by considerable structural distortions between the participating countries, creating a painful asymmetry between the different currencies. Especially France and Italy suffered considerably from currency depreciation in times of recession and growing unemployment.

In France, the economic downturn was aggravated by the new macroeconomic policies of the Socialist government. Planning to re-institute Keynesian policies, the new government had tried to stimulate internal demand and long-term employment through a number of measures, but the changes only worked to increase the recession. In order to realign under the EMS system, France needed to devalue the Franc in three political and economically painful steps between 1981 and 1983. By 1983 it had become clear that the choice was between exiting the EMS and completely revising French macro-economic policy. Advocates rallied into two camps either supporting EMS and a policy of a '*Franc fort*' or continuing the Keynesian measures without European constraints. Ultimately going with the 'Europeans', Mitterrand decided on 21 March 1983, to keep the Franc in the EMS, at the cost of new draconian economic measures accompanied by the third devaluation of the franc, and to abandon his Keynesian policies. This famous 'U-turn' which followed the 'Mitterrand experiment' was the single most important decision point of the Mitterrand Presidency, the turning point that allowed a continuation of European monetary integration.

After this experience of being dependent on the rigorous politics of the German *Bundesbank*, the French goal became to control German monetary dominance by creating a common European Central Bank. The proposals of Edouard Balladur gathered initial support from Italy and the German foreign minister Hans-Dietrich Genscher and were elaborated by a committee headed by Jacques Delors. The German Chancellor Helmut Kohl, however, remained unconvinced and the UK rejected the idea outright. In the absence of Franco–German agreement, EMU might never have succeeded, had it not been for the political earthquake that shook Germany in 1989: the fall of the Berlin wall (Cameron 1996).

The bilateral negotiations that thereafter took place between Helmut Kohl and François Mitterrand are often referred to as the 'grand bargain', exchanging French support for German reunification against German support of EMU. This perspective is probably oversimplified (Dyson and Featherstone 1999), but what is certain is that EMU would have never been possible without the tenacious insistence of France. Mitterrand not only rallied his European partners around the Delors plan, he also assured that definite dates would be committed to for the launching of the different phases. Mitterrand and Kohl launched a joint initiative to achieve political union and EMU by 1993, even though these dates were later adjusted to a more realistic time frame. French diplomacy was vital for making EMU a viable political objective.

Increasing tensions between contradictory goals

The period leading up to 1992 was undoubtedly one of the most important ones in the history of the EU and the Franco–German tandem was essential in determining the direction it was going to take. However, the intense work towards deeper integration had been a violation of the sovereignist values of France. Among many French citizens, the feeling came up that too much integration ran counter to more immediate French interests. The 1990s were therefore marked by a slowing down of pro-European initiatives. On the other hand, the fall of the Soviet Union forced France to reconsider its role in the new world order. As in the early post-war period, this meant a turn towards Europe. However, since integration had already advanced considerably, it had become difficult to function as a 'French' Europe, with the EU enlarged to fifteen states. The most recent difficulties of European foreign policy during the Iraq crisis testify to these tensions.

The Maastricht aftermath

Despite the unanimity of French negotiators, the ratification of the Maastricht Treaty (the Treaty on European Union—TEU) proved to be difficult (Appleton 1996). In a tense domestic context—the Left had been beaten in regional elections in early 1992 and had to prepare for the 1993 legislative election—Mitterrand decided to submit the decision to a public referendum. France ratified the TEU in September 1992 by the smallest possible margin of 51.05 per cent. The small margin illustrates how Europe, and especially the criteria for EMU, had become associated with unemployment in the minds of many French citizens. Starting with the early 1990s, euro-scepticism became a common electoral stance for French politicians, and not just for demagogues like Jean-Marie Le Pen of the Front National.

Throughout the 1990s, France remained conspicuously cautious about European affairs, careful to demonstrate that the EU would not impose undesirable outcomes onto French domestic politics. The difficult discussions around the agricultural issue at the Uruguay Round of the GATT might have been partially due to this development. On another occasion, Lionel Jospin insisted on a review of the EMU Stability Pact in June 1997, and pushed for the adoption of a separate resolution on growth and employment by the European Council, a central pillar of French domestic politics. The Amsterdam Treaty of 1997 was signed by an enlarged EU in an atmosphere of dampened enthusiasm.

Nonetheless, the European Union had established itself as a political reality. Most notably, two ethical issues marked the end of the 1990s: the scandal surrounding the Santer Commission in early 1999, and the boycott of Austria in January 2000, which was incited largely through French activism. Following the coalition of the Austrian Right with the extreme right party FPÖ of Jörg Haider, France led the European countries to publish a declaration in which the EU threatened sanctions against Austria.

On most other issues, such as the new requirements for a European Union enlarged to twenty-five states, France has been rather reactive. Jacques Chirac's contributions to the Nice Council have been criticized and it was the German foreign minister, Joschka Fischer, and not a Frenchman, who relaunched the debate about the architecture of European integration.

Redefining Europe's role in the new world order

Having lived with the WEU defence arrangement of 1954 throughout the Cold War, France started to think about a new solution for European defence soon after the collapse of the Soviet Union. Mitterrand's proposal of a European Confederation of the whole of the continent had quickly been rejected by the Eastern European states, which preferred the idea of future membership of the EU and of NATO to an alliance with Russia.

Searching for alternatives, Mitterrand met with Helmut Kohl during the summer of 1991 to present the idea of transforming the infant Franco–German brigade created in 1986 into a 'Franco-German army with a European vocation'. The two heads of state agreed in principle, but Helmut Kohl insisted on formally informing Washington. On the same day, the UK and Italy presented a joint Anglo–Italian declaration on the security and defence of Europe based not on a separate European defence, but on the supremacy of NATO, and thus the US. Germany and France immediately distributed their counter-proposition based on the WEU, inviting the other European countries to join the future Franco–German division in order to constitute a European corps. With the Maastricht Council in view, the European powers and the US forged a compromise at the NATO summit in Rome in November 1991.[4]

Interestingly, the most important advance came from an unusual Franco–British initiative. Reflecting upon the Balkan disaster at a meeting St Malo in Brittany, British Prime Minister Tony Blair and Jacques Chirac proposed a European Rapid Reaction Force, upon which Germany eventually embarked. At the Cologne meeting of the European Council in 1999, the WEU's Military Staff was abandoned and the remaining political functions were moved to Brussels and integrated within the EU. Even though the policies are required to be compatible with NATO policies, European defence is today an independent European policy area under the control of the European Institutions and includes humanitarian and rescue tasks, peacekeeping tasks and combat-force tasks in crisis management.

Despite this recognized European defence identity, foreign and security policy remains the most contentious area of European coordination. Although France has pursued this goal since the early 1950s, it continues to view it as a necessary extension of French policy, not a constraint upon its sovereign decisions. France tried to conduct its foreign policy through Europe in the aftermath of the Balkan crisis by proposing a stability plan for Central and Eastern Europe. However, the EU did not prevent an embarrassing division between member states concerning the recognition of Croatia and Slovenia, a lack of coordination and inertia.

More noteworthy still was the EU schism in 2003 over the US war on Iraq. Continuing the old Franco–German alliance, Gerhard Schröder's clumsy affirmations against a war in Iraq comforted Jacques Chirac's opposition to it. Aware of the German position, France knew that it would speak up as part of the Franco–German couple. The situation is paradoxical. While most observers argue that the Franco–German position has driven a wedge into Europe, others argue that the sudden Franco–German agreement countering the US position promises further deepening of European integration and establishes Europe as a pole in world politics.

What is certain is that foreign policy continues to be a matter considered vital to national sovereignty. As much as France wants Europe to grow closer together, it will not cede its decision-making power. Another lesson from the Iraq crisis is that the two

---

[4] The Maastricht Treaty negotiated in December 1991 finally formalized European defence as an integral part of a CFSP, but delegated its operation to an external organ, the WEU.

French ambitions for Europe—extending French interests and integrating further—are more and more contradictory as the EU evolves. In spite of Jacques Chirac's sharp critique of the Eastern countries' opinion on security matters, an enlarged EU will only make common positions more difficult.

Institutional and policy adaptation in France

Having examined the significance of France for Europe, we now try to understand how the EU affects and transforms French institutions and policy-making. As the recent proliferation of studies on the Europeanization showed (Ladrech 1994; Cole and Drake 2000; Guyomarch 2001), the impact has been considerable, but became especially visible in the last decade. In the following section, we will investigate the adjustment process by looking at three related but distinct categories.

First, we look at the changes in fixed structures (that is the *legal and institutional arrangements* in France), while at the same time examining how these structural adaptations affect political relations and responsibilities. Second, we try to give an overview of the very complex re-orientation of French *public policies* increasingly subject to guidelines or pressures from the EU. Last, we examine the normative adjustment and the reorientation of political ideas by looking at the re-organization of *public opinion and political cleavages* in France.

Formal structures

Formal structures in France have changed in several ways. First, the EU treaties and legislation have led to direct adaptation of the French constitution and French law. Second, they have required the reorganization of French political institutions. Third, the interplay of the different layers of government, most notably at the regional level, has become more complex.

Direct constitutional and legal adaptation

Until 1992 the European treaties had no specific impact on the French constitution. Under the French constitution of 27 October 1946, the Treaty of Rome was classified as an international treaty. The Fifth Republic's constitution of 1958 went little further, stipulating merely a procedural innovation with the possible use of a public referendum for the ratification of a treaty.[5] The ratification of the Treaty on European Union, however, required a constitutional revision, especially due to its provisions on EU citizenship and the right of EU citizens to participate in French municipal elections. Called upon by the President, the Constitutional Council agreed in April 1992 to modify the Constitution. After heated political discussion, the modifications were adopted by both assemblies of the Parliament, and then submitted to a public

[5] The referendum has been used twice under the Fifth Republic in relation to European integration: once in 1972 for the ratification of the first enlargement and once in 1992 for the ratification of the Maastricht Treaty. It will be used again for the ratification of the Constitutional Treaty in 2005.

referendum with the ratification of the Maastricht Treaty. Through the revision, an explicit reference to obligations linked to EU membership is now in the French constitution. Surprisingly, a second revision was found to be necessary for the Schengen agreement under the Balladur government, even though France had ratified the agreement in 1985 and the application convention in 1990, a ratification that had been judged constitutional by the Constitutional Council in 1991. A third constitutional revision took place in the context of the ratification of the Amsterdam Treaty. It inscribed an even closer cooperation between the government and the national parliament, thus permitting parliamentary control on European white papers, green papers or the agenda of the Commission.

The modifications in 1992 represented a qualitative jump: European treaties had moved beyond the status of international agreements (Oberdorff 1994). The constitutional amendment thus provided for further European integration in the future, and was hence dubbed by some French lawyers the French '*constitution européenne*'. From 1992 on, the French constitution ceased being an 'untouchable dogma' that existed independently of European integration.

Since treaties and European secondary legislation—regulations and directives—obtained priority over national laws in 1989 with the Nicolo case of the Conseil d'Etat, the superiority of European law on national law is now fully recognized. Generally, transposition is a shared competence of the government and of the parliament. The 1958 Constitution, however, limited the law-making competence of parliament more than in other European countries, leaving mainly the executive to transpose EU directives through decrees or ordinances. However, the parliament lately became more and more active, transposing directives by means of legislation (Rozenberg and Szukala 2001). Moreover, the transposition process has been facilitated through two prime-minister circulars in 1992 in order to be able to meet the implementation deadlines of the EU, after it had been repeatedly criticized for its long delays.

An important factor in this development is the fact that the European Court of Justice (ECJ) can be utilized by European citizens against national legislation or regulation. ECJ rulings condemning France are thus another important motor for change within France. With some notable exceptions, the French administration has been quite compliant with rulings of the ECJ. Through its reliance on jurisprudence, European integration contributed to the transformation of political legitimacy, which no longer solely derives from majority rule, but also from fundamental principles—invoked from the European Convention on Human Rights, for example—and from a system of judicial recourse largely open to citizens against member states, in the quality of rights. Europe is not the only source of this transformation, as the Constitutional Council also gained a significant influence at the domestic level since the early 1970s. Unlike the ECJ, however, it cannot at this stage be accessed directly by citizens. This new reliance on jurisprudence constitutes one of the most remarkable changes within the French political system.

Reorganization of governmental structures

The most important innovation brought about by European integration is the interministeral coordination, which is assured by a body directly linked to the Prime Minister, the *Secrétariat Général du Comité Interministériel pour les Questions de Coopération Economique Européenne* (SGCI). As the task of the EU grew, coordination became crucial between the French civil servants working on the preparation of negotiations, the strategic calculations on the part of the Foreign Affairs Ministry, and the implementation work of the concerned ministries. Supervised by the European adviser of the Prime Minister, the SGCI acts as a crucial link between the administration in Paris and the French permanent representative in Brussels. The Minister of European Affairs, a Junior Minister in the Ministry of Foreign Affairs, is closely associated with the coordination of the SGCI (Lequesne 1993).

The fundamental role of the SGCI facilitated a growing importance for the Prime Minister. Originally, the Prime Minister had no official function in European affairs, since foreign affairs were supposed to be the exclusive domain of the President. In the European Council, France was the only member normally represented by its head of state rather than its head of government. The first Prime Minister to ever participate in a European Council was Pierre Mauroy as late as 1983. During the first cohabitation period under Mitterrand, the Prime Minister and the President sat together at almost every meeting. All subsequent Prime Ministers have influenced key European decisions. This growth in importance illustrates that EU policy is nowadays increasingly equated to national policy issues rather than to foreign policy.

Parallel to the loosening up of a vertical governmental hierarchy, the Parliament increasingly affirmed its place in European affairs. On the one hand, this happened through the transposition of European legislation as mentioned above. On the other hand, the Parliament also formally asked to be associated more closely with the decision-making process in the Council in 1992. To their indignation, the passing of information to members of the *Sénat* and the *Assemblée Nationale* sometimes took several months. In extreme cases, some propositions were even transmitted from the SGCI after the EU Council had already adopted them in Brussels. With the modification of the Constitution in 1992, the government was then obliged to refer proposals to Parliament, if they contain provisions which are matters for statute law. The revision of the Constitution in January 1999 and a circular of the Prime Minister on 13 December 1999 finally assured the information of Parliament for all relevant texts, if the Council of State deemed them so, within a deadline of one month.

In summary, the shift of the status of EU affairs from foreign policy to issues of national concern manifests itself in (1) a greater role of the Prime Minister, (2) a change from a vertical to a more horizontal hierarchy within the executive, (3) greater clout for the Parliament, and (4) the re-organization of task-related institutions. Most of these adaptations correspond to a shift in the status of the European question from a foreign affairs issue to a supranational dimension of subject-specific policy stakes.

French regions in a multilevel system

The multilevel system of governance of the EU is often presupposed to have created a 'Europe of regions'. Since France is the archetype of a centralized state, it is the most interesting test for this hypothesis. It is true that the EU's regional policy has to a large extent replaced France's regional policy. However, the EU's willingness to empower regions by giving them a greater role in the management of structural funds has not had as large an effect as one could imagine. The transformations that one can observe are as much a result of EU regional policy as they are of the parallel attempts of the French state to decentralize (Balme and Jouve 1996).

For a number of reasons, French regions did not become fully fledged political actors within the European policy network. In the wake of decentralization, the central government progressively changed its mode of leadership and embraced a more contractual way of dealing with local communities. Since 1982, the central government used its resources, its expertise and a network of the *préfectures* and the *sous-préfectures* to keep a hand on local development. Departments and regions alone often lacked the human and financial resources to handle such issues. The implementation of the *Contrats de Plan Etat Région* in the 1980s paved the way for the management of Community Support Framework and Operational Programmes, brought about by the EU in its structural funds reform in 1988. Even though the EU wanted to deal directly with the regions, the central government secured its control over information circuits and budgetary procedures so that it became an inevitable partner in the European regional policy networks. Moreover, French regions failed to exploit all the resources the EU offered them. Due to a lack of administrative and political capacities, in some cases even a lack of political legitimacy, the regions were not able to fully commit themselves to Community initiatives, such as the programme designed to stimulate interregional cooperation (known as Interreg), or even to maintain a permanent representation in Brussels.

Compared to historical conditions, French regions gained greater autonomy and access to the public sphere created by the EU. However, the grasp of the central government in key policy networks is still significant and the emergence of a more federal system, like the German *Länder* or the Spanish regions, is highly unlikely.

Public policy adjustment

The impact of the EU on French public policies is quite certain, but systematic conclusions are difficult, as most analyses remain based on specific case studies (for example Palier 2000; Schmidt 2001). Analysing recent policy changes, we give an overview of the general impact of the EU on domestic public policy, without suggesting that the EU is the only reason for domestic changes. The Europeanization of public policy is in our view more relevant when considered as the interface between European and domestic policy-making, leading to a wide range of possible situations, from joint consolidation to mutual exclusion. We argue that EU policy-making is a facilitator and a powerful lever for French policy reforms.

In order to clarify the nature of the changes, we broadly follow the categorization developed by Theodore Lowi in constitutive, regulative, distributive, or redistributive policy types (Lowi 1972). We take constitutive policies to designate policy domains that make up the essence of the state, sovereignty policies, or *politiques régaliennes*, such as constitutional reforms, justice, defence and security, and borders control. Regulative policies determine the conditions, results or standards of issue areas, such as working conditions, sanitary standards or environmental law. Distributive policies are policies that use the state's resources to furnish a universal access to basic needs for the whole of society, such as public schools, public health, public transports or roads. Redistributive policies, by contrast, are policies aiming to help one particular part of society, such as specific industrial sectors, people living under the poverty threshold or the unemployed for instance.

All policy types can be found in French politics, and a mix of different policy instruments covers most policy sectors. However, France largely developed distributive policies, notably with a specific conception of public services ('*services publics*'), well beyond that of universal welfare, to include a high degree of interventionism in the industrial sphere. Infrastructure services, such as gas and electricity, railroads, postal services, telecommunications, or air transport have been state monopolies. The priority of distributive policy areas was even fixed in the preamble of the French constitution of 1946, which states that 'all good, all business, of which the exploitation acquires the characteristics of a national public service or a monopoly *de fait* must be collectively owned'.

The EU transformed domestic public policies by reorienting the general mix of policy types in three ways. First, the EU, marked by regulative governance, promoted a recourse to regulative policies especially in moderately and highly integrated policy areas (Majone 1996). For example, most formally state owned industrial sectors underwent privatization and regulation through independent authorities, such as the Regulation Authority of Telecommunications (ART). Second, by capping the possibility of high public spending, the EU forced an orientation away from very general distributive policies to more targeted, redistributive policies. Third, as integration proceeded further, all European member states opened some of their sovereign policies to the European realm. This does not necessarily mean that they 'gave up' sovereign to the EU, as some of these policy areas are governed by intergovernmental cooperation or regulative agencies more than by supranational institutions. The fact that domestic politics loses its monopoly in controlling sovereignty policies does not equate with the growth of a European state. Border controls are the most striking example, but justice and defence are also more and more striving for a European coherence.

The turn towards regulative policy-making has been noted by several authors and it often equated with the '*tournant néo-libéral*' in France (Jobert 1994). However, the change is not exclusively market-orientated, as a large number of redistributive policies persist and continue. The French State continues to have a firm role in framing, conditioning, and balancing the market. The policy types, however, with which it aims to do so, have changed under the influence of the EU.

Public opinion and political cleavages

The last section revolves around political ideas and perceptions. How has European integration affected French political cleavages and public opinion? To address this issue, we consider support for European integration in public opinion, participation in European elections and ratification of European Treaties, changes in the partisan system and new opportunities for protest movements.

Support for European integration

Regarding public opinion and European integration, Eurobarometer surveys show that France stands globally very close to the European average. In 2002, 52 per cent of French respondents think that French membership to the EU is a good thing (EU15 55 per cent), and 71 per cent are in favour of the Euro (EU12 71 per cent). France is therefore at the midpoint between strong supporters of the EU, such as Belgium or

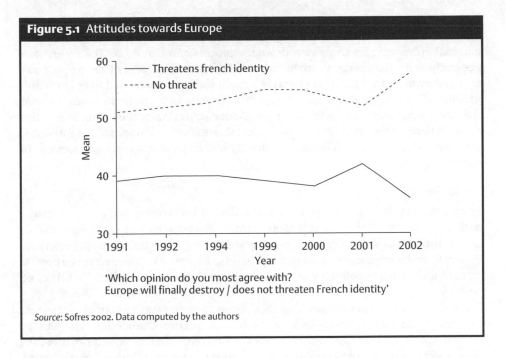

Figure 5.1 Attitudes towards Europe

'Which opinion do you most agree with?
Europe will finally destroy / does not threaten French identity'

Source: Sofres 2002. Data computed by the authors

Italy, and the most Euro-sceptical countries like the UK, Finland, Sweden, and Austria (CEC 2002). The SOFRES surveys, conducted since the early 1990s to measure the perception of European integration as a threat for national identity, also affirm a general acceptance of the EU (SOFRES 2002; see Figure 5.1). Over the last decade, trust in EU integration regularly increased, with a slight inflexion in 2000 caused by the approaching Euro. With confidence in the Euro increasing, the single currency seems now to have further fostered confidence in the EU.

An analysis of EU-related voting further helps us to understand support for European integration. Like in other European countries, turnout in European elections has always been lower than in national polls, and followed the same pattern of decline. Several overlapping factors can be considered to explain this situation. Low interest in European affairs and a general crisis of political representation both contribute to this low turnout. Moreover, EU institutions are complex and not very well understood by citizens. Even an increase in the competencies of the EP did not reverse or limit the decline in turnout. A last factor lies in the electoral rule and in the framing of the campaign. The proportional rule in a national district leaves voters in total uncertainty about the final composition of the Parliament, not to speak about its impact on the designation of the Commission formed by national governments. It also imposes that national (rather than European) parties compete in the campaign. Consequently, European campaigns highlight national issues, making European elections secondary national elections without much political consequence—seemingly redundant and of little relevance. Participation therefore relies mainly on a sense of European civic duty.

A more salient European issue was the Maastricht referendum in 1992. Turnout remained low in the ballot, but the campaign hosted a vivid debate between supporters and opponents, culminating with a TV debate confronting President François

Mitterrand with the Gaullist Philippe Séguin. The result was a tight majority for 'yes' (51 per cent), which sent the message to the political elite throughout Europe that national public opinion could slow down the process of integration. 'Yes' voters were generally from the modern, urban, educated, and well-off part of the population, opposed by more traditional segments of French society, who tended to be rural, sub-urban, and popular, and severely affected by economic and social crisis. Furthermore, the referendum was a means for leaders and citizens to criticize the liberal orientation of the EU even if they did not necessarily feel threatened by European integration. As we shall see below, the referendum indirectly had tremendous consequences on the partisan system.

The partisan system

Europe has not led to a complete reorientation of the French party system: major national political parties are still there, European elections and campaigns mainly host national issues, and European matters are not very salient in domestic elections. However, had European integration not progressed, we would not observe the present state of French party politics, even though change has been an indirect result of EU politics.

Consider ideological changes. The most dramatic one was the U-turn of the *Parti Socialiste (PS)* in 1983, from national Keynesianism to European monetarism. Europe did not 'cause' this change. Rather, it was the fiasco of previous policies that led the liberal wing of the party to impose its view. Europe was not an inevitable constraint, it was used by the *PS* as a political opportunity. Other parties were affected in similar ways. The *Parti Communiste (PC)* was forced to abandon its categorical rejection of the single market project, if it wanted to remain a potential coalition partner. The Gaullist party *RPR*, leader of the right-wing coalition, equally mellowed its position. Having vigorously contested the European and Atlantic policy of Valéry Giscard d'Estaing in the 1970s, Jacques Chirac had to distance his party from the historical stance of de Gaulle on national sovereignty. By the mid-1990s, the *RPR* shared the positions of the *PS* on the single market and later on the single currency. Competing for international credibility and domestic leadership, the two presidential parties had converged on the same policy stance.

This convergence in turn created tensions within the two major French political parties. The Socialists faced the internal opposition of the left-wing *CERES* led by Jean-Pierre Chevènement and finally the exit of the latter in 2000. In the presidential election of 2002, his candidacy in the name of the *Pôle républicain* contributed to the defeat of Lionel Jospin. The *RPR* saw severe internal competition during the nineties, notably between Edouard Balladur and Jacques Chirac and between Alain Juppé and Philippe Séguin. The most traditional Gaullists left the party in 1999 to create the *RPF* around Charles Pasqua. The European issue was not the only cause of these intra-party divisions. Nevertheless, policy adjustments of major parties undoubtedly nourished internal ideological *aggiornamentos*, political tensions, and changes in partisan organizations.

European integration also altered the coalition possibilities between parties. Similar to the convergence between the *PC* and the *PS* mentioned above, the *RPR* and the *UDF* have largely converged on nearly all issues when compared to the early 1980s. This convergence largely contributed to the feasibility of the creation of the *UMP* in 2002, a very large right-wing party agglomeration supporting Jacques Chirac's presidency around both parties.

Another major change of the French party system is the introduction of proportional rule brought since 1979 by European elections. This was a political opportunity for small and new parties like *Les Verts* and the *Front National* to get public attention and mobilize resources. After 1986, regional elections adopted the same proportional rule and thus continued the tendency. As a consequence, the partisan system has become wider and more fragmented than it used to be. Old Trotskyist organizations like *Lutte Ouvrière* and the *Ligue Communiste Révolutionnaire*, and different '*souverainistes*' candidates seized European elections to get access to the public sphere. The Maastricht referendum revealed that there was a political space available to contest the forms of European integration, and parties left outside governmental coalitions widely used this ideological 'niche'.

The new cleavage did not become dominant, and did not simply erase the old left/right alignment, mainly because there is neither a unified pro-European pole nor a homogeneous anti-European coalition. Changes are indirect, but nevertheless significant. Convergence of governmental parties at the centre, coupled with radicalization at the extremes, keep the public from the relevant political debate on European issues. This is obviously hazardous for European citizenship, but even more so for national citizenship, as it contributes to a general crisis of political representation. The results of the presidential election of April 2002, qualifying Jean-Marie Le Pen for the second round, epitomize this trend.

Social movements and protests

One last issue for considering the impact of European integration on French political cleavages is social movements and protest politics. Has European integration affected the French pattern of social conflicts? Did it open new motives for political mobilization and protest? Did it renew the relations between the state and social movements?

Consider actors from traditional socioeconomic organizations, including labour unions, business organizations, and farmers' unions. From Tocqueville to Tilly and Crozier, France has traditionally been depicted as the homeland of revolution and protest politics with little room for collective bargaining and consensual decision-making. Over the last two decades, French unions have naturally been concerned with the accomplishment of the single market and the developments of social policy at the EU level. The *CFDT* trade union organization in particular was close to the ideas of Jacques Delors, and within the European confederation, the *ETUC*, a strong supporter of the Social Dialogue. The European strategy of the *CFDT* was part of a more reformist orientation of the union at the domestic level, and of its willingness to negotiate with business organizations or with the government rather than to oppose reforms through calls for strikes and mass demonstrations. Conflicting with more traditional views of other union organizations, the *FO* and the *CGT*, this attitude undermined unions' solidarity and capacity for collective action. During the great strikes of 1995, the tensions culminated and even divided the *CFDT* internally, leading to the formation of the new, more radical union *SUD*. Despite these difficulties at the domestic level, the EU institutions continued to be a forum for more consensual approaches and the *CFDT* remained active within them. In March 1999, the *CGT* finally joined the *ETUC*, having been the last large union in the EU not to join. The event is remarkable, showing that the *CGT*, close to the *Parti Communiste*, finally acknowledged the legitimacy of the single market and the policy relevance of EU institutions like the Social Dialogue.

In the same vein, the French business organisation *MEDEF* was traditionally renowned for its social conservatism and reluctance to engage in collective bargaining with unions. During the last decade, this attitude has been changing. First, *MEDEF* recognized the importance of the European Social Dialogue, and was active within the European industrialists's organization, *UNICE*, in defining more cooperative positions. Second, at the domestic level, *MEDEF* promoted a strategy of 'social refoundation' under the Jospin government, calling for a re-launch of collective bargaining to contain the so-called '*dirigisme*' of the French state in social policy. At both the European and the national level, the threat of social legislation brings business organizations to accept or promote collective bargaining, because the results are less uncertain and unfavourable than those of radical pro-labour state legislation. The *MEDEF* strategy corresponds to the evolution of the *CFDT* mentioned above. Social dialogue did not just die with the end of Keynesianism, and it is somewhat counter-intuitive and noteworthy to observe this tentative move towards more consensual industrial relations coupled with the liberalization of French capitalism.

Turning now to agriculture, its importance within French economy, society, and politics overall explains why the CAP was promoted by French governments since the 1960s. French farmers are largely unionized, and agriculture policy comes close to sectoral neo-corporatism (Muller 1984). The dramatic changes of the sector motivated frequent protest movements of farmers, in France or in Brussels. Interestingly, the transformation has led to a diversification of the movement. Traditionally, the largest farmers' union, the *FNSEA*, has been very influential and was closely associated to the making of governmental policies. Their close connection to decision-making has led to the creation of an alternative organization, the *Confédération paysanne* led by José Bové. This more radical movement would then organize at the European level, and progressively penetrate the EU policy communities.

Other French movements have benefited from the European sphere as well. The movement of the unemployed began during the 1990s at the domestic level in order to demand better unemployment benefits independently from workers unions. The French movement was the initiator of the massive mobilisation in Amsterdam in 1997 and in following European summits. It was successful in promoting the employment issue on the European agenda and contributed to its inclusion in the Amsterdam Treaty, even though the effects remain limited (Chabanet 2002). One could also argue that Europe had a decisive effect on the ecology movement. Over the last two decades, the environment has moved from an ill-defined social movement to a political party, for the first time participating in a governmental coalition through the Greens between 1997 and 2002. Domestic protest regarding the environment no longer opposes industrial policies in the name of ecology, as was the case in the 1970s with the French nuclear plants programme. On the other hand, the institutionalization of the ecology movement has created opposition from a newly formed hunters movement, contesting the European legal ground for hunting regulation.

To summarize the transformation of political cleavages, we observe the convergence of policy positions of major actors of the political system. This is true for governmental parties, large labour unions and business organizations, farmers' unions, and environmental groups. Domestic factors also contribute to these changes. Still national consensus is often a pre-condition for access to influence at the European level, and European institutionalization thus nourishes a convergence of policy positions of major domestic political actors. Borrowing from Peter Mair (2000), we name this trend the 'cartellization' of the system of political representation, including political parties and major interest groups. Referring to the consensus or to the declining conflict between actors, cartellization also implies that policy convergence reduces political competitiveness and offers less clear alternatives to public opinion. It therefore undermines the relation between political supply and demand, between elites and citizens, and between the political system and society. As a result, new lines of cleavages have emerged, between protest and governmental parties, between well-established interest groups and more radical organizations contesting the system.

Conclusion

We briefly conclude our analysis with the following remarks. First, from the diplomatic point of view, the Mitterrand–Kohl relationship probably marked the end of thirty years of Franco-German centrality in deepening European integration. Due to the obvious economic, diplomatic, and demographic importance of both countries, this axis will remain crucial. Nonetheless, a distinct part of European history, the overcoming of the Second World War aftermath in Western Europe, is now over. European stakes have moved further east, in the context of enlargement, and further west, where global security and trade issues require a rethinking of transatlantic relations. These developments imply a decline of French leadership in European integration, made evident by the difficult leadership of the French presidency at the Nice summit in December 2000. Once the UK enters the Euro zone, the deterioration of French leadership would be even more inevitable. From this perspective, the Franco-German coalition forged in the context of the Iraq War of 2003 may be understood as an attempt to re-establish their leadership in European diplomacy. The effectiveness and the robustness of this recent enterprise remains a topic for discussion.

Concerning the Europeanization of the French polity, policy paradigms, policy instruments, and policy rules have considerably evolved under the influence of the EU over the last two decades. The transformation of political representation, albeit significant, remains more limited. We therefore suggest that Europeanization should mainly be understood as the transformation of relations among domestic actors, rather than as the transnationalization of domestic politics. In the French case, the main effects of these transformations lie in the European mainstreaming of public policies, the convergence of policy positions, and the cartellization of major political actors. This in turn yields new lines of cleavages and political contention.

Finally, it is necessary to underline that the changes depicted here are not just adaptation to external constraints. Policy adjustments do occur, sometimes with difficulties, to obey European directives. But in the large majority of cases, competition, currency, agriculture, or trade for instance, European constraints are just the feedback of commitments domestic actors have been pushing hard to promote at the European level. European rules are not independent from domestic actors, certainly not from governments. In this perspective, European institutions may be understood, like central banks or constitutional courts, as agencies externalizing political commitments of domestic actors, voluntarily engaged in self-binding strategies. Adjustment 'to' Europe may be better understood, in the case of France, as modernization 'through' Europe.

Further reading

Recent works specifically addressing the role of France in the EU and the effect of European integration on France are Dreyfus *et al.* (1993), Guyomarch *et al.* (1998), and Gueldry (2001), but general writings on French politics are also instructive. The most comprehensive French analysis is d'Arcy and Rouban (d'Arcy and Rouban 1996). For historical details, see Bossuat (1996). Some of the more recent books on the Franco–German axis are Cole (2001), Hendriks (2000), Calleo and Staal (1998), or Pedersen (1998). Ladrech (1994) wrote one of the first articles on Europeanization in France. Recent studies include Cole and Drake (2000), Guyomarch (2001) and Guyomarch *et al.* (2001).

Weblinks

A very extensive bibliography on France in the European Union is maintained by Osvaldo Croci 'The European Union: a bibliography (5.6 France)', available online at <**http://www.mun.ca/ceuep/EU-bib.html**>. Information and updates on all French governmental institutions can be found at the site 'Governments in the WWW' maintained by Gunnar Anzinger <**http://www.gksoft.com/govt/en/fr.html**>. The gateway to relations with France from the EU's website is <**http://www.europa.eu.int/ abc/governments/ france/index_en.htm**>.

References

Appleton, A. (1996), 'The Maastricht Referendum and the Party System', in J. T. S. Keeler and M. Schain (eds), *Chirac's Challenge: Liberalization, Europeanization, and Malaise in France* (New York: St Martin's Press, 301–24).

d'Arcy, F., and Rouban, L. (eds) (1996), *De la Ve République à l'Europe* (Paris: Presses de Sciences Po).

Balme, R., and Jouve, B. (1996), 'Building the Regional State: Europe and Territorial

Organization in France', in L. Hooghe (ed.), *Cohesion Policy and European Integration: Building Mulitlevel-Governance* (Oxford: Oxford University Press), 219–56.

Bossuat, G. (1996), *L'Europe des Français, 1943–1959: la IVe République aux sources de l'Europe communautaire* (Paris: Publications de la Sorbonne).

Calleo, D. P., and Staal, E. R. (1998), *Europe's Franco-German Engine* (Washington, DC: Brookings Institution Press).

Cameron, D. R. (1996), 'National Interest, the Dilemmas of European Integration, and Malaise', in J. T. S. Keeler and M. Schain (eds), *Chirac's Challenge: Liberalization, Europeanization, and Malaise in France* (New York: St Martin's Press).

CEC (2002), *Eurobarometer 58*. Autumn. Brussels: European Commission Publication. <http://europa.eu.int/comm/public opinion>.

Chabanet, D. (2002), 'Les Marches européennes contre le chômage, la précarité et les exclusions', in R. Balme, D. Chabanet, and V. Wright (eds), *L'action collective en Europe. Collective Action in Europe* (Paris: Presses de Sciences Po), 461–93.

Cole, A. (2001), *Franco-German Relations* (Harlow: Longman).

Cole, A., and Drake, H. (2000), 'The Europeanization of the French polity: continuity, change and adaptation', in *Journal of European Public Policy* 7/1, 26–43.

Daniel, L., and Aron, R. (eds) (1956), *La Querelle de la C.E.D.: essais d'analyse sociologique* (Paris: A. Colin).

Dreyfus, F. G., Morizet, J., and Peyrard, M. (1993), *France and EC Membership Evaluated* (London: St Martin's Press).

Dûchene, F. (1994), *Jean Monnet: The First Statesman of Interdependence* (New York: Norton).

Dyson, K., and Featherstone, K. (1999), *The Road to Maastricht: Negotiating Economic and Monetary Union* (Oxford: Oxford University Press).

Favier, P., and Martin-Roland, M. (1990), *La Décennie Mitterrand* Vol. I Les ruptures (1981–4) (Paris: Seuil).

Fursdon, E. (1980), *The European Defense Community: A History* (London: Macmillan).

Gillingham, J. (1991), *Coal, Steel, and the Rebirth of Europe, 1945–1955* (Cambridge: Cambridge University Press).

Grant, C. (1994), *Delors: Inside the House that Jacques Built* (London: Nicholas Brealey Publishing).

Gueldry, M. R. (2001), *France and European Integration: Toward a Transnational Polity?* (Westport, CT: Praeger).

Guyomarch, A. (2001), 'The Europeanization of Policy-Making', in A. Guyomarch, *et al.* (eds), *Developments in French Politics 2* (London: Palgrave), 116–35.

Guyomarch, A., Machin, H., Hall, P., and Hayward, J. (eds) (2001), *Developments in French Politics 2* (London: Palgrave).

Guyomarch, A., Machin, H., and Ritchie, E. (eds) (1998), *France in the European Union* (London: Palgrave).

Hendriks, G. (2000), *The Franco-German Axis in European Intergration* (Cheltenham: Edward Elgar).

Jobert, B. (1994), *Le tournant néo-libéral en Europe: idées et recettes dans les pratiques gouvernementales* (Paris: Harmattan).

Ladrech, R. (1994), 'Europeanization of Domestic Politics and Institutions: the case of France', in *Journal of Common Market Studies* 32/1, 69–88.

Lequesne, C. (1993), *Paris–Bruxelles: comment se fait la politique européenne de la France* (Paris: Presses de Sciences Po).

Lowi, T. (1972), 'Four Systems of Policy, Politics and Choice', in *Public Administration Review* 32/4, 298–310.

Mair, P. (2000), 'The Limited Impact of Europe on National Party Systems', in *West European Politics* 23/4 (October), 27–51.

Majone, G. (1996), *Regulating Europe* (London: Routledge).

Mitterrand, F. (1986), *Réflexions sur la politique extérieure de la France: introduction à vingt-cinq discours, 1981–1985* (Paris: Fayard).

Muller, Pierre (1984), *Le technocrate et le paysan* (Paris: Les Editions ouvriéres).

Oberdorff, H. (1994), 'Les incidences de l'Union européenne sur les institutions françaises', in *Pouvoirs* 69/spécial.

Palier, B. (2000), 'Does Europe matter? Européanisation et réforme des politiques sociales des pays de l'Union européenne', in *Politique européenne* Septembre/2: 7–28.

Pedersen, T. (1998), *Germany, France, and the integration of Europe: A Realist Interpretation* (New York: Pinter).

Peyrefitte, A. (1994), *C'était de Gaulle* (Paris: Fayard).

Rozenberg, O., and Szukala, A. (2001), 'The French Parliament and the EU: Progressive Assertion and Strategic Investment', in A. Maurer and W. Wessel (eds), *National Parliaments on their Ways to Europe: Losers or Latecomers?* (Baden-Baden: Nomos), 223–50.

Schmidt, V. A. (2001), 'Europeanization and the Mechanics of Economic Policy Adjustment', in *European Integration online Papers (EIoP)* 5/6 <http://eiop.or.at/eiop/texte/2001-006a.htm>.

SOFRES (2002), *Evolution du clivage gauche-droite depuis 10 ans* (Paris: <http://www.sofres.com/etudes/pol/140202_clivage_n.htm>).

Sotou, G. H. (1996), *L'Alliance Incertaine: les rapports politico-strategiques franco-allemands, 1954–1996* (Paris: Fayard).

Chapter 6

The United Kingdom:
A *Europeanized* Government
in a *non-Europeanized* Polity

David Allen

Contents

Summary

Britain's relationship with the EU, it is argued in this chapter, has been characterized by partial Europeanization. The British ruling elite, notably the civil service, has been Europeanized. However, the political parties have been characterized by internal divisions on European integration, while public opinion has been amongst—if not *the*—least supportive of integration amongst the member states. The chapter first of all explores the history of Britain's relationship with the integration process. It then turns to Europeanization, exploring in turn the impact of the EU on British politics, its policy machinery and policy content, highlighting the differing levels of accommodation with European integration.

Introduction

This chapter reviews the British experience of EU membership; its central argument is that, whilst the British government and significant sections of the British ruling elite have become 'Europeanized' (Rosamond, 2001: 195–6), the same can not be said of the wider British polity. Although in 1975 the British people voted in a referendum (Butler and Kitzinger 1976) by two to one to remain within the European Economic Community, the Blair government, despite the prime ministers' initial optimism, clearly did not have any confidence in either of its first two terms in office that it could achieve a similarly positive response in a referendum on British membership of the single currency. Although Britain has been a member of the European Union for more than thirty years (it was significant that the thirtieth anniversary of membership passed unnoticed and uncelebrated on 1 January 2003) it remains an uncertain member state; uncertain about the advantages of membership, uncertain about its relationship with the other leading member states, and uncertain about the direction that it would like the European Union to take following its eastern enlargement (Allen 2003b; Menon, 2004). These uncertainties about the consequences and future of EU membership all essentially relate to the failure of successive British governments to build a supportive consensus amongst the British public for the EU policies that they wish to pursue. Although there have been significant differences in the negotiating *style* of British governments towards the EU since 1973 there have always been significant continuities in the *substance* of British policy—not least a preference for an intergovernmental European Union of 'independent' states. This preference has led governments of both political persuasions to distort and emphatically reject all notions of a 'federal' European Union, and to discourage any serious internal discourse concerning the European *finalité* (Serfaty 2003); the result has been an ongoing external perception of British 'awkwardness' reinforced by continuing internal indications of public indifference and hostility to the EU.

The chapter is divided into four sections dealing with the evolution of Britain's European diplomacy, the impact of EU membership on British politics, the impact of EU membership on the institutions and procedures of British government and the impact of EU membership on the substance of British policy in key sectors.

Britain's European diplomacy

In 1950 when the European Coal and Steel Community (ECSC) was first proposed, the British government decided that, whilst it supported the idea, it did not consider that it would be appropriate for Britain to become a member of a supranational organization. The British government had been prepared to participate in a number of European organizations but only after the principle of intergovernmentalism, supported by voting procedures requiring unanimity, had been established. Additionally the Attlee government felt that Britain, with its continuing global interests and responsibilities, should not be restricted to regional status.

In the original six member states of the EU the foundations of statehood had failed in the preceding decade and there was an understandable predisposition to contemplate new ways of managing intra-European relationships. In Britain, the only European state to enter the Second World War voluntarily and to emerge victorious, there was no such urge to challenge its internal arrangements and external alliances that had emerged seemingly unscathed from the Second World War.

The fact that it was a Labour government that turned down the opportunity to be part of the European experiment from its inception was significant. As well as harbouring continuing global pretensions, Labour was suspicious of the ideological basis of the ECSC initiative. After all what was proposed was not a European Coal and Steel Company but a free market in coal and steel and this understandably did not appeal to a government that had just spent the previous five years nationalizing the 'commanding heights' of the economy including the coal and steel industries. Britain's response to the ECSC was to say that this was a good idea but not for Britain and this view was maintained once the Conservatives returned to power in 1951 despite the fact that Churchill had raised the hopes of his fellow European statesmen with his speeches in favour of a United Europe whilst in opposition. Nevertheless, Britain's response to the ECSC was essentially positive in that no serious attempt was made to prevent the Six from progressing their plans; however, there was a suggestion (to be repeated over the ensuing years) that any European organization that did not have Britain as a member might struggle to succeed.

This proved to be the case with the French proposal for a European Defence Community (EDC) that came hard on the heels of the ECSC in 1952. Britain favoured the idea of a supranational army but it soon became clear that Britain had no intention of joining such an organization. Then, as now, a credible European military force required, at a minimum, the participation of both Britain and France, although, of course, for France the main purpose of the EDC was not military effectiveness but restraint of Germany. Thus one of the reasons for the failure of the EDC was Britain's refusal to join. Its demise left the problem of an acceptable framework for German rearmament unresolved until the British government successfully proposed an alternative institutional solution—Western European Union (WEU). The government saw this as the triumph of pragmatic intergovernmentalism over idealistic supranationality. This then became a significant factor when the Six sought to revive the European idea with a plan to use the ECSC model to create a general common market. This time the British response was negative from the very beginning (Young 1999: 71–98); Britain challenged the idea of supranational regional trade arrangements by first of all proposing global free trade and, when that was rebuffed, by establishing a rival (intergovernmental) European organization—the European Free Trade Association (EFTA). Britain initially rejected the European Economic Community (EEC) on the grounds that pooled sovereignty and the creation of European institutions were unnecessary to achieve the agreed objectives of security and prosperity. The British government argued for traditional intergovernmentalism and clearly believed that, without British participation, the EEC was unlikely to succeed.

When the EEC produced more impressive results than EFTA (although both did well) the British government reversed its position and in 1961 Harold Macmillan applied to join the EEC in company with Denmark, Ireland, and Norway. This dramatic shift in policy had both domestic and international roots. At home, Macmillan, a pro-European who had replaced Anthony Eden in 1957 following the Suez débacle, saw EEC membership as a distraction from domestic troubles and as a chance to keep the Tories in power (Young 1999: 99–145). Internationally, the application suggests a realization that the other 'circles' of British influence—the Commonwealth and the special relationship with the United States were no longer realistic alternatives to EEC membership. Macmillan himself had spoken of the 'winds of change' that were blowing across Africa and transforming the Commonwealth, and Suez raised doubts about the reliability of the United States as a global partner.

The Macmillan application to join the EEC was less than wholehearted; an attempt to 'reverse' almost unnoticed into Europe. Partly because of the lack of a supportive domestic consensus and partly because of EEC inexperience, the initial negotiations were based on an assumption that Britain and the EEC were equals and that both might be required to make concessions in order to achieve a successful enlargement. It soon became clear that the British government wished to change the very nature of the EEC in a way that would challenge French leadership of that organization and this proved too much for the French President. In 1963 De Gaulle unilaterally rejected Britain's application for membership, implying amongst other things that Britain would act as a 'Trojan horse' allowing the US to gain unwanted access to the EEC; in 1967 De Gaulle repeated the exercise when he rejected an application from the Labour government led by Harold Wilson. France sought to counter-balance its rejection of Britain's application by reinforcing its own special relationship with Germany. From 1963 until the present-day one of the key objectives of Britain's European diplomacy has been to create either a bilateral or multilateral alternative to the Franco-German integrative motor.

The 1960s were a period of retrenchment for British diplomacy in response to harsh evidence of Britain's declining international economic and political influence. The devaluation of the pound, the forced military withdrawal from East of Suez and the realization that Britain, in common with the EEC states, had little interest or ability to fight alongside the US in Vietnam, meant that EEC membership became increasingly attractive and associated with notions of modernization and renewal. From 1967 Britain actively sought EEC membership under both the Wilson and Heath governments. Edward Heath's determination to secure British membership was reinforced by the first significant rejection by a post-war British prime minister of the primacy of the special relationship with the United States. Heath accepted the French argument that a choice needed to be made between the US relationship and EEC entry; Heath's period in office is notable both for the success of the entry negotiations and for a significant downturn in UK–US relations. Subsequent British governments have rejected the notion that EU membership requires neglect of the 'special relationship' although all British prime ministers since 1973 have at one time or another faced difficulties in managing and balancing the transatlantic and European dimensions of British diplomacy.

What is strange about the relationship between the British conception of the imperatives of the special relationship and policy towards the EU is that it has never really been reciprocated in the United States. It is hard to think of an American administration since 1945 that has ever sought to put pressure on Britain to make the choice between Europe and America; on the contrary most American leaders have gone out of their way to stress that Britain is primarily of interest to the US as an influential member of the EU. It is successive British governments unilaterally who have attached continuing significance to the connection between their relationship with the US and their relationship with the EU. For Heath it implied rejection of the special relationship, for Thatcher it implied the opposite and for Wilson, Callaghan, Major, and Blair it has been a continuing source of difficulty.

No sooner had Heath secured Britain's entry to the EEC in 1973 than he found himself ejected from office and replaced by Harold Wilson and eventually James Callaghan.

Primarily for domestic reasons the Wilson government undertook an essentially spurious 'renegotiation' of the terms of EU membership (Allen 2004: 53–7), culminating in a successful recommendation to the British people to vote for their acceptance in the 1975 referendum. Between 1974 and 1979 Labour found itself increasingly at odds with its European partners over the future direction of the EEC whilst at the same time sharing with them a short-term willingness to break EU state aid rules in the face of an international economic recession. The Callaghan government demonstrated a singular lack of enthusiasm for active participation in the supranational common market but a growing fondness for the intergovernmental procedures underpinning the system of diplomatic exchanges known as European Political Cooperation (EPC); the result was that British policy towards Europe drifted even whilst a British President of the European Commission (Roy Jenkins) worked with the leaders of France and Germany to advance the cause of monetary cooperation.

It was not until Mrs Thatcher gained office in 1979 that a clearly definable EC strategy emerged. Between 1979 and 1984 the British government sought to restrain plans to revive the EC until the question of Britain's net EU budget contribution was addressed. Mrs Thatcher wanted 'her money back' and she was prepared to prevent further integration until her demands were met. In 1984, following several acrimonious short-term budget settlements, a settlement was agreed at Fontainbleau. Opinion is divided about the background to this agreement, which saw Britain granted a rebate on its gross contribution to the budget based on a formula designed to last for a significant period rather than just one year (in fact successive British governments have been able to retain this rebate over the years in the face of strenuous efforts to end it). Those who saw the budget settlement as a triumph for British diplomacy are challenged by those who saw Britain's hasty acceptance of the rebate as a belated recognition that its EC partners had had enough of British obstructionism and would choose to go ahead (with the revitalization of the EC) without Britain if necessary. In other words acceptance of the 1984 budget deal could be seen as a recognition (that was not then followed through) that the game was up for a British blocking strategy.

It was certainly the case that Mrs Thatcher was one of the architects of the policy that underpinned the mid-1980s revival of the EC's fortunes; the Single Market Programme was advocated by Thatcher and taken forward in the Delors Commission by a British Commissioner, Lord Cockfield. To facilitate the Single Market Programme the British government signed up to the Single European Act and thus to a reformed EU decision-making system which combined qualified majority voting in the Council with significant legislative powers for the European Parliament. Mrs Thatcher's miscalculation arose from the dynamic effect of the SEA and the SMP on the evolution of the EC. She believed in the Single Market but she did not accept the logic, so successfully exploited by Delors, that called for further integrative measures—most obviously economic and monetary union. As Delors, with the support of France and Germany, pushed ahead, so Mrs Thatcher sought to revert to the policy of resistance. It was however too late for this and by the end of the 1980s it was clear that the rest of the EC intended to move ahead with or without Britain. The result in Britain, albeit not just for European policy reasons, was the removal of Margaret Thatcher by her own Cabinet; this was greeted with relief by Britain's EC partners and by pro European forces within the UK. Both made the mistake of seeing Thatcher's hesitations about the future direction of the EC as unique to her rather than, as they were, an extreme version of a more deep seated and ongoing British unease about further integration.

Nevertheless, the Major government promised and at first delivered a new approach. Where Thatcher swept out of European meetings, John Major remained stubbornly determined to place Britain 'at the heart of Europe' and to insist on full account being taken of Britain's concerns. Thus it was that Britain achieved a significant measure of success at the Maastricht negotiations which produced the Treaty on European Union. There, Major's stubbornness, supported by the hostility of his party back home, ensured that Britain managed to preserve the pillar structure of the Union and thus limit the spread of supranationalism. In addition Major won serious consideration of the concept of subsidiarity, the right to 'opt in' to EMU at a time of Britain's own choosing and to opt-out of the Social Chapter. In terms of European diplomacy John Major was probably right to proclaim on his return from Maastricht that it was 'game set and match' to Britain (Seldon 1997: 243). However, he probably overestimated his domestic position when he confidently predicted that that British ratification of the TEU would soon follow.

Shortly after the April 1992 election, as the UK Presidency approached, it did seem as if the European tide was turning in Britain's favour. With the TEU agreed in a manner acceptable to Britain the next big project for the EU was likely to be enlargement to include the rest of EFTA and eventually the newly liberated states of Eastern Europe and the former Soviet Union. EU enlargement has always been a major diplomatic objective for Britain. The issue has usually found Britain at odds with France and allied with Germany. Britain and France usually agree that enlargement inhibits the 'deepening' of the EU—both believe that 'wider equals weaker' and this has led Britain to advocate enlargement and France to oppose it. Thus Britain naturally favoured its own application and was supported by Germany but opposed by France. A similar line-up has applied to all subsequent enlargements including the latest in 2004.

Major's election victory in 1992 and various governmental changes in Britain's EU partner states meant that the British government was in a relatively strong position and no longer as isolated on EU matters as it had been. The EU's immediate agenda, which included the completion of the single market as well as enlargement, suited British tastes and it seemed as if the negativism vis-à-vis the EU of the Thatcher years was finally over. But then it all began to unravel; first as the Danes voted to reject the Maastricht Treaty and then as Britain unceremoniously departed from the Exchange Rate Mechanism (ERM) in September 1992. These events served to undermine the domestic base of Major's European diplomacy as they gave succour to the Eurosceptics in his party.

Thus events conspired against the Major government's attempts to normalize Britain's relations with its European partners. At Edinburgh in December 1992, collective fear for the future of the Union ensured a degree of success for an otherwise ill-fated British Presidency (see Ludlow 1993). This success came about as the other member states rallied round to agree on a financial perspective for 1993–1999 that retained the UK rebate, as well as on EFTA enlargement and on a reinterpretation of the TEU that was designed to help the Danes vote for it in a referendum and the British Parliament to ratify it. The atmosphere of agreement and solidarity was however illusory and between 1992 and 1997 Britain once again became isolated in its European diplomacy. Unlike Mrs Thatcher however, John Major found himself without friends at home and abroad. The Conservative government's open support for the re-election of George Bush Senior in 1992 meant that the incoming Clinton administration was not prepared to offer Major the sort of transatlantic solidarity in the face of European adversity that Mrs Thatcher had enjoyed.

As the Major government became increasingly weakened by the attacks of the Eurosceptics at home, things went from bad to worse at the European level. The much lauded new Common Foreign and Security Policy (CFSP) almost immediately unravelled as the member states found themselves pursuing individual and contradictory policies with regard to events in former Yugoslavia whilst, inside the EU, Britain found itself at odds with its partners over the institutional arrangements for the 1995 enlargement, over the appointment of a new Commission President in 1994–5 and in 1996 over the BSE issue. In 1996 it fell to the Italian Presidency to initiate the next IGC and the rest of the EU found itself facing once more a hostile and intransigent Britain. Every proposal for reform of the Treaties was rejected and as the BSE crisis worsened the British began a period of non-cooperation in the Council of Ministers. Where once (in 1965–6) the French had succeeded in changing the course of European integration by refusing to attend the Council the British succeeded only in creating further antagonisms by turning up but then refusing to endorse any action requiring unanimity. The policy of non-cooperation was short lived but by the time that the BSE crisis was over it was clear to Britain's partners that no new Treaty could be agreed until either the Major government was removed or (less likely) returned by the British electorate with a new mandate.

In 1997 the Blair government was elected with an overwhelming majority and once again an incoming British prime minister sought to distinguish his approach to the EU from that of his predecessors by promising both the British electorate and Britain's EU partners a fresh approach. At Amsterdam shortly after his election Blair opted into the Social Chapter, went along with a degree of communitization of the Justice and Home Affairs (JHA) pillar and a significant extension of qualified majority voting. When both France and Germany intervened to veto the application of QMV to areas of policy where they had their own domestic concerns it became clear that they had been 'free riding', that is hiding behind Britain's obstruction of further integration.

Despite Amsterdam Blair then proceeded to disappoint his EU colleagues by rejecting, in the autumn of 1997, the opportunity to move quickly towards British participation in the single currency, preferring instead to adopt a policy of 'prepare and decide' (even if this was an advance on the previous administration's policy of 'wait and see'). Britain's rising profile and status within the EU was therefore limited by London's reluctance to fully embrace the Euro. The 1998 UK Presidency presented a difficult challenge to Blair's desire to exercise leadership in the EU as it was inevitably dominated by the need to oversee preparations for the introduction of the single currency in 1999. Still wary of Britain, and despite Blair and Brown's hopes to the contrary, the Eurozone countries decided to exclude Britain from their 'Euro' deliberations prior to meetings of the Ecofin Council. In so doing they made it clear that, whilst they welcomed the changed British attitude, they were not going to be led anywhere by a non-participant in the single currency.

This provides the context for Britain's subsequent and rather surprising defence initiative agreed with France at St Malo in 1998 which eventually led to the establishment of the Rapid Reaction Force (RRF) within the framework of a European Security and Defence Policy (ESDP). This move, which led to a rehearsal of familiar arguments between those who saw EU defence as threatening NATO and those who saw it enhancing it, is significant because it has been seen through to a sort of conclusion (EU forces have been deployed in Bosnia, Macedonia, and Central Africa) despite the differences that existed between Britain, France, and Germany over Iraq. The advances that have been made on the defence front do represent a significant change of direction by Britain.

Blair's ambition for Britain to be a 'pivot' or a 'bridge' between the EU and the US was always likely to be challenged once the Clinton administration was replaced by that of George W Bush. The immediate reaction to 9/11 saw Britain quite comfortably participating in a coordinated and sympathetic EU response but, as the US began to put serious pressure on its European allies over first Afghanistan and then Iraq, a more familiar British position re-emerged. Faced with a choice between supporting Bush's determination to bring down Saddam Hussein by force and aligning itself with the opposition to this course of action that was led within the EU by France and Germany, Britain once again went with the US. This time, however, Britain was less isolated than on previous occasions with both Spain and Italy providing a measure of support from the EU15 along with most of the (then) applicant states from Eastern Europe and the former Soviet Union.

Despite the frictions that arose during 2003 over the war in Iraq, significant efforts were made in the latter part of the year to both patch up the internal EU divisions and to collectively repair the damage to EU–US relations, in both cases easing Britain's position. The differences over the war in Iraq, combined with the problems that arose over France and Germany's unilateral rejection of the agreed rules of the Stability and Growth Pact and the failure of the IGC under the Italian Presidency to agree a new Treaty, all suggested that France and Germany's ability to drive the EU forward was diminished. For several years Blair had sought to take on the Franco-German duo both by attempting to divide them and by seeking new bilateral relationships within the EU. Thus Germany is a natural partner for Britain over CAP reform, restricting the EU budget, enlargement and some (but not all) aspects of institutional reforms (Grabbe and Munchau 2002). The defence initiative found Britain engaged with France with Germany an initially reluctant onlooker. Blair has also engaged Spain and, more controversially, Italy, as partners in the drive to make Europe competitive whilst the Labour government worked hard with both the Swedish and Danish Presidencies to maintain the enlargement momentum when it looked like faltering in 2001–2.

However Britain's new found allies will have been disappointed by indications that Britain, France, and Germany are developing a realization that a *directoire* of three— whether it be on defence issues, the Lisbon process or the EU's relationship with Iran—may be the answer to a perceived lack of direction in the enlarged EU. It is, however, too early to argue that Britain has finally found a permanent place amongst the leaders of the European Union. British European diplomacy will continue for some time in the future to be constrained by a lack of a domestic consensus for any-thing other than pragmatic and piecemeal adjustment within the EU—an inability to participate in the Euro is the most obvious and fatal manifestation of this constraint. Britain has signed and ratified a number of EU treaties and it has taken its turn at running a number of Council Presidencies but in all cases cautious pragmatism has prevailed over either vision or effective leadership. Given the abject failure of the

Blair government to project domestically the 'case for Europe' it is hard to imagine that things will be very different in the immediate future.

The EU and British politics

The European Union has had a major impact on British politics but to date no government or opposition has been able to create a lasting permissive domestic consensus for the policies towards the EU that they wish to pursue. Thus all governments since 1979 have fundamentally supported British membership of the EU but have fallen foul in one way or another of domestic public opinion. Similarly, there have been significant periods of time when leading parties in opposition have sought to build a consensus around a fundamental challenge to British membership but they have fared no better. When Labour in opposition drifted under the leadership of Michael Foot towards advocacy of a Eurosceptic position in the early 1980s they were regarded as unelectable, as were the Conservatives under William Hague in the late 1990s. Thus the British people seem reluctant to support either a government that advances Britain's role in the EU or one that seeks to significantly limit it.

By the late 1960s both major political parties (the Liberals under a variety of guises have always supported an active British membership of the EU) had sought membership whilst in office. However, even before entry was achieved the European question proved internally divisive with significant minorities in both the Conservative and Labour parties opposing the views of the party leadership. The European issue has always proved to be a challenging one for Britain's two leading political parties as its internally divisive tendencies have intersected with a fundamentally adversarial political system with the result that the two major parties have always resisted making Europe a significant electoral issue. Thus, in Britain, the debate about Europe, such as it is, has essentially taken place within, rather than between, the major political forces and parties (George 1998). The British have always struggled to fit the European debate into their adversarial political culture and the result has been an understandable reticence to argue publicly about the pros and cons of membership, let alone the desired direction of European integration. (Britain's European diplomacy has often been seen as confrontational to the extent that it reflects the adversarial approach to politics that characterizes political debate in the UK.) European issues have always been important in British politics and they have had a significant impact on the fate of the last two British Prime Ministers before Tony Blair. Nevertheless the EU has rarely featured strongly in national election campaigns (Geddes 2004: 214) and it languishes at the bottom of most candidates' political agendas at election time. In the June 2004 European elections, however, the success of the UK Independence Party (with 16 per cent of the vote on the British mainland and taking twelve of the seventy-five seats) signalled a heightened level of electoral salience which may impact upon future national elections. The announcement of a referendum on the EU Constitutional Treaty, plus the long-standing commitment to holding a referendum on membership of the Euro, may sustain the new electoral salience of the European issue.

Thus, politics in Britain did not show any early signs of potential Europeanization. Those who advocated membership avoided, where possible, serious public debate about the advantages and disadvantages but they were not entirely alone in this. The West European states that created the European Community lacked prestige, but they enjoyed governments whose leaders were confident that their electorates would endorse the deals that they made with one another. This bore some similarity with how Britain negotiated its way into the EEC in 1973, with Parliament alone endorsing the relevant Treaties. The electorate as a whole only gained a say after the event as a result of divisions within the Labour Party. In the Referendum of 1975 the Labour government gained overwhelming support for its 'renegotiated terms' even though the negotiations had produced no change whatsoever to the Accession Treaty. This was essentially also how Margaret Thatcher approached the debate about the revival of the EEC that culminated in the Single European Act. She was prepared to bargain hard at the European level for her limited vision of Europe, but she expected the British people to accept whatever deal she struck—as they did.

John Major's approach to the Maastricht negotiations was slightly less confident, because he understood that he would be closely scrutinized, not so much by the broad British electorate or the official opposition, but by disgruntled members of his own party, many of whom were unable to come to terms with Mrs Thatcher's departure. In particular he was able to use this domestic unease as a bargaining tool when it came to issues such as subsidiarity and federalism—the dreaded 'f' word.

Thanks to Mrs Thatcher's success in arguing that a federal Europe symbolized the relentless advance of a European superstate, any British government now faces an enormous challenge in separating the two ideas. Blair's awareness of this problem is to be seen in his strange portrayal of the EU that is 'a superpower but not a superstate' (Blair 2000). However, the image of the latter is still strong and a real barrier to any informed discussion in Britain about the future of Europe. Ironically, the British may be forced to reconsider their view of federalism as a consequence less of the debate about the future of the EU than of Blair's constitutionally significant moves to advance devolution in Britain. The Blair government has begun a process that could well result in Britain's own evolution from a unitary to a federal state.

The twelve leaders who negotiated the Maastricht Treaty more than a decade ago did not anticipate the problems that would be encountered in getting the Treaty ratified at home. Following the Danish rejection and French hesitancy, John Major was forced to endure 18 months of misery as he battled to persuade the House of Commons to ratify the treaty. In preparing both the Amsterdam and Nice Treaties, British politicians (like most of their EU counterparts) were concerned about a potentially adverse reaction at home.

The result is that British politicians, like their counterparts in the other EU member states, now know that they are addressing two audiences—each other but also their domestic electorate. This explains in part the Major government's spectacularly negative public performance at the 1996 Intergovernmental Conference (IGC), Blair's negativity about EU defence at Amsterdam and his backtracking in the Convention on the Future of Europe and the 2003 IGC as the endgame of treaty negotiation approached (Menon 2004).

Thus the British government's position in the debate over the EU must now take into account domestic forces as much as the views of other EU member states, a significant departure from earlier periods. In 1997 the Labour Party restricted itself to a cautious manifesto commitment promising to hold a referendum on the single currency (a promise repeated in 2001) and to lead reform efforts in the EU. Although the Labour Party had a more constructive agenda than its predecessors, there was little European policy debate during or after either general election in 1997 and 2001. In effect, both political parties have reversed their positions. During the 1980s the Labour Party was torn apart over the issue of policy toward Europe, with almost fatal consequences as the pro-European right wing of the party departed to form the Social Democratic Party. This left Mrs Thatcher to preside over a fundamentally pro-European government while gaining considerable political capital from her obstruction of wider EU ambitions. By the end of her premiership, however, she had become much more resistant to further integration.

In the 1990s Labour sought, won, and retained power by shifting to a pro-European stance as the Conservative Party enthusiastically embarked on a fatal internal battle over Europe. As a result, New Labour has a large majority of predominately pro-European MPs and Cabinet ministers, in contrast to the Conservative Party, which is dominated by the Eurosceptic Right and whose opposition to British membership of the Euro is in danger of sliding into opposition to EU membership itself. Labour's problem is with the electorate, whose acquiescence will be needed in a referendum on the Euro and, as Tony Blair has announced, on the Constitutional Treaty that was agreed in June 2004. Persuading the House of Commons to agree to a new European treaty is the least of the government's problems; Britain's European future is dependent on a positive popular vote on the treaty.

Since 1997 the Blair government has shown an awareness of the need to relate its European ambitions to the interests of its citizens. Blair correctly understands that the legitimacy crisis that the EU has been experiencing in recent years is a barrier to his European ambitions, and that the British people must somehow be persuaded to love the EU or at least not dislike it. Public opinion about the EU is, and always has been, negative with European views often argued passionately but usually held weakly. In the regular Eurobarometer polls published by the Commission over the years since British entry, Britain has always come at or close to the bottom of any ranking of member states by enthusiasm for the EU or belief that the EU has done any material good (Geddes 2004: 211–24). In all recent polls significantly more than half of the British population opposes entering the Euro, either ever or in the foreseeable future, although paradoxically a similar percentage usually express the belief that eventual entry is inevitable, suggesting that the British people are actually indifferent to the issue.

These figures may give the impression that the electorate is open to persuasion about an issue it cares little about, but the image of an all-powerful, predominantly anti-European media would seem to counter that view (Wilkes and Wring 1998).

Undoubtedly, the British popular press has done little to inform the public debate about the EU. The Murdoch-owned News International Group broadly supported Labour in the 1997 election, but it has not softened its opposition to the EU in general and the Euro in particular. Indeed, most of the tabloid press remains hostile to the EU and seeks mainly to sensationalize rather than impartially report the activities of the various European institutions (Wilkes and Wring 1998). The *Sun* and the *Daily Mail* continue to wage a nationalistic campaign against Brussels and all things foreign, while the *Daily Telegraph, The Times*, and the *Sunday Times* report the EU from a sceptical perspective. Of the daily broadsheets, only the *Financial Times*, the *Guardian*, and the *Independent* offer in-depth and broadly sympathetic reporting on the EU; the weekly *Economist* does so as well. Much has been said about the alleged power of the British press to affect government policy, and the government is certainly sensitive to the press's ability to influence its overall popularity. Other analysts have made the point that the main impact of a more intrusive press is to divert ministers' attention from substantive policy matters to mere policy presentation (Coles 2000: 100) and this is certainly borne out by the recent experience of the British government's shifting views on the Convention and the IGC (Menon 2004).

Evidence suggests, however, that, when the government is clear about its European policy direction, the press will usually follow. This was the case when John Major won the 1992 general election on a manifesto designed to put Britain at 'the heart of Europe', an idea that provoked moderation in the media's Thatcher-inspired Euroscepticism. The British press once again took up the cudgels on Europe only after Major's government lost its authority. In the light of this experience, Blair's pro-European colleagues constantly urge him to take the lead on Europe, forcing the press to follow him, and Labour initially made serious efforts to improve the British public's perception of Europe. The 1998 British EU Presidency (Ludlow 1998) set itself the unusual priorities of dealing with unemployment, crime, and the environment in a bid to relate the EU to the public's major concerns. However, the determination of the Blair government to create a domestic consensus has not been sustained or successful. Twice now the urgency of the need to carry the public with it on Europe has passed as decisions have been taken to postpone the Euro referendum. Blair has made numerous public announcements to the effect that the government intends a Step Change in its approach to the EU and to promoting the public image of the EU but to date, whilst the style of British policy has clearly changed this has not been backed up by any significant change in public attitudes towards the EU.

To say that the British people have not yet adjusted to British membership of the EU and to say that British politics remains relatively non-Europeanized is not to say that membership of the EU has had no impact on British political life. No British general election has been contested over or decided by the issue of Europe because the British people continue to retain or reject governments on the basis of judgements about the broad management of the British economy and the more specific management of public services such as education, social services, and health (all significantly areas where British governments along with their European partners have been determined to retain national competence rather than transfer responsibility to the EU level).

Nevertheless the question of Europe has clearly impacted on British politics in between elections. In the end her European policy contributed to Mrs Thatcher's downfall, John Major's government first triumphed and then faltered before being fatally wounded by the European issue and Tony Blair, once so cocksure and optimistic about Europe, has once more been forced to downgrade his ambitions. Blair's failure to carry the British people on Europe accounts for his probable failure in Europe—a Europeanized government forced to cut its cloth to suit a non-Europeanized polity.

Even the elections to the European Parliament that have been held every five years since 1979 have failed to rouse much interest amongst the British people. Turnout has always been low (never more than 40 per cent and in 1999 only 24 per cent) compared to both the EU average (only in 1999 did that average dip below 50 per cent) (Geddes 2004: 118) and compared to turnout in British General Elections. The elections are accorded a low priority by the major political parties who prefer to spend their limited resources on national, regional, and even local elections rather than European elections. Furthermore, 'European' issues are rarely debated at the hustings. Instead, European elections in the UK turn into national by-elections with those who do turn out to vote using the opportunity to express their frustrations with the government in office.

Until 1999 the use of the 'first past the post' simple majority system of voting in single member constituencies meant that Britain (the only member state not to use a system of Proportional Representation) was significantly out of step with its partners predominately returning members drawn from the two major political parties. All this changed in 1999 when Labour introduced, as promised, a system of proportional representation. Under this system Britain was divided up into large multi-member regional constituencies and for the first time the Liberal Party had (ten) MEPs elected, and several minority parties such as the Greens and the UK Independence Party also achieved a measure of success. In this way the EU did indeed make a small impact on British politics.

Britain and the European Union: institutional adaptation

In contrast to the problems of adaptation demonstrated by the wider British society over the years, Britain's governance institutions are generally perceived to have made a successful adaptation to accommodate EU membership. Most observers would claim that the adjustment has been steady and incremental rather than radical but some would argue that, since the election of the Blair government in 1997, the pace of institutional change has both quickened and deepened (Bulmer and Burch 2003).

For Britain EU membership presented a potential coordination problem and raised the question of how governmental procedures would deal with the 'blurring' of the boundaries between the domestic and the foreign. In many ways EU business is primarily domestic policy negotiated and implemented in partnership with foreigners. For Britain membership had implications for all its major institutions and procedures; the office of prime minister, the cabinet system, the 'pecking order' of government departments, the civil and diplomatic services, the legislative, budgetary, and scrutiny powers of the Parliament, the principle of sovereignty, the judiciary, the electoral system, and the relationship between the various parts of the United Kingdom.

British government had to develop effective procedures for both projecting to and receiving from the EU. British adaptation has been pragmatic and effective on a day-to-day basis but the system has been criticized, especially by Britain's partners within the EU, for its failure to develop long-term strategies built around a clear vision of the European future. British negotiators, both politicians and officials are seen as formidable negotiators and effective lobbyists in Brussels. Most British governments have entered office determined to 'start afresh' with the EU but most have at one time or another been branded as 'awkward' by their partners. This is partly to be explained by the failure of successive governments to create a supportive domestic consensus, partly by a consistent antipathy to supranationality and talk of federalism but also by a certain 'style' which is a product of the British policy and political process. British negotiators at all levels have never been willing to subsume their concern about the specifics of policy or institutional development to a general enthusiasm for European integration. In addition, and more positively perhaps, British awkwardness can be explained by a seriousness of intent to both implement and enforce any agreements that are reached.

Britain's policy towards the EU is coordinated in at least three different places; the Cabinet Office, whose European Secretariat has in recent years been headed by the Prime Minister's personal adviser on EU matters, the Foreign and Commonwealth Office and UKREP—Britain's Permanent Representation to the EU based in Brussels. At the heart of the British system of government is the cabinet system presided over by a prime minister who is constitutionally regarded as being no more than *primus inter pares* but who is often perceived to have ambitions to make the British system more presidential, in particular by building up his or her office in Downing Street.

At the centre, the prime minister plays a growing role, partly out of choice and partly because the EU itself is increasingly driven by the European Council where the prime minister meets with his fellow leaders from the other EU member states. Prime ministers with a keen interest in the EU such as Margaret Thatcher and Tony Blair have chosen to enhance the power of Downing Street on EU matters whereas Harold Wilson, James Callaghan, and John Major were more content to leave the direction of EU business in the hands of their foreign secretaries and thus the Foreign and Commonwealth Office (FCO). Under Blair in recent years, the Downing Street Office has grown steadily to support the direct involvement of the prime minister in foreign policy in general and the EU in particular. Blair has been criticized by those (Owen 2003) who fear that the erosion of collective cabinet decision-making impacts adversely on the quality of Britain's EU policy. Whilst the cabinet as a decision-making forum on Europe has undoubtedly been diminished under Blair, the Treasury, and the Chancellor, Gordon Brown, have exercised significant countervailing power by maintaining a stranglehold over British policy on the Euro.

Whilst membership of the EU has enabled the British prime minister to enhance his power, the Foreign Secretary has struggled (with a degree of success to date) to maintain FCO control over contacts, both formal and informal, between the British government and its EU partners (Allen 2003a). A great deal of EU business concerns single government departments such as the Department of Trade and Industry (DTI) or the Department for the Environment, Food and Rural Affairs (DEFRA) and under the British system they are, in the main, left alone to determine British interests and negotiate the detail of policy. The Foreign Office plays a key coordinating role and, in recent years, it has been organized on functional as well as geographical lines. This coordinating role is nowadays much prized by the FCO which has always resisted more radical suggestions that EU policy should be entrusted to a Ministry for Europe.

Similarly successive foreign secretaries have resisted the idea that the post of Minister for Europe (currently a junior ministerial appointment under the direction of the foreign secretary) should be elevated to cabinet rank. Whilst the FCO might relish the prospect of having two seats in the Cabinet, the foreign secretary is understandably reluctant to contemplate the downgrading of his own role that this might imply.

The British cabinet rarely discusses EU business; at political level this is mainly done in a sub-committee of the cabinet chaired by the foreign secretary. Most business is carried out at official level within the European Secretariat of the Cabinet Office which provides a forum in which any interdepartmental disputes on EU policy are ironed out (Forster and Blair 2002). A particular feature of this process is an inter-departmental meeting held each Friday in the Cabinet Office which is also attended by the British Ambassador (Permanent Representative) to the EU—the only ambassador in the British diplomatic service who gets to return to London each week to participate in the writing of his own instructions! The work of UKREP is generally admired within the British system although senior officials are sometimes heard to complain that the British EU Ambassador both represents Britain in Brussels and Brussels in Britain.

EU membership has always involved a few key ministries such as the FCO, the DTI, the Treasury, and DEFRA and it could be argued that several of these owe their continued existence to their EU related role. For instance the DTI valued its essential role in the negotiation of the Single Market at a time when the Thatcher administration did not believe that government had any real role to play in either trade or industry. Even the FCO has shifted from regarding EU business as a rather tiresome activity to seeing it as a core part of its continuing *raison d'être* (Allen 2003a). In recent years the Home Office has seen its EU role rapidly expand as issues such as immigration, asylum, and counter-terrorism have come onto the EU agenda. It remains to be seen whether the British Ministry of Defence, which is traditionally closest to the US Pentagon, now develops a greater EU persona as ESDP develops.

The British civil service had little difficulty in handling EU business in Britain but resisted at first the idea that British officials might move effortlessly between London and Brussels. The result was that at first a number of British officials who did choose to take up the posts made available in the Commission or the secretariats of the Council, Parliament, and Court found their way back to Britain effectively blocked. The choice seemed to be a 'zero-sum' one and the result was that many disaffected British civil servants remained in Brussels whilst in other member states their opposite numbers returned to their national capitals to add their Brussels expertise to national decision-making capacities. Things have now changed in Britain and with the introduction of a European dimension to both the home and diplomatic 'fast stream' Britain now seeks to 'place' some of its best officials in Brussels for a while before bringing them back to enhance Britain's national bureaucratic capacity. In recent years British officials like David Williamson (Secretary-General of the Commission under Delors) or John Kerr (Secretary to the Convention on the Future of Europe) have come to hold influential roles in EU institutions.

The British legal system appears to have experienced little difficulty in adapting to the introduction of Roman-based EU law to operate alongside English and Scottish law with their different traditions. British judges seek the guidance of the European Court of Justice (ECJ) on matters concerning EU law without apparent resentment (in recent times the only senior Law Lord to speak out against what he saw as the imposition of an alien legal culture was Lord Denning), British law firms have developed respected and highly profitable EU legal practices and British Ministers have accepted ECJ judgements even when they have gone significantly against their estimation of British interests.

The British Parliament has adapted less easily than the core executive to the interaction of EU business. On paper, Britain has the second most effective system for parliamentary scrutiny of EU legislation after Denmark. When Britain first joined the EU, the then government pledged that it would never agree to legislation in the EU Council of Ministers that had not first been considered by the British Parliament. Successive governments have adhered to this and all EU legislative proposals are sent to the House of Commons European Scrutiny Committee with an explanatory memorandum. The Scrutiny Committee, which has two standing committees, assesses the legal and political implications of each proposal, decides which ones should be debated in the House and monitors the activities of British ministers in the Council. The problem with this system is that it is swamped by the sheer volume of EU legislation that it has to process and by lack of time. This is often made worse by delays in making English translations of original French documents available. However, these problems are not regarded as serious because national parliamentarians do not seem to be that interested in tackling the detail of EU law at this stage preferring instead to rely on the government to act in the Council. Those who are exercised about Britain's membership of the EU tend to hold their fire for the big set piece debates that occur when new Treaties are ratified and national MPs show little interest in the detail of EU business or in the activities of their colleagues in the European Parliament. In the House of Lords, the European Union Select Committee with its numerous sub-committees, conducts very effective inquiries into EU issues, takes evidence from every incoming EU Presidency and from the Minister for Europe after every European Council meeting. The Lords Committee is one of the best and most respected sources of information on the EU and its policies in Britain.

Since 1997 there have been a number of significant constitutional changes, some of which are indirectly linked to EU membership and all of which will, in time, impact on Britain's relationship with the EU. The most important of these changes (which also include the introduction of Proportional Representation for the 1999 elections to the European Parliament) is devolution. In Britain there has been a significant devolution of governance to Scotland, Wales, and Northern Ireland and there are plans for this to be extended to the English regions. At present, although significant powers have been transferred to the devolved authorities, British EU policy is determined in London and there are complex agreements and procedures that are designed to ensure that devolved interests are considered by the government of the UK. Scotland and Wales have stepped up their representation in Brussels even though formal relations continue to be conducted through UKREP. At present the new system would seem to be working well and a taste of devolved power has not given rise to demands for independence which would lead to individual membership of the EU for Wales, Scotland and Northern Ireland. However, to date, the political composition of the devolved administrations has not been radically different to the party in power in London. It remains to be seen whether a British form of 'cohabitation' would raise difficulties for the UK position in Brussels.

What is emerging though is another tier of government in Britain which when combined with British participation in the European Union suggests that Britain is now a full participant in what can be described as a system of multilevel governance in Europe. Britain has learned to effectively project itself at the EU level and as a result of this and of its size and influence has become one of the EU's leading member states with the institutional apparatus to sustain this. British officials and politicians now play a significant role in all the EU institutions and procedures both formal and informal. Countless British officials, representatives and citizens also play significant roles in the EU's policy networks and epistemic communities. The British government is an effective player at the EU level and it has a good reputation for the implementation and enforcement of EU legislation yet it still has not yet succeeded in persuading the wider British public that Europeanization is a good thing. Because of this limiting factor the institutional adaptation supports British tactics at the EU level but has not yet provided the basis for an effective long-term strategy.

Britain and the European Union: policy adaptation

It is perhaps an indication of Britain's relatively flat EU learning curve that the issues that first caused the UK difficulties in its relationship with the European Union persist as negative factors for the British public. For most British citizens, the EU raises the issue of cost whether it be the overall cost of membership as indicated by Britain's continuing role as a major net contributor to the EU budget or the specific costs that policies like the common agricultural and fisheries policy are believed to have inflicted on Britain over the years of membership. Rarely are the less tangible benefits of the single market programme, the enhanced trade negotiating power or the more recent advances in justice and home affairs highlighted or discussed as benefits of EU membership.

In the case of the budgetary arrangements and the CAP Britain paid the price of late entry. Had Britain managed to enter the EU in 1963 then the arrangements would most certainly have been different. The CAP was designed by officials conscious at the time of Europe's inability to feed itself. The objective was to support farmers and increase supply by guaranteeing a price and supporting that price with the concept of Community preference to be enforced by protective levies on agricultural imports. In Britain, agriculture had been traditionally subsidized in a different way with selected farmers receiving direct payments that enabled consumers to enjoy the lowest prices available on the world market. Adjusting to the CAP meant higher prices for British consumers with just a few, already wealthy, British farmers benefiting from the high guaranteed prices. The CAP has proved difficult to reform over the years but the British view has eventually begun to prevail and now informs plans to break the link between subsidies and production.

In addition to the problems that the CAP presented, in the 1990s the UK faced two severe agricultural crises during both of which the government and the media were inclined to scapegoat the EU. The BSE crisis of the mid-1990s saw Britain misleading its EU partners, reacting against legal restraints on exports imposed by the Commission and eventually pursuing a policy of non-cooperation in the Council of Ministers (Westlake 1997). In 2001 the foot and mouth outbreak led to the European Commission once again been criticized for its ban on the movement of livestock.

The Common Fisheries Policy, which is based on the principle of equity of access for all EU boats into EU waters, and which now uses a system of restrictive quotas to try and preserve EU fish stocks, has always been regarded with suspicion in the UK. The Common Fisheries Policy was the one part of the *acquis communitaire* that Britain never really accepted because it was so obviously only agreed by the Six in 1970 in order to gain access to the fishing grounds of the then applicants—Britain, Norway, Ireland, and Denmark. The principle of equity of access led to the Norwegian decision not to join the EEC in 1973 and in Britain it has always been held primarily responsible for the depletion of fish stocks in what were once British but are now EU waters.

The budgetary issue arose from the early decisions to give the EU its own resources based initially on monies raised by the common external tariff and the agricultural levies and to spend those resources primarily on agricultural support. In both cases Britain was destined to lose out and this provided the basis for Mrs Thatcher's famous demand that she 'wanted her money back'. Despite the rebate that she eventually won Britain remains the second largest net contributor to the EU budget with a net contribution that has fluctuated in recent years between £2 billion and £4 billion.

The EU budget has always been small representing in total around 1 per cent of EU GDP as compared to the 44 per cent of UK GDP that is taken by the UK budget. Similarly Britain's net contribution has never been economically or fiscally significant but it has always been politically significant and responsible for a negative view of the cost of EU membership. The problem is that the direct costs are much easier to calculate than the indirect benefits. Because it is a net contributor, the UK is in the forefront of those member states who are most keen to resist any significant expansion of the EU budget.

Many would argue that the British budgetary problem was also responsible for the establishment and subsequent rapid development of the EU's other major area of expenditure—the Structural Funds. In the 1970s the EU was stimulated to develop its regional policy by a desire to find a policy that Britain might benefit from given that at the time some 80 per cent of the EU budget was taken up with agricultural support that did not favour British producers. Since then as the structural funds have grown in significance, Britain has managed to take full advantage of grants aimed both at regions such as the Scottish Highlands and Islands where GNP per capita was below the EU average and those, like Merseyside, which contain industries in decline. Britain has been an enthusiastic recipient of EU regional funds but the British government has always resisted some of the integrative objectives of these funds. Thus London resisted for some time the application of the principle of additionality preferring to regard European funding (via a system known as 'EUROPES') as an alternative rather than an addition to UK funding. Similarly, attempts by the Commission to encourage the development of 'multilevel governance' by involving and empowering local and regional government in EU structural policy making and implementation have been strongly and effectively resisted by London.

Britain's interest in membership of the EU has always been primarily for economic reasons and the establishment of first of all a common market and then, after 1986, of a single market has been and is one area of EU activity that has always had Britain's unqualified support. This is hardly surprising as over 50 per cent of Britain's trade is now with the EU and the Blair government makes constant reference to the fact that membership directly accounts for some 3 million jobs and a substantial proportion of Britain's overall income. In recent years the British government has been to the fore in advocating and supporting the EU's drive to create a more competitive single market by 2010. Here, though, the preferred method is the more flexible open method of coordination which involves peer review, benchmarking and the search for best practice rather than an extensive programme of EU legislation. The British, with their antipathy to a further extension of supranational law, prefer a method of policy cooperation that places the primary responsibility on the member states rather than the Commission or the Court of Justice.

Britain's enthusiasm for the single market and for a more competitive market can be perceived as a fondness for 'negative integration' by which is meant the removal of barriers. British governments have always had trouble with the idea of 'positive' integration by which is meant the creation of common (interventionist) policies at the EU level. Thus, whilst competition policy has been seen as useful in order to maintain the freedoms of the market, attempts to develop social policy have often been seen in Britain as unnecessarily interventionist. This is partly a resistance to further integration and partly a resistance by Conservative governments to 'supranational socialism'. Mrs Thatcher saw these two things coming together in Jacques Delors's advocacy of a Social Charter and this led her to complain in her speech at Bruges that 'we have not successfully rolled back the frontiers of the state in Britain only to see them reimposed at a European level' (Young 1999: 479). The Social Charter was thus seen by both Margaret Thatcher and John Major as an attempt to further both integration and intervention. Although Tony Blair reversed the Social Chapter opt-out in 1997 both he and Gordon Brown have been keen to essentially continue the Thatcher objective of resisting further EU regulation of British working practices.

There are several areas of policy—the environment, women's rights, consumer affairs—where the EU can be seen to be the main driver of British domestic policy providing a supranational framework for the development of a national policy. This is most obvious in environmental policy where the EU's six environmental action programmes have had a major impact on British approaches to the management of waste and to air and water quality. Geddes argues that in this sector Britain has become significantly pro-active and policy-shaping in stark contrast to its initial rather sceptical and defensive position (Geddes 2004: 136). At times British ministers with responsibility for policy in one of these relatively new areas of government activity have found themselves amongst 'friends' in the EU Council of Ministers in contrast to a relatively isolated role within the British cabinet.

At Maastricht, John Major also negotiated the right to delay opting in to economic and monetary union and the creation of a single currency—an EU objective that has caused Britain difficulties ever since it was first mooted at The Hague European Summit of 1969. Britain's suspicions about EMU stem from a concern about both its potential political and economic impact on British sovereignty and independence. Quite apart from technical concerns about the 'fit' between the British economy and those of the major EU member states, Britain has always worried about the link between EMU and further integration. Britain only reluctantly joined the European Monetary System in 1978 but, thanks to Mrs Thatcher's resolute opposition, did not join the Exchange Rate Mechanism until 1990. As such Britain joined at the wrong time and at the wrong rate and the result, which has scarred British views about EMU ever since, was a humiliating departure on 'Black Wednesday' (16 September 1992).

As discussed above, the question of Euro membership is a political one as much as an economic one and there remains little prospect of it being seriously considered in the future if the British government remains convinced that the opinion polls are correct and that it has no prospect of winning a referendum on the issue. In the mean-time whilst the value of the Euro (an important virility test in British eyes) rose in 2003–4 after a shaky start in 1999, the inability of several of the leading countries within the Eurozone to stick to the rigid criteria for Stability and Growth that they had insisted upon, meant that British hesitancy seemed increasingly justifiable inside Britain if not amongst Britain's partners.

Finally, mention should be made of Britain's engagement with EU policies within the two intergovernmental pillars of the TEU. The development of policies in the field of Justice and Home Affairs, initially resisted by the Major government, now presents some real opportunities for a country which, as a potential terrorist target, has an increasing pragmatic interest (especially since the events of 9/11) in the security advantages to be had from cooperation in the areas of counter terrorism, drug trafficking, major crime, asylum and immigration. However, Britain continues to hesitate about full participation in the Schengen arrangements because it continues to believe that its island position ensures the continuing effectiveness of border controls (for people if not goods). Nevertheless, in a short period of time the British Home Office has evolved from being a British government department with minimal EU involvement to being one with a European dimension to almost all aspects of its responsibilities.

One of the major reasons for the original Six finally welcoming and accepting Britain's EU membership bid relates to the external dimension of European integration and it was an awareness of its own diminished role in the world that was one of the major factors that explained Britain's turn to Europe after 1961. With regard to EU competence in trade, aid, and development, Britain has always been a major player in the evolution of policy. The EU is the world's largest trading bloc and the world's largest provider of development aid. In particular, since the end of US hegemony in the global economic system, Britain has seen clear benefit from being a part of one of the trio of major players (the US and Japan being the other two) that govern the contemporary international economic system. Britain has consistently argued for a liberal approach by the EU towards international trade negotiations seeking in particular to keep the single market open to the outside world as well as internally. In recent years, Britain's anxiety to reform the CAP has been partly related to its internal costs but mainly related to a British desire to remove a problem from the EU's external trade negotiating position. If the EU is to secure access to the world market for services that is comparable to the access that it currently enjoys for its goods then it will have to stop subsidising agricultural exports and do away with its protectionist agricultural policies.

When Britain joined the EU in 1973 the EU's aid and development policy was primarily targeted at francophone Africa. British membership extended this as did the subsequent membership of Spain and Portugal. Britain has always been a firm supporter of the pooling of a certain amount of national aid as EU aid, and Britain has supported the idea of collective decision making and of the effectiveness of multilateral aid programming. What the British have never accepted is the way that European Commission administers EU aid arguing instead that this would be better done by an independent EU agency.

Britain has always been a keen advocate of the principle of EPC and the CFSP and has been in the forefront of those countries determined to make the established intergovernmental procedures work more effectively. Whilst Britain remains determined to maintain a separate national foreign policy and diplomatic service it long ago recognized the fact that the EU is Britain's 'point of departure' when it comes to foreign policy rather than the first thing that Britain bumps into. Britain, like most of the EU's major powers, had had occasion to break with or prevent EU unity on import-ant foreign policy positions (Iraq being the most recent and dramatic of examples) but the strength of the CFSP is illustrated by the speed with which bruised feelings are repaired and the search for common positions resumed.

Britain of necessity is a major player in any external position adopted by the EU and it is an essential player in any attempt to give European foreign policy a defence dimension. For the most part Britain's role in the CFSP/ESDP has been both significant and constructive and reflects the fact that, ever since its inception in 1969, successive governments have placed a high value on European cooperation in foreign and security policy.

Conclusions

The broad conclusion of this chapter is that Britain does indeed have a Europeanized government operating in a still non-Europeanized polity. To this extent despite his clearly stated initial ambitions Prime Minister Blair has failed to date in his bid to once and for all resolve the question of Britain's participation in the European integrative experiment (Stephens 2004; Peel 2003; Prowse 2003). In 1997 Blair came to power seemingly determined to make a significant difference to Britain's relationship with the EU primarily by creating the domestic consensus necessary to underpin Britain's whole-hearted and complete participation in, and leadership of, the European Union. However, despite many announcements of a determination to once and for all engage the British public in a positive appreciation of the advantages of EU membership, the Blair government has been no more successful in this endeavour than its predecessors.

Thus Britain's future in the European Union remains uncertain as does the future of the European Union itself. But for the vital question of British membership of the Euro one might have been able to argue that Britain and the EU have both been moving towards one another in recent years. Under Blair, Britain has become more EU-friendly and since the mid-1990s the EU has become more intergovernmental and more conducive to the British approach. However, the continued failure to 'sell' the EU to the British people means that there is still no sign of a consensus in favour of normalizing Britain's relationship with the EU. By 2004 the question of Euro mem-bership, which Blair had sought to isolate from other aspects of the EU discourse, was significantly entangled with concerns about the future direction of the EU. Towards the end of the Convention on the Future of Europe, the Blair government was forced to harden its previously cooperative position in response to a hostile domestic response to the ideas under consideration (Menon 2004: 2 and 38–40). Blair's decision to hold a referendum on the Constitutional Treaty, agreed in June 2004, has raised the political stakes considerably. While Blair seems to have decided to resolve Britain's commitment once and for all, he has also made himself hostage to the vagaries of a hostile domestic public opinion. In 1998 Menon and Wright (1998) contrasted the negativity of public perceptions of Britain's place in Europe with the generally held external perception of Britain as an effective member of the EU exerting a growing influence on its evolution. How long can a British government that is clearly 'European' continue to operate effectively in the EU when domestic opinion and the domestic media remain so stubbornly 'non-European'?

Further reading

Hugo Young (1999) has written an excellent politico-historical account of Britain's relationship with the EU. The book can be supplemented from 1999 to 2003 by reference to Young's *Guardian* journalism on the same subject which can be found at <http://www. guardian.co.uk/hugoyoung>. Geddes (2004) provides a useful single-authored overview of the impact of membership on British politics whilst the collection edited by Baker and Seabright (1998) contains more specialized articles on particular aspects of the relationship. George (1998) is an excellent chronological account of the evolution of Britain's EU membership up to the end of the Major administration and there are several recent publications that deal with the Blair administrations (Bulmer 2000; Deighton 2001; Rosamond 2002, Allen 2003b, Menon 2004). Forster and Blair (2002) and Bulmer and Burch (2003) provide a good overview of the impact of EU membership on British policy-making.

Weblinks

The FCO website <http://fco.gov.uk> has a very useful section on Britain and the EU and all of Prime Minister Tony Blair's speeches on Europe can be found at <http://www. pm.gov.uk>. The Federal Trust <http://www.fedtrust.co.uk/policybriefs> is a good source on the British debate about the EU whilst SOSIG <http://sosig.ac.uk> is an extensive database for all social sciences in Europe. Most British newspapers have websites with links to material on Britain and the EU—particularly recommended are the *Guardian* <http://politics. guardian.co.uk>, the *Financial Times* <http://www.ft.com> and the *Economist* <http://www. economist.com>. The Political Studies Association of the UK has a comprehensive website including a section dealing with Britain <http://www.psa.ac.uk/ www/uk_ polgovt.htm>.

References

Allen, D. (2003a), 'The Foreign and Commonwealth Office: Adapting to Change Within a Transformed World', in B. Hocking and D. Spence (eds), *Integrating Diplomats: Foreign Ministries in the European Union* (Basingstoke: Palgrave).

Allen, D. (2003b), 'Great Britain and the Future of the European Union: Not quite there yet', in S. Serfaty (ed.), *The European Finality and its National Dimensions* (Washington, DC: Center for Strategic and International Studies), 77–105.

Allen, D. (2004), 'James Callaghan', in
K. Theakston (ed.), *British Foreign Secretaries since 1974* (London: Routledge).

Baker, D., and Seawright, D. (eds) (1998),
Britain For and Against Europe: British Politics and the Question of European Integration (Oxford: Oxford University Press).

Blair, T. (2000), Speech to the Polish Stock
Exchange, 6 October, <http://
www.number-10.gov.uk/> (Speeches).

Bulmer, S., and Burch, M. (2003), 'The
Europeanization of UK Government: From
Quiet Revolution to Explicit Step-Change'.
Paper presented at UACES/ESRC Seminar on
Europeanization, University of
Sheffield, 19 September 2003,
<http://www.shef.ac.uk/ebpp/index.html>.

Bulmer, S. (2000), 'European policy: fresh start
or false dawn?', in D. Coates and P. Lawler
(eds), *New Labour in Power* (Manchester:
Manchester University Press), 240–53.

Butler, D., and Kitzinger, U. (1976), *The 1975
Referendum*, 2nd edn. (London: Macmillan).

Coles, J. (2000), *Making Foreign Policy: A Certain
Idea of Britain* (London: John Murray).

Deighton, A. (2001), 'European Union Policy',
in A. Seldon (ed.), *The Blair Effect: The Blair
Government, 1997–2001* (London: Little
Brown and Co.), 307–30.

Forster, A., and Blair, A. (2002), *The Making of
Britain's European Foreign Policy* (London:
Longman).

Geddes, A. (2004), *The European Union and
British Politics* (Basingstoke: Palgrave).

George, S. (1998), *An Awkward Partner: Britain in
the European Community*, 3rd edn. (Oxford:
Oxford University Press).

Grabbe, H., and Munchau, W. (2002), *Germany
and Britain: An Alliance of Necessity* (London:
Centre for European Reform).

Ludlow, P. (1993), 'The UK Presidency: A View
from Brussels', *Journal of Common Market
Studies*, 31/2, 246–60.

Ludlow, P. (1998), 'The 1998 UK Presidency: A
View from Brussels', *Journal of Common
Market Studies*, 36/4, 573–83.

Menon, A., and Wright, V. (1998), 'The
Paradoxes of "Failure": British EU
Policy-Making in Comparative
Perspective', *Public Administration and
Public Policy*, 13/4.

Menon, A. (2004), *Leading from Behind: Britain
and the European Constitutional Treaty* (Paris:
Notre Europe, Research and European
Issues No 31, January).

Owen, D. (2003), 'Two-Man Government',
Prospect, 93, December, 14–16.

Peel, Q. (2003), 'The failure of Blair's
European policy', *Financial Times*,
6 May.

Prowse, M. (2003), 'Blair has failed to
prepare the ground for an integrated
Europe', *Financial Times*, 7 June.

Rosamond, B. (2002), 'Britain's European
Future', in C. Hay (ed.), *British Politics Today*
(Cambridge: Polity), 185–215.

Seldon, A. (1997), *Major: A Political Life*
(London: Weidenfeld & Nicolson).

Serfaty, S. (ed.) (2003), *The European
Finality Debate and its National Dimensions*
(Washington, DC: Center for Strategic
and International Studies).

Stephens, P. (2004), 'Blair's big failure
on Europe', *Financial Times*,
24 February.

Westlake, M. (1997), 'Mad Cows and
Englishmen—The Institutional
Consequences of the BSE Crisis; Keynote
Article, in *The European Union 1996;
Annual Review of Activities, Journal of
Common Market Studies, Annual Review*
(September 1997), 11–36.

Wilkes, G., and Wring, D. (1998), 'The British
Press and European Integration:
1948–1996', in D. Baker, and D. Seawright
(eds), *Britain For and Against Europe: British
Politics and the Question of European Integration*
(Oxford: Oxford University Press),
185–205.

Young, H. (1999), *This Blessed Plot: Britain and
Europe from Churchill to Blair* (London:
PaperMac).

Chapter 7

Italy and Spain: A Tale of Contrasting Effectiveness in the EU

Federiga Bindi with Manuela Cisci[1]

Contents

Summary

Italy and Spain are two southern member states that joined the European integration process in the aftermath of fascist rule, and with a view to building international credibility. For both states integration offered opportunities: for Italy an alternative to governmental instability at home; for Spain, a means for achieving economic modernization. This chapter compares how the two states have adapted their institutional machinery to EU membership, examining central government, the parliaments, and the regions. After exploring the European diplomacy of the two states, the chapter compares how far and how well they have adapted to the process of European integration; and to what extent this has contributed to changes at the domestic level.

[1] I would like to thank Nadia Desai for her lingustic support.

Introduction

This chapter will compare Italy and Spain in relation to their EU membership. Reasons for membership will be discussed first, followed by an analysis of the support of both public opinion and political parties vis-à-vis the process of European integration. The institutional frameworks and the role of the different actors in the management of European affairs will then be compared, followed by the 'European diplomacies' of the two countries—that is their negotiating style and techniques within the European Union decision-making processes. The chapter argues that Spain has been more effective than Italy at projecting its interests in Brussels and sets out the basis for this argument.

History and politics of the European issue

Motivations for membership

At the time of the Schuman Declaration, in May 1950, Italy was a former fascist dictatorship, with an agriculture-based economy and high rates of unemployment. Due to the political uncertainties, foreign financial help had been slow to arrive. In Prime Minister De Gasperi and Foreign Minister Sforza's minds, ECSC membership was to offer security to the newborn Italian democracy. The decision to join was therefore a political decision of the government supported by many political leaders but opposed by other influential actors, such as the Socialist and Communist parties and the steel industry.

Spain's accession took place some thirty years after Italian membership. Yet, the circumstances show some similarities. Spain was a poor, mainly agriculture-based country marked by forty years of Franco's dictatorship and subsequent international isolation. The first agreement with the European Communities (EC), on the progressive reductions of obstacles to trade, dates from 1970; membership of the Council of Europe from 1977; the agreement for the free circulation of goods between EFTA and Spain dates from 1979; NATO membership dates from 1982. The negotiations for EC membership—officially opened on 17 October 1978—lasted for nearly a decade, the membership treaty being signed on 12 June 1985. Concerns about Spanish accession came in fact from Italy and France—afraid that EC funding to Spain's agriculture would be diverted at the expense of their own agricultural economies—and from Germany and the UK, which opposed any rise in agricultural expenditure. Nevertheless, the EC's political commitment to enlargement eventually over-rode these detailed concerns.

The foreign policy context

Since the beginning of the Italian Republic, the mainstreams of foreign policy have been pro-US and pro-European values, as the Christian Democratic (DC) party in government and its President (and Prime Minister), Alcide De Gasperi, believed that

Italy could better defend its national interests within a policy of European solidarity. The efforts thus went in the direction of reintegrating Italy into international institutions as soon as possible. Hence Italy was included both into the Bretton–Woods agreement (1946) and as a member of the IMF (1947). By accepting the Treaty of Paris as a defeated country with no concession to nationalism and to 'national pride', in July 1947 Italy could take part in the negotiations for the Marshall Plan (thus being a founding member of OEEC in 1948) and in 1949 in those for the Council of Europe. With the signature and the Parliament's ratification of the North Atlantic Treaty (18 March 1949), Italy had officially moved on from its military defeat in the Second World War After De Gasperi's death (1954), a 'de-politicization' of Italian Foreign policy took place: pro-European and pro-American values remained at the centre of Italian foreign policy, but its conduct witnessed an increased role of 'technicians'—diplomats and bureaucrats—while politicians would rather deal with domestic matters.

When politicians have to decide on allies, they tend to choose actors on the basis of the perceived political proximity: in the past, the usual allies of Italian governments were Christian Democratic-led countries such as Germany and the Benelux. With the arrival of the 'Olive tree' centre-left government (1996–2001), this long-term pattern shifted. The main allies became Blair's UK Labour government or the socialist government of Antonio Guterres's Portugal. For Berlusconi's centre-right government (2001 onwards), the major ally became José Maria Aznar's centre-right Partido Popular (PP) government in Spain. This development signalled a shift in the traditional pro-European stance of Italian governments towards a more nationalist attitude. Two questions are raised. First, whether, given the economic, cultural and societal differences from the new partners, such alliances really served Italian interests. Secondly, whether the recent nationalist stance is helping or damaging the defence of Italian interests. An example is given by the 2003 Italian Presidency, which was marked by the failure to approve the EU Constitutional Treaty (subsequently approved in June 2004 under the Irish presidency). There was in fact a political decision on the part of the Presidency not to negotiate the new Treaty at the Brussels December 2003 European Council and one of the reasons recalled by Mr Berlusconi for doing so was the wish not to displease his good friend Aznar. Only a matter of months later, in March 2004, Aznar lost the national election—held under the shadow of a terrorist atrocity in Madrid—to the socialists.

The rationale behind the Spanish choice of allies is, not surprisingly, the pursuit of national interests. In particular, Spain has been very active in defending its prerogative (and funds) as a 'poor' country, while at the same time working to enhance its political status of an 'almost big' country. For instance, during the negotiations leading to the Nice Treaty, Spain promoted an alliance with the other Cohesion Fund countries, while at the same time allying with Poland in defending its 'almost big' status in terms of voting rights in the Council. In this context, political proximity is also used by Spanish leaders when useful, as was the case by the socialist prime minister, Felipé Gonzales (1982–96) in order to get support for Spanish accession to the EC.

One special mention concerns the Spanish–Portuguese relationship. During the dictatorships period (1930s to mid-1970s), no institutional relations existed between the two countries, despite some cooperation within the UN and the signature of a *Pacto Iberico* granting mutual help. Following the EFTA–Spain treaty on the free circulation of goods (1979), exchanges started to take place between the two countries. Yet Spain and Portugal held separate negotiations for EC membership, also making a point of signing the accession treaties in two distinct places and moments. EU membership has enhanced both economic and political cooperation: since 1998, the Spanish and the Portuguese Premiers meet every semester to discuss matters of importance to the two countries and to coordinate actions; common interests shall thus be jointly defended.

Public opinion and political parties

Support for the EU is generally widespread in both countries—with the exception of extreme left parties, and of a more nationalist point of view of conservative political forces. Both Italians and Spanish are considered to be supporters of the process of European integration. However, whilst in Italy the support of the process of European integration corresponds to a lack of confidence in the Italian institutional and political system, in Spain the support for European integration is coupled rather with a self re-evaluation and a perception of the centrality of Spanish interests within Europe.

The Italian system has been characterized by two features—the comparative weakness of the prime minister and the relative strength of the second chamber (the Senate)—which have contributed to governmental instability. As this situation developed over the years the EC began to be perceived as the only possibility to bring order into the national system. Thus the demand for supranational structures corresponded to a demand for repairing the inefficiencies of the Italian system. On the other hand, the EC has at times been used by Italian politicians to legitimize their own actions, or to justify unpopular policies, notably fiscal and monetary measures. As two illustrative headlines from leading Italian newspapers show: 'The Twelve ask us for tears and blood' (*La Repubblica*, 5 May 1992); 'Privatization? It is imposed by the EC' (*Corriere della Sera*, 3 August 1992).

As for the attitude of the political parties vis-à-vis integration, except for the period right after the war, all the major parties gradually became supporters of the process of European integration. To Christian Democrats (DC) pro-European and pro-US values were the basis of foreign policy. Socialists (PSI) and Communists (PCI), initially opposed to the EC, changed position over the years. The invasion of Hungary in 1954 marked the change for the PSI, which abstained on the ratification vote for the EEC Treaty and voted in favour of EURATOM. The PCI remained against the EC until the end of the 1960s, when it shifted its broad policy away from following a Moscow line towards so-called Euro-communism. Thus it started to change perspective when the first Communists were appointed to the European Parliament (1969) and it embraced pro-European values by the time of the first direct elections to the European Parliament (1979). As a result, gradually the EC became a non-issue in the Italian political arena. In the words of the former foreign minister, Giulio Andreotti, '[the EC] is a great tradition . . . of both cultural and political families of the [Italian] Nation'.[2] According to former Ambassador Sergio Romano (1994: 114): 'Italians are pro-European in the same way they are catholic: Europe has become a sort of religious icon in front of which politicians briefly kneel before talking about other things'.

[2] Quoted in *Dossier Europa*, 6.90, 8.

In Spain, since EC membership, two parties have been in government: the socialist PSOE (Felipé Gonzales 1982–96 and José Luis Rodríguez Zapatero, 2004–) and PP (José Maria Aznar, 1996–2004). European integration has enjoyed a large consensus among political parties, yet their attitude regarding Community affairs has been quite reactive and their participation limited. Membership meant, for political elite and public opinion alike, the return to the Western world from which the country felt excluded. Accession to the EC was supported almost unanimously by all political parties and societal actors.

The institutional framework

Institutions at the national level

The main institutional difference between Italy and Spain lies in executive–legislative relations. Thus, while Italy has been characterized by an Executive lacking cohesion and dominated by the Legislative, Spain's Executive is strong, prevailing over the Legislative. The position of the President of the Council also differs: a *primus inter pares* in Italy, a predominant figure in Spain. We offer a sketch of the institutional set-up in general in order to explain how European policy is handled.

The 1948 Italian Republican Constitution, after the troubled fascist period, was the result of many political compromises. Italian society is pluralist and the Constitution reflects that. The Constitution designed weak institutions and strong parties, as it was believed that the system would work because of the strength and authority injected from outside by the parties. Parties are thus not only involved in policy-making, but they also appoint the ministers and decide upon state secretaries, chairmen and members of the boards of any public company or body and, of course, public departments. According to Cotta (1990: 76) the Italian parliament is 'a highly polycentric institution not easily amenable to majoritarian decisions and to firm leadership by Cabinet'. Because of *perfect bicameralism*—the *Senato* (Upper Chamber) and the *Camera* (Lower Chamber) perform identical functions and share legislative power. Parliamentary procedures assign the government a marginal role in parliamentary work, while maximizing opportunities for influence in the setting of the agenda and in the legislative process for individual deputies and minor groups. All this tended to shape an organizational and procedural model whereby the Parliament acts as legislator and neglects control and scrutiny functions. In the beginning this was meant to reduce confrontation and incorporate opposition parties in the democratic system. Over the years it has reduced the Parliament's performance and effectiveness. In addition, the pure proportional electoral system produced a very fragmented party system, with at least eight national parties represented in Parliament at any given time, and very little stability. The new electoral system introduced in 1994[3] has not

---

[3] According to the new electoral law, in the Chamber of Deputies 75% of the MPs are to be elected on a majoritarian system, while the remaining 25% are still to be distributed on a proportional basis. The former electoral law was purely proportional.

reduced the number of parties: in the 1996–2000 Legislature some forty different political groups were represented in Parliament, with an eight-party coalition in government. In the Legislature from 2000 the number of parties is twelve, plus the linguistic minorities.[4] As a result, the over fifty-five Cabinets of the Republic have been large and unstable four–five party coalitions, with some of the parties (notably the DC) further subdivided into powerful 'correnti' (streams), each one with its own agenda and leaders.

The Italian President of the Council is appointed by the President of the Republic and can take office only after having obtained a vote of confidence from the Parliament. In principle he selects his Ministers. However, in doing so he has to respect the 'suggestions' of party leaders. Only the 'Amato I' Government (1992–3)—and to some extent the Berlusconi II Government (2001–)—have not respected this unwritten rule. The Council of Ministers—in principle a collegial body—was in fact not thought of as an effective centre for policy coordination: the level of collegiality has usually been low, while inter-ministerial competition has always been high. The mechanism allowing for an easy use of the non-confidence vote further weakened the Italian Government. In Giuliano Amato's (1994: 225) words:

'Italy is an excellent example of the theory of involution expounded by Mancur Olson: a vital system that becomes progressively rigid, incapable of correcting its increasing entropy, and unable to keep up with the need of change, is finally destroyed by the impact on its corrupted tissues of newly emerging counter-forces.'

Since the XIV Legislature (2001 onwards), the number of ministries was cut to 12,[5] while the powers of the President of the Council, as well as its operative tools, have been sensibly extended. Berlusconi has been trying to extend to the maximum the powers given by the Constitution and the law to the President of the Council. Despite this, though, his government has been suffering like its predecessors from inter-ministerial and inter-party competition. The difference is that from the mid-1990s onwards, there has been a reduction in Parliament's turnover. Whilst there have been five different governments in the years 1996–2004,[6] the Legislative has finally completed its natural cycle of five years. It is unsurprising that this institutional situation impacts upon the conduct of Italian European policy.

In Spain the 1978 Constitution made the monarch Head of the State, but his role is that of a moderating and arbitrating power, with the primary function of symbolizing the Spanish State. Because of his role in stabilizing Spanish democracy, King Juan Carlos has acquired a legitimacy and status that surpasses that of the Monarchy itself. However, political responsibility falls entirely on the Government.

The Spanish Constitution was careful in vesting the President (in constitutional terms the Prime Minister does not exist, rather the President of Government or President of the Council of Ministers) with special authority. The President of

---

[4] Cf. <http://www.camera.it/dati/leg14/datistatistici/attivitalegislativa> as of 3 Jan. 2003.

[5] Yet in the Berlusconi II Government one finds 14 Ministers, plus 8 Ministers without Portfolio and 6 Junior Ministers. See <http://www.governo.it/Governo/Ministeri/ministri_gov.htlm> as of 3 Jan. 2003.

[6] Four 'Olive Tree' governments—Prodi, D'Alema I, D'Alema II, Amato II—and one 'Polo delle Libertà'—Berlusconi II.

Government is not responsible to the monarch, but rather to the electorate through the Parliament. The Parliament (*Cortes Generales*) is a bicameral body with a weak upper house (Senado)—of whose 257 members 208 are directly elected and 49 are appointed as regional representatives—and a lower house (*Congresso de los Diputados*) whose 350 members are elected by proportional representation. Whereas the Italian institutional system stressed popular sovereignty and proportional representation in an attempt to balance powers between the Executive and Legislative, the Spanish model placed major emphasis on strong and stable governments. The Spanish Legislative–Executive relationship has been defined as the most pro-government of Europe. Parliament was important during the transition to a democracy, and then slowly lost its previous central role.

The Spanish President of Government is charged with the formation and leadership of the Government. The Premier has virtually free hands over the structure and appointments to Cabinet (although the number of Ministers with Portfolio can only be changed by the Cortes). It is he—rather than the entire government—that must have the confidence of the Cortes, in order to govern, as expressed in a vote of investiture. The President can demand a vote of support at any time, while for a vote of no-confidence a constructive censure motion on the German model is required, including the nomination of an alternative candidate for the Presidency. Since 1978 the custom has been that of considering the leader of each party as the candidate for the Presidency; this has reinforced the political leadership of the Premier. Standing at the centre of Spain's political system, the President of the Government has extensive means and is backed by a wide staff of advisers.

Regional authorities

In October 2001 the Italian Constitution was modified providing Italy with a federal framework. Article 5 of the Constitution enshrines both the principles of national unity and autonomy: the Republic is one and indivisible but local autonomies are recognized and promoted. Italy is subdivided into Municipalities, Provinces, and Regions, to which the reform added the so-called 'metropolitan cities', that is the biggest cities of the country that now have a special status.

The Constitution distinguishes the five 'special Regions' (*Regioni a Statuto speciale*) from the 'normal' regions (*Regioni a Statuto ordinario*): geographical, historical, and ethnical differences are the basis on which Val d'Aosta, South Tyrol, Friuli, Sicily, and Sardinia have been given special status and wider powers. Every Italian Region has a directly elected assembly (*Consiglio regionale*), provided with legislative powers and an executive body (*Giunta regionale*), chaired by its President. All regions have legislative and administrative powers, but the *Regioni a Statuto speciale* enjoy exclusive legislative competencies as compared to the concurrent legislative competencies characterizing the other Regions. While the *Regioni a Statuto speciale* were created at the same time as the Constitution was written by means of constitutional law, the *Regioni a Statuto ordinario* were formed only at the beginning of the 1970s. They, too, have their own Statute, but it does not have the same legal strength of the *Statuti speciali*.

Before the 2001 Constitutional reform, the Italian institutional framework was based on the hierarchical supremacy of the central government over regional authorities. In law-making regions had to respect the principles fixed by central legislative power, while central Government's decentralized authorities checked the administrative acts of the Regions. The constitutional reform has created a new philosophy, namely that the Italian Constitution no longer enumerates regional competencies but the State ones. Regions can now act in every area that the Constitution does not specifically attribute to the State.

The importance of the seventeen Spanish *Comunidades Autonomas* in the institutional framework was heightened by comparison with that of the Italian Regions due to the influence that the political parties of the historical nationalities, the nationalist parties of the Basque Country and Catalonia, were able to exercise during the process of drawing up the Constitution, claiming wide autonomy from the central power. As it was not possible to give the whole of Spain such a large measure of independence, the Spanish Constitution did not create a decentralized structure, but rather laid down the rules to be followed in order to voluntarily and gradually institute *Comunidades Autonomas* (autonomous communities). This system has created a strongly asymmetrical, decentralized State. There are seventeen *Comunidades Autonomas*; all have both legislative (exclusive and concurrent) and administrative powers but with different levels of independence from the central Government. The Basque Country, Catalonia, and Galicia have the widest autonomy, followed by Andalucia; then there are Valencia and the Canary Islands and finally, all the remaining *Comunidades*.

The relationship between *Comunidades Autonomas* and central Government is not a pure hierarchical relationship, as it was in Italy before the constitutional reform, it is more correct to say that it is based on the division of competencies between them. The *Comunidades Autonomas* have to respect the legislative norms fixed by the central Parliament only in those areas where they do not have exclusive competencies.

EU policy-making

The relationship between European law and national law

The Italian Constitution does not mention the European Communities. Article 11 of the Constitution—foreseeing the possibility for the State to delegate powers to international organizations—was introduced with an eye on the newborn United Nations, which Italy joined in 1955. At their creation the European Communities were thus understood as classical international organizations, producing international law. For a long time both legal doctrine and the Italian Constitutional Court's rulings thus supported the principle of the separation between the two juridical systems—the EC and the Italian one—notwithstanding the quite different views of the ECJ, which had established the principle of the supremacy of EC law.[7] In 1973, the Italian Constitutional Court recognized the principle of supremacy of EC law over national law, yet with limits,[8] and it was only in 1984 that the conflict between the Italian

---

[7] See the ECJ's rulings in *Costa v ENEL* (n. 14 of 7 Mar. 1964); and *Simmenthal* (9 Mar. 1978).

[8] Ruling 183 of 1973. Cf. also *Industrie Chimiche Italia Centrale c/ Ministero del Commercio con l'Estero*, n. 232 of 30 Oct. 1975.

Constitutional Court and the ECJ finally came to an end, with the *Granital c. Ministero delle Finanze* ruling.[9]

The transposition of EC directives into national law takes place in Italy through the unusual means of the annual so-called 'Community Law' (*legge comunitaria annuale*), created with Law 86/1989, also known as '*Legge La Pergola*'. While in the past, implementation of EC norms relied on a variety of techniques, the 'Community law' provides a specific and systematic method for the harmonizing of domestic regulations to EC norms. The 'Community law' is only partially an instrument for immediate implementation. Rather, it is a device for programming and rationalizing the various sets of implementing measures. By 31 of March of each year, the government—namely the Minister for EU Affairs—submits to Parliament a bill including all EC norms in need of national implementing measures. The law allows different techniques to be chosen for direct and indirect implementation: (a) Parliamentary abrogation or modification of existing domestic legislation; (b) delegation of legislative powers to the government; (c) authorization to the Government to adopt regulations in subject areas beforehand regulated by primary sources; and (d) administrative acts. The 'Community law' also provides a strict regulation of the timing of its presentation, while the rules of procedure of the Parliament regulate the discussion, with the aim to have it approved within the year. The *Legge La Pergola* was designed to improve the transposition rates of European legislation in Italy. It brought in a more systematic approach but, if the annual 'Community law' itself became held up in parliament, the consequences for transposition could be serious (Giuliani and Piattoni 2001: 118).

In the 1978 Spanish Constitution, Articles 93–6 are devoted to international treaties; thus they were used as the basis for Spanish integration into the EC system. Article 93 allows Spain to delegate powers to international institutions or organizations. Although it does not specifically mention the EC, it legitimized Spain's accession into the EC. Article 95 imposes a Constitutional reform when the State signs an international treaty that is divergent from the Constitution, and Article 96 settled that approved international treaties become an integral part of national law. Thus some of the conflict between the legal systems, as experienced in Italy, could be avoided. Efforts to improve Spain's record in implementing European legislation have been undertaken, including through a monthly report on overdue measures, made by the Secretariat of State for EU Affairs (SSEU), which is responsible for EU policy coordination within the Ministry of Foreign Affairs (Morata 1988: 105–6; Basabe Lloréns 2003: 180).

The Minister of Foreign Affairs and the Prime Minister

In Italy, the assimilation of the Communities as a classical international organization led to the attribution of the main role in dealing with European affairs within the government to the Ministry of Foreign Affairs (MAE). Until the 1999 reform of the Government, the organization and distribution of tasks within and among the Ministries were based on old laws dating back to the origins of the Italian State in the mid-1800s. In January 2000, a much-awaited reform of the Ministry of Foreign Affairs took place. Before the reform the MAE was composed of six thematic

---

[9] Ruling 170 of 8 June 1984, where the Constitutional Court finally declared that national judges have to apply EC norms whenever they conflict with national legislation.

Directorate-Generals (DGs), each provided with a European desk, while the overall coordination on European issues was undertaken by the Political Affairs DG. Today, the Ministry of Foreign Affairs is subdivided into five geographical and seven thematic DGs, amongst which one finds both a DG of 'European Countries' (DGEC), and a DG of 'European Integration' (DGEI). While DGEC deals with bilateral issues, DGEI handles multilateral European questions (chiefly but not exclusively the European Union). DGEI is also charged with the spreading of information coming from the COREPER and the Commission to the other branches of the Italian public administration. The duties of the Minister of Foreign Affairs in relation to the EU are manifold: the Common Foreign and Security Policy (CFSP), the political and economic external relations of the EU, as well any EU treaty negotiations. However, since 1999, the Presidency of the Council is responsible, too, for the 'participation of the Italian State in the EU' and for the 'actuation of EU policies'. Acting in coordination, the Presidency of the Council and the Foreign Ministry should thus ensure the promotion of the Italian positions within the European institutions. In doing so, they are supported respectively by the Undersecretary of State for Foreign Affairs charged with European Affairs and by the Minister for EC Policies.

The Undersecretary of State for Foreign Affairs charged with European Affairs (*Sottosegretario agli Esteri con delega per gli Affari Europei*) has, on paper, wide tasks. S/he is in fact charged with the following of European bilateral relations, with participation in the EU, the OECD and the Council of Europe. S/he is part of the delegation attending the EU General Affairs Council and the European Councils. However, s/he cannot act independently from the Minister.

The Ministry for the Coordination of EC Policies was created in 1980 within the Presidency of the Council. Its lack of resources was such that it was once defined by Grottanelli de Santi (1992: 186) as the Cinderella of the Italian Ministries. Thus, in 1995, it was suppressed and its tasks attributed to the Undersecretary of State for Economics; in 1996, they were further shared between the Undersecretary of State at the Presidency of the Council and the Undersecretary of State for Foreign Affairs charged with European Affairs. In 1998, the renamed Minister for Community Policies was re-introduced and given enhanced means and political role. Yet, from a formal point of view, the Minister's tasks were not changed over the years. They concern above all the transposition of EC directives into national law. In addition, the Minister shall: deal with the ECJ cases concerning issues of national interest; promote the professional training of public officials in EU affairs; spread information on the EU; promote Italian citizens in the EU institutions; represent Italy in the Council for the Internal Market; coordinate *with* the different sectors of public administration and social partners on EU Politics. This task is to be addressed by means of an ad hoc meeting of the State-Region Conference (*Sessione Comunitaria della Conferenza Stato-Regioni*). However, the use of the word 'with' is not casual, since the Ministry never had the authority to coordinate other ministries. In addition, the Minister is not part of the delegations attending the General Affairs Council, nor of the European Council, a fact that has at times undermined its role both domestically and at the European level. The fortunes of the Department for Community Policies have varied over the years: it is only from 1998 that it was given substantial new means and resources.

In Italy there is no permanent body charged with the inter-ministerial coordination of European affairs, such as exists in France with the *Secrétariat général du Comité*

Interministériel pour les questions de coopération économique européenne (SGCI) or with the (much smaller) Cabinet Office European Secretariat in Britain. Intra- and inter-ministerial coordination thus remain unsolved problems in the Italian Government. In the functional ministries, the level of intra-ministerial coordination on European affairs varies from no coordination at all (the Ministry of Environment), to little coordination (Ministries for Telecoms, Health, Treasury, and Transport), to the only example of effect-ive coordination: the Ministry of Finances and Treasury, where a 'Unità di indirizzo' has been set up in 1999 at the Director General's level to coordinate EU and international issues. EU and international affairs are thus generally considered issues to be dealt by the Minister's *cabinet* (that is ministerial advisers). Coupled together, the lack of intra-ministerial coordination and inter-ministerial rivalry have prevented any attempt at creating a body entrusted with inter-ministerial coordination on EC affairs.

Within the Spanish Government, the central role in European affairs is more clearly assigned, going to the Ministry of Foreign Affairs. The Ministry of Foreign Affairs is responsible for the Permanent Representation in Brussels and for inter-ministerial coordination on the EU (all three pillars are coordinated by the Ministry). Within the Ministry, the leading role is played by the State Secretary for the European Union (SSEU). The *State Secretary* oversees sectoral policies; maintains relations with the Permanent Representation in Brussels and with the Ministries in Madrid; moni-tors institutional policy-making, legal affairs, co-ordination of sectoral information (that is the preparation of the General Affairs Council) as well as horizontal tasks; and serves as Head of Delegation in intergovernmental negotiations. He is assisted by the Secretariat General for Foreign Policy and the EU and by the Technical Office: yet, it suffers from limited personnel and scarce resources. The *State Secretary* and the Ministry of Foreign Affairs are at the centre of a three-tier national system of policy coordination over EU issues:

- The Interministerial Committee for European Affairs, created in 1985, is led by the State Secretary for the European Union and is entrusted with the task of coordination. It is not a decision-making or strategic planning arena, rather a forum for the exchanging of information, as it meets at a more junior level than originally intended. It should be noted that specialized units for EU affairs only exist in some functional Departments: Agriculture, Public Works and Transports, Industry and Energy and Environment.

- The Delegated Committee of the Government for Economic Affairs, in which both the State Secretary and the Ministry participate, intervenes to solve prob-lems that were left unsolved at the previous level;

- The Council of Ministers (that is the cabinet) may also decide the Spanish position on the most important questions.

The President of the Government can impose decisions but rarely does so due to hesitance at entering the daily policy-making of the Union and in the routine coordi-nation of EU affairs. However, Gonzales, Aznar, and lately Zapatero, have all taken charge of controversial issues and matters of strategic importance. Despite this, most of the coordination is done informally by the Secretariat General for Foreign Policy and the EU, which is staffed, in order to enhance communication, by official experts on EU affairs coming from different departments. Finally, another important Committee is the Inter-ministerial Committee for Proceedings before the ECJ, chaired by the State Secretary. It includes a Solicitor from the State Legal Service, and members from the office of the President of the Government, the Ministry of Economy and Finances, the Ministry of Public Administration (when regions are involved). It follows all actions brought against Spain, as well as those which might affect Spanish interests, including preliminary rulings filed by Spanish Courts.

The role of the national parliaments

According to Rometsch and Wessels (1996: 354), until the end of the 1990s, the Italian Parliament displayed a 'low level of Europeanization', in terms of structural adaptation, energies devoted to EC law scrutiny, and activism in pressing for a greater role vis-à-vis the government. As mentioned in relation to EC law, European affairs were, for a long time, assimilated into foreign policy. In 1968, the Senate created an ad hoc body, the *Giunta per gli affari delle Comunità europee* (committee for EC affairs), with only fact finding and consultative functions and whose impact on parliamentary activities has been limited. It was in the aftermath of the SEA, in light of the need to cope with the flood of EC directives for achieving the Single Market, that a number of reforms took place. In 1987 the *Fabbri Law* and in 1989 *La Pergola Law* provided the basic framework for domestic EC-related decision making. Both the Senate (in 1988) and the Chamber of Deputies (in 1990) revised their rules of procedure, introducing specific mechanisms for the handling of European affairs. For the first time, permanent committees were empowered to address to the Government resolutions expressing their positions on EC Commission proposals. In 1990, the Chamber set up a *Commissione speciale per le politiche comunitarie* (special committee for EC affairs). Both were ad hoc committees, equal to the standing committees in size, structure, and functions, but without full legislative power. The permanent committees thus had the primary responsibility for reviewing proposals for European legislation in their subject area.

On the basis of the Fabbri Law (1987), the government was to transmit all proposals for regulations, directives and decisions within thirty days from their reception, as well as the legal acts adopted by the Community institutions, together with a short assessment of their impact on the domestic legal order. Furthermore, the La Pergola Law (1989) provided for enhanced parliamentary access to written information on Community developments. The government was to present a report to Parliament every six months on Italy's participation in Community policies, and a general annual report focusing on the progress made by the European Community towards the achievement of the Internal Market, paying special attention to the effects of regional policies and to the national management of structural funds, as well as to the WEU and the Council of Europe. The most important innovation in those years was, however, the aforementioned annual 'Community Law' created by the La Pergola Law.

In the second half of the 1990s new significant reforms took place with regard to the role of the Parliament in European affairs. In August 1996, the ad hoc committee of the Chamber of Deputies was transformed into the (standing) XIV Committee—EU Policies. With the 'Community Law 1995–97', the Parliament's scope of action in European affairs was expanded, obliging the Government to submit to it all proposals concerning the EU. In 1998, the law ratifying the Amsterdam Treaty enacted a protocol that brought legislative initiatives from the EU's third pillar into the committee's remit. Finally, the 'Community Law 1998' better regulated the reports on EU affairs, which the Government was thenceforth to present annually to the Chambers. In general terms the goals of the reforms were twofold, and run parallel with the reform of the Government's structure from 1999 onwards. First, they aimed to update the instruments for dealing with European affairs, so as to promote a pro-active and anti-cipatory style of policy making and to establish a stricter link between the negotiating and implementing phases of the EC policy making cycle. And, second, they were to modify the Parliament's philosophy when dealing with European affairs, by introduc-ing the issues of quality and of coherence in legislation. However, notwithstanding the so-called 'perfect bicameralism' of the Italian Parliament, as far as control over EU affairs is concerned there is a clear imbalance between the two Chambers. While in the Chamber of Deputies the XIV Committee now coordinates the other standing commit-tees and is in charge of the examination of the 'Community law', in the Senate the *Giunta* is still a consultative body.

The Spanish Parliament does not play a major role in EC/EU affairs in legislative terms, apart from its participation in the formal transposition of EC directives into domestic law. Its role in EU affairs is limited to a loose supervision and monitoring of the Government's action in the EC/EU decision-making on a strictly reactive basis. The *Cortes*, over the last few years, has increased the number of reports, resolutions, requests, oral or written questions to the Government, in order to contribute to the formation of national preferences. Yet, they do not condition the positions defended by the Spanish national delegates at the EU level. In general terms, the position of the Spanish Parliaments with regard to EU affairs is thus more reactive and supervisory than proactive and agenda-setting.

Within the *Cortes*, a Joint Committee of the Congress and the Senate was established in 1986 (*Comisión Mixta para la Unión Europea* or Joint Committee for the EU). It succeeded the Joint Committee for the European Communities created in 1985. The *Joint Committee* is composed of an equal number of Senators and Deputies, reflecting the proportional-ity of political forces in the two Chambers. A member of the main opposition party, usually a leading personality, chairs it.[10] The Secretariat is shared with the Standing Committee for Foreign Affairs of the Congress of Deputies. The mixed committee is not a legislative committee and is not involved in preparing legislation; its tasks tend to be more of study and control. Secondary legislation enacted in pursuance of EC law has to be examined by the regular standing committees of a legislative nature. In practice, the Mixed Committee stimulates the involvement of other committees by adopting and passing to them their conclusions, opinions, and motions. Information from sectoral Ministries and the European Commission is channelled by the Foreign Ministry to the Mixed Committee. In case a subcommittee is formed to monitor a specific policy or issue, it can adopt a report that is presented to the Government, but without any legally binding effect. The Mixed Committee meets on average once a month.

Since the first Spanish EC Presidency of 1989, the plenary session of the Congress of Deputies holds a meeting after gatherings of the European Council in order to get informed about its results, a session that has become the major EU-related activity at parliamentary level. The SSEU appears bi-monthly before certain bodies of the Mixed Committee and the Senate's Budget Committee. In addition, most of the sectoral

---

[10] For example, Marcellino Oreja, Isabel Tocino, Pedro Solbes, and Josep Borrell.

committees of the Congress also organize hearings and raise questions in order to control the application and enforcement of EC legislation in their respective fields.

The role of the regions and of the autonomous communities

For a long time, the Italian Regions had a very weak role in European affairs, both in the making and transposition of EC law. Neither the Constitution nor the Regional Statutes regulated regional participation on European affairs. Thus, the regions were not considered able to participate in the formulation of the European policies and, at times, their powers of acting for the implementation of European law were absorbed by the central Government.

The first law dealing with the regions' role in European affairs dates from 1987. It recognized the regions' right to directly enact regulations in their fields of competence, while the state established the rules to apply in the absence of regional legislation. In 1987, the *Fabbri Law* gave the regions the right to directly enforce directives, provided that they fell within their fields of competencies and that they could be enacted with an administrative act. Only the *Regioni a Statuto speciale* were able to directly enforce directives requiring a legislative act. Such prerogative was given also to the *Regioni a Statuto ordinario* only in 1998 (Law 128/1998). In 1989, the *La Pergola Law* had stated in fact that the Government was to fix the principles that the regions had to respect in enforcing directives each year. Finally, the reform of the Constitution gave the regions concurrent (with the State) legislative powers in relation to EC affairs, also affirming their ability to take the initiative and to execute EC acts.

The powers of the regions in European policy-making were even less than in its transposition. In 1988, the *Conferenza Stato-Regioni*, was established. In recent years it has become the forum for regions and central government to discuss European issues. Since 1996 (law 52/1996), regions are allowed to set up offices in Brussels, while in 1998, the Community Law provided for greater regional participation in EU policy-making. Finally, the 2000 Constitutional reform, with the new Article 117, granted regional participation in Italian EU policy-making in areas of their own competencies. Such a change in the role of the Italian Regions in EU affairs is linked to EU regional policy developments, that transformed the Regions from passive into active participants. The elaboration of the National Plan, necessary for obtaining EC Structural Funds, requires the participation of the Regions. Together with the government, they have to determine eligibility and use of EU funds. However, apart from isolated successes EU Funds are mainly an unsuccessful story in Southern Italian regions, due to the inability of the latter to conduct long-term planning and to use funds in their entirety.

The presence of regional representatives in European institutions is still limited. In the elections for the European Parliament, the electoral system—setting macro-regional electoral constituencies—gives candidates from more populated regions an advantage over those coming from scarcely populated ones (for instance, in the constituency 'Islands', the difference between Sicily and Sardinia). National legislation granting the systematic participation of regional representatives in the working groups of the Commission or of the COREPER is still missing. Likewise, regional representatives are not part of the national delegations sitting in Council working groups. The reform of the Constitution may however open new possibilities in such cases. Finally, regional representatives are present in the Committee of the Regions.

Yet, only twelve seats out of twenty-four are attributed to the regions, the remaining ones being given to representatives of provinces and of municipal authorities.

The Spanish Constitution does not deal with the participation of the Autonomous Communities in European affairs. Yet, a number of regional Statutes affirm the duty of the Government to inform (in the Canary Islands case to consult) them about the negotiation of international treaties affecting their competencies[11] and affirm the right of the *Comunitades* to execute international treaties when falling within their competencies. For instance, the Autonomous Communities were informally consulted during the accession negotiations.

The lack of a clearly defined system of State and regional competencies caused several judicial conflicts between central and local government regarding the enforcement of European acts. In order to improve the situation, the Spanish Constitutional Tribunal settled the principle of no alteration of internal competencies,[12] according to which the Spanish Autonomous Communities implement EC policies in their own areas of competence. Moreover, the Tribunal recognized in the 'principle of collaboration' established before Spanish EC membership, the correct standard for regulating the central State-Autonomous Communities relationship in European affairs.[13] In order to enact this, some measures were taken. Created in 1987, and further regulated by law 30/1992, are three permanent bodies (*Conferencias Sectoriales*) for consultation between the central state and the Autonomous Communities. One of them, the *Conferencia Sectoriale para assuntos relacionados con las Comunidades europeas* (Conference for EC Affairs) is responsible for European issues. Created in 1988 and further regulated by law 2/1997, the conference is active both in the execution and in the formulation of EC law. Finally, the Autonomous Communities are also called to cooperate with the Government in the definition of the plan required to obtain Community funding, as well as in its management. In doing so, Spanish authorities have been far more successful and efficient than Italian ones; indeed EU funding has made a major contribution to Spain's development.

The representation of the Spanish regions in the European institutions is only slightly different from the Italian situation. Each Autonomous Community elects its own representatives to the Committee of the Regions and regional representatives sit in the Commission working groups and committees. Finally, regional representatives can represent the State in the Council.

European diplomacy

Negotiation techniques and EU alliance-building

Stanley Hofmann (1966) introduced the distinction between *high politics* and *low politics* in the EC policy process. In the Italian case such a distinction is useful: Italy has been generally passive in low politics (that is the day-to-day politics of the EU), while it has

[11] Statutes of: Andalucia Art. 23, Asturias Art. 40, Canaries Art. 37, Cataluña Art. 27, Madrid Art. 33, Murcia Art. 33, Basque Countries Art. 20.
[12] Constitutional Court, ruling 252/1988.   [13] Ibid.

been fundamental in the high politics, as illustrated by the 'constitutional choices' of Europe. In the early 1990s, two studies of the Italian Senate's *Giunta per gli Affari Comunitari* (Senato 1991) and of the Chamber of Deputies' *Commissione speciale per gli Affari Comunitari* (Camera dei Deputati 1993) underlined the absence of Italy in the shaping of European norms, and in general terms the lack of a pro-active Italian strategy in the EU. Italian politicians have never considered EU issues a priority. Yet, in high politics, Italy's role proved crucial in many important phases of the process of European integration. Two Italian Presidencies—those of 1985 and 1990—are worth recalling. In 1985, the Italian Presidency supported the Commission's request of convening an Intergovernmental Conference (IGC) on institutional reform and other issues, making it their priority. To achieve it, the Socialist President of the Council, Bettino Craxi and the Christian Democrat Foreign Minister, Giulio Andreotti, worked on their respective European political counterparts. However, at the Milan European Council (28–29 June 1985), the UK, Danish and Greek governments opposed the call for an ICG. To avoid deadlock, the Italian Presidency took the unprecedented decision to ask for a formal vote,[14] thus outvoting the three resisting countries. In the 1990 Presidency, the goal was to reach a compromise on monetary union (EMU) and to call for two separate IGCs; one on EMU and one on Political Union. After extensive bilateral meetings,[15] the *Rome I* informal European Council (27/28 October 1990) was organized: notwithstanding the UK's opposition;[16] Minister Carli's proposal on EMU was approved. The British Prime Minister, Margaret Thatcher (1993: 763–5) argued in her memoirs that a 'Florentine trap' had been set up by the President of the Council, Giulio Andreotti, with 'his own MEPs' and 'other Christian Democratic parties'. At the *Rome II* European Council (14/15 December 1990) the two ICGs where thus formally convened.

Spain was rather quick in adapting to the new EC/EU negotiating reality. The defence of the national interest has been a key issue since membership. To pursue it, Spain does not hesitate in using veto-power if so needed (contrary to Italy), as well as negotiating techniques such as cross-table bargains. Despite its 'almost big' status, Beyers and Dierickx (1998) show how Spain's consistency and credibility in negotiations made it one of the most wanted partners in the Council. Spain's membership also brought new areas of interest into the Community: European Aid to South America for instance doubled in the period 1991–5. Spain held its first Presidency in the second half of 1989 with good results, the second one in 1995 and the third one in 2002. The last two ones especially have been marked by a high level of activism; it was for instance in November 1995 that the Barcelona Process on the EU's Mediterranean policy was launched.

---

[14] The convention up to that point was not to vote in the European Council but to operate by consensus.

[15] For instance with the socialist leaders Mitterrand (France) and Gonzales (Spain) and the encounters with Christian Democrats leaders (six EC leaders were Christian-Democrats: Andreotti (Italy), Ruud Lubbers (The Netherland), Jacques Santer (Luxembourg), Wilfred Martens (Belgium), Constantine Mitsotakis (Greece), and the German Chancellor Helmut Kohl.

[16] In informal Councils there are no formal conclusions so it was mentioned at the press conference that the report was approved by 'all but one', a clear reference to the UK.

Spanish leaders also give great attention to nominations to top European posts. Spain has had, among others, three Presidents of the European Parliament, one Vice-President of the Commission, one President of the Court of Justice, plus Javier Solana—first Secretary General of NATO and then 'Mr CFSP'. Solana, a socialist, was named by the centre-right Government of Aznar, suggesting that national interests come before political affiliation. The contrast with the Italian case was demonstrated with nominations for the post of United Nations High Representative for Bosnia in 1997. The Italian centre-left government proposed an internationally-unknown MP, Mr Migone, against the former Spanish Secretary of State and Foreign Minister Carlos Westendorp. The latter was nominated.

The Italian government's attitude vis-à-vis top EU posts still recalls La Palombara's (1967) *clientele* as Euro-jobs are considered interim positions for national politicians waiting to go back into the national political arena. As Altiero Spinelli (1991: 314) noted in his diary in the 1960s: 'Nenni [then PSI leader]. . . asks me to help find an international post with a good salary for Cattani, who lost the elections . . . the Italian government . . . considers EC posts as positions to be given according to the rules of *sottogoverno*' (the colonization of political offices through party patronage). Thirty years after, Letta (1997: 80–1) recalled 'it is time to change the idea that one gets a post in Bruxelles either because defeated at home or as a political retirement'. In addition, sudden departures from the Commission, like that of Commission President, Franco Malfatti, (1972) or the Environment Commissioner, Carlo Ripa di Meana, (1992)—both to become national Ministers—have undermined Italian credibility. When Italians are named in top international posts, it is essentially due to their personal prestige rather than to a national interest choice on the part of the government. For example, Renato Ruggero, former WTO Director General, succeeded thanks to the support of Henry Kissinger and the past FIAT President, Gianni Agnelli. Romano Prodi was supported by the D'Alema Government for the post of President of the Commission (1998) for domestic political reasons, as Massimo D'Alema—who had replaced him as President of the Council—felt more secure with the Olive Tree leader away in Brussels.

On the other side of the coin, Italy's best top EU officials are scarcely known at home. Numerically, Italians are well represented in the European Commission but this is due to a large number of Italians holding C-and D-level posts in the European Commission, a result of the past Italian emigrations to Belgium. Overall, at the more senior B level (assistants) and A level (management functions), Italians hold the average number of the other three 'big' countries.[17] However, Italian EU officials—unlike other cases, including the Spanish—are usually left alone in the delicate passage from the A4 to the A3 level, when the nomination becomes political.

Italy and Spain: allies or rivals?

One might expect a stricter cooperation among EU member States that share similar socio-economic interests, such as Spain and Portugal. The Nordic countries managed

---

[17] In Spring 2002, an internal document of the Ministry for Foreign Affairs, counted for Italy 2 Director Generals (as opposed to 6 of the UK, France, and Germany); 4 Deputy Director Generals, 20 Directors (against 22 French, 22 British, 18 Germans); 24 A2 (France had 28, Britain 25).

under the 1999 Finnish Presidency to put as a permanent item on the European Council's Agenda the issue of the 'Nordic dimension'. A similar cooperation does not exist among the Southern European countries. Several Italian observers agree on the fact that priority should be given to the Southern and namely Mediterranean countries of the EU, but there appears to be no will to create a 'Southern European alliance'. Beyers and Dietrickx (1998: 289–317) show extensive interactions among Southern European representatives in the Council: yet, such collaboration—though successful when put into place (see Bindi 1999)—is casual rather than intentional. Spain does lead a coalition of member States who are major recipients of Cohesion Funds. Italian-Spanish annual summits are held, but despite some closeness between Berlusconi and Aznar, until the latter lost office, it is not possible to declare the existence of a special partnership between the two countries.

Conclusion

What comparative conclusions can we make about the engagement of Italy and Spain in the EU? They are clearly two important southern member states, which utilized European integration—at different stages of its development—to establish their - international credentials after fascist rule. They have also seen the EU as a means for achieving economic modernization and have regarded participation in the Euro as an important prize. They are both states contending with asymmetrical regionalism in their constitutional arrangements. Finally, and perhaps more controversially, we suggest they are member states in the second rank of influence in the EU, behind France, Germany, and the UK. In the case of Spain it is not, of course, a large state according to the key indicators of population, voting weight in the Council and so on. In the case of Italy, however, governmental instability and the failure to have as effective a voice in the EU as the 'big three' states is to blame. There is a notable contrast in the effectiveness of the European diplomacy of the two states. In reviewing this chapter we organize our conclusions around three themes: the definition of national interests; negotiating strategies; and the adaptation of national institutions. They represent three key determinants of a member state's effectiveness in the EU.

Definition of national interests: In Italy the very notion of 'national interest' has had a negative connotation because of the stress placed on it during the Fascist period. Italy's membership of the ECSC was dictated by the need to recover 'international respectability' and, coupled with a similar strategy within other multilateral frameworks, it served the objective. However, this was done by adopting a sort of 'penitent' attitude—appropriately for a Catholic country such as Italy!—within which there was no space for stressing national interests. The idea of the need to defend national interests was finally and controversially put back on the political agenda in the mid-1990s by the *Berlusconi I* government and later accepted also by centre-left governments, in particular since D'Alema's premiership (1998–2000).[18] Yet, there is in

---

[18] The parallel with the increased reference to national interests under Chancellor Schröder's government is a notably comparison here (see Chapter 4).

Italian political culture an unresolved major problem. In many Italian politicians' minds the fundamental distinction between private interests—whether it be personal or party ones—and public interests is still blurred; a dangerous overlap exists between the two. In such conditions, the 'rational' definition of national interests can prove difficult.

At the time of EC accession, Spain was exiting from a much longer dictatorship and international isolation but, as a former 'glorious' Empire. It had a very different attitude towards national interests. If Italian politicians had difficulties even mentioning national interests, for Spain they have been at the forefront since the beginning (see, for instance, Gonzales Sanchez 1992). Possibly, the long period of negotiations also helped in getting used to defending national interests within the EC decision-making processes.

From a procedural point of view, the definition of national interests presupposes the existence of specific procedures, in particular the existence of a good level of both intra-ministerial and inter-ministerial coordination. This is a weak point for both countries, though particularly critical in Italy. In Italy, in fact, the rivalry among Ministries is particularly acute due to the large (and litigious) coalition governments. It also results in intra-ministerial competition, that is between the Minister and (his) Under Secretaries of State and expands top-down all along the scale. The remedy found in keeping an informal coordination process among diplomatic advisers to the Ministers does not solve the problem, as the number of issues dealt with at the technical level in the EU is now too many. Moreover, centralizing coordination at the Cabinet level jeopardizes continuity due to the frequent Government turnovers. The lack of a clear definition of national interests, coupled together with the absence of intra- and inter-ministerial coordination means, in practical terms, that it is not rare for Italian national officials to attend meetings in Brussels without having a clear position at all. In Spain coordination exists but it is more a forum for consultation than for decision-taking. Yet some informal adjustments have been put in place to enhance inter-ministerial cooperation such as the fact that the members of the Secretariat General for Foreign Policy and the EU come from different Ministries in order to facilitate communication.

Negotiating strategies: Italian and Spanish officials and diplomats are equally good at negotiating, but this is undermined by the absence of proper instructions from the national Ministries. When this is coupled with government instability, it can undermine the negotiating stance of national representatives, as research conducted by Beyers and Dierickx (1998) shows for case of Italy, while they also show how Spain is now one of the best regarded partners by other EU members.

One instrument Italy and Spain are both unable to use in negotiations is the possibility to call for Parliamentary scrutiny reserve in Council negotiations, a tool that—if used to the absolute and rigid extent like Denmark does—can be an impediment in negotiations. However, if applied with discretion like by other member states (for example the UK), it can greatly support negotiators. In Spain the absence of this bargaining instrument is explained by the constitutional framework that designed a strong Executive over a weak Parliament. In Italy—where the constitutional design was contrasting—the Parliament's lack of leverage can be explained by the low level of interest on the part of national politicians in EU technical affairs.

Adaptation of national institutions: The most striking feature of the Spanish political system is the centralization of powers and the dominance of the Executive—and within it of the President of the Government—a characteristic that according to Ignacio Molina (2000) has been reinforced by the process of European integration. In Italy the Executive, and in particular the President of the Council, have also been reinforced by the process of European integration. Since the mid-1990s, some Presidents of the Council (namely Prodi, D'Alema and Berlusconi) have used the EU to improve their standing at home. Of them, though, Mr. Berlusconi took it to a new level by assuming for eleven months the tasks of both President of the Council and Foreign Minister. The person finally chosen as new Foreign Minister, Mr Frattini, was judged as a mere executor of the Presidency of the Council's decisions (Pistelli and Fiore 2004: 141). Berlusconi also brought to the limit the personalization of foreign policy, creating criticism that personal friendship was coming before the geopolitical interests of the country (see Pistelli and Fiore 2004: 142; also Andreatta 2003). As a result, and with the Ministry of Foreign Affairs having its hands tied, the 2003 EU Presidency was far less successful then previous ones, concluding with the failure to achieve agreement at the Brussels European Council of December 2003 on the the EU Constitutional Treaty. It was, overall, a clear break with the tradition of political negotiations and compromise that had been the positive characteristics of Italian Governments in the past.

Our conclusion, therefore, is that the two states are in the second rank of influence in the EU. Spain appears to have better adapted to the EU and to be 'fitter' for handling EU decision-making procedures than Italy is. This is the result of a combination of variables, in particular: political culture, institutional framework, and procedures. In general terms, Italian weaknesses in dealing with EU affairs are linked to the fact that Italian diplomacy is dependent on domestic politics, rather than on a rational calculation and prosecution of domestic needs and interests. Overall, it is a tale of contrasting effectiveness on the part of the European diplomacy of the two states.

Further reading

The English language literature on Italy and Spain in the EU is quite limited, chiefly being confined to single chapters in edited collections. An exception is Francioni (1992), although this volume is dated and needs to be treated with caution on the detail. Spain is better served with the publication of Closa and Heywood (2004). A special issue of *Journal of European Public Policy* (2004) deals with the Europeanization of politics and policy in Italy. Of the chapter studies, Basabe Lloréns (2003) and Molina (2000) deal with the policy process in the Spanish government. Gallo and Hanny (2003), Della Cananea (2000) and Giuliani and Piattoni present the equivalent picture for Italy. For more on the respective parliaments, see Basabe Lloréns and Gonzales Escudero (2001) for Spain and Bindi and Grassi (2001) for Italy.

Weblinks

The official EU gateway to Italy is at <http://www.europa.eu.int/abc/governments/italy/index_en.htm>. That for Spain is located at <http://www.europa.eu.int/abc/governments/spain/index_en.htm>. The Spanish foreign ministry site is located at <http://www.mae.es>; its Italian counterpart at <http://www.esteri.it>. Another useful weblink for these two states relates to the Euro-Mediterranean partnership <http://www.europa.eu.int/comm/external_relations/euromed/index.htm>.

References

Amato, G. (1994), 'Italy: The Rise and Decline of a System of Government', *Indiana International & Comparative Law Review*, 4/Winter 225-30.

Andreatta, F., *La politica internazionale nell'era della globalizzazione*, (2003) RISP, fascicolo: 1, vol. 33, 3-29.

Basabe Lloréns, F. (2003), 'Spain: the emergence of a new major actor in the European arena', in Wessels, Maurer and Mittag, 184-215.

Basabe Lloréns, F., and Gonzales Escudero, M. T. (2001), 'The Parliament of Spain: Slowly Moving onto the European Dirction?', in A. Maurer, and W. Wessels (eds), *National Parliaments on their Ways to Europe: Losers or Latecomers?*, Schriften des Zentrum für Europäische Integrationsforschung (ZEI) (NOMOS Verlagsgesellschaft).

Beyers, J., and Dierickx, G. (1998), 'The Working groups of the Council of the European Union: Supranational or Intergovernmental Negotiations?', in *Journal of Common Market Studies*, 36/3 September 289-317.

Bindi, F., and Grassi, S. (2001), 'The Italian Parliament: From Benevolent Observer to Active Player', in A. Maurer, and W. Wessels (eds), *National Parliaments on their Ways to Europe: Losers or Latecomers?*, Schriften des Zentrum für Europäische Integrationsforschung (ZEI) (NOMOS Verlagsgesellschaft).

Bindi, F. (1999), L'influenza italiana nei processi decisionali UE, in *Europa-Europe*, Anno VIII, 3 Roma.

Closa, C., and Heywood, P. (2004), *Spain and the European Union* (Basingstoke: Palgrave Macmillan).

Cotta, M. (1990), 'The Centrality of Parliament in a Protracted Democratic Consolidation: the Italian Case' in U. Liebert, and M. Cotta, *Parliament and Democratic Consolidation in Southern Europe* (London: Pinter).

Della Cananea, G. (2000), 'Co-ordination of EU Policy Making in Italy', in H. Kassim, B. G. Peters, and V. Wright (eds), *The National Co-ordination of EU Policy—The Domestic Level*, (Oxford: Oxford University Press).

Francioni, F. (ed.) (1992), *Italy and EC Membership Evaluated* (London: Pinter Publishers).

Gallo F., and Hanny, B. (2003), 'Italy: Progress behind complexity', in Wessels, Maurer, and Mittag, 271-97.

Giuliani, M., and Piattoni, S. (2001), 'Italy: Both Leader and Laggard', in Zeff and Pirro, 115-42.

Gonzales Sanchez, E. (1992), *Manual del negociador en la Comunidad Europea* (Madrid: Officina de Information Diplomatica).

Grottanelli de Santi, G. (1992), 'The Impact of EC Integration on the Italian Form of Government', in Francioni, F. (ed.), *Italy and EC Membership Evaluated* (London: Pinter Publishers).

Hoffmann, S. (1996), 'Obstinate or Obsolete? The Fate of the Nation-State and the Case of Western Europe?', in *Daedalus* Summer 862–915.

Journal of European Public Policy (2004), special issue entitled 'Europeanisation and the Italian political system: Politics and Policy', guest-edited by Fabio Franchino and Claudio M. Radaelli 11/6.

La Palombara, J. (1967), *Clientela e parentela. Studio sui gruppi di interesse in Italia* (Milano: Comunità).

Letta, E. (1997), *Euro Sì. Morire per Maastricht* (Roma-Bari, Laterza).

Molina, I., 'Spain,' in H. Kassim, B. G. Peters, and V. Wright (2000), *The National Coordination of EU Policy. The Domestic Level* (Oxford: Oxford University Press).

Morata, F. (1988), 'Spain: Modernization through Integration', in K. Hanf and B. Soetendorp (eds), *Adapting to European Integration: Small States and the European Union* (Harlow: Longman), 100–115.

Pistelli, L., and Fiore, G. (2004), *Semestre Nero* (Roma: Fazi Editore).

Romano, S. (1994), *L'Italia scappata di mano* (Milan: Longanesi).

Rometsch, D., and Wessels, W. (1996) (ed.), *The European Union and Member States. Towards Institutional Fusion?* (Manchester: Manchester University Press).

Spinelli, A. (1991), *Diario Europeo / II* (Bologna: Il Mulino), 314.

Thatcher, M. (1993), *The Downing Street Years* (London: Harper Collins).

Wessel, W., Maurer, A., and Mittag, J. (eds) (2003), *Fifteen into One? The European Union and its Member States* (Manchester: Manchester University Press).

Zeff, E., and Pirro, E. B. (eds) (2001), *The European Union and the Member States: Cooperation, Coordination and Compromise* (Boulder CO: Lynne Rienner Publishers).

Chapter 8
The Benelux Countries: Identity and Self-interest

Erik Jones

Contents

Summary

The Benelux states engaged with the integration process from the outset. Each of the three states—Belgium, The Netherlands and Luxembourg—did so for rather different reasons. Over the subsequent half-century their interests in the integration process have adjusted, not least because of the consequences of participation. The chapter utilizes the notions of identity and self-interest to explain their original motivation, their evolving interaction with the EU, and the effects of Europeanization upon the three states, their institutions and policies.

Introduction

The purpose of this chapter is to analyse the relationship between the European Union and the Benelux countries—meaning Belgium, the Netherlands, and Luxembourg. The argument is that for each of these countries, participation in European integration originated as an act of national self interest. However, it developed into a facet of national identity. Along the way, conceptions of self-interest changed as well. The process is untidy and yet the general principle is straightforward. Participation in Europe changes the member states even as the member states create and change the institutions of Europe. The end result of this circular relationship is ambiguous. Belgium, the Netherlands, and Luxembourg are transformed but they do not disappear. They share a common identity and yet they remain different countries, each distinctive in its own way. I argue that each country's distinctiveness is grounded in its historical pathway into, and through, the integration process.

The chapter is organized in five sections. The first analyses integration in the Benelux as a harbinger or precursor for integration in Europe. The second examines the preferences and politics of the Benelux countries as participants in European integration up to the mid-1960s. The third sets out the domestic distributive consequences of participation from the 1960s onward. The fourth looks at the institutional implications, again from the 1960s onward. The fifth returns to the question of preferences and politics and concludes with some suggestions about what the experience of the Benelux countries implies about the process of Europeanization more generally.

Identity and self-interest

As a starting point, it is worth noting that the choice to treat the Benelux countries as a single unit for analysis is more reflective of the need to hold down the number of chapters in this volume than of any strong assertion that the Benelux countries are all alike. Nevertheless, the choice to group the Benelux countries together is not arbitrary. Belgium, the Netherlands, and Luxembourg share the same geographic space— known generically as the 'Low Countries'. They have shared a special economic relationship for more than half a century. And, of Europe's smaller countries, they have the longest experience of integration.

Still, the irony is that the three countries are actually very different from one another. Take language, for example. Like most countries in Europe, the Dutch speak a single language—called 'common civilized Dutch'—albeit with a moderate-to-strong dialectical variation from south to north and from west to east. People from Amsterdam (which is toward the northwest) can understand people from Maastricht (which is in the southeast), however the people from Maastricht can make it difficult if they choose. The Belgians are divided by language, with the northerners speaking Flemish varieties of the Dutch and the southerners speaking Walloon French.[1] The capital of Belgium, Brussels, is officially a bilingual city French/Dutch. Even there, however, visitors are quick to note that the shopkeepers tend to prefer one language over another. Finally, the Luxembourgers are polyglot. They are educated in French and German, they use French as their official language, and they speak their own

---

[1] There is also a very small community of German speakers in the easternmost part of Belgium who were ceded to the country as part of the territorial settlements at the end of the Second World War.

German dialect—Lëtzebuergisch—at home. This multilingual education is actually a clever strategy for keeping Lëtzebuergisch alive. So long as everyone is equally well trained in French and German, no-one need feel they are disadvantaging their children by speaking to them in dialect.

Political identity

The point to note is that such linguistic differences are more political than 'organic'. The people who live in the Low Countries have long spoken a variety of languages and dialects—just as everywhere else in Europe. However, in contrast to countries such as France, Germany, or Italy, the Low Countries were never subject to linguistic homo-genization as a group—and not for want of opportunity. At the start of the nineteenth century, the Great Powers cobbled together the Low Countries under the Kingdom of the Netherlands in order to create a viable buffer between France and Germany. It was the end of the Napoleonic Wars, the Concert of Europe was just asserting itself, and the 'balance of power' provided the organizing principle for the European state system. A single Kingdom of the Netherlands could not defend itself against a resurgent France or a united Germany. However, it could do reasonably well against a downtrodden France and a fractious cluster of German principalities. Hence the Dutch king, William of Orange, set about unifying the different parts of the Low Countries economically, politically, and, after 1819, culturally and linguistically as well (Bernard 1961).

The problem was that the Belgians did not enjoy being under the tutelage of the House of Orange, for religious as well as linguistic reasons. The Belgians were more Catholic than Protestant in addition to being more likely to speak French than Dutch. For their own part, the Luxembourgers preferred existence as a sovereign duchy than as a dependent province. Culturally, they felt more attuned to France or Germany than to the Netherlands. The Belgian revolt of 1830 put an end to the United Kingdom of the Netherlands and the Treaty of London in 1839 restored the sovereignty of the Grand Duchy of Luxembourg. Luxembourg and the Netherlands remained in a per-sonal union, with the King of the Netherlands being also Grand Duke of Luxembourg. However, by the end of the nineteenth century even this union fell apart as a woman (Wilhelmina) ascended to the Dutch throne but was prevented from becoming Grand Duchess. (Up to that point the rules governing succession in the Luxembourg permit-ted only men to inherit titles; within less than two decades, the rules were changed to extend this privilege to women as well.) The House of Orange retained control over the Grand Duchy, but along a different branch of the family from that residing in The Hague. In this way, the last vestiges of the post-Napoleonic Kingdom of the Netherlands were undone, and the promise of economic, political, and cultural unification along with them (Bernard 1961; Weil 1970).

Environmental self-interest

The Low Countries chose not to remain unified and yet they could not escape the dictates of geography or of the European state system (Eyck 1959). They preferred not to live together, but they could not prosper easily alone. Hence, for much of the early twentieth century, relations between the three small countries alternated between cordial and fractious. Throughout, it was self-interest that drove the countries together and identity that pushed them apart. To give an example, the people of Luxembourg acknowledged that they would have to join in an economic union with some larger country in order to remain viable after the First World War. Given the choice in referendum, however, the Luxembourg population voted over-whelmingly for union with France. Britain resisted such a union and France demurred. Belgium offered the only other alternative, and the 1922 economic union between Belgium and Luxembourg was the result (Bernard 1961: 690–1; van Meerhaeghe 1987).

The Benelux as an organization has similar origins. During the Second World War, the political leaders of the three small countries found themselves together in exile in London. They realized that some formal relationship between their economies would be better than going it alone. And yet they feared that domestic opposition would scupper any attempt to negotiate a union during the period of reconstruction that was sure to follow the war. Hence they decided to negotiate the terms of the Benelux union before the war ended and under the exceptional power they retained as leaders in wartime. In this way, the union would be a *fait accompli* (Spaak 1969: 150–2). As it turned out, their reasoning was well founded. Not only did the Benelux countries implement their union only slowly after the war, but they also had to fend off a num-ber of competing but less universally acceptable proposals from France and Italy—with names such as 'Fritalux' or 'Finebel' (Milward 1984: 306–16).

As a 'union', however, the Benelux has been something of a disappointment. The customs union between the three countries was successful both in opening Dutch markets to exports from Belgium and Luxembourg after the Second World War and in providing a favourable context for the belated industrialization of the Netherlands. The currency union proved less robust. The parity between the Belgian and Luxembourgish francs remained fixed per their earlier agreement, but the exchange rates between the franc and the Dutch guilder moved already by the end of the 1940s. Finally, the elaboration of common Benelux political institutions had little if any suc-cess. As a symbol or aspiration, the proposal to deepen the institutions of the Benelux in the 1960s may be said to have encouraged greater enthusiasm for integration via the European Community. But as a practical venture it offered few tangible results (Weil 1970: 224–31).

Unity with diversity

The development of the Benelux was tightly circumscribed by the differences in the identities of the three countries and by the overlap in their self-interest. Admitting that, however, should not imply that either identity or self-interest have proved immutable. On the contrary, the promotion of the Benelux greatly increased the pace of exchange between the Low Countries—tightening cultural as well as economic bonds (Samoy 1981). The fact that it makes sense today to group the Benelux countries together is testament to the impact that the experience of their union has had on the development of their separate national identities. Whatever the limits of the union between them, the Benelux countries are now more than just Belgium, the Netherlands, and Luxembourg. They are 'Benelux countries' and as such can be treated as a case group.

Preference and policy

The overlap in self-interest lies at the heart of the Benelux approach to Europe up through the 1960s. For all three countries, the top priority was to ensure that they would benefit from market access. The problem is that as small countries they were more dependent upon access to European markets than any of the larger countries of Europe (France, Germany, Italy, and the United Kingdom) were dependent upon the provision of exports from the Low Countries. As a result they had little leverage to secure their self-interest against the wishes of their larger neighbours. Of course, the Benelux countries were not unique in this dependence. Virtually all of the small countries of Europe shared the problem of needing large country markets more than large countries needed them (Katzenstein 1985). However, four geographic factors—one common, and three particular—make the position of the Low Countries somewhat unique. The common factor is position: The Low Countries nestle between France, Germany, and Britain. As a result, they were (almost) symmetrically dependent in a number of different directions. It was not enough for these countries to have access to one large country or another. Their self-interest was to have access to them all.

The three specific factors appertain to each of the Low Countries. Belgium included the earliest industrialized zone on the continent—predominantly located in the French-speaking south of the country—and so was economically dependent upon mature industries such as coal, steel, and textiles, for which the danger of market protectionism is particularly acute. A similar point can be made for Luxembourg, however with the proviso that the Grand Duchy's economy was so small as to rely almost wholly upon coal extraction and metal processing. Meanwhile, the Dutch economy centred on agriculture, fishing, and commerce. In addition to the country's large production of meat and dairy products, the harbours at Rotterdam and Amsterdam provided the principal gateway from the Atlantic seaways to the European continent. Hence the Low Countries all required access to trade to differing degrees and for different reasons (Eyck 1959).

Multilateral market access

The first major experiment with trade integration came already in the 1930s. Within the context of the League of Nations, the Low Countries joined with the Nordic countries (Denmark, Finland, Sweden, and Norway) in a tariff alliance—called the Oslo Alliance after the Norwegian capital city where the treaty was signed. The goal of this alliance was to arrest the movement toward trade protection that coincided with the onset of the Great Depression. The small countries agreed to consult with each other over trade restrictions between themselves and to work together in their tariff negotiations with the larger countries of Europe. The result was less than hoped for. The larger countries refused to join in the Oslo alliance and worked actively to promote its disintegration. By the end of the 1930s, the Oslo alliance was in tatters (Van Roon 1989).

Despite this failure, however, the importance of institutionalized collective action became a cornerstone for the foreign economic policy of the Low Countries

(Eyck 1959: 84). The alliance of small countries may have failed, but at least it offered a chance of success. Moreover, politicians in the Low Countries made a direct connection between the failure of international economic relations and the breakdown of international security. Such reasoning is evident in the recollections of Paul-Henri Spaak (1969: 148–9), a long-time Foreign Minister of Belgium and one of the principal architects of European integration:

In 1942, my thinking could be stated precisely as follows: 'There is no political solution without an economic solution and vice-versa. In the world of tomorrow, particularly in the Europe of tomorrow, and even more particularly for the small countries of Europe, the problems of security and prosperity will be indissolubly mingled.'

Spaak went on in his recollections to argue about the need for the creation of supranational authority over the national governments of Europe—replacing 'nationalism' per se with a type of enlightened 'internationalism'. However, his admiration for supranationalism was less widely shared within the Low Countries than was his commitment to the need for collective action between countries. If there is a common characteristic to the lesson-learning of the inter-war period, it was that regional integration should be institutionalized around national self-interest in order to succeed. The Benelux is a case in point that has already been touched upon. However, it is worth outlining the economic situation at the end of the Second World War in order to illustrate the type of economic exchanges that international integration makes possible.

Market access and trade lay at the core of the Benelux as an economic bargain. At the end of the Second World War, Belgium and Luxembourg had large supplies of coal and steel that the Netherlands could use for reconstruction. The problem was that the Netherlands had little to offer in exchange. Even worse, Belgium and Luxembourg had ample foreign exchange reserves while the Netherlands did not. By implication, any trade between Belgium or Luxembourg and the Netherlands would result in a bilateral imbalance that the Netherlands could not finance. Yet Belgium and Luxembourg needed to sell their coal and steel and the Netherlands needed to buy them. The Benelux promised to square the circle by guaranteeing market access in both directions—skewing Dutch exports toward Belgium and Luxembourg in order to enable the Dutch to finance imports from its two southern neighbours. The result was never entirely effective, and hence the breakdown in the fixed exchange rate between the franc and the guilder by the end of the 1940s. However, the trade diversion did take place and economic connections within the Benelux tightened rapidly (Economic Recovery Program 1949).

The Schuman Plan

The imprint of national self-interest can also be found in the different reactions of the Low Countries to Robert Schuman's May 1950 proposal to create a European Coal and Steel Community (ECSC). As major coal and steel producers, Belgium and Luxembourg were clearly affected by the proposal. However, the implications for the two countries were very different. Belgian diplomats expressed concern that their older industries would be among the first to be phased out as a result of European competition. Given that these industries were located in the French-speaking south of the country, such competition would invariably feed into growing political tension between Walloons and Flemings. Hence the Belgians agreed to the Schuman Plan only reluctantly and on condition that they be allowed to subsidize coal and steel producers beyond the levels provided by the ECSC and that they also be permitted to opt out of the agreement in the event that the domestic implications proved unmanageable (Milward 1992: 46–83).

By contrast, Luxembourg diplomats focused on the planning side of Schuman's proposal. Their concern was that Belgium would use the excuse of the ECSC to undermine the privileged access that Luxembourg producers had to Belgian markets under the terms of the 1922 economic union between the two countries. The justification for this concern was that privileged access through the Belgium–Luxembourg Economic Union had skewed the export orientation of Luxembourg industries and so made them excessively dependent upon Belgian markets. (Here already we can see how the experience of integration has changed the calculation of self-interest.) At the same time, the Luxembourgers noted that the powers of the High Authority—the supranational body responsible for administering the coal and steel pool—would give it effective control over the mainstay of the Grand Duchy's economy. Hence they demanded guarantees that they would not lose their existing market advantages and that their sovereignty would not be unduly eroded by the High Authority.[2]

The reaction of the Netherlands to the Schuman Plan was also ambivalent. Although supportive of the ideal of an integrated European market, the Dutch were deeply suspicious of the delegation of national responsibilities to a supranational agency such as the proposed High Authority. Such an agency would be likely to be coopted to serve the interests of large countries rather than small, and would offer little or no protection to Dutch national interest in any event. Hence the Dutch insisted on the creation of an intergovernmental Council of Ministers to oversee the actions of the High Authority and to safeguard the national interest of the member states (Griffiths 1980: 278–279).

Towards the Common Market

Despite the ambivalence of the Low Countries regarding the ECSC, their enthusiasm for European economic integration was unmatched. The Dutch were particularly energetic in coming up with ideas. Soon after the announcement of the Schuman Plan, the Dutch Foreign Minister, Dirk Stikker, proposed that the countries of the Organization for European Economic Cooperation (OEEC—an institutional precursor to the OECD) engage in an aggressive liberalization of European trade by sector. Weeks later, his counterpart at the Dutch Ministry of Agriculture, Sicco Mansholt, proposed the creation of a European Agricultural Community along much the same lines as the ECSC. Neither of these proposals came to fruition—although the

---

[2] Evidence for this point can be found in a brilliant website assembled by University of Leiden Professor Richard Griffiths. The commentary on the site is available only in Dutch; the documents are in original languages. The specific document used here is a memorandum to the Luxembourg Minister of Foreign Affairs and dated 7 December 1950. The URL for the website is <http://esf.niwi.knaw.nl/esf1997/projects/schuman/we/welkomframe.html>.

Mansholt proposal arguably survived in the Common Agricultural Policy (CAP) of the European Economic Community (EEC) if only insofar as Mansholt himself was the first European Commissioner for Agriculture (Milward 1984: 446–54). Such failings only underscore a harsh reality identified by Charles Kindleberger (1986: 298) in his analysis of the Great Depression: Even 'the most sensible proposals emanating from small countries are valueless if they lack the capacity to carry them out and fail to enlist the countries that do'.

The experience of a further Dutch initiative bears this out. During the ill-fated deliberations over the creation of a European Defence Community (EDC 1951–4), another Dutch Foreign Minister, Willem Beyen, proposed that the members of the ECSC form a common market. His reasoning echoed the sentiments of his Belgian counterpart, Paul-Henri Spaak (cited above). Security integration must be underpinned by economic integration in order to function, because only economic integration can ensure the political union of those countries aspiring to create an EDC. More important, however, the Beyen Plan signalled the determination of the Netherlands to keep the issue of market access on the European agenda. And while the collapse of the EDC brought down the Beyen Plan as well, the proposal to create a European customs union and common market remained embedded in the integration process (Griffiths and Milward 1986).

Within less than a year from the end of the EDC deliberations, the members of the ECSC agreed to return to the question of market access. In their declaration at Messina (1955) they announced:

The governments of the Federal Republic of Germany, Belgium, France, Italy, Luxembourg and the Netherlands believe the time has come to take a new step on the road of European construction. They are of the opinion that this objectives should be achieved first of all in the economic sphere.

They believe that the establishment of a united Europe must be achieved through the development of common institutions, the progressive fusion of national economies, the creation of a common market, and the gradual harmonization of their social policies.[3]

Support for supranational authority

The progression from the Messina declaration to the Treaty of Rome is well known and fits comfortably within the national interest of the Low Countries as described above. However, one element of initial Low Country preference remains to be explained. During the ECSC, both Luxembourg and the Netherlands expressed concern about the supranational High Authority—with the Netherlands insisting even that the ECSC be endowed with an intergovernmental Council of Ministers. As Richard Griffiths (1980: 279) notes: 'Interestingly, there is no sign, at this early stage, of the belief in supranationalism that was later to become the hall-mark of the Dutch approach.'

The change in attitudes centres around the negotiation of the French Fouchet Plan (1960–2) and the concomitant first British application for EEC membership (1961–3).

---

[3] The text of the Messina Declaration can be found at another website hosted by Richard Griffiths. The URL is <http://www.let.leidenuniv.nl/history/rtg/res1/messina.htm>.

The two episodes are not directly linked. However, they are connected through the relationship between the larger and smaller member states. The Fouchet Plan was a French proposal to broaden the scope of European integration into a number of different functional areas—foreign policy, defence, economics, and culture—each of which would be endowed with its own administrative organization much like the European Commission served the common market. The centre of gravity in this new system would be the Council of Ministers and by implication the separate supra-national authorities would have little scope for autonomy. This arrangement would seem to be in keeping with Dutch attitudes as revealed in the ECSC negotiations and yet the Netherlands emerged as an immediate and steadfast opponent of the proposal (Silj 1967).

Dutch opposition rested on two concerns. First, European defence cooperation would undermine relations between Europe and the United States within the North Atlantic Treaty Organization (NATO) and it would also undermine cooperation with Britain, which was in NATO and the Western European Union (WEU)—effectively the European pillar of NATO—but which was not a member of the EEC. Second, any organization dependent upon a Council of Ministers that included only the six orig-inal EEC member states could too easily devolve into a Franco-German condominium at the expense of the smaller countries. This position is entirely consistent with the earlier objection to the ECSC. Having a supranational agency that is implicitly captive to the interests of large countries is bad for small country interests. Having an intergovernmental arrangement that is explicitly dominated by large countries is worse.[4]

The Dutch strategy for opposing the Fouchet Plan had two components: support for British entry in the EEC; and insistence that the European Commission remain the singular and encompassing supranational authority for the Community. Initially, the Dutch were isolated in their opposition. Although they would have preferred to have Britain in the EEC and to retain a strong supranational check on Franco-German dominance, Belgium and Luxembourg were initially willing to support the Fouchet Plan. However, as French opposition to British entry became clear and as De Gaulle became more demanding in the Fouchet negotiations, Belgium and Luxembourg swung their support behind the Dutch (Silj 1967; Jones 1993: 114–21).

The Fouchet negotiations collapsed and the EEC moved into a period of conflict and relative stagnation—marked by the French vetos of British accession (1963 and 1967), the empty chair crisis (1965), and the Luxembourg compromise (1966). However, the Low Country position within the EEC was secure. France and Germany did not dominate the Council of Ministers. The Commission was strong enough to check the Council but not so strong as to override the national interests of even the smaller member states. And progress toward the extension of market access across a wide range of sectors was running ahead of schedule. The question to consider then is what impact this had on the Benelux.

---

[4] As Christian Franck (1983: 86–7) points out, this interpretation does not rely on an implicit understanding among the smaller countries. Indeed, the advantage of supporting the Commission against the Council is precisely that it supports small country interests even when a coalition of the smaller states cannot be formed.

Distribution and adjustment

The economies of the Benelux countries changed dramatically during the period from the 1960s to the 1990s. In Belgium, the balance of wealth shifted from South to North, with the Flemish-speaking provinces becoming the new centre of gravity for politics and economics. Meanwhile, the mature industries of the Walloon South stagnated and coal mining disappeared entirely. Luxembourg developed as a financial centre, it attracted a large immigrant workforce, and it consolidated its position as host to a number of large European institutions. The Netherlands enjoyed a brief period of manufacturing success but then returned to its origins as a predominantly service-sector economy. At the same time, Dutch agriculture flourished and consolidated, becoming not only among the most productive food exporters in Europe but also one of the most heavily capitalized.

The difficulty lies in determining how much (if any) of such transformations should be attributed to European integration per se. The balance of wealth and power in Belgium was shifting northward before the onset of the Second World War and per capita income grew faster in Flanders than in Wallonia from 1948 to 1959 (Chaput and de Falleur 1961: 186). The migration of foreign workers to Luxembourg is a long-standing development as well. What is more, any progress that the Grand Duchy has made as a financial centre is at best only equal to (at least in relative terms) that achieved by Switzerland and Liechtenstein despite their being outside the European Community (now Union). Finally, the renewed service sector emphasis of the Dutch economy only mirrors developments elsewhere. Hence if there is a clear beneficiary of European integration it is Dutch agriculture. Given the role that the Dutch played in shaping the CAP, it would be surprising if it were otherwise.

The difficulties of estimating the precise impact of Europe are not unresolvable. But their resolution is more complicated than necessary to chart the broad contours of the EU–member state relationship. Indeed, the scholarly literature has focused primarily on three questions: Has European integration benefited capital more than labour? Does it constrain macroeconomic strategies to focus on stability rather than growth? Or is the effect of European integration really to enhance rather than to diminish the capabilities of the member states? The first two of these questions are independent but complementary. Europe can be either pro-capital or pro-stability without necessarily implying the other, and it can be both pro-capital and pro-stability without giving rise to contradiction. The third question is exclusive because it changes the frame of reference. If Europe enhances the capabilities of the nation-state, then the state can be pro-capital or pro-stability, but European integration cannot. Otherwise, so soon as state policymakers changed their attitudes toward either capital–labour relations or the trade-off between growth and stability, they would find their autonomy constrained by Europe and not enhanced.

Integration and business

Paulette Kurzer (1988; 1993; 1997a) is the most forceful proponent of the argument that European integration has privileged capital over labour, particularly as it applies to Belgium and the Netherlands. The force of her claim rests on three propositions. First, market access facilitates the direct foreign investment of large multinational corporations, many of which were attracted to the Low Countries at the start of the European Communities in the 1960s. Roughly one-quarter of all United States investment into the EEC during the 1960s went into the Low Countries, and foreign direct investment into Belgium accounted for as much as a half of the country's net capital formation (Van Rijckeghem 1982: 592–3). These foreign firms represented a new political force for the governments of the Low Countries to have to take into consideration. Second, market access works the other way as well, making it easier for domestic firms to move their production facilities abroad without losing their position with domestic consumers. In this way, domestic firms became politically more powerful because they could use the threat to move production abroad as a lever to manipulate government policy. Third, the liberalization of international capital flows in the late 1970s and 1980s strengthened the first two forces by making it easier for firms to enter the Low Countries and easier for them to exit as well. Beyond that, capital market liberalization also gave rise to 'international finance' as a separate power with which the governments of the Low Countries had to contend. Banking became an economic mainstay in Luxembourg during the 1980s (Hey 2003: 81), and banking interests moved to the centre of monetary policymaking in Belgium and the Netherlands as well (Kurzer 1988).

Kurzer (1993) uses this argument about the pro-business bias of European integration to explain why social democracy in the Low Countries has fared less well than it has in either Austria or Sweden. As business and financial interests have grown in importance, the rights and privileges of the working classes have been downgraded. This is most evident in the pressure to reform public expenditures and labour market regulations. It is also evident in the gradual shift in the distribution of value-added from labour to capital that took place in Belgium and the Netherlands during the 1980s and 1990s.

A pro-stability bias?

The macroeconomic constraints implied by European integration emerge from similar factors and particularly from the free movement of capital across national borders. The force of the argument derives not from the intentions of any specific group—say, business versus labour. Rather it emerges from the unintended consequences of the capital flows themselves. Mobile capital creates volatility in foreign currencies, international trade, public expenditure, and national output. This volatility in turn has profound implications for virtually everyone in society (Strange 1986; 1997). The European response to this volatility has been to tighten the institutions for exchange rate coordination, first through the European Monetary System (EMS) and later through the creation of a single European currency, the euro.

Kenneth Dyson (2000) argues that one effect of monetary integration is to change the structure of policy-relevant values in participating countries. The politicians and policymakers who join the monetary union do more than just reject the volatility of international capital markets and they do more than simply aspire to stability per se. Such politicians and policymakers ultimately come to embrace the particular notion of stability that underwrites the European single currency and to accept the importance of adhering to rules and procedures in order to bring that stability about. Specifically: they accept the numerical ceilings for acceptable debts (60 per cent of gross domestic product (GDP)) and deficits (3 per cent of GDP) as set down in the excessive deficits procedure of the Treaty on European Union; they accept the medium-term commitment to achieve a budgetary position that is close to balance or in surplus as required in the Stability and Growth Pact (SGP); and they accept the multilateral enforcement and monitoring procedures that underwrite these commitments (Jones 2002b: 35–57).

Dyson (2002: 359–66) leaves open whether this conception of stability necessarily privileges business over labour. Indeed he suggests that the opposite may be the case. The goals and procedures that underwrite European stability may be more useful for shoring up the welfare state than for dismantling it. What matters for Dyson is simply that the commitment to stability is normative and recursive. The more countries want rule-based stability, the more they come to believe in its necessity.

Writers like Kurzer (1997b) and Verdun (2002) are sceptical that any such pro-stability bias in the Low Countries actually emanates from the process of European integration. They admit that Belgium and the Netherlands are committed to macroeconomic stability and to fixed exchange rates. However, they note that these commitments pre-date the process of integration in Europe. Hence, they suggest, it is more likely that Belgium and the Netherlands inculcated these values at the European level than the other way around. What is more, both Kurzer and Verdun note that fiscal policy was never so tight in Belgium or the Netherlands as the architects of the EMS and the single currency would have liked. Any reform of the welfare state that did take place emerged only piecemeal, and was not part of some wholesale conversion to the values of macroeconomic stability as set out in the European Union's excessive deficit procedure or SGP.

Rescuing the nation state

This debate over the normative influence of monetary integration brings discussion of the Low Countries into the framework suggested by Peter Katzenstein (1985). In his *Small States and World Markets*, Katzenstein argues that small states like the Low Countries survive (even flourish) in world markets by combining international integration with domestic forms of compensation, which is to say a strong welfare state. The Low Countries fit this pattern very closely. As they entered into first the Benelux and then the European Communities, all three countries established domestic institutions to protect both labour and industry from the shocks and volatility that are inherent in opening up to world markets. In other words, the social welfare institutions in these countries exist to compensate for the costs of integration. Hence there is no surprise in finding that the Low Countries would be slow to implement welfare state reform even as integration progressed.

The interesting question is how the Low Countries have managed the tensions between integration in world markets and generous welfare state institutions. Here we should accept that Kurzer's argument about the pro-business bias of European integration has some merit. The competitive forces both in European and world markets do pose a number of challenges for the functioning of welfare state institutions. Demographic changes, ranging from declining birth rates to increasing life-spans, pose problems as well. To assume that Belgium and the Netherlands could avoid having to respond would be unrealistic (Hemerijck and Visser 2000). Even tiny Luxembourg is not impervious to the inexorable forces for welfare state reform (Osborn 1999).

At least part of the answer to the question of reconciling integration and the welfare state was found in using the requirements for integration in Europe as an excuse for undertaking otherwise necessary reforms. Hence, coalition governments in both Belgium and the Netherlands justified fiscal consolidation as being necessary to prepare for entry into the single currency (Jones 1998a; 1998c). To an even greater extent, however, the answer was found in pursuing ever deeper forms of European integration in order to stave off the requirements for domestic economic or political adjustment. This is the essence of Alan Milward's (1992) argument about the *European Rescue of the Nation State*. And it has particular resonance for the Benelux.

The Low Countries used market access to increase export earnings and promote industrialization. They used exchange rate coordination to stabilize the foreign trade developed within the Common Market. They supported the elimination of non-tariff barriers to trade in the 1980s in order to foster greater European competitiveness versus third countries such as the United States or Japan. They saw capital market liberalization as a means to escape the liquidity constraints operating on small countries. And they relied on monetary integration to moderate the volatility implied by liberalized capital markets. At each step in the process, the goal was not to strip away the powers of the state. Rather it was to strengthen the capabilities of the state initially to expand, then to protect, and then shore up the provision of social welfare. That some welfare state reform took place should not necessarily imply that an adverse European bias is at work. It may only suggest that the strategy of pursuing integration was insufficient to the challenge at hand (Jones forthcoming).

Institutions and adaptation

The problem with assertions that European integration has somehow 'rescued' the Benelux countries is that they gloss over the many and difficult adjustments required within the integration process. In general terms, countries must adapt to the institutions, norms, and procedures of multilateral decision-making. In specific terms they must implement and enforce the legislation passed at the European level. Neither aspect of adjustment is easily accomplished, and both strain domestic political institutions and practices (Peterson and Jones 1999: 37–41).

By most accounts, the Benelux countries have been much better at the general than at the specific. While widely regarded as effective negotiators, neither Belgium nor Luxembourg has amassed a strong record in the transposition of European Union (EU) legislation into national law (Beyers, Kerremans, and Bursens 2001: 72–3). Poor transposition used to be a problem in the Netherlands as well, but was eliminated through an overhaul of Dutch implementation procedures at the start of the 1990s (Harmsen 1999: 101–2). The conclusion to draw from this is simply that being a good European citizen does not come naturally even in the smallest member states or in those with the longest record of participation.

The challenge is to identify the magnitude of adjustment implied by the integration process, the structure of the political interests surrounding the adjustment process, and the resulting pattern of adaptation. In the scholarly literature, such concerns are bracketed within the larger context of 'Europeanization'—understood broadly to encompass virtually the whole of the EU–member state relationship (cf. Olsen 2002). This literature focuses predominantly on institutional concerns. From this institutionalist perspective, the magnitude of adjustment derives from the 'goodness of fit' between national and European institutions (Börzel 2002). The structure of political interests is contextually specific (Börzel 1999: 577–80). And the pattern of adaptation depends upon a 'logic of appropriateness' inherited from pre-existing political and social institutions (Harmsen 1999: 85; see also Petersen 1998).

Goodness of fit

The Benelux countries would seem to be a good fit with the practice of policymaking at the European level. Among students of comparative politics, Belgium and the Netherlands illustrate type cases for consensual democracy. Luxembourg also has a strong reputation for institutionalized consensus building. And, the European Union relies on consensus as well. With its complex legislative procedures, super-majoritarian voting rules, and multiple reinforcing political cleavages, the European Union is arguably even more dependent upon consensus than any of the member states—the Benelux countries included.

The irony is that consensus politics is more problematic than helpful in dealing with the European Union. Consensual institutions imply that a large number of actors must be involved in the formation of any national position. The coordination of these many views is a daunting challenge in its own right. The reconciliation of competing interests is more problematic still. Such coordination is possible, but it is complex (Beyers, Kerremans, and Bursens 2001). Hence private interests in the Netherlands prefer to lobby the European Union outside the official channels managed by the government (Van Schendelen 1993). Private interests in Belgium channel their demands directly through the country's Permanent Representative, who helps them to network with other interested parties at the European level and without recourse to the Belgian state (Pijnenburg 1993: 171–2). Such broad use of the Permanent Representative is not necessarily a weakness. However, it does imply that Belgium has to take great care in the selection and maintenance of its representation to the EU despite the fact that the Belgian Ministry of Foreign Affairs is only blocks away from the European Commission (Kerremans and Beyers 2001).

Excessive resort to consensus also has a negative effect on the ability of the Benelux countries to implement EU legislation. The more complicated the mechanism for transposing European legislation into national law, the slower the process of transposition and the more susceptible it becomes to backlog. This is the most often cited explanation for the relative failings of Belgium on the implementation side of its relations with Europe (cf. Kerremans and Beyers 1998). Legislative complexity also used to be a major factor behind the weakness of implementation in the Dutch case (Hoetjes 1996: 164).

As in the Netherlands, the Belgian government attempted to streamline its procedures in order to improve performance (de Wilde d'Estmael and Franck 1996). However, it was unable to overcome the demand by different groups in Belgian politics for adequate representation. The Netherlands was more successful. Yet this success in reforming the implementation of EU legislation has given rise to concern in the Netherlands that the state is infringing on the rights and privileges of civil society. Whether such concerns will become problematic remains to be seen. Whatever the outcome, moving away from consensus does impose a cost. And the more deeply consensus is embedded in the country, the higher the cost becomes. Hence, 'in the Netherlands . . . it is the autonomy of society, not the sovereignty of the state, which may ultimately prove to be the faultline at which supranational integration could stumble' (Harmsen 1999: 105).

The difficulty in Luxembourg is not too much consensus so much as it is too few people. The small number of government officials actually makes it much easier to coordinate policies through the state. However, it also makes it more difficult to transpose and implement EU legislation in a timely manner. Luxembourgish officials have to run to stay in place. Hence, their relatively poor performance actually constitutes quite an achievement. In contrast to the attitudes prevalent among Belgian bureaucrats, the Luxembourgers are pleased with their record for transposition (Beyers, Kerremans, and Bursens 2001: 88 n. 49). The point remains, however, that the fit between Luxembourgish and European institutions is not as good as the simple correlation of consensual characteristics would suggest.

Interest and institutional context

But institutions can be changed. The difficulty is that most institutional innovations—in the Benelux countries as elsewhere—take place for reasons that have little to do with the process of European integration. Some such developments may complement Europeanization. Others may work against it. For example, each of the three Benelux countries has undergone an important transformation during the past four decades. Belgium has witnessed the rise of linguistic conflict and the subsequent federalization of political authority. The Netherlands has experienced a pluralization of domestic politics and a weakening of formal political institutions. Luxembourg has seen its economy change over from a heavy reliance on steel manufacturing to an equally heavy reliance on banking and finance. The question to consider is whether these changes have made it easier or more difficult for the governments of the Benelux countries to participate in the European Union.

The federalization of Belgium has certainly made matters difficult. This is true in part because a federal Belgium includes many more formal actors who wish (indeed, who are obliged) to be involved in the process of European integration. On those matters where the Belgian regional governments are sovereign, such as public transport, the regional governments actually represent the Belgian 'state' (Franck, Leclercq, and Vandevievere 2003). However, it is also true because politicians in the regional governments have attempted to use the European Union as a lever in the competition for national resources. At one point during the 1990s, for example, a Flemish bus manufacturer (Van Hool) tried to overturn a Walloon public procurement decision on the grounds that it violated European law. The fact that the European Commission agreed with Van Hool and its representative in the Flemish regional government only made matters more and not less complicated. The Commission had no powers to direct the Walloon regional government and could only refer matters to the courts. Meanwhile, the Belgian federal government could not intervene because public procurement is a matter of regional authority. By the time the European Court of Justice intervened, the procurement process was already completed (Jones 1998b: 154).

The pluralization of Dutch politics has had a more ambivalent effect. During the early years of European integration, politics in the Netherlands was controlled by political parties rather than by the government per se. Political elites commanded a certain deference from the electorate and, correspondingly, had a reasonable amount of leeway in conducting multilateral negotiations. With the pluralization of Dutch politics, however, the control of the political parties has weakened and the deference accorded to political elites has evaporated. By implication, the government has become relatively stronger and more decisive. However, the electorate has become less docile and more challenging. The strength of the government makes it possible for the Netherlands to be more successful in implementing EU legislation as suggested above. However, the weakening of elite control has given rise to increasing electoral volatility. The May 2002 elections witnessed unprecedented turmoil in Dutch politics because the right-wing politician Pim Fortuyn, the leader of the populist movement known as the List Pim Fortuyn, was assassinated on the eve of voting (Jones 2002a). And the campaigns leading up to the January 2003 elections saw a growing ambivalence among many political parties in their attitudes toward European integration.

The growth of the Luxembourgish financial industry is problematic as well. Much of the money deposited in Luxembourg comes from the other member states of the European Union. The motivation of the depositors is to avoid paying tax. Hence much of the European Union would like to see Luxembourg change its regulations as they apply both to banking secrecy and to the taxation of interest income. Because it fears such changes would drive away business, the Luxembourg government refuses. How long they can continue to refuse and still remain in the good graces of the European Union remains to be seen (Hey 2003: 80–3).

Idiosyncrasy and persistence

In the previous example, the politics of Luxembourg has altered very little over time. Industrial dependence has changed over from industry to banking, but the political constitution of the country has changed little if at all. Meanwhile, Belgium has transformed itself from a centralized unitary state into a decentralized federation, and the Netherlands has moved from a highly structured consociational democracy to a highly volatile pluralist one. The question to consider is which of these cases is the odd one out. Put another way, all three of the Benelux countries have participated in European integration during the past half century and only Luxembourg remains politically unchanged: Does that make Luxembourg the exception or the norm?

The question hinges on a false dichotomy. The reality is that all three Benelux countries are equally idiosyncratic in their political development. The reason is that political development is sensitively dependent upon initial conditions, on context, and on what institutionalists refer to as historical path dependence. This is why attention needs to be paid to their respective historical experiences of the integration process. Despite the common forces of Europeanization, the politics of European countries have grown little more alike if at all. Indeed the developmental trajectories followed by European countries over the past decade are almost all different from one another (Anderson 2002).

Perhaps the Benelux countries remain different because of their participation in the European Union. Of course, it would be convenient if the persistence of idiosyncracy could be marked down to the work of factors external to the process of European integration. Then we could retain a convergent notion of Europeanization while at the same time conceding the divergent effect of exogenous factors or stochastic shocks. However, it may be true that European integration is itself a source of diversity. This could happen if European integration were to make it possible for countries to sustain outmoded industrial sectors, such as coal in Belgium. It could happen through incentives to specialize according along lines of comparative advantages, such as agriculture in the Netherlands. Or it could happen by removing the institutional supports for an area of existing specialization, such as finance in Luxembourg. Diversity could also take the form of encouraging political centralization (Netherlands), decentralization (Belgium), or overload (Luxembourg). The end result of such forces would be to make the Benelux countries less alike and not more; rendering them less likely as objects for analysis as a group.

Conclusion: self interest and identity

More than ever in their history, however, the Benelux countries share a common identity—as Benelux countries and as EU member states. This common identity does not transcend national self-interest. But it does shape conceptions of self-interest. To give an example, much of the political ambivalence toward European integration expressed by Dutch political parties in the Autumn of 2002 was directed at the Common Agricultural Policy. Their concern was not that the CAP would be reformed, but rather that the reforms would not be sweeping enough. Far from being worried about the state of their farmers, Dutch politicians are concerned about the costs and distortions that will arise from the enlargement of the European Union to the East.

This common identity is experiential and not accidental. It does not emerge despite the diverse effects of European integration. Rather it is a result of the common need to manage these effects. Europeanization is nowhere the same. The fact that Europeanization is a challenge to be dealt with is. The Benelux countries have a long history of advocating and participating in European integration. That history began as an act of self interest. But that history soon took on a meaning and significance all its own. Just as the political development of the Benelux countries is historically path dependent, their identities are grounded in past experience. No matter what the material effects of that experience, the fact remains that European integration has been shared as a process. The fact that participation in Europe offers advantages has been shared as well. And so has the fact of Europeanization itself. In this sense, integration in Europe has been much more powerful as a source of identification than was union within the Kingdom of the Netherlands. As a result, Belgium, the Netherlands, and Luxembourg share a common identity even while they remain different countries, each distinctive in its own way.

Further reading

Finding literature on the Benelux countries and the EU is not entirely straightforward. Interested students are likely to have to scour the large body of comparative edited volumes (like this one) for relevant chapters. Surveys of the individual countries are to be found in Wessels, Maurer, and Mittag (2003); of Belgian European policy-making at home (Kerremans 2000); of the Belgian and Dutch representations in Brussels (respectively Kerremans and Beyers 2001; Soetendorp and Andeweg 2001). An alternative collective appraisal of the three countries is offered by Beyers, Kerremans, and Bursens (2001).

Weblinks

Basic political data is relatively easy to come by. The University of Florida maintains a web portal <**http://web.uflib.ufl.edu/docs/EUguide/EUgovs.html**> with information about all current European Union member states that leads to information about their relations with the European Union, their governments, elections, leaders, and political parties. The European Union has a similar portal <**http://europa.eu.int/abc/ governments/index_en.htm**> but it is slightly less user-friendly. Finding statistical information on the Benelux countries is relatively easy. Most of the major international organizations provide data that is freely downloadable. For example, the United Nations Economic Commission for Europe <**http://www.unece.org**> has social, demographic, and some basic economic data, while the the European Commission offers access to its much more detailed annual macroeconomics database going back to 1960 <**http://europa.eu.int/comm/economy_finance/indicators/annual_macro_economic_ database/ameco_en.htm**>. A few of the international organizations also provide more in-depth analysis of current events, both political and economic. The International Monetary Fund (IMF –<**http://www.imf.org**>) is the best resource in this area, with freely downloadable country reports on all member countries.

References

Anderson, Jeffrey J. (2002), 'Europeanization and the Transformation of the Democratic Polity, 1945–2000', *Journal of Common Market Studies* 40/5 (December), 793–822.

Bernard, Henri (1961), *Terre commune: Histoire des pays de Benelux, microcosme de l'Europe*, 2nd edn. (Brussels: Éditions Brepols).

Beyers, Jan, Kerremans, Bart, and Bursens Peter (2001), 'Belgium, the Netherlands, and Luxembourg: Diversity among the Benelux Countries', in Eleanor E. Zeff and Ellen B. Pirro, (eds), *The European Union and the Member States: Cooperation, Coordination, and Compromise* (Boulder, CO: Lynne Rienner Publishers), 59–88.

Börzel, Tanja A. (1999), 'Towards Convergence in Europe? Institutional Adaptation in Germany and Spain', *Journal of Common Market Studies* 37/4 (December), 573–96.

Börzel, Tanja A. (2002), 'Pace-Setting, Foot-Dragging, and Fence-Sitting: Member State Responses to Europeanization', *Journal of Common Market Studies* 40/2, 193–214.

Chaput, Gilberte, and de Falleur Richard (1961), 'Le produit intérieur brut des régions en 1948 et 1959', *Cahiers économiques de Bruxelles* 10 (April), 179–208.

de Wilde d'Estmael, Tanguy, and Franck, Christian (1996), 'Belgium', in Rometsch, Dietrich, and Wolfgang Wessels, *The European Union and the Member States: Towards Institutional Fusion?* (Manchester: Manchester University Press), 37–60.

Dyson, Kenneth (2000), *The Politics of the Euro-Zone: Stability or Breakdown?* (Oxford: Oxford University Press).

Dyson, Kenneth (2002), 'Conclusions: European States and Euro Economic Governance', in Kenneth Dyson (ed.), *European States and the Euro: Europeanization, Variation, and Convergence* (Oxford: Oxford University Press), 335–66.

Economic Recovery Program (ERP 1949). *Belgium and Luxembourg Country Study* (Washington DC: Economic Cooperation Administration).

Eyck, F. Gunther (1959), *The Benelux Countries: An Historical Survey* (Princeton NJ: D. Van Notrand Company).

Franck, Christian (1983), 'Belgium: Committed Multilateralism', in Christopher Hill (ed.), *National Foreign Policies and European Political Cooperation* (London: George Allen & Unwin for the Royal Institute of International Affairs), 85–105.

Franck, C., Leclercq, H., and Vandevievere, C. (2003), 'Belgium: Europeanisation and Belgian Federalism', in Wessels, Maurer, and Mittag, 69–91.

Griffiths, Richard T. (1980). 'The Netherlands and the EEC', in Richard T. Griffiths (ed.), *The Economy and Politics of the Netherlands since 1945* (The Hague: Martinus Nijhoff), 277–303.

Griffiths, Richard T., and Milward, Alan S. (1986). 'The Beyen Plan and the European Political Community', in Werner Maihofer (ed.), *Noi si mura: Selected Working Papers of the European University Institute* (Florence: European University Institute), 595–621.

Harmsen, Robert (1999), 'The Europeanization of National Administrations: A Comparative Study of France and the Netherlands', *Governance* 12/1 (January), 81–113.

Hemerijck, Anton, and Visser, Jelle (2000), 'Change and Immobility: Three Decades of Policy Adjustment in the Netherlands and Belgium', in Maurizio Ferrera and Martin Rhodes (eds), *Recasting European Welfare States* (London: Frank Cass), 229–56.

Hey, Jeanne A. K. (2003), 'Luxembourg: Where Small Works (And Wealthy Doesn't Hurt)', in Hey, Jeanne A. K. (ed.), *Small States in World Politics: Explaining Foreign Policy Behavior* (Boulder CO: Lynne Rienner Publishers), 75–94.

Hoetjes, Bernard J. S. (1996), 'The Netherlands', in Dietrich Rometsch and Wolfgang Wessels (eds), *The European Union and the Member States: Towards Institutional Fusion?* (Manchester: Manchester University Press), 155–84.

Jones, Erik (1993), 'Small Countries and the Franco-German Relationship', in Patrick McCarthy (ed.), *France-Germany, 1983–1993: The Struggle to Cooperate* (New York: St Martin's Press), 113–38.

Jones, Erik (1998a), 'Belgium: Keeping Up with the Pack', in Erik Jones, Jeffry Frieden, and Francisco Torres (eds), *Joining Europe's Monetary Club: The Challenges for Smaller Member States* (New York: St Martin's), 43–60.

Jones, Erik (1998b), 'From Depillarization to Decentralization and Beyond: The Gathering Storm in Belgium', *Dutch Crossing* 22/1 (Summer), 139–60.

Jones, Erik (1998c), 'The Netherlands: Top of the Class', in Erik Jones, Jeffry Frieden, and Francisco Torres (eds), *Joining Europe's Monetary Club: The Challenges for Smaller Member States* (New York: St Martin's), 149–70.

Jones, Erik (2002a), 'Politics Beyond Accommodation? The May 2002 Dutch Parliamentary Elections', *Dutch Crossing* 26/1 (Summer), 61–78.

Jones, Erik (2002b), *The Politics of Economic and Monetary Union: Integration and Idiosyncrasy* (Lanham: Rowman and Littlefield).

Jones, Erik (forthcoming), *Economic Adjustment and Political Transformation in Small States* (Lanham: Rowman and Littlefield).

Katzenstein, Peter (1985), *Small States in World Markets: Industrial Policy in Europe* (Ithaca NY: Cornell University Press).

Kerremans, Bart (2000), 'Belgium', in H. Kassim, B. G. Peters, and V. Wright, (eds), *The National Co-ordination of EU Policy: The Domestic Level* (Oxford: Oxford University Press), 182–200.

Kerremans, Bart and Beyers, Jan (1998), 'Belgium: The Dilemma between Cohesion and Autonomy', in Kenneth Hanf and Ben Soetendorp, (eds), *Adapting to European Integration: Small States and the European Union* (London: Longman), 14–35.

Kerremans, Bart and Beyers, Jan (2001), 'The Belgian Permanent Representation to the European Union: Mailbox, Messenger, or Representative?', in Hussein Kassim, Anand Menon, B. Guy Peters, and Vincent Wright (eds), *The National Coordination of EU Policy: The European Level* (Oxford: Oxford University Press), 191–210.

Kindleberger, Charles P. (1986), *The World in Depression, 1929–1939* (revised and enlarged edn Berkeley: University of California Press).

Kurzer, Paulette (1988), 'The Politics of Central Banks: Austerity and Unemployment in Europe', *Journal of Public Policy* 7/1 (January–March), 21–48.

Kurzer, Paulette (1993), *Business and Banking: Political Change and Economic Integration in Western Europe* (Ithaca NY: Cornell University Press).

Kurzer, Paulette (1997a), 'Decline or Preservation of Executive Capacity? Political and Economic Integration Revisited', *Journal of Common Market Studies* 35/1 (March), 31–56.

Kurzer, Paulette (1997b), 'Placed in Europe: The Low Countries and Germany in the European Union', in Peter Katzenstein (ed.), *Tamed Power: Germany in Europe* (Ithaca NY: Cornell University Press), 108–41.

Milward, Alan S. (1984), *The Reconstruction of Western Europe, 1945–1951* (London: Routledge).

Milward, Alan S. (1992), *The European Rescue of the Nation-State* (London: Routledge).

Olsen, Johan P. (2002), 'The Many Faces of Europeanization', *Journal of Common Market Studies* 40/5 (December), 921–52.

Osborn, Alan (1999), 'Banking on the Euro', *Europe* 384 (March), 8–9.

Petersen, Nikolaj (1998), 'National Strategies in the Integration Dilemma: An Adaptation Approach', *Journal of Common Market Studies* 36/1 (March), 33–54.

Peterson, John and Jones, Erik (1999), 'Decision-making in an Enlarging Europe', in *Two Tiers or Two Speeds? The European Security Order and the Enlargement of the European Union and NATO*, James Sperling (ed.) (Manchester: Manchester University Press), 25–45.

Pijnenberg, B. (1993), 'Belgium: Federalized EC Lobbying at Home', in M. P. C. M. Van Schendelen (ed.), *National Public and Private EC Lobbying* (Aldershot: Dartmouth), 155–81.

Samoy, Achille G. (1981), 'La création de l'union économique Benelux', *Studia Diplomatica* 34/1–4, 179–98.

Silj, Alessandro (1967), 'Europe's Political Puzzle: A Study of the Fouchet Negotiations and the 1963 Veto', *Occasional Papers in International Affairs 17* (December) (Cambridge MA: Center for International Affairs).

Soetendorp, B. and Andeweg, R. (2001), 'Dual Loyalties: the Dutch Representation to the European Union' in H. Kassim, A. Menon, B. G. Peters, and V. Wright, (eds), *The National Co-ordination of EU Policy* (Oxford: Oxford University Press), 211–28.

Spaak, Paul Henri (1969), *Combats inachevés: De l'indépendence à l'alliance* (Brussels: Librairie Arthème Fayard).

Strange, Susan (1986; 1997), *Casino Capitalism* (Manchester: Manchester University Press)

van Meerhaeghe, M. A. G. (1987), 'The Belgium–Luxembourg Economic Union', *SUERF Series 54 A.* (Tilburg, The Netherlands: Société Universitaire Européenne de Recherches Financières).

van Rijckeghem, Willy (1982), 'Benelux', in Andrea Boltho (ed.), *The European Economy: Growth and Crisis* (Oxford: Oxford University Press), 581–609.

Van Roon, Ger (1989), *Small States in Years of Depression: The Oslo Alliance, 1930–1940* (Assen: Van Gorcum).

Van Schendelen, M. P. C. M. (1993), 'The Netherlands: Lobby It Yourself', in M. P. C. M. Van Schendelen (ed.), *National Public and Private EC Lobbying* (Aldershot: Dartmouth), 131–54.

Verdun, Amy (2002), 'The Netherlands and EMU: A Small Open Economy in Search of Prosperity', in Kenneth Dyson (ed.), *European States and the Euro: Europeanization, Variation, and Convergence* (Oxford: Oxford University Press), 238–54.

Weil, Gordon L. (1970), *The Benelux Nations: The Politics of Small-Country Democracies* (New York: Holt, Rinehart, and Winston, Inc).

Wessels, W., Maurer, A., and Mittag, J. (2003), *Fifteen into One? The European Union and its Member States* (Manchester: Manchester University Press).

Chapter 9
The EU and the Nordic Countries: Organizing Domestic Diversity?

Morten Egeberg

Contents

Summary

This chapter covers the Nordic member states Denmark, Finland, and Sweden, as well as the 'associated' countries Norway and Iceland, although the latter are not formal members of the EU. It presents the history and politics of the European issue in these countries, their efforts at influencing EU level policy-making, and how the EU level impacts on their politics, institutions and policies. Two perspectives are introduced in order to interpret EU–member state relationships. From an intergovernmental perspective, a member country is supposed to act coherently on the European scene, and its integrity is not seriously threatened by international cooperation. However, from an organizational perspective, international and supranational institutions *might* be organized in such a way that they encourage cooperation and conflict *across* nation-states, for example, along sectoral, functional, partisan, and ideological lines. Research shows that European integration in many situations strengthens national coherence and consistency. However, under certain conditions, national political systems might slightly disintegrate domestically. Here we explore this paradox in the Nordic context.

Introduction

The Nordic countries are located at the edge of Europe. However, their political, economic, cultural, and social life have for centuries been heavily influenced by developments taking place on the European continent or the British Isles. Not only massive wars, but also numerous less dramatic events have made the European context highly relevant to the everyday life of the Nordic peoples. For example, for hundreds of years, government officials from Nordic countries have travelled around Europe to learn about institutional arrangements that could be imported to their respective home lands (Knudsen 2002), and architecture and furniture reflecting different periods of European style may be found in the most northern periphery. Naturally, the extent to which Nordic countries have made their impact felt in other European countries has been relatively modest. However, for instance, Sweden's involvement in continental wars and conquering of Baltic and German territories in the seventeenth century were not insignificant at the time. Later on, in the period following the Second World War, the Nordic welfare state model may be said to have enjoyed some attraction from areas outside the Nordic region. Nordic economies, although not that big, also became relatively prosperous and thus interesting from a broader European perspective.

The Nordic countries got involved in the European integration process at different points in time, and to different degrees. Denmark became a member of the European Community (EC) already in 1973, while Finland and Sweden joined in 1995. Iceland and Norway, on the other hand, became in 1994 associated with the European Union (EU) through the European Economic Area (EEA) agreement which in fact makes the two countries part of the internal market. A section of this chapter will deal with some of the backgrounds for these different paths to involvement in the European integration project. Thereafter, the main parts follow; first, focusing on how the Nordic countries strive to impact on decision processes at the EU level, and how they organize their 'inside-out' (bottom-up) processes, and, second, how the EU directly affects their national level ('outside-in' or top-down processes). But, first of all, in the next section, two theoretical perspectives will be outlined in order to give us some background for interpreting the relationships between the EU and its Nordic member states. One basic idea here is that if profound transformation of the European political order is really going on, this will be reflected in the way patterns of conflict and cooperation develop. Arguably, if such patterns *along* national boundaries are significantly complemented by such patterns *across* state borders, then deep change is in fact taking place. Thus, European integration might well be accompanied by a certain disintegration of the political system at the national level. The extent to which this may actually happen is here supposed to depend on the kind of institutions that emerge at the EU level, and *how these institutions are organized*. In the conclusion, the empirical parts will be confronted with the theoretical perspectives. One final observation is in order here. In dealing with three member states, as well as discussing Iceland and Norway, there is an inevitable selectiveness in the empirical material covered. The section on 'further reading' provides guidance on complementary material.

Theorizing the relationship between the EU and its Member States

There are several contending theoretical angles from which the EU-member countries relationship might be approached. Each perspective has its own expectations about the actual functioning of the European political order. From an *intergovernmental* perspective, member countries act internationally as coherent entities coordinated and led by their respective national governments (for example Moravcsik 1998). Thus, the interests of different sub-national regions, branches of government and interest groups are all seen as forged into a common national position that the government advocates in its dealing with other countries. Representatives of national governments arrive at the international scene 'pre-packed' with national preferences and identities that only exceptionally might be reshaped significantly at the international level. International organizations are basically seen as arenas for solving collective problems among nation-states; thus, such organizations have no profound independent impact beyond the authority delegated to them by the constituent member states (Moravcsik 1998). It follows that patterns of cooperation and conflict are supposed to *coincide with* national boundaries. Finally, intergovernmentalists tend to see compliance with, or defection from, agreed treaties and conventions as a question of control of national implementation through rewards or punishments (Moravscik 1998).

Institutional perspectives highlight the crucial role that institutions might play at the EU as well as the national level. First, institutions such as the European Commission, Parliament, and Council are thought to have an *independent* impact on actors' preferences and identities, as well as on EU policies (Bulmer 1994; Aspinwall and Schneider 2000; Olsen 2000). Thus, according to this view, a state centric political order might be transcended in some way or another, something which is not quite foreseeable from an intergovernmental perspective. Second, administrative institutions at the national level may, under certain conditions, distort or seriously hamper implementation of EU policies. This may happen if such policies are incompatible with established institutional core values. If, on the other hand, EU policies are deemed appropriate in relation to a country's administrative traditions, national adaptation of policies and institutions is supposed to take place on a routine basis without much delay (Olsen 1992; Knill 2001a).

The *multi-level governance* approach offers first and foremost a more accurate account of the actual functioning of the European system of governance. The perspective's explanatory ambition is less clearly articulated. It portrays the EU as a highly complex machinery characterized by multiple levels of governance and multiple channels of interest representation in which sub-national regions and national interest groups occasionally bypass national governments in order to have a say at the EU level (Kohler-Koch 1996; Hooghe and Marks 2001).

An *organizational* perspective on EU governance can be seen as a complementary approach that may help to clarify the conditions under which the system will tend to operate according to a basically intergovernmental logic or not (Egeberg 2004). Thus, EU institutions may be structured in ways that underpin and accentuate a state centric order rather than challenge it. Clearly, the set-up of the Council of the EU, like that of classic international organizations, neatly reflects the territorial composition of the system. The structure thus embodies a pattern of cooperation and conflict that coincides with national boundaries and may be expected to mainly sustain national identities among policy makers. However, the sectoral and functional specialization of the Council at the ministerial and working group level may, in addition, evoke sectoral and functional allegiances among participants, that is allegiances that cut *across* state borders (Hayes-Renshaw and Wallace 1997; Egeberg 1999).

The Commission divides its work according to sector or function. Thus, from an organizational perspective, we expect cleavages to emerge along sectoral lines rather than territorial lines (Egeberg 2004). For example, when the Commission worked out its white paper on the Union's transport policy, a clash was observed between the transport department and the environment department; the latter accusing the former of not paying enough heed to environmental concerns (*European Voice*, 31 May–6 June 2001). Similarly, the European Parliament organizes itself mainly according to non-territorial criteria, namely those of ideology (party) and sector (standing committee) (Hix 1999). By this, the Parliament provides an unprecedented arena for transnational party politics, that is politics which involves European level federations of, for example, centre-right or socialist parties.

From an organizational perspective, the unparalleled high level of transnational interest group activity, organized along sectoral or functional lines, found in the EU (cf. Andersen and Eliassen 2001; Greenwood and Aspinwall 1998; Mazey and Richardson 1996), is supposed to be due to the way the Commission and the Parliament structure their work. Their sectorally organized departments and committees create 'natural' points of access for interest groups organized according to the same criteria, points that are not that easily spotted in bodies composed of national governments, for example, Coreper or the European Council. Thus, EU institutions facilitate coalition building among similar groups *across* member states, for example industrial or environmental groups.

From an organizational point of view, the advanced division of labour found among EU institutions (executive, legislatures, court, bank, etc.) creates itself a more complex pattern of cooperation and conflict in the system. Since decision makers develop loyalties to their respective institutions, inter-institutional conflicts are also supposed to increasingly supplement intergovernmental ones (Egeberg 2004). For national governments, the (at the international level) unique split between the Council and the Commission means they are in a sense forced to assume two different roles. On the one hand they are expected to serve their respective nations at home and vis-à-vis the Council. However, on the other hand, they have in a sense become part of the EU administration in its policy preparatory and implementation stages. In practice this means participating in (preparatory) expert committees in the Commission and being monitored by the Commission in their implementation work. Finally, an organizational perspective explicitly draws attention to *organizational* characteristics of national institutions, not only their culture and traditions, when national coordination and implementation processes are to be accounted for (Kassim *et al.* 2000; Caporaso *et al.* 2001; Knill 2001a).

The history and politics of the European issue

None of the Nordic countries was among the founding members of the EC. Denmark, Norway, and Sweden instead joined the European Free Trade Association (EFTA), in which the UK was the leading country, from its start in 1960. Iceland became a member of this organisation in 1970. While the EC, and even its predecessor the European Coal and Steel Community (ECSC) of 1952, had a genuine political vision for its future development, EFTA was from the beginning defined as a mere economic project (Urwin 1995). Its objectives were limited to the elimination of tariffs on most industrial goods among its member states. Thus, EFTA membership seemed compatible with the formal neutrality status of states like Sweden, Austria, and Switzerland. Finland, however, in the shadow of the former Soviet Union, did not feel free to join until 1986. Also, EFTA became an alternative for those countries that shared the British scepticism towards a closer union, and that also adhered to the UK's more 'Atlantic line' in their foreign and security policies (that is Norway and Denmark) (Urwin 1995; Eriksen and Pharo 1997).

Compared to Norway, Denmark, with its highly competitive agricultural industry, was, probably in all terms (not only geographically), closer to continental Europe (Eriksen and Pharo 1997). When Denmark, as the first Nordic country, together with the UK, in 1961 applied for full membership in the EC, an application from Norway was submitted the year after. France, however, vetoed further negotiations, and the same happened in 1967 when these countries had again applied for full membership of the Community. In the meantime, Nordic cooperation across several policy areas had progressed considerably. Through a network of committees officials had, over time, quite pragmatically, succeeded in harmonizing a considerable number of laws; for example, a common labour market had been established and people were allowed to cross borders without carrying their passport with them (Laursen 1998). After having been rejected by the EC for the second time, then, the Danes initiated a further strengthening of the Nordic alternative by proposing the erection of a Nordic economic cooperation regime (NORDØK). Events in the wider European context soon put an end to this initiative, however. The EC now welcomed new applications for membership, and Denmark and Norway also this time followed the UK in their third attempt (Tamnes 1997). The result was that the UK, Ireland, and Denmark became full members of the Community from 1973. Norway remained outside due to a referendum in which the government's recommendation to enter the EC was turned down by a relatively narrow majority of 53.5 per cent of the voters (cf. Pesonen et al. 1998, and Table 9.1). During the negotiations, the future of the Norwegian fishery regime and non-competitive agriculture were among the hardest issues to solve. The result of the referendum showed that the government had not succeeded

Table 9.1 The Nordic referendums on membership in the EC/EU

Country	Date	Type	'Yes' %	Turnout
Norway	25 Sept. 1972	Consultative	46.5	79.2
Denmark	2 Oct. 1972	Binding	63.4	90.4
Finland	16 Oct. 1994	Consultative	56.9	74.0
Sweden	13 Nov. 1994	Consultative	52.3	83.3
Norway	28 Nov. 1994	Consultative	47.7	89.0

Source: Pesonen et al. 1998: 16–17.

in convincing the voters entirely on these points. In addition, there was an enduring, underlying broad scepticism towards becoming part of a 'union' once more (Tamnes 1997). It seemed as if both the union with Denmark (1380–1814) and the union with Sweden (1814–1905) were still present in a negative way in the collective memory of the Norwegian people.

Also the Danish government referred the membership decision of 1972 to the people; in fact it was required by the constitution to do so. A majority of 63.4 per cent then approved the proposal (cf. Table 9.1). As members of the EC/EU, the Danes have, however, all the time been among the most sceptical to further deepening of the Community/Union (von Dosenrode 1998). Thus, the Maastricht Treaty, which emphasized more intense cooperation in the areas of foreign and security policy, justice and home affairs, and in addition set a timetable for the introduction of the economic and monetary union, became hard to swallow for the Danes. In 1992 a 51 per cent majority voted against the agreement (Pesonen et al. 1998). However, the European Council in Edinburgh in 1992 allowed Denmark to opt out of currency union, any future common defence policy and any institutionalization of European citizenship. Subsequently, a second Danish referendum produced a positive result of 57 per cent.

The fall of the Soviet Union and the disintegration of the Warsaw Pact opened new windows of opportunity for the neutral states Finland, Sweden, and Austria, which had abstained from membership in the EC/EU because of its genuine political ambitions and close links with NATO (Ekengren and Sundelius 1998; Jenssen et al. 1998). For Finland, it was a high priority to create as many strong ties as possible to the 'Western bloc'. In addition, Finland, and Sweden as well, experienced serious economic problems in the early 1990s. Against this background, the new 'single market EC' emerged as an increasingly attractive alternative (Jenssen et al. 1998). The first stage was an agreement between the EC and EFTA in 1992 on the EEA, which in fact made the EFTA countries part of the EC's internal market. However, almost simultaneously to this event, Sweden and Finland both submitted membership applications to the EC (Pesonen et al. 1998). Afraid of becoming politically and economically marginalized, Norway followed shortly after (Tamnes 1997). The accession negotiations were completed in March 1994, soon after the EEA agreement had come into force. All countries arranged a referendum on the membership issue that same year.

Table 9.1 shows that 56.9 per cent supported membership in Finland, 52.3 per cent did the same in Sweden, while only a minority of 47.7 per cent approved Norwegian participation in the EU. Thus, a Norwegian government had suffered a defeat on the issue for the second time. Part of the explanation may be found in the fact that the Norwegian economy was not in the same bad shape as the Finnish and Swedish economies, due to the revenues from petroleum resources. However, this very popular explanation of the deviant case of Norway should not be assigned too much weight. The reason is that the voting pattern was amazingly similar to the pattern that emerged in the 1972 referendum, that is at a time when the so-called 'oil adventure' had not yet started. On both occasions, a centre-periphery dimension, both in geographical and social terms, was highly present: the pro-votes were first and foremost found in the southern and most densely populated urban areas and among the more wealthy, better educated and male parts of the population (Jenssen et al. 1998; Tamnes 1997).

The Norwegian voting pattern in 1994 was not only mirroring the 1972 referendum; it was also quite similar to the pattern found in the Finnish and Swedish 1994 referendums (Jenssen et al. 1998). Thus, when Sweden happened to become a member of the EU, while Norway did not, this might well be due to the more extensive centralization policy that had been exercised in Sweden for a long time. In all three countries, EU membership was first and foremost discussed as a domestic issue in the sense that the main question raised was: 'What is in the country's best interest?' Only marginally did the debate touch upon issues like the organization of the European system of governance or its future development (Jenssen et al. 1998; Johansson 2002).

The EU members Denmark and Sweden are not part of the Economic and Monetary Union (EMU). The EFTA countries Iceland and Norway (and Liechtenstein) had to build their relationship to the EU on the EEA agreement which had come into force from January 1994. The EEA countries are made part of the EU's internal market, and this means that they have to incorporate all EU legislation of relevance to the market project (that is the bulk of the Union's directives and regulations). Important exemptions were, however, made as regards agriculture and fisheries. On the other hand, other fields of cooperation were added, such as research, education, culture, environment, and consumer affairs. Like Denmark, Finland, and Sweden, Iceland and Norway are also signatories to the Schengen agreement on police and border control cooperation. In addition, Norway has established close cooperation with the EU on CFSP (Claes and Fossum 2002).

Although being obliged to incorporate the EU's internal market legislation into their national legislation, the EEA countries enjoy rather limited rights of participation in the legislative process. Officials from EEA countries may attend relevant preparatory committees in the Commission as well as a number of comitology (implementation) committees. It follows, however, from the non-membership status that EEA nationals are absent from both the College of Commissioners, the European Parliament, and the Council of the EU. From an organizational perspective, one could hypothesize that the EEA countries, due to their exclusion from the Council, could become less coordinated and integrated domestically (Egeberg and Trondal 1999). On the other hand, political parties may not have the same opportunities for transnational coalition building and,

Table 9.2 Nordic countries: formal forms of association to the EU

	EU member	Schengen	CFSP	EMU	EEA
Finland	X	X	X	X	
Sweden	X	X	X		
Denmark	X	X			
Norway		(X)	(X)		X
Iceland		(X)			X

(X): Limited access to the policy making process.

thus, potentially bypassing their governments, in these countries. Table 9.2 summarizes the Nordic countries' various formal forms of association to the EU. Taking into consideration the 'opt-outs' among the member states and the peculiar agreements of the EEA countries, 'differentiated integration (or membership)' might possibly be a more proper term than the simple 'membership-non-membership dichotomy' (Stubb 1996; Egeberg and Trondal 1999).

Bottom-up processes: aiming at influencing EU level policy-making

For analytical purposes it may be wise to distinguish between bottom-up and top-down processes in order to understand EU–member states dynamics. In practice, however, the two are interwoven in a highly complex manner. For example, bottom-up processes, in which national actors strive to have an impact on EU level policy making, are themselves profoundly shaped by the institutional configuration and opportunity structure found at the EU level (cf. Chapter 1 in this volume; Hix and Goetz 2000). With this in mind, this section will focus on the efforts of the respective national governments, parliaments, political parties and interest groups to influence EU level policy making. The next section on top-down processes will deal explicitly with how the EU level impacts on politics, institutions, and policies at the national level.

Nordic governments

Due to the EU's broad agenda, most central government units in the Nordic countries are affected by the Union's activities (Lægreid et al. 2002). In order to cope with the European challenge, increased personnel resources have been allocated to this task, however, the institutional structure has remained basically unchanged.

Like in other non-Nordic member states, the typical organizational solution seems to have been to integrate EU-related tasks into those units that already deal with the respective issue areas (Jacobsson et al. 2001). Thus, for example, EU transport infrastructure issues have been assigned to the unit in national transport ministries that deal with these kind of issues on a daily basis. This practice expresses clearly that EU politics is, to a very large extent, also domestic politics: it is hard to see how EU issues could be meaningfully put into separate units, or concentrated in, for example, the foreign ministry. In many ministries and agencies, however, an 'EU coordinator' has been appointed in order to have a person dedicated to monitoring the flow of EU-related issues within the institution (Lægreid 2001).

The most visible organizational change that has taken place in the Nordic governments probably is the erection of committee structures for coordinating national EU policies. Denmark, already an EC/EU member from 1973, naturally first embarked on this road. At the lowest level are the thirty-five (at the beginning, eighteen) Special Committees, largely reflecting the remits of the Commission's directorates general (von Dosenrode 1998; Pedersen 2000; Christensen 2002). For example, the Special Committee on Environment is chaired by the Ministry of Environment and has representatives from the most affected ministries, agencies, and also interest groups (see below). The Ministry of Foreign Affairs may participate on all committees. The respective lead ministries are in charge of drafting a proposal on what should be the Danish position on Commission policy initiatives, and, in most cases, the national position is agreed upon at the Special Committee level (Pedersen 2000). If conflicting views can not be reconciled at this level, however, the dispute is referred to the level above, the so-called EU Committee. It is composed of the secretaries general of the nine most affected ministries and chaired by the foreign ministry's top official. Finally, at the political level, the ministers most concerned have their Cabinet committee on EU affairs. In practice, most conflicts that are not solved at the Special Committee level have to be referred further to the Cabinet Committee for a final decision, probably because they are of a highly politicized nature (Pedersen 1996).

In order to prepare and coordinate the negotiations on the EEA Agreement, Norway in 1988 established a coordination structure that is a blueprint of the Danish arrangement (Sverdrup 1998). However, since Norway did not become a member of the EU, and, therefore, was not entitled to participation in the Council of the Union, the level of activity never reached the same level as in the Danish apparatus (Egeberg and Trondal 1999). Also the Finns erected a quite parallel coordination structure, consisting of thirty-eight groups at the lowest level (Lægreid 2001). Only the Swedes went their own way in this respect, relying on a more ad hoc and informal network of committees, although with a permanent coordinating committee in the Ministry of Foreign Affairs. At the political level, a group composed of state secretaries from the most affected ministries convenes regularly (Ekengren and Sundelius 1998; Lægreid 2001).

An observation pertaining to most member states is that prime ministers play an increasingly central role in EU matters, a tendency reflected in growing organizational resources for their offices. In general, however, foreign ministries retain an important role, although in all the member states they find themselves in a position of relative decline (Kassim *et al.* 2000). This development mirrors the fact that most topics on the EU's agenda deal with highly domestic issues in the sense that these are issues normally taken care of by others than foreign ministries. The fact that this organizational adaptation has not taken place earlier tells a lot about the inherent robustness of existing institutional arrangements. It may, however, also reflect that, at least some, governments have been eager to retain a definition of EU relations as 'foreign policy' and in this way signalling their support to a basically intergovernmental, nation-state based, political order. While pursuing *national* interests is at the core of foreign ministries' mission, prime ministers are, arguably, more used to launch *party* political programmes, for example, on the role of the public sector in the economy. Accordingly, among the Nordic member states, the transfer of responsibility for coordinating EU policies from the foreign ministry to the prime minister's office has been more significant in Finland and Sweden than in Denmark; probably the most EU sceptical of the three (Jacobsson et al. 2001; von Dosenrode 1998).

We have just learned how the Nordic countries have set up an apparatus within their national administrations in order to coordinate their respective policies towards the EU. It remains to be seen, however, whether these arrangements actually result in coherent action or not. Empirical studies show that the extent to which a member state behaves consistently in its relationship to the Union depends heavily on the kind of EU institution it deals with. Thus, Table 9.3 reveals big differences between Commission-related behaviour and Council-related action respectively.

Those attending meetings in Council working parties clearly have to consult the ministry of foreign affairs (MFA) or other relevant ministries on which policy position to take much more frequently than those on Commission expert committees. It is also much more common for the former to have clear instructions about how to behave. In fact, it seems to be a matter of routine to endow participants with a clarified mandate before they attend Council meetings while this appears to be far from the case in relation to the Commission. This pattern is strongly confirmed by studies that

Table 9.3 Percentage of Scandinavian national officials who agree on the following assertions:

	Domestic officials		Permanent representatives	
Assertions	EC	WP	EC	WP
'I have to coordinate with the MFA or with other central coordinating units'	15	49	19	57
'My position has been coordinated with all relevant ministries'	26	61	29	74
'I have clear instructions as to what positions to follow in EU committees'	27	64	24	59

Note: The table is based on 209 returned questionnaires from Danish, Norwegian, and Swedish officials participating in expert committees in the Commission (ECs) and Council working parties (WPs) respectively. (WPs are only relevant for Danish and Swedish respondents.) 'Domestic (home-based) officials' were drawn from two sectors; environment and the occupational health and safety sectors. 'Permanent representatives' were drawn from the three countries' staff at the Permanent Representations in Brussels.
Source: Trondal 2001: 158, 163.

also cover several non-Scandinavian member states, as well as other policy sectors (Egeberg 1999; Egeberg et al. 2003). Thus, as argued in the theoretical part of this chapter, the Council setting, due to its territorial structure, seems to foster policy coordination and consistency at the national level, that is domestic integration. Accordingly, Jacobsson (1999) observed that the Swedish accession to the EU entailed an increased demand for *Swedish* policy positions: through EU participation, sector experts not used to think in terms of national interests became aware of their *national* identities. Also as hypothesized, however, the separate executive role assigned to the Commission tends to split national administrations so that they also assume the role as part of the EU administration as far as policy development and implementation are concerned. Member state officials (never executive politicians) are invited to particip- ate in committees, and their travel and accommodation costs are covered by the Commission. These officials furnish the EU executive with valuable expertise and information on their respective governments' policy orientations within various policy fields, thus contributing to the *Commission*'s policy work. Studies reveal that national civil servants show a lot of confidence in the Commission officials with whom they interact (Egeberg 1999; Egeberg et al. 2003; Trondal 2001: 214). That national officials participate in a partly uncoordinated and independent way in this arena is also substantiated by the findings presented in Table 9.4. Again, Trondal's (2001) results from his Scandinavian study are paralleled by those from research including also other member countries (Egeberg 1999; Egeberg *et al.* 2003).

It may seem, however, as if Norwegian civil servants behave slightly differently. A study based on interviews with Commission officials who had served as committee chairpersons reported that Norwegian participants tend to be more concerned with making their national views heard than with contributing to common European solu- tions (Gudmundsen 2002). Although this kind of approach may be seen as somewhat inappropriate in this particular setting, it is nevertheless highly understandable since the Commission represents the only official channel through which Norwegian interests can be presented on a routine basis. If Norway acts as a lobbyist; however, it is also to some extent treated like a lobbyist: it carries the costs of participation itself,

Table 9.4 Percentage of Scandinavian national officials who perceive colleagues from other countries as 'independent experts' or 'government representatives'

	Domestic officials		Permanent representatives	
Colleagues' roles:	EC	WP	EC	WP
Mainly 'independent experts'	32	16	32	12
Mixed roles	38	16	41	5
Mainly 'government representatives'	30	68	27	83

Note: See Table 9.3
Source: Trondal 2001: 208.

and Norwegian (and other EEA) committee participants are usually seated together with interest groups and other private lobbyists in an open space *within* the rectangular meeting table. In spite of some observed efforts at coordinating and pursuing Norwegian national interests already at the Commission stage, however, the overall impression seems to be that also the Norwegian executive functions in a rather compartmentalized way and without much attention from its political masters in its relation to the Commission (Veggeland 2000). While the Council structure provides a countervailing and integrating force within the member states, this is not the case for the EEA countries. Thus, the administrative systems of the latter may become relatively more disintegrated and fragmented in their relationships to EU institutions (Egeberg and Trondal 1999; Gudmundsen 2002).

Clearly, in general, role perceptions are more diffuse and relaxed in the Commission committees than within the Council structure (cf. Table 9.4). The considerable representation of expert orientations may be encouraged by the sectoral and functional organization of the Commission. In the Council context, the 'government representative' role dominates, although there apparently is some room for other allegiances as well, particularly among domestic sector personnel. This may be due to the functional and sectoral specialization of the working party system.

Does the EU level participation of Nordic governments matter? Do they succeed in making their views heard? According to their own judgement, they have, on the average, been relatively successful. More than half of the most affected ministry and agency departments report that their influence on policy-making in the Commission and the Council has been substantial (Esmark 2001: 127). However, there are huge differences among the states. First, the non-member Norway (and probably Iceland as well) lags far behind in this respect. This certainly pertains to Council policy making processes to which the EEA countries have no official access, although one has tried to compensate slightly for this by installing regular meetings between Norway, Denmark, and Sweden in advance of ministerial and Coreper meetings (Gudmundsen 2002; Larsen 2001: 184). It also, however, relates to Commission decision making, even if the Commission provides the only arena for the involvement of EEA countries on a regular basis in the EU's policy making processes. The reason could be that EEA countries lack the 'access points' that member states may have via their respective compatriots found at the College, cabinet and administrative levels. Although Commission personnel at all levels are supposed to act on behalf of the Commission (and they increasingly seem to do so) and not on behalf of their country of origin, they, nevertheless, tend to facilitate interaction with their respective compatriots; for example for linguistic reasons (Nugent 2001). Even participation in expert committees is seen as far less influential by Norwegian respondents than by their Nordic counterparts (Esmark 2001). This may be partly due to the fact that participants from EEA countries may lack some of the strong personal ties that member state officials might be able to build up. The latter, who also see each other frequently at Council working party meetings, have more opportunities for informal networking outside the conference rooms (Trondal 2001: 138).

Second, influence appears to be unevenly distributed not only between member states and EEA countries, but also among member governments themselves. A significantly higher proportion of Danish administrative units assess their impact as satisfactory compared to their counterparts in the other Nordic member countries

(Esmark 2001). In this case, the underlying dimension is probably length of membership. Having been a member for thirty years, the Danish executive has been in a position to accumulate considerable knowledge on how the EU system works, and to develop a wide net of informal and personal relationships. Obviously, this pays off with respect to power and influence in the Union's decision making processes. Although not that influential, the Swedish government seems, nevertheless, to have championed policies on transparency, the environment and employment with some success (Miles 2000; Johansson 2002).

Nordic parliaments

While national governments have their well-defined points of access to the EU level of decision making in the Council structure, national parliaments lack institutional arenas in which to operate at the Union level. Arguably, the main reason is that the EU's (quasi-) federal structure resembles first and foremost the German polity, which is characterized by a second legislative chamber composed of representatives of the regional (constituent) *governments* rather than of the regional parliaments, as we find in Austria. Given the strong role of the nation-state in people's mind, it may be democratically justifiable that national governments rather than parliaments take care of the 'sub-territorial' representation at the EU level. After all, only national *governments* are entitled to speak on behalf of countries as such. In the European Parliament, however, voters are directly represented via political parties, as is the case in (the first chamber of) national parliaments.

On this background, the role of national parliaments in EU policy-making depends on the extent to which they are able to influence their respective governments and hold ministers accountable as regards EU-related decision-making. The role of national parliaments thus has to be *indirect* under the current institutional conditions. In order to have as much influence as possible, however, all Nordic member state parliaments have assigned responsibility to a particular committee in this respect. The Danish parliament's European Affairs Committee dates from 1973 when Denmark entered the Community and has, in general, been seen as a successful device for parliamentary control. It convenes every week ahead of meetings in the EU's Council of Ministers, and is entitled to impose instructions on ministers on how Danish interests are to be interpreted and pursued. The committee routinely receives legislative proposals from the Commission and the agenda of the Council of Ministers. It may request a memorandum from the government on any case it wishes. These memoranda provide information on a directive's content, legal basis, relation to existing Danish law, and financial and economic consequences (von Dosenrode 1998).

The Swedish Parliament's Advisory Committee on European Affairs was modelled on the Danish committee in most respects. The government's positions in up-coming Council sessions are presented and discussed, but the committee is not entitled to instruct ministers (Ekengren and Sundelius 1998). Contrary to the Danes and the Swedes, the Finns chose to charge an already existing parliamentary body, the Grand Committee, with the main responsibility for EU-related matters. Also, the standing committees of the Finnish parliament were afforded an influential role from the very beginning. Draft legislation from the Commission is simultaneously forwarded to the Grand Committee and to one or several specialized committees. The latter, in which detailed, sectoral knowledge is often available, prepare an opinion, and the Grand Committee seldom deviates from it. The Grand Committee does not share the Danish committee's right to impose a clear mandate on ministers. However, since the Grand Committee does not have to rely on the government for 'expert' knowledge to the same degree as the other parliaments' EU committees, it is considered to be the most influential among them (Raunio and Wiberg 2000; Hegeland and Neuhold 2002).

Concerning the EEA countries Iceland and Norway, the parliaments do not even have an indirect role to play at the EU level. Since the governments of these states are not allowed to participate in the Council, the usual occasions for bringing parliaments in are simply not there. However, the EEA Committee that was set up in the Norwegian parliament prior to the 1994 referendum in the event that Norway joined the Union is still there. The committee consists of the members of the Foreign Affairs Committee, complemented by the Norwegian representatives to the EEA Joint Parliamentary Committee. The EEA committee may be consulted by the government regarding policy issues in which the government strives to influence EU decision-making more informally. However, the committee's main function is related to implementing EU legislation at the national level. The Icelandic parliament has assigned EU-related tasks to its Foreign Affairs Committee (Raunio and Wiberg 2000).

Nordic political parties

Modern governments are party-based. In that sense, political parties connect to the international level when governments act internationally. In this case, however, parties are not represented in their own right. National political parties, including Nordic ones, have, however, for a long time taken part in transnational party federations and cooperation with sister parties in other countries. This kind of networks has made national parties less dependent upon information and ideas provided by their respective governments and embassies, bodies that might be under the control of rival parties (Heidar and Svåsand 1997). Arguably, the EU has profoundly changed the role and relevance of transnational party cooperation. Direct elections to the European Parliament (EP) from 1979, and extended use of the co-decision procedure (involving both the EP and the Council) in EU policy-making, have provided an unprecedented arena for European level party politics. The Nordic Council and the parliamentary assemblies of organizations like the Council of Europe and NATO may have facilitated transnational cooperation among parties. However, it is probably right to say that the rather modest role assigned to these parliamentary assemblies in the decision making process has created few incentives for real coordination among national parties.

Political parties from the Nordic member countries are affiliated to all the major party groups in the EP; the group of socialists and social democrats, the group of christian democrats and conservatives, the group of liberals and the group of left wing socialists. The Norwegian social democrats and conservatives take part in their respective European federations, but obviously not in these federations' counterparts in the EP; that is the EP party groups (Heidar et al. 1997). Among the factors explaining the involvement of national parties at the European level are their organizational resources, their attitudes on European integration and the availability of a relevant 'party family' (Bille and Christoffersen 1997). Over time, Nordic parties have devoted more personnel resources to their international activities, and, among these activities, participation in the EP has achieved the absolutely highest priority (Bille and Christoffersen 1997; Jerneck 1997).

EP party groups are remarkably cohesive. They are less cohesive than party groups in the legislatures of the member states, but more unitary than parties in the US Congress (Raunio 2002). Although the formation of transnational party groups benefits from secretarial and financial resources made available by the EP, EP group chairs dispose of few rewards and punishments. For example, they do not control or even influence candidate selection. Instead, common positions emerge through consensual decision making, with groups working hard to hammer out positions that are acceptable to all or nearly all parties in the group (Hix 1999; Raunio 2002). In practice, then, EP party groups are the central mechanisms for structuring debate and coalition-formation in the EP. Since the EP is dominated by two groups; the European Peoples Party (christian democrats/conservatives) and the Party of European Socialists (social democrats and socialists), voting most commonly reflects the left-right dimension (Hix 1999). The important implication is that national parties become parts of transnational ideological coalitions *across* member countries. Opposition parties thus also have their own route to EU policy making, bypassing their own governments. This kind of transnational role assumed by national political parties can be most clearly observed among Danish parties, the Nordic parties supposed to be most familiar with Union politics (Heidar et al. 1997).

Nordic interest groups

National interest groups have multiple tracks to EU level policy making. First, they may work indirectly through their governments. Secondly, they may contact EU institutions directly in order to present their concerns. However, since EU institutions, and particularly the Commission, for obvious reasons prefer to deal with European level groups, a third option is to go indirectly through such a European association in which the national group is a member (Mazey and Richardson 1996). Interest groups in the Nordic countries use all these routes. Historically, there have been, across policy fields, relatively strong ties between national authorities and different kinds of interest organizations. EU-related issues seem to have been incorporated into these already established relationships. In Denmark, interest groups have also become formal members of the government's coordination committees for EU-related issues, that is the Special Committees (see above) (Pedersen 2001; Christensen 2002). We might expect national groups to work through their governments in situations where they perceive their interests to be nationally based.

Nordic member country associations are directly represented in the Economic and Social Committee (ECOSOC) of the Union. For example, Swedish interest groups dispose of twelve of the 222 seats in ECOSOC. ECOSOC is, however, considered to be too peripheral in the EU decision making process, and too cumbersome as well, to be of any real interest (Karlsson 2000). When it comes to membership in European level groups, a study of Danish national associations (N = 1316) unveiled that 36 per cent were members. Membership was, however, rather unevenly distributed among groups: while about half of the economic (business and labour) interest groups were members, this holds for only 27 per cent of associations within other areas of societal life. The former conceive of themselves as much more affected by the Union's policies than the latter, however (Sidenius 1998). European level associations also normally welcome the participation of groups originating from non-member countries. Thus, Norwegian interest organizations share this channel of representation with member country associations.

Transnational federations of interest groups have existed for a long time, and their activity covers much more than the EU. However, parallel to what was argued as regards political parties, the political relevance of EU institutions tends to encourage the formation of more governable transnational associations than usually found. Since most interest groups are organized along sectoral and functional lines, they also easily identify their 'counterparts' within the sectorally and functionally arranged Commission, or in the specialized committees of the EP. The above study of Danish national interest groups showed that going through European level associations in order to promote their interests is clearly more common than working through Danish authorities (Sidenius 1998). A clear majority of those being members of European level associations considered these to be important both as regards the supply of information and regarding their ability to impact on EU policy making. Moreover, an overwhelming majority states that European level associations have increased in importance since 1985 (Sidenius 1998). Increased importance may be partly due to an enhanced ability to formulate coherent positions on Commission policy proposals. For example, a general tendency within business organizations to base membership on individual companies rather than on national associations, and to introduce majority voting rather than to require unanimity, have been highly conducive to this development (Knill 2001b). Still, however, a lack of resources and autonomy make European level associations less governable than comparable national organizations (Greenwood 2002). Nevertheless, interest groups might, like political parties (see above), forge viable coalitions *across* member countries through their European level associations. Since most groups champion sectoral and functional interests, coalitions may come to encompass sectorally or functionally based divisions of the Commission, and/or the relevant sectorally specialized committee of the EP.

Top-down processes: how the EU impacts on the domestic level

Becoming a part of the EU (in one way or another) alters profoundly the institutional frame within which a country finds itself. In this section we ask what the consequences are for 'domestic' politics, the structuring of particular institutions, and the policies being adopted.

How domestic politics is affected

How the Union impacts on 'domestic' politics has already been extensively dealt with in the previous section. As already argued, bottom-up and top-down processes are in practice highly interwoven. The politics of 'up-loading' policies to the EU level (cf. the previous section) can only be adequately accounted for by taking into consideration the institutional context present at the EU level. The most important observation made so far is that the existence of EU level institutions may foster new patterns of cooperation and conflict; patterns that cut *across* national political systems. First, we have seen that the division of work between the Council and the Commission has imposed two separate roles on national governments. According to the one role, executives are supposed to serve their respective parliaments and pursue what has been defined as national interests. The other role makes national administrations almost a part of an 'EU administration', expecting them to deliver both policy-relevant expertise and efficient implementation.

Second, it has been observed that the embryonic bicameralism of the EU legislature offers no direct point of access to the decision making process for national parliaments. Arguably, this strengthens national governments in relation to parliaments since the former also have 'their' institution at the Union level; that is the Council. Third, we have seen that reforms of the EP have been highly conducive to developing more coherent and governable EP party groups. Thus, ideological cleavages along partisan lines that cut across member countries occur more often than before. Although national parliaments may see their legislative role diminished, political parties, in position as well as opposition, are offered additional arenas at the European level. And, finally, it has been advocated that the significance of EU institutions, and the fact that the Commission, and, partly the EP, are organized according to sector and function, has encouraged the formation of more governable EU level interest groups. As a consequence, transnational sectoral and functional coalitions emerge with higher frequency. Thus, although EU level policy-making has narrowed the scope for government-group negotiations at the national level, Union institutions provide new channels and venues for organized interests.

Institutional adaptation at the national level

According to a broad survey study of Danish institutions, European integration has primarily left its marks on central government; very little institutional adaptation seems to have occurred at the regional and local level (Beck Jørgensen 2002). As far as the central level is concerned, however, the EU is considered to be an important trigger behind organizational and procedural reforms, and, particularly so in the relatively new member states Finland and Sweden, in which the EU is in fact seen as the main 'change agent' (Lægreid 2001). In the 'bottom-up section' we have already seen how the Nordic governments on their own have coped with the European project institutionally. EU related issues have, as a main rule, been incorporated into already existing administrative structures, although additional personnel resources have been provided. The most visible voluntary adaptation has probably been the erection of committee structures for coordinating EU-related national policy-making. Similarly, the parliaments in Denmark, Norway, and Sweden have, as shown, established European affairs committees.

Although EU policies in most areas have to be implemented by the constituent governments themselves, it is probably right to say that the Commission has not yet formulated a common, full-fledged public administration policy (Sverdrup 2002). There certainly are some EU standards pertaining to 'good administration', for example merit-based recruitment, due procedures, and implementation capacity (Goetz 2001). This kind of requirement may represent a serious challenge to many new applicant countries, however, they hardly form a workable template for administrative design in the more advanced member states (Olsen 2003). Nevertheless, if one takes a closer look at some of the directives, one will, within certain areas, find rather precise guidelines on administrative arrangements; for example on the set-up of regulatory agencies in the transport, communication, and foodstuff sectors. And monopolies, like the state alcohol monopolies in Finland, Norway, and Sweden, are at the outset banned by EU law. While import monopolies were abolished, those on retailing survived due to public health concerns (Ugland 2002).

The main conclusion to be drawn from studies of institutional adaptation in Denmark and Norway seems to be that Europeanization has been incremental and step-wise, and heavily constrained by existing administrative traditions (Sverdrup 1998; Pedersen 2002). However, older institutions display more robustness than younger ones, and highly integrated and coherent policy sectors are less subject to change than those with the opposite characteristics (Marcussen and Ronit 2002; Ugland 2002). Studies of Swedish adaptation, on the other hand, reveal some clash between EU style and Swedish administrative culture. The high pace of decision making in the Council has, according to Ekengren and Sundelius (1998), challenged the Swedish logic of appropriate procedure. There is simply not time available to erect committees broadly composed of experts and affected parties in order to provide an extensive policy report.

Policy adaptation at the national level

While the responses of national institutions to the EU's development seem in general to diverge considerably, observers seem to agree that significant policy convergence takes place simultaneously (Olsen 2003). If true, this may represent a challenge to institutional and organizational theory since it usually postulates there is a clear relationship between structure and decision behaviour. However, it might very well be that national institutions still primarily match *national* and 'bottom-up' policy making processes (which are probably seen as more important) rather than 'top-down' implementation processes. In that case, the observed mismatch makes sense.

Research shows that the average deficit in transposition of Community legislation into national legislation in the period from 1997 to 2001 has decreased from 7.5 per cent to 2 per cent. The Nordic countries, member states as well as non-members, are performing even better with a deficit of less than 1 per cent (Sverdrup 2004). Regarding conflicts over non-implementation, the Nordic states pursue a more consensus seeking approach, with limited use of courts, than the EU average. This pattern may be due to a more consensual policy style supposed to be found in general in the Nordic countries (Sverdrup 2004; Richardson 1982).

No policy sector in the Nordic countries seems completely unaffected by the EU. However, the extent to which policy adjustment has taken place varies a lot across areas. Focusing on pillar I issues, the Union has left its marks most clearly on agricultural, transport, communication, industry, energy, and environmental policies (Lægreid 2001). As a consequence, market solutions have probably become more prevalent in the communication, transport and energy sectors (Claes and Tranøy 1999). Since the EEA agreement leaves out agriculture and fisheries, the EEA countries are obviously not particularly affected in these areas. However, in all other respects, it makes little policy difference if a country is a full member state or an EEA country (Claes and Tranøy 1999). The same is probably true as regards Schengen policies. Concerning pillar II issues, the Finnish and Swedish policy of 'non-alignment' has, according to observers, been subject to remarkable changes subsequent to the countries' involvement in the CFSP (Miles 2000).

Conclusion

We have seen that, in most cases, the Nordic countries' relationship to the EC or EU has been a highly contentious issue. Two countries are not full members, and 'opt-outs' prevail among member states. Notably, Denmark and Sweden are not in the euro-zone, whereas Finland is. Political parties, interest organizations, and councils of ministers (cabinets) have been deeply split, also internally, on the European issue. Thus, the usually more pro-integrationist elites have been afforded narrow mandates for acting at the EU level. Except for Finland, therefore, the Nordic countries are for the most part associated with the more reluctant Europeans. The distinctive Finnish enthusiasm and involvement on all dimensions can probably be accounted for by taking into consideration the 'special relationship' with the former Soviet Union during the cold war. In that sense accession opened up a new era for Finnish foreign policy. The presence of a broad consensus behind European policy—with no political party opposing membership of EMU—sets Finland apart from Sweden and Denmark (see Tiilikainen 2003).

When we in this chapter ask whether European integration integrates or disintegrates countries domestically, we are not thinking of whether the EU generates conflicts or not among domestic political actors; it certainly does. What we have in mind is whether a political system that becomes part of a larger whole continues to act relatively coherently in relation to its environments, or, whether new patterns of cooperation and conflict that cut *across* national boundaries emerge. According to an intergovernmental perspective, nation-states will be able to aggregate divergent interests internally and to 'upload' these in a consistent manner, and, may even be strengthened in this role. Thus, the expectation is that European integration fuels domestic integration simultaneously. From an institutional and multi-level governance perspective, on the other hand, preference and identity formation is a 'two-way process', and transnational coalitions that bypass national governments might well emerge. From an organizational perspective, however, both developments are plausible, depending on the institutional constellation present at the EU level.

Clearly, the EU Council represents an integrating force at the domestic level. In the Nordic member countries on which we have data, Council participation is characterized by national coordination among government departments, parliament, and interest groups. Had it not been for the fact that the EU also consists of institutions based on non-territorial principles of specialization, intergovernmentalists would have been mainly right. First, the pure existence of the Commission and its executive functions assign an additional role to national governments; namely that of becoming part of a *European* administration as well. In this capacity, we have seen that Nordic officials experience ambiguous role expectations and tend to act relatively independently from national coordinators. Second, due to the sectoral and functional organization of the Commission, it seems to underpin administrative segmentation at the national level, and encourage transnational coalitions of interest groups. From the available data, we have seen that Nordic organized interests increasingly prefer to approach EU level policy making through their respective European level associations. And, third, due to the growing role of the EP, Nordic political parties get more involved in transnational party coalitions. In sum, there are thus clear signs that European integration also might decompose national political systems. As argued in the introduction, one could indeed perceive of profound transformation of the existing state order as precisely the process whereby EU institutions manage to redirect patterns of cooperation and conflict so that these patterns also cut across national borders. Looking for institutional or policy convergence or divergence across countries in this respect might be less fruitful. After all, national institutions and policies have for centuries been more or less Europeanized *within* a Westphalian political order of sovereign states.

Parallel to observations made in other member states, policies tend to converge more than institutional forms in the Nordic states (both members and non-members) as well. For example, the coordination structures installed by governments and parliaments are not exactly the same. In these respects it doesn't seem to matter whether a country is a full EU member or not. However, we have seen that a state's form of association with the Union does have a say as far as participation and influence at the EU level are concerned.

Acknowledgement

I am grateful to Ulf Sverdrup and other colleagues at ARENA for their comments.

Further reading

Jenssen *et al.* (1998) covers much of the history and politics of the European issue in the Nordic countries. Jacobsson et al. (2001; 2003) compare EU adaptation by the governments of Denmark, Finland, Norway and Sweden. Amongst the chapter-studies available on particular countries and their relationships to the EU are: Ekengreen and Sundelius (1998) on Sweden; Sverdrup (1998) on Norway and von Dosenrode (1998) on Denmark. The literature on Finland is a little sparser but see Tiilikainen (1998). Also see the chapters on Denmark, Finland and Sweden in Wessels, Maurer and Mittag (2003).

Weblinks

Access to the Danish Government with links is available at <http://www.statsministeriet.dk>; access to the Finnish Government with links is at <http://www.statsradet.fi>; the Icelandic Government site is at: <http://www.brunnur.stjr.is>. The Norwegian Government site is accessed via <http://www.odin.dep.no>. Finally, access to the Swedish Government is at: <http://www.sweden.gov.se>. Another useful site is that of the European Free Trade Association (EFTA): <http://www.efta.int>. Finally, a fuller set of links can be obtained from the EU gateway to member states at: <http://europa.eu.int/abc/ governments/index_en.htm>.

References

Andersen, S. S., and Eliassen, K. (2001), 'Informal Processes: Lobbying, Actor Strategies, Coalitions and Dependencies', in S. S. Andersen, and K. A. Eliassen (eds), *Making Policy in Europe* (London: Sage).

Aspinwall, M., and Schneider, G. (2000), 'Same Menu, Separate Tables: The Institutionalist Turn in Political Science and the Study of European Integration', *European Journal of Political Research*, 38, 1–36.

Beck Jørgensen, T. (2002), 'Forvaltningsinternationalisering i dag. En oversigt over former og udbredelse', in Marcussen and Ronit.

Bille, L., and Christoffersen, C. (1997), 'De danske partiers internationale forbindelser' in Heidar and Svåsand.

Bulmer, S. J. (1994), 'The Governance of the European Union: A New Institutional Approach', *Journal of Public Policy*, 13, 351–80.

Caporaso, J. A., Green Cowles, M., and Risse,T. (eds) (2001), *Europeanization and Domestic Change* (Ithaca NY: Cornell University Press).

Christensen, J. G. (2002), 'Den fleksible og robuste forvltning', in Marcussen and Ronit.

Claes, D. H., and Fossum, J. E. (2002), 'Norway, the EEA and Neo-Liberal Globalism', in

S. Clarkson, and M. G. Cohen (eds), *Governance on the Edge: Australia, Canada, Mexico and Norway under Globalism* (London: Zed Books).

Claes, D. H., and Tranøy, B. S. (1999) (eds), *Utenfor, annerledes og suveren? Norge under EØS-avtalen* (Bergen: Fagbokforlaget).

Egeberg, M. (1999), 'Transcending Intergovernmentalism? Identity and Role Perceptions of National Officials in EU Decision-Making', *Journal of European Public Policy*, 6, 456–74.

Egeberg, M. (2004), 'An Organisational Approach to European Integration. Outline of a Complementary Perspective', *European Journal of Political Research*, 43, 199–219.

Egeberg, M., Schaefer, G. F., and Trondal, J. (2003), 'The Many Faces of EU Committee Governance', *West European Politics*, 26 (July), 19–14.

Egeberg, M., and Trondal, J. (1999), 'Differentiated Integration in Europe: The Case of EEA Country, Norway', *Journal of Common Market Studies*, 37, 133–42.

Ekengren, M., and Sundelius, B. (1998), 'Sweden: The State Joins the European Union', in Hanf and Soetendorp.

Eriksen, K. E., and Pharo, H. Ø. (1997), *Kald krig og internasjonalisering, 1949–1965. Norsk utenrikspolitisk historie, Bind 5* (Oslo: Universitetsforlaget).

Esmark, A. (2001), 'Mod en transnational forvaltning?', in Jacobsson *et al.*

Goetz, K. H. (2001), 'Making Sense of Post-Communist Central Administration: Modernization, Europeanization or Latinization?', *Journal of European Public Policy*, 8, 1032–51.

Greenwood, J. (2002), *Inside the EU Business Associations* (Basingstoke: Palgrave).

Greenwood, J., and Aspinwall, M. (1998) (eds), *Collective Action in the European Union. Interests and the New Politics of Associability* (London: Routledge).

Gudmundsen, J. O. (2002), 'Statskonsult on Improving Performance in EU Committees: EEA EFTA Participation in the Shaping of EEA Legislation', *Efta Bulletin*, no 1, 2001.

Hanf, K., and Soetendorp, B. (1998) (eds), *Adapting to European Integration. Small States and the European Union* (London: Longman).

Hayes-Renshaw, F., and Wallace, H. (1997), *The Council of Ministers* (New York: St Martin's Press).

Hegeland, H., and Neuhold, C. (2002), 'Parliamentary Participation in EU Affairs in Austria, Finland and Sweden: Newcomers with Different Approaches', *European Integration online Papers (EioP)*, 6 <http://eiop.or.at/eiop/texte/2002-010a.htm>.

Heidar, K., Pettersen, H. C., and Svåsand, L. (1997), 'Internasjonalt partisamarbeid', in Heidar and Svåsand.

Heidar, K., and Svåsand, L. (1997) (eds), *Partier uten grenser?* (Oslo: Tano).

Hix, S. (1999), *The Political System of the European Union* (Houndmills: Macmillan Press).

Hix, S., and Goetz, K. H. (2000), 'Introduction: European Integration and National Political Systems', *West European Politics*, 23, 1–26.

Hooghe, L., and Marks, G. (2001), *Multi-level Governance and European Integration* (Lanham: Rowman & Littlefield).

Jacobsson, B. (1999), 'Europeiseringen och statens omvandling', in K. Goldmann, J. Hallenberg, B. Jacobsson, U. Mörth, and A. Robertson, *Politikens internationalisering* (Lund: Studentlitteratur).

Jacobsson, B., Lægreid, P., and Pedersen, O. K. (2003), *Europeanisation and Transitional States* (London: Routledge).

Jacobsson, B., Lægreid, P., and Pedersen, O. K. (2001) (eds), *Europaveje. EU i de nordiske centralforvaltninger* (Copenhagen: Jurist- og Økonomforbundets Forlag).

Jenssen, A. T., Gilljam, M., and Pesonen, P. (1998), 'The Citizens, the Referendums and the European Union', in Jenssen *et al.* (1998).

Jenssen, A. T., Pesonen, P., and Gilljam, M. (1998) (eds), *To Join or not to Join: Three Nordic Referendums on Membership in the European Union* (Oslo: Scandinavian University Press).

Jerneck, M. (1997), 'De svenska partiernas utlandsförbindelser—från internationalisering til europeisering?', in Heidar and Svåsand.

Johansson, K. M. (2002) (ed.), *Sverige i EU* (Stockholm: SNS Förlag).

Karlsson, M. (2000), 'Swedish Interest Groups and the EU', in Miles.

Kassim, H., Peters, B. G., and Wright, V. (2000) (eds), *The National Co-ordination of EU Policy. The Domestic Level* (Oxford: Oxford University Press).

Knill, C. (2001a), *The Europeanisation of National Administrations. Patterns of Institutional Change and Persistence* (Cambridge: Cambridge University Press).

Knill, C. (2001b), 'Private Governance across Multiple Arenas: European Interest Associations as Interface Actors', *Journal of European Public Policy*, 8, 227–46.

Knudsen, T. (2002), 'Fra Politicus til Politicus? Forvaltningsinternationalisering i et historisk perspektiv', in Marcussen and Ronit.

Kohler-Koch, B. (1996), 'The Strength of Weakness: The Transformation of Governance in the EU', in S. Gustavsson and L. Lewin (eds), *The Future of the Nation-State* (London: Routledge).

Larsen, G. (2001), 'Nordiske og internasjonale relasjoner', in Jacobsson *et al.*

Laursen, J. (1998), 'Det nordiske samarbejde som særvej? Kontinuitet og brud, 1945–73', in J. P. Olsen and B. O. Sverdrup (eds), *Europa i Norden. Europeisering av nordisk saamarbeid* (Oslo: Tano).

Lægreid, P. (2001), 'Organisasjonsformer: Robusthet og fleksibilitet', in Jacobsson et al.

Lægreid, P., Steinthorsson, R. S., and Thorhallsson, B. (2002), 'Europeanization of Public Administration: Change and Effects of Europeanization on the Central Administration in the Nordic States', *Paper presented at the EGOS Colloquium*, Barcelona.

Marcussen, M., and Ronit, K. (2002) (eds), *Internationaliseringen af den offentlige forvaltning i Danmark—robusthed og fleksibilitet* (Århus: Århus Universitetsforlag).

Mazey, S., and Richardson, J. (1996), 'The Logic of Organisation: Interest Groups', in J. Richardson (ed.), *European Union: Power and Policy-Making* (London: Routledge).

Miles, L. (2000) (ed.), *Sweden and the European Union Evaluated* (London: Continuum).

Moravcsik, A. (1998), *The Choice for Europe. Social Purpose and State Power from Messina to Maastricht* (London: UCL Press).

Nugent, N. (2001), *The European Commission* (Houndmills: Palgrave).

Olsen, J. P. (1992), 'Analyzing Institutional Dynamics', *Staatswissenschaften und Staatspraxis*, 3, 247–71.

Olsen, J. P. (2000), 'Organising European Institutions of Governance. A Prelude to an Institutional Account of Political Integration', in H. Wallace (ed.), *Whose Europe? Interlocking Dimensions of Integration* (London: Macmillan).

Olsen, J. P. (2003), 'Towards a European Administrative Space?', *Journal of European Public Policy*, 10, 506–31.

Pedersen, O. K. (2001), 'Interesseorganisationer og europæisk integration', in Jacobsson *et al.*

Pedersen, O. K. (2002) (ed.), *EU i forvaltningen—Broen fra Slotsholmen til Bruxelles* (Copenhagen: DJØF Forlag).

Pedersen, T. (1996), 'Denmark', in D. Rometsch, and W. Wessels (eds), *The European Union and Member States. Towards Institutional Fusion?* (Manchester: Manchester University Press).

Pedersen, T. (2000), 'Denmark', in Kassim *et al.*

Pesonen, P., Jenssen, A. T., and Gilljam, M. (1998), 'To Join or not to Join', in Jenssen *et al.*

Raunio, T. (2002), 'Political Interests: The EP's Party groups', in J. Peterson, and M. Shackleton (eds), *The Institutions of the European Union* (Oxford: Oxford University Press).

Raunio, T., and Wiberg, M. (2000), 'Parliaments' Adaptation to the European Union', in P. Esaiasson, and K. Heidar (eds), *Beyond Westminster and Congress: The Nordic Experience* (Columbus: Ohio State University Press).

Richardson, J. (1982) (ed.), *Policy Styles in Western Europe* (London: Allen & Urwin).

Sidenius, N. C. (1998), 'A Collective Action Problem? Danish Interest Associations and Euro Groups', in Greenwood and Aspinwall.

Stubb, A. C-G. (1996), 'A Categorization of Differentiated Integration', *Journal of Common Market Studies*, 34, 283–95.

Sverdrup, U. (1998), 'Norway: An Adaptive Non-Member', in Hanf and Soetendorp.

Sverdrup, U. (2002), 'Towards a European Union Public Administration Policy' (Oslo: ARENA manuscript).

Sverdrup, U. (2004), 'Compliance and Conflict Management in the European Union' *Scandinavian Political Studies*, 27, 23–43.

Tamnes, R. (1997), '*Oljealder 1965–1995*'. Norsk utenrikspolitikks historie bind 6 (Oslo: Universitetsforlaget).

Tiilikainen, T. (1998), *Europe and Finland, Defining the Political Identity of Finnland in Western Europe* (London: Ashgate).

Tiilikainen, T. (2003), 'Finland: smooth adaptation to European values and institutions', in Wessels, Maurer and Mittag, 150–65.

Trondal, J. (2001), *Administrative Integration across Levels of Governance. Integration through Participation in EU Committees* (Oslo: ARENA Report 01/7).

Ugland, T. (2002), *Policy-Recategorization and Integration—Europeanization of Nordic Alcohol Control Policies* (Oslo: ARENA Report 02/3).

Urwin, D. W. (1995), *The Community of Europe. A History of European Integration since 1945* (Harlow: Longman).

Veggeland, F. (2000), 'Delegering, låring og politisk kontroll: Norges deltakelse i EU-komiteer påveterinær- og næringsmiddelområdet', *Internasjonal politikk*, 58, 81–112.

von Dosenrode, S. Z. (1998), 'Denmark: The Testing of a Hesitant Membership', in Hanf and Soetendorp (1998).

Wessels, W., Maurer, A. and Mitley, J. (eds) (2003), *Fifteen into One? The European Union and its Member States* (Manchester: Manchester University Press).

Chapter 10

The Europeanization of Austria and Ireland: Small can be Difficult?

Gerda Falkner and Brigid Laffan

Contents

Summary

Ireland and Austria are two of the smaller member states that joined the integration process at one of the enlargement rounds (in 1973 and 1995 respectively). This chapter offers a comparison between the two states' relations with the EU. It looks at the politics of the European issue in the two states, as well as at the issue of institutional adaptation to EU membership. An exploration of the adaptation of domestic policies to EU membership is confined to one symbolic issue that brings the two states together: their differing traditions of neutrality in international relations.

Introduction

This chapter analyses the adaptation of Austria and Ireland to European integration and to their engagement with the structures and processes of the European Union. Both a top-down perspective and the bottom-up perspective are used. In other words, we examine not only how the EU impacts on formerly national policy fields and political structures but also how the member states try to influence the EU (Börzel 1999). We understand Europeanization as an 'incremental process reorienting the direction and shape of politics to the degree that EC political and economic dynamics become part of the organizational logic of national politics and policy-making' (Ladrech 1994: 69).

Austria and Ireland are in many respects very different countries. When Ireland joined in 1973, it was poor, rural although rapidly urbanizing, and conservative. When Austria joined in 1995, it was highly industrialized (with some problematic agriculture in the alpine regions), wealthy, and therefore immediately a net contributor to the EU budget. A social democratic party had been the senior partner in government (if not governing alone) since 1970. Further differences with continuing significance relate to the state structure, Austria is a federal and Ireland a unitary state. Moreover, Austria has traditionally featured one of the most corporatist public–private interaction patterns in Europe, whereas public–private concertation, known as social partnership, emerged in Ireland much later.

However, there are also similarities—even beyond size. In the first place, Ireland and Austria perceive themselves as neutral countries (for sure, with quite different concepts of neutrality that were furthermore not stable over time). Both applied for EU membership on the basis of an elite consensus directed at opening up the domestic systems, and notably the economies, to international competition and liberalization. The EU was used and accepted as an external justifier for modernization not only in the 1990s, when its liberalization-aimed *acquis communautaire* had grown enormously, but already when Ireland made its first application for membership in 1961. EU membership was for Ireland bound up with its national project of modernization.

The outline of this chapter is as follows: 'The European issue before and after membership' deals with how the European issue was and is discussed in both countries (including the pre-accession phase). 'Institutional adaptation' analyses potential institutional misfits and change in Ireland and Austria. 'Policy adaptation' focuses on policy adaptation. The conclusions argue that both member states found themselves at a critical juncture in their relations with the EU, Austria in 2000 with a right-wing populist party in government and Ireland in 2001 following the rejection of the Nice referendum by the Irish electorate. Before all this, however, we start with the question of membership.

The European issue before and after membership

The European issue in Ireland

Serious engagement with the European Union began for Ireland at the end of the 1950s. In the mid-1950s Ireland found itself relatively isolated during the OEEC-based talks for a free-trade zone on trade liberalization that led to the European Free Trade Association (EFTA).[1] A stagnant economy, continuing high levels of emigration, trade dependence on the United Kingdom led to a reassessment of Ireland's domestic economic paradigm. The Secretary of the Finance Ministry, Ken Whitaker, penned what was known as the 'Grey Book' in which he argued strongly for the liberalization of the national economy and internationalization. In the new Irish Prime Minister, Sean Lemass, who took up office in 1959, he found a receptive political ear. Together they moulded a deep transformation of Irish economic policy. Ken Whitaker fought the inter-ministerial battles against those who feared change. Sean Lemass proved capable of persuading his party, Fianna Fail (largest party in Ireland), of the need for change and he advocated the case for domestic preparation for EU membership right though the 1960s. Ireland made its first application for membership in July 1961 but did not join until 1973. The length of time it took to secure membership was due to events beyond Ireland's control. Notwithstanding the delay, preparations for membership continued. Ireland signed the Anglo-Irish Free Trade in 1965, and joined the IMF and the GATT by the end of the decade. Liberalization and inward investment began to transform Ireland from an agricultural and dependent economy into an industrialized one (Laffan 2003).

Following the successful negotiations the accession treaty was put to the Irish people in a referendum in 1972. It was passed by a majority of 83 per cent. Membership of the Union was clearly the 'settled will' of the Irish people. An important feature of Ireland's engagement with the EU was the absence of splits in the main parties on the issue. The two centre-right parties—Fianna Fail and Fine Gael—supported membership and the Labour party opposed. In an election in 1973, just after accession, Labour joined with Fine Gael in a coalition government. The Labour party accepted the verdict of the electorate and settled quickly into engagement with EU institutions. This meant that Irish governments and their officials could start Ireland's engagement with the Union within a broad political consensus. They did not have to look over their shoulders to a hostile parliament or electorate. A second feature of Ireland's engagement was the dominance of economic issues and concerns. Ireland did not fight in the Second World War and as an island state did not share the historical experience or geopolitical environment of the continental small states. Successive Irish governments aimed to position Ireland as a constructive, pragmatic player in the Union rather than as a committed multilateralist. Thus, Irish politicians rarely used the rhetoric of integration in their pronouncements on the Union. The support of the Irish public for Ireland's membership of the EU remained solid. Three subsequent referendums—Single Act, Treaty on European Union and Treaty of

---

[1] Ireland did not join EFTA, but Austria was a founding member.

Amsterdam—were endorsed by the Irish electorate. The rejection of the Nice Treaty in June 2001 was thus a major shock to the Irish political class, its partners in Europe and the candidate states in central Europe. In a low turnout of just over 34 per cent of the electorate, the treaty was rejected by 54 per cent to 46 per cent (see Table 10.1). Ireland's stable European policy was loose of its moorings.

The European issue in Austria

Although Austria is a recent EU member, the European issue has a long-standing history. By the time of the first European integration efforts at the end of the 1940s and the beginning of the 1950s, the then occupied country of Austria was faced with a clear conflict of objectives between its interest to participate in (Western-) European cooperative organzations, above all the Marshall Plan and a desire not to cause confrontations with the Soviet Union and thereby endanger Austria's aspirations for the restoration of state sovereignty. Finally, Austria committed itself in the 'Moscow Memorandum' which involved declaring permanent neutrality following the Swiss model. Subsequently, the Soviet Union agreed to the Austrian Independence Treaty (*Staatsvertrag*) on 15 May 1955.

During the 1950s, neutrality and membership of the European Communities were generally seen as incompatible. Despite its frequently discussed close economic cooperation with the EC six in the sector of coal and steel and concerns of being disadvantaged in matters of supply and export in these industries, Austria decided to restrict itself to a tariffs agreement with the ECSC. It stayed away from the negotiations of the Treaties of Rome despite Spaak's invitation addressed to all OEEC-countries to participate. However, when the European Free Trade Area (EFTA) was established in 1960 for the seven OEEC countries that did not form part of the EEC, Austria became a founding member alongside Great Britain, Denmark, Norway, Portugal, Sweden, and Switzerland.

During the second half of the 1980s, Austrian EC-related policy made a complete U-turn. Above all, the EEC's Internal Market Programme revived Austrian debates on a rapprochement with the EU.[2] Already before the publication of the European Commission's White Paper on the Internal Market, two professors of international law declared for the first time (their expertise was paid for by the Association of Austrian Industry, VÖI) that EU membership was not to be considered in conflict with Austrian neutrality. Full membership was first demanded by the (then liberal and pro-European) Freedom Party and by the Association of Industrialists (VÖI), in spring 1987. The ÖVP followed suit in early 1988. The Social Democrat Chancellor Vranitzky gave a statement to that effect in summer 1988. Soon thereafter, the international law department of the Foreign Ministry (*Völkerrechtsbüro*) advocated membership with a reservation on grounds of neutrality (*Neutralitätsvorbehalt*), and the social partners welcomed EC membership in a joint report 'assuming that Austrian permanent neutrality would be upheld in all aspects and secured' (Sozialpartnerstellungnahme 1989: 11).

A further crucial step was the government's report to Parliament of 17 April 1989 which recommended membership under the conditions of upholding neutrality, federalism, the Austrian social system, an offensive environmental protection policy,

---

[2] For details on the Austrian path towards membership see Luif (1995).

Table 10.1 Recent referenda on EU-related issues in Austria and Ireland

	Referendum topic (date)	Result	turnout
Ireland	Nice Treaty I (June 2001)	rejected by 54% to 46%	34%
Austria	EU membership (12 June 1994)	accepted by 67% to 33.4%	82%
Ireland	Nice Treaty II (19 October 2002)	accepted by 63% to 37%	48%

an area-wide peasant agriculture[3] and, finally, of solving the problem of transit traffic through the endangered Alpine regions. On 17 July 1989, the formal letter of application was submitted in Brussels. However, negotiations on the European Economic Area (EEA) were already under way, and the forthcoming Maastricht Treaty furthermore delayed any immediate follow-up to this desire of membership.

Formal accession negotiations between the EC and Austria began on 1 February 1993. The relevant *Commission Opinion* (Europäische Kommission 1992) had positively underlined the political stability and economic health of the applicant, while fearing that neutrality might hamper the development of a European Foreign and Defence Policy. Against this background, it came as a great surprise that neutrality was not a controversial issue in the ensuing negotiations. By contrast, agriculture, real estate markets and transit proved to be the trickiest chapters in the Austrian case. Membership negotiations with Austria were concluded after 13 months only, on 1 March 1994. Negotiations of this third EC widening round were significantly eased by the fact that the EEA agreement had already transferred sizeable parts of the EC's economic *acquis* to the EFTA states.

Institutional adaptation

Ireland

Ireland's institutional adaptation to EU membership was relatively smooth. The core constitutional features of Irish government, collective responsibility of the Cabinet and ministerial responsibility at a departmental level were not altered by EU membership. Ireland was a highly centralized unitary state with weak local government and a non-existent regional tier. Thus European policy was the responsibility of central government. Membership did, however, alter the relationship between the Executive and Parliament (Oireachtas) as the latter no longer had the sole law making power. This required an amendment to the Irish constitution that formed part of the 1972 referendum.

---

[3] This expressed that an industrialization of agriculture was not desired in Austria where small units and family management were still common.

Central government and administration

The focus in Ireland was on achieving membership of the Union with the result that very little attention was paid to how EU issues would be managed following membership. The lead ministry on integration was the Finance Ministry but the Foreign Ministry managed to have its minister lead the accession negotiations, albeit flanked by the secretaries of four ministries—Foreign Affairs, Finance, Agriculture and what was then called Industry and Commerce. The underlying inter-ministerial battle between Finance and Foreign Affairs was not settled until 1973 when a government decision gave day to day responsibility for the coordination of EU business to Foreign Affairs. Foreign Affairs issued the first memorandum on the management of EU affairs in September 1973. The memorandum established the principle of the 'lead ministry' which remains at the core of the Irish system. The European Communities Committee, the main inter-ministerial coordination device, had been in operation as the Committee of Secretaries from the 1950s onwards. At the outset, it met at secretary level but was quickly delegated to the next tier in the administrative hierarchy—assistant secretaries and chaired by Foreign Affairs. It met monthly. A large number of interministerial committees were established at that time but remained dormant. The small size of the Irish bureaucracy, the intimacy of the culture and the ease of personal relations meant that informal consultation and contact within a shared normative framework was the dominant mode of interaction in the Irish system. The focus was on issues of key interest to Ireland—regional policy, agriculture, the budget and ensuring that the costs of EC regulation could be borne by the Irish state and the private sector. The Irish Presidency in 1975 marked the end of Ireland's apprenticeship in the system.

The management of EU affairs was subject to some change since 1973 (Laffan 2001 a, b, and c). The progressive Europeanization of many areas of public policy ensured that all ministries have an EU dimension and almost all have staff in the permanent representation in Brussels. In 1987 the Government altered the format of the key interministerial committee. It was chaired by a Minister of State based in the prime minister's office. Thus the chair and servicing of this committee moved from Foreign Affairs to the Taoiseach's department. This signalled the growing involvement of the prime minister in EU business. That said, the bulk of the EU cadre remained in Foreign Affairs. The International/EU division in the prime minister's office had only six staff. The preparation of Ireland's first national development plan was the responsibility of a Committee of Ministers and Secretaries although in reality it consisted of the Prime Minister and senior civil servants drawn from the key ministries. Throughout the 1990s there were many ad hoc interministerial groups depending on the EU agenda— IGCs, budgetary bargains and so on. By the end of the 1990s, the system became more institutionalized with the establishment of a Cabinet sub-committee that actually meets once a month and a senior officials group (SOG) that prepares the work of the Cabinet committee and engages in strategic thinking about Ireland's place in the Union. This brings together the most senior officials in the EU cadre below the level of heads of ministry. A number of interministerial committees such as one on the Future of Europe, the 2004 presidency and JHA became operational in 2001/2.

Parliament

In response to the legislative power of the Union, the Irish parliament established what was known as the Joint Committee on Secondary Legislation in 1974 to oversee the implementation of EC law in Ireland by means of ministerial order. The committee's members were drawn from the lower tier (Dáil) and the upper tier (the senate). The Committee was co-terminous with the life of the parliament and fell into abeyance when an election was called. It had to be re-established by each new parliament. Its terms of reference were broadened over time but its ability to hold the Irish government accountable was limited. It had weak administrative back up and limited research capacity. Moreover, there was no tradition of parliamentary committees in Irish political culture. Irish parliamentarians carry a heavy constituency load and tend to be more focused on local and domestic issues rather than European ones. That said the Joint Committee on Secondary Legislation was an important experiment in the use of committees and influenced later parliamentary reform that was characterized by the establishment of a broad range of committees. The work of the Joint Committee was subsumed into a newly established Foreign Affairs Committee in 1993 but this was later split in 1997 into a Foreign Affairs Committee and a European Affairs Committee. Although the resources of the committees were enhanced, it could not be argued that Ireland was characterized by strong parliamentary oversight of EU affairs.

The question of parliamentary accountability emerged as a salient issue during the Nice I referendum in 2001. It was raised, in particular, by a former Attorney General (chief law officer of the state) who was very critical of the weakness of parliamentary scrutiny. Tackling the parliamentary deficit was one of three governmental responses to the rejection of Nice. The Senior Officials Group and Foreign Affairs were given responsibility for designing new processes and procedures for executive/parliamentary relations. The new procedures came into operation in autumn 2002. They are designed to give the European Affairs Committee far more systematic information on the flow of EU policy. Each ministry must prepare a 'note' on all new Commission proposals and ministers and officials must go before the Committee. The new procedures will further codify how EU business is managed in Ireland and are likely to have as significant an impact on the management of EU business within government as on executive parliamentary relations.

The regions

Ireland's size and the importance of the county as a source of identification militated against the emergence of a strong tier of regional government. Furthermore, a centralized administration and a highly localized political culture ensured that regions would not develop as meaningful political or administrative arenas. The organization of the state below the level of central government by ministries and state agencies was characterized by ad hoc special designations driven by the imperatives of the ministry or agency with little attention to the consequences in spatial terms on the ground. The fact that Ireland was designated as one region for the purposes of structural funds meant that the Commission's primary interface was with central government, particularly the Finance ministry. EU funding did, however, have an impact on territorial politics in Ireland. The growth of EU largesse inevitably raised expectations as different parts of the country fought for a piece of the Brussels pie. Moreover, the Commission's preference for 'partnership' began to make itself felt. In 1987, eight regions were established as part of the implementation of the first national development plan. The regions consisted of two committees, one drawn from the elected politicians in participating local authorities and another from state agencies and local government officials. These committees did not have a decisive say on the distribution of EU monies but were largely a response to the Commission's demands. The negotiation and implementation of the second development plan (1992–9) was characterized by enhanced local involvement in the plan. There was a growing commitment to supporting the response of local community groups in urban and rural Ireland to the economic devastation of the 1980s and there was a proliferation of local community groups throughout the country.

The regional issue re-emerged in 1997–9 when it became clear that Irish per capita incomes had converged with the EU average and that Ireland would no longer be considered an objective one region. The decision on regionalization was related to the Agenda 2000 negotiations in that it was a response to Ireland's changing eligibility for structural fund monies. Within the Government and the Fianna Fail party, there was a very contentious debate. Many Fianna Fail deputies from the non-objective one constituencies were fearful of the public finance implications of the decision for their regions. In November 1998 the Government finally took a decision to divide the country into two regions, the East which would not get objective one status and the Border, Midlands, and Western region, known as the BMW region, where average per capita incomes were just under 75 per cent. The Government's planned regionalization was accepted by Eurostat but without the inclusion of two counties in the original decision of the government. There was some disquiet in Brussels about subsidy shopping. The two regions are unlikely to survive beyond 2006 when Ireland will lose objective one status entirely.

Private interests

Unlike Austria, Ireland did not have a tradition of corporatism but it did have a pluralist system of interest mediation that deepened with urbanization and economic development. The key Irish interests—the employers and farmers—established offices in Brussels from the outset and were fully engaged in their respective EU wide confederations and federations. Irish trade unions did not have sufficient resources to have a permanent presence in Brussels but were active in the European Trade Union Confederation (ETUC). With the expansion of mobilization in the Union following the Single Act, the economic interests were joined in Brussels by women's groups, environmentalists, anti-poverty networks, and consumer organizations. The Irish voluntary sector has been particularly active in European networks and well plugged into Commission committees and observatories. The most significant impact of EU membership on interest mediation in Ireland was, however, generated by pressures in the domestic political economy.

Ireland's economic performance in the 1980s was particularly bad. On every single indicator—unemployment, inflation and budget deficits—Ireland held the worst position on EU wide league tables. Ireland's economic and social strategy and its prospects were in ruins. Fuelled by a palpable sense of national crisis, the Irish political and economic class found the institutional and cultural capacity to reverse the trend. The core of the new approach was known as social partnership. It began in 1987 with the Programme for National Recovery (1987–90) and was followed by a number of subsequent programmes. The programmes involved agreement between employers, trade unions, farming interests, and the Government on wage levels in the public and private sectors and on a wide range of economic and social policies. The content of all programmes was negotiated in the context of EU developments and the need to ensure that Ireland adjusted to the demands of economic integration. The ability to move from adversarial relations to partnership was in considerable measure due to EU engagement. The employers and trade unionists learnt the value of partnership when exposed to continental European practices and not just the British adversarial system in industrial relations. The partnership approach together with an expansion of EU spending programmes in Ireland and a significant increase in US investment produced the much-needed recovery from the disastrous early and mid-1980s. From 1992 onwards, Ireland consistently out-performed its EU partners in terms of economic growth, employment creation and the growth of exports and thus caught up with the richer parts of Europe.

Austria

Austria is a particularly challenging case regarding top-down impact on the national political system. From the viewpoint of the traditional Austrian 'model' of a political system, EU membership was expected to have significant consequences on several basic features. To counterbalance the predicted effects, a number of steps were taken or attempted (some significant, some rather symbolic) to protect, in particular, the traditional roles of parliament, the regions (*Länder*) and the social partners from being eroded in the multi-level system.[4]

Central government and administration

Looking back at the membership negotiations and summarizing their experiences, Austrian diplomats admitted that their EU counterparts had been much better versed in bargaining (Luif 1995: 119, with further references). Before formal membership as of 1 January 1995, Austrian representatives experienced some training in EU-internal diplomacy since they were allowed to participate in all kinds of meetings, as 'active observers'.

Following membership, Austrian EU diplomacy has been fully developed. The domestic handling of EU affairs is based on the 1994 inter-party 'Europe Agreement' between the SPÖ[5] and ÖVP[6] (for more detail see Müller 2000). The lead ministry which represents the Republic in the EC Council and which coordinates the domestic process of decision-making is selected on the basis of an agreed list and of giving priority to the ministry which undertakes the main public expenditure for the relevant task. While membership triggered no changes to the overall structure of government departments, EU adhesion has initiated a moderate modernization process in public administration. The need to employ travel-ready personnel with good language and negotiation skills needed more flexible employment contracts than the civil service had before, and some unusually fast-track careers (even for women) were made on the basis of 'European' qualifications.

A unique case concerning EU-related diplomacy in both the bottom-up and the top-down directions was the issue of Austrian government formation in 2000 and the

---

[4] For a full analysis of these aspects see Falkner (2000).
[5] Austrian Social Democratic Party.   [6] Austrian People's Party.

EU reaction to this (Falkner 2001a). A few days before the new Austrian centre-right government between Christian Democrats (ÖVP) and the Freedom Party (FPÖ) was formally agreed on 4 February 2000, the Portuguese EU Council Presidency issued a statement 'on behalf of 14 Member States'. It announced that

the governments of the fourteen Member States will not promote or accept any official bilateral contacts at political level with an Austrian government integrating the FPÖ; there will be no support for Austrian candidates seeking positions in international organzations; Austrian Ambassadors in EU capitals will only be received at a technical level.

At that time, the Treaty on European Union (TEU) included only provisions on the suspension of membership rights in the case of 'the existence of a serious and persistent breach' of basic principles. It is important to note that this procedure was at no point initiated against Austria since it was almost uncontested among the EU fourteen that Austria was not 'in serious and persistent breach' of the Treaties' basic principles. The other governments were, however, concerned that this might be the case at some point in the future, under a government including the FPÖ—a legitimate concern in a European Union where the members of national governments make up the main decision-making body and can block many crucial initiatives, often even unilaterally. From this perspective, reacting to the formation of the new Austrian government made sense.

However, arguments have been put forward that question the wisdom of the specific form of reaction. Considering the EU provisions in force, it would have been a clear breach of the Treaty provisions if 'EU sanctions' had been imposed on Austria. Many even thought that the Fourteen's multiple 'bilateral' action was premature because the Union's basic rules do not only contain the clear procedures for potential sanctions outlined above, but also provisions on the respect of the national identities of the member states (Art. E TEU), on abstaining from any measure which could jeopardize the attainment of the objectives of the Treaty (Art. 10 TEC), and, very prominently, on non-discrimination for reasons of nationality (for example Art. 12 TEC). From this perspective, the Fourteen's 'bilateral' measures seemed questionable at least in the spirit of the Treaties. Furthermore, their design was criticised for the initially open-ended character and the lack of an exit option other than a breakdown of the Austrian centre-right government. The Presidency, an institution of the Union and the Communities, was used to proclaim the multi-national (but not 'European') decision (on legal aspects see Pernthaler and Hilpold 2000). Contentwise, the second measure (non-support of Austrians in international organzations) has been discussed most controversially since one of the EU's major policies is non-discrimination on grounds of nationality. Point two of the 'sanctions' could, however, affect persons who had never in their life voted for the FPÖ or who had even protested against the centre-right government.

Five months after the imposition of the 'sanctions', the Fourteen developed an ad hoc exit strategy based on a report by three 'wise men' who criticized the FPÖ (for example for methods of campaigning and for intimidation of political critics via litigation in court) but confirmed the general opinion that the new government had not acted against European values (see further reading recommendations, at the end of the chapter). On that basis, the 'sanctions' were immediately lifted without follow-up procedure or qualification. What this episode actually meant for both Austria and the EU remains to be seen in the longer term (for early analysis, see Schneider 2000). It should be mentioned, however, that the Austrian government threatened to hold a referendum on blocking EU reforms if the sanctions continued, and that it came out of this episode domestically rather stronger and more unified than was initially the case. The same is true for the ÖVP and the breakdown of the centre-right government in autumn 2002. After serious internal upheavals within the Freedom Party (the FPÖ members of government were sidelined by more right-wing and 'Haiderist' members in an extraordinary party convention), the ÖVP became the strongest Austrian party with seventy-nine seats in Parliament (SPÖ: 69; FPÖ: 18; Greens: 17). That the ÖVP was therefore in a rather more powerful position than before in the ÖVP–FPÖ government formed in late February 2003 meant that it could pursue its European integration stance more easily than before. By the time of the new government formation (that happened to fall into the crucial phase of the ten accession treaty preparations in Brussels), the ÖVP indeed had enough leverage to have its pro-enlargement policy accepted by the to-be coalition partner.

Parliament

During the years preceding Austrian accession to the EU, studies on the likely effects predicted manifold changes due to the significant differences between the political system of the EU, on the one hand, and Austria, on the other (see notably Gerlich and Neisser 1994). A focal point of these studies was the expectation that the government and the administration would gain in political weight to the detriment of parliament. A change in terms of the horizontal distribution of functions was expected since the government was to have its action capacity increased via privileged access to EU decision making, at the expense of a decisive say for political representatives who are directly legitimated.

Even the constitution was changed to give the directly elected first chamber of the Austrian parliament powers to control the government in EU affairs that even exceed the Danish example (for an international comparison see Bergman 1997; Morass 1996). Article 23e of the Federal Constitution provides that the *Nationalrat* must be informed in good time about all EU-related projects by the responsible minister. On projects leading to mandatory law in areas which before would have needed national legislative scrutiny (this is notably the case when new EC Directives or Regulations are negotiated), the *Nationalrat* may issue an opinion which will bind the Austrian members of government in EU-level negotiations and votes.[7]

It is important to note that the accession-related constitutional reforms stem from a period when the Austrian grand coalition government did not have the two-thirds majority needed to adopt laws of constitutional quality in parliament (1994–6). The members of the minor Green and Liberal parties asked for far-reaching parliamentary participation and control. The latter were not a core feature of the Austrian political culture at all, which has certainly contributed to the very low number of binding opinions issued by the Austrian *Nationalrat* (only thirty-four by Summer 2001, see Blümel and Neuhold 2001: 319). In practice, the Austrian parliament has not been able to control government effectively in EU affairs (Falkner 2000).

---

[7] Exceptions exist for 'compelling reasons of foreign or integration policy'.

The regions

Austria is a federal state with nine provinces (*Länder*). Although the legislative powers of the *Länder* were already quite limited before 1994, EEA and subsequently EU membership eroded them even more. That the level of decision making would change from *sub*national to *supra*national was not the only concern of Austrian *Länder* politicians and political scientists dealing with matters of federalism. Another issue was that the decision-makers at the supranational level would not be representatives of the *Länder*, since there is no co-decision power for the subnational regional entities at the EU level.

In turn, a reform of the national distribution of competencies between the central and the regional level was demanded (Dachs 1994) to counterbalance losses of the *Länder* in the multilevel political system of the EU, but was never adopted. At least, the participation of *Länder* (and, to some extent, even districts) in domestic EU-related decision-making has been regulated in Article 23d of the Austrian Constitution and in a special state–*Länder* agreement. The procedure resembles the participation of the *Nationalrat*. In practice, however, unanimity is a big hurdle and binding opinions of the *Länder* are very rare (Steiner and Trattnigg 1998: 164). Furthermore, the deadlines and time pressures of Euro-politics impinge on the *Länder* even more than on actors at the federal level.

Another concession to the *Länder* gained during the pre-accession phase is that they can directly participate in EU negotiations. If issues within their realm of domestic legislative responsibility are discussed, the government may include a *Länder* nominee in the Austrian delegation. This representative may, however, only act in cooperation with the responsible member of the government (see Art. 23d Paragraph 3 of the Austrian Constitution).

Private interests

The most widely discussed and supposedly most 'typical' feature of the Austrian political system is corporatist cooperation of the centralized peak associations of labour and management with the state in shaping public policies. In the Austrian case, both the structural (the interest group set-up) and the procedural dimensions (involvement in policy-making) of corporatism are extremely well developed. There are a number of quite hierarchically organized 'chambers' (for business, labour, agriculture, etc.), that is interest groups set up by Austrian law where membership is obligatory. The classic social partner institutions in Austria are thus the Chamber of Business (*Wirtschaftskammer Österreich*), the Chamber of Labour (*Bundesarbeitskammer*), the Conference of Presidents of the Chambers of Agriculture (PRÄKO) and the encompassing Austrian trade union confederation (ÖGB). These pillars of 'social partnership' cooperate formally (for example in a plethora of working groups) and informally with the other political institutions, on a daily basis. It is not uncommon that draft legislation is negotiated between the social partners and/or the relevant ministry before being 'rubber-stamped' in parliament.

EU adhesion was not expected to put an end to this pattern of corporatism (or social partnership), but to change it in a 'substantial and speedy' way (for example Tálos 1994: 179). As a *direct* effect of membership, the issues prone to joint decision-making by the Austrian social partners and 'the state' would be less numerous since decisions would be shifted to the EU level. As an *indirect* effect, pluralist patterns of interest group behaviour at the European level ('lobbying') were expected to trickle down into the Austrian system.

The major interest groups feared that 'significant parts' of their powers in national policy-making would be transferred to Brussels (Sozialpartnerstellungnahme, 1989 no. 976: 157).[8] As early as 1989, a party agreement between SPÖ and ÖVP promised that the long-standing practice of social partner participation in the shaping of Austrian social and economic conditions would be upheld even during EU membership. The 1994 'Europe Agreement' between the Austrian coalition parties allocated specific participation rights at the European and the domestic[9] levels to the four social partner institutions. The four major associations were even promised 'equal' participation in the various EU decision-making bodies and committees.[10] Soon after the Austrian adhesion, however, the government qualified its concession. It argued that, according to EU rules, only government representatives are officially part of national delegations. For special cases, the responsible Minister nevertheless agreed to include social partner representatives in the national delegation, although without the right to speak (Karlhofer and Tálos 1996: 141).

Nevertheless, the social partners were rather content with their role in the shaping of Austrian positions for the EU Council during the early years of EU membership (Eder and Hiller 1998). Subsequently, however, differences between policy areas further increased (Kittel and Tálos 1999)[11] and (much more important in that respect than EU membership itself) the concertation-adverse centre-right government since 2000 affected Austrian social partnership (Tálos and Kittel 2001).

Policy adaptation

Already at the time of Irish accession in 1973, policy adaptation to EC requirements was by no means insignificant. However, joining in the mid-1990s meant that Austria had to conform to more than 4,000 EC regulations and approximately 1,200 EC Directives (Heinisch 2001: 271) which touched almost all policy areas.

For reasons of space, we shall only discuss one policy issue that is of great importance for both Ireland and Austria: neutrality, which is a kind of 'touchstone' for both countries (or, in the latter case, at least was a touchstone by the time of application and entry).

Ireland

Traditionally Irish neutrality was a contingent and ambiguous political concept moulded by historical experience and the centrality of the relationship with Britain.

---

[8] All translations from German language documents are by Gerda Falkner.

[9] During the preparation of Austrian EU positions, the social partner associations participate in relevant meetings, which are organized at the sub-ministerial, departmental and cross-ministerial levels (Kittel, Bernhard, and Tálos, Emmerich (1999)).

[10] '[G]leichberechtigte Teilnahme an der österreichischen Entscheidungsvorbereitung und Entscheidungsfindung im Rahmen der EU' (pt. 13a).

[11] Social affairs is the field with best practice from the economic interest groups' point of view, contrary to finance and agriculture.

Successful neutrality in the Second World War, which was a very potent experience and symbol of Irish sovereignty, made neutrality a 'sacred cow' in Irish society. The justification for non-membership of NATO in 1949 was that membership might imply recognition of the border between the Republic and Northern Ireland. Ireland remained a non-member of NATO but Irish neutrality was not seen as an impediment to membership of the Union in 1961. In fact, the then prime minister, Sean Lemass, said that Ireland would be prepared to join a defence arrangement, if that formed part of the evolving Union. That said, neutrality has been an issue in every Irish EU referendum and successive Irish governments have been very cautious in supporting the emergence of an EU security pillar and a European defence policy. Governments have stressed that Irish neutrality has not been eroded by the cumulative development of the Common Foreign and Security Policy (CSFP) and the European Security and Defence Policy (ESDP).

Just like in Austria (see below), the ambiguous nature of Irish neutrality has led to heated debates between successive Irish Governments and the pro-neutrality lobby. The debate is characterized by more heat than clarity because security in Ireland is discussed in the absence of an external threat to the Irish state. The debate is about beliefs, values, and perceptions of Ireland rather than cool analysis of security in Europe and globally. A long tradition of UN peacekeeping has an important impact on public opinion.

Although CFSP and the ESDP did not feature in any significant way in the Treaty of Nice, concern about neutrality was the third most important reason for voting 'no' in the first Nice referendum. In developing a strategy to tackle the fallout from Nice, the Government decided that it would need to address concerns about neutrality. The response had three elements:

1. A national declaration by Ireland at the Seville European Council in June 2002.
2. A declaration of the European Council at Seville.
3. A constitutional prohibition on Ireland joining a European common defence.

The Irish declaration confirmed that involvement in the CFSP did not 'prejudice its traditional policy of military neutrality' and the European Council declaration noted the Irish declaration and set out its interpretation of the provisions in the TEU dealing with a common defence. The constitutional amendment prohibits Ireland from adopting a decision of the European Council to establish a common defence if such a common defence were to include Ireland. If in future an Irish Government wants Ireland to participate in a European common defence, it will have to have another referendum. Given the manner in which neutrality re-emerged as an issue in the second Nice referendum and the concern, particularly among women, about defence, the declarations and the constitutional amendment were probably necessary for the success of the second referendum.

Austria

In Austria, accession had been considered impossible for reasons of foreign and security policy, for decades, but then neutrality was the most surprising chapter of the EU–membership negotiations. The debates preceding the 1989 application had been based on the assumption that there would be exemptions and specific provisions in the membership treaty securing that the special status of Austria could be upheld in full (see above). Even the formal letter containing the Austrian membership applications for any of the three European Communities had contained a reservation on neutrality. The EC opposed these reservations and feared that the permanent neutrality status might hamper the development of a common foreign and security policy since the latter needed unanimous approval. However, the negotiations on this chapter were concluded in a surprisingly short time since Austria reinterpreted its concept of neutrality (Luif 1995: 309). It was in practice agreed that the meaning of the Austrian neutrality status should be reduced to the military core of the old concept. This excluded a number of economic and political duties that had formerly been a generally accepted part of 'permanent neutrality'. In 1993, the Austrian cabinet issued a declaration to support the Foreign Minister in the negotiations:

the Federal Government proceeds from the assumption that Austria is not obliged to participate militarily in wars, not obliged to accede to military alliances and to establish military bases of foreign states on its territory. This Austrian position will have to be cleared up by appropriate domestic legal regulations' (quoted from Luif 1995: 309).

However, many argued that changing the Austrian law on neutrality which was not only of constitutional character but also highly valued by the citizens, would in practice have meant not joining the Union (ibid.). For this reason, even those EU member states that would in theory have liked to see a formal and far-reaching commitment of the applicants to the future development of a joint foreign and security policy finally gave in to those who advocated a pragmatic approach.

The Austrian accession treaty[12] included a joint declaration of the by 1995 new members on foreign and security policy. Austria, Finland, and Sweden agreed to be able and ready, from the time of their accession, to participate fully and actively in the EU's Common Foreign and Security Policy as defined in the Treaty on European Union. In the negotiations, Austria declared that this participation would be in accordance with domestic constitutional law and that relevant adaptations were to be accomplished under new framework conditions, in the context of EU accession.[13] Significantly, the question posed to the Austrians in the membership referendum did not mention the issue of neutrality at all. The Austrian law on neutrality has not been formally changed during or after the membership negotiations but, as outlined, the concept of neutrality has been incrementally reinterpreted to such a large extent that a fundamental change in substance cannot be neglected. During 2001, the SPÖ (in opposition for the first time since 1970) was still split on the neutrality issue. At the same time, even NATO membership was already being discussed on a daily basis in Austria. In December 2001, a new security doctrine was adopted in the Austrian parliament by the governing coalition parties. It characterizes Austria as non-aligned, but no longer as neutral. One argument is that by the very fact of having cooperated in the framework of the EU's Common Foreign and Security Policy, the status of permanent neutrality according to international law would already have been changed.

---

[12] Document annexed to III–176 *BlgNR* XVIII GP. This passage is quoted in Luif, Paul (1995).
[13] Government initiative proposal on changes to the constitution with a view to membership, *Regierungsvorlage zum Beitrittsverfassungsgesetz*, 1546 *BlgNR* XVIII GP, 9.

In December 2002, the by far largest Austrian party, the ÖVP, even advocated Austrian membership in a Euro-defence-zone in the context of the EU's constitutional debate.

Outlook: a critical juncture?

The analysis in this chapter suggests that the fit between domestic institutional patterns and the EU was mostly unproblematic in Ireland, but not in Austria. On the level of policy adaptation, both countries used the EU as a means to modernize and liberalize the economy. With regard to foreign policy and particularly neutrality, which is a controversial issue in both of these small member states, there is another parallel development. Politicians in both countries seem more ready to give up their respective concept of neutrality and to participate in a European foreign and defence policy than their citizens (or, at least, important sub-groups within the country). Again in both countries studied here, the recent past can be interpreted as having led to critical junctures, involving conflict with the EU and threats of defection.

In Ireland, a pragmatic political and administrative culture buttressed by a consensus about the importance of the EU to Ireland led to a process of incremental adjustment and adaptation. The Irish state elite set out to position Ireland as a constructive player committed to the Union. This should not be interpreted however as a willingness to embrace a 'maximalist' approach to the constitutional development of the Union. The protection of domestic autonomy in key policy areas, notably taxation, and a concern about the potential for excessive EU regulation, has led successive governments to seek to protect domestic space and autonomy in EU negotiations.

The most fundamental challenge to *Ireland* from EU membership was learning how to live with economic liberalization and the domestic constraints imposed by internationalisation. It took the shock of the 1980s to bring home to the Irish political elite that sound domestic management was essential if the benefits of participation in the larger market were to bear fruit. By the early 1990s, Ireland had adjusted to the European political economy and the promise of membership was fulfilled. Economic catch-up, the core goal of economic policy from the 1950s onwards, was finally realized. Paradoxically, once it was achieved the road-map for Ireland's engagement in the Union was no longer so clear. The tone of pronouncements on Europe began to change, at least those emanating from some leading politicians. This was exacerbated by the budgetary conflict between the Government and the Commission in 2001 concerning Irish budgetary policy. The Commission was no longer seen as Ireland's best friend and there was an emerging sense that the EU was no longer as central to Ireland as it once was.

It took the shock of the rejection of the Nice Treaty to underline the continuing importance of the Union to Ireland. The Government, administration and the peak economic groups reacted by preparing the ground for a re-run of the referendum. The Government embarked on a three pronged approach involving the establishment of a National Forum on Europe, enhanced parliamentary scrutiny and the declarations on neutrality. The Government sought to assure its partners in the Union and the candidate states that Ireland remained a committed member of the Union. The second Nice referendum was characterized by extensive mobilisation of the 'yes' groups in Ireland. The Government, the pro-Nice opposition parties and the key interest organizations all ran very effective campaigns. They were joined by a civil society alliance—the Irish Alliance for Europe—that managed to mobilize a broad cross-section of Irish society. The second referendum was passed by a decisive majority of 62 per cent. The 'no' vote increased by some 400 votes whereas the 'yes' vote increased by just under 500,000.

The second referendum confirmed the underlying support of Irish public opinion for EU membership and its recognition of the centrality of the EU to Ireland's economic and political prospects. It has not, however, resolved the challenge facing the Irish political class as they grapple with changes to Ireland's position in the Union, the arrival of many more small states and the pressure for further constitutional change. Moreover, the Government and the wider political class now know that it cannot take the electorate for granted and that it must begin to communicate politically about Europe. Otherwise it faces a difficult political battle in the inevitable referendum following the conclusion of the next treaty, a constitutional treaty.

The *Austrian* political elites, by contrast, knew from the very beginning that significant misfit existed in a number of fields. On the institutional level, concessions were made to parliament, to the regions, and to the social partners in order to counterweight their loss of direct influence under the condition of EU membership. Most of them seem rather symbolic, in practice, for the domestic countersteering measures to expected Europeanization effects were in no field really successful. Among the reasons are (to different degrees in various sub-fields) EU-level specifics (EC Council or working group decisions are rather intransparent and not easily controlled from the lower levels), domestic culture (for example coalition discipline in parliament in practice impedes exercising strict control over governmental EU policy) and the ÖVP–FPÖ government's preferences. It may also have played a role that everyone got used to the way in which EU-decisions are made as well as to the functional 'needs' of efficient participation therein, and that promoting diverging domestic patterns against the normal 'European' way of doing things is even more difficult than before 1995.

On the policy level, too, Austria adapted to EU patterns, and the implementation performance is rather good, in general terms (Falkner 2001b). Only in comparatively few issue areas, above all on Alpine transit, has the level of dispute between Austria and the EU been persistently high. It should, however, be noted that Austria, in contrast with Ireland, has a strong party that is not too sure if the EU really is 'A Place We Belong'. Against this background, discrepancies between the EU's and the 'Austrian' standpoint (be it the nationwide agreed view or only a particularistic opinion) tend to be used, in a popularistic way, to raise Euro-scepticism. This feature of domestic politics (also known from, for example, the Italian case) should be taken seriously in terms of the future of European integration.

In both Austria and Ireland, one can therefore conclude that state adaptation was rather successful, but that the same cannot be said about societal adaptation. This is all the more worrying since recently, both Austria's and Ireland's EU memberships have been characterized by frictions. Most importantly, Irish budgetary policy and Austrian government formation were harshly criticized by the EU (see above). In both countries, public opinion showed strong reactions to that treatment. While the Irish voted against the Nice Treaty, Austrians considered EU membership hardly worthwhile[14] and were extremely sceptical towards the 2004 enlargement.[15] The Freedom Party even threatened to initiate a referendum on EU enlargement and/or to voice a veto, but this plan was finally dropped. When the centre-right coalition had broken down after an intra-party clash in the FPÖ, and was re-built in 2003, the ÖVP seems to have had enough leverage to have its own EU-related policy options dominate during the crucial phase of the signature of the accession treaties in Brussels. In any case, both Austria and Ireland were reluctant to divert funding to the CEECs.

Quite obviously, 'benign neglect' is no longer a term that captures the public attitudes vis-à-vis the EU in Ireland and Austria which are now 'small but difficult' members.

Further reading

Most studies of these two states' relations with the EU are offered in chapters of edited collections like this one. On the Europeanisation of Austria, see Falkner (2000). Muller (2000) and Höll, Pollack and Puntscher-Riekmann (2003) present explorations of the European policy-making machinery in Austria. Luif (1998) examines Austria in the context of a collection on small member states in the EU. Studies of Ireland's European policy-making machinery are available in Laffan (2001c; 2003). For an analysis of the Irish economy's place in the EU, see O'Donnell (2000). Also see Department of the Taoiseach (2003) for an official review of policy priorities ahead of the 2004 presidency. The two member states' implementation performance is discusssed in Falkner *et al.* (2005).

Weblinks

On Austria official governmental information is available at <http://www.austria.gv.at/e/>, with official statistics at <http://www.statistik.at/index.shtml>. The Report on Austria of 8 September 2000 by the 'wise men' Martti Ahtisaari, Jochen Frowein und Marcelino Oreja <http://www.mpiv-hd.mpg.de/de/Bericht-EU/index.cfm>. For analysis of Austrian European European policy see the site of ECSA–Austria, Österreichische Europaforschungsgesellschaft, <http://fgr.wu-wien.ac.at/ecsa/ecsa-e.htm>. Also useful are

---

[14] Only 38% of Austrians thought by May 2001 that their country had on balance benefited from being a member of the EU (peak: 83% of Irish people; lowest rate: 27% in Sweden; European Commission 2001). It is true that Austrians have been quite critical ever since they joined the EU, but in 1999 (i.e. before the 'sanctions') at least 42% had answered favourably.

[15] Only 33% of respondents supported the forthcoming widening of the European Union to the east and south which would include a number of Austrian neighbours. This is the lowest rate throughout the EU. In Ireland, a majority of 59% supported further widening of the Union. There is evidence that the further away the applicant countries are, the more enthusiastic Europeans are with regard to including them: 70% of respondents agreed to enlargement in Greece (European Commission 2001).

EIoP, European Integration online Papers, and European Research Papers Archive, both edited under the auspices of ECSA-Austria <**http://eiop.or.at/erpa/eiop.htm**>.

On Ireland official government information is available at <**http://www.irlgov.ie**>, with offical statistics <**http://www.cso.ie/**>. Other useful sites are those of the Irish Institute of European Affairs <**http://www.iiea.com**> and of the National Forum on Europe <**http://www.ForumonEurope.ie**>.

References

Bergman, Torbjörn (1997), 'National parliaments and EU Affairs Committees: notes on empirical variation and competing explanations', *Journal of European Public Policy*, 4/3, 373–87.

Blümel, Barbara, and Neuhold, Christine (2001), 'The Parliament of Austria: Big Procedures with Little Implications', in Andreas Maurer and Wolfgang Wessels (eds), *National Parliaments on their ways to Europe: Losers or Latecomers?* (Baden-Baden: Nomos), 304–30.

Börzel, Tanja A. (1999), 'Towards Convergence in Europe? Institutional Adaptation to Europeanization in Germany and Spain', *Journal of Common Market Studies*, 37/4, 573–96.

Dachs, Herbert (1994), 'EU-Beitritt und die Bundesländer', in Peter Gerlich and Heinrich Neisser (eds), *EU-Beitritt als Herausforderung* (Wien: Signum), 185–208.

Department of the Taoiseach, (2003), *Ireland and the European Union: Identifying Priorities and Pursuing Goals* <http://www.gov.ie/taoiseach>.

Eder, Martina, and Hiller, Karin (1998), 'Sektorstudie Sozialpolitik', in Gerda Falkner, and Wolfgang C. Müller (eds), *Österreich im europäischen Mehrebenensystem: Konsequenzen der EU-Mitgliedschaft für Politiknetzwerke und Entscheidungsprozesse* (Wien: Signum), 39–78.

Europäische Kommission (1992), *Die Erweiterung der Gemeinschaft: Aufgaben und Herausforderungen. Stellungnahme der Kommission zum Beitrittsantrag Österreichs* (Bulletin der Europäischen Gemeinschaften (Beilage 4)).

European Commission (2001), *Eurobarometer. Public Opinion Analysis.* in DG Press of the European Commission (ed.), Brussels.

Falkner, Gerda (2000), 'How Pervasive are Euro-Politics? Effects of EU Membership on a New Member State', *Journal of Common Market Studies*, 38/2, 223–50.

Falkner, Gerda (2001a), 'The EU14's "Sanctions" Against Austria: Sense and Nonsense', *ECSA Review* (*Journal of the European Community Studies Association USA*), 14/1, Winter 2001, 14–20.

Falkner, Gerda (2001b), 'The Europeanisation of Austria: Misfit, Adaptation and Controversies'. *European Integration online Papers* (*EIoP*), 5/no. 13, available <http://eiop.or.at/eiop/texte/2001-013a.htm>.

Falkner, G., Treib, D., Hartlapp, M., and Leiber, S. (2005), *Complying with Europe. EU Minimum Harmonisation and Soft Law in the Member States* (Cambridge: Cambridge University Press).

Gerlich, Peter, and Neisser, Heinrich (eds) (1994), *Europa als Herausforderung. Wandlungsimpulse für das politische System Östereichs* (Wien: Signum).

Heinisch, Reinhard (2001), 'Austria: Confronting Controversy', in Eleanor E. Zeff and Ellen B. Pirro (eds), *The European Union and the Member States. Cooperation, Coordination, and Compromise.* (Boulder, CO/London: Lynne Rienner), 267–84.

Höll, Otmar, Pollack, Johannes, and Puntscher-Riekmann, Sonja (2003), 'Austria: domestic change through European integration', in Wessels, Maurer, and Mittag 337–54.

Karlhofer, Ferdinand, and Tálos, Emmerich (1996), *Sozialpartnerschaft und EU. Integrationsdynamik und Handlungsrahmen der österreichischen Sozialpartnerschaft* (Wien: Signum).

Kittel, Bernhard, and Tálos, Emmerich (1999), 'Interessenvermittlung und politischer Entscheidungsprozeß: Sozialpartnerschaft in den 1990er Jahren', in Ferdinand Karlhofer, and Emmerich Tálos (eds), *Zukunft der Sozialpartnerschaft: Veränderungsdynamik und Reformbedarf* (Wien: Signum), 95–136.

Ladrech, Robert (1994), 'Europeanisation of domestic politics and institutions: the case of France', *Journal of Common Market Studies*, 32/1, 69–88.

Laffan Brigid (2001a), 'Rapid Adaptation and Light Co-ordination', in O'Donnell R. (ed.), *Europe: The Irish Experience* (Dublin: IEA), 125–47.

Laffan Brigid (2001b), *Organising for a Changing Europe: Irish Central Government and the European Union*, Dublin (Trinity Blue paper).

Laffan Brigid (2001c), 'National Co-ordination in Brussels: The Role of Ireland's Permanent Representation', in Kassim H., Menon A., Peters G., and Wright V., *The National Co-ordination of EU Policy: The European Level* (Oxford: Oxford University Press), 277–96.

Laffan Brigid (2003), 'Ireland: Modernisation via Europeanisation', in Wessels W., A. Mauer, and J. Mittag, *Fifteen into one? The European Union and its Member States*, (Manchester: Manchester University Press), 248–70.

Luif, Paul (1995), *On the Road to Brussels. The Political Dimension of Austria's, Finland's and Sweden's Accession to the European Union* (Wien: Braumüller).

Luif, Paul (1998), 'Austria: Adaptation through Anticipation', in Hanf and Soetendorp 116–30.

Morass, Michael (1996), 'Österreich im Entscheidungsprozess der Europäischen Union', in Emmerich Tálos and Gerda Falkner (eds), *EU-Mitglied Österreich. Gegenwart und Perspektiven: Eine Zwischenbilanz* (Wien: Manz), 32–50.

Müller, Wolfgang C. (2000), 'EU Co-ordination in Austria: Challenges and Responses', in Hussein Kassim, Guy B. Peters, and Vincent Wright (eds), *The National Co-ordination of EU Policy: The Domestic Level* (London: Macmillan).

O'Donnell, Rory (2000), *Ireland in Europe: the Economic Dimension* (Dublin: Institute of European Affairs).

Pernthaler, Peter, and Hilpold, Peter (2000), 'Sanktionen als Instrument der Politikkontrolle—der Fall Österreich', *Integration*, 23/2, 105–19.

Schneider, Heinrich (2000), 'Österreich in Acht und Bann—ein Schritt zur politisch integrierten "Wertegemeinschaft"', *Integration*, 23/2, 120–48.

Sozialpartnerstellungnahme (1989). '*Österreich und die Europäische Integration*'.

Steiner, Gerhard, and Trattnigg, Rita (1998), 'Sektorstudie Umweltpolitik', in Gerda Falkner and Wolfgang C. Müller (eds), *Österreich im europäischen Mehrebenensystem* (Wien: Signum), 139–71.

Tálos, Emmerich, and Falkner, Gerda (1996), 'Österreich in der EU: Erwartungen—Gegenwart—Perspektiven', in Emmerich Tálos, and Gerda Falkner (eds), *EU-Mitglied Österreich. Gegenwart und Perspektiven* (Wien: Manz), 287–312.

Tálos, Emmerich, and Kittel, Bernhard (2001), *Gesetzgebung in Österreich* (Wien: WUV/Universitätsverlag).

Chapter 11

Greece and Portugal: Convergent or Divergent Europeanization?

Béatrice Hibou

Contents

Summary

This chapter compares the integration of two relatively small southern member states of the EU. They both joined the European Union in the 1980s and shared some common challenges. These included a certain degree of refocusing from previous international orientations and the processes of economic modernization and administrative adaptation to the EU. The availability of EU funding was an important facilitator for the two states' integration. The chapter demonstrates that the two countries' experiences of Europeanization have followed distinct pathways, conditioned by history as well as the economic and social circumstances of the country concerned.

Introduction

Greece's and Portugal's European integration processes have often been compared due to a certain number of features they have in common: small peripheral states, lower economic development and low industrialization, lower standard of living than the EU average, recent democratization, southern European location and accession in the 1980s to the European Community. And often, at least until the late 1990s, they were held up as the couple that perfectly epitomized the bad and good pupil of Europe. But, in addition to the fact that this sort of judgment can always be reversed—Portugal being singled out by the Commission in 2001 for breaching the Stability Pact rules on monetary union—approaching European integration in this way presents a number of pitfalls. First, analyses in terms of good and bad pupil (or, by the same token, in terms of convergence and divergence) do not help to grasp the complexity and ambivalence of integration processes, no matter which member state is analysed. All the themes developed in this chapter tend to show that institutional adaptations and the reorientation of economic policies have followed different paths and it is difficult to set a general course. Second, apparent similarities should not conceal specific national trajectories and hence the distinct nature of each country's European integration process. Many analyses, in almost exclusively examining the recent phenomenon of 'European compliance', often underestimate the differences that arise from extremely diverse economic, social, and political histories. The examples below suggest on the contrary that the political and social signification of member state Europeanization depends to a great extent on the specific, historically constructed perceptions they have of European issues. Third, the influence of European construction on the small peripheral countries is generally thought to be much greater than that exercised on Europe's large, central, more developed countries. This is probably true if one sticks to the formal definitions of economic policies, to the apparent (re)modelling of certain institutions, to dominant discourses and the vocabulary used to legitimate public action. But, if one looks at how policies are actually implemented and especially, if one seeks to detect the socio-political significations and the ways national actors understand Europeanization, then the 'European constraint' seems just as ambivalent in Greece and Portugal as in France, England, or Germany.

The politics of Greek and Portuguese accession

By comparison to the recent enlargement processes toward the East, the relative speed and 'simplicity' of Portugal's negotiation process (1980–5) and especially Greece's (1975–80) are striking. The *acquis communautaire* was already the cornerstone of these negotiations, but in retrospect, the constraints it ended up exerting were fairly weak, for three reasons.

The primacy of politics, first of all: for the Community authorities, the aim was to demonstrate unflagging support for the first democracies of the 'third wave', by not taking into account, in the very terms of accession, their respective economic and social situations, whatever they might be. For instance, a 1976/7 Commission report clearly stated that Greece was absolutely not prepared economically to enter the Community, but that it would be integrated nevertheless on the basis of a purely political decision. The perception of these countries as basically Western, liberal societies with market economies, despite the momentary divergence of their political trajectory, laid the groundwork for this position.

Favourable economic assessments, next: due to the little economic weight of Greece and Portugal, the budgetary impact of extending European mechanisms to these two countries seemed negligible and unproblematic. Furthermore, without similar experiences, the difficulties of adaptation and the financial costs of the 'catching up' process were vastly underestimated. This was particularly true for Greece, and negotiations were more rigorous with the countries of the Iberian peninsula. Moreover, the vague idea circulated that association agreements (1962 for Greece and 1972 for Portugal) and mainly Portugal's membership in EFTA had already played a role in the economic rapprochement and opening of these countries to Europe.

Last, a historical period of optimism: at the end of the 1970s and in the early 1980s, the elites in power shared all the more evident optimism for European institutions and processes since they envisaged them partially as substitutes for the declining economic dynamism of the old continent. Not to mention that the ambiguities and uncertainties of enlargement had yet to appear in full, particularly because the threshold effect for the number of member states had yet to be reached.

It can thus be noted in retrospect that discussions between applicants and the Commission were relatively easy and swift. Agricultural negotiations were without a doubt the thorniest problem. But there again, the relative difficulty of the Portuguese negotiations and the slow pace at which they took place were largely due to the fact that the Commission had decided that the two Iberian countries had to negotiate accession and enter Europe simultaneously. Negotiations hinged mainly on implementation deadlines, temporary derogations, and transitional periods, not on the content of the *acquis communautaire*, including for the agricultural policy, even while its unsuitability to southern Europe agrarian and rural conditions, particularly in Portugal, was being acknowledged at that very time. Neither Greece nor Portugal defended an original position, a social or economic model, or specificity. But the similarities stop there. In Greece, accession occurred without a broad consensus, even despite a strong cleavage between political parties (Karamanlis's New Democracy and the PC and Papandreou's PASOK) and within the population, a cleavage that leaned more in favour of opponents to integration. In Portugal, on the other hand, European integration came about without mobilizing the people, but without great opposition either, in that it was the fruit of a convergence between elites, since all political parties, except for the PCP, agreed that this option was the country's inescapable (and desirable) future.

Negotiation processes already revealed certain features of the Greek and Portuguese ways of being European. For both countries, the most important discussion points had to do with financing and reducing institutional constraints, thereby unveiling a primarily instrumental vision of Europe. The tradition of small dependent countries can explain this absence of a clear and original vision, as well as the determined quest for additional resources. It also helps understand why the two countries sought more to obtain deadlines, exemptions, and budgetary extensions than to influence the logic and concept behind the European process (on Greece, see Tsalicoglou 1995; Verney 1993). But entering Europe also involves rethinking and redefining borders, and in this realm the positions were easily perceived. In Greece, the most sensitive nego-tiation points became salient quickly and virulently, with regard to Turkey and, to a lesser extent, the Middle East. In Portugal on the other hand, the strategy was more unspoken and less direct. But the Portuguese authorities constantly sought to set themselves apart from the parallel process undertaken by Spain, appearing as the well-behaved and docile children of the accession process and defending a certain vision of national independence and sovereignty (particularly with regard to its neighbour), for instance in delaying the opening of strategic sectors to European competition.

The ambiguity of being European

Portugal's and Greece's position in Europe are extremely ambiguous: both fully fledged members and in a dependent, even third-worldist posture; both entirely in Europe and on the outside. The problem is not one of a lack of adaptation, a lack of Europeanness or even European immaturity. This ambiguity illustrates at once the multiple facets of being in Europe, the fluidity and the blurring of Europe's social, political, and existential frontiers and the ambivalence of what it means to belong to Europe.

External links

Portugal and Greece are European countries: that is taken for granted today. But this belief is a recent one, and fluctuations in perceptions illustrate how fluid the bound-aries of major civilizations and political spaces can be. Historically, European borders shifted because, basically, they do not constitute a geographic line of demarcation. They cannot thus be understood solely in legal and administrative terms. The bound-aries are sociological and existential, and thereby highly dependent on socio-political transformations and historical contingencies. The definition of Europe has constantly changed, not only 'because of' small peripheral countries like Greece and Portugal. Britain, too, was long perceived as being outside of Europe (this was true up through the 1940s), whereas Turkey was considered a European power (until the 1920s).

Without reviewing the history of these two countries in detail, it is helpful to rapidly recall a few major characteristics of their formation that highlight this ambi-guity. Although Greece was born out of the Greek revolt against the declining Ottoman Empire (1821), the creation of Greece (1830), and the country's unification (1830–1926) were only materially made possible through the military, political and economic intervention of the major European powers. Contemporary Greece is largely an offspring of European nationalism and romanticism, and a very European interpretation of Hellenism. But at the same time, it has glorified its own way of being oriental and lays claim, no doubt ambiguously but nevertheless incessantly, to its

Byzantine, and more recently, to its Ottoman heritage. It has rediscovered the Balkan side of its identity, just when the Balkans are considered to be at Europe's doorstep. And the anti-Western and third-worldist tradition was long fed by the dictatorship and later by populist parties starting with Andreas Papandreou's PASOK. This explains why it took the impact of structural funds, cohesion funds, the CAP and even more so, historical contingencies (the fall of the Berlin Wall and the Balkan crisis) for perceptions and feelings about Europe to alter significantly, without, however, erasing the ambivalence of belonging to Western Europe.

Despite appearances, Portugal's European trajectory is almost as tortuous. Of course the Portuguese have constantly repeated that their country is the oldest nation-state in Europe whose current borders are the most stable on the continent. Portugal long-developed privileged ties with old European powers (Flanders, France, England) and participated in some of the most fundamental episodes in European history, among them the new world conquest. At the same time, Portugal built itself up in opposition to Europe by long giving preference to its empire and colonial relations. It also structured itself in opposition to Spain with the economic, political and military support of England, at the time considered non-European. Its relations with the United States were quite close until the 1960s, and since then, Portugal has remained one of the EU's most Atlantic-oriented member countries. The discrepancy between a very ambiguous, even hostile discourse toward Europe and the true nature of their relations cannot be ignored: the gap widened into an abyss in the 1960s. But this contradiction itself is indicative of the uncertainty of Portugal's Europeanness until the end of the 1960s. Portugal's turn toward Europe, which occurred in the 1950s, was primarily the product of material and pragmatic evolutions such as emigration to Europe (whereas the migratory flow had previously been toward Brazil), the flow of direct foreign investment and European tourists and the gradual marginalization of trade flows with the colonial empire. EFTA membership in 1959 and the association agreement with the EEC simply rounded off this turn of direction.

Dependence

Greece and Portugal have in common, historically, the fact that both are small peripheral countries with respect to Europe. They are geographically peripheral, of course, but especially economically and politically. This situation resulted in a historical dependence on Europe, and consequently gave rise to a tradition of coping with this dependence. It was mainly starting in the eighteenth century that Portugal experienced a long period of backwardness. The country was unable to keep up with the quick pace of development in Europe and the United States in the nineteenth century, and trapped itself into a relationship of foreign debt and financial and technological dependence on France and especially Great Britain, which had, moreover, dominated it economically since at least the eighteenth century. As for Greece, it was born dependent, so to speak. The country has almost always been financially, economically and technologically dependent on Great Britain, France, Germany and the United States, and it did not undergo intensive development until the 1960s. This long history of dependence is reflected still today especially by the vigour of dependentist thought in both Portugal and Greece, as can be seen in the preponderance of discourse on the need for modernization, development, and the ambition to catch up (on Greece see

Mouzelis 1986; Featherstone 1998). European integration can in fact be interpreted as a new form or a reactivation of dependence, as suggests the absence of any original contribution to the functioning of Europe on the part of either country. This tendency has been perpetuated in recent years, particularly through negotiations on eastern enlargement, which both countries view as a financial threat (because structural funds will necessarily decrease after 2006). Portugal, moreover, considers that enlargement places it even more on the geographic periphery. The summits, in Nice (June 2000), Ghent and London after the 11 September attacks, exacerbated the sensitivity of the EU's small peripheral countries because of a perception that the large member states predominated.

However, this apparent consistency conceals very different perceptions, understandings and strategies due, first, to their different geographic positions and, second, to their long histories, which have nothing in common. Whereas Portugal was once a 'great nation' (even more so in terms of its self-image) and intensely resented its economic 'decadence', the onset of which it dates to the Treaty of Methuen with England signed in 1703, Greece, to ensure its very existence, has always been obliged to rely on the major powers. From an economic standpoint, foreign influence was therefore greater in Greece: The League of Nations played a much greater role there in the 1920s and 1930s in defining and implementing financial reforms than it did in Portugal. Similarly, French, German, and Italian legislation were more directly and more forcibly imported. Today, these different histories and perceptions of dependence are reflected by often opposite stands taken on European issues. Greece, which generally aligns itself on all economic topics (including those that affect it directly and almost exclusively, such as the tobacco and cotton policies), has up until recently been vehemently opposed to any compromise on issues that touch on its national identity, such as relations with Turkey or the Balkans, countering with obstructionist threats and unconstructive criticism. On the other hand, Portugal has rarely opposed Community decisions, including on thorny subjects affecting it such as Spain's membership of the Community or privileged relations with the Portuguese-speaking world, preferring to play on ambiguities in implementing directives and the division of competences between the national and European level. This position has also been reflected in the swift and sweeping ratification of directives, even if follow-up and actual applications are quite at variance with the spirit of them.

Unequivocal membership

Economic dependence, dependentist thought and sometimes even an outsider's vision of Europe in no way prevent Greece and Portugal from being full members of the Community. Not only has the two countries' participation in the daily workings of European bodies become general practice, but above all, the European presidencies have fully played their role of identification and belonging, mainly in these past years (first semester 2000 for Portugal, first semester 2003 for Greece). Similarly, their participation in the single currency (in 1999 for Portugal, in 2000 for Greece) did not require as much number-juggling as it did for other European countries, whatever the detractors of the PIGS (Portugal—Italy—Greece—Spain) or the 'Club Med' may believe. Recently, Portugal has been particularly active in defending the interests of 'small' countries, especially in Nice, and Greece has played a decisive role in the evolution of the Union's relations with Turkey, especially during preparation for the Copenhagen summit. Generally speaking, the two countries actively defend their interests and their dossiers, for instance during negotiations on Agenda 2000 to preserve cohesion funds or in support within the constitutional Convention for reinforcing the Commission's powers with respect to the 'big' countries. As participation in Europe starts to lose its obvious advantages, particularly financial ones, and evolutions grow more complex, Greece and Portugal are asserting themselves and becoming more active, either to maintain the status quo (structural funding, the CAP and the Council voting system), either to combat the spectre of directorship by the big countries, or yet again to contribute to the debate on the redefinition of Union boundaries, particularly on its southern flank.

Last but not least, Greece's and Portugal's unequivocal membership is illustrated by their total adhesion to 'European norms', often in a fairly idealized form, since it is so difficult to define them. Their objective dependence is thus reflected by the widespread propagation of a very pessimistic, critical and normative view of themselves (even if it is not shared by all), with respect to a certain image they have constructed of Europe. It is by this standard that they deem their civil service to be backward, inefficient and corrupt, their economy underdeveloped and their labour management defective: without a rigorous analysis having necessarily been undertaken on what these European norms are.

Managing dependence as EU member states

The so-called 'European constraint' must be analysed in this context. Despite the peripheral location of these two countries, the magnitude of dependentist thought with its explicit acknowledgement of 'backwardness', the determination to catch up and modernize, the instrumentalization and idealization of European 'norms', it is misleading to speak of a European straitjacket. Discourse, texts and principles of legitimacy are not everything. In concrete terms, European integration of its member states is also shaped by a particular tradition of international integration, the relationship to Europe and the way dependence is handled, as well as by a specific understanding of European issues.

Europeanization and economic nationalism

The combination of objective dependency and a dependentist view of the world on one side and a certain nationalism on the other, explain that the inevitable internationalization of the Portuguese and Greek economies was done reluctantly and consequently in a defensive manner. This is true of both countries, even today. But here again, history has left a different imprint on the two countries' opening processes.

In word, mind, and partly in deed, Portugal until the late 1960s shut itself up in a backward-looking vision of its grandeur, withdrawing into itself and its declining empire that was gradually slipping away, dominated by a protectionist and nationalist vision of its economy. Even if the autarchic discourse was far from actual behaviour, and if the choice to join Europe was enthusiastic and genuine (at least from 1977 on and up until recently), the country's political and economic elites harboured this fear of opening and internationalization, essentially from an economic standpoint, because culturally, they have always been open to the outside, particularly Europe. Such discrepancies (economic/socio-cultural; discourse/politics; perceptions/reality) and dual positions (protectionism and openness) today are reflected in a two-sided behaviour: on one hand, a genuine Europeanization and considerable Hispanization of the economy and, on the other, the persistence of a protectionist and nationalist discourse, reflexes contrary to the principles of the single market that are sometimes acted upon, and a perception that openness is dangerous and must be controlled.

On the other hand, Greece, since independence, has been divided over its relation to other countries. Some interests, and not the least of them, have always been open to the outside and have always played the international card: already in the 1830s–1840s, ship owners, large trading firms, and private shareholders of the National Bank were involved in international activities and transactions, in conjunction with certain arms of the nascent state. Others, on the contrary, strongly resented this foreign domination, recommending a protectionist policy reverting to the national economy. Up until today, Greece's economic history has largely been one of swinging back and forth and a particularly flagrant economic and financial dualism in the way it has handled international integration.

Neighbours rediscovered

Until recently, no dynamic action has allowed Greek or Portuguese companies to gain a significant foothold abroad, no more in Europe than elsewhere. It is, moreover, fairly significant that banks and businesses in these two countries are so little and poorly represented in European bodies in Brussels, and that in the rationale of modernization and globalization, they do not show preference for the European market. The behaviour of Greek companies is beginning to change, favoured as they are by their regional environment and their tradition of a greater familiarity with international markets, but here again, it is not the heart of Europe that is targeted but its periphery. In Greece as in Portugal, Europeanization has meant more the rediscovery of its neighbours, Spain for Portugal, the Balkans for Greece, than the discovery of Europe as a whole. This has had major consequences in terms of dynamics in that, historically, Portugal has always feared Spanish domination whereas the Greeks, even before they had formed a homogeneous polity and an independent nation-state, had had a tendency to dominate their immediate neighbours.

In Greece, Europeanization has above all meant the rediscovery of the Balkans and the countries of Eastern Europe. 'Rediscovery', because these ties have always existed, even if the entrance of these countries in the Soviet bloc after the Second World War had weakened them. To some degree, this historic moment can be interpreted as the adoption of a new posture: the usual intermediary between Europe and the Balkans. This turnaround is easily explained by the fall of the Berlin Wall, then the wars in the former Yugoslavia. But it was made possible by a set of conditions, beginning with the historic ties between these countries, their geographic proximity and the sweeping privatization and liberalization policies in the former socialist countries. And by a constraint: unable to conquer other markets due to their relative archaism, their lack of competitiveness and their weak capital base, it was the only geographical area Greek businesses could prospect in. This is true of the banks, which, like their Greek clients, invested in Macedonia, Bulgaria, Albania, and Romania, and have projects in Turkey. Greek businesses in these countries are a step ahead of the banks, particularly for having reactivated former networks of acquaintances: students who could not afford to study in French, German, Italian, or British universities and who went on to study in Zagreb, Bucharest, Belgrade, or Budapest; trade networks linked to Greek immigration; Greek communities who had sought asylum in the Soviet bloc after the civil war when the communists were crushed, and so on. The opening of the Greek entrepreneurial sector, still marginal but already dynamic, flows directly from the new way in which Greece projects itself in the region, both as a Balkan country in Europe and a European country in the Balkans. This rediscovery, however, reflects the ambiguity of Greece's standing in Europe: both on the inside and out, a reflection of how the Balkan countries perceive their position with respect to an ambiguous European policy, and just as the Europeans from the 'centre', in other words the countries of the EU, view this region (Wallden 1999).

The main orientation of Portuguese investments abroad might cast doubt on their relevance to Europe, for they are primarily made in either captive markets (Angola, Mozambique, emigrant Portuguese community and, in more competitive conditions, Brazil) or markets with a low potential (tiny niches in Eastern Europe). It is striking to note how marginal, in terms of both amounts and location, investments are abroad and especially how weak Portugal's presence is in the European Community.

On the other hand, relations with Spain have been totally transformed by the simultaneous Europeanization of both Iberian peninsula countries. With the advent of democracy in Portugal, then Spain, and especially negotiations with the EC, the rapprochement between these two countries quickly resulted in the signature of a treaty of friendship and cooperation in 1977 that brought an end to isolationism. A bilateral Portuguese–Spanish trade agreement (1980) later organized the dismantling of customs and legal barriers. Every year an Iberian summit takes place. This event is not purely rhetorical but genuinely attempts to overcome divergences (for instance over water and management of shared rivers), define common strategies within the EU with regard to cross-border cooperation and common infrastructures as well as other multilateral organizations, and even initiate cooperation policies, modelled after the Ibero-American summits. Their bilateral political relations have definitely been pacified, even if Spain continues to consider its neighbour as too small to be viewed as 'strategic', and if Portugal continues to exploit the syndrome of the 'little' partner. By choosing to deal with Madrid via Brussels, Lisbon has thus managed to normalize its relations with its age-old enemy, at least from a political and security standpoint. For Portuguese nationalism continues to be expressed, albeit *mezza voce*, but it is nevertheless articulated in economic matters: the theme of Spanish invasion is still alive. Spain's role in Portuguese foreign trade, once insignificant, has indeed become essential: from 0.9 per cent in 1960, 4.2 per cent in 1973, 14 per cent in 1990 to 21.1 per cent in 1998. By 1994 Spain had become Portugal's primary trading partner. Spain now has more than 20 per cent of the Portuguese market, although Portugal's market share in Spain is only 6 per cent; there is still an imbalance in favour of Spain in the high technology sectors. For Portugal, relations with Spain are without a doubt *the* main issue of Europeanization and globalization, whereas the opposite is obviously not the case.

Europe as a means of finance

Traditionally, Greece's and Portugal's trade balances are in deficit, the balance of payments being ensured by a wide variety of external financing. In both countries there is in fact a sort of myth of the external windfall, a myth of 'invisibles': in all political and economic situations, the arrival of external resources prevented massive debt (even if Greece found itself in default on payments in the nineteenth century) and total dependence. EU membership can thus be interpreted as keeping with this tradition: a new source of external windfalls.

Of course, this has not been a conscious strategy or policy devised by the successive governments in Greece and Portugal, in other words a talent for resourcefulness and survival. It instead stems from a constantly recurring situation produced by various action rationales (survival, enrichment, chance, economic calculation, independence, social mobility) and various actors (migrants, settlers, capitalists, investors, traders). In any event, at least since the nineteenth century, the external deficit has been covered by fortunate contingencies that only rarely involved strategies of planning, economic modernization, industrialization or the quest for foreign markets. For Portugal, it involved emigration to Brazil and emigrants' remittances, the return on Portuguese investments abroad, especially in Brazil, re-exportation of colonial products, re-exportation of European products, usually illegally, to Spain, and, in the 1960s, emigration to Europe, emigrant remittances, and tourism. For Greece it involved emigration to Europe, the United States and Australia, return on Greek investments abroad and a portion of ship owners' profits, and more recently, tourism.

Membership of the European Community was a new opportunity for all these actors and a new environment for these rationales of action through European transfers (structural funds, cohesion funds, the CAP), the rise in direct foreign investment (even if it must not be overestimated, especially in Greece where it has always been minimal, but also in Portugal) and the conquest of new markets (less so, in fact, for exports than for re-exports and services, especially in Greece's case). Furthermore, participation in the single currency has created a new context, favourable to deficit countries in the short term, since the euro allows greater deficits without immediate consequences and to some extent numbs the economic and political decision-makers. Both a constraint and an opportunity, a straitjacket and a factor of laxity, an incentive to act yet to wait and see. European integration means all this at once.

Migratory flows and the new European order

Traditionally countries of emigration, Greece and Portugal became countries of immigration in the 1990s, a trend that has now been amply documented. This reversal has been analysed as the sign of European normalization, a reflection of the modernization of the Greek and Portuguese economies, the expression of a convergence process going on inside Europe. But this blanket interpretation is unsatisfactory. Here again, the historic modalities of international integration of the Greek and Portuguese populations have to a large extent oriented and fashioned recent migratory movements.

In Greece, immigration (to a large extent illegal) grew significantly in the 1990s due to events in neighbouring countries. Figures vary according to the source and counting methods, but anywhere between one to 1.2 million legal and illegal, permanent and seasonal migrants are estimated. According to the OECD, the illegal foreign population makes up 12 per cent of the working population. These are mainly Albanians, Bulgarians, and Romanians as well as Polish, other east bloc citizens, and more recently, Egyptians, Filipinos, Turks, Chinese, and Pakistanis. But Greece is not only a host country, it is also and above all a transit country. Both the frontier between the East and West and an intermediary for the Balkans, becoming part of the EU and, particularly, one of the Schengen countries, has overwhelmingly resulted in making the country a gateway to the Union through which one usually passes illegally.

Studies by Portuguese sociologists have recently shown the full complexity of the new migratory configuration in Portugal. Certainly the country has become a country of immigration, but it has not lost its emigration tradition as a result, or to be more precise, it has recently renewed it. Here again the weight of history is crushing: the immigrants are mainly Portuguese-speaking Africans and Brazilians; Portuguese emigrants are once again headed in the very large majority for France, Germany, and Switzerland. But the weight of European integration is equally a factor: the tightening of borders and free internal circulation have worked together to reactivate the advantage of Portuguese labour in new forms (temporary workers, subcontractors, service providers) and in new modalities (by taking advantage of lower social costs and salaries in Portugal). Portuguese-speaking immigrants are now to a great extent illegal, given the primacy granted to Schengen and Europe to the detriment of the paternalistic and colonialist rationale. The arrival of 'non-traditional' migrants (Moldavians, Ukrainians, Chinese, Indians, and Pakistanis) is particularly influenced by the slackness in border controls and certain 'loopholes' in integrating European legislation into the Portuguese system (Baganha 2001).

The restructuring of state intervention

European membership means, particularly for Greece and Portugal, both the strengthening of the state and a change in its methods of intervention. This has been widely recognized today, and is usually demonstrated in a global, quantitative, and technical fashion by examining how the CAP, structural funds, technical standardization procedures, administrative upgrading, and the adoption of directives have been reflected in the state's budget and civil service. The points made below will also underscore another aspect of these transformations, the political dimension, and show how they all fit into the history and specificity of Greek and Portuguese modes of government.

Increased public spending

The first area in which state intervention was restructured is finance. Although Greece and especially Portugal entered Europe at the time when economic liberalism was on the upswing, their integration very quickly led to an increase in public spending. In both countries, prior to the switch to democracy and entrance into Europe, the weight of the state in the economy was fairly small in financial terms, and the budgetary policy followed then was characterized by a fairly low balance between spending and revenues. Whereas public spending was only 21 per cent in Greece (1958) and Portugal (1960), it was about 40 per cent for the Community as a whole. These figures were approximately 30 per cent and 45 per cent respectively at the end of the 1970s: due to their political history, Greece and Portugal did not have a welfare state characteristic of the other European countries. Since the fall of the Colonels and the Carnation Revolution, the policy pursued by the new governments, whose objective was to reintegrate the population excluded during the dictatorship, therefore involved a catching-up process that European integration merely accelerated: in 1985 and 1991 respectively, Greece and Portugal joined the rest of Europe with budget expenditures amounting to slightly over 50 per cent of their GDP.

The relationship between changes in budget expenditure and European integration is ambiguous. There is no doubt that budgetary policies both in Greece and Portugal were mainly shaped by national constraints (political and social aims of the PASOK government in the early 1980s in Greece and the post-revolutionary governments in Portugal). But these turned out to be perfectly compatible with the European welfare-state norm. Naturally, this convergence is not to be exaggerated. Greece and Portugal reoriented their budgetary policy toward the European norm precisely at the time when member states had begun converting to liberal policies. The system set up so far turned out to be highly inefficient and very costly. The rise in expenditures was also largely due to an increase in public sector employees. But it is interesting to note that although they began at a much lower level than the Community (−11 points in 1979 in Greece; −10 points in 1985 in Portugal), budget expenditures reached the Community average in less than six years. Greek and Portuguese policies—by distributing purchasing power via salary increases that were much higher than the increase in productivity as well as advantageous reforms of the retirement system, health care system, and social welfare system in general—unquestionably accelerated the harmonization of consumer habits and living standards, even if this occurred regardless of criteria of rationalization and financial viability and at the expense of increasing debt.

At the same time, the specific European institutional mechanisms had a direct effect on state financial measures, if only through the management of agricultural funds and structural and cohesion funds. In fact, net transfers amounted to very high percentages of the GDP, especially with the entrance of the Iberian countries into the Community (see the data in Table 11.1).

The influence of European integration was and remains dual as regards agricultural subsidies in the context of the CAP. There was indeed a significant rise in support for agriculture up until the early 1990s; the weight of public interventionism in this area increased as a consequence. But government efforts triggered by adopting the Common Agricultural Policy were not sustained over time. On the contrary, already in the late 1980s, a substitution effect was taking place to the benefit of European funds, which amounted to over 90 per cent of agricultural subsidies. This reflects an undeniable retraction of national institutions in this sector and the virtual absence of a specific agricultural policy.

Analysis of the financing of public investment is very similar, except that European aid is less substantial, slower to be set up and the withdrawal of the state is less significant. But without a doubt, joining Europe was synonymous with the reinforcement of public action in the public investment sector.

Table 11.1 Net European transfers in % GDP since accession

	1981	1982	1983	1984	1985	1986	1987	1988	1989	1990	
GREECE	0.3	1.2	2.0	1.7	2.1	2.9	3.0	2.9	3.8	3.4	
PORTUGAL						0.6	1.0	1.6	1.6	1.4	
	1991	1992	1993	1994	1995	1996	1997	1998	1999	2000	2001
GREECE	4.4	4.1	4.3	4.3	4.3	4.1	3.8	3.9	3.6	3.3	3.5
PORTUGAL	3.6	3.8	3.8	3.4	3.1	3.2	2.9	3.1	2.7	1.9	1.5

Sources: J. Spraos, 'EU transfers and Greece's real exchange rates: a naked view', in Ralph C. Bryant, Nicholas C. Garganas, and George S. Tavlas (eds), *Greece's Economic Performance and Prospects* (Athens/Washington, Bank of Greece/The Brookings Institution, 2001), 281–321; José das Silva Lopes, *A Economia Portuguesa desde 1960* (Lisbon, Gradiva, 1996); *Eurostat*.
Note: n/a denotes data not available.

Changing fields of intervention

In addition to these quantitative transformations, at the same time and much more significantly, the fields of state intervention changed. Like in all other European countries, a huge task of bringing regulations up to European norms was undertaken. In certain areas this effort was more intense than in other European member states given the late entry of Greece and Portugal into the Community and the lack of a tradition of public action in various fields. Such was the case of social policy (health care, education, retirement, child labour), social dialogue (bargaining structures were set up, as well as an economic and social council and an ombudsman), but also, more implicitly, in the areas of regulations and economic incentives (industrial policies, environmental policies).

In Portugal the Carnation Revolution had already made huge leaps possible in terms of employment policies, even if the texts were and still are only marginally implemented. With European integration, innovation took place more in the field of social policy and the fight against exclusion and poverty. Support measures for struggling businesses and nationalizations had become incompatible with the Community's liberal philosophy, which is even more true of the Union. State intervention was therefore redirected at pursuing privatizations (after a revision of the Portuguese Constitution in 1989) and the definition of new industrial policies on the basis of investment incentives and subsidies (particularly European subsidies with the PEDIP projects). In Greece, a similar restructuring in favour of social policies occurred. But industrial policies were virtually non-existent, and the economy was very clearly reoriented toward the service sector. It is interesting to note in this regard that since Greece joined the EU, it is mainly civil service administrations, considered 'non-productive', that have grown (public works, education, health care, public administration, real estate, and related activities).

These modifications are all the product of a more or less faithful adaptation to Community regulations. But European integration also triggered specific restructuring on the part of the public authorities, a function of specific national perceptions and preoccupations. Such was the case of Portugal's policy of safeguarding national interests (for instance with acquisition of equity or heterodox interpretations of regulations and legislation). This was also the case of Greece's policy of intermediation and construction of a regional pole (by setting up specific bodies, financing mechanisms, studies, prospecting and consulting, etc.).

Problems of administrative adaptation

In that European membership first and foremost translates as additional public spending and an extension of the fields of government intervention, it goes without saying that national administrations have played and continue overwhelmingly to play a fundamental role in the adaptation process. As a sort of filter that largely conditions the modalities of European influence, they thereby constitute one of the main channels through which national characteristics are expressed.

The consequences and ups and downs of administrative adaptation depend, like everywhere, on the nature, history and functioning of national civil service bodies. Greece and Portugal share (certainly with other member states as well) a common trait in this domain: the lack of a technocratic tradition.

In Portugal, despite the absolutism of the late seventeenth century, the process of bureaucratic centralization that followed the fall of the old regime in 1820 and the restructuring of the civil service in the mid-nineteenth century, the civil service was never conceived as a high place of knowledge and authority. Even under the Salazar dictatorship, during which the civil service played a much more important role than in the past, there were very few technocrats even if, at the time, the senior civil service enjoyed a certain prestige and constituted a real means of social advancement. But this configuration was weakened by the very hierarchical and arbitrary functioning of the civil service and by the competition exercised by other loci of power (the *gremios*, corporatist bodies, informal networks linking the political and financial spheres). The revolutionary period and the liberal turn taken in the 1980s contributed to denigrating the state such that today the civil service is to a large extent perceived as resistant to change, a sphere of clientelism and a mere source of low but steady income (Oliveira Rocha 1998). Greece's history differs considerably but arrives at a similar perception: the civil service is seen as providing access to a steady income, but not as a place of prestige and even less as an instrument by which to serve the public. Greece's administrative apparatus was fashioned partly according to a certain Ottoman tradition (delegation, patrimonialized, and considerably fragmented civil service) and a strong dependence on the superpowers (weight of the League of Nations and certain Western bureaucracies) such that the national civil service has never been recognized as a fundamental instrument of state power. In both countries, the traditional public function is characterized even today by a lack of knowledge and professionalism.

But Community regulations and financing are demanding in terms of public administration. The lack of a technocratic tradition potentially increases the role of Europe in transformations of the administrative apparatus in countries such as Greece and Portugal. To accomplish this, a preliminary set of Community measures has aimed at improving the functioning of the civil service and continues to do so. Portugal and Greece have thus benefited from technical programs financed by Europe such as

'Politia' to improve the quality of the civil service and 'Taxis' to computerize the tax administration. Other projects have involved training civil servants, improving the administration and computerizing services, particularly customs, the revenue service, control of agricultural aid, and statistics. There have been marked improvements, especially in personnel management: recruitment was professionalized in the 1990s in both Greece and Portugal with a reform of the competitive exams; in Greece, the Supreme Council for Personnel Selection was created in 1995 to avoid politicization, etc. But these reforms are very slow in producing a more efficient administration, and are often confined to small niches (a given department of the revenue service, an exemplary project such as the 'Citizens' Centre' in Portugal). Not to mention that some transformations are illusory, such as the countless computerization programs that are sometimes incompatible among one another or between services, and always subject to the civil servants' good will (as was the case of tax inspections in Greece) (Spanou 2003).

But Europe has a much greater influence on national administrative structures through another mechanism: Brussels' demands as regards the management of European funds. For instance, structures under ministry supervision have been specially created or adapted to manage Community financing that could not be handled by routine administrative procedures. Moreover, personnel training programs foster a certain transfer of experience and technical knowledge: after spending a few years in Brussels as civil servants or experts, the personnel return to their home country with specialized Commission skills that they should theoretically adapt by suggesting modifications of legal frameworks, pilot projects and studies. These consultants are only rarely incorporated into the civil service. More often, they remain in hybrid structures alongside the traditional administration. In both cases a sort of parallel administrative or para-administrative structure is created that is supposed to improve the workings of the civil service, with priority given to European funds, but that is also spread to other areas of public action.

This process was implemented in the late 1980s in Portugal with the creation of para-public entities to manage European funds (INGA and IFADAP for agricultural policy, coordination commissions to manage structural funds in the context of Community support frameworks), but quickly spread to other sectors such as public works, transportation, and education, such that alongside the traditional administration, a series of agencies, institutes, and jobs developed with more flexible rules of operation, particularly for finance and accounting, and often more professional and better paid staff. For at the same time, the development of contract jobs within the administration allowed it to recruit skills (that is of computer programmers and other specialists) that were previously inaccessible. On the other hand, it was not until the late 1990s that Greece adopted this model, following serious dysfunctions in administering European funds and in reaction to repeated pressures from Brussels. But now, given the slowness of civil service reform, the Simitis and Karamanlis governments in Greece have resolutely opted for this model—even if the decision remains largely implicit: to create a new civil service, *ex nihilo*, with a private status although under public supervision, on the basis of a competitive exam open to young people who have often graduated from schools abroad, with an experience of Europe, generally from the private sector or the institutions in Brussels. This new parallel civil service creams off the best elements of the public sector and the authorities manage to pay them accordingly. Since it had been unable to manage a tentacular and inefficient public administration, this option reflects the will, for the first time in Greece's history, to build a competent civil service, a will that largely stemmed from a constraint turned into an opportunity.

This model is just emerging in Greece, particularly in professional training, the management of unemployment and social aid, and the promotion of public works under the third Community support framework. But it is gradually spreading to areas that are very much the preserve of the state, such as the traditional civil service (Civil Service Ministry complaints department). This model, it would appear, at least in the political discourse and spirit, is promised a great future in Greece. On the other hand, it is already in crisis in Portugal, for a variety of reasons: misuse of these hybrid entities; continuation of former practices (traditional clientelism, corporatist equilibrium, changes in rentier practices, even simple corruption); overly generous recruitment policy; creaming off skills and requirements without spill-over, leaving the traditional civil service to its routines, its habitual functioning, its lack of professionalism, even its incompetence.

The process of Europeanization thus implies—both implicitly, even unconsciously (European regulation, norms production, 'new' ways of posing the problems) and very consciously (explicit programs to improve the civil service, computerization, organization of the management of European funds)—transforming the way national administrations function. But when it is remembered how state apparatuses went through the economic and political upheavals of the last century, and in particular how little thought was given to the conversion process from dictatorships and populism, one can only expect very slow and minor effects of European integration. In Greece as in Portugal, the routine functioning of the civil service remains fairly unaffected by Europeanization on the whole. Despite the (partial) renewal of civil servants and the recruitment of young graduates, despite the emergence of a parallel administration, both civil services remain loci of power, rent-seeking and obstacles, instead of being loci of skill, a place to reflect on public affairs and design strategies and policies. The administrative machine is highly inefficient, incapable of controlling, even less of sanctioning, and totally lacking authority among private actors and the political class, but conversely, not a vehicle for conveying political decisions and demands from private actors.

Changing modes of government

The arduous transformation of the administrative apparatus is only one aspect of the modification of modes of government stemming from European integration, but not exclusively so. Though full detail is impossible here, it is important to underline four characteristics.

Politicized centralization

One trend that appears clearly in both Greece and Portugal is a politicized process of centralization. European pressure for decentralization was strong enough in both countries to provoke institutional change, but it turned out to be so removed from the internal concerns and demands of the two countries, both small and highly central-ized, that circumvention strategies dominated the establishment of these new regu-latory bodies. Faced with demands for decentralization, particularly in the management of European transfers, in both countries there has been what can simply be called pseudo-decentralization. As regards Community funds, fairly formal decentralized echelons and regional commissions have been set up, but due to the increasing complexity of financial circuits, the low level of competence of the new institutions and, *a contrario*, the preeminence of historic institutions, the effect of this new config-uration has been an even greater involvement of the central administrations. For those involved, it is even hard to know precisely how things are divided among the echelons, and this indirectly encourages the centralization of decision-making. Even when an area is decentralized, financial decisions often continue to be centralized because responsibility remains at the ministerial level. In Portugal, in the agricultural sector, at the regional level there has been duplication of a mini-ministry with its various depart-ments. But with the centralizing tendency quickly winning out, any project, however small, must be approved both by the regional commission and a commission in Lisbon.

The Portuguese rejected outright the project of political decentralization presented by the government by referendum on 8 November 1998. The rejection of this form of administrative–political reorganization explains, by contrast, the difficulties encoun-tered in decentralization requested by Europe for the management of Community funds. In Greece, there was indeed an apparent increase in decentralization in 1997, with the election of prefects to administer the departments and groups of townships. But this reform was virtually thwarted by the implementation of regionalization, in other words the creation of thirteen regions (or 'peripheries') that are actually totally dependent on the central level of administration. Especially, decentralized budget allocations are distributed at the regional rather than the departmental level. The recentralization of public action has been further reinforced by serious deficiencies in equipment, skills, and the quality of staff. Paradoxically, with regard to the period prior to accession, there has even been greater centralization in some sectors, such as support for agriculture.

Aside from obvious political considerations, the reluctance to decentralize can be explained by an overdose of reform. Traditional civil services are already up against a variety of reforms and must learn European regulations and standards. Decentralization is clearly not a priority for these historically highly centralized administrations. For even if there are significant regional differences in both Greece and Portugal, they are not expressed as a demand for greater administrative, financial and political autonomy, but in a much more fluid manner, through networks of influence.

There are two other manifestations of centralization that are not, in fact, specific to Greece or Portugal. First, the concentration of powers around the Prime Minister: the need to represent a national position in the European Council reinforces this. And at the same time, the negotiation process in Brussels encourages a (re)centralization of gov-ernment decisions. Second, there is an increasing distinction between the civil service elite that centralizes analyses and decision-making on European subjects (and other subjects as well) and the rest of the administration which acts almost as a counter-weight. For instance, in Portugal, the GPPA (the agri-food planning and policy board that implements Community policy guidelines) centralizes all agricultural policies and is particularly effective, especially since 1999. But alongside this dynamic agency, the central administration acts as a hindrance due to its unwieldy size (about 40,000 civil servants) and the lack of mid-level supervision. A large majority of the civil servants are posted to Lisbon, whereas their new tasks should induce them to move to the regional structures. Without devolving responsibility and making actors accountable for their initiatives, it is difficult to modernize national agricultural policy and implement guidelines developed by competent teams, for instance on the policy of quality products, appellation and certification (cheese, olive oil, meats, etc.). Another example of this centralization can be seen in the way public authorities negotiate at the European level. In Greece and Portugal, this negotiation process was extremely centralized at the time of accession and has been afterwards. The tiny government elite that negotiates in Brussels is considerably out of touch with the population as well as the huge body of civil servants in charge of putting guidelines into practice within the administration.

In any event, in both cases, there is a strengthening of the dominant historical trend in the modes of government in Greece and in Portugal: a politicized centralism, more so in Greece than in Portugal.

Delegation and privatization

At the same time, the state is tending to delegate, even privatize, which by no means counteracts the preceding trend of centralization, but is instead a very particular way of doing it. Delegation to private entities, associations, businesses that are more or less controlled by public entities, independent agencies, and institutes has become a widespread phenomenon in Europe since the 1990s. This same trend can be seen both in Portugal and Greece, but the modalities, fields of application, visibility and signification of each are highly specific. The decision to delegate—or 'outsource' in the jargon in Brussels—became systematic in Portugal at the end of the 1980s and in Greece in the mid-1990s. It was justified on the basis of the public administration's mediocrity and rigidity, the incapacity of the current staff to implement reforms and overcome bureaucratic obstacles, the lack of a public service mentality, but also the insufficiency of intermediary bodies. For outsourcing and privatization can take on various forms.

The outsourcing option is not only a specific choice of administrative organization. It also reflects a change in modes of government. In fact, these agencies, institutes and establishments are hybrid entities, being both public and private, centralized, and independent. Most of all, they are much less subject to control than traditional administrations. Not only do they have to set up procedures likely to function properly in the European context quickly, but they must also enlist technical and professional skills for negotiations, decision-making and new systems of government which are not necessarily available in traditional administrations. The private sector is thus systematically called on to develop organizational, professional, and technical skills in relation to furthering European integration.

This evolution is entirely positive with regard to the functioning of these entities and the service offered: the staff can therefore be considerably more skilled, their qualifications better adapted to the services requested, and recruitment, day-to-day operations, and funding is handled in a much faster and more efficient manner. This said, the development of outsourcing has two adverse effects.

First, it does not reform the civil service, so duplication is instituted as a means of state intervention. The institutions that really function on the idealized model of independence and competence are entities created *ex nihilo*, such as ombudsmen or certain private organizations in charge of managing European funds. On the other hand, pseudo-restructurings often occur, particularly when nearly all the staff moves from a ministerial department to an entity coming under private law. This was the case of the OPEKEPE (Organization for the distribution of European agricultural subsidies), created in 1998 in Greece to manage the EAGGF Guarantee Section after the DIDAYEP (Board for the management of agricultural markets) was criticized for laxity by the European authorities. The OPEKEPE did not come into effect until 2001 and still has not managed to function with all its prerogatives. Even when the delegated administration functions properly, the proliferation of entities makes coordination among them difficult, thereby crippling the administration and often preventing effective control of these organizations by their supervisory body. Such is the case for instance with the agricultural bureaucracy in Portugal: there are twenty-seven agencies that come under the Agriculture Ministry, including the IFADAP (National Institute for the Support of Agriculture and Fishing) which manages the EAGGF Guidance Section and the INGA which manages the EAGGF Guarantee Section, which are virtually states within the state. But the same is true in the areas of social facilities (twenty-two institutes) and cultural programmes (eighteen institutes).

Second, the outsourcing option is often tantamount to privatization in that the national agency calls on private competencies to implement its policies. This practice fits within very specific economic-political systems: both in Portugal and Greece, there is a de facto reinforcement of the symbiosis between public and private, between the political–administrative sphere and the economic sphere characteristic of the political economy of each country. This symbiosis is certainly conducive to defining national strategies such as the defence of national interests in Portugal or the constitution of a new sphere of regional influence in Greece, as well as an acceleration of decision-making processes. But at the same time, it fosters clientelism, corruption, and tolerance of illegal, even criminal behaviour. For the outsourcing or privatization option must be understood in very different terms with regard to the development of independent authorities and autonomous regulation agencies: Portugal and Greece have no tradition in this area and these entities are weak, very recent and enjoy little respect (except for the central banks, but only since the late 1990s).

Another variant of the privatization process resides in a much less resolute and anticipated evolution: the unorganized and unmanaged transfer of competences of public entities to private entities. For instance, in both Portugal and Greece, the CAP brought an end to advisory services and the decline of agricultural engineers within ministries and its decentralized departments. This staff became absorbed by administrative tasks (follow-up and monitoring of cases of notified aid of European subsidies). Consequently, the work of informing, advising, and consulting has been left to the private sector, to agricultural and fertilizer supply salesmen, large agri-food companies that consume these supplies and consultancy firms often staffed, even started, by the very civil servants who were dispossessed of their former tasks! With the rapid development of structural funds, and European funds in general, consultancy firms, and to a lesser extent, development agencies have multiplied and have become major economic actors in both countries. This form of outsourcing and privatization is essential to the creation of intermediary bodies, inexistent in Greece as well as Portugal, all the more so since the administration has little capacity for analysis and academic research does not take any particular interest in these fields. Since a study must be conducted prior to any European financing, this preliminary work is delegated to private entities. But in highly politicized societies and administrations, it is easy to imagine the connivance that goes on between these firms and the public agencies that benefit from European funds. There again, outsourcing strengthens the symbiosis between public and private, between the economic sphere and the political-administrative sphere. The last example is provided by the services offered by volunteer organizations and NGOs in setting up actions financed by the EU. This is particularly relevant in areas such as the environment, the fight against poverty, advocacy of equal opportunities for women, integration of minorities and the fight against sexual abuse of women and children. In Greece and Portugal, which historically have always suffered from a lack of volunteer culture and have not strictly speaking experienced the welfare state, these activities came about at the instigation of Europe.

With respect to Greece's and Portugal's historic trajectories, these evolutions represent both a contrast and a certain continuity. In Greece, especially, it is the first time a strategy has been elaborated for building a competent administration, based on knowhow, technique and expertise. However, in Portugal, and in Greece as well, the outsourcing and privatization process underway combines with the historical closeness, even symbiosis, of relations between public and private interests, economic-financial interests on one hand, and political-administrative interests on the other.

Political culture

The state and the administration in Greece and Portugal are often analysed in normative and negative terms: weak state, inefficient administration, widespread clientelism and corruption, lack of civic-minded traditions, etc. This sort of judgment can be found in European analyses of these two countries' institutional adaptation to Europe: Greece and Portugal (sometimes with Italy and Spain) are said to have behaviour that is shiftier, more fraudulent, wasteful, corrupt, illegal, etc. than the other member states. Due to these institutional problems of adaptation, Europeanization is said to have more difficulty permeating society, and there is more fraud, more irregularity, and a more systematic lack of compliance with directives. This said, some European Commission documents, particularly from the European Anti-Fraud Office, suggest that such conclusions are not necessarily accurate: even if it is important to examine with caution the highly political and therefore necessarily negotiated findings of studies and research based on data supplied by governments that are more or less concerned with the truth of the statistics and more or less reliable, Portugal and Greece do not seem to be the worst offenders of all the member states, especially in recent years. Both in terms of implementing directives (France especially appears, particularly in recent years, to be more problematic), occurrences of fraud (for instance on VAT or customs where the problem is an overall one, tied in with organized crime and the difficulty all member states have of adapting their systems to the dismantling of borders) or irregularities in the use of funds (with Great Britain and Germany being particularly accused). According to the annual Commission report on monitoring the application of Community law, the two countries indeed ranked poorly in the early 1990s (Greece, last in terms of referral to the Court of Justice and reasoned opinions; Portugal, next to last in terms of formal notices), but their position has improved considerably, particularly Portugal's (way ahead of France and Belgium in terms of referral to the Court).

Implementation gaps

The sizeable gaps often noted in Greece and Portugal between EU texts and their application, as regards, for instance, labour law, social rights, but also taxation and the courts, reflect an implicit model of the ideal legal-rational state. Contrary to what is often asserted, this is not on account of a congenital difficulty peripheral societies have in adapting to European norms (these gaps being recurrent in the history of both countries), or on account of cultural factors or signs of under-development. Research in historical sociology suggests instead that this characteristic is rooted in the political and social history of Greece and Portugal. These 'gaps' are modes of government in themselves: it is in the in-between, in the interstices of what is legal, authorized, accepted or tolerated that state power is situated, and not primarily in the enactment of a law. Under such conditions, the gaps between texts and practices, or non compliance of Portuguese and Greek reality to European 'norms', cannot be analyzed in terms of institutional lack of adaptation, lagging behind or immaturity.

Tolerance for a so-called informal economy, tax evasion, undeclared employment, contraband and counterfeiting, their social legitimacy and the centrality of behaviour on the fringe of legality should not be considered as archaïsm, remnants of bygone economies and political societies that have not been entirely Europeanized. On the contrary, recent developments suggest that Europeanization perpetuates and reactivates this behaviour. The multiplication of decision-making bodies that European construction has created has had its effect: The emergence of a new echelon, Europe, has caused a new space to materialize, with new actors, new relationships, and hence new opportunities, including that to play on the various levels and scales and therefore on loopholes or the complexity of legislation or regulations. These phenomena can be found in all member states. On the other hand, others are specific to cohesion countries. European subsidies have been interpreted occasionally as the flip side of tax evasion: as many opportunities not to pay oneself, but to get the state or Europe to pay. In that case too, Europeanization has reinforced rather than reduced marginally legal behaviour. Likewise, European funds have been oriented toward infrastructures and construction work, sectors conducive to undeclared work. This trend has been reinforced in recent years: The conjunction of growth and the rise in the standard of living (these also tied to European transfers) and the tightening of controls at the borders of northern European countries have directed illegal immigration toward the southern European countries. But beyond these unintended effects, a lack of coherence in Community decisions can fuel fringe activities. Such is the case of adopting a single market and free circulation of capital without harmonizing taxation and social policies at the same time. Thus Portugal has specialized in exporting a very peculiar commodity: companies offer the services of unskilled labour in construction and the service sector, that is paid much less and enjoys much lower social coverage because all these costs are paid in Portugal. There is not exactly infringement of the law, but rather a play on the various legislations with ill-defined borders, a game that further blurs the distinction between legal and illegal. In the so-called peripheral countries, Europe also often turns a blind eye on practices of which it theoretically disapproves.

European bureaucracy has often neglected its original institutional role and behaved with the laxity characteristic of traditional financial backers. Greece and more recently Portugal have been criticized for misappropriation, or at least inappropriate use of European funds and delays. And a European-style delinquency is developing, due both to the huge flow of European funds and the formalism of Community mechanisms. Responsibility for such behaviour should thus be attributed to the bureaucracy in Brussels as well, it having been particularly lax, at least up until recent years. This laxity is easy to explain: a desire for 'success'; abuses tolerated because they come from small countries; a question of interests, large construction projects being particularly profitable to three major European countries: France, Germany, and Italy.

In short, the gaps between texts and practices, the rhetoric of fraud, undeclared labour, and a parallel economy are good indicators about modes of government. Europeanization does not basically alter the specific understanding of them; it only changes the way it is expressed, for instance by bringing the question of tax evasion to the political forefront.

Conclusion: neither convergence nor divergence

Under such conditions, it is impossible to reason in terms of convergence or divergence. Economic and social actions can only 'adapt' in various and hybrid ways and take their own shape. This shape is naturally outlined by European incentives, but primarily along lines circumscribed by national historic trajectories. The point here is of course not to deny the influence of Europe on the major economic issues (inflation, budget, debt) or the major orientations of economic policy (mainly monetary policy, but also liberalization of trade, finance, and services). It is instead to underline that the disembodied data conceal micro- and macroeconomic practices and political and social practices that differ considerably from one country to the other.

Furthermore, advocates of European integration should remain cautious as to the benefits of first the Community, then the Union, on the catching-up, convergence and harmonization processes. When economic performance (growth, buying power, productivity) in the 1950s and especially the 1960s is compared with recent performance, the European era comes up short, despite the amount of net transfers received by Greece and Portugal: Growth in the 1960s had a much greater impact on the convergence of Greek and Portuguese economies than did joining the European Communities (see Table 11.2).

In general, the relationship between the European integration process and political and economic change is far from unambiguous. The very same European norms and criteria can be adopted in pursuit of vastly differing internal logics. Whether this attitude is conscious or not, it should be pointed out that the European authorities require and evaluate technical criteria alone. This prevents them from understanding and influencing the political rationales underlying such reforms, rationales that are sometimes diametrically opposed in spirit to the norms the authorities are trying to impose. An example of the importance of national interpretation and comprehension

Table 11.2 Economic growth in Greece and Portugal since the 1950s

	Greece	Portugal	EC—12
Growth rate GDP			
1950–1960	6.0	4.1	5.1
1960–1973	7.6	6.9	4.7
1973–1994	2.1	2.5	2.1
Growth rate GDP/inhabitant			
1950–1960	5.0	3.6	4.3
1960–1973	7.0	6.9	3.9
1973–1994	1.4	1.9	1.7
Growth rate overall productivity			
1960–1973	2.8	5.0	3.3
1973–1993	0.0	0.6	1.2

Source: Jose da Silva Lopes, *A Economia Portugesa desde 1960*, Lisbon, Gradiva, 1996.

can be seen in the 'Ahmed Rezala' case, the suspected murderer (the 'train killer') who fled to Portugal where the government refused to extradite him to France. What was viewed in France and Europe in general as a violation of the principle of legal cooperation, in other words analysed under the heading 'Justice and Home Affairs', was experienced and interpreted in Portugal not only in terms of national sovereignty but of the very legitimacy of power. In fact, the abolition of the death penalty in 1864 and of life imprisonment in 1884 were symbolic and founding acts of the Portuguese liberal tradition and constitute obligatory references for Portuguese democracy, precisely because they ground the regime that came out of the Carnation Revolution in history. It is in this regard that analyses in terms of European influence, even constraint, violation or respect for European norms reach their limits: they conceal the fact that behind technical terminology and legal classifications are internal historical political rationales and registers of legitimation and subjectivation of power.

One cannot, without twisting the facts, find uniformity, unity or meaning in the changes noted since Greece and Portugal joined Europe: Europeanness is, to some degree, devoid of meaning, in that European integration cannot be boiled down to a project, that the evolutions that have occurred cannot be assessed normatively and that Europe cannot determine social practices on its own and give an overall meaning to the events underway. Belonging to Europe, for Greece and Portugal, like for all the other member states, should be taken to be the contingent result of multiple processes that doubtless are the product of a technocratic project, itself multidimensional, but also of complex historical trajectories involving both innovation and disintegration.

Further reading

On the history of the Portuguese membership to the EU, see de Vasconcelos & Seabra (2000) and contributions to Royo and Manuel (2004). On EU policy-making within Portugal, see Seabra (2003). On relations between the Greek and Portuguese administration and the EU, see Frangakis and Papayannides (2003). On the political economy of Greece and Portugal, see Bryant, Garganas, and Tavlas (2001) and Corkill (1999).

Weblinks

The obvious starting points are the two government web portal: for Greece <**http://www.government.gr**> and for Portugal <**http://www.portugal.gov.pt**>. In relation to the two economies, see the Bank of Greece: <**http://www.bankofgreece.gr**> and the Bank of Portugal: <**http://www.bportugal.pt**>. A useful website on the Europeanization of Greece is offered by the Hellenic Centre for European Studies <**http://www.ekem.gr**>, which has a number of on-line papers on the subject.

References

Baganha, M. I. (2001), 'A cada Sul o seu Norte: dinâmicas migratorias em Portugal', in B. de Sousa Santos (org), *Globalização: Fatalidade ou Utopia* (Porto: Afrontamento) 135–59.

Bryant, R. C., Garganas, N. C., and Tavlas, G. S. (eds) (2001), *Greece's Economic Performance and Prospects* (Athens: Bank of Greece and Washington: The Brookings Institution).

Corkill, D. (1999), *The Development of the Portuguese Economy. A Case of Europeanization* (London: Routledge).

Featherstone, K. (1998), 'Europeanization and the Centre-Periphery: The Case of Greece in the 1990s', *South European Society and Politics*, 13/1, 23–39.

Frangakis, N., and Papayannides, A. (2003), 'Greece: a never-ending story of mutual attraction and estrangement', in Wessels, Maurer, and Mittag, 166–83.

Mouzelis, N. (1986), *Politics in the Semi-Periphery: Early Parliamentarism and Late Industrialism in the Balkans and Latin America* (London: Macmillan).

Oliveira Rocha, J. A. (1998), 'La fin de l'Etat administratif au Portugal', *Revue française d'administration publique*, no. 86, April–June, 219–27.

Royo, S., and Manuel, P.C. (eds) (2004), *Spain and Portugal in the European Union: The First Fifteen Years* (London: Frank Cass).

Spanou, C. (2003), 'L'administration grecque en mutation: le double défi de la démocratisation et de l'européanisation', *Pôle Sud*, no. 18, May, 51–62.

Seabra, M. J. (2003), 'Portugal: one way to Europeanisation', in Wessels, Maurer, and Mittag, 355–68.

Tsalicoglou, I. (1995), *Negotiating for Entry: The Accession of Greece to the European Community* (Aldershot: Dartmouth).

de Vasconcelos, A., and Seabra, M. J. (eds) (2000), *Portugal, a European Story* (Cascais: Principia).

Verney, S. (1993), 'From the "Special Relationship" to Europeanism: PASOK and the European Community', in R. Clogg (ed.), *Greece 1981–89: The Populist Decade* (London: Macmillan).

Wallden, S. (1999), 'Greece and the Balkans: Economic Relations', in V. Coufoudakis, H. Psomiades, and A. Gerolymatos (eds), *Greece and the New Balkans: Challenges and Opportunities* (Flushing, NY: Center for Byzantine and Modern Greek Studies), 71–122.

Chapter 12

The New Member States and the EU: Responding to Europe

Klaus H. Goetz

Contents

Summary

Compared to the EU-15, the ten new EU member states are characterized by distinct patterns of integration and Europeanization. Their experiences so far have been shaped by a phased process of gaining entry to the EU and 'anticipatory and adaptive Europeanization'. The capacity of the new members to influence the integration process is limited as a consequence of their diverse interests and weak intraregional coordination amongst the Central and Eastern European states. Europeanization has affected polity, politics, and public policies, but such effects have been shallower than in long-standing member states.

Introduction

What is distinct about the experiences of integration and Europeanization of the ten states that have become members of the EU in May 2004 when compared to the other countries and regions analysed in this volume? Three considerations stand out:

- *The nature of the new members' relationship to the EU*: When the new members—Cyprus, Czech Republic, Estonia, Hungary, Latvia, Lithuania, Malta, Poland, Slovakia, Slovenia—acceded to the EU on 1 May 2004, this marked the culmination of a long-drawn-out process. Cyprus and Malta had association agreements with the EU since the early 1970s and had applied for EU membership already in 1990. The Central and Eastern European countries successively followed suit between 1994 and 1996. From 1991 onwards, they had developed institutionalized ties to the EU in the form of the 'Europe agreements', which 'provided for cooperation in political, economic, cultural and other areas—including a large degree of liberalization of trade in non-agricultural goods—and for the adoption of important parts of EU rules and policies (. . .) The preamble of the agreements recognized membership as the wish of the associated states, without affirming it as the aim of the EU' (Avery 2004: 35). For the majority of countries, accession negotiations started in March 1998 (negotiations with Latvia, Lithuania, Malta, and Slovakia were opened in February 2000) and negotiations were closed in April 2003 (see Tables 12.1A and B).

  The experience of integration and Europeanization of the ten new members has, therefore, so far been one of a phased process of gaining entry to the EU, on the one hand, and 'anticipatory and adaptive Europeanization' (Ágh 2003), on the other. The nature of their relationship to the EU has been that of applicants, candidates, negotiating partners, and acceding countries rather than of full members. The patterns of Europeanization that have emerged up to now are likely to reflect their 'outsider' status. Thus, they have, so far, been primarily 'downloaders' of EU law, policies and practices, 'policy-takers', with only limited opportunities for 'uploading' country-specific preferences and priorities as 'policy-makers'. Accordingly, 'impositional' Europeanization is more likely than in member states that have been able to influence, if not determine, the *acquis communautaire*. Following full membership, this pattern is set to change, especially in policy areas of central concern to the new members. Yet, as the experience of Southern enlargement during the 1980s suggests, their 'uploading' efforts are bound to remain selective for the foreseeable future, reflecting their status as medium-sized, small or even micro-states (with the obvious exception of Poland).

- *The nature of the EU's approach to the new members*: The run-up to May 2004 differed decisively from previous enlargements of the EU. There were a number of key differences. First, there was an extended period of gradual approximation and adaptation, which lasted for some fifteen years. Second, there was a much greater emphasis on the adoption and full implementation of the *acquis* prior to accession than had been the case in the 1980s, when Greece, Portugal and Spain had joined. Third, the detailed attention paid to domestic institutional capacity to implement the *acquis* was distinctive. Fourth, wide-ranging conditions for membership had been set out in the form of the 'Copenhagen criteria' adopted

Table 12.1A Dates of association agreements, Europe agreements, and official application for EU membership

	Europe agreement signed	Europe agreement came into force	Official application for EU membership
Czech Republic	October 1993	February 1995	January 1996
Estonia	June 1995	February 1998	November 1995
Hungary	December 1991	February 1994	March 1994
Latvia	June 1995	February 1998	October 1995
Lithuania	June 1995	February 1998	December 1995
Poland	December 1991	February 1994	April 1994
Slovakia	October 1993	February 1995	June 1995
Slovenia	June 1996	February 1999	June 1996
	Association agreement signed	**Association agreement came into force**	
Cyprus	December 1972	June 1973	July 1990
Malta	December 1970	April 1971	July 1990

Source: own compilation on the basis of:
<http://europa.eu.int/comm/enlargement/pas/europe_agr.htm> (accessed 21 Feb. 2004)
<http://europa.eu.int/scadplus/leg/en/lvb/e40001.htm> (accessed 21 Feb. 2004).

in 1993, which included 'stability of institutions guaranteeing democracy, the rule of law, human rights and respect for and protection of minorities; the existence of a functioning market economy, as well as the capacity to cope with competitive pressure and market forces within the Union; the ability to take on the obligations of membership including adherence to the aims of political, economic and monetary union'. Fifthly, an informal *acquis* had emerged, that is a set of norms and expectations against which the applicants would be measured that were not part of the legal obligations of membership that applied to the EU-15. Also new was the creation of an elaborate machinery for monitoring and assessing the candidates' progress on their way towards meeting the accession criteria. Finally, there was a reliance on conditionality (Grabbe 2002; Smith 2003), whereby progress on the way to full entry was linked to meeting often highly specific conditions, targets, and deadlines.

This distinct approach to enlargement reflected concerns of both the EU Commission and the EU-15 member states over the consequences of adding ten new member states. These concerns centred on the functioning of the institutions of the EU, notably the Council of Ministers, but also the Commission

Table 12.1.B Dates of the adoption of accession partnerships and the opening and closing of membership negotiations

	Adopt accession partnership	Open negotiations	Close negotiations
Cyprus	March 2000	March 1998	April 2003
Czech Republic	March 1998	March 1998	April 2003
Estonia	March 1998	March 1998	April 2003
Hungary	March 1998	March 1998	April 2003
Latvia	March 1998	January 2000	April 2003
Lithuania	March 1998	January 2000	April 2003
Malta	March 2000	January 2000	April 2003
Poland	March 1998	March 1998	April 2003
Slovakia	March 1998	January 2000	April 2003
Slovenia	March 1998	March 1998	April 2003

Source: own compilation on the basis of:
<http://europa.eu.int/comm/enlargement/negotiations/index.htm> (accessed 21 Feb. 2004)
<http://europa.eu.int/scadplus/leg/en/lvb/e40001.htm> (accessed 21 Feb. 2004)
<http://europa.eu.int/abc/history/2000/index_en.htm> (accessed 21 Feb. 2004)
<http://europa.eu.int/scadplus/leg/en/s40000.htm#CH> (accessed 21 Feb. 2004).

and, to a lesser extent, the European Parliament; the tensions between widening and the prospects of a further deepening of integration; and, perhaps most significantly, the question of how the political, economic, and security interests of existing member states and their power in the EU could be safeguarded. In a nutshell, the EU strategy was to ensure that the political, economic and social costs of domestic adaptation to the EU would largely accrue prior to full membership, so as to minimise the burdens on the enlarged EU-25.

■ *The nature of the new members' relationships to each other*: Although there are important commonalities in their experiences of integration and Europeanization, the new members do evidently not form a cohesive group. Malta and Cyprus have not much in common, beyond their status as Mediterranean islands. The Central and Eastern European accession countries are, in themselves, a heterogeneous grouping, including the Baltic states, which emerged from the break-up of the Soviet Union; Slovenia, which declared its independence from Yugoslavia in 1991; the Czech Republic and Slovakia, which became sovereign states in January 1993; Hungary and Poland. With the exception of Poland, all are medium-sized, small, or micro states, and they differ significantly in terms of key socioeconomic data (see Table 12.2). Political ties amongst the Central and Eastern European countries

Table 12.2 Basic socioeconomic data for the new members

	Land area km 2 2002	Population in 1000s, 2001	Unemployment rate in % 2002	Inflation rate in % 2002	GDP per capita in PPS* 2001	Annual growth of GDP % 1999	Annual growth of GDP % 2001
Czech Republic	78866	10283	7.3	1.4	13700	0.5	3.3
Estonia	45227	1634	9.1	3.6	9240	−0.6	5.0
Cyprus	9251	762	5.3	2.8	17180	4.8	4.1
Latvia	64589	2355	12.9	2.4	7750	2.8	7.7
Lithuania	65300	3478	13.1	0.4	8960	−3.9	6.0
Hungary	93930	10188	5.6	5.2	12250	4.2	3.7
Malta	316	393	7.5	2.2	—	4.1	0.8
Poland	312685	38638	20.0	1.9	9410	4.1	1.1
Slovenia	20273	1992	6.4	7.5	16210	5.2	3.0
Slovakia	49035	5397	19.4	3.3	11200	1.3	3.3

* PPS (Purchasing Power Standards): The artificial common currency unit used in the EU to express the volume of economic aggregates for the purposes of cross-country and regional comparisons.

Source: own compilation of table from European Commission, *Towards an Enlarged European Union* (EC/Eurostat, Apr. 2003). <http://europa.eu.int/comm/enlargement/docs/pdf/eurostatapril2003.pdf> (accessed: 23 Feb. 2004).

are weak, and, in some cases, strained, not least because of the existence of ethnic minorities in neighbouring countries (the relationship between Slovakia and Hungary may serve as an example). Attempts to strengthen such bonds, including the formation of the 'Visegrad group' of the Czech Republic, Hungary, Poland, and Slovakia have had only very limited success.

Helen Wallace (2001) has stressed the importance of functional, territorial, and affiliational linkages in understanding the historical trajectory of European integration in Western Europe with a 'distinctive pattern of integration: multi-framework, multi-layer, multi-lateral and multi-purpose' (p. 12). This pattern is contrasted to that found in Central and Eastern Europe with 'a segmented history, followed by recent attempts to define European engagement by achieving incorporation within the west European-defined transnational system. This move "towards" western Europe is now beginning, but only beginning, to be flanked by more local patterns of linkage. There are also tragic instances of de-linkage where (joint functions) tasks, territory and (affiliation) trust are all contested' (p. 11). One immediate consequence for the integration process is that the diversity of interests, preferences and priorities of the new members 'hit' the EU in an unmediated way, since little, if any, effective intraregional aggregation of positions appears to take place. The manner in which the accession negotiations were conducted did little to encourage the applicants to coordinate their views. Thus, 'the "bilateral nature" of the process (. . .) was an important structural factor of the negotiations (. . .) it rendered it difficult for the applicant countries to present a common front to the EU' (Avery 2004: 39). This weakness of intraregional cooperation and coordination does not mean that the new member states are condemned to being weak 'uploaders' in the EU policy process, but it certainly makes for turbulence and unpredictability.

In addition to these factors fostering distinct patterns of integration and Europeanization in the new member states, two further aspects ought to be noted at the outset:

■ *The nature of the new members' relationships to existing member states*: The horizontal dimension of European integration consists, at its core, of a series of 'special relationships', of which the Franco-German alliance has, perhaps, been the most celebrated. Enlargement has added decisively to this tapestry of special relationships, some of which are historically and politically highly charged. One need only mention the relationships between Poland and Germany; Cyprus and Greece; Hungary, Slovenia and Austria; or Malta, Italy and the UK (on the latter see Baldacchino 2002). These ties indicate a potential for interstate cooperation and strategic alignment, but, in some cases, they also mark a source of conflict. Inevitably, they promote further bilateralization and multilateralization of relationships amongst the EU member states.

■ *EU integration as part of a broader dynamic of state and nation-building, domestic transformation, and Western integration*: EU integration and Europeanization in the ten accession states can only be properly understood if they are considered in the context of the broader political and economic transformations that these countries have been undergoing over the last fifteen years or so. Three such transformations stand out. First, since the late 1980s, the Baltic states, the Czech Republic, Slovakia, and Slovenia have experienced historically momentous processes of state-building, and, in some cases, nation-building. In the cases of Cyprus and Malta, too, integration, on the one hand, and state and nation-building, on the other, have been closely intertwined (Cini 2001). Second, in the Central and Eastern European members, their integration policies strongly interacted with a post-Communist dynamic of democratization, marketization, and liberalization. Third, EU integration proceeded alongside, and was influenced by, the accession countries' selective integration into other forms of international cooperation, notably through membership in the Council of Europe, the OECD and, most importantly, NATO (see Table 12.3). These 'grand' transformations unfolded contemporaneously and had a mutual influence on each other.

To draw attention to specific features and basic conditions of integration and Europeanization does not mean to ignore important precedents and parallels both with previous enlargements—the integration dimension—and the Europeanization experiences of the EU-15, especially if one takes account of developments outside the North-Western core of the founding members. For instance, post-war Germany provides a paradigm for understanding the connection between state (re-)building and integration,

Table 12.3 Dates of membership of new EU members in major international organizations

	Council of Europe	NATO	OECD
Cyprus	May 1961	—	—
Czech Republic	June 1993	March 1999	December 1995
Estonia	May 1993	April 2004	—
Hungary	November 1993	March 1999	May 1996
Malta	April 1965	—	—
Latvia	February 1995	April 2004	—
Lithuania	March 1993	April 2004	—
Poland	November 1991	March 1999	November 1996
Slovakia	June 1993	April 2004	December 2000
Slovenia	May 1993	April 2004	—

Source: own compilation on the basis of:
<http://www.coe.int/T/e/com/about_coe/member_states/default.asp> (accessed 21 Feb. 2004)
<http://www.nato.int/issues/enlargement/index.htm> (accessed 21 Feb. 2004)
<http://www.nato.int/docu/update/1999/0310e.htm> (accessed 21 Feb. 2004)
<http://www.oecd.org/document/58/0,2340,en_2649_201185_1889402_1_1_1_1,00.html> (accessed 21 Feb. 2004).

and the Southern enlargements to Greece, Portugal, and Spain of the 1980s illustrate the linkage between democratization, liberalization, and integration. Spain also provides a case study of how EU integration and integration into the Western military alliance of NATO were linked, even at a time when defence and foreign security were outside the EU *acquis*. Weak horizontal ties, too, are nothing new in the EU. Greece has long served as an example, and, perhaps more surprisingly, Portugal and Spain have often been said to have a 'back to back' rather than 'face to face' relationship. Moreover, some of the specificities of the experiences of the countries considered here are bound to be of a transitional nature, whilst others are likely to persist in the medium and long term. Nonetheless, as argued in the Conclusion, the new member countries, whilst forming a heterogeneous grouping, add decisively to existing diversity in the EU, so that experience of integration and Europeanization of the North-Western founder members of France, Germany, and the Benelux countries, in particular, is becoming ever more exceptional (Dyson and Goetz 2003a), whilst, at the same time, losing some of its ideational attraction as a template to be followed by more recent members.

The specific, although not necessarily unique, facets of integration and Europeanization in the new member states also have implications for the analytical lenses employed in studying domestic polity, politics and public policy effects of accession. Two deserve highlighting:

■ Discussions of Europeanization 'Eastern-style' have tended to stress the 'hierarchical' and 'impositional' aspects of domestic 'adaptation', fostered by 'conditionality' (Grabbe 2002; Smith 2003). 'Top-down'—as opposed to 'bottom-up'—dynamics are often seen to play a more prominent role in shaping Europeanization in the recent accession states when compared to the long-standing members. As noted earlier, there has been immense pressure on the part of the EU to ensure the full adoption and 'effective and efficient' implementation of the *acquis* prior to membership, and there are examples of intensive involvement of the EU in promoting institutional change even in areas such as the establishment of civil service systems where formal EU competences are minimal (Dimitrova 2002; Scherpereel 2003). Yet, this hierarchical perspective on Europeanization should not obscure the 'usage' of EU integration (Jacquot and Woll 2003) by domestic actors for their own purposes. More recent work on Europeanization in Western European countries has emphasized 'the use that domestic actors make of the EU in order to legitimate policy reforms, to develop new policy solutions, and to alter policy beliefs' (Dyson and Goetz 2003b: 18). But these 'usages' are not restricted to the policy dimension; they can also, for example, be observed in the field of electoral and party competition, where the politics of Euroscepticism has emerged as an influential force in several of the new members (Taggart and Szczerbiak 2004). There is, as yet, little systematic research on this bottom-up dimension of Europeanization in the new member states (but see Featherstone 2001), though there is no reason to doubt its importance.

■ Drawing on the insights of the Europeanization literature that focuses on Western Europe, a strong case can be made that the institutional and policy effects of accession, in particular, have been more immediate than in other parts of the EU (Grabbe 2001; Goetz 2001). Oft-cited reasons include, *inter alia*, the weakness of institutional 'cores' in the post-Communist states—notably those that only came into being after the fall of Communism—which are less likely to offer resistance to 'adaptive pressures' than the deeply embedded state institutions of Western European countries; evident crises of performance and legitimacy of domestic institutions, which encourage policy transfer and learning from foreign experiences; the existence of institutional and policy 'voids', so that Europeanization involves not so much adaptation, but rather the *ab ovo* creation of new actors, institutions, and policies.

On the other hand, however, and this is less often remarked upon, there are equally good arguments to suggest that Europeanization effects, whilst more immediate, may also be less profound and that patterns of 'institutionalization for reversibility' prevail (Goetz 2002). Thus, the new members had little incentive to invest in 'deep' Europeanization that would 'lock in' specific institutional and policy arrangements prior to full membership precisely because of their weak uploading capacity as *demandeurs*. They could hope that, as full members, they would be able to challenge, or escape altogether, some of the constrictions that a negotiation process, which was structured to favour the existing members, had imposed on them. 'Rationalist' arguments suggesting a pattern of wide-ranging, but relatively shallow, effects are underscored by more constructivist understandings of Europeanization, which stress the importance of learning and socialization and note that institutions are not just constructed around interests, but norms and values. In the new member states, such learning and socialization effects are likely to be, up to now, less deep because of their shorter period of intensive engagement with the EU and, for most of the time, an 'outsider' status; and less extensive, since, as discussed below, active engagement with the integration process has, up to now, been restricted to a fairly narrow group of political, administrative and economic élites. Under conditions of shallow institutionalization, fluidity, and uncertainty (on the latter see Grabbe 2003: 318 ff.), strategic interest-based 'rational' behaviour by domestic actors is more likely than action according to a 'logic of appropriateness'. As Schimmelfennig (2003) has shown both need to be considered in understanding decision-making about enlargement; both should also be kept in mind when one tries to explain differing trajectories of Europeanization in the new member states.

The history of the European issue

The story of the evolution of the European issue in the accession countries can be told from two perspectives: an enlargement perspective; and a domestic politics perspective, which concentrates on the domestic circumstances that have shaped the quest for EU integration. The first perspective—enlargement—has tended to dominate so far, not least because this story is in some respects easier to tell, with clear landmark decisions along the path to full EU membership. The main steps on the part of the EU towards the integration of the ten new members are well-documented (see, for example, Mayhew 1998; Cremona 2003; Cameron 2004). After the fall of Communism, there was an early wave of goodwill and of help and assistance, which was partly bilateral and partly channelled through the European Union. In the pronouncements of both the EU and the leaders of existing member states, but also the new post-Communist political élites, an early linkage was established between democratic transition and consolidation and European integration. Democracy was confirmed as a key condition for eventual EU membership (on the evolution of this condition see Verney 2002); at the same time, and not least with reference to the historical experiences of Germany, Italy and the Southern enlargements of the 1980s, the contribution of integration to underpinning a successful regime transition was underlined.

The chronology of enlargement differed somewhat from country to country, but the main sequence of events varied little, at least as far as the Central and Eastern European countries were concerned: early assistance after the fall of Communism; the conclusion of 'Europe agreements' with the post-Communist states from 1991 onwards; the development of a 'pre-accession' strategy on the part of the EU from 1993; applications for EU membership between 1994 and 1996 (Malta and Cyprus had applied for membership in 1990); the development of a 'reinforced' accession strategy from 1997; the conclusion of 'accession partnerships'; the opening of accession negotiations in March 1998 (or February 2000 in the cases of Malta, Slovakia, Latvia, and Lithuania); the conclusion of the negotiations in spring 2003, following the European Council in Copenhagen of December 2002; the signing of the Act of Accession in April 2003; and accession in May 2004. The last of the annual pre-accession 'country reports', monitoring the countries' preparations for membership, were published in November 2003, but despite the many severely critical remarks that had survived the politicized editing process, enlargement had turned from a distant aspiration to a certainty. The overall trajectory of the EU's decision-making vis-à-vis the accession states can be described as the evolution of an increasingly differentiated 'composite policy' (see Sedelmeier and Wallace 2000, where a concise overview of the main stages of the evolution of the EU approach can be found). In this composite policy, 'decisions about the macro level of policy, to determine the overall objectives and parameters of policy' needed to be coordinated with 'decisions about the specific detail and substance of policy, generally dealt with by the various policy-makers that have the relevant technical expertise and decision-making competences' (ibid.: 429).

The thrust of the EU's approach changed markedly over time, as its position became more elaborated and differentiated. Whilst initially the approach was principally enabling and assistance provided was to some extent 'demand-driven', the 'reinforced accession strategy' launched at the 1997 Luxembourg European Council, was, at heart, about ensuring the full adoption and implementation of the *acquis* by the prospective new members. The provision of pre-accession funding through the PHARE, ISPA and SAPARD instruments was 'supply-led', for although the Central and Eastern European accession countries played a role in the definition of the projects for which these funds were to be used, the EU authorities defined their objectives and had to authorize their use (see Table 12.4).[1] The 'accession partnerships', concluded as part of the

---

[1] ISPA: Instrument for Structural Policies for Pre-accession covering transport and the environment; PHARE: an assistance programme launched in 1989 for Hungary and Poland only, but subsequently opened to all ten CEE applicants (i.e. the eight new member states, Bulgaria and Romania); SAPARD: Special Assistance Programme for Agriculture and Rural Development.

Table 12.4 Allocations for PHARE, SAPARD and ISPA, 2000 to 2002 (in Euro millions)

	PHARE	SAPARD	ISPA	Total
Czech Republic	296.3	68.8	217.4	2482.5
Estonia	96.2	37.8	88.5	222.5
Latvia	107.3	68.2	141.3	316.8
Lithuania	340.9	93	163.9	624.8
Hungary	360.3	118.8	272.9	752
Poland	1404.5	526.5	1076.4	3007.4
Slovenia	103.7	19.8	52.2	176.2
Slovakia	238.4	57.1	94.7	440.2
Total	4909.2	1623.0	3214.1	9486.6

Note that Cyprus and Malta received pre-accession funding under different budgets.

Own Table compiled from European Commission, *The General Report on Pre-accession Assistance, Phare, SAPARD, ISPA in 2000* (SEC 2002), 18. European Commission, *The General Report on Pre-accession Assistance, Phare, SAPARD, ISPA in 2001* (SEC 2003), 22. European Commission, *The General Report on Pre-accession Assistance, Phare, SAPARD, ISPA in 2002* (SEC 2003), 24.

same strategy, provided 'rather little scope for the candidates themselves to shape their pace and content, causing considerable criticism that the language of partnership disguises rather thinly the imposition of EU priorities' (Sedelmeier and Wallace 2000: 452). Tellingly, 'from a legal point of view, they are not agreements but unilateral acts' (Maresceau 2003: 31). Overall, as accession approached, the European Commission, largely driven by the demands of existing member states, notably those sharing borders with the accession countries and the major net contributors and net recipients of the EU budget, increasingly hardened its stance on the comprehensive pre-accession adaptation. At the same time, the financial conditions of the first years of full membership worsened considerably between what had been agreed at the 1999 Berlin European Council and the deal that was offered at the conclusion of the negotiations (see Table 12.5):

in the field of regional policy they represented only 137 euros per head of population for the new members in 2006, compared with 231 euros per head for Greece, Spain and Portugal and in the field of agriculture they were based on a phasing-in of the EU's scheme of 'direct payments' to farmers commencing at 25 per cent in 2004 and rising to 100 per cent over a long transitional period of ten years (Avery 2004: 54).

This increasingly 'self-interested' approach on the part of the EU and its most powerful member states was, at least in part, informed by the universally recognized need to synchronize political, institutional and policy reforms in the prospective new

Table 12.5 Financial framework for enlargement 2004–6—indicative allocation of commitment and payment appropriations in Euro millions

	COPENHAGEN PACKAGE		
	Appropriations for Commitments[1]	Appropriations for Payments[2]	Total
Cyprus	607.7	498.8	1,106.5
Czech Republic	4,612.7	2,918.6	7,531.3
Estonia	1,020.4	576.2	1,596.6
Hungary	5,100.5	3,095.5	8,196
Latvia	1,638.6	879.5	2,518.1
Lithuania	2,676.8	1,560.4	4,237.2
Malta	360.1	300.4	660.5
Poland	19,264.3	11,274.2	30,538.5
Slovakia	2,602.9	1,480.2	4,083.1
Slovenia	1,261.7	892.8	2,154.5
Total	40,851	25,142	65,993

[1] Commitment appropriations are payments covering several years as part of a multiannual programme.

[2] Payment appropriations refer to spending for the current year.

Source: own compilation on the basis of:
<http://europa.eu.int/comm/budget/pdf/financialfrwk/copenhagen_package/webtablesEN.pdf>
(accessed 21 Feb. 2004).

members with institutional and policy reforms in the EU so that both sides would be 'ready for each other'. The Treaties of Amsterdam and Nice, agreed in 1997 and 2000, respectively, and the Constitutional Treaty, agreed in principle by the member governments in June 2004, constituted important milestones in reforming the EU itself, so as to increase its own 'absorption' capacity and ensure its future functioning. Western politicians were also sensitive (or had to be seen to be sensitive) to public opinion in their own countries, which, in several key member states, was far from universally supportive of enlargement (see Table 12.6).

Compared to the enlargement perspective, the evolution of the domestic histories and politics of EU integration in the ten new members is more difficult to sketch, but one key commonality may be noted. This has been the existence of a solid domestic élite consensus in favour of EU integration, which, despite contestation from directly

Table 12.6 Public opinion in existing member states on accession detailed by accession countries

	B		DK		D		GR		E		F		IRL		I		L		NL		A		P		FIN		S		UK	
	+	−	+	−	+	−	+	−	+	−	+	−	+	−	+	−	+	−	+	−	+	−	+	−	+	−	+	−	+	−
Czech Republic	41	43	67	21	43	40	61	20	55	17	33	52	57	17	57	27	58	29	54	30	41	43	47	26	61	23	72	16	38	31
Slovakia	38	45	61	25	37	44	58	24	53	18	26	56	51	20	51	31	49	36	48	34	41	43	43	29	53	30	69	18	32	36
Poland	44	41	73	18	39	46	61	23	54	19	40	47	64	15	60	25	56	32	51	35	34	39	49	25	55	30	72	18	44	28
Hungary	44	41	68	21	56	29	62	22	52	20	35	50	59	17	61	25	58	28	54	30	66	23	49	26	70	18	71	18	42	29
Slovenia	35	48	53	30	49	30	57	25	52	20	23	59	50	21	48	34	46	38	39	41	54	33	43	29	42	39	62	24	31	36
Estonia	40	43	74	17	35	41	55	27	51	20	24	58	52	20	43	38	52	32	51	31	42	36	42	30	73	17	74	16	32	35
Latvia	41	42	74	17	36	40	53	27	51	20	24	58	50	22	42	38	52	31	50	31	41	35	41	30	64	24	73	17	33	34
Lithuania	37	45	73	18	41	38	53	28	51	21	25	57	50	20	43	37	50	32	48	32	40	37	42	29	63	25	72	17	31	36
Cyprus	48	37	51	32	38	40	51	21	51	21	33	52	65	15	54	29	56	29	53	28	48	33	45	28	55	31	66	21	50	24
Malta	52	33	64	21	45	34	52	20	52	20	36	49	66	14	65	20	64	22	59	23	53	29	47	27	57	26	71	16	56	19

Enlargement, which countries should join, % by country

Source: own compilation of table from Eurobarometer 58 (Mar. 2003), 87–8.

Table 12.7 Membership: a 'good thing' or 'bad thing'? (% by country)

	A good thing	A bad thing	Neither good nor bad	DK/DA
Cyprus	59	11	26	4
Czech Republic	44	15	34	7
Estonia	38	16	37	8
Hungary	56	10	24	10
Latvia	46	16	31	7
Lithuania	55	9	29	7
Malta	55	17	22	7
Poland	52	13	28	7
Slovakia	58	8	31	4
Slovenia	50	8	37	5

Source: own compilation of table from European Commission, *Candidate Countries Eurobarometer 2003.4* (Feb. 2004). <http://europa.eu.int/comm/public_opinion/archives/cceb/2003/cceb2003.4_full_report.pdf> (accessed 23 Feb. 2004).

affected interests, such as agriculture or the coal and steel industries, was not fundamentally challenged, with the exceptions of Malta and, for a while, Slovakia. For example, the Eurosceptical musings of former Czech Prime Minister and now President, Václav Klaus (Brugge 2003), did little to slow down the integration process (although they may well have helped to delay domestic institutional and policy reform). Public opinion surveys and, in particular, the results of the accession referenda held in 2003 underscored that the political élites in the accession countries had managed to carry the people with them—no mean feat in the often sharply partisan settings of post-Communist politics (see Tables 12.7 and 12.8). With the exception of Malta, there were no knife-edge referenda results, although there was considerable variation in voter turnout (Szczerbiak and Taggart 2004). What is, perhaps, in the longer term more significant than the results of the accession referenda is the fact that all bar one of the new members felt it necessary to hold such referenda (and several are committed to hold referenda on the future European Constitution). This provides an indication that as integration progresses it cannot be restricted to an elite project, but is reliant on the active support of the citizens of the new members.

Table 12.8 Results of Accession Referenda

	Date	Result %		Turnout %
		Yes	No	
Czech Republic	13–14 June 2003	77.3	22.7	55.2
Cyprus	—			
Estonia	14 September 2003	67	33.16	64.02
Latvia	20 September 2003	67	32.3	72.5
Lithuania	10–11 May 2003	89.92	8.85	63.37
Hungary	12 April 2003	83.76	16.24	45.62
Malta	8 March 2003	53.6	46.4	91
Poland	7–8 June 2003	77.45	22.55	58.85
Slovenia	23 March 2003	89.61	10.39	60.29
Slovak Republic	16–17 May 2003	92.46	6.20	52.15

Source: own compilation of table from Gallup Europe, 'Enlargement Poll Monitor'
<http://www.gallup-europe.be/epm/default.htm> (accessed 23 Feb. 2004).

Negotiating accession and beyond

The scope for substantive bargaining between the EU and the prospective member states was strictly limited from the outset. The *acquis* was declared sacrosanct, and the Commission's strategy was to allow transitional arrangements only where the financial costs of its full implementation immediately upon accession would be prohibitive, as applied most notably in the field of environmental policy. This does not mean, however, that the negotiations amounted to little more than window dressing. There were intensive discussions over the timing and sequencing of national measures for the transposition of EU legislation into national law, the opening and closing of the thirty-one policy 'chapters' around which the negotiations were structured, and, in particular, over what constituted satisfactory adoption and effective implementation of the *acquis*. Recent research on transposition and implementation of EU legislation in the EU-15 highlights that there is a considerable degree of discretion and interpretation when it comes to determining what constitutes compliance (Börzel 2003; Falkner et al. 2004). This was also evident in the wide-ranging annual progress reports (see Fig. 12.1), which seemed, in many instances, based on highly subjective assessments and were themselves subject to intense discussions between the EU authorities and the

Figure 12.1 Abridged reproduction of a table of contents in a European Commission 'Regular Report on Progress towards Accession'

Table of contents

Figure 12.1 *(Continued)*

Source: <http://europa.eu.int/comm/enlargement/report2002/cz_en.pdf> (accessed 21 Feb. 2004).

applicants, within the Commission and between the latter and the member states (notably those holding the Presidency of the Council). The European diplomacy of the accession states was, therefore, for the most part about what could be regarded as acceptable domestic institutional and policy responses. There were, of course, exceptions where matters of 'high politics' were involved. Examples included the highly conflictual relations between Slovakia and the EU between 1994 and 1998 under the leadership of Prime Minister Mečiar (Malová and Rybář 2003); the intense high-level international diplomacy surrounding the resolution of the partition of Cyprus (Nugent 2000); or the thorny issue of citizenship policies and the protection of national minorities in the Baltic states (Gelazis 2003).

In the diplomacy of the accession states, size, and tactical and strategic calculations mattered. Poland is generally regarded as having been the most assertive negotiator, safe in the knowledge that there would be no enlargement without it. This assertive stance has, of course, continued since. Thus, Poland was one of the signatories of the 'Letter of Eight' of January 2003, which supported the US position on Iraq, a stance that brought it in direct and open conflict with France and Germany. In December 2003 it was Poland, together with Spain, that was widely held responsible for the failure to agree on a European Constitution at the Rome European Council. Already in 2000, William Wallace (2000: 537) predicted that 'Polish governments are likely to prove as important players as Spanish, with as determined a commitment to the promotion of their perceived interests'. The approach of the EU and key member states, notably

France and Germany, during the accession negotiations, may help to explain this conflictual diplomacy. Prior to the conclusion of the accession negotiations, Attila Ágh (2003: 152), one of the most perceptive analysts of Central and Eastern European politics, noted that Poland might follow in the footsteps of Spain as a 'very tough negotiating partner', 'if the incumbent members socialize the new members again to a heavy fight for their national interests through the merciless use of their political and economic overweight in the closing accession negotiations in Copenhagen'. Viewed from this perspective, Polish intransigence in Rome may have been the price the old member states have had to pay for the manner in which they shaped the conditions of membership.

Patterns of Europeanization I: polity and politics

What domestic effects associated with EU integration may be observed so far in the new member states? And how have these effects been produced? As far as the EU impact on the polity—the public institutions of the state—is concerned, the experience of Western Europe would suggest that governmental-administrative institutions and here, in particular, linkage institutions at the central level of government, have been most immediately affected. Linkage refers to 'the institutional arrangements that link national executives and EU authorities and the institutional practices that have evolved at the national level to support national-EU connections' (Goetz 2000: 212). In the context of the accession states, this has meant, up to know, particularly those governmental and administrative actors, structures, and procedures that were in charge of the accession negotiations; the transposition of the *acquis*; and the management of pre-accession funds. There is already a good deal of research on this issue, with work on Hungary (Ágh 2003: 91 ff.), Slovenia (Fink Hafner and Lajh 2003), Lithuania (Nakrosis 2003), Poland (Zubek 2002), and comparative studies covering a range of countries, including the Czech Republic, Estonia, Hungary, Poland and Slovenia (Lippert et al. 2001; Laffan 2003). As in Western Europe (Kassim et al. 2000; Wessels et al. 2003), the new member states differ as regards the degree to which linkage functions have been concentrated within specialized units or dispersed (polycentrism); patterns of interministerial coordination; and the role of the chief executive and his/her staff in domestic-EU linkage. For example, in the Slovenian case,

despite the *formally* crucial role assigned to the Government Office for European Affairs in managing EU issues (. . .) *in practice* a relatively *polycentric model* developed (. . .) In the vertical coordination, the *Prime Minister* played the key co-ordinating role in cases of politically sensitive questions. The *Negotiating Team* as an expert group ensured the prevalence of expertise over political and factional interests in the negotiating process, and the *Council of Ministers* played the role of the ultimate national executive unit for EU affairs' (Fink Hafner and Lajh 2003: 166; emphases in the original).

By contrast, in Poland, after a prolonged period during the 1990s, when 'the Polish core executive lacked sufficient resources to effectively direct, coordinate and advise line ministries in the transposition process' (Zubek 2002: 6), there was a major shift towards a much more centralized approach in 2000, which included 'strong leadership from the prime minister and the minister for European affairs' and 'reinforced central and hierarchical coordination mechanisms' (ibid.: 11).

Some observers have argued that the creation of specialized executive units dealing with accession, transposition, and pre-accession funds has fostered fragmentation at the level of central government, as such units constitute organizational 'islands of excellence' or 'enclaves' (Goetz 2001; Nunberg 2000); certainly, dealing with EU business has, on the whole, tended to increase the autonomy of executive actors. For example, a recent study of Czech civil servants concerned with EU accession has found that involvement in EU business brings a 'significant degree of institutional autonomy towards domestic politics since civil servants tend to be more sensitive to signals from the EU institutions than those from their political leadership. This sensitivity is most pronounced with those who are most exposed to the EU' (Drulák, Česal, and Hampl 2003: 651).

There are several reasons to explain why there has been a pronounced tendency to the emergence of distinct 'EU core executives', which are, to a greater or lesser extent, separated from the rest of the administration. Negotiating entry and ensuring legal transposition of the entire *acquis* posed challenges of a different quality and magnitude from those associated with day-to-day EU business in long-standing member states. It was much more akin to the 'high politics' of shaping member states' basic relationships with the EU than the 'low politics' surrounding individual policy decisions. In this connection, it is worth recalling that even in Germany, which has a low degree of centralization and hierarchical coordination in EU matters (Goetz 2003), the range of actors is radically reduced and the core executive dominates when fundamental issues, notably treaty revisions, are at stake. The EU itself insisted on dealing with a small range of authoritative interlocutors, stressing the need for an effective lead from the centre. It commissioned the SIGMA (Support for Improvement in Governance and Management in Central and Eastern European Countries) unit at the OECD to develop 'baselines' for the effective interministerial coordination and the progress reports regularly commented on this issue. Perhaps most crucially, centralization is a less challenging form of coordination than network-based solutions, which require higher levels of stability, predictability, and trust amongst actors than tend to obtain in many Central and Eastern European executives, in particular (Dimitrov, Goetz, and Wollmann 2005).

Other dimensions of state organization where the EU influence has been documented in some detail include the development of the civil service (Bossaert and Demmke 2003; Dimitrova 2002; Verheijen 2002; Scherpereel 2003), and decentralization and regionalization (Brusis 2002; Hughes, Sasse, and Gordon 2001; Keating and Hughes 2003). As regards the former, major efforts were made from the mid-1990s to promote civil service reform in the post-Communist countries, not least through the formulation of 'baselines' for civil service development, which were developed by OECD–SIGMA on behalf of the EU. These baselines strongly favoured the establishment of career civil services based on the principles of a Weberian depoliticized bureaucracy. Technical and financial assistance was made available to the CEE applicant states to develop their civil service systems, both through the SIGMA programme and through PHARE projects. The need for the adoption of a comprehensive set of civil service legislation, and its effective implementation, was regularly emphasized in the annual progress reports on accession.

Nonetheless, despite such a targeted approach to shaping state organization, the results, in terms of creating non-politicized civil service systems, appear to have been, at best, modest, especially where legislation owed more to external exhortations than a domestic reform consensus (Meyer-Sahling 2004). This was, for example, the case in the Czech Republic, which was the last amongst the CEE accession states to adopt a civil service law in 2002, despite repeated and detailed interventions by EU actors for many years (the law is expected to come into force in January 2005) (for a detailed analysis see Scherpereel 2003). Even this law, in the view of SIGMA, falls far short of what is desirable. Thus, SIGMA's (2003: 5) Public Service and Administrative Framework Assessment for the Czech Republic noted that although the law was 'a positive step towards bringing the Czech civil service system closer to those of the EU Member States',

the law has many shortcomings, inconsistencies, and confused wording and structure, which may multiply interpretation issues and implementation problems (. . .) It is (. . .) unlikely that civil servants as defined by this law will be in place before 2008 (. . .) the positive effects of this law, if any, will begin to be seen only in five to eight years, which represents an unforeseeable future.

In a similar manner, the EU sought to promote effective decentralization of the administrative systems of the post-Communist states and was generally in favour of strengthening subnational governments at local and regional levels. To be sure 'the perception that the European Commission required the establishment of political regions is as false in central and eastern Europe as in the west' (Keating 2003: 57); but, 'the Phare programmes and the early phases of adaptation to the EU involved an expectation that there would be widespread regionalization in candidate countries' (ibid.: 58). However, recent work on administrative and political decentralization and regionalization in the region notes, 'how divergent endogenous interests and pressures triumphed over external convergence pressures, and resulted in a diversity of institutional outcomes' (Hughes 2003: 190).

Drawing on the insights of the comparative Europeanization literature lack of institutional convergence despite common external pressures and the very limited success of institutional transfer, as in the case of the civil service, are scarcely surprising. Even those who stress the relevance of institutional 'misfit' in triggering Europeanization (Börzel, in this volume) are quick to point out that associated adaptive pressures are mediated through domestic actors and institutions, which are of principal importance in shaping national institutional trajectories. Power asymmetries during the accession negotiations between the EU and existing members, on the one hand, and the applicants, on the other, do not necessarily imply that Europeanization follows a top-down logic. Rather, as noted earlier, they may encourage 'institutionalization for reversibility'—as EU pressures lessened, and once accession was 'in the bag', domestic preferences could strongly reassert themselves, with the result that, as in Hungary (Ágh 2003: 113 ff.) administrative and political decentralization and regionalization initiatives are effectively stalled.

Turning to integration effects on politics—electoral behaviour, parties, and party systems—again we know from the comparative Europeanization literature that effects vary very considerably amongst the longer-standing member states. In some, such effects are pronounced (see, for example, Egeberg, in this volume); in others, such as Germany, they are strictly limited (Anderson, in this volume). In Malta, the Labour Party has adopted a strongly Eurosceptic stance and campaigned vigorously against accession (Cini 2001; Pace 2002); the results of the accession referendum underlined the degree of division on the issue amongst the Maltese people. In Central and Eastern Europe, too, Euroscepticism 'is already an integral party of the party systems' (Taggart and Szczerbiak 2004: 24), with high party-based Euroscepticism particularly pronounced in the Czech Republic, Estonia, Hungary, Latvia, and Slovakia. Interestingly, 'soft Euroscepticism seems to be expressed by some mainstream parties' and it 'is expressed by opposition parties and by parties in government' (Taggart and Szczerbiak: 15). However, given the fluidity of party systems in parts of Central and Eastern Europe, the future persistence of these orientations is far from certain and there are important precedents of parties, such as the Greek Socialists, that have converted from an initially strongly Euro-critical stance to staunch supporters of integration.

Patterns of Europeanization II: public policy effects

There can be no doubt that the adoption of the *acquis* has had profound policy effects across a very wide range of domestic public policies in the accession states, even tough legal transposition does not equal effective implementation. The transposition of the *acquis* has meant the export of a highly evolved and differentiated policy regime to a set of countries the majority of which are at a significantly lower level of socio-economic development than the EU average. The full consequences of such an ambitious exercise will only become fully apparent in the coming years, as the political focus moves from transposition to effective implementation, and as the new members become subject to the normal compliance procedures applying in the EU.

Optimists expect accelerated modernization in the economic and social systems of the new members and stress its benefits; pessimists emphasize that most new member states still have a steep mountain to climb before they catch up with the less prosperous of the existing member states and highlight the potential for economic and social dislocation that their integration into the EU entails. Can policy regimes that were developed for some of the most socioeconomically advanced countries in the world be transferred to Central and Eastern Europe, in particular, without massive domestic disruption? In addressing this question, the experience of the Southern European countries, most notably Greece, but also Portugal and Spain, is of special relevance. It points to the likelihood of persistent compliance problems in key policy areas; suggests that socioeconomic convergence will be a matter of decades, not years; underlines the importance of large-scale financial transfers, notably through the EU cohesion policy, to foster convergence and to cushion the domestic effects of market liberalization (as noted earlier, it is extremely unlikely that the EU will agree to transfers to the new members comparable in magnitude to those that have gone to Southern Europe in the past); and raises the possibility of a Europeanization pattern that, as in Southern Europe, might be characterized by the co-existence of 'dynamism, asymmetry, and fragmentation' (Featherstone and Kazamias 2001: 3).

The expectation of a distinct, though not necessarily unique, pattern of integration and Europeanization for the longer term is reinforced by the fact that most of the ten new member states will, for the foreseeable future, remain outside the Euro zone. Under the terms of accession, they are expected to join at a future date to be determined the Exchange Rate Mechanism II, which links the currencies of member states that are not part of the euro area to the euro. They are committed to adopt the euro, if they have fulfilled the Maastricht criteria. Early adoption of the single currency seemed a top priority of the new members, but EU Finance Ministers and the European Central Bank already made it clear in the spring of 2003 that the ten accession states, for their own interest, might be best advised not to adopt the euro for several years. Since then, economic and fiscal data in the majority of cases have worsened, so that the head of the EU Economic and Finance Committee warned the eight Central and Eastern European countries in September 2003 to relinquish their hopes of early entry to the euro area. Whilst they will soon be subject to many of the disciplines and coordinating mechanisms associated with ERM II, the new members will not be participants in the 'Euro-12' Council as such, remaining outside the decision-making core of monetary politics in the EU.[2] Thus, a pattern of 'differential' membership will be strengthened, and, in a vital area of EU policy-making with a profound influence on wider economic and fiscal policy, they will remain 'policy-takers' rather than 'policy-shapers'.

Thus far, policy effects have mainly been debated in the cases of a broad range of economic policies (reflecting their centrality in the integration project and their close interconnection with post-Communist liberalization, privatization, and marketization); environmental policy (not least because in this field the need for transitional arrangements was obvious given the costs associated with the implementation of the EU's regime); agricultural policy (the EU's most costly policy and, given the importance of the rural economy for many of the new members, especially Poland, politically highly sensitive); and cohesion policy. However, in policy terms, there has been a further feature that set apart the 2004 accessions from previous enlargements: the high profile accorded to justice and home affairs. In part, the prominence of justice and home affairs does, of course, reflect the rapid extension and intensification of the *acquis* in these areas; but it is also owed to the domestic security concerns that many of the EU-15 associate with enlargement, including, for example, illegal immigration and people smuggling, asylum, drug trafficking, organized crime, and effective controls of the EU's borders. The prospect of enlargement, and the security fears it has conjured up, have had a decisive 'feedback' effect on EU policy, as, for instance, the plans for a European border police demonstrate.

It is too early to reach any definitive conclusions about policy effects in the new members. But at least as far as the majority of CEE members is concerned, the pattern that is emerging suggests that enlargement has added decisively to the diversity of EU–member state relations. This growing diversity is grounded in (i) the major question marks over the capacity, and, in some instances, willingness on the part of the

---

[2] The Euro-12 Council is an informal meeting of ministers of those countries participating fully inside the Euro-zone. The new states are not the only ones not to participate in this body, since Denmark, Sweden, and the UK are also absent because they have not adopted the Euro as their currency.

new members to ensure compliance; (ii) the existence of transitional arrangements affecting both the implementation of the *acquis* in the new member states, the EU funding regime, and restrictions on the freedom of movement of labour imposed by existing member states; (iii) the exclusion of most new members from the single currency for the foreseeable future; and (iv) the intense involvement of the EU in citizenship, minority politics and inter-community relations which has no precedent in the EU-15. The mixture of features differs from country to country, but their cumulative effect is unmistakable.

Conclusions

What lessons does the experience of integration and Europeanization of the EU-15 hold for the new members? What will the new members add to EU-member state relations? Finally, what are the implications of enlargement for our understanding of Europeanization, in particular?

The contributions to this volume provide ample evidence for the existence of differential forms of EU membership and differential patterns of Europeanization. The member states participate in the EU in different forms and with differing intensities, and they exhibit a high degree of variation in the incidence and strength of Europeanization effects, most markedly as regards electoral behaviour, political parties, and party systems (Ladrech, in this volume). There are noteworthy parallels in accounts of integration and Europeanization in Southern Europe, on the one hand, and CEE, in particular, on the other. They include selective 'uploading'; selective 'downloading'; asymmetry and fragmentation in domestic responses to EU integration; and the close interaction between integration and Europeanization, on the one hand, and democratization and modernization, on the other.

Turning to our understanding of EU–member state relations, the new member states heighten the *problematique* of large states versus small and even microstates in the EU. Power asymmetries are set to become more pronounced, and are heightened by the fact that intraregional ties are weak or more or less non-existent. The proliferation of small states in the EU largely undermines calls for subsidiarity; it also involves a further pluralization of EU–member state relations. It is already evident that enlargement has further promoted the search for intensified cooperation amongst the core member states, as recent Franco-German initiatives underscore. Thus, 'the "shrinking" core may turn out to be a "harder core"' (Dyson and Goetz 2003a: 376).

Finally, the experience of the new members shows that 'misfit' is not a necessary precondition of Europeanization in polity or policy terms, and carries no explanatory power when it comes to politics. Both institutional settings and policy regimes in Central and Eastern Europe, in particular, have been very fluid, a fact that static accounts of match and mismatch find difficult to accommodate. They privilege a top-down view of Europeanization, and neglect 'bottom-up' Europeanization through domestic institutional and policy entrepreneurs. In settings where institutions are far from fixed and their socializing effects generally limited, actors matter.

Further reading

For accounts of events leading up to the 2004 enlargement of the EU see Baun (2000), Cameron (2004), Mayhew (1998), Papadimitriou (2002) and Torreblanca (2001). For in-depth studies of how the new members have responded to accession see Ágh (2003) on Hungary; Cordell (2000) on Poland; Pettai and Zielonka (2003) on the Baltic states; Rupnik and Zielonka (2003) on the Czech Republic and Slovakia; Fink Hafner and Lajh (2003) on Slovenia; several articles on Malta in South European Society and Politics, 2002, Volume 7, No 1; Featherstone (2001) on Cyprus. Grabbe (2003) and Goetz (2001) discuss Europeanization in post-Communist contexts.

Websites

Comprehensive information on the EU's approach to enlargement can be found on relevant pages at the sites of the European Commission <http://www.europa.eu. int/comm/enlargement/index_en.html> and of the European Parliament <http://www. europarl.eu.int/enlargement/default_en.htm>. The site of the Commission also contains links to the official websites of the ten new members focusing on accession <http://europa.eu.int/abc/governments/index_en.htm>. The site of the Centre for European Reform contains up-to-date analyses of accession-related information <http://www.cer.org.uk/enlargement/index.html>. The Organizing for EU enlargement project, conducted by academics from six countries, focuses in particular on executive adaptation in Estonia, Hungary and Slovenia, but with comparison to more established members (Finland, Greece, and Ireland), see <http://www.oeue.net>.

References

Ágh, A. (2003), *Anticipatory and Adaptive Europeanization in Hungary* (Budapest: Hungarian Centre for Democracy Studies).

Avery, G. (2004), 'The Enlargement Negotiations', in F. Cameron (ed.), *The Future of Europe: Integration and Enlargement* (London: Routledge), 35–62.

Baldacchino, G. (2002), 'A Nationless State? Malta, National Identity and the EU', *West European Politics*, 25/4, 191–206.

Baun, M. J. (2000), *A Wider Europe: The Process and Politics of European Union Enlargement* (Lanham: Rowman & Littlefield).

Börzel, T. A. (2003), 'Guarding the Treaty: The Compliance Strategies of the European Commission', in T. A. Börzel and R. A. Cichowski (eds), *The State of the European Union. Volume 6: Law, Politics, and Society* (Oxford: Oxford University Press), 197–220.

Brugge, P. (2003), 'Czech Perceptions of EU Membership: Havel vs. Klaus', in J. Rupnik and J. Zielonka (eds), *The Road to the European Union. Volume 1: The Czech and Slovak Republics* (Manchester: Manchester University Press), 180–98.

Brusis, M. (2002), 'Between EU Requirements, Competitive Politics, and National Traditions: Re-creating Regions in the Accession Countries of Central and Eastern Europe', *Governance* 15/4, 531–59.

Cameron, F. (ed.) (2004), *The Future of Europe: Integration and Enlargement* (London: Routledge).

Cini, M. (2001), 'The Europeanization of Malta: Adaptation, Identity and Party Politics', in K. Featherstone and G. Kazamias (eds), *Europeanization and the Southern Periphery* (London: Frank Cass), 261–76.

Cordell, K. (ed.) (2000), *Poland and the European Union* (London: Routledge).

Cremona, M. (ed.) (2003), *The Enlargement of the European Union* (Oxford: Oxford University Press).

Dimitrov, V., Goetz, K. H., and Wollmann, H. (2005), *Governing after Communism: Institutions and Policy* (Lanham: Rowman & Littlefield).

Dimitrova, A. (2002), 'Enlargement, Institution-Building and the EU's Administrative Capacity Requirement', *West European Politics*, 25/4, 171–90.

Drulák, P, Česal, J., and Hampl, S. (2003), 'Interactions and Identities of Czech Civil Servants on their Way to the EU', *Journal of European Public Policy*, 10/4, 637–54.

Dyson, K. and Goetz, K. H. (2003a), 'Europeanization Compared: The Shrinking Core and the Decline of "Soft" Power', in Dyson and Goetz (eds), *Germany, Europe and the Politics of Constraint* (Oxford: Oxford University Press), 349–76.

Dyson, K., and Goetz, K. H. (2003b), 'Living with Europe: Power, Constraint and Contestation', in Dyson and Goetz (eds), *Germany, Europe and the Politics of Constraint* (Oxford: Oxford University Press), 3–35.

Falkner, G., Hartlapp, M., Leiber, S. and Treib, O. (2004), 'Non-compliance with EU Directives in the Member States: Opposition through the Backdoor?, *West European Politics*.

Featherstone, K. (2001), 'Cyprus and the Onset of Europeanization: Strategic Usage, Structural Transformation and Institutional Adaptation', in K. Featherstone and G. Kazamias (eds), *Europeanization and the Southern Periphery* (London: Frank Cass), 141–62.

Featherstone, K., and Kazamias, G. (2001), 'Introduction: Southern Europe and the Process of "Europeanization" ', in

Featherstone and Kazamias (eds), *Europeanization and the Southern Periphery* (London: Frank Cass), 1–22.

Fink Hafner, D., and Lajh, D. (2003), *Managing Europe from Home: The Europeanisation of the Slovenian Core Executive* (Ljubljana: Faculty of Social Sciences).

Gelazis, N. M. (2003), 'The Effects of EU Conditionality on Citizenship Policies and the Protection of National Minorities in the Baltic States', in V. Pettai and J. Zielonka (eds), *The Road to the European Union. Volume 2: Estonia, Latvia and Lithuania* (Manchester: Manchester University Press), 46–75.

Goetz, K. H. (2000), 'European Integration and National Executives: A Cause in Search of an Effect', *West European Politics*, 23/4, 211–31.

Goetz, K. H. (2001), 'Making Sense of Post-Communist Central Administration: Modernization, Europeanization or Latinization', *Journal of European Public Policy*, 8/6, 1032–51.

Goetz, K. H. (2002), 'Europeanisation in West and East: A Challenge to Institutional Theory'. Paper prepared for 1st Pan-European Conference on EU Politics, Bordeaux, 26–28 September.

Goetz, K. H. (2003), 'The Federal Executive: Bureaucratic Fusion versus Governmental Bifurcation', in K. Dyson and K. H. Goetz (eds), *Germany, Europe and the Politics of Constraint* (Oxford: Oxford University Press), 57–72.

Goetz, K. H., and Wollmann, H. (2001) 'Govermentalizing Central Executives in Post-Communist Europe: A Four-Country Comparison', *Journal of European Public Policy*, 8/6, 864–87.

Grabbe, H. (2001), 'How Does Europeanization Affect CEE Governance? Conditionality, Diffusion and Diversity', *Journal of European Public Policy*, 8/6, 1013–31.

Grabbe, H. (2002), 'European Union Conditionality and the *Acquis Communautaire*', *International Political Science Review*, 23/3, 249–68.

Grabbe, H. (2003), 'Europeanization Goes East: Power and Uncertainty in the EU Accession Process', in K. Featherstone and C. Radaelli (eds), *The Politics of Europeanization* (Oxford: Oxford University Press), 303–27.

Hughes, J. (2003), 'Regional Convergence and Divergence in an Enlarged EU', in M. Keating and J. Hughes (eds), *The Regional Challenge in Central and Eastern Europe: Territorial Restructuring and European Integration* (Brussels: Lang), 183–91.

Hughes, J., Sasse, G., and Gordon, C. (2001), 'Enlargement and Regionalization: The Europeanization of Local and Regional Governance in CEE States', in H. Wallace (ed.), *Interlocking Dimensions of European Integration* (Basingstoke: Palgrave), 145–78.

Jacquot, S., and Woll, C. (2003), 'Usages of European Integration: Europeanization from a Sociological Perspective', *European Integration online Papers*, 7/12.

Kassim, H., Peters, P. G., and Wright, V. (eds) (2000), *The National Co-ordination of EU Policy: The Domestic Level* (Oxford: Oxford University Press).

Keating, M. (2003), 'Regionalization in Central and Eastern Europe: The Diffusion of a Western Model?', in M. Keating and J. Hughes (eds), *The Regional Challenge in Central and Eastern Europe: Territorial Restructuring and European Integration* (Brussels: Lang), 51–67.

Keating, M., and Hughes, J. (eds) (2003), *The Regional Challenge in Central and Eastern Europe: Territorial Restructuring and European Integration* (Brussels: Lang).

Laffan, B (2003), 'Managing Europe from Home: Impact of the EU on Executive Government: A Comparative Analysis', Research project report (draft), EU Fifth Framework Programme.

Lippert, B., Umbach, G., and Wessels, W. (2001), 'Europeanization of CEE Executives: EU Membership Negotiations as a Shaping Power', *Journal of European Public Policy*, 8/6, 980–1012.

Malová, D., and Rybář, M. (2003), 'The European Union's Policies towards Slovakia: Carrots and Sticks of Political Conditionality', in J. Rupnik and J. Zielonka (eds), *The Road to the European Union. Volume 1: The Czech and Slovak Republics* (Manchester: Manchester University Press), 98–112.

Mayhew, A. (1998), *Recreating Europe: The European Union's Policy Towards Central and Eastern Europe* (Cambridge: Cambridge University Press).

Meyer-Sahling, J. (2004), 'Civil Service Reform in Post-Communist Europe: The Bumpy Road to Depoliticisation', *West European Politics*, 27/1, 71–103.

Nakrosis, V. (2003), 'Assessing Governmental Capacities to Manage European Affairs: The Case of Lithuania', in V. Pettai and J. Zielonka (eds), *The Road to the European Union. Volume 2: Estonia, Latvia and Lithuania* (Manchester: Manchester University Press), 104–39.

Nugent, N. (2000), 'EU Enlargement and the "Cyprus Problem" ', *Journal of Common Market Studies*, 38/1, 131–50.

Nunberg, B. (2000), *Ready for Europe: Public Administration Reform and European Accession in Central and Eastern Europe* (Washington, DC: World Bank).

Pace, R. (2002), 'A Small State and the European Union: Malta's EU Accession Experience', *South European Politics & Society*, 7/1, 24–42.

Papadimitriou, D. (2002), *Negotiating the New Europe: The European Union and Eastern Europe* (Aldershot: Ashgate).

Pettai, V., and Zielonka, J. (eds) (2003), *The Road to the European Union. Volume 2: Estonia, Latvia and Lithuania* (Manchester: Manchester University Press).

Rupnik, J., and Zielonka, J. (eds) (2003), *The Road to the European Union. Volume 1: The Czech and Slovak Republics* (Manchester: Manchester University Press).

Scherpereel, J. A. (2003), 'Appreciating the Third Player: The European Union and the Politics of Civil Service Reform in East-Central Europe'. Paper presented at the Annual Meeting of the American Political Science Association, Philadelphia, August.

Schimmelfennig, F. (2003), 'Strategic Action in a Community Environment: The Decision to Enlarge the European Union to the East',*Comparative Political Studies*, 36(1/2), 156–83.

Sedelmeier, U., and Wallace, H. (2000), 'Eastern Enlargement: Strategy or Second Thoughts?', in H. Wallace and W. Wallace (eds), *Policy-making in the European Union*, 4th edn. (Oxford: Oxford University Press), 427–460.

SIGMA (2003), *Czech Republic. Public Service and the Administrative Framework Assessment 2003* <http://www1.oecd.org/sigmaweb/PDF/assessments/Candidates2003/CzechCivServ200603.pdf>.

Smith, K. (2003), 'The Evolution and Application of EU Membership Conditionality', in M. Cremona (ed.), *The Enlargement of the European Union* (Oxford: Oxford University Press), 105–139.

Szczerbiak, A., and Taggart, P. (eds) (2004), 'Choosing Union: The 2003 EU Accession Referendums', special issue of *West European Politics*, 27/4.

Taggart, P. and Szczerbiak, A. (2004), 'Contemporary Euroscepticism in the Party Systems of the European Union Candidate States of Central and Eastern Europe', *European Journal of Political Research*, 43/1, 1–27.

Torreblanca, J. E. (2001), *The European Union and Central Eastern Europe* (Aldershot: Ashgate).

Verheijen, T. (2002), 'The European Union and Public Administration Development in Central and Eastern Europe', in R. Baker (ed.), *Transitions from Authoritarianism: The Role of Bureaucracy* (Westport CT: Praeger), 245–59.

Verney, S. (2002), 'Creating the Democratic Tradition of European Integration: The South European Catalyst', in H. Sjursen (ed.), *Enlargement and the Finality of the EU* (Oslo: ARENA, Report No. 7/2002), 97–127.

Wallace, H. (2001), 'Introduction: Rethinking European Integration', in H. Wallace (ed.), *Interlocking Dimensions of European Integration* (Basingstoke: Palgrave), 1–22.

Wessels, W., Maurer, A., and Mittag, J. (eds) (2003), *Fifteen Into One? The European Union and its Member States* (Manchester: Manchester University Press).

Zubek, R. (2002), *Europeanizing from the Centre? Core Executive Configurations and Transposition of Community Legislation in Poland, 1997–2002.* Paper presented at the EGPA 2002 Conference, Potsdam.

Part III

Europeanization

Introduction

The shift of policymaking from the national to the EU level led scholars to examine the dynamics of the member states' actors and institutions, as well as interest representation in the multilevel governance polity. It offers the opportunity to measure the consequences of the shared engagement of European, state as well as sub-national institutions in the regulation of economic and social activities. States institutions include parliaments but also courts, because conflicts around the implementation of legal norms is part of the EU game. In a multilevel governance system, power is diffuse and it is difficult to rank levels of authority. In particular, the state institutions no longer have the monopoly of exercising political authority. If state institutions and actors are no longer exclusive actors, they remain nevertheless dominant. In some respect, one might even wonder if European negotiations do not enable certain governmental agencies, national parliaments, or national judges to maximize their power by inserting themselves into functional networks at the EU level.

The institutions of the member states also derive power from their strong involvement in the implementation of EU policies: policies which remain differentiated from one territory to another (see Part 2). This fact makes it necessary to take some distance from the hypothesis that the EU is the locus of a reconstruction of legitimate political community which has superseded the state. Contrary to what has been said by some scholars, there is no 'fusion' between the EU and the national institutions (Wessels, Maurer, and Mittag 2003). The interactions correspond more to what Helen Wallace has called a 'moving pendulum' (Wallace 2000: 45). Its movements are shaped by the context in Western Europe, by the array of policy functions needing attention, and by the purposes and predicaments of national actors. EU institutions provide the means by devising collective policy responses. How they operate is influenced by the interests, and the ideas coming from the member states' agendas. Differentiation is particularly obvious for national parliaments. The mechanical equation by which the projection of national parliaments in the EU polity is enough to enable them automatically to achieve control in relation to the central state institutions must be avoided. It is the political autonomy negotiated beforehand with the state within national constitutional frameworks that enables national parliaments to Europeanize with greater or lesser success.

The Europeanization of national interest groups and political parties has also to be studied on a comparative basis. For interest groups, the EU offer what Robert Ladrech calls in his chapter 'changing opportunity structures'. This situation contributes to destabilize national corporatist systems through the potential that private actors have to project themselves onto EU institutions and to form new institutions. Nevertheless, interest groups' activities outside the domestic level also remain conditioned by the domestic interest intermediation systems, which are very different from one member state to another. More than the interest groups, political parties remain strongly embedded in national strategies, because of the lack of a European party government. As Peter Mair showed, despite the existence of transnational party federations at the EU level national party programmes are little influenced by the EU (Mair 2000).

The Europeanization of national policies has been addressed in a wide range of ad hoc studies as well as a small number of more systematic analyses. Simon Bulmer and Claudio Radaelli do not try to chart all the empirical findings of this research but, rather, attempt to offer a differentiated explanation of the mechanisms by which national policy is Europeanized.

Studying the EU–member state relationship on a comparative basis also makes it important to reflect on the Europeanization of national economies. Thus it is important to understand the conflict that frequently arises between the sovereignty of national territories on one hand, and the construction of a single market on the other. Since the 1980s, the market norm and the single currency have established themselves as essential frames of reference for the economic policies of member states. In macroeconomic policies, but also in telecommunications, transport, or energy policies, the rules of the internal market and of Economic and Monetary Union have come to destabilize economic practices and social orders inherited from national welfare states. Although the states have not lost their capacity to oppose the effects of the internal market and of the Economic and Monetary Union (some states, of course, are not participating in the single currency), government economic policies, business practices, and industrial relations must now act within the limitations of what is allowed under European economic governance. It does not mean, however, that a unified system of economic governance has replaced totally the former national economic systems. As Vivien Schmidt demonstrates, the European movement towards more convergence is compatible with different national models of capitalism, resulting from the historical trajectories, institutional patterns and political cultures of the member states (Schmidt 2002).

References

Mair, Peter (2000), 'The limited impact of Europe on national party systems', *West European Politics*, 23/4, 27–51.

Schmidt, Vivien (2002), *The Future of European Capitalism* (Oxford: Oxford University Press).

Wessels, Wolfgang, Maurer, Andreas, and Mittag Jürgen (eds), *Fifteen Into One? The European Union and its Member States*, (Manchester: Manchester University Press, 2003).

Wallace, H. (2002), 'The Policy Process: A Moving Pendulum', in H. Wallace and W. Wallace (eds), *Policy-Making in the European Union*, 4th edn. (Oxford: Oxford University Press), 39–64.

Chapter 13

The Europeanization of Member State Institutions

Hussein Kassim[1]

Contents

Summary

The impact of the EU on domestic institutions has been complex and far reaching. As well as the cross-national differences that arise from the impact of integration on states with contrasting constitutional arrangements, legal traditions, and political cultures, domestic institutions have been affected very differently. The effect on central governments has been the most dramatic and the most ambivalent: Union membership imposes constraints and burdens that are often onerous, but at the same affords new opportunities and makes available new resources. Integration has reinforced the decline of national legislatures, while national courts at all levels have assumed new functions and become part of a wider Community of law. The consequences for sub-national governments, by contrast, defy easy generalization. Interaction between the EU and member state institutions is similarly complex, with linkages and inputs varying by type and by state.

[1] I should like to thank Simon Bulmer and Dionyssis G. Dimitrakopoulos for useful comments on an earlier version of this chapter. All errors that remain are my own.

Introduction

EU member states are embedded in a 'system of shared decision-making and collective governance', the defining characteristic of which is 'the enmeshing of the
national and the European' (Laffan *et al.* 2000: 74). Although political debate (and
much of the academic literature) focuses on the constraints that Union membership
imposes, integration has also created 'new structures for opportunity' (Hix and Goetz
2000: 12), new possibilities to influence the economic and political environment in
Europe, and a new space for political action above and beyond the national level
(Favell 1998).

This chapter examines the impact of European integration on national institutions,
and their interaction with the Union.[2] It puts forward three arguments. The first is
that the EU's effects on domestic institutions have not been uniform and that their
differential impact can be explained in terms of factors at both EU and national levels.
With respect to the former, national institutions are assigned different roles within
the EU system. They intervene at different stages of the policy process, have access
to different channels and pathways, and command different resources. National
governments occupy the most privileged position. They negotiate treaty reform at
Intergovernmental Conferences (IGCs), set the medium-term goals of the Union in
meetings of the European Council and adopt EU legislation in the Council of the
European Union. National parliaments, by contrast, have no direct role in EU decision-
making processes, while the Committee of the Regions limits the participation of
sub-national bodies to a consultative role in a limited number of policy areas. National
courts, meanwhile, are participants in a continuous 'inter-institutional dialogue' with
the European Court of Justice (Stone Sweet 1998). The role of the institutions and their
relative position in the domestic polity is also important. The performance of 'specific
socio-political functions such as judging or legislating' and the fact that institutions
are subject to 'the demands of specific political constituencies' (Mattli and Slaughter
1998: 255) account for the differences in the way that they interact with the EU.

The second argument is that national context matters. National differences are
evident both in the EU's impact on member state institutions and their interaction
with the Union (Rometsch and Wessels 1996; Wessels, Maurer, and Mittag 2003). The
structure of the domestic polity, as well as policy style and popular and elite attitudes
towards integration, present quite different opportunities and constraints, and mediate the Union's impact differently. The extent to which parliaments assert themselves
vis-à-vis their respective governments in EU matters, for example, depends on domestic factors, such as the constitutional provisions that govern executive–legislature
relations, institutional culture, the nature of the party system, parliamentary norms
and practices, and the size of the parliamentary workload (Norton 1996: 9–11). In

---

[2] The EU's impact is also felt beyond its borders. For its effects on Central European
states before they became EU members, see Lippert et al. 2001, and for its impact on non-
members, see Fischer et al. (2002) on Switzerland and Claes (2002) on Norway. Also see
Chapter 9 in this volume.

the case of courts, by contrast, national policy preferences, legal culture and legal doctrine account for variation in the terms of legal integration (Mattli and Slaughter 1998: 265–76). Differences in domestic structures also account for cross-national variation in the arrangements put in place by national governments to manage their EU policies (Kassim 2001), as well as, to a significant extent, the mobilization of subnational authorities at the level of the Union (Rometsch and Wessels 1996). So diverse are member state systems that attempts to distinguish between broad sub-types—for example, between unitary and federal states—are likely to be confounded by the sheer range of national differences.

Finally—and less of an argument than a reminder—the relationship between the EU and member state institutions is a two-way interaction. The top-down dynamic is an important dimension of integration, but the bottom-up flow is no less significant. Not only can national influences be detected in the design of EU bodies, but member state institutions are players at the EU level (in other words, the Union is not exogenous to national political systems),[3] they have a considerable impact on the operation of EU institutions (the effect is most apparent with respect to the Council and the Commission), and the institutional, administrative and judicial capacities of the Union as a system are set by the respective capacities of national institutions (Metcalfe 1992).

The discussion below is organized into five sections. The first looks at central governments. Parliaments are investigated in the second section, sub-national authorities in the third, and courts in the fourth. Conclusions are set out in the fifth.

National governments and the EU

The nature of the EU's impact on national governments as actors is strongly contested. While intergovernmentalists (Moravcsik 1993; 1998; Milward 2000; Hoffmann 1966; 1982) argue that governments both control and are strengthened by European integration, neofunctionalists (Haas 1958; Stone Sweet and Sandholtz 1998), new institutionalists (Pierson 1996; Pollack 1997) and multilevel governance theorists (Marks, Hooghe, and Blank 1996) recognize the continuing importance of national governments, but emphasise the constraints that the Union imposes on them. The Union's effects on governments as administrations is less hotly disputed, though there are differences concerning its relative importance as a source of administrative change.[4] With respect to the interaction between member states and the EU, there is general agreement that national governments are the most powerful member state institutions in Brussels and that they dominate, even if they do not absolutely control, the relationship between the Union and the national polity, and domestic EU policy making.

---

[3] I am grateful to Dionyssis G. Dimitrakopoulos for this point.

[4] According to one view, EU impact has been minimal, when compared with other sources of change, such as new public management reform and privatization (Wallace 1996; Goetz 2000; Page 2003). Another view holds that integration may not have brought about a fundamental transformation, but has nevertheless led to important changes at the administrative level (Knill 2001; Kassim and Menon 2003a; 2003b).

The impact on national governments

EU membership locks national governments into a system of collective governance, circumscribing their autonomy, but at the same time affords new opportunities. The European Union makes it possible for governments to achieve collectively what they can no longer they achieve individually. It provides an instrument for managing the externalities that arise from regional interdependence (Moravcsik 1993; 1998), an arena for finding solutions to transnational problems, such as environmental pollution, drug trafficking, and illegal immigration, and an on-going forum within which governments can address matters of common concern without incurring repeated set-up costs each time a new problem arises.

The EU also affords individual governments the means of attaining goals that would otherwise not be possible. As policy entrepreneurs or 'policy leaders' (Héritier *et al.* 1996), governments can use the EU as a channel to influence policies pursued in the rest of the Union in ways that are favourable to their domestic constituencies—for example, by avoiding the imposition of adjustment costs on firms that may arise if rules are introduced at the EU level that differ from national regulations or by exporting their domestic model to Brussels to give their nationals a competitive advantage.[5] It is worth noting, though, that the pro-market bias of the treaty and the support it gives to negative integration (the removal of barriers to competition) is not neutral. Rather, it favours states that pursue liberal, as opposed to statist, economic policies.

A further benefit to governments arises from the 'nesting' of the domestic arena inside the EU framework. Governments are best placed to win the 'two-level game' (Putnam 1988), since they can appeal to the constraints imposed by other governments as a justification for presenting a limited set of policy options at home.[6] Moreover, 'by according governmental policy initiatives greater domestic political legitimacy and by granting them greater domestic agenda-setting power . . . the institutional structure of the EC strengthens the initiatives and influence of national governments by insulating the policy process and generating domestic agenda-setting power for national politicians' (Moravcsik 1993: 473–524). Governments can, at least in countries where public opinion is favourable to integration, override domestic opposition by citing demands made by Brussels.

The constraints on governments arise in a variety of forms and operate at different levels. Power-sharing with other governments and with EU institutions is perhaps the most fundamental. Executive power is shared with the Commission, legislative power with the European Parliament (Hix 1999: 25, 32, and 56). Moreover, the supranational institutions—the Commission and the Court—exercise important powers that undermine 'member state institutional autonomy' (Schmidt 1999: 20). Its formal monopoly over policy initiation, strategic location in the policy process, and privileged access to

---

[5] A rather spectacular case of a government successfully multilateralizing its policy preferences is air transport liberalization, where the UK sought in the 1980s to use Community competition rules to relax the restrictive regulations that governed European aviation (see Kassim and Stevens, forthcoming).

[6] They can also take advantage of the fact that negotiations take place behind closed doors, beyond the scrutiny of parliament and the media, to press for measures that they would not be prepared to support publicly.

information enables the Commission, for example, to exert an important influence over policy and grants it a structural advantage in decision making. Meanwhile, the Court, through the constitutionalization of the treaties (see below)—a process neither anticipated nor supported by the member states—has created a Community legal system, which significantly restricts the actions and choices available to national governments.[7] Indeed, Hoffmann and Keohane conclude that '[o]f all Community institutions, the Court has gone furthest in limiting national autonomy by asserting the principles of superiority of Community law and of the obligation of member states to implement binding acts consistent with Community Directives' (1991: 278).

Furthermore, although the supranational institutions were created by the member states as 'agents' to carry out functions that are time-consuming, call for technical expertise or require intervention by an impartial authority (see Moravcsik 1993; 1998; Pierson 1996; Pollack 1997; see also Kassim and Menon 2003a), government 'principals' have been unable to prevent them acting independently. On the one hand, the Commission and the Court developed interests that did not coincide with those of governments, but which they were able to pursue, using the resources entrusted to them. On the other, governments, constrained by short-time horizons associated with the electoral cycle, the high barriers to institutional reform and informational asymmetries that favour the supranational institutions, have found it difficult to re-assert their control (Pierson 1996; though see Kassim and Menon 2003b).

The obligations of membership can also severely restrict governments' freedom of action. Although the extent to which states could be authors of their own destinies in an increasingly interdependent world is overestimated by critics of integration, who contrast the restrictions imposed on states by the EU with an (imagined) freedom outside it, there is little doubt that the EU imposes significant constraints on governmental autonomy. As treaty signatories, member states must accept the primacy of EC over national law (Raunio and Hix 2000: 154), as well as all existing and future Community legislation, and the obligation to agree common policies and participate in various forms of joint action. With the expansion of the Union's competencies— Hix and Goetz (2000: 4) report that '80 per cent of all rules governing the production, distribution and exchange of goods, services, capital and labour in the European market' are decided in Brussels—the scope for discretionary action on the part of government across a broad range of policies has diminished. The constraints imposed on governments have been apparent since the 1950s, but they have become more visible, more far-reaching and more controversial since the mid-1980s. The EU has emerged as an increasingly important political arena, a source of binding rules and regulations, and a body with significant funds for distributive and redistributive purposes.

These developments have important consequences for the ability of national governments to originate policy preferences. As a result of EU rules, governments cannot, to take but a few examples, run 'excessive' public deficits, offer regulatory protection or financial support to companies anointed 'national champions', or reserve coastal fisheries for their nationals, while Community rules proscribing the use of certain policy instruments, such as state aid, have compelled governments to abandon not only traditional policy goals, but entire industrial strategies—though

---

[7] See Mattli and Slaughter (1998); Alter (1996).

the precise impact depends, of course, on the degree of congruence between pre-existing national policies and EU policy developments. One paradox is that, as a neoliberal regime has emerged in Brussels in the wake of the SEA, traditional supporters of integration, such as France, have been forced to undertake extensive reform and radical revision of traditional policies as a consequence of policies decided by the Union, while the Euro-cautious UK has had to make relatively few policy sacrifices (see Menon and Wright 1996).

The fact that national governments occupy key positions at all levels of decision making—and that their centrality has become more deeply entrenched since Maastricht (Kassim and Menon 2004)—does not, however, compensate for the loss of policy control that they have experienced. Collectively, governments may be 'masters of the Treaty' (Wessels 2001) and sit at 'the decisionmaking centre of the Community' (Wessels 1991), but individually they have little say over the pace of integration or the determination of EU policy. The increased use of qualified majority voting in the Council, for example, prevents any single government from blocking the adoption of regulations or directives to which it is opposed (Garrett and Tsebelis 1996). With the national veto effectively obsolete, governments must ally with other actors to form a 'winning coalition' or a blocking minority if they are to exert any influence over final outcomes, and compromise is usually necessary to avoid isolation. Barriers at the 'heroic' level of decision making are similarly high. Treaty reform requires the unanimous assent of member states (Pollack 1997). Moreover, experience demonstrates that even the negotiation of an explicit opt-out does not guarantee a government escape from the obligations imposed by newly negotiated treaty provisions (Schmidt 1999).

A further difficulty is that states find the EU a challenging environment in which to operate, particularly since at the Union level they lack the resources—authority, agenda control, party discipline, established networks, and administrative tradition—that enable them to dominate the domestic arena (Wright 1996; Kassim *et al.* 2000). Several features make the EU a difficult arena to negotiate. First, the EU system is

fluid, ambiguous, and hybrid . . . not based on a single treaty, a unitary structure, or a single dominating centre of authority and power . . . [but] built on several treaties and a complex three-pillar structure . . . [where] the pillars are organized on different principles and supranational/intergovernmental mixes' (Olsen 1997: 165).

Second, institutional fragmentation and organisational density are high with successive treaty revisions apparently moving the EU further in the direction of ever greater complexity (Maurer 2002: 5). Third, the legislative procedures of the EU are labyrinthine, while the policy process involves multiple actors, who interact across different levels—the European, the national and the sub-national—and are subject to different imperatives and 'rules of the game' at each. The policy menu is long, ever changing, and more varied than at the national level—a further complicating factor—and the EU policy process unusually open (Peters 1994; Wright 1996). Finally, sectorization is strongly pronounced (Mazey and Richardson 1995) with each policy sector exhibiting a particular logic and conflict potential. Governments have responded by putting in place dedicated systems designed to ensure a flow of information between the national capital and Brussels, and that national interests are appropriately defended (see below).

EU membership also carries certain obligations. At Union level, governments must participate in various fora, decision-making bodies and committees, the most important of which are the European Council and the Council of the European Union. The demands on human resources are significant. The need to be represented at more than 300 Council working groups (General Secretariat of the Council 1996: 91–105) places considerable strain on national administrations not only because of the pressure on personnel—2,596 working days were spent in these meetings in 1996 (General Secretariat of the Council 1999)—but also on account of the difficulties involved in ensuring that officials comply with ministerial guidelines. In addition, governments must take their turn to run the Council Presidency for a six-month term—an increasingly onerous responsibility. At member state level, meanwhile, national administrations operate as part of the EU administration, assuming, in ensuring the implementation of EU policy, an extra role in addition to their national responsibilities. The demands of this task should not be underestimated. The volume of EU legislation in force has increased significantly since the early 1980s, growing from 4,566 in 1983 to 9,767 in 1998 (Wessels *et al.* 2003: 6). As well as monitoring the implementation of the *acquis communautaire*, with the attendant implications for human resources, national administrations may have to employ unfamiliar instruments or apply measures that run counter to traditional policy orientations.

As well as its impact on governments as actors, EU membership has had organisational consequences. Though there are some commonalities, as with the mechanisms developed to manage the national coordination of EU policy, there is little evidence of convergence around a single administrative model. Administrative change in response to the pressures of EU membership has been 'incremental', 'path dependent . . . along the lines of previously established patterns', and driven by 'learning', whereby 'member states come to identify the pressure that they face, but then go on to "respond" *individually*' (Dimitrakopoulos and Pappas 2003: 442). National administrations have created new bodies and introduced new arrangements to manage government input and representation in EU institutions. The importance of 'getting it right in Brussels' to ensure that policy outcomes are favourable, avoid decision or rulings that are politically embarrassing, especially now that 'Europe' has become a salient domestic issue, or gain a share of the spoils, creates strong incentives for governments to establish effective coordination procedures to make sure that national interests are effectively represented. All EU member states have put in place an apparatus to fulfil this purpose, though the costs of operating this machinery are high, while managing coordination at, as well as across, two levels—the national and the EU—places considerable strain on scarce institutional resources, which the different, often contradictory, logics that prevail in each arena, further exacerbates (Wright 1996).

The EU can also be a cause of administrative re-organization in a variety of forms. New member states, for example, have found it necessary to create new ministries soon after their accession to the Union. While Portugal had no environmental ministry when it joined the Union, Greece had no department for overseas development. New structures were rapidly established by both soon after they became EU member states. New legislation may also require administrative change. As Knill observes (2001: 3)

a regulation may call for the creation of new structures (e.g. an environmental agency), the centralisation or decentralisation of regulatory processes (e.g. by introducing uniform reporting requirements to a central authority), or it may demand horizontal organizational change (e.g. by requiring the coordination of previously distinct administrative tasks).

Where a regulation calls for a specific administrative style, such as regulatory intervention, or for administrative interest mediation, domestic arrangements will have to be adjusted (Knill 2001: 214–15).[8] Change of a different sort involves cases where the EU alters the relative status of parts of government. A notable example is the Dutch prime minister, whose domestic position has been significantly enhanced as a consequence of the coordinating role played by the prime minister in EU affairs. Its most important impact is also, however, the most general. The work of virtually every ministry now has a 'European' dimension, which has to be appropriately handled.

As noted above, relations between governments and the EU do not flow in one direction only. Not only do EU institutions bear the imprint of national administrative traditions (Stevens and Stevens 2000), but national administrations are a ubiquitous presence in the EU system (Kassim and Wright 1991; Kassim 2003), and their functioning affects the speed and effective operation of EU institutions. This is most apparent with the Council, where decisions can be held up if member states are slow to define where they stand.[9] More broadly, without its own field services, the EU is dependent upon national administrations for the transposition, implementation and enforcement of Union legislation. The capacity of the EU as a system is, therefore, more or less a reflection of the capacities of both domestic political systems and state-level bureaucracies. With respect to the former, it might have been expected that the ECJ-upheld principle of institutional autonomy, 'the right of member states to perform the tasks that stem from membership of the EU on the basis of their own constitutional rules' (Dimitrakopoulos 2001a: 444) would lead to significant differences between the way that EU law is transposed in member countries. However, as Dionyssis Dimitrakopoulos has argued, 'analysis of the national mechanisms and procedures . . . demonstrates remarkably similar patterns' (ibid). The administrative dimension is more problematic. Since EU policies need to be implemented consistently across the whole territory of the Union if they are to be genuinely common, any weaknesses in national administrations are a matter of general concern, as they are likely to limit the overall effectiveness of the EU system (Metcalfe 1992).[10]

Interaction with the EU

In the interaction between the EU and the member states, central government is the dominant actor in representing national interests in Brussels and in defining and delivering policy responses to EU initiatives (see Table 13.1 below; see also

[8] One example comes from EU-funded regional policy projects, where the Commission's insistence since 1989 that member states comply with EU procurement law has forced governments to change their procedures.

[9] Concern about national arrangements for the coordinating input into the EU policy process, particularly in view of enlargement, led the Heads of State and Government at the Helsinki European Council to take a decision to review the systems put in place by the member states (European Council, Presidency Conclusions 1999).

[10] See Spanou (1998) for a discussion of the implications for EU policy of weaknesses in Greece's public administration.

Table 13.1 National Coordination Systems: sample from among the EU-15

	Type of coordination system	Coordinating structures	Coordination initiated by	Lead departments
Austria	Comprehensive decentralized	▪ Weekly coordination meetings, involving responsible departments, Länder and social partners ▪ Federal Government	Ministry of Foreign Affairs	Responsible ministry, including Ministry of Foreign Affairs; PM's office coordinates European Council preparation
Belgium	Comprehensive decentralized	▪ Permanent Representation ▪ Inter-departmental conferences (sectoral) ▪ Cabinet (or cabinet sub-committee on foreign policy)	Ministry of Foreign Affairs, Permanent Representation Federal Government or Sub-national Authorities	Permanent Representation Directorate for European Integration and Coordination in Ministry of Foreign Affairs
Denmark	Comprehensive centralized	▪ Specialized sectoral committees, reporting to EU Committee ▪ Government Committee on Foreign Policy	Specialized committee	EU Committee, supported by Ministry of Foreign Affairs
France	Comprehensive centralized	▪ Arbitration can be effected, under PM's authority at SGCI level (inter-departmental), by PM's *cabinet* (private offices of ministers involved) and by PM personally at cabinet committee	SGCI	SGCI in PM's office
Germany	Comprehensive decentralized	▪ EU units in government departments ▪ Meetings of directors-general and monthly meetings of secretaries of state discuss issues that cannot be resolved by lead ministry ▪ Bilateral meetings between ministers in federal government	Responsible ministry	Responsible ministry Monthly meetings of secretaries of state chaired by deputy minister for European affairs with vice-president from Ministry of Finance and administrative support from Ministry of Foreign Affairs

Table 13.1 (*Continued*)

	Type of coordination system	Coordinating structures	Coordination initiated by	Lead departments
Greece	Comprehensive decentralized	■ Flexible inter-departmental arrangements ■ Ministry of Foreign Affairs ■ Relevant ministries with Permanent Representation	Permanent Representation	Ministry of Foreign Affairs
Ireland	Selective centralized	■ Department of Foreign Affairs with lead ministry ■ Ministerial Committee for European Affairs	Relevant ministry	Coordination assured by group of senior civil servants from ministries concerned, chaired by PM's department
Italy	Comprehensive decentralized	■ Ministry of Foreign Affairs and Prime Minister	Ministry of Foreign Affairs, EU Department in PM's office	Ministry concerned, but EU Department in PM's office and Ministry of Foreign Affairs have general responsibility
Netherlands	Comprehensive decentralized	■ Interdepartmental working group (BNC) and lead ministry ■ Contact between lead ministries ■ Weekly instruction meeting for instructions to Coreper ; coordination Committee (CoCo), chaired by Secretary of State for European Affairs to resolve problems, with sensitive issues discussed by cabinet committee on EU affairs (REIA) ■ Cabinet	Ministry of Foreign Affairs	BNC, instructions meeting and CoCo chaired by Ministry of Foreign Affairs REIA chaired by PM's office Cabinet committee chaired by PM's office

Country	Type		Ministry of Foreign Affairs / Responsible department	
Portugal	Selective centralized	■ Ministry of Foreign Affairs and permanent representation ■ Inter-departmental committee for Community affairs (CIAC), in which ministries and autonomous regions represented: sub-committees can be created to consider specific issues ■ Cabinet committee	Ministry of Foreign Affairs	CIAC, chaired by Minister of Foreign Affairs
Spain	Selective centralized	■ Ministry of Foreign Affairs ■ Inter-departmental Conference for EU Affairs (CIAUE), chaired by Prime Minister's office ■ Delegated Government Commission for Economic Affairs ■ Conference for EU-related matters (includes autonomous communities)	Secretariat of State for European Affairs, Ministry for Foreign Affairs (SEAE)	CIAUE, chaired by Secretary of State for European Affairs; secretariat from Ministry for Foreign Affairs
Sweden	Comprehensive centralized	■ Responsible department takes lead ■ EU committee composed of secretaries of state, in which all departments represented ■ Government	Responsible department	EU unit of Foreign Ministry, PM's office, and EU Committee, chaired by secretary of state for EU questions
United Kingdom	Comprehensive centralized	■ Responsible ministry initiates consultation with other interested departments ■ Ministerial Committee on European Policy (EP) ■ Ministerial Committee on Defence and Overseas Policy (DOP)	Responsible department	European Secretariat in the Cabinet Office oversees coordination with Foreign and Commonwealth Office and Permanent Representation and organizes *ad hoc* inter-departmental meetings, when necessary. Weekly meeting between Head of European Secretariat and UK Permanent Representative

Source: Kassim et al. (2000; 2001), Council of the European Union (2001).

Kassim et al. 2000; 2001). The national coordination systems put in place by the member states share several features:

- Heads of government play a central role and have, with the strengthening of the European Council, become ever more deeply involved in business.

- Foreign ministries continue to occupy a key position, particularly in operating communications infrastructures, but, as well as having their monopoly broken by the IT revolution, they are increasingly overshadowed by prime ministers, challenged by finance ministers, and bypassed by line ministries with technical expertise.

- Interdepartmental coordination in EU matters is managed by specialist mechanisms, such as the General Secretariat of the Interministerial Committee (SGCI) in France, the European Secretariat of the Cabinet Office in the UK, and the Secretariat of State for the European Union (SSEU) in Spain, located close to the Prime Minister or in the ministry of foreign affairs.

- special EU policy units have been set up in line ministries.

- all member states maintain a permanent representation in Brussels, which is the main locus for national coordination at the EU level.

However, there are also significant differences. While in some member states (for example Denmark, Portugal, Spain), the foreign ministry is the leading actor, elsewhere responsibility is shared with the economics or finance ministry (for example Germany, Greece), with the Prime Minister's Office (Italy) or the Cabinet Office (the UK). In France, by contrast, it is the SGCI, responsible to the Prime Minister rather than the ministry for foreign affairs that sends instructions to the Permanent Representation. More fundamentally, national coordination systems vary along two main dimensions. The first is the nature of the coordination ambition. Some countries attempt to monitor Commission activity and intervene on all fronts, while others concentrate attention on areas that are salient domestically. The second is the extent to which decision making is centralized, for example, in specialist units located in the prime minister's office or the ministry for foreign affairs, or decentralized to individual ministries. Simplifying, these differences reflect different national attitudes towards integration—countries which have a preference for intergovernmentalism are more likely to adopt a comprehensive (defensive) strategy—and features of the domestic polity—directive coordination is only possible in a strongly centralized state; a more decentralized, even ministerial, approach to coordination is likely to be found where coalition governments are common or in federal states (Kassim 2003).

Among these differences, the dominant position of central government is a common feature. With few exceptions, such as Belgium, where the six sub-national authorities are co-equal partners of the federal government (Kerremans 2000), national governments control the coordination process. They take the lead in defining policy and they operate the diplomatic network that links the national capital with other member states and with Brussels. They possess the vital assets lacked by other member state institutions—information and access—but, crucially, are recognized at the EU level as *the* representatives of their national populations.

Parliaments and the EU

The weakness of national parliaments that has been a feature of post-war democracies in Western Europe has been reinforced by European integration. Although, as Tapio Raunio and Simon Hix (2000) point out, it is a mistake to blame the European Union for 'deparliamentarianization' (Wessels and Rometsch 1996) when the shift of power from legislatures to executives has largely been brought about by other factors, there is little doubt that parliaments have been among the losers of integration (Maurer and Wessels 2001a; Maurer 2001; Maurer 2002b). Parliaments are weak both as players at the EU level and as domestic actors in the formation of national preferences and the scrutiny of governments in matters concerning the Union (Maurer 2001). In terms of interaction, their ability to influence governments in matters of EU policy varies between member states, but is generally limited, even though there has been a modest resurgence since Maastricht. Pre-existing constitutional arrangements largely account for the variation.

The impact on national parliaments

The most obvious impact of EU membership on national parliaments has been an increase in their workload. During 2003, for example, 1080 documents were examined by the UK House of Commons Select Committee on European Scrutiny (2004: para 2). The volume of EU documentation is significant—von Beyme estimated that 20 per cent of legislation adopted by the Bundestag between 1983 and 1994 originated in Brussels (cited in Raunio and Hix 2000: 153)—but so is its nature. EU work is complex and highly technical with parliamentarians aware that developing a specialism in EU affairs is unlikely to advance their careers.

More broadly, European integration has weakened parliaments in four ways. First, the transfer of competences from the national arena to EU level has removed decision making across a wide range of activities from the purview of national legislatures. Policy is made in a distant forum, where parliaments are not present and have little influence. As one commentator has observed:

the EU is structurally embedded into the domestic systems. This inter-penetration alters the parameters for parliaments, which have traditionally sought to control their governments. For they are now operating in a situation where the source of legislation is partially external, and where they cannot legally bring about any alternation in the *acquis* or even promote alternative policies or laws which could conflict with those of the EU (Newman 1996: 189, cited by Raunio and Hix 2000: 154).

Second, the Union's decisional processes disadvantage national parliaments. Not only do legislatures lack a formal role in EU decision making—'governments, and not legislatures, are the national bodies striking bargains at the European level' (Raunio and Hix 2000: 145)—but the requirements imposed by Council negotiations, the fast-moving and technical nature of EU business, and the institutional density of the Union create formidable barriers to effective parliamentary scrutiny and control. Qualified majority voting is a particular problem, since it removes the requirement that policy outcomes receive the assent of national parliament (see Norton 1996; Marquand 1981: 226).[11] Third, the EU privileges executives over legislatures, offering them opportunities to bypass parliamentary control. Dimitrakopoulos (2001a) has shown, for example, how control over the implementation of EU legislation— through the use of delegated legislation to transpose directives—enables executives to circumvent parliamentary scrutiny. Fourth, parliaments lack the resources and the independence needed to scrutinize effectively the action and activity of their governments in Brussels. The regular contact that takes place between EACs through COSAC (see below), ties between national MPs and MEPs based on party, and establishing their own offices in Brussels—the case with the Danish and Finnish parliaments, the UK House of Commons, and the French Senate—have only marginally improved the position of parliaments. In addition, the same factors responsible for their domestic decline are also at work in EU matters: modernization has concentrated expertise in the executive branch, while party discipline ensures the subordination of parliament in votes concerning 'Europe' as surely as in domestic policy.

Though the impact of integration on legislatures has generally been negative, it is important to recognize that some parliaments have fared better than others. 'Path dependence' is again in evidence with the effects of integration on legislatures varying according to their strength in the domestic polity (Dimitrakopoulos 2001b; see also see Norton 1996: 187–9). The effect of integration in countries where the legislature is weak or subordinate (for example in France) has been felt less intensely than those where the parliament is strong (for example in Denmark and Italy). In the UK, where integration threatens parliamentary sovereignty, the impact has been especially dramatic (Craig 1991).

Moreover, since Maastricht, parliaments have been strengthened (Norton 1996; Raunio and Hix 2000; Maurer 2002; Maurer and Wessels 2001). During the 1990s, in response to the widening and deepening of EU competencies, 'most parliaments in Europe established institutions and mechanisms that forced governments to explain their EU policies and actions in the European arena to parliaments' (Raunio and Hix 2000: 163). As a result, the position of parliaments has improved 'through more effective overall scrutiny of government, particularly better access to information' (ibid).[12] Raunio and Hix argue that 'the driving force behind this partial reassertion has been the desire by non-governing parties and backbench parliamentarians to redress the "information gap" between governing elites and the parliamentary rank-and-file' (ibid). Examination of the role of parliaments in EU policy-making at member state level seems to confirm this view.

Interaction with the EU

Interaction between parliaments and the EU is limited to three areas: treaty ratification, the transposition of EU legislation, and the scrutiny of ministers. In each case the

---

[11] It is worth recalling that it was not until 1999 that the Council was obliged to publish the results of votes under QMV (Maurer 2002: 7 n. 2).

[12] Indeed, 'in some countries', they contend, 'European integration has been a catalyst in the re-emergence of parliaments' (2000: 143).

room for manoeuvre is narrow (Maurer 2002: 6–7). With respect to the first, they can answer 'yes' or 'no'; and in relation to the second, they can be circumvented by government (as noted above). Parliamentary involvement is greatest in regard to the third, but even here the extent to which legislators can affect the behaviour of members of the executive branch is limited, relatively recent and differs between states.

In the early days of the European Communities, the involvement of national parliaments in Europe-related policy was extremely limited, despite the fact that the European Parliament was composed of national parliamentarians. Community matters were handled by foreign affairs committees or committees in the upper house, as in the Netherlands, Germany, and Italy.[13] Specialist committees were established by the parliaments of the acceding states in 1973, but it was not until the SEA increased the volume and the scope of Community legislation that national legislatures developed 'greater specialisation, greater activities, and made some attempt to integrate MEPs into their activities' (Norton 1996: 179–82; Maurer 2002: 19). Whereas historically bills with a Community dimension were discussed by functional standing committees, specialist European Affairs Committees (EACs) became a more general feature from the late 1980s. Calls for greater parliamentary involvement increased in the run-up to the Maastricht IGC. The presidents of national parliaments began to meet regularly from 1989 and the EACs to meet at six monthly intervals within the Conference of Representatives of European Affairs Committees (COSAC), and on the eve of the IGCs an informal conference of parliaments (the *Assises*) took place in Rome, though this proved to be a one-off.

In response to this pressure, and at the suggestion of the British and French governments, the Heads of State and Government adopted two declarations with the Treaty on European Union: the first, Declaration No. 13, called for 'greater involvement of national parliaments in the activities of the European Union', better exchange of information, reciprocal facilities and regular meetings between national parliaments and the European Parliament, and for governments to ensure that national parliaments 'receive Commission proposals . . . in good time for information of possible examination'; the second, Declaration no. 14, invited 'the European Parliament and the national parliaments to meet as necessary as a Conference of the Parliaments' to be consulted on the main features of the European Union. The two declarations expressed different views about the role of national parliaments and the level at which they should operate (Norton 1996: 183). The first looks to a strengthening of legislatures at the domestic level, the second for a collective role for national parliaments at the EU level. Subsequent developments have been moved in the direction of the first. Initiatives in support of formalized collective involvement have so far failed. Disagreements over the form that such a body should take (see Maurer 2002: 11–13, 27–9), the problem of conflicting mandates with the Council and the European Parliament as representative bodies of EU states and the peoples of the EU respectively, and the implications of creating yet another body to participate in an already complex policy process, have so far proved insurmountable obstacles. The masters of the treaty have in practice opted for *democratization*—strengthening the European Parliament—rather than *parliamentarianization*—involving national parliaments (Maurer 2002). Though

---

[13] Belgium, where the relevant committee was located in the lower house from 1962 until 1979, is an exception (Norton 1996: 177).

the draft constitutional treaty adopted in June 2004 envisions an enhanced role for legislatures, it does so as a device to police subsidiarity, giving parliaments the power of referral rather than a direct role in policy.[14]

It is at the national level, specifically in the scrutiny of government action in EU matters, that the power of parliaments has increased since Maastricht. The Protocol on National Parliaments agreed at the Amsterdam IGC specified which documentation was to be supplied by governments to parliaments, even if, as in the case of Declaration no. 13, no legal obligation was imposed (Maurer 2002: 11).[15] Also, both the Council and the Parliament amended their internal rules so as to recognise national parliaments and COSAC as consultative bodies in the EU decision-making process (Maurer 2002: 21).

Though cross-national differences remain, the role of national parliaments in EU matters has been strengthened (see Table 13.2). In some countries (for example France and Germany), the constitution was amended to oblige governments to keep their parliaments fully informed and, in the case of Austria, to allow the main parliamentary committee, as well as party leaders, the right to sit in cabinet meetings where EU matters are discussed (Maurer 2002: 21).[16] In others—Belgium, Spain, Ireland, the Netherlands, and Portugal—special laws or conventions have been signed, which strengthen government accountability to parliament. EACs have multiplied, and become more influential, even if their composition varies—MEPs are represented in committees in the Belgian federal parliament, the German Bundestag, and the Greek and Irish legislatures (Raunio and Hix 2000: 157)—some meet more frequently than others, and the range of their responsibilities differs considerably. Other differences relate to the range of documents they are entitled to see, at what stage of the EU policy process they intervene, and, most importantly, their influence over the position that their government takes in the Council. Only the Hauptausschuß in the Austrian Nationalrat (lower House) and, with respect to matters that fall within the exclusive competence of the Länder, the Ausschuß für Fragen der Europäischen Union in the German Bundesrat (upper house) yet approach the status of Denmark's legendary European affairs committee, the Europaudvalget (formerly, the Committee for Relations with the Market), which has the power to mandate the negotiating position of Danish ministers in the Council. This is not to say, however, that other EACs, for example, in the Finnish and Swedish Parliaments, the UK House of Commons, and the German Bundestag, are not without some policy-affecting influence (Maurer and Wessels 2001b: 20; Bergman 1997: 377).

In practice, it remains unclear whether those parliaments that have the formal authority to give instructions to government are significantly more powerful than their counterparts in other member states. The prerogative is not used frequently, but even when it is the complexity and secrecy of Council negotiations make it difficult to

---

[14] The relevant provisions are to be found in Part IV of the draft constitutional treaty in the Protocol on the role of National Parliaments in the European Union and the Protocol on the Application of the Principles of Subsidiarity and Proportionality.

[15] These provisions have been retained in the Protocol on the Role of National Parliaments in the European Union, appended to the draft constitutional treaty.

[16] See Article 88 (4) of the French Constitution and Article 23 of the Basic Law in Germany respectively.

Table 13.2 European Affairs Committees in National Legislatures (Eu-15 only)

Member state	Chamber	Name of committee	Date est'd	Composition	Competence (pillars)	Frequency of meetings	Degree of control
Austria	Nationalrat Bundesrat	Hauptausschuβ EU-Ausschuβ	1994 1995	MPs	I, II, III I, II, III	X2 p/m No regular meetings	Strong Weak
Belgium	Chambres des Représentants Sénat	Comié d'avis federal charge de questions europeennes	1985	MPs + MEPs	I	X1 p/m	Weak
Denmark	Folketinget	Europaudvalget	1972	MPs	I, II, III	X1 p/w	Strong
Finland	Eduskunta	Suuri valiokunta	1995	MPs	I, II, III	X2 p/w	Moderate
France	Assemblée Nationale Sénat	Délegation de l'Assemblee Nationale pour l'UE Délégation du Sénat pour l'UE	1979 1979	MPs	I I	X1 p/w X1 p/w	Weak Weak
Germany	Bundestag Bundesrat	EU- Ausschuβ Ausschuβ fur fragen der Europaischen Union	1991 1957	MPs + MEPs	1, II, III 1, II	X1 p/w	Moderate Strong
Greece	Vouli Ton Ellinon	Epitropi Evropaikon Yrothesseon	1990	MPs + MEPs	I	Every 3 weeks	Weak
Ireland	Dáil Éireann Seanad Éireann	Joint Committee on European Affairs	1995	MPs + MEPs	I, II, III	No regular meetings	Weak
Italy	Camera dei Deputati Senato della Repubblica	Commissione Politiche dell' Unione Europea Giunta per gli Affari della Comunità europea	1990 1968	MPs	I I	Up to X2-3 p/w No regular meetings	Weak Weak

Table 13.2 (Continued)

Member state	Chamber	Name of committee	Date est'd	Composition	Competence (pillars)	Frequency of meetings	Degree of control
Luxembourg	Chambres des Députés	Commission des Affaires étrangères et communautaires	1989	MPs	I, II, III	On occasion of important Council meetings	Weak
Netherlands	Tweede Kamer	Algemene Commissie voor EU-Zaken	1986	MPs	I, II, III	X1 p/w	Weak
	Eerste Kamer	Vaste Commissie voor Europese Samenwerkings-organisaties	1970	MPs	I, II, III	X1 p/w	Weak
Portugal	Assembleia da Republica	Comissão de Assuntos Europeeus	1987	MPs	I	X1 p/w	Weak
Spain	Congresso de los Diputados Senado	Comisión Mixta para la Unión Europea	1985	MPs	I	X1 p/w	Weak
Sweden	Riksdagen	EU-nämnden	1994	MPs	I	X1 p/w	Moderate
United Kingdom	House of Commons	Select Committee on European Legislation	1974	MPs	I, II, III	X1 p/w	Moderate
	House of Lords	Select Committee on the European Communities	1974		I	X2 p/m	Weak

Sources: Raunio and Hix (2000); Maurer (2002; 1995); Bergman (1997).

discern whether a government has stuck to the position laid down by parliament. Moreover, even where they are subject to a specific parliamentary mandate, governments simply may not be able to carry the day. Indeed, member states may be at a distinct disadvantage if parliaments are able to force governments to uphold a position that denies them room for manoeuvre in the endgame of negotiations.

In short, parliaments may have been strengthened since Maastricht, but they remain weak.

Sub-national Authorities

Sub-national authorities—sub-national states, regions, and municipalities—show the greatest diversity in impact and interaction among member state institutions. These differences reflect the variety of both the territorial models—federal, devolved, regionalized unitary, decentralized unitary, and centralized unitary (Loughlin 2000: 24–32)—and the local government systems in place across the Union, but the picture is further complicated by differences between sub-national actors within the same state (Hooghe 1996; Balme and Le Galès 1997; Smith 1995).[17] As with national governments, the EU has imposed new constraints on sub-national authorities, but it also offers them new possibilities for action and new channels of influence.

Impact on sub-national authorities

The most general effect of European integration on sub-national authorities is also perhaps the most radical. As a system of shared governance, the Union challenges the territorial exclusivity that defined the traditional state, reconfiguring territorial relations within member countries. With the migration of decision-making authority from national capitals to Brussels, the state is no longer in all instances the supreme authority within its borders. As a result the hierarchical relationship between central government and sub-national authorities has been loosened. Sub-national actors now operate within a broader political system that transcends national borders and in which they are able to develop and pursue projects independently of the national capital.[18] Like other domestic interests, they are able to make direct contact with their counterparts abroad, as well as with EU institutions, without having to channel their demands through central government (Marks 1992: 217; Hooghe 1996).

A second effect concerns how the EU has affected the way in which sub-national authorities carry out their routine functions. The Union has increasingly impinged on sub-national governments since the mid-1980s. As Peter John observes, '[i]f the

[17] Moreover, EU action can be contradictory (Thielemann 2002; Wishlade 2003). While the Union's regional policy has a decentralizing dynamic, the implementation of competition policy, particularly in the area of state aid, has imposed severe constraints on the ability of national governments to pursue regional development policies.

[18] State-bound centre-local relations are no longer the only game in which sub-national authorities are engaged, but instead, the relationship has become, to paraphrase Peter John, one of three dyads (2000: 879).

requirements for contracting public services are [taken into account], there was no area of local and regional government that was not affected by European regulation by the early 1990s' (2000: 879). The precise impact of the EU has varied both between policy areas and between member states, with the most powerful sub-national authorities and those with the broadest responsibilities—in Germany, Belgium, Spain, and the UK—most strongly affected.

EU intervention has taken a variety of forms. Regulatory action has been important, but the development of structural and cohesion funds has turned the Union into a redistributive actor (Hix 1999), where Brussels decides the criteria according to which revenue collected from the member states is allocated to sub-national territorial units. The availability of structural funds and cohesion funds creates a strong incentive for sub-national authorities to engage in 'grantsmanship' and to lobby for favourable rule changes at the EU level. Regional and local governments have responded, albeit to varying degrees, by seeking to influence decision making via their national governments, or by acting alone or with others in Brussels.

The effect of the EU's regional policy has been especially notable. The Union's structural and cohesion policies have enhanced the opportunities for sub-national governments to become involved in policy formulation. The 1998 reform of the structural funds, for example, added 'partnership' between national government and private and public authorities, including sub-national governments, to the principles of programming, concentration and conditionality that governed the structural funds. This change reflected a desire on the part of the Commission to ensure that sub-national authorities were involved in the formulation and implementation of national programmes. Although the reform succeeded in extending participation, it did not necessarily increase the power of sub-national authorities vis-à-vis central government. The latter remained firmly in control of EU regional policy making at both Union and domestic levels (see Anderson 1990; Bache 1998; Bache and Jones 2000; Pollack 1995) with two exceptions. The first is Community initiatives, where the Commission can direct funding to programmes that it favours, provided that money is spent in line with the broad priorities approved by the member states.[19] The second is 'seed corn' funding, which is used to create and sustain trans-regional networks. Recite (Regions and Cities of Europe), launched in 1991 with the aim of encouraging co-operation between regions, is a much-cited example (Hooghe 1996: 189).

The EU's impact in the member states has been felt very differently from country to country, reflecting pre-existing variations in the territorial distribution of power. The different models presented a contrasting range of vulnerabilities and sensitivities, allocated varying levels of resource, and established quite different capacities for action on the part of sub-national authorities. Those with the broadest responsibilities and the highest status—the so-called, 'constitutional regions' (Scott 2002)—are, as noted above, the most exposed to EU action, but they also have the most resources to mobilize in pursuit of their demands. For example, the German Länder have been able to exploit the position that they enjoy under the Federal Republic's system of administrative federalism, as well as the federal government's liability for the

[19] Examples include Intereg (promotion of cross-border cooperation), Urban (urban regeneration), and Equal (combating discrimination in the labour market).

implementation of EU legislation, to ensure that their demands are listened to in Berlin (Wessels and Rometsch 1996: 345). They also warned the German government at Maastricht that, unless it succeeded in securing a greater role for regions in the decision-making system of the Union, they would veto the resultant treaty. The creation of the Committee of the Regions, as well as the inclusion of a provision in the treaty (Article 146) that allowed the inclusion of regional officeholders in national delegations at meetings of the Council, came about as a result of this pressure, though subsequent efforts have been less successful.[20] Other territorial models do not offer sub-national authorities the same opportunities to exert influence. In Spain, for example, the Senado is not a territorial chamber. Autonomous communities use other channels to press their demands.

Interaction with the EU

The pattern of interaction linking sub-national actors to the EU is best captured by the concept of 'multi-level governance', which Gary Marks defines as:

a system of continuous negotiation among nested governments at several territorial tiers— supranational, national, and local—as a result of the broad process of institutional creation and decisional re-allocation that has pulled some previously centralised functions of the state up to the supranational level and some down to the local/regional level (1993: 392).

As Liesbet Hooghe argues, the involvement of sub-national authorities in EU policy making renders obsolete a narrowly state-centric conception of the Union, while the notion of a 'Europe of the Regions', which envisages 'a European federation compounded of smaller, more natural units (regions) built around a strong supranational core' (Hooghe 1995: 177), overstates the extent to which sub-national units are in competition with central government. Multilevel governance, or 'Europe *with* the regions', by contrast, recognizes the importance of sub-national authorities as a tier of government additional to the national and supranational levels.

At the same time, Hooghe acknowledges two important qualifications (1995: 178). First, sub-national mobilization is very uneven across the Union. The extent to which regions or municipalities have become organized varies not only between member states, but also within them (see also John 2000). The same finding is reported by other authors, who do not subscribe to the multilevel governance approach. Richard Balme and Patrick Le Galès (1997), for example, distinguish between 'bright stars' and 'black holes', while Andy Smith's (1995) discovery of sharp differences between regions in France led him to problematise the issue of why regions mobilize. Second, coverage of the EU is unequal. Regions enjoy greater access than local authorities, wealthier regions are better represented than poorer regions, and only a minority of regions are represented in Brussels, accounting for 40–45 per cent of the EU's population (Hooghe 1996: 186). Similarly, John (2000) points out that only 40 per cent of the Union's population are covered by the structural funds. For both

---

[20] See, for example, Political Declaration by the constitutional regions of Bavaria, Catalonia, North Rhine-Westphalia, Salzburg, Scotland, Wallonia, and Flanders, 28/May/2001 <http://europa.eu.int/futurum/documents/contrib/dec280501_en.htm> or AER, Position on the draft Constitutional Treaty and the IGC, 02/Oct./03 <http://www.are-regions-europe.org/COMMUN/A211a1.html>.

reasons—the unevenness and the inequality of mobilization—generalisations about the so-called 'third level' are problematic.

Where it exists, sub-national mobilization takes a variety of forms: institutionalized and non-institionalized, collective and individual (Hooghe 1996). The Committee of the Regions (CoR) is the most open institutionalized channel for the representation of sub-national interests at EU level, but its powers are limited and it has been beset by internal differences.[21] Unlike the European Parliament, which adapted its internal procedures to maximise its bargaining strength in inter-institutional negotiations, the CoR has yet to demonstrate an ability to act strategically to increase its influence. Other institutionalized channels are more limited in scope. Regional ministers are permitted to participate in the Council of Ministers, as noted above, but in practice only the German Länder, Belgian regions and communities, and members of the Scottish executive have used this channel, and, since they attend as members of national delegations, they have no independent voice. A second channel is through the partnership arrangements that form part of the structural funds policy discussed above. However, the committees in which sub-national actors participate play a bureaucratic rather than a political role and operate within a 'strict national mould' (Hooghe 1996: 182).

Institutionalized channels at the national level are similarly uneven. Though central government dominates national EU policy making, in some federal states sub-national authorities exert influence in both heroic and routine policy making (see Kassim et al. 2000, 2001). For example, in Belgium and Germany EU treaty reform must be approved by the regions and the communities and the Länder (via the Bundesrat) respectively. In addition, regional observers are attached to the permanent representations of Austria, Belgium, and Germany, and regions play a formal role in co-ordination machinery in Austria, Belgium, and Germany, and are represented in those of Spain and Italy (Kassim and Peters 2001).

Non-institutionalized channels take both collective and individual forms. With respect to the former, the key organizations are: the Assembly of European Regions (AER), founded in 1985, whose members come from elected regional parliaments; the Council for European Municipalities and Regions (CEMR), originally the Council of European Municipalities dating from 1951 and which assumed its current form in 1984; the Standing Conference of Local and Regional Authorities of Europe (CLRAE); and the International Union of Local Authorities (IULA). These bodies are important interlocutors of the Commission and can be influential during IGCs. The difficulties of devising common strategies limit their effectiveness as campaigning organizations, but they provide an important information-gathering service for their members. In addition to these general organizations, there are numerous trans-regional networks of varying size and type, some of which receive Community funding. Examples include: the 'Four Motors' group, which brings together four of the most powerful regional economies in Europe—Baden-Württemberg, Catalonia, Lombardy, and the Rhone Alps; Euroceram, representing regions with ceramics interests; and Eurocities, which has a membership of sixty large cities and exists to exchange knowledge and experience between members (Greenwood 1997: 233–6).

---

[21] The Committee of the Regions replaced the Consultative Council of Regional and Local Authorities (CCRLA), the members of which were appointed by the Assembly of European Regions (AER) and the Council for European Municipalities and Regions (CEMR).

In terms of individual action, many sub-national authorities have a direct presence in Brussels. Their regional offices act as informal embassies (Hooghe 1996), though as Marks et al. have shown (1996; 2002) their precise functions, as well as the resources at their disposal, vary considerably. Their number grew dramatically from two in 1985 to 54 in 1993 (Hooghe 1995: 185), 135 in 1996 (Greenwood 1997: 228), and 218 (European Commission 2004: 22).[22] When broken down by member state—the UK has the largest number (30), followed by Italy (28), Germany (26), France (23), and Spain (19), while Greece and Luxembourg have none—it becomes clear that the propensity to establish regional offices cannot be explained simply in terms of national territorial structure. Several factors are at work: rivalry between regions in federal states; national politics—Thatcherite centralization accounts for what John calls 'counteractive Europeanization' as 'local authorities sought a new role and engaged with more sympathetic political actors at the supranational level' (2000: 884); culture—the 'tendency for the more bureaucratised and professionalised local authorities in the north to set them up, whereas local representatives in the more clientelistic systems . . . rely on their informal contacts' (John 2000: 888); and entrepreneuralism—the desire of some cities and regions to move into the orbit of the EU with a view to gaining access to opportunities that are unavailable to them in the domestic arena (Balme and Le Galès 1997).

National courts

The constraints imposed on national governments by the EU's development as a 'Community of law' have already been noted, but the legal systems of the member states have also been significantly affected. National courts have been drawn into a Community-wide legal order with the European Court of Justice at its apex and converted into enforcers of EU law. At the same time, they have participated in and contributed to, albeit with varying levels of enthusiasm, to the creation and development of this system.

Impact on national courts

The founding treaties imposed a new set of responsibilities on national courts. While the European Court of Justice (ECJ) was to be responsible for resolving legal disputes at the Community level—that is those that arise between EU institutions and the member states, and between member states—national courts were entrusted with the task of ensuring member state conformity with EU law (Stone Sweet 1998). Moreover, '[i]n its jurisprudence, the Court has sought to enlist national judges in a working partnership to construct a constitutional, rule of law Community . . . [whereby], national judges become agents of the Community order' (Stone Sweet 1998: 163–4), as 'Community judges'. The Court relied heavily on the willingness of

---

[22] Their creation is an expression of paradiplomacy, where sub-national authorities represent their interests independently of central government.

national judges to follow its rulings, but also to use the Article 234 (ex. 177) 'preliminary ruling' procedure,[23] which permits a national court to request the ECJ's opinion when a case raises an issue that requires interpretation of the Treaty. '[N]ational courts and the European Court are thus integrated into a unitary system of judicial review' (Weiler 1991: 2420).

Fundamental changes have also resulted from 'constitutionalization', the process whereby 'the EC treaties evolved from a set of legal arrangements binding upon sovereign states, into a vertically integrated legal order that confers judicially enforceable rights and obligations on all legal persons and entities, public and private within EC territory' (Stone Sweet 1998: 160). As a consequence—and in contrast to the doctrine of *lex posteriori*, according to which in international law treaty obligations can be overridden by laws that are subsequently adopted by the legislature—national judges 'treat EC law as if it were a source of law that is superior to, and autonomous from, national statutes, and capable of being applied, directly, within the national legal order, by national judges' (Stone Sweet 1998: 161). However, national courts take contrasting views on the two principles, enunciated by the Court in two leading cases, *Van Gend en Loos v. Nederlandse Administratie der Belastingen*, and *Costa v. ENEL*,[24] on which the Community of law is founded. The first is the doctrine of *direct effect*, whereby Community legal norms grant individual citizens rights that can be invoked against their own governments in national courts. The second is the doctrine of *supremacy*, according to which any Community norm takes precedence over any national law that conflicts with it, whether or not that law was adopted before or after the Community norm.

Though they differ in their reasoning and in the terms on which they accepted these principles (see below), national courts have in general responded positively to the ECJ's 'gambit' (Stone Sweet 1998).[25] Of the many explanations put forward to account for the willingness of the national courts in this regard (Mattli and Slaughter 1998; Craig 2003), two are particularly persuasive and can be seen as complementary. The first is the 'judicial empowerment thesis', associated with Stein (1981) and Weiler (1991; 1994), which asserts that 'judges work to enhance their own authority to control legal . . . outcomes, and to reduce the control of other institutional actors' (Stone Sweet 1998: 164). The second is an approach consistent with neofunctionalist arguments (see Burley and Mattli 1993; Stone Sweet 1998), which contends that, once the Court afforded them the opportunity, private actors pursued their interests before national courts, using Community norms to challenge national laws through the preliminary ruling procedure. The power of national courts was increased as cases involving direct effect and supremacy were pleaded before them, turning them into

---

[23] Federico Mancini and David Keeling summarize, as follows: 'If the doctrines of direct effect and supremacy are . . . the 'twin pillars of the Community's legal system', the [preliminary ruling] reference procedure . . . must surely be the keystone in the edifice; without it the roof would collapse and the two pillars would be left as a desolate ruin' (quoted in Alter 2001: 209).

[24] Cases 26/62 [1963] ECR 1 and 6/64 [1964] ECR 585 respectively.

[25] One effect, as Alter points out, was increased workload: '[A]llowing private litigants access increases the number of actors who can raise legal challenges, and thus the number of cases a court has to hear' (Alter 2001: 218).

Community courts in their own right. Lawyers specializing in EC law were 'willing advocates' in the process (Craig 2003: 32).[26]

The bases on which national courts have accepted the supremacy of EU law and the terms of its application vary significantly (Mattli and Slaughter 1998a, 1998b; Craig 2003).[27] Courts in Belgium and the Netherlands based their judgments on reasoning that is close to the ECJ's own, as expressed in *Costa v ENEL* (Case 6/64); namely, that

by creating a Community of unlimited duration, having . . . powers stemming from a limitation of sovereignty, or a transfer of powers from the States to the Community, the Member states have limited their sovereign rights, albeit within limited fields, and thus have created a body of law which binds both their nationals and themselves.

In France, by contrast, the highest civil court, the Cour de Cassation, accepted the supremacy of Community law in 1975, but based its decision on Article 55 of the French Constitution, which recognises the superior authority of treaties or agreements duly ratified. The highest administrative court, the Conseil d'Etat, did not reach this conclusion until 1990, while the Conseil Constitutionnel ruled in 1992 that there are limits to France's acceptance of supremacy. In Italy, the Constitutional Court initially held that where two norms clashed the one that was adopted later in time should take precedence—this was the decision which led eventually to the ECJ's ruling in the *Costa* case—but modified its position in 1984, when it recognized the primacy of Community legislation, where no threat is posed to the fundamental values of the Constitution.

In Germany, the Federal Constitutional Court first accepted the ECJ's claim, but retreated in 1974 on the grounds that the transfer of competence to an international organization must not contravene the underlying principles of the Basic Law. Its concern about the protection of the rights of individuals was linked to the absence of a codified charter at Community level. However, in 1986, the FCC ruled that so long as the EC ensured effective protection of fundamental rights, the FCC would no longer review Community legislation against the Basic Law. Since then, however, in its 1993 'Maastricht judgment', the FCC has ruled that the Basic Law limits the transfer of powers to the EC and that it (the FCC) has the power to declare acts of the EC *ultra vires* where they stray beyond it. Finally, although in the UK the doctrine of direct effect was accepted by British courts on accession to the Community, supremacy was problematic because it conflicted with parliamentary sovereignty. Since any treaty given force by being incorporated in an Act of Parliament could be superseded by any

[26] The 'inter-court competition' approach, developed by Karen Alter argues that different courts have different interests in legal integration and that lower courts are more likely to use ECJ jurisprudence as a way of asserting their power vis-à-vis higher courts, whereas higher courts have an interest in 'thwarting the expansion and penetration of EC law into the national legal order' (Alter 1998: 242). For a different view, which emphasises the power of the member states in relation to the European Court of Justice, see Garrett and Weingast (1993).

[27] Mattli and Slaughter (1998) have suggested that the timing and scope of acceptance has been influenced by three factors: national policy preferences concerning the desirability of European integration; national legal culture (for example professional values, modes of legal reasoning, understanding of the role of courts in relation to legislative bodies, etc); and specific national legal doctrines (for example monism or dualism). However, they concede that these factors do not provide a wholly satisfactory explanation.

later Act of Parliament, the 1972 Act of Accession was apparently as vulnerable as any other Act. The leading decision was made in 1990. Following a reference from the House of Lords, the ECJ ruled in *R v Secretary of State for Transport, ex p. Factortame Ltd (no. 2)* that the Merchant Shipping Act of 1988 was in breach of EU law (Craig 1991). The House of Lords accepted this judgment, arguing that there was no conflict with parliamentary sovereignty, because in adopting the 1972 Act the UK Parliament had accepted the EU legal system of which the supremacy doctrine is a part. It followed that any future parliament could repeal the 1972 Act.

The above discussion makes it clear that the EU has not only had an impact on national courts, but that national courts 'asked questions which the Commission or a member state would never ask', enabling the ECJ 'to comment on national policy and to expand the reach and scope of European law' (Alter 2001: 22).

Interaction with the EU

At the heart of the EU's legal order is a 'set of institutionalised dialogues between supra-national and national judges' (Stone Sweet 1998: 305). The interchange has become increasingly intense, particularly since the late 1970s.[28] In the 1980s, the number of references for preliminary ruling per annum fell below the 100-mark only once, and for much of the 1990s was consistently above 140 (Stone Sweet and Brunell 1998: 74). By 2003 the figure was 233 (*ECJ* 2004: 216) However, beyond a general increase across time and the older members making more references in each period than the member states that joined later, there are significant differences in the extent to which national courts use the Article 234 system. Explaining cross-national variation has so far proved elusive (though see Stone Sweet and Brunell 1998; Chalmers 2000), but Hix (1999: 114) makes two interesting observations. First, with each enlargement, the larger member states made more references than the small states—France, Germany, and Italy made more than the Benelux countries, the UK more than Denmark and Ireland, and Spain more than Portugal. Secondly, UK courts make relatively few references (see Golub 1996).

Conclusion

The impact on member state institutions of their location within a system of a system of collective governance has been extremely far-reaching. Domestic institutions have assumed new responsibilities and obligations. In some areas, their freedom of action has been circumscribed, but these losses must be set against the new opportunities that have been created and the new channels that have opened to all, but national parliaments.

The impact of integration has not been uniform, however, and there is no sign of an 'ever greater convergence' of national political systems. Although in some respects central governments feel their constraints more keenly than other bodies, they are also

---

[28] For a study of preliminary references by topic between 1961 and 1995, see Stone Sweet and Brunell 1998.

the most powerful actors within the EU system and have greater opportunities to pursue their favoured projects. National courts have assumed a new function as part of the system of Community law to which they belong, while sub-national governments have experienced both the effects of regulation and the opportunities deriving from the territorial redefinition that has taken place in the Union. Only national parliaments seem not to have benefited. Despite a modest revival since Maastricht, they remain marginal actors in relation to EU affairs at both Union and national levels. Their inability to scrutinize governments effectively raises important questions about accountability and the democratic credentials of national EU policy-making systems (see Katz 1999).

National differences are also evident. Differences in the way that constitutions allocate power and responsibility between branches of governments domestically produce a pattern of strong national differentiation in terms of the resources available to institutions and their vulnerability to encroachment by the EU. These factors affect both the inclination and the capacity of domestic institutions to mobilize. This point is illustrated well by the experiences of national parliaments, where in general the more powerful they have been in the pre-existing domestic system, the more assertive and influential they have been in relation to the EU. This point also applies to sub-national authorities and the constitutional balance between central and sub-central government. Both at EU and national level, the so-called 'constitutional regions' have been more influential than their counterparts elsewhere in the Union.

Finally, while attention in the EU literature, particularly on Europeanization, focuses on the implications of action in Brussels for domestic actors, it should not be forgotten that national institutions play an important part not only in shaping outcomes at the EU level, but also in determining the capacities—administrative, legal and political—of the Union as a system. The functioning of EU institutions and the ability of the Union to deliver along all three dimensions depend, fundamentally, on the operation and effectiveness of member state bodies at both the supranational and the domestic levels.

Further reading

Wessels, Maurer, and Mittag (2003) provide a comprehensive examination of the impact of the EU on member state institutions, with chapters on the EU-15 and a conceptual overview. Goetz and Hix (2000) take a thoughtful, and sceptical, approach to the Europeanization of national political systems.

On individual institutions, Goetz (2000) offers one of the few discussions of how executives have been affected by the EU, while Knill (2001), Dimitrakopoulos and Pappas (2003) and Page (2003) take very different approaches to the Europeanization of national administrations. Maurer (2001; 2002), Maurer and Wessels (2001), and Raunio and Hix (2000) are the best places to begin reading on national parliaments, Hooghe (1995) and John (2000) are excellent on regions and local government respectively, and, on national courts, Craig (2003) and Slaughter, Sweet, and Weiler (1998) are extremely valuable—the first a single chapter overview, the latter a sophisticated conceptual treatment. On the interaction between the EU and national levels, Kassim, Peters, and Wright (2000) and Kassim, Menon, Peters, and Wright (2001) examine how member states coordinate EU policy at national and EU level.

Weblinks

There are few websites on the Europeanization of member state institutions, but contributions to the Convention on the Future of Europe at <**http://european-convention.eu.int/**> often highlight institutional dynamics. Also see the EU's gateway to member states <**http://europa.eu.int/abc/governments/index_en.htm**>.

References

Alter, K. (1998), 'Who are the "masters of the Treaty"? European governments and the European Court of Justice', *International Organization*, 52/1, 121–47.

Alter, K. J. (1996), 'The European Court's Political Power', *West European Politics*, 19/3, 458–87.

Alter, K. L. (2001), *Establishing the Supremacy of European Law* (Oxford: Oxford University Press).

Anderson, J. J. (1990), 'Skeptical Reflections on a Europe of Regions: Britain, Germany, and the ERDF', *Journal of Public Policy*, 10/4, 417–47.

Bache, I. (1998), *The Politics of European Union Regional Policy: Multi-Level Governance or Flexible Gatekeeping* (Sheffield: UACES/Sheffield Academic Press).

Bache, I., and Jones, R. (2000), 'Has EU Regional Policy Empowered the Regions? A Study of Spain and the United Kingdom', *Regional and Federal Studies*, 10/3, 1–20.

Balme, R., and Le Galès, P. (1997), 'Stars and black holes: French Cities and Regions in the European Galaxy', in M. Goldsmith and K. K. Klausen (eds), *European Integration and Local Government* (Cheltenham: Edward Elgar), 63–76.

Bergman, T. (1997), 'National parliaments and EU Affairs Committees: notes on empirical variation and competing explanations', in *Journal of European Public Policy*, 4/3, 373–87.

Burley, A. M., and Mattli, W. (1993), 'Europe before the Court: a political theory of legal integration', *International Organisation*, 47/1, 41–76.

Chalmers, D. (2000), 'The Positioning of EU Judicial Politics within the United Kingdom', in K. H. Goetz and S. Hix (eds), 'Europeanised Politics? European Integration and National Political Systems', special issue of *West European Politics*, 23/4, 169–210.

Claes, D. H. (2002), 'The process of Europeanization—the case of Norway and the Internal Energy Market' (University of Oslo: ARENA Working Papers, WP 02/12).

Council of the European Union (2001), *Preparing the Council for Enlargement, Part III: Summary of Coordination Systems for EU Matters in the Member States* (Brussels, 7 June 2518/01).

Craig, P. (1991), 'Sovereignty of the UK Parliament after *Factortame*', *Yearbook of European Law*, 11, 221–55.

Craig, P. (2003), 'National Courts and Community Law', in J. Hayward and A. Menon (eds), *Governing Europe* (Oxford: Oxford University Press), 15–35.

Dimitrakopoulos, D. G. (2001a), 'The Transposition of EU Law: "Post-Decisional Politics" and Institutional Autonomy', *European Law Journal*, 7/4, 442–58.

Dimitrakopoulos, D. G. (2001b), 'Incrementalism and path dependence: European integration and institutional change in national parliaments', *Journal of Common Market Studies* 39/3, 405–22.

Dimitrakopoulos, D. G., and Pappas, A. G. (2003), 'International Organizations and Domestic Administrative Reform', in B. G. Peters and J. Pierre (eds), *Handbook of Public Administration* (London: Sage), 440–50.

European Commission (2004), *Inforegio panorama* (European Commission: Brussels, 13 April) <http://europa.eu.int/comm/regional_policy/sources/docgener/panora_en.htm>.

European Council, Presidency Conclusions (1999), *Presidency Conclusions: Helsinki European Council, 10 and 11 December 1999* <http://europa.eu.int/council/off/conclu/dec99/dec99_en.htm>.

European Court of Justice (2004), *Annual Report 2003* (Luxembourg: Office for the Official Publications of the European Communities).

Favell, A. (1998), 'The Europeanisation of immigration politics', European Integration On-line Papers (EioP), 2:10 at <http://eiop.or.at/eiop/texte/1998-010a.htm>.

Fischer, A., Nicoloet, S., and Sciarini, P. (2002), 'Europeanisation of a Non-EU Country: The Case of Swiss Immigration Policy', *West European Politics*, 25/4, 143–70.

Garrett, G., and Tsebelis, G. (1996), 'An institutional critique of intergovernmentalism', *International Organization*, 50/2, 269–99.

Garrett, G., and Weingast, B. R. (1993), 'Ideas, interests and institutional constructing of the EC's internal market', in J. Goldstein and R. Keohane (eds), *Ideas and Foreign Policy* (Ithaca NY: Cornell University Press), 173–206.

General Secretariat of the Council (1999), *Review of the Council's Work in 1996* (Luxembourg: Office of Official Publications of the European Communities).

General Secretariat, of the Council of the European Union (1996), *Council Guide: Vol. I. Presidency Handbook* (Luxembourg: Office for Official Publications of the European Communities).

Goetz, K. H. (2000), 'European Integration and National Executives: a Cause in Search of an Effect', in K. H. Goetz, and S. Hix (eds), 'Europeanised politics? The Impact of European Integration on Domestic Politics', special issue of *West European Politics*, 23/4, 211–31.

Goetz, K. H. and Hix, S. (eds) (2000), 'Europeanised politics? The Impact of European Integration on Domestic Politics', special issue of *West European Politics*, 23/4.

Golub, J. (1996), 'The politics of judicial discretion: rethinking the interaction between national courts and the European Court of Justice', *West European Politics*, 19, 360–85.

Greenwood, J. (1997), *Representing Interests in the European Union* (Basingstoke: Macmillan).

Haas, E. B. (1958), *The Uniting of Europe* (Stanford CA: Stanford University Press).

Héritier, A., Knill, C., and Mingers, S. (1996), *Ringing the Changes in Europe* (Berlin: Walter de Gruyter).

Hix, S. (1999), *The Political System of the European Union* (Basingstoke: Macmillan).

Hix, S., and Goetz, K. H. (2000) 'Introduction: European Integration and National Political Systems' in K. H. Goetz, and S. Hix, (eds) 'Europeanised politics? The Impact of European Integration on Domestic Politics', special issue of *West European Politics*, 23/4, 1–26.

Hoffmann, S. (1966), 'Obstinate or obsolete? The fate of the nation state and the case of Western Europe', *Daedalus*, 95, 892–908.

Hoffmann, S. (1982), 'Reflections on the nation state in Europe today', *Journal of Common Market Studies*, 21, 21–37.

Hoffmann, S., and Keohane, R. O. (1991), 'Institutional Change in Europe in the 1980s' in R. O. Keohane & S. Hoffman (eds), *The New European Community* (Boulder CO: Westview Press), 1–40.

Hooghe (1995), 'Subnational Mobilisation in the European Union', *West European Politics*, 18/3, 175–98.

Hooghe, L. (1996), *Cohesion Policy and European Integration* (Oxford: Oxford University Press).

House of Commons Select Committee on European Scrutiny (2004), *The Committee's work in 2003. Eighth Report: the Committee's work in 2003*, (HC 42–viii, 03 02 2004).

John, P. (2000), 'The Europeanisation of Sub-national Governance', in *Urban Studies*, 37/5–6, 877–94.

Kassim, H. (2001), 'Introduction: Coordinating National Action in Brussels', in H. Kassim, A. Menon, B. G. Peters, and V. Wright (eds), *The National Coordination of EU Policy: The European Level* (Oxford: Oxford University Press), 1–46.

Kassim, H. (2003), 'The National Co-ordination of EU Policy: Must Europeanisation Mean Convergence?', in Kevin Featherstone and Claudio Radaelli (eds), *The Politics of Europeanisation: Theory and Analysis* (Oxford: Oxford University Press), 83–111.

Kassim, H., and Menon, A. (2003a), 'The Principal-Agent Approach and the Study of the European Union: Promise Unfulfilled?', in E. Jones and A. Verdun (eds), 'Political Economy and the Study of European Integration', special issue of *Journal of European Public Policy*, 10/1, 121–39.

Kassim, H., and Menon, A. (2003b), 'Les Etats membres de l'UE et la Commission Prodi' *Revue française de science politique*, 53/4, August, 491–510.

Kassim, H., and Peters, B. G. (2001), 'Conclusion: Co-ordinating National Action in Brussels—a Comparative Perspective', in H. Kassim, A. Menon, B. G. Peters, and V. Wright (eds), *The National Coordination of EU Policy: The European Level* (Oxford: Oxford University Press), 297–342.

Kassim, H., Menon A., and Wright, V. (eds) (1996), *The European Union and national insustrial policy* (London: Routledge).

Kassim, H., and Stevens, H. M. G. (forthcoming), *The EU's Air Transport Policy: Europeanization and its Limits* (Basingstoke: Palgrave).

Kassim, H. and Wright, V. (1991), 'The role of national administrations in the decision-making processes of the European Community', *Rivista Trimestrale di Diritto Pubblico* (with Vincent Wright), 832–50.

Kassim, H., Menon, A., Peters, B. G., and Wright, V. (eds) (2001), *The National Co-ordination of EU Policy: the European Level* (Oxford: Oxford University Press).

Kassim, H., Peters, B. G., and Wright, V. (eds) (2000), *The National Co-ordination of EU Policy: The Domestic Level* (Oxford: Oxford University Press).

Katz, R. S. (1999), 'Representation, the Locus of Democratic Legitimation, and the Role of the National Parliaments in the European Union', in R. S. Katz and B. Wessels (eds), *The European Parliament, the National Parliaments and European Integration* (Oxford: Oxford University Press), 21–44.

Kerremans, B. (2000), 'Belgium' in H. Kassim, B. G. Peters, and V. Wright (eds), *The National Co-ordination of EU Policy: the domestic level* (Oxford: Oxford University Press), 182–200.

Knill, C. (2001), *The Europeanisation of National Administrations*, (Cambridge: Cambridge University Press).

Laffan, B., O'Donnell, R., and Smith, M. (2000), *Europe's Experimental Union* (London: Routledge).

Lippert, B., Umbach, G., and Wessels, W. (2001), 'Europeanization of CEE executives: EU membership negotiations as a shaping power', *Journal of European Public Policy*, 8/6, 980–1012.

Loughlin, J. (2000), 'Regional Autonomy and State Paradigm Shifts in Western Europe', in *Regional and Federal Studies*, 10/2, 10–34.

Marks, G. (1992), 'Structural policy in the European Community' in A. Sbragia (ed), *Euro-Politics* (Washington, DC: Brookings Institution).

Marks, G. (1993), 'Structural Policy After Maastricht', in A. Cafruny and G. Rosenthal (eds), *The State of the European Community* (New York: Lynne Rienner), 391–410.

Marks, G., Haesly, R., and Mbaye, H. A. D. (2002), 'What Do Subnational Offices Think They Are Doing in Brussels?' *Regional and Federal Studies*, 12/3, 1–23.

Marks, G., Hooghe, L., and Blank, K. (1996), 'European integration from the 1980s', *Journal of Common Market Studies*, 34/3, 341–78.

Marquand, D. (1981), 'Parliamentary Accountability and the European Community', *Journal of Common Market Studies*, 19/3, 221–236.

Mattli, W., and Slaughter, A-M. (1998), 'The Role of National Courts in the Process of European Integration: accounting for Judicial Preferences and Constraints' in A-M. Slaughter, A. Stone Sweet and J. H. H. Weiler (eds), *The European Court and National Courts—Doctrine and Jurisprudence* (Oxford: Hart Publishing), 253–76.

Maurer, A. (2001), 'National Parliaments in the European architecture: from Latecomers Adaptation to Permanent Institutional Change', in A. Maurer and W. Wessels (2001), *National Parliaments on their Ways to Europe: Losers or Latecomers?* (Baden-Baden: Nomos Verlagsgellschaft), 27–76, available on-line at <http://aei.pitt.edu/archive/00001476/>.

Maurer, A. (2002), *Les rôles des Parlements nationaux dans l'Union européenne: Options, Contraintes et Obstacles*, contribution to the Convention on the Future of Europe, available on-line at <http://europa.eu.int/ futurum/documents/other/ oth010302_fr.pdf>.

Maurer, A., and Wessels, W. (2001), *National Parliaments on their Ways to Europe: Losers or Latecomers?* (Baden-Baden: Nomos Verlagsgellschaft), available on-line at <http://aei.pitt.edu/archive/00001476/>.

Maurer, A., and Wessels, W. (2001a), 'Main Findings' in A. Maurer and W. Wessels (2001), *National Parliaments on their Ways to Europe: Losers or Latecomers?* (Baden-Baden: Nomos Verlagsgellschaft), 17–26, available on-line at <http://aei.pitt.edu/archive/00001476/>.

Mazey, S., and Richardson, J. (1995), 'Promiscuous policymaking: the European policy style?', in C. Rhodes and S. Mazey (eds), *The State of the European Union: vol. III, Building a European Polity?* (Harlow: Longman), 337–59.

Menon, A., and Wright, V. (1998), 'The paradoxes of "failure": British EU policy making in comparative perspective', *Public Policy and Administration*, 13/4, 46–66.

Metcalfe, L. (1992), 'International policy coordination and public management reform', *International Review of Administrative Sciences*, 60, 271–90.

Milward, A. S. (2000), *The European Rescue of the Nation-State*, 2nd edn. (London: Routledge).

Moravcsik, A. (1993), 'Preferences and Power in the European Community: A Liberal Intergovernmentalist Approach', *Journal of Common Market Studies*, 31/4, 473–524.

Moravcsik, A. (1998), *The Choice for Europe. Social Purpose and State Power from Messina to Maastricht* (Ithaca, NY: Cornell University Press).

Newman, M. (1996), *Democracy, Sovereignty and the European Union* (London: Hurst and Company).

Norton, P. (1996), 'Conclusion: Addressing the Democratic Deficit', in P. Norton (ed), *National Parliaments and the European Union* (London: Frank Cass), 177–93.

Norton, P. (1996), 'Introduction: Adapting to European Integration', in P. Norton (ed), *National Parliaments and the European Union* (London: Frank Cass), 1–11.

Olsen, J. P. (1997), 'European Challenges to the Nation State', in B. Steunenberg and F. van Vught (eds), *Political Institutions and Public Policy* (Amsterdam: Kluwer Academic Publishers), 157–88.

Page, E. C. (2003), 'Europeanization and the Persistence of Administrative Systems', in J. Hayward and A. Menon (eds), *Governing Europe* (Oxford: Oxford University Press), 162–76.

Peters, B. G. (1994), 'Agenda setting in the EU', *Journal of European Public Policy*, 1/1, 9–26.

Pierson, P. (1996), 'The path to European integration: a historical institutionalist analysis', *Comparative Political Analysis*, 29/2, 123–63.

Pollack, M. A. (1995), 'Regional actors in an intergovernmental play: the making and implementation of EC structural policy', in C. Rhodes and S. Mazey (eds), *The State of the European Union: vol. III, Building a European Polity?* (Harlow: Longman), 361–90.

Pollack, M. A. (1997), 'Delegation, agency and agenda setting in the European Community', *International Organization*, 51/1, 99–134.

Putnam, R. D. (1988), 'Diplomacy and domestic politics: the logic of two-level games', *International Organization*, 43/2, 427–60.

Raunio, T., and Hix, S. (2000), 'Backbenchers Learn to Fight Back: European Integration and Parliamentary Government', in K. H. Goetz, and S. Hix (eds), 'Europeanised politics? The Impact of European Integration on Domestic Politics', special issue of *West European Politics*, 23/4, 142–68.

Schmidt, V. (1999), 'European "Federalism" and its Encroachments on National Institutions', *Publius: The Journal of Federalism*, 29/1, 19–44.

Scott, A. (2002), ' "Constitutional" Regions and the European Union', paper presented as evidence to Richard Commission, Aberystwyth, October.

Slaughter, A-M., Stone Sweet, A., and Weiler, J. H. H. (eds) (1998), *The European Court and National Courts—Doctrine and Jurisprudence* (Oxford: Hart Publishing), 305–30.

Smith, A. (1995), 'Going beyond the democratic deficit: the European Union and rural development in networked societies', *Regional and Federal Studies*, 5/1, 45–66.

Spanou, C. (1998), 'European integration in administrative terms: a framework for analysis and the Greek case', *Journal of European Public Policy*, 5/3, 467–84.

Stein, E. (1981), 'Lawyers, judges and the making of a transnational constitution', *American Journal of International Law*, 75/1, 1–27.

Stevens, A., and Stevens, H. (2000), *Brussels Bureaucrats?* (London: Palgrave).

Stone Sweet, A., and Sandholtz, W. (1998), 'Integration, Supranational Governance, and the Institutionalization of the European Policy', in W. Sandholtz and A. Stone Sweet (eds), *European Integration and Supranational Governance* (Oxford: Oxford University Press), 1–26.

Stone Sweet, A. (1998), 'Constitutional Dialogues in the European Community', in A-M. Slaughter, A. Stone Sweet, and J. H. H. Weiler (eds), *The European Court and National Courts—Doctrine and Jurisprudence* (Oxford: Hart Publishing), 305–30.

Stone Sweet, A., and Brunell, T. L. (1998), 'The European Court and the national courts: a statistical analysis of preliminary references, 1961–95', *Journal of European Public Policy*, 5/1, 66–97.

Thielemann, E. R. (2002), 'The Price of Europeanization: Why European Regional Policy Initiatives Are a Mixed Blessing', *Regional and Federal Studies*, 12/1, 43–65.

Wallace, H. (1996), 'Relations between the European Union and the British Administration', in Y. Mény, P. Muller, and J-L. Quermonne (eds), *Adjusting to Europe* (London: Routledge), 61–72.

Weiler, J. H. H. (1991), 'The transformation of Europe', *Yale Law Journal*, 100/8, 2405–83.

Wessels, W. (1991), 'The EC Council: The Community's Decisionmaking Center', in R. O. Keohane and S. Hoffmann (eds), *The New European Community* (New York: Westview), 133–54.

Wessels, W., and Rometsch, D. (eds) (1996), *The European Union and Member States. Towards Institutional Fusion?* (Manchester: Manchester University Press).

Wessels, W. (2001) 'Nice Results: The Millennium IGC in the EU's Evolution', *Journal of Common Market Studies*, 2001, 39/2, 197–219.

Wessels, W., Maurer, A., and Mittag, J. (2003), 'The European Union and the Member States: analysing two arenas over time', in Wessels, Maurer and Mittag (eds), *Fifteen Into One? The European Union and its Member States* (Manchester: Manchester University Press), 3–28.

Wishlade, F. G. (2003), *Regional State Aid and Competition Policy in the European Union* (The Hague: Kluwer Law International).

Wright, Vincent (1996), 'The National Co-ordination of European Policy-Making Negotiating the Quagmire' in J. Richardson (ed), *European Union. Policy and Policy-Making* (London: Routledge), 148–69.

Chapter 14
The Europeanization of Interest Groups and Political Parties

Robert Ladrech

Contents

Summary

Political parties and interest groups are not immune from the process of Europeanization. Both are key actors in their respective domestic environments. Each, however, responds differently in kind to the adaptational pressures exerted by European integration. Interest groups have more opportunities to exploit the multi-level governance structure of the EU than do political parties. Both, no matter the activities in which they engage in with supranational actors and institutions, are constituted and thereby conditioned in terms of their central goals by their primary environment, the domestic level. Interest groups' activities outside the domestic level are conditioned by the domestic interest intermediation system, and political parties are constrained from exercising power beyond the national political system by the lack of a European party government. Both actors, though, have sought to promote their interests at multiple levels of decision making, thus demonstrating the Europeanization process.

Introduction

Political forces such as parties and interest groups are key actors in Western representative democracies. They are also present in the multi-level EU system, although their role departs in some significant ways in comparison with that in the member states. Whereas EU policy-making has been described as 'governance without government', interest groups have been able to pursue various channels of influence at multiple levels. 'Party government', on the other hand, has not been associated with the EU at this stage in its institutional and political development, and consequently parties have had to make do with less satisfactory alternative approaches to representing their constituencies interests. It is not surprising, therefore, that there is a long history and abundant literature associated with the EU-level activities of interest groups, the structures and activities of Euro-groups, and the general impact of the EU on interest intermediation. There is, as it follows, a much shorter history (and therefore literature) on political parties' involvement in EU affairs, at both the national and European level of organization. In both cases, we should expect to see some form of adaptation by parties and interest groups as a result of their countries' embeddedness in the multi-level EU system. This chapter presents an analysis and evaluation of the degree to which Europeanization may have altered the roles of these political forces in the EU, both at the EU and domestic levels. In view of the historic debates concerning the constitutionalization of the EU, for example, in the Convention on the Future of Europe, the significance of parties and interest groups may well be directly affected. Therefore understanding their present role in the EU, in particular the pressures to adapt to the increased influence of the EU since the 1980s, is of utmost importance regard to questions of EU legitimacy and democratic accountability.

Europeanization, as understood in this volume, is a term describing an adaptive process on the part of organizations and other actors (Radaelli 2000) to the impact of European integration, but also the European-level system-forming contribution by national actors. It not only reflects changes in national actors' preferences and relations with domestic institutions (top-down), but also their involvement and activity beyond the national arena, both transnational and supranational (bottom-up). However, the European political system, such as it exists, creates variable opportunity structures for national non-state actors. This is to say that EU institutions alone, however receptive they may or may not be to parties and interest groups, do not in themselves generate the type of activity, nor create non-state supra- and transnational actors, that significantly impact domestic actors such that they have become less influential in their respective domains. Furthermore, domestic environmental factors, for example, institutional, organizational, etc., quite apart from EU inputs, contribute to the motivations, constraints, and advantages/disadvantages of non-state national actors as they calculate targeting time and resources at the European level. A cost–benefit analysis alone, therefore, does not explain the presence of national actors at the European level (Cram 1998). Although a more careful analysis will demonstrate distinct differences between the fortunes of political parties and those of interest groups, suffice it to say that the Europeanization of political forces has not altered the basic functions and fundamental legitimacy of domestic actors, however much their European-level counterparts may have developed over the past decades.

Lastly, although 'bottom-up' Europeanization can be considered a key dynamic in the creation of European level party and interest organizations, 'top-down' Europeanization has not altered the fundamental interactive balance of forces in which the domestic actor remains the most influential. It is certainly the case that the European level counterpart has witnessed a qualitative enhancement in its policy and decision-making input, but it would be more accurate to claim that this is so within their European level environment. That is to say, the development of European parties—both transnational party federations as well as European Parliament parliamentary groups—and Euro-level interest groups, are indeed real 'players' in EU decision and policy-making, but this role has not resulted in a corresponding diminution in their national counterparts' legitimacy vis-à-vis their national decision-making authorities. In other words, a zero-sum situation has not occurred.

Europeanization and political forces

As discussed in the opening chapter of this volume, 'Europeanization' is a term used to describe a process of change in the behaviour (and possibly structure) of a range of actors, be they individuals, organizations, or institutions. Change is omni-directional, that is, the European integration process has generated political and economic dynamics at all territorial levels—sub-national, national, and supranational, such that the term 'multi-level' refers to actual linkages and relations among and between actors in all of these arenas (Hooghe and Marks 2001). Changed circumstances, whether it is formal, such as EU directives and regulations, or new sources of financing as in the case of EU regional policy, are among some of the well-documented factors precipitating changed strategies for interest satisfaction. Domestic political competition, interest group lobbying on national governments, self-promotion for enhanced influence by the European Parliament, all of these examples and more have contributed toward institutional changes at the European level. Yet, how does one determine what particular set of factors is responsible for any one behavioural change? For example, the enhancement of EU regional policy in the late 1980s had actors both supranational (Commission) and national (Spain and Portugal, among others) championing it, yet its effects stimulated in many respects sub-national mobilization, which introduced an additional dimension. Many other examples could be chosen, but the main point is that the complexity of the EU system obscures simple mono-causal pathways. The variety of channels open to actors, but also fluidity in the patterns of institutional behaviour, has meant that a 'snap-shot' view of the EU system may not be representative of general dynamics and trends. One has also to incorporate the variation among member states such that certain propensities for action on the part of actors such as interest groups results from specific domestic institutional properties (Schmidt 1997). For all of these reasons, 'bottom-up' and 'top-down' characterizations of Europeanization serve basically a heuristic function, though certainly case studies can trace initial statutory changes and alterations in strategies.

The interactive dimension outlined in the opening chapter reflects the reality of Europeanization, for the EU has reached a stage in which its presence or influence is now part of the panoply of factors that automatically informs the strategic development of certain organizations. In regards to studying the effects of Europeanization on political forces, what we can more readily discern and evaluate is the change of position or relevance in their respective environments, that is, the extent to which adaptation has altered the system functions of the specific actor.

How does one conceptualize the 'environments' that political forces operate in, especially in the context of Europeanization? Here the multi-level governance thesis lends a useful perspective. The multi-level governance thesis suggests that the site of political power and especially decision making cannot be confined to the national level any longer, and that relations among and between actors at the supranational, national and sub-national levels are part of an incremental process of polity creation. Additionally,

political arenas are interconnected rather than nested. While national arenas remain important arenas for the formation of national government preferences, the multi-level governance model rejects the view that subnational actors are nested exclusively within them . . . National governments do not monopolize links between domestic and European actors. In this perspective, complex interrelationships in domestic politics do not stop at the national state but extend to the European level. (Hooghe and Marks 2001: 4).

Although the importance of national arenas for the formation of national government preferences is a valid observation, we must also bear in mind that the role or function an actor such as an interest group or political party plays in this formation establishes and determines their organizational identity. Furthermore, system properties—whether national, sub-national or supranational—condition actors' own perspectives on strategy, that is, what is or is not possible. Thus, while the multi-level governance thesis is helpful in drawing attention to the fact that political arenas are interconnected rather than nested, and the consequent opportunities this opens up for the actions of actors at all levels, we should also understand that actors 'belong' to the level in which they were founded. Their 'home territory' still counts, for at the most elemental level, their respective 'missions' derive from factors peculiar to their primary environment. This pertains to the supranational level as well.

This leads finally to a consideration of the function that specific actors play in their primary environment (level). What is clear from a comparison of the EU with national political systems is that there is a significant difference that has direct consequences for the interactive relationship between interest groups and political parties at both levels. The European level is constituted—in both formal and informal meanings—by a unique combination of supranational and intergovernmental logics, whereas member states, however much Europeanization is reflected in altered institutional approaches, adaptive behaviour by non-state actors, etc., remain constituted—constitutionally and practically—as the principal arena for their nationally constructed/constituted actors. Although this may appear as a statement of the obvious, it leads to the following contention: actors at the European level reflect the duality of the EU, that is, supranational and intergovernmental logics, and as such, their developing role at the European level is formally mediated by actors from both levels; whereas national actors, although their domestic environment has become increasingly permeable to EU inputs, adapt according to a logic solely corresponding with the institutional dynamics of their respective national system which itself may experience change. The implications of this situation are that national actors have, in a sense, a privileged position at the European level that is not replicated for European-level actors at the national level. European-level actors have not become a viable substitute to national political representation, nor has the development of interest representation at the EU level decreased the legitimacy of political representatives at the national level. Furthermore, transnational political parties and transnational interest groups remain agents of their constituent member organizations, although the balance between supranational and intergovernmental logics may shift.

The multi-level governance thesis is useful in shedding light on another aspect of the 'longer range' of activities in which political forces are engaged. The other levels of activity, although different from the central, constituting level, provide potentially freer room for manœuvre, and indeed, may be used in two-level gamesmanship. This seems obvious in the case of interest groups, where the additional resources and/or allies might bring pressure upon a particular national government. It is less obvious for political parties, but the development of the two largest transnational party federations, the Party of European Socialists and the European People's Party-European Democrats, allows an additional platform to interact with other government players when in opposition. Thus Europeanization presents innovative opportunities to wield power denied or temporary blocked at the domestic level.

Parties and interest groups

Parties and interest groups have fundamentally different opportunities and constraints in regard to actions beyond the domestic level. These differences also have direct consequences for the development at the European level of Euro-groups and Euro-parties and their national counterparts' adaptation to the EU and the implications of this in their domestic settings. First and foremost, parties seek to form governments, and the means to this end is contesting elections. Although the financing of parties varies throughout the EU, from support from affiliated organizations and individual membership to public (state) financing, a key activity of parties involves participating in elections. Winning office and/or influencing policy depend to a large degree on forming and developing a secure resource base, and the overwhelming source of such maintenance is *national*.[1] Resource transfer from the EU to national parties in any significant sense does not occur, and this simple fact explains the lack of incentive by national parties to expand their presence and activities at the European level. We might add that votes are nationally derived as well, thus grounding the actions of parties all that much more firmly in a domestic basis. National parties are also limited in terms of institutional entry points at the European level, with the European

---

[1] At the Nice summit in 2001 a declaration was agreed on regulating the financing of transnational party federations and party groups in the European Parliament under Article 191 TEC. There is explicit prohibition on transferring EU funds to national parties.

Parliament (EP) as the sole hospitable institution, although the larger party families have attempted to project collective interests through meetings ahead of the European Council. This being said, however, the supranational identity of the EP (or the character of the European Council for that matter) advantages no single national party.

Interest groups, on the other hand, are much less encumbered than parties in the source of their financing and in the scope of their activities. Financial support obviously derives from members, whether this is trade unions or manufacturers' associations (associational groups) or business corporations (institutional groups). However, the EU can be a source of funding, and not simply resources such as regional aid. The Commission, in its attempt to encapsulate as many interests as possible in its policy development, offers incentives and funds for groups to present their views in Brussels. Aspinwall and Greenwood (1998), for example, note the relatively high percentage of funds for public interest groups in particular. The Council and Parliament are also inviting targets for organized groups. In other words, however episodic the mobilization of resources at the EU may be, there is an inviting set of institutions to present one's case as it arises. Furthermore, unlike parties, the measure of success—that is, the acquisition of new benefits/resources or maintenance of such for members, is not solely dependent on national government largesse. Even in statist systems, certain interests may ally with EU policy intentions in order to circumvent national government opposition. The central point is that in comparison to political parties, interest groups have a much wider repertoire from which to choose tactics and strategies. In this sense the multi-level structure of the EU system represents the opportunity of potential channels to key decision makers and resources. Parties, on the other hand, are heavily domestic-bound in relation, having no direct benefactor at the European level.

Taking into consideration the above discussion, we can analyse the extent to which Europeanization of parties and interest groups has resulted in fundamental change in their position with respect to their operating environments. First, we investigate change in *authoritativeness*, that is, has their function in the national political system demonstrated any shift, formal or informal, that would suggest a diminution of their role. This assumes that Europeanization of institutions, such as legislatures and

---

Box 14.1 Europeanization and Political Forces: a framework for analysis

Change in *authoritativeness*: has their function in the political system—national or supranational—changed? Examples: European Commission reaches out to interest groups, making them indispensable to EU policy-making; national parliamentary scrutiny diminished due to EU level bargaining activity of national executives.

Change in role of actors *articulating* interests to government, national or supranational? Examples: Narrower range of economic policy competence for national government reduces parties' links with business groups and trade unions; expansion in number and specialization of Euro-level interest groups creates more pluralist Euro-environment.

Change in the *interactive* relationship between Euro-level and national parties and interest groups. Examples: National parties and parliamentary groups involving their respective MEP's more closely in national decision-making; increase in *ad hoc* coalitions reduces dependency on federal-type Euro-interest groups.

executives, may have changed, and marginalizing them in the process. Second, as both parties and interest groups *articulate* the interests of their members, is there any evidence that this function has been lost, however partially, to another actor, in this case a European-level actor? Third and finally, has the balance in the *interactive* relationship, which we assume began as one of unequal status, that is, Euro-groups and parties as simply the European level agents of national principal actors, unable to pursue independent agendas, changed in any way?

Changing opportunity structures: interest groups

The EU creates varying opportunity structures for parties and interest groups, between the two types of organizations as well as among them. Interest groups, as mentioned above, have a much longer history than parties in investing at the EU level, and indeed, the EU, especially the Commission (more latterly the EP), has been ardent in its calls to private and semi-public actors for attention and involvement. Without retracing the history of the EU, it is worth noting at the outset that a common or single market was intended to effect change in the business/economic sphere exactly for the purpose that economic actors could better advance their interests. Questions relating to the removal of tariffs, market opening, deregulation both nationally and internationally, etc., was never left up to one solitary actor, and so from the beginning a competition of sorts developed to 'guide' European economic integration. The point is that interest groups, especially producer groups, from agriculture to steel, had an *incentive* to promote their interests, or in the case of steel in the 1980s, to protect their interests. As the EU became more and more of a key player in the decisions affecting the livelihood of these interests, their lobbying evolved in such a way as to pressure the points of contact and influence that existed in the EU system.

Yet Europeanization and national interest group behaviour is not so straightforward a phenomenon as one might expect. There are a number of reasons why the open channels fostered by the Commission might not have significantly altered national interest group lobbying tactics. To begin, member states have created their own systems of interest intermediation, and not to push the point too strongly, these systems have peculiarly national characteristics. This obvious fact is not confined to a simple acknowledgement of the differences between pluralist, neo-corporatist and statist systems. Rather, it is to suggest that patterns of relations, sources and maintenance of financial capability, privileged networks, customs, etc., all make up the bundle of factors which define each national system. With this in mind, however 'intrusive' the EU has become into each national system, an adaptive response to European integration, that is, Europeanization, is conditioned by the present and future relations each actor maintains in their domestic level (Beyers 2002). Thus Europeanization is not an automatic process, and organizations chose to ignore the European level of influence based upon a variety of risk factors. However, it is important to stress this point, that as national actors are part of their national arenas, organizational innovation and development in response to the EU is complementary, not alternative, to their on-going domestic pursuit of interest satisfaction.

With regard to interest groups, a number of factors maintain the ties that bind them to the national level, and are themselves significant in any fundamental change in the relationship interest groups have with national governments. These 'ties' are not necessarily constraints; rather they are part of the domestic environment that governs the strategic development of these groups. As such, they are 'givens' in the organizational life of interest groups. The first of these factors is the possible existence of privileged relationships with political actors such as parties. This benefits interest groups whatever the type of system, although pluralist systems would seem to accentuate the benefit. Obvious couplings include trade unions with social democratic parties and business groups and farmers' associations with agrarian/conservative/ Christian Democrat parties. Second, regarding influencing decision-making at the EU level, 'partisan-friendly' national governments are also an asset in Council of Ministers dynamics, and may serve as an expedient way to protect the status quo at home. National agricultural interests are an especially noteworthy example of this fact. Third, the extra-national environment may not provide sufficient allies necessary for supranational mobilization, no matter the receptiveness of other potentially relevant actors and institutions. The case of public utilities in France, that is, preserving a regulated and monopolistic advantage, is an example of this situation where both a sympathetic ear in Brussels or a 'critical mass' among other similar national organizations was absent. Last, organized interest groups may experience a rate of success or satisfaction that neutralizes any attempts to alter national dynamics, whatever might be the potential added benefits. In this case, we might label this predisposition 'conservative'. Taking all four factors into consideration, the picture that emerges is one of familiarity with a tried and true cast of national actors and institutions that preclude moves that might engender unintended and negative consequences. Inputs from the EU into any national system must therefore either import statutory changes having direct and significant consequences for interest groups, or else present a policy change either hostile to the maintenance of national benefits or else of such positive enhancement as to be explicit and obvious to most members of an interest organization.

As much as the EU may be receptive to the participation of interest groups, there are also certain problematic aspects regarding their abilities to engage at the EU level. First, there is the simple fact of resources. Lobbying EU institutions and actors, necessitating added personnel, is a realistic option only for well-endowed single entities or else business associations (Greenwood 1997). Second, affiliating with related Euro-groups does not necessarily resolve the resource problem by incorporating an economy of scale, for the needs of any one national member of a transnational interest association may have such unique characteristics as to make the more generalist orientation of a Euro-group of no great assistance. Last, although the incentive to promote or protect interests by lobbying the EU may be apparent, the investment of resources by national interest groups is complementary to their on-going activities at the domestic level. This is because the EU, depending upon the policy, may be targeted as and only when it is required (and this may still entail only an intensified link with the appropriate Euro-group). This is a prime difference between domestic interest groups and their Euro-level counterparts. National actors approach the EU in a problem-solving manner, accessing the appropriate contacts as and when they are needed. National organizations, by and large, are not permanent actors at the EU level, apart from exceptionally large enterprises, and these are usually of a multinational character. They are not embedded in this system as they would be in their respective national systems, and therefore incentives to participate in the EU level of policy-making are of a different nature than their involvement in national environments (Aspinwall and Greenwood 1998).

Interest groups for which the European level is their primary operating environment are nevertheless tied to national arenas, although we can distinguish between types of Euro-groups, those representing nationally constituted interests and those seeking to represent issues of a clear transnational significance. The former would include trade associations, manufacturers, etc., and the latter organizations represent, *inter alia*, women's and environmentalist concerns. In the case of the former, Euro-groups project the sectoral interests of their members, acting as the lobbying eyes and ears of the national members. With the latter, the Euro-group seeks to assist national affiliates by providing information and lobbying on their behalf. These types of groups often have, compared to the former group, much less of an 'organic' tie with the national affiliates, that is, they are 'virtual' lobbies, speaking on behalf of a 'public good.'

Assessing the Europeanization of interest groups

We can now assess how the process of Europeanization has altered certain characteristics of interest groups, both national and European. The first area to look for change is their position of *authoritativeness* in relation to their primary operating environment. Has their role diminished or enhanced as a result of institutional change? Is change related to actions on their own instigation, that is, adaptation, or were they the recipients of statutory amendments to their organization and activities?

Are national interest groups any less significant or legitimate as interlocutors between individuals and group interests and the primary target of their activities, namely the national government? National systems of interest intermediation may have indeed experienced some evolution due to the impact of European integration (Scharpf 1999), and this is represented primarily by the growing competence of the EU in selected policy areas. We must distinguish, however, between changes in the fortunes of particular sectoral interests which may be due to wider causes, such as internationalization and subsequent competition due to reduced tariff barriers, etc., and that produced by changes in both the place and cast of key decision makers. EU institutions acquiring or sharing competences over previously nationally determined policy areas may cause deterioration in special domestic relationships (or policy communities/networks), whether in neo-corporatist or pluralist environments, as some change in the number of actors may alter the competitive edge for some. On the other hand, the existence of a receptive Commission, etc., may enhance the bargaining position of formerly marginal groups. It is fair to say that although the EU has had an effect in national systems of interest intermediation, national interest groups as a whole have not been disenfranchised. Two reasons explain the endurance of the authoritativeness of national interest groups. First, as explained elsewhere, national interest groups have had the incentive to protect and promote their concerns, and there has been considerable success on their part from lobbying Brussels. This has not been confined solely to business groups, as EU legislation in the area of the environment (see, for example, Fairbrass and Jordan 2001) attests. From this perspective, Europeanization has meant a diversification of group strategies, appropriating the required resource or influencing the relevant decision-making body as they have moved onto the supranational level. Thus the permeation of the domestic sphere by EU inputs does not necessarily lead to a diminishment of the capacity of interest groups to secure their goals.

The second reason has to do with change in national systems *per se*, that is, how Europeanization has altered them from within. Whether from the need to coordinate in a more efficient manner etc., national administrations have had pressure to adapt to EU legislation which both ensures a smooth translation of EU directives and regulations into national law, as well as to coordinate various units of government in such a way as to support national executive actions at the EU level (Kassim 2000). This phenomenon has not meant a structural change in the linkages between government and domestic organized interests. On the contrary, the need for information, coupled with the fact that domestic and sub-national actors may develop relations with EU actors, has led some national governments to monitor rather than ignore the activities of these actors. In the longer run, however one may label a particular national system—pluralist, neo-corporatist, or statist—the expectation of convergence around one model, stimulated by adaptation to a single model of EU state-society relations, is unlikely, and instead 'moderate diversity' at the meso-level may be a more accurate description. According to Falkner, this is characterized by the 'co-existence of different types of policy networks within the same political system. While *intra-system diversity* of public–private interaction may even increase, this development is likely to be accompanied by a *trend towards inter-system convergence* in specific policy areas, as a consequence of Europeanisation' (2001: 94). This process does not inherently undermine the relations of organized interests, broadly categorised, and their respective national governments.

The second area to evaluate is the position of national interest groups as representatives or interlocutors between individuals and groups and the national government. Have national interest groups, either industry-specific or associations, become marginalized or has the system of national interest intermediation become more pluralist in the sense that European level actors compete with their national counterparts? If we are asking whether or not a change of magnitude with structural ramifications for different national political systems has occurred, such that national interest groups' role has ebbed due to state attention becoming diverted to a different set of actors, then the verdict is no. This is not to say, however, that the activities of Euro-groups do not themselves become involved in national affairs. For the set of Euro-groups who lobby on issues of a public interest, for example environmental issues, groups such as the European affiliate of the Friends of the Earth are crucial in transmitting information from the European level to their various national members. In this sense, having a European level counterpart assists weak national actors when they present their case to national authorities. In other cases, Euro-level industry groups have increasingly aimed their lobbying strategies to include national governments, which may be in a position to affect positions in Council of Minister deliberations. It is certainly the case that Euro-groups are not confined to the EU institutional system for their activities, and permeation of a national system therefore means it is open to more than simply the outputs of EU legislation. Following the perspective of the multi-level governance model, as well as the 'network governance model' (Kohler-Koch 1999), boundaries are not strict confinements of actors' pursuits at any level. But the integrity of the levels remains, and although Europeanization may result in some degree of convergence at the meso level, the role of interest groups in general remains a defining characteristic of the representative system in each of EU member states. When the term 'democratic deficit' is employed, national interest groups are not usually included as actors finding their channels or linkages with authoritative decision makers reduced. On the contrary, interest groups persist as key players in national politics. Although, as Mazey and Richardson (2001: 233) state, '[e]ven when an interest group and a national government are on the same side (often not a reasonable assumption), the group cannot rely on a national government to be able to deliver under QMV', national governments remain intimately involved in interest group preference formation and indeed legal identity. National governments are no longer the only game in town for domestic interest groups, but they remain the *primus inter loci* for them. As Aspinwall suggests, 'it appears that a positive sum game is emerging in which interests have a greater say in Brussels while also retaining their historically specific roles in the member states' (1998: 212).

Thirdly, has the interactive relationship between national and supranational interest groups changed over time? Have supranational actors developed interests and goals independent, and even at odds, with their national counterparts? The interest group field at the European level has certainly matured, alongside the enhancement of the EU's policy competences. Aspinwall characterizes the situation in the following way:

In the tug of war with national advocacy systems, EU-level groups are using increasingly sophisticated means to attract allegiance, including group specialisation, diversification of political objectives, and temporary alliances. In addition, both the groups themselves and the EU institutions are socialising private interests to the efficacy of Euro representation' (1998: 196).

Europeanization is manifest at the European level in the case of Euro-groups, and their role has become integral to EU policy-making. Even more, the 'technical nature and interrelatedness of regulatory issues, and the role of the member states in its formulation and subsequent administration, mean they have more input at both the European and national levels' (Aspinwall 1998: 197). As Eurogroups have become crucial for policy development at the EU level, and expanded both in numbers and range of policy issues, the amount of information and resources (of a technological nature) open to national groups has also increased. A paradoxical relationship of sorts has consequently developed. On the one hand, increased organizational resources and specialization of Euro-groups has entrenched their position in Brussels. Specialization, however, means more choice in the type of Euro-group to join, and motivates domestic groups to engage in multiple memberships, even moving about based on the more useful Euro-group or policy network.[2] This 'promiscuity' (Mazey and Richardson 2001: 227), together with easier and less costly means to secure information regarding EU decision-making by national groups, means that the interactive relationship, although it too can be said to have matured, has not resulted in fundamental shifts in the sense that Euro-groups are no longer agents of the national affiliates. It would be more accurate to say, rather, that a learning process—a component of the

---

[2] This suggests a phenomenon closer to what Warleigh (2000) terms a 'policy coalition'.

Europeanization process—has resulted in more sophisticated calculations by actors at both levels, with interdependency decreased slightly.

Changing opportunity structures: political parties

It has been suggested that 'in the advocacy void created by the absence of strong EU-level political parties, interests have been able—and encouraged—to express views on issues of relevance' (Aspinwall 1998: 197). The absence of 'strong EU-level parties' has been long remarked, especially by those lamenting the uncertain legitimacy of the EU. If parties have a crucial role to play linking voters with governing decision-makers, as well as with opposing or countervailing political forces, that is, a govern-ment opposition, it would seem that the absence of parties is a contributing factor in the 'democratic deficit'. Yet we have three sets of party actors in the EU, namely, national parties, party groups in the European Parliament, and transnational party federations. When the phrase 'strong EU-level parties' is mentioned, there is an implicit acknowledgement of a certain function to be played, in a certain type of institutional environment. To put it bluntly, there is the assumption that European elections should link voters with a European Parliament, which itself would operate in an inter-institutional EU system in which its role would replicate that of a national parliament (with the Commission reproducing the role of a national executive). Until this 'parlia-mentarization' of the EU takes place, 'strong EU-level parties' would be unable to exist, having no apparent function. Therefore, according to this perspective, national parties are confined to their respective national arenas, and the two Euro-level party organi-zations find themselves ineffective in filling the 'advocacy void'. Is this the case, or has the process of Europeanization resulted so far in some development of 'partyness' in the EU system? Or, to put it another way, is there evidence of party actors taking part in EU multi-level governance? If so, what are the consequences for national parties?

The first question to answer is in what ways has Europeanization resulted in opportunities and/or constraints for parties? Unlike interest groups, the EU system has a profoundly different institutional logic for parties, and although we will note

---

Box 14.2 Types of Party actors

National parties: operating in domestic political systems, aiming to win elections and/or influence national public policy.

European Parliament (EP) party groups: parliamentary party groups composed of national delegations elected in European elections every five years; Member's of European Parliament (MEP's) sit according to party family, for example, Green, Socialist, Christian Democrat, etc. They operate and organize the EP's work through committees etc.

Transnational party federations: 'parties of parties', with national parties composing the membership. Organized according to party family: Party of European Socialists, European Green Party, European People's Party-European Democrats (conservative and Christian Democrats), Groups of the United Left (Communists), etc.

'top-down' as well as 'bottom-up' Europeanization dynamics, there is not the kind of hospitable EU-level institutional 'goodness of fit' (Risse, Cowles, and Caporaso 2001) for parties as there has been for interest groups to pursue goals. Further, the relationship between Euro-parties and their national counterparts is fundamentally different than for interest groups. To the extent that we assume organizations seek to adapt to their environments, the differences between national political systems and the EU have resulted in dissimilar party organizational actors. The consequence for the relationship between sets of Euro-parties and national parties is that a mixed supranational–intergovernmental logic governs the relationship, with intergovernmental (that is national) influence predominant.

To begin, we should note that Europeanization, in the sense of 'bottom-up' dynamics, has not resulted in national parties lobbying either individually or in a Euro-group vis-à-vis the European Commission, as the putative executive. And in fact one would not expect this as a party behaviour; rather, some form of executive–legislative relationship between the EP and Commission would be closer to a traditional interaction in which party numbers in the EP would determine roles of government and opposition behaviour. This is, of course, not the case among these EU institutions, and the lack of such a readily identifiable form of 'government' at the EU level is a contributing factor to the weak association of average national party members and voters with EU institutions.[3] Without an elected Commission (executive), the work of the EP in the legislative dimension nevertheless proceeds in important ways, for instance in the scrutiny of EU institutions. However, its role as the body to which the Commission is accountable is, at best, underdeveloped.[4] This is the first, very basic point to bear in mind, that is, the EU level does not correspond to the familiar system in which all national parties in competitive liberal democracies operate. Consequently, any involvement would either have to be according to this level's own institutional dynamics, or else be generally absent.

Second, the two Euro-level party actors are themselves quite different in organization and function. The first, the EP party groups, do exist and function in a clearly demarcated institutional environment, the EP, which has defined sets of rules governing their activities (Kreppel 2002). It would be fair to say that the work of the EP depends on the tactics and interactions of the party groups, in particular the largest ones for staffing positions such as President, but most are involved in the committee work of the EP, one of its most significant contributions to the EU legislative process. On the other hand, transnational party federations, although they have experienced organizational development during the 1990s—notably the Greens, Liberals, Socialists, and Christian Democrats/conservatives (Johansson and Zervakis 2002), remain on the margins of EU politics (see Ladrech 2000 for the case of the Party of European Socialists in policy-making matters). Transnational party federations are caught up in a transnational limbo, so to speak, in which they are organizationally speaking 'parties of parties',[5]

---

[3] It also explains to a degree the continuing nature of European elections as 'second-order'. See Reif and Schmitt (1980).

[4] The resignation of the Santer Commission in 1999 represents one of those defining episodes that incrementally alter this relationship in favour of the EP.

[5] Some, such as the European People's Party (EPP), have an individual membership option, but this has yet to produce any noticeable internal dynamics in the EPP.

that is, the membership is composed of national parties, but they also depend on resources that derive from their respective EP party group.[6] They exist primarily as organizational platforms for the projection of collective national party leaders' concerns. On the one hand, they serve as a partisan-hospitable meeting point for national parties to discuss common matters, perhaps even introducing and/or influencing perspectives on European level issues. On the other hand, unlike the EP party groups, they have no 'purpose-built' institutional link with any of the EU bodies.

Third, if a prime function of parties is to link voters with government, then both Euro-party types fail. Although Members of the European Parliament (MEPs) are elected, these elections have been described as 'second-order', and in fact, it is the case that they are scarcely European, for national parties display relatively 'little genuine interest in European elections . . . especially among party leaders. This is natural, for the primary channel for influencing EU policy is by holding executive office at the national level, not through winning seats in the Parliament' (Raunio 2002a: 271). Transnational party federations hold even less interest for average party members and voters, for their 'mission' is ill-defined in that they have no specifically formal function within the EU system.[7] Decisions by the executive bodies of these 'parties' are also not ratified by national party members or voters. Delegates to the congresses of these parties are usually appointed as well, such that a democratic or grassroots mandate is missing. In the end, it is safe to say that although these two party organizations share some attributes normally associated with political parties, they are quite removed from the functions linked with parties in national systems, though the work of the EP party groups in the operation of the EP is important.

Finally, the linkage with the national party, for both party organizations, is extremely significant, because it is a key factor in explaining the degree to which Europeanization is reflected in changed circumstances for these actors. In a word, national parties are in a position to act as a *constraint* on the development of both types of party organization. In the case of EP party groups, the national delegation is a crucial actor in the formation and operation of party groups, going so far as to contest and consequently arrange the distribution of positions in committees, etc. National delegations, of course, take their cues from the national party, whether in government or the opposition. In this manner, the national party plays an indirect role in the activities of the EP. As was noted above, national parties run European election campaigns, and just as important for the staffing of the EP, the list of candidates is determined by national parties. This power of selection, another source of national influence on EP affairs, means that MEPs have an incentive to remain in good standing with their national party if they wish to be re-elected. Finally, national political dynamics may dictate the professional career patterns of MEPs (Scarrow 1997), such that they may be called upon to fill an important position in national politics as it may arise. These three aspects of indirect national influence on EP party groups through

---

[6] The draft statute on the financing of such parties was presented at the Nice intergovernmental conference, but this still awaits ratification at the time of writing.

[7] The manifestos on which national parties campaign are drafted and approved at congresses of the transnational parties. However, in most cases, these documents are ignored by the parties themselves. See Pennings (2002) for a discussion of the diversity of policy positions in these manifestos.

national party constraints on MEPs represent a conditional factor in the Europeanization process. However much the EP itself may strengthen its position within the EU policy-making process, and the implications of this in relation to increased lobbying by other forces, for example, interest groups, national governments, etc., the consequences for the development of party groups remains tempered by national considerations.

As for the transnational party federations, their environment—neither national nor supranational—and the lack of a specific 'target' to focus their actions, has meant that they remain, at best, projections of national party leaders' partisan aspirations at a European level. Bearing in mind that whatever issue a particular transnational party federation may pursue has been developed as a result of negotiation by all party leaders representing an entire party family, quite often the agenda items of these party actors is very general indeed. The supranational-intergovernmental logic in regards to transnational party federations is entirely tilted in favour of national actors.

Europeanization understood in its 'bottom-up' dimension is variable according to the particular type of party actor. For EP party groups, their development has been dependent on that of the EP itself, and over the course of the 1990s their role in the EU policy-making process increased. We can state then that their systemic function has witnessed a development consistent with notions of Europeanization. At the same time, the national considerations mentioned above condition their specific institutional attributes, and on occasion this indirect influence can have significant repercussions.[8] As for transnational party federations, although they have a function to play concerning national party leaders (see Hix 1996), and have experienced modest organizational development, their potential as effective European level actors remains unfulfilled.

As for national parties and 'top-down' Europeanization, the picture is mixed. On the one hand, conceiving national governments as *party government* means that any increase in the EU's policy competence in areas formerly under national control has an indirect effect on the range of policy issues that parties can legitimately claim to be able to resolve (Ladrech 2000; Mair 1995; 2001). As a result of the last stage in the introduction of Economic and Monetary Union (EMU), it could be said that an entire realm of economic policy-making has been taken out of the hands of party-political considerations. On the other hand, European integration has not resulted in any direct, explicit constitutional changes that impact the role of parties within their national environments. Thus national elections, legislative–executive relations, and other functions and activities normally associated with parties have not been formally disadvantaged (nor advantaged for that matter). Indirectly, however, European elections add another dimension to intra-system competitive dynamics, even if they do not impact national party systems to any great degree (Mair 2001). We might also note that national parliamentary party groups have suffered from the ability of national executives to enjoy a privileged relationship with EU actors and decision making, a feature of the national dimension of the 'democratic deficit' (Ladrech 1993) in which the scrutiny power of national parliaments is reduced. 'Top-down' Europeanization can

---

[8] In the case of the vote on investing the Santer Commission in 1995, the Spanish Socialist delegation heeded Madrid's insistence on departing from the EP Socialist Groups anti-Santer position.

be said, therefore, to have an effect on national parties in an indirect manner, that is, to the extent that national systems of governance have reduced their policy scope and have augmented the position of national executives vis-à-vis national parliaments.

Europeanization and political parties, in its broadest reading, fundamentally departs from the experience of interest groups in the confinement of the two main party actors within their respective levels. EP party groups are only involved in national settings in two types of activity, through the output of their EP voting behaviour and relations between national delegation and their national party. Relations with national parliamentary groups occurs, but not on a widespread basis. In both of these types of activity, the national party or government leadership is in a position to influence the EP national delegation, that is, the Euro-level actors are in a dependent relationship with the corresponding national actor. As we have seen, EP partisan activity is not a prime concern of national party leaderships, and although this may mean a certain amount of latitude for EP national delegations, ultimately the national party can sanction MEP's. We can say, therefore, that EP party groups do not have any noticeable effect in national arenas. As for national parties, although they have the opportunity to influence the EP's legislative behaviour through their national delegation, this influence is dissolved in the large number of partisan groups even within national delegations. In the third and fourth European legislatures, 1989–99, the British Labour Party delegation within the Socialist Group was much larger than the rest (owing to the use of first-past-the-post voting for British MEPs), and this conferred upon it certain privileges such as chairs of committees, secretary-general of the Group, etc. Despite this advantage, intra-group negotiation was still necessary as this plurality of seats was counterbalanced by all of the other delegations. Apart from the EP, national parties have attempted to use their transnational party federations, or at least the meetings of its party leaders, to push certain agendas (Johansson 1999; 2002). Yet, as noted above, this type of activity is marginal to the normal operation of the EU policy-making process. Party actors as government ministers have a route to EU decision-making in the Council of Ministers, or even the European Council, but national rather than partisan dynamics dominate their behaviour. In the end, national parties continue to focus their attention and operations in the national arena, as all of the rewards and resources are still located in this sphere.

Assessing the Europeanization of political parties

Has the authoritativeness of national parties diminished as a result of Europeanization? There has been some change, namely an erosion in the legitimacy of parties as purposive actors, and the enhancement of the role of interest groups in influencing national government (and national-preference formation for EU bargaining purposes). Parties, through election campaigns, promise to deliver a set of policies distinguishable from their competitors. As the scope of what national government can accomplish narrows, this indirectly affects parties in terms of what they can promise. For those parties in more statist systems, this phenomenon challenges them to redefine their programmatic understanding of the use of government as a tool for policy change. A further aspect of European integration, the emphasis on coordination with other non-national actors, also dilutes somewhat the use of government to produce significant alterations in public policies. One could say that it narrows the policy space between the centre-left and centre-right on a host of different issues, especially economic. An indirect effect of this trend may be growing voter disillusionment with electoral politics. Another change in the situation of national parties is their relationship with interest groups. Parties represent channels of influence for allied interest groups in government policy-making. If the ability of parties to present policy packages clearly favourable to certain interests that have been historically aggregated by the relevant party decreases, the incentive for interest groups to continue to support parties with resources may decline, due to their increased capacity to access information and lobby non-national actors such as the European Commission and EP (Raunio 2002b). In other words, the different relationships and networks that make up national systems of interest intermediation may evolve in such a way as to slightly downgrade the position of parties, and increase the role of interest groups with national administrations, not the least of which for the reason that they are less confined to the national level and are consequently useful as holders of information in the policy development stage as it pertains to issues with a EU component.

Along these lines, the ability of parties to articulate and aggregate the demands and interests of voters is weakened. This occurs for two reasons. First, as the policy-making capacity of national government declines in some areas (Scharpf 1994), parties are either forced to remain silent on issues that they have no means to influence, or develop a discourse that has relevance in linking national needs to some form of multi-level action (Schmidt 2002). This of course presupposes that parties acknowledge the authority of the EU in certain areas and attempt to link their agendas with change at the EU level. This has not occurred, as witnessed by the absence of truly European issue campaigns during European Parliament elections, or visibility of national ministers and government positions in EU bargaining and negotiations. Thus parties find themselves in an ever-increasing dilemma as to how to articulate or represent interests in a meaningful manner.

Finally, has the interactive relationship between national and European level party actors changed in any substantial ways? The confinement to levels, as mentioned above, puts a limit on the possible degree of change. Nevertheless, there is evidence of national parties taking their MEP's more seriously in the form of integrating their delegations' leadership within the national party's executive bodies.[9] Furthermore, as MEP's expertise and information on policies with a EU competence become more widely recognized in national parties and national parliamentary groups, relations between them and national parliaments have evolved (Raunio and Hix 2001). In addition, regional parties have resorted to joining or creating their own EP party group as a means to enhance their stature and resources through the EU's emphasis on sub-national representation and its Cohesion policy (De Winter and Gomez-Reino 2002). Though these changes are minor, they reflect Europeanization in the sense that national parties are seeking to improve their position vis-à-vis the EU level by accessing and improving their means to 'insider' information through their own agents.

[9] This is the case with the British Labour Party, in which the leader of Labour's EP delegation is automatically included on its national executive committee (NEC). For a theoretical discussion of the relationship between national parties and their EP members, see ESRC grant No R000239793, 'The Europeanisation of National Political Parties', Poguntke, Aylott, Ladrech, Luther, grantholders.

Conclusions and outlook

Europeanization as it has been employed in this volume describes a process of adaptation and evolution, that is, national actors adapting to the influence of the EU and European level actors evolving in accordance with the transfer of competences from the national to the supranational level. These twin dimensions of Europeanization do not unfold in isolation from one another, and indeed analysing the interactive dimension sheds light on the factors promoting and controlling the adaptive and evolutionary process. What seems clear is that for interest groups, the EU is indeed a multi-level system in which they are relatively free to pursue their goals with the appropriate partner and/or institution. The EU system has been a key factor in the motivation of national interest groups to both form Euro-level associations and for themselves to directly lobby EU institutions. The fact that the EU, especially the Commission, was hospitable to various interests has 'played a key role in stimulating the emergence of a fully fledged EU interest group intermediation system' (Mazey and Richarson 1999: 105). Multi-level governance 'works' if the levels are not closed, but instead are open planes of competition and contestation in which various actors can creatively pursue their goals. As we have seen, the channels by which interest groups can simultaneously engage with national, sub-national and supranational institutions and actors does not render them 'rootless'; on the contrary, the Europeanization process has meant that the different levels are complementary (if not interwoven), and the level from which they originate continues to structure the goals and strategies of various interests.

The nature and logic of the institutional arenas in which parties seek to achieve their goals correspond less to the multi-level governance thesis. National parties are indeed affected by the increases in the EU's scope of policy competence, but in an indirect manner through the exercise of party government and their linkages with domestic interest groups and voters. Yet their goals, rewards, and resources are fundamentally confined to their national arena. In the same manner, EP party groups are creatures of the European Parliament, and while the relationship between the EP and national parliaments remains 'uncoupled', EP party groups' activities will not have much of an impact in domestic systems, much less in the party life of their national counterparts. Transnational party federations have yet to develop beyond a form of national party elite interaction, and consequently the emergence of a European party system (not to be confused with the party system within the European Parliament) remains to be created, one possible means by which European voters might have the opportunity to influence EU policy-making.

Parties and interest groups, traditionally understood by their organization and activities, are not the only political forces that have experienced a 'turn towards Europe.' Imig and Tarrow (2001) present evidence of new strategies and targets of action by social and protest movements. The EU also represents a political opportunity structure for movements such as refugees, environmental and women's, as well as a target for protests by farmers and trade unions (that is, outside the 'normal' forms of lobbying). National organizational, cultural, political, and institutional features explain the chances of European-level associations among these groups, and in some instances the aim of protests at national targets represents a claim against EU policies. Political forces, out of self-preservation as well as promotion of their interests, have sought out the best means to adapt to the multi-level nature of the EU. European integration has not resulted in the end of the nation-state, but national actors must nevertheless accommodate new environmental variables in the pursuit of their goals. Some actors (interest groups) are better able to exploit the new environment, mostly as a means to complement whatever is the primary arena of their activities. For others (parties), for whom the primary objective is, generally speaking, to form party *government*, the European system of *governance* rests uneasily with their capacity to adapt to a multi-level system.

Finally, we turn to the challenge facing the ten states which joined the EU in 2004. Parties and interest groups in the new member states will experience many similar dynamics as described above. However, there is an additional element regarding the nature and activities of parties and interest groups in the eight former communist countries that joined in May 2004. In the ten years or more since their governments applied to join the EU, and bearing in mind the enormous efforts to integrate the acquis communautaire into their social, economic and legal systems, post-communist party organisations and interest groups have developed with the goal—amongst others—to enter the EU. For parties, membership was crucial in transnational party federations, not only for the technical advice—and in some cases financial resources—but also for the legitimacy that affiliation with long-established government parties in the west would bring. Interaction with Western party leaders, many of whom are prime ministers, will have aided in accelerating the socialization of east-central European political elites to EU politics and bargaining. Interest groups—as well as most elements of civil society—will also have developed their organizational profile during the massive transformation of the state-owned command economy to market-driven dynamics. During this transformation, applicant governments were assisted by such EU programmes as PHARE etc., and expertise on the EU policy-making process was transmitted. The result is that the impact of enlargement onto the existing EU in terms of additional actors with far different backgrounds is less than if EU actors and institutions had not 'reached out' to them in the 1990s. The integration of post-communist parties and interest groups into the EU decision-making process is therefore affected by the external efforts to assist in training and the internal/domestic stability of the respective countries as they evolve norms and processes that allow a good 'fit' with the EU.

Further reading

The literature on interest groups and the EU is abundant, and could be traced back to the early neo-functionalist theorists. Nevertheless, a good place to begin is Mazey and Richardson (1993), followed by Greenwood (1997) and Greenwood and Aspinwall (1998). Europeanization, national interests and the EU is explored in Cowles, Caporaso and Risse (2001). European integration and national political systems is analysed in Goetz and Hix (2001), and more specifically Europeanization and parties is the topic of a special issue of *Party Politics* (2002). On parties and the EU more generally, see Hix and Lord (1997).

Weblinks

The most relevant web links are those of the individual interest groups and political parties. Thus, for interest groups, see <http://www.unice.org> for the website of the Union of Industrial and Employers' Federations; <http://www.etuc.org> for the European Trade Union Confederation; <http://www.beuc.org> for the European Consumers Association; and <http://www.socialplatform.org> for the Platform of European Social NGOs. Each of the transnational party federations also have websites: <http://www.pes.org> for the Party of European Socialists; <http://www.epp-eu.org> for the European People's Party (Christian Democrats); <http://www.eldr.org> is the website of the European Liberal Democrats; and <http://www.europeangreens.org> is that of the European Federation of Green Parties.

References

Aspinwall, M. (1998), 'Collective attraction—the new political game in Brussels', in Greenwood and Aspinwall 196–213.

Aspinwall, M., and Greenwood, J. (1998), 'Conceptualising collective action in the European Union: an introduction', in Greenwood and Aspinwall 1–30.

Beyers, J. (2002), 'Gaining and seeking access: The European adaptation of domestic interest associations', *European Journal of Political Research*, 41/5, 585–612.

Cowles, M., Caporaso, J., and Risse, T. (2001) (eds), *Transforming Europe: Europeanization and Domestic Change* (Ithaca NY and London: Cornell University Press).

Cram, L. (1998), 'The EU institutions and collective action: constructing a European interest?', in Greenwood and Aspinwall, 63–80.

De Winter, L., and Gomez-Reino, M. (2002), 'European Integration and Ethnoregionalist Parties', *Party Politics*, 8/4, 483–503.

Fairbrass, J., and Jordan, A. (2001), 'Protecting biodiversity in the European Union: national barriers and European opportunities?', *Journal of European Public Policy*, 8/4, 499–518.

Falkner, G. (2001), 'Policy Networks in a Multi-Level System: Convergence Towards Moderate Diversity?', in Goetz and Hix, 94–120.

Goetz, K., and Hix, S. (2001), *Europeanised Politics? European Integration and National Political Systems* (London: Frank Cass).

Greenwood, J. (1997), *Representing Interests in the European Union* (London: Macmillan).

Greenwood, J., and Aspinwall, M. (1998) (eds), *Collective Action in the European Union* (London: Routledge).

Hix, S. (1996), 'The transnational party federations', in J. Gaffney (ed.), *Political Parties and the European Union* (London: Routledge), 308–31.

Hix, S., and Lord, C. (1997), *Political Parties in the European Union* (Basingstoke: Macmillan).

Hooghe, L., and Marks, G. (2001), *Multi-Level Governance and European Integration* (Lanham MD: Rowman & Littlefield Publishers).

Imig, D., and Tarrow, S. (2001) (eds), *Contentious Europeans: Protest and Politics in an Emerging Polity* (Lanham MD: Rowman & Littlefield Publishers).

Johansson, K-M. (1999), 'Tracing the Employment Title in the Amsterdam Treaty: Uncovering Transnational Coalitions', *Journal of European Public Policy* 6/1, 85–101.

Johansson, K-M. (2002), 'Party Elites in Multilevel Europe: The Christian Democrats and the Single European Act', *Party Politics* 8/4, 423–40.

Johansson, K-M., and Zervakis, P. (2002) (eds). *European Political Parties Between Cooperation and Integration* (Baden-Baden: Nomos Verlag).

Kassim, H. *et al.* (2000) (ed.), *The National Co-ordination of EU Policy: The Domestic Level* (Oxford: Oxford University Press).

Kohler-Koch, B. (1999), 'The Evolution and Transformation of European Governance', in B. Kohler-Koch and R. Eising (eds), *The Transformation of Governance in the European Union* (London: Routledge), 14–36.

Kreppel, A. (2002), *The European Parliament and Supranational Party System: A Study in Institutional Development* (Cambridge: Cambridge University Press).

Ladrech, R. (1993), 'Parliamentary democracy and Political Discourse in EC Institutional Change', *Journal of European Integration*, 17/1, 53–69.

Ladrech, R. (2000), *Social Democracy and the Challenge of European Union* (Boulder CO and London: Lynne Rienner Publishers).

Mair, P. (1995), 'Political Parties, Popular Legitimacy and Public Privilege', in J. Hayward (ed.), *The Crisis of Representation in Europe* (London: Frank Cass).

Mair, P. (2001), 'The Limited Impact of Europe on National Party Systems', in Goetz and Hix, 27–51.

Mazey, S., and Richardson, J. (1993) (eds), *Lobbying in the European Community* (Oxford: Oxford University Press).

Mazey, S., and Richardson, J. (1999), 'Interests', in L. Cram, D. Dinan, and N. Nugent, 105–29.

Mazey, S., and Richardson, J. (2001), 'Interest groups and EU policy-making: organisational logic and venue shopping', in J. Richardson (ed.), *European Union: Power and Policy-Making* (London: Routledge), 217–38.

Party Politics (2002), special issue 'Europeanization of Party Politics', in R. Ladrech (ed.).

Pennings, P. (2002), 'The Dimensionality of the EU Policy Space: The European Elections of 1999', *European Union Politics*, 3/1, 59–80.

Radaelli, C. (2000), 'Whither Europeanization?: Concept Stretching and Substantive Change', *European Integration online Papers (EioP)* <http://eiop.or.at/eiop/texte/2000-008a.htm>.

Raunio, T. (2002a), 'Political Interests: The EP Party Groups', in J. Peterson and M. Shackleton (eds), *The Institutions of the European Union* (Oxford: Oxford University Press), 257–76.

Raunio, T. (2002b), 'Why European Integration Increases Leadership Autonomy within Political Parties', *Party Politics*, 8/4, 405–22.

Raunio, T., and Hix, S. (2001), 'Backbenchers Learn to Fight Back: European Integration and Parliamentary Government', in Goetz and Hix, 142–68.

Reif, K., and Schmitt, H. (1980), 'Nine Second-Order National Elections: A Conceptual Framework for the Analysis of European Election Results', *European Journal of Political Research*, 8/1, 3–44.

Risse, T., Cowles, M., and Caporaso, J. (2001), 'Europeanization and Domestic Change: Introduction', in M. Cowles, J. Caporaso, and T. Risse (eds), *Transforming Europe: Europeanization and Domestic Change* (Ithaca NY and London: Cornell University Press), 1–20.

Scarrow, S. (1997), 'Political Career Paths and the European Parliament', *Legislative Studies Quarterly*, 22/2, 253–63.

Scharpf, F. (1994), 'Community and Autonomy: Multi-level Policy-Making in the European Union', *Journal of European Public Policy*, 1/2, 219–42.

Scharpf, F. (1999), *Governing in Europe: Effective and Democratic?* (Oxford: Oxford University Press).

Schmidt, V. (1997), 'European integration and democracy: the differences among member states', *Journal of European Public Policy*, 4/1, 128–45.

Schmidt, V. (2002), 'Does Discourse Matter in the Politics of Welfare State Adjustment?', *Comparative Political Studies*, 35/2, 168–93.

Warleigh, A. (2000), 'The hustle: citizenship practice, NGOs and "policy coalitions" in the European Union—the cases of Auto Oil, drinking water and unit pricing', *Journal of European Public Policy*, 7/2: 229–43.

Chapter 15

The Europeanization of National Policy[1]

Simon J. Bulmer and Claudio M. Radaelli

CONTENTS

Summary

Europeanization has had a profound impact upon the public policy functions of the member states. However, the impact has not been uniform. Member states have lost much of the scope for independent action in some areas, such as monetary policy or trade. In others the impact has been much more fragmented: on areas such as health care or employment policy. Between these two extremes lie the majority of policy areas. In reviewing this subject matter we explore the dynamics of Europeanization: what are the processes involved and the effects produced? We then relate the processes and effects to categories of policy in order to map the Europeanization of public policy.

[1] Earlier versions of this chapter were available on-line in the Queen's University Belfast Europeanization papers and (in Romanian) at: <http: //www. studiidesecuritate.ro/ index. html>.

Why Europeanization?

Although both the general notion of 'Europeanization of member states' and the more specific idea of 'Europeanization of domestic policy' are not new, in recent years there has been an exponential growth of research projects adopting this perspective (Cowles, Caporaso, and Risse 2001; Featherstone 2003). Some aspects of what goes under the label of Europeanization are more often than not a simple re-branding of classic research themes. However, there are also substantive reasons for the growth of interest in this topic. They refer both to the evolution of European integration and to the internal dynamics of research agendas in political science and public policy analysis. Let us look at the changing nature of integration in the European Union (EU) first and then consider the internal dynamics.

There are at least four macro-dynamics in 'the real world out there' that stimulated a redirection of the intellectual debate toward Europeanization. One is the institutionalization of the single market. Although the EU is in a sense still completing the internal market, the sheer volume of EU directives, regulations, and jurisprudence affecting domestic markets increased dramatically from the Single European Act (1986) onwards (see Fligstein and McNichol 1998: 75–85).

The second reason refers to the advent of Economic and Monetary Union (EMU). Not only has EMU created a single currency and interest rate regime across participant member states (the euro-zone) but it has heightened still further the degree of interdependency amongst other policies. Within the Euro zone, the 'culture of stability' enshrined in EMU has provided direction to the debate on major issues such as labour market reforms and changes in national pension regimes. The consequences are not confined simply to the character of national policy but also affect the process by which it is formulated. Thus employment policy has become more subject to EU-wide considerations as a consequence of EMU. At the same time there is also evidence that EMU may have changed the 'game' of politics in some countries, by empowering certain actors and disempowering others (Dyson and Featherstone 1999).

Europeanization is not simply the product of a widening in the array of policies carried out at EU level. It also occurs as a result of processes that are more market-driven: a third macro-dynamic. A process that ran parallel to the creation of the single market was an emergent pattern of regulatory competition. Although we still do not know very much about regulatory competition in Europe (Sun and Pelkmans 1985), there are political preoccupations concerning its unforeseen (and for some people undesirable) consequences. Mutual recognition and competition policy—this is the political argument—have locked domestic choices into a web of regulatory competition. A number of European policy-makers think that 'excessive' regulatory competition may have already spawned a race-to-the-bottom, detrimental to the cause of the welfare state and the European social model. It is interesting to observe that the *Foreign Affairs* article by Krugman (1994) on the 'obsession with competitiveness' was extremely well received in Europe. So much so that Rudolf Scharping (at that time chairman of the German Social Democrats), writing in the same journal a few months later, turned Krugman's academic analysis into a plea for immediate action against the 'market for tax evasion' and other monsters created by excessive competition

(Scharping 1994: 193). Europeanization may thus be a process whereby national policies adjust to seek competitive advantage within a broad EU policy context. In other words the adjustment of national policy is not simply to some EU requirement but in this case to a market dynamic unleashed by the global economy but 'framed' by a set of EU rules.

A final key dynamic that is currently to the fore with the ongoing process of enlargement. Although this process has not yet concluded, since absorption of the new states is ongoing and further applications are pending, the negotiations with candidate countries can be seen as a colossal exercise in policy transfer. The EU was trying to export the *acquis communautaire* lock, stock, and barrel. Additionally, the EU was making an effort to transfer rules and norms of democratic behaviour to new member states, going well beyond the domain of the single market. The Copenhagen criteria (1993) governing accession identified standards that would-be members had to meet with regard to the rule of law, democracy, human rights, as well as on economic adjustment. Not only was the EU engaged in a formidable export of its regulatory pillar, it was also seeking to transfer the normative pillar (see Laffan 2001 on the relations between these pillars of the EU). Insofar as Europeanization has the EU as its source, enlargement represented the largest example of this process. The 'Europeanization effect' was therefore very strong externally—at least until the accession of most of those states to the EU in May 2004, at which point the process became, for them, internal.

The accumulated effect of these developments prompts the question: what is left for national public policy? Virtually every policy area is now affected to a greater or lesser extent by the EU. The ramifications of this development reach well beyond the bounds of this chapter. They include, not least, the question 'what is left to be decided by national politics and, specifically, domestic elections'? National elections are still contested on the basis of policy choices, but policies are substantially decided in Brussels. At the same time, it is argued that there is no real political debate at the EU level on policies, because the EU policy process is technocratic (Mair 2001). This political asymmetry is a major reason for concern about the hollowing out of elections as a tool to decide the content of public policy.

Looking at these changes to Europe, it is little surprise that there has been an increased academic interest in Europeanization (see Featherstone 2003: 5). And this is precisely what has happened over the last few years. Having spent intellectual energy in seeking to understand the 'nature of the beast', that is, the nature of European integration, political scientists have now realized that a EU political system is in place, produces decisions, and impacts on domestic policies in various guises. Hence the focus has shifted to studying those impacts. Additionally, Europeanization intrigues political scientists because it is a model-building exercise. The challenge is to model the impact of European integration on domestic policy, knowing that at the same time domestic politics is a major factor at work in EU political change (Olsen 2002). The boundaries between cause and effect, independent and dependent variables are blurred, as is demonstrated in Tanja Börzel's discussion of Europeanization as uploading and downloading (see Chapter 3). And if this is not enough to make the modelling of Europeanization complex, there are two further problems. One is that neither the EU nor the member states are static, so Europeanization is a matter of reciprocity between moving features. The second is that attribution of domestic change to the EU is not always easy, since globalization is also a force at work. Europeanization thus offers the opportunity to take a fresher look at domestic policy change caused by open and interdependent markets. Classic international political economy has dealt with the implications of globalization for domestic policy choices, often emphasizing the constraints that are imposed. New research agendas associated with Europeanization raise other questions:

- Is Europeanization a bastion against globalization (in this case understood as 'Americanization')?

- Is Europeanization (as opposed to globalization) a convenient discourse for legitimising domestic reform (Hay and Rosamond 2002)? Put another way, is Europeanization a manifestation of globalization?

- Or is it a 'mix' of both of these that is dependent on the particular circumstances within individual member states (also see Hay and Rosamond 2002)?

Types of Europeanization

Having explained why Europeanization of policy is a hot topic, one needs to understand it. Elsewhere in this volume a range of definitions has been utilized. In this chapter we understand it in a relatively broad manner, as set out in Box 15.1. This definition is important because it identifies a number of features of Europeanization that we will deploy in the empirical part of the chapter. It highlights three particular features of Europeanization:

- It can derive from different stages and forms of the policy process: policy formulation (construction); putting policy into practice (institutionalization); and in a much less structured manner (diffusion), where the EU's role may be quite limited.

- Europeanization is not simply about formal policy rules but about less tangible aspects, such as beliefs and values.

- The concept of Europeanization is about the *impact* of European policy within member states. It thus entails two steps: adoption at EU level and then incorporation at the domestic level. The former step alone is only part of the story. That is why Europeanization and EU policy-making are distinct from each other conceptually.

Box 15.1 A definition of Europeanization

Europeanization consists of processes of (a) construction, (b) diffusion and (c) institutionalization of formal and informal rules, procedures, policy paradigms, styles, 'ways of doing things', and shared beliefs and norms which are first defined and consolidated in the EU policy process and then incorporated in the logic of domestic (national and sub-national) discourse, political structures, and public policies.

How can we move from these preliminary observations to something more analytical: something that allows us to understand the dynamics of the Europeanization process? One way is to look at the different modes of EU policy-making, as identified in the existing literature.[2] However, these modes have not been devised with Europeanization in mind and fall foul of the concerns raised in the third bullet point above. Our preference is to devise a typology that is built on analytical categories which target the research questions of Europeanization studies.

Drawing upon the work of Fritz Scharpf (1997), Christoph Knill (2001) and Bulmer and Padgett (2005), we identify four characteristic patterns of governance in the European Union, each associated with a particular type of policy. As with any framework with only four patterns, we should point out that this simplifies what is a more complex situation. We then seek to identify the analytical core, the mechanism of Europeanization and the explanatory factors that apply to each of the four patterns. Later in the paper we go on to utilise these categories to explain 'the real world' of the Europeanization of national policy. Let us look at each of the four patterns of governance in turn.

Governance by negotiation

The European Union is in a constant state of negotiation across multiple policy areas: everything from fisheries through foreign policy to immigration. The EU's authority varies considerably across the range of policy areas: from having exclusive authority (for instance, on the internal market) to having limited powers of setting targets (employment policy). However, in each case where the EU takes a decision—whether legally binding or a mere declaration—it is the culmination of a process of negotiation. The analytical core concerning how such decisions come about derives from the long-standing debate about the relative authority of the supranational institutions and the member states.

How does governance by negotiation relate to Europeanization? The answer to this question lies in the fact that European policy does not emerge from thin air but derives from a process, namely that of negotiation. The member governments are central to this process: either by being directly seated at the negotiating table or by means of having set the terms under which power has been delegated to such supranational bodies as the Commission or the European Court of Justice. The typical form that Europeanization takes at this stage is the 'uploading' that is outlined by Tanja Börzel in Chapter 3. National policy models or rules are inserted into EU-level negotiations, with the most likely outcome being a synthesis, although very occasionally one state may be especially influential. An example of the latter was in environmental emissions policy, specifically with the large combustion directive. As Albert Weale puts it 'the relevant official . . . was simply given the agreed German large combustion ordinance and told to translate it into Euro-speak' (1996: 603). It then became the basis for negotiation amongst governments. More typically, however, EU policy templates

---

[2] One categorization of policy-making is that proposed by Helen Wallace, and comprising five variants: the Community method, the EU regulatory model, multilevel governance, policy coordination and benchmarking, and intensive transgovernmentalism (Wallace 2000: 28–35).

are a synthetic construction arising from different national approaches and the inevitable horse-trading during negotiations.

In the initial negotiating phase, namely where policy is under construction, the explanations for the extent of Europeanization lie in the extent of convergence of preferences on the part of the member states, the voting rules in the Council, and the learning that takes place over repeated sessions of negotiation. The potential for the Europeanization of national policy is greatest where the member governments are able to agree policy because their interests converge. It is also greatest where they are encouraged by Council rules to avoid unanimous voting and the use of national veto power. In consequence, individual members are much less likely to pursue obstructionist negotiating strategies in the Council of Ministers, for fear that they will be overruled. Finally, repeated negotiations may encourage the construction of a shared understanding of the issues. Some policy areas require several rounds of legislation as part of a process of building up a shared understanding of new arrangements, for instance in the case of air transport liberalization's three packages (Armstrong and Bulmer 1998: 169–97). The creation of a shared understanding of policy through learning on the part of the participants is important for the potential for the success of Europeanization when policy comes to be put into practice. In each of the three factors, where the converse conditions apply, the prospects for Europeanization of national policy are likely to be much weaker.[3]

We have included this form of Europeanization in the chapter for the sake of completeness in understanding the process. However, we are not suggesting that Europeanization is synonymous with European integration or EU policy-making. Rather, we are making clear that the process of agreeing EU policy is inextricably linked with the prospect, later in the policy process, that a change in policy will ensue at the national level. If national policy is to be Europeanized, EU policy must have an impact at the domestic level. In moving to this next stage in the policy process, we explore the different patterns of governance whereby EU policy is put into practice at domestic level: governance by hierarchy and facilitated coordination.

Governance by hierarchy

Governance by hierarchy relates to those circumstances where the supranational institutions have a considerable amount of power delegated to them. The institutions concerned are the Commission, the Council and the European Court of Justice (ECJ). At the end of the negotiation phase of governance (see above) the Council typically has agreed European legislation which needs to be put into practice in the member states. A set of 'command and control' mechanisms comes into play at this stage. These mechanisms derive from the uniquely supranational character of the EU and help to assure that agreements are put into effect by the member states. The enforcement mechanisms are designed to build trust by limiting the scope for individual

---

[3] It is worth pointing out that EU governance by negotiation is not always consistent with the patterns predominating in individual member states. France and the UK have strong traditions of political confrontation. For them Europeanization requires some kind of cultural shift towards negotiated governance.

states to cheat on the negotiated agreements. The exact character of the mechanisms and the consequent explanations of the dynamics of Europeanization vary according to what are known as positive and negative integration (Pinder 1968). We explore each of these in turn.

Positive integration

Positive integration requires the introduction of an active, supranational policy. Typically, the EU has negotiated a policy template, and the task is to put it into operation in the member states. In economic policy areas positive integration often entails market-correcting rules. That is to say, policy is designed to limit damaging effects of market processes: through pollution control, social policy, regional policy, veterinary policy to accompany the Common Agricultural Policy (CAP), and so on. In policy areas such as these the EU has to go through often arduous negotiations in order to agree the policy rules. But what is of key interest here is that the agreed policy template has to be 'downloaded' to the member state level. The Commission has to ensure that legislation is properly implemented, and it can refer laggard governments to the ECJ if necessary. The supremacy of European law is indicative of the hierarchical nature of arrangements. There is a pronounced coercive dimension in these arrangements, and it is the member governments that have to ensure that market-correction is put into practice effectively.

Negative integration

By contrast with positive integration, negative integration relates to areas where the removal of national barriers suffices to create a common policy. National legislation is often not required to put policy into practice. Indeed, in some cases even European legislation is unnecessary, since the rules may be embedded in the treaties themselves. The Commission is delegated extensive powers and the jurisprudence of the ECJ can be relied upon to enforce the framework of rules, such as those set down in the supranational treaties. Negative integration is typically concerned with 'market-making'. In other words, EU-level rules are designed to allow the efficient functioning of the market. A classic case is the EU's competition policy, which specifies what is admissible in terms of mergers or joint ventures between companies, pricing and market-sharing agreements between them and so on. Where there is doubt about the admissibility of an arrangement, the companies concerned must seek approval from the EU authorities. Similar arrangements obtain in the single market, where discrimination by nationality is outlawed, whether through through physical barriers (border controls), fiscal ones (tax regimes) or technical ones. In particular sectors of the economy, special rules may be needed in order to facilitate 'market-making'. Thus, there are special policy arrangements for areas such as telecommunications, energy, air transport, postal services, and so on. In these cases measures of positive integration are needed initially but the aim is still to allow markets to function subject to oversight, normally by the Commission.

The market that is created in this way has two dimensions. It is, first, a market amongst economic actors. Secondly, it is a market amongst differing national regimes. If the UK regime for the financial services sector or the new media is perceived as creating a better environment for the flourishing of business, then other member states may find they have to adjust their national set of rules. In short, the market-making character of negative integration creates a much more horizontal process of policy adjustment associated with Europeanization. In negative integration it is the competition amongst rules or amongst socio-economic actors that accounts for Europeanization rather than the need for national policy to comply with EU policy templates, as under positive integration.

Facilitated coordination

Facilitated coordination relates to those policy areas where the national governments are the key actors. This situation obtains where the policy process is not (or is negligibly) subject to European law; where decisions are subject to unanimity amongst the governments; or where the EU is simply an arena for the exchange of ideas. In practice these circumstances apply in such areas as foreign policy, police cooperation, and the whole range of policies covered by what is known as the Open Method of Coordination (OMC). In these areas agreements predominantly take two forms: political declarations or 'soft law'. Soft law relates to rules of conduct that are not legally enforceable but none the less have a legal scope in that they guide the conduct of the institutions, the member states and other policy participants (Wellens and Borchardt 1980: 285; see also Snyder 1994). Political declarations are often explicitly made in order *not* to have legal scope, such as in conclusions reached at the end of European summit meetings.

Whichever of these forms the agreements take, the supranational institutions have very weak powers: they cannot act as strong agents promoting Europeanization. Nevertheless, that does not mean that no Europeanization takes place, but simply that it is much more voluntary and non-hierarchical. If the member states cannot reach an agreement on policy, such as occurred in 2003 with foreign policy owing to the fundamental divisions on how to deal with the Iraqi regime of Saddam Hussein, then policy is not Europeanized. On the other hand, the exchange of practice on employment policy may lead to the cross-fertilization of ideas and learning. This is why this form of policy is concerned with the convergence of ideas. The lack of supranational powers in these policy areas explains the horizontal pattern of Europeanization. This pattern has prevailed in the Common Foreign and Security Policy (CFSP). Whilst many commentators have focused on the institutional short-comings of the CFSP, a strong 'coordination reflex' (procedural learning) developed (for example see Glarbo 1999: 643-5) and in some areas of policy a shared set of policy understandings has emerged, for instance over the Palestinian issue. These developments did not come about because of hierarchical governance but because of 'horizontal' exchanges between member government and the resultant learning of shared policy principles.

To summarize this section, we have identified three modes of governance in the EU, and they intersect with different types of policy to produce different mechanisms of Europeanization (see Table 15.1). These mechanisms may be vertical (uploading or downloading) or horizontal. In other words, Europeanization follows no single 'logic'.

Table 15.1 Governance, policy and the mechanisms of Europeanization

Mode of governance	Type of policy	Analytical core	Main mechanism
Negotiation	Any of those below	Formation of EU policy	Vertical (uploading)
Hierarchy	Positive integration	Market-correcting rules; EU policy templates	Vertical (downloading)
Hierarchy	Negative integration	Market-making rules; absence of policy templates	Horizontal
Facilitated coordination	Coordination	Soft law, OMC, policy exchange	Horizontal

Understanding the dynamics of Europeanization

We now turn our attention to the *interpretations* of the dynamics of Europeanization. At this stage we omit detailed consideration of Europeanization by negotiation, since this form is essentially a synonym for European integration or policy-making: a topic which has been covered extensively elsewhere (for example see Wallace and Wallace 2000). However, what we do wish to point out is that an absence of learning at this stage of the policy process—that is of all the member states developing a shared understanding of policy goals—may be storing up problems such that the Europeanization process is more fragile later on. We also draw attention to the evidence from some areas of market integration that the process of EU-level policy negotiation may bring forward domestic reforms already under consideration. There is evidence of this Europeanization-effect in the liberalization of the telecommunications and electricity sectors, where some states accelerated domestic reform in order to synchronize it with EU policy developments.[4] The main effects of Europeanization, however, are felt in connection with the other three modes of governance.

Goodness of fit

Let us start with the 'goodness of fit' argument, which was advanced by Risse, Cowles, and Caporaso (2000). They argued that, in order to produce domestic effects, EU policy must be somewhat difficult to absorb at the domestic level. If the policy of country A fits in well with EU policy, there will no impact: things can go on as they were before.

---

[4] This evidence has been revealed in a study of utilities regulation—undertaken by Simon Bulmer, David Dolowitz, Peter Humphreys, and Stephen Padgett and funded by the UK Economic and Social Research Council ('The European Union as a Medium of Policy Transfer: Case Studies in Utility Regulation', award no. L216252001-A).

At the other extreme, where country A has a policy which is completely different from the EU policy, it would be almost impossible to adapt to Europe. They argued that the impact of Europeanisation will be most pronounced in cases of moderate goodness of fit (Börzel and Risse 2003; Cowles et al. 2001). Domestic institutions play a key role in absorbing, rejecting, or domesticating Europe. Indeed, the 'goodness of fit' explanation is rooted in new institutionalist approaches to political behaviour.[5]

We argue that the 'goodness of fit' argument is valid under certain conditions (namely, the presence of EU policy templates or models). As such, it best applies to one type of policy—positive integration—rather than offering a general explanation. Let us see what the problems are if, following the suggestions of those who have put forward the 'goodness of fit' interpretation, one tries to use it as a general explanation of Europeanization. 'Goodness of fit' assumes a clear, vertical, chain-of-command, in which EU policy descends from Brussels into the member states. Domestic institutions are like rigid posts channelling the impact of Europe. But we know of cases in which EU policy has been an absolute innovation for domestic institutions. EU environmental policy started before Spanish environmental policy became a reality. The same applies to the transfer of competition policy to some candidate countries. To speak of 'goodness of fit' between EU policy and non-existent domestic policy is unconvincing.

More importantly still, the 'goodness of fit' explanation may be a special case rather than a general explanation). As shown by Mark Thatcher (2004) in the case of telecommunications, governments have been under little adaptational pressure from EU regulation. Yet they have used European policy to justify and legitimate change. Governments already seeking reform have been able to use European policy as an opportunity, rather than responding to a 'pressure'. The effects of this type of Europeanization have been large in terms of the clash between the reformers and the advocates of the status quo in telecommunications. But these effects are not captured by the 'goodness of fit' argument. Héritier and Knill (2001) have presented empirical evidence of European policies leading to domestic reforms even in the absence of adaptational pressure. Their argument is that European policies can be exploited by national actors engaged in policy reforms even if European and national arrangements are compatible. The implication is that adaptational pressure is not a necessary condition for Europeanization to cause domestic change or that adaptational pressure is politically constructed.

Other authors have observed that adaptational pressure is not the best predictor of how a country responds to Europeanization. A country can be under strong adaptational pressure, yet it can implement EU policy without too many problems, as shown by the implementation of the packaging waste directive in the UK (Haverland 2000). The intervening variable in this process is the presence or absence of institutional veto points, as argued by Haverland (2003). Institutional veto points available to those opposing EU policy can make Europeanization very problematic even in the case of

---

[5] The type of new institutionalism usually deployed is usually termed 'historical institutionalism'. Other analysts adopt a more sociological approach, for example arguing that Europeanization operates via socialization effects, for example (Börzel and Risse 2003). It is possible to envisage a more rationalist variant of new institutionalism being applied, although the 'snapshot' analysis—as opposed to historical institutionalism's 'movie' approach—militates against its utility somewhat.

low adaptational pressure. Conversely, in the absence of veto points, it is quite possible for large adaptational steps to be taken.[6]

The 'goodness of fit' interpretation works well in cases where EU policy prescribes a model or a template of how a country should go about putting policy into practice. However, one drawback of the 'goodness of fit' explanation is that it is couched in a 'vertical' (chain-of-command type) view of Europeanization. It best corresponds, therefore, to governance by hierarchy and patterns of positive integration. But, as Table 15.1 indicates, this represents only one of the mechanisms of Europeanization, so what of the horizontal variants?

Regulatory competition

One of these variants is regulatory competition in the shadow of EU negative integration. In this case a policy template is either absent or plays a limited role. A range of actions (such as discrimination between residents and non-residents) are prohibited by EU law and some key principles are established by the jurisprudence of the European Court of Justice, most importantly mutual recognition. Countries can play the regulatory competition game in different ways. They can be more or less aggressive, for example. But this game is always 'horizontal'; that is, one country versus the others in the 'race' for highly skilled labour and capital. Fitting in with EU models plays a limited role.[7]

Despite the importance often attributed to regulatory competition, the fact is that studies of competition amongst rules have been few and far between. Indeed, there are some significant problems to be tackled in conducting such projects. Arguably the most significant is to isolate the impact of European market rules from those emanating from the global economy. Let us take a hypothetical example of how Europeanization impacts upon regulatory competition in the telecommunications sector. Two counter-arguments would need to be isolated first of all, namely: (a) competition amongst rules is a product of global regulatory competition, and the EU does not matter; (b) national traditions of regulation are so embedded in their domestic context that adaptation may not give rise to convergence: whether in response to EU or global stimuli (see as illustrations Héritier et. al. 2001; Teubner 2001). Without being able to isolate these other explanations it would be difficult to demonstrate that Europeanization is the explanation for regulatory competition in the first place.

In reality what we find in seeking evidence of the impact of Europeanization upon competing regulatory regimes is pretty mixed. A well established literature sets out how the EU, through its internal market programme, provided for mutual recognition (see, for instance, Egan, 2001). However, the impact of mutual recognition on (competing) regimes of national standards has received much less treatment. In those sectors, such as telecommunications or electricity, where specific legislation was introduced to facilitate liberalization, we find Europeanization studies concentrating

---

[6] The role of veto players is acknowledged in recent versions of the 'goodness of fit' explanation. See Börzel and Risse (2003).

[7] This circumstance only arises when legislation is needed in order to attain a liberalized market, such as has occurred in the telecommunications and electricity sectors. In such circumstances adaptation to an EU template may be needed during these transitional stages.

on the policy templates that were introduced with a view to phasing in competition rather than on any competition amongst rules subsequently unleashed (Schneider 2001; Héritier et. al. 2001; Bulmer, Dolowitz, Humphreys and Padgett, 2003). In one of the rare exceptions, Susanne Schmidt explores the consequences of opening up the internal market to competition in the insurance and road haulage sectors (Schmidt 2002). Her findings are that there has been relatively little use of regulatory competition in these sectors. In her case-study states (France and Germany) she found that liberalization of the sectors had led to major domestic change but, alas, found little evidence of competition amongst rules. Our evidence-base on this form of Europeanization remains negligible.

Learning

Learning is an important dimension in all stages of Europeanization, including negotiation. However, it becomes an especially important feature where the EU does not work as a law-making system but, rather, as a platform for the convergence of ideas and policy transfer between member states. This is especially the case with the open method of coordination (OMC). However, intergovernmental forms of EU policy-making are decades old and soft-law has been known to legal scholars for a long time (Snyder 1994). Indeed, the OMC itself, as defined by the Lisbon Council in the year 2000, is more an attempt to provide a definition to modes of policy-making that emerged in different policy areas in the 1990s than a dramatic innovation. Be that as it may, what is the OMC?

The OMC is a means of spreading best practice and achieving convergence towards the EU's goals. The idea is to use the EU as a transfer platform rather than a law-making system. Thus, the OMC should assist member states in developing their own policies. As such, it hinges on horizontal mechanisms of governance rather than on the vertical imposition of models coming from Brussels. The 'method' is defined by the following characteristics: EU guidelines combined with specific timetables; action to be undertaken at the national and regional level; benchmarking and sharing of best practice; qualitative and, when appropriate, quantitative indicators; 'period monitoring, evaluation, and peer review organized as mutual learning processes' (Presidency Conclusions, Lisbon European Council, 23–24 March 2000). OMC introduces into the political sphere some of the practices of the business sector, such as benchmarking. In some policy areas (that is, immigration and social policy) the method works in conjunction with traditional EU legislative instruments. In other areas, however, the method enables the EU to enter new policy domains, where no legislation is operating and where the member states think that there is no scope for legislative action at the EU level.

Scholars looking at the OMC as an emerging governance architecture stress its potential for policy learning (de la Porte and Pochet 2002; Mosher and Trubek 2003). Some authors have argued that the major impact of this mode of policy-making is at the ideational level (Bertozzi and Bonoli 2002; Radaelli 2003). Policy-makers engage in the definition of criteria of best practice and, as in the case of taxation, worst practice. They also accept the principle of peer review of their policies. Criteria and peer review are fundamental instruments of ideational convergence. In areas in which it is either impossible or politically too sensitive to say what the EU 'model' should be, policy-makers seek to develop some ideas of how to improve their policies and notions of good and bad policy. They develop common benchmarks. They also elaborate a common vocabulary. Thus in areas previously impenetrable to Europeanization, 'communities of discourse' with their own vocabulary, criteria, and belief systems are emerging. The OMC now covers several policy areas, such as asylum policy, the information society and the European research area.

As a recent development the OMC inevitably receives a great deal of attention. However, longer-standing patterns of intergovernmental policy-making have been subject to similar types of dynamic. Like the OMC they feature a prominent role for national ministers and officials, with the supranational institutions playing a relatively small role. European law is largely absent as a policy instrument, with 'soft law' and political agreements predominant. Similarly, there are relatively discrete communities of policy-makers concerned with a particular set of issues. Whether it be CFSP, Justice and Home Affairs, or even the cooperation amongst central bankers in the European Monetary System, the same horizontal dimension applies to the Europeanization process. In other words, if Europeanization occurs, it is a process of learning amongst national elites. The EU simply provides the arena. Indeed, the trans-governmental cooperation need not be across all EU member states, as the Schengen process demonstrated, when a sub-set of states cooperated on JHA business outside the formal EU framework (den Boer and Wallace 2000; Monar 2002: 188).

The key question is how powerful is Europeanization in the case of governance by coordination? How far can it go? Longer-established forms, such as the Schengen process or the EMS, reveal that the Europeanization process was such that member governments—or most of them—were prepared to go one step further, and transfer some of these policies to governance by hierarchy. That occurred when, respectively, some aspects of the Schengen Treaty were brought into the Treaty of the European Community under the terms of the 1997 Treaty of Amsterdam (see Monar 2002), and when the steps were taken to create EMU. However, the CFSP shows that member governments are very reluctant to forgo their own powers, as revealed by the failure to agree a common policy in the early 1990s on the Yugoslav crisis or in 2003 on Iraq.

With the OMC it is unclear what pattern of development will transpire. The main point to bear in mind is that the expectation on which the whole OMC is based is that ideational convergence will produce policy change at the domestic level. The EU is a platform for learning about good policy practice. Then—the argument goes on—policy-makers with the same 'Europeanized' ideas will learn and change their domestic policies accordingly. Of course, policy-makers can also learn without the OMC. In the absence of collective learning platforms such as the OMC, however, policy-makers typically learn through crisis and sustained policy fiascos. The advantage of the OMC is that it can enable policy-makers to learn ahead of failure (Hemerijck and Visser 2001).

The relationship between ideational convergence, learning, and policy change is rather problematic. People may adopt the same language and talk in terms of the same criteria without necessarily taking the same decisions. To make things more complicated, decisions may not be followed by actions, or may be followed by unforeseen actions, 'deviant' administrative behaviour, and 'creative' bottom-up interpretations of decisions (Brunsson 1989; Pollitt 2001). The 'linear causal relationship between the formation of a European ideational consensus and local action' has also been questioned by projects on areas outside the OMC, such as regional policy (Kohler-Koch 2002).

Briefly, the jury is still out on the issue of the results achieved by the OMC and soft-law in general. One point is clear, though. The potential of the OMC is all in terms of creating ideational convergence and learning (with the aspiration of improvement to domestic policy); not necessarily in terms of creating the basis for hard law in the future. The OMC is not a poor substitute (under conditions of political necessity) for hard law, but a radically different way forward for Europeanization. Those who criticize the OMC for its lack of sanctions do not understand its mechanisms. The method is based on changes in the cognitive frameworks used by policy-makers to understand and assess reality. This potential for learning does not hinge on sanctions but on conviction. A separate, empirical question concerns whether learning actually occurs.

It would be wrong to assume that when the EU does not work in a law-making mode, horizontal mechanisms are all about deliberation, participatory governance, and cooperation. Networks can be more hierarchical than one would imagine (see the evidence presented by Kohler-Koch 2002 on networks of regional policy). Collective learning can be a very political exercise. Competitive benchmarking can be used to establish hierarchies of national practice. A key question for the future, therefore, is whether the OMC will Europeanize the national models of capitalism by forcing convergence towards the Anglo-Saxon model. This is unlikely, considering the resiliency of different models of capitalism in Europe (Hall and Soskice 2001; also Schmidt in this volume). However, the OMC was introduced by the Lisbon Council as a means to the end of making Europe the most competitive knowledge society in the world. Thus the aspiration is that the OMC will improve the competitiveness of Europe, although not necessarily in an Anglo-Saxon direction.

Researching Europeanization

What we have established thus far in this chapter is that Europeanization is more variegated in nature than how it was explained in the early stages of its exploration. However, this inevitably comes at a cost: that of simplicity. Owing to its variegated character it is not easy to provide a single research strategy or analytical framework to analyse the impact of Europeanization on different types of policies.[8] The first type of policy—positive integration—lends itself to research designs informed by new institutionalism. This is the predominant framework deployed in the first major collection of studies of Europeanization, although the role of domestic actors is also taken into account (Cowles, Caporaso, and Risse 2001). Institutions are seen as mediating pressures from the EU and shaping the consequent impact in terms of

---

[8] We omit once again Europeanization at the negotiation stage. The research methodologies and analytical tools available for such cases are essentially those to hand for studies of policy- and decision-making. See Wallace and Wallace (2000) and Peterson and Bomberg (1999) for coverage of them.

domestic change. A similar admixture of institutional and actor-centred analysis is to be found in the study by Héritier *et al.* of the EU's impact on domestic transport policy across the member states (2001). In the case of negative integration, where we have limited policy templates, a similar approach can be pursued. However, in view of the expected impact here of a competition amongst rules, it would seem particularly appropriate to apply a more rationalist framework, emphasising the strategic calculations of actors in responding to the opportunities available to them in the context of liberalized markets. In reality, we still await the emergence of such analyses. The third type of policy, that is, facilitated coordination, is arguably the most difficult to assess. Research strategies on this type need to be extremely sensitive to the local context. They also need to avoid the fallacy of assuming a linear relationship between the emergence of ideas of good practice or policy at the EU level and domestic policy change. The question is how does one know if changes in domestic policy are the result of the engagement in the European policy process and not the product of other variables at work at the domestic level?

The more traditional forms of intergovernmental cooperation are perhaps easier to research by process tracing, monitoring shifting national policy positions in light of repeated negotiations within, say, CFSP on some aspect of foreign policy, such as the Middle East. This task has been attempted by Alistair Miskimmon and William Paterson in respect of German foreign and security policy during the 1990s (Miskimmon and Paterson 2003). Their framework comes from the same institution-alist tool-kit as that used by Cowles, Caporaso, and Risse (2001) but includes cognitive dimensions, too. This use of the cognitive dimension forms a bridge with some of the considerations which come into play when exploring Europeanization in the OMC.

When it comes to isolating the impact of Europeanization upon policy areas covered by the OMC, one needs a focus on the local level, not on Brussels. The idea is to look at the problems, resources, and ideas most relevant to policy-makers 'at the hub of the problem' and then examine to what extent the ideational resources made available by the OMC do or do not matter in the games domestic actors play. Systematic research on the OMC is still in its early stages. However, research on cohesion policy provides evidence that one may find widely shared European ideas and norms at the local level, yet their support cannot be traced back to origin with the EU (Kohler-Koch 2002). The implication is that there is 'a European space of ideas that stretches beyond the realm of EU policy-making' (Kohler-Koch 2002: 9).

Kohler-Koch's statement alerts us to the role of contextual variables at work in Europeanization processes and to the importance of looking for Europeanization beyond the narrow space of EU policy-making processes. This is a difficult task. Bilateral relationships, notably between France and Germany, have served to generate policy models or ideas that have then been adopted at EU level, such as the European Monetary System. And one of the most interesting findings of research on the Europeanization of policies in candidate countries is that the EU is only one of the actors promoting Europeanization. Organizations such as the Council of Europe are also deeply involved (perhaps to a higher degree than the EU) in the transfer of European models, as shown by Harcourt's study on media policy regulation in four candidate countries (Harcourt 2003). More broadly, the Council of Europe's role in Europeanization has perhaps been under-estimated; see Lovecy's exploration of gender mainstreaming in Europe (2002).

Enlargement is a process characterized by the asymmetry of power—rooted in conditionality for accession—between the EU and candidate countries. The major mechanisms of policy transformation in candidate countries include the provision of models, financial and technical aid, advice and twinning, and benchmarking (Grabbe 2003). All three types of policy portrayed in Table 15.1 are involved in these mechanisms. The EU has made use of asymmetric power to Europeanize the policies of candidate countries. Yet the use of power is also constrained by uncertainty, as shown by Grabbe (2003). There is uncertainty about the content of the EU policy agenda in areas such as social policy, justice and home affairs, and taxation. There is uncertainty about whom to satisfy: the Commission, the Council or specific governments. And there is uncertainty about standards and thresholds, that is, what degree of compliance will really count as the candidates 'meeting the EU conditions' in the economic domain?

There are also forms of radical uncertainty, when candidate countries have to draft major legislation in haste (for example, competition policy or the regulation of utilities), under pressure from both the EU and US providers of models, with limited knowledge and expertise in house. Radical uncertainty can make it impossible to map out neat policy strategies. Under these conditions, what comes out as Europeanization may be nothing but the outcome of political expediency and contingency and it may not be deeply rooted (see also the chapter by Klaus Goetz in this volume).

On balance, asymmetric power is the major force, but one should not underestimate the counter-forces produced by uncertainty. Consequently, policy emulation (of EU models) in candidate countries can be highly selective (Jacoby 2001; 2002). Candidate countries may import, imitate, and absorb EU policies creatively. Leaders in the former communist states in Eastern and Central Europe have distinguished between those aspects of EU policy which were useful for domestic political purposes and those which were politically damaging or useless. Imitation had a political logic (Jacoby 2001: 173; Olsen 2002). More importantly still, candidate countries played a game of catch-up with the EU via the negotiation of the chapters of the *acquis communautaire*. But occasionally, they also played a leap-frogging game. Not only can the advantages of relative backwardness—to paraphrase Gerschenkron (1962)—show how to avoid the mistakes of the past, but candidate countries can find creative solutions to cope with the puzzles posed by the *acquis communautaire*.

The Europeanization of public policy can take different forms. In principle, it can impinge on all the basic elements of the policy process, such as actors, resources, and policy instruments. Additionally, Europeanization can affect the policy style, for example by making it more or less conflictual, corporatist, or pluralist, or more or less regulative. This kind of effect potentially has major implications, such as by rebalancing the power of national policy actors and policy-makers. Finally, it can impact on the cognitive and normative dimensions. Changes of cognitive and normative frames (Surel 2000) may trigger transformative effects on all the elements of policy. For example, they may alter the interpretation of a political dilemma facing a political party. Or they may impact on the perception of what is at stake in a policy controversy. They may even transform the interests and preferences upon which negotiations are structured. Policy discourses can be decisive in terms of securing legitimacy for choices in line with EU policy (Schmidt 2001). To conclude, research designs should be clear on the type of impact that is to be measured. They should distinguish between impacts on the elements of the policy process, impacts on cognitive and normative frames (a topical issue for research on the OMC), and impacts at the level of actual policy results (or, simply, what goes under the label 'policy change').

Empirical overview

How can we bring together the analytical discussion in this chapter with some suggestive characterization of the Europeanization of national policy? We cannot possibly do this in great detail, given that there are twenty-five member states, each with a different story in many different policy areas. Detailed accounts must be the province of case studies. However, we seek to map our typology onto the EU's policy areas by way of concluding (see Table 15.2).

- Positive integration, with its utilization of policy templates to achieve market-correcting goals, has the most coercive form of Europeanization. Backed up by European law, measures have a formal expectation that they will be put into effect in the member states. Amongst the policy areas concerned are the Common Agricultural Policy, EMU, social and environmental policies. In each case the supra-national character of policy provides the adjustment pressure behind adaptation. The potential for regulatory intrusion is high. In these cases the goodness of fit argument seems to be the default interpretation: how well does the EU policy template match up with the existing domestic policy? What adjustments are necessary?

- Negative integration uses policy templates in a limited sector-specific way. They are designed to bring about an internal market of the kind that exists in the general market for goods and services as a result of the treaties, and as understood from the mid-1980s onwards. Here also European legal measures spell out policy requirements. However, regulatory intrusion is less than in positive integration, since the whole idea of policy is to allow markets to function. In the transitional phase of legislation, some member states will be faced with the need to adjust policy following the goodness of fit explanation. However, once the transition is

Table 15.2 Europeanization and policy illustration

Type of policy	Illustrative policy areas	'Default' explanation of Europeanization
Positive integration	Environment, social policy, EMU, CAP	Goodness of fit
Negative integration	Internal market in goods and services, utilities sectors (for example telecommunications, electricity), corporate governance	Regulatory competition
Coordination	CFSP, third pillar, OMC policies (for example employment, social inclusion, pensions, enterprise policy, asylum policy)	Learning

complete, regulatory competition should become the key dynamic. Member states (or even sub-national entities) will seek to position themselves competitively. The internal market and the utilities sectors (telecommunications, transport, electricity) should be exemplars here. The conundrum thus far is that there has been no in-depth study of regulatory competition as a means of Europeanization. Arguably it is in the competition amongst EU regions to attract inward investment that a kind of regulatory competition is most prominent.

■ Coordination comes about in those policy areas where the EU is itself weak, thus severely limiting the scope for coercion. Policy is made through intergovernmental negotiations or looser exchanges. Legal measures are downplayed in favour of political declarations, targets and so on. A whole host of policy areas is covered by the term coordination, including more recent developments under the OMC: the CFSP, the third pillar, economic policy, employment policy, social inclusion, research and development and so on. Whether coordination occurs in longer-standing areas of policy cooperation, such as foreign policy, or through newer ones, such as the OMC, the process is essentially horizontal and dependent on learning. In older forms the learning is typically part of agreeing a European policy intergovernmentally. In the OMC the learning is much more ad hoc, with the EU serving as an arena within which member governments may find policy solutions to domestic problems.

Our brief section on empirical illustration must carry with it a health warning. First, there is no clear delineation of competences between the EU itself and the member states, although the situation will be clarified as and if the Constitutional Treaty is ratified. This means that there is as yet no orderly designation of policy areas to particular levels of government, such as was set out in the German Basic Law of 1949, nor an immediate correspondence between policy area and mode of governance. In consequence, some policy areas are quite difficult to assign to one of our three categories. Taxation policy, for instance, entails some elements of positive integration (for example regarding Value Added Tax regimes), some competition amongst national regimes in accordance with negative integration (for example on savings or corporation taxation) and a means of monitoring *harmful* tax competition through coordination. Another illustration is environmental policy, where there is a mix of policy instruments, including directives and non-binding codes. In some cases, therefore, it is the policy issue rather than the policy area that is the more suitable basis for classification. Second, we underline that Table 15.2 refers to the *default* patterns of Europeanization. As we already noted in discussion above, deviant cases will always exist.

Conclusion

The European Union has had a very significant impact upon the policies of the member states. It has also impacted upon near-neighbours, such as states in the European Economic Area, and outside Europe, for instance on the recipients of aid programmes. This chapter, however, has been concerned only with the member states. Over the last decade the EU's impact has become a focus of attention for academic scholars, taking the debate beyond its long-standing concerns with (largely 'bottom-up') processes of integration and policy-making. The debate has now become a fully fledged one at the start of the twenty-first century.

Empirical studies of Europeanization can be organized in various ways: by the member state or by the policy/issue area concerned. In this chapter we have not sought to concentrate on summarizing empirical studies, for that would probably result in a bewildering array of findings. Instead we have sought to concentrate on the dynamics, processes and effects involved by developing typologies and classifications derived from patterns of governance within the EU. We have argued that governance by negotiation—the agreement on EU policy—bears upon the Europeanization process. The identification of a set of 'default' explanations of Europeanization effects draws upon recent analytical and empirical work in the area. With the ongoing institutional, policy (and now constitutional) reform process over the period since the Single Act of 1986, not to mention successive waves of enlargement, studying the empirical effects of the Europeanization process looks likely to be a similarly long-term pursuit on the part of students of the EU. In the cases of regulatory competition and coordination, the empirical analyses of Europeanization are pretty much still on the starting-grid. Analyses deploying the goodness of fit explanation have set off from pole-position at speed. However, the intellectual history of Europeanization is still short and the likely prospect of one interpretation predominating is improbable.

Further reading

For reviews of the Europeanization literature, see Olsen (2002), Featherstone (2003), and Börzel (this volume). On different modes of policy-making in the EU, see Wallace (2000) and Scharpf (1999). On explanatory accounts of Europeanization, including its causal mechanisms, see Cowles, Caporaso, and Risse (2001); Knill (2001); and Haverland (2000). For a collection of papers on markets and regulatory competition in Europe, see Radaelli (2004). On the Open Method of Coordination, see de la Porte and Pochet (2002), Mosher and Trubek (2003); Zeitlin and Trubek (2003).

Weblinks

There are few websites devoted to Europeanization as such. However, the following academic sites are valuable for bringing together on-line papers on the subject <**http://www.arena.uio.no/**>; <**http://www.qub.ac.uk/ies/onlinepapers/poe.html**>. These and other papers may also be found through the following on-line paper gateway <**http://eiop.or.at/erpa/**>. Owing to the diffuse nature of Europeanization there are hardly any 'official' websites of relevance. One exception is the European Commission's scoreboard on the implementation of the single market, an indicator of the extent of Europeanization. It can be found at <**http://europa.eu.int/comm/internal_market/en/update/score/index.htm**>.

References

Armstrong, K., and Bulmer, S. (1998), *The Governance of the Single European Market* (Manchester: Manchester University Press).

Bertozzi, F., and Bonoli, G. (2002), 'Europeanisation and the convergence of national social and employment policies: What can the open method of coordination achieve?', Paper prepared for the ECPR joint sessions of workshops, Turin, 22–27 March 2002.

Börzel, T., and Risse, T. (2003), 'Conceptualising the domestic impact of Europe', in K. Featherstone and C. M. Radaelli (eds), *The Politics of Europeanization* (Oxford: Oxford University Press).

Brunsson, N. (1989), *The Organization of Hypocrisy. Talk, Decisions and Actions in Organizations* (Chichester and New York: John Wiley and Sons).

Bulmer, S., Dolowitz, D., Humphreys, P., and Padgett, S. (2003), 'Electricity and Telecommunications: Fit for the European Union?', in K. Dyson and K. Goetz (eds), *Germany, Europe and the Politics of Constraint* (Oxford: Oxford University Press), 251–69.

Cowles, M. G., Caporaso, J., and Risse, T. (2001) (eds), *Transforming Europe: Europeanization and Domestic Change* (Ithaca NY and London: Cornell University Press).

de la Porte, C., and Pochet, P. (2002) (eds), *Building Social Europe through the Open Method of Coordination* (Brussels: European Interuniversity Press).

Den Boer, M., and Wallace, W. (2000), 'Justice and Home Affairs: Integration through Incrementalism?', in Wallace and Wallace (2000), 493–519.

Dyson, K., and Featherstone, K. (1999), *The Road to Maastricht: Negotiating Economic and Monetary Union* (Oxford: Oxford University Press).

Egan, M. (2001), *Constructing a European Market* (Oxford: Oxford University Press).

Featherstone, K. (2003), 'In the name of Europe', in K. Featherstone and C. M. Radaelli (eds), *The Politics of Europeanisation* (Oxford: Oxford University Press).

Fligstein, N., and McNichol, J. (1998), 'The Institutional Terrain of the European Union', in W. Sandholtz and A. Stone Sweet (eds), *European Integration and Supranational Governance* (Oxford: Oxford University Press), 59–91.

Gerschenkron, A. (1962), *Economic Backwardness in Historical Perspective: A Book of Essays* (Cambridge MA.: Harvard University Press).

Glarbo, K. (1999), 'Wide-awake diplomacy: reconstructing the common foreign and security policy of the European Union', *Journal of European Public Policy*, 6/4, 634–51.

Grabbe, H. (2003), 'Europeanisation goes East: power and uncertainty in the EU accession game', in K. Featherstone and C. M. Radaelli (eds), *The Politics of Europeanisation* (Oxford: Oxford University Press).

Harcourt, Alison (2003), 'The regulation of media markets in selected EU Accession States in Central and Eastern Europe', in *European Law Journal*, 9/3, 316–40.

Haverland, M. (2000), 'National adaptation to European integration: The importance of institutional veto points', *Journal of Public Policy*, 20/1, 83–103.

Haverland, M. (2003), 'The impact of the EU on environmental policies', in K. Featherstone and C. M. Radaelli (eds), *The Politics of Europeanisation* (Oxford: Oxford University Press).

Hay, C., and Rosamond, B. (2002), 'Globalisation, European integration and the discursive construction of economic imperatives', *Journal of European Public Policy* 9/2, 147–67.

Hemerijck, A., and Visser, J. (2001) 'Learning and mimicking: How European welfare states reform', typescript.

Héritier, A., and Knill, C. (2001), 'Differential responses to European policies: A Comparison', Héritier *et al.* 257–94.

Héritier, A., Kerwer, D., Knill, C., Lehmkuhl, D., Teutsch, M., and Douillet, A-C. (2001), *Differential Europe. The European Union Impact on National Policymaking* (Lanham MD: Rowman and Littlefield).

Jacoby, W. (2002), 'Ordering from the Menu: How Central and East European states cope with EU demands for institutional reform' Paper prepared for the ECPR Workshop 4 on Enlargement and European Governance, ECPR Joint Session Workshops, Turin 22–27 March.

Jacoby, W. (2001), 'Tutors and Pupils: International Organizations, Central European Elites, and Western Models' *Governance* 14/2.

Knill, C. (2001), *The Europeanisation of National Administrations. Patterns of Institutional Persistence and Change* (Cambridge: Cambridge University Press).

Kohler-Koch, B. (2002), 'European networks and ideas: Changing national policies'?, *European Integration on line Papers* (EioP) vol. 6/6, <http://www.eiop.or.at/eiop/texte/2002-006a.htm>.

Krugman, P. (1994), 'Competitiveness: A Dangerous Obsession', *Foreign Affairs*, 73/2: 28–44.

Laffan, B. (2001), 'The European Union polity: a union of regulative, normative, and cognitive pillars', *Journal of European Public Policy* 8/5, 709–27.

Lovecy, J. (2002), 'Gender Mainstreaming and the Framing of Women's Rights in Europe: the contribution of the Council of Europe', *Feminist Legal Studies* 10, 271–83.

Mair, P. (2001), 'The limited impact of Europe on national party systems' in K. H. Goetz and S. Hix (eds), *Europeanised Politics? European Integration and National Political Systems* (London: Frank Cass), 27–51.

Miskimmon, A., and Paterson, W. (2003), 'Foreign and Security Policy: On the Cusp Between Transformation and Accommodation', in Dyson and Goetz, 325–45.

Monar, J. (2002), 'Institutionalizing Freedom, Security and Justice', in J. Peterson and M. Shackleton (eds), *The Institutions of the European Union* (Oxford: Oxford University Press), 186–209.

Mosher, J., and Trubek, D. (2003), 'Alternative Approaches to Governance in the EU: EU Social Policy and the European Employment Strategy', *Journal of Common Market Studies* 41/1, 63–88.

Olsen, J. (2002), 'The Many Faces of Europeanization', *Journal of Common Market Studies*, 405, 921–52.

Peterson, J., and Bomberg, E. (1999), *Decision-Making in the European Union* (London: Palgrave).

Pinder, J. (1968), 'Positive integration and negative integration: some problems of economic union in the EEC', *The World Today* 24/3, 89–110.

Pollitt, C. (2001), 'Convergence: The useful myth?' *Public Administration*, 79/4, 933–47.

Radaelli, C. M. (2003), 'The code of conduct in business taxation: Open method of coordination in disguise?', *Public Administration* 81/3, 513–31.

Radaelli, C. M. (2004), 'Markets and Regulatory Competition in Europe', special issue of *Journal of Public Policy*, 24/1.

Risse, T., Cowles, M. G., and Caporaso, J. (2001), 'Europeanization and Domestic Change: Introduction', in Cowles, Caporaso and Risse, 1–20.

Scharpf, F. W. (1997) *Games Real Actors Play. Actor-Centred Institutionalism in Policy Research* (Boulder CO: Westview Press).

Scharpf, F. W. (1999), *Governing in Europe: Effective and Democratic?* (Oxford: Oxford University Press).

Scharping, R. (1994), 'Rule-Based Competion', *Foreign Affairs*, 73/4: 192–4

Schmidt, S. (2002), 'The impact of mutual recognition—inbuilt limits and domestic responses to the single market', *Journal of European Public Policy* 9/6, 935–53.

Schmidt, V. (2001), 'The politics of economic adjustment in France and Britain: when does discourse matter?' *Journal of European Public Policy*, 8/2: 247–64.

Schneider, V. (2001), 'Institutional Reform in Telecommunications: The European Union in Transnational Policy Diffusion', in Cowles, Caporaso, and Risse (2001), 60–78.

Snyder, F. (1994), 'Soft law and institutional performance in the European Community', in S. Martin (ed.), *Essays in Honor of Emile Noel* (Dordrecht and London: Kluwer), 197–225.

Sun, J.-M., and Pelkmans, J. (1985), 'Regulatory competition in the single market', *Journal of Common Market Studies*, 33/1, 67–89.

Surel, Y. (2000), 'The role of cognitive and normative frames in policy-making', *Journal of European Public Policy*, 7/4, 495–512.

Teubner, G. (2001), 'Legal Irritants: How Unifying Law Ends up in New Divergencies', in P. Hall and D. Soskice (eds), *Varieties of Capitalism. The Institutional Foundations of Comparative Advantage* (Oxford: Oxford University Press), 417–41.

Thatcher, M. (2004), 'Winners and Losers in Europeanization: Reforming the national regulation of telecommunications', *West European Politics*, 27/1, 29–52.

Wallace, H. (2000), 'The Institutional Setting: five variations on a theme', in H. Wallace and W. Wallace (eds), *Policy-Making in the European Union*, 4th edn. (Oxford: Oxford University Press), 3–37.

Wallace, H., and Wallace, W. (eds) (2000), *Policy-Making in the European Union*, 4th edn. (Oxford: Oxford University Press).

Weale, A. (1996), 'Environmental rules and rule-making in the European Union', *Journal of European Public Policy*, 3/4, 594–611.

Wellens, K., and Borchardt, G. (1980), 'Soft Law in European Community Law', *European Law Review*, 14/5, 267–321.

Zeitlin, J., and Trubek, D. M. (eds) (2003), *Governing Work and Welfare in a New Economy: European and American Experiments* (Oxford: Oxford University Press).

Chapter 16

The Europeanization of National Economies?

Vivien A. Schmidt

Contents

Summary

With the ever-quickening pace of European monetary and market integration, epitomized by the completion of the Single Market project in 1992 and the inception of the Single Currency in 1999, the European Union has sought to build a single European economy out of the diverse national economies of its member states. The main questions addressed in this chapter are: How successful has the EU been in promoting this goal? How much convergence has occurred, and how much divergence remains?

The chapter answers these questions by examining the development of Europe's national economies from the postwar period until today, using in illustration the three largest and arguably most different countries: Britain, Germany, and France. The chapter begins with a discussion of the three main post-war varieties of capitalism, next outlines the impact of globalization and Europeanization, and then considers the changes in government policies, in business practices, and in industrial relations. In conclusion, the chapter speculates on future patterns of political economic development in the European Union.

Introduction

Globalization has over the past decade and more attracted all the headlines with regard to economic change. It has often been characterized as a juggernaut sweeping away national differences, with the competitive pressures resulting from the internationalization of the financial markets and trade ensuring the replacement of national varieties of capitalism with a one-size-fits-all neoliberal version; with the rise of supranational trade organizations and treaties undermining national sovereignty by reducing government autonomy in decision making and control over economic activities in the national territory; and with the circulation of neoliberal ideas pushing out contrary views and eliminating differences between governments of the right and left.

But if all this were true for globalization, then it would have to be doubly true for Europeanization. This is because European integration, as a regional variant of globalization, has gone much further in terms of the Europeanization of financial markets and trade, of the Europeanization of decision-making, and of the circulation of neoliberal ideas than anything linked to globalization. The EU has created a liberalized regional economic zone that has subjected its member states to much greater competitive pressures in the capital and product markets than those experienced by advanced industrialized countries subject only to globalization. The development of the European Union as a supranational set of institutions has diminished EU member states' national sovereignty far more than any global set of institutions. And the EU has actually put into effect neo-liberal ideas that are often more talk than action in countries influenced by global forces alone. In consequence, Europeanization has produced much more dramatic change for EU member states than globalization has for any advanced industrialized nations including EU member states.

But Europeanization has not been subject to the same polemics or confrontations as globalization—we do not find the same numbers of demonstrators at the European Council meetings that we find in Seattle or Genova, nor of pamphlets and books on the evils of Europeanization to match those on globalization. Why? Because Europeanization has brought significant economic enhancement as well as competition, with the single market and the single currency providing greater economic stability and growth than might have been the case if European countries had been subject to globalization alone. Moreover, in exchange for the loss of governmental autonomy and control, European member states have gained a kind of shared supranational authority and control that goes way beyond anything experienced by countries part of only global or other regional trade associations. Finally, as a set of ideas, Europeanization has mostly been a positive force, serving in the national discourse to legitimize changes—not just as a blame shifting device but as an empowering force for national actors seeking to reform.

As a regional variant of globalization, therefore, the experience of the EU can tell us much about the potential challenges for advanced industrialized democracies worldwide if and when global and other regional institutions reach the level of maturity of

EU ones. For Europe itself, it already tells us that whatever the pressures for convergence, countries will remain highly differentiated. In consequence of common EU policies and an integrating European economy, as this chapter argues, national government policies, although more similar as a result of monetary convergence, financial market liberalization, business deregulation, and labour market decentralization, are not the same. National business practices, although more competitive in inter-firm relations and more dependent upon the financial markets for capital, continue to differ. And national industrial relations, although more flexible and decentralized, remain highly differentiated.

This chapter will show that national political economies, although all moving toward greater market orientation, continue to be distinguishable into not just one neo-liberal version of capitalism, as much of the globalization literature assumes (for example Greider 1997; Ohmae 1990), nor towards two varieties, as recent firm-centred approaches to capitalism suggest (Hall and Soskice 2001), but at least three varieties of capitalism, differentiable along lines of development from the original post-war models (Schmidt 2002; Coates 2000). Market capitalist countries such as Britain and Ireland to a lesser extent, with post-war market-driven inter-firm relations and market-reliant management–labour relations assured by a 'liberal' state, have gone even further in this direction. Managed capitalist countries such as Germany as well as smaller European countries such as the Netherlands, Sweden, Denmark, and Austria, with post-war collaborative inter-firm relations and cooperative labour-management relations facilitated by an 'enabling' state, have retained their overall outlines, despite changes at the edges. And state capitalist countries such as France and to a lesser extent Italy,[1] with the post-war 'interventionist' state organizing inter-firm collaboration, directing business investment, and imposing management–labour cooperation, have transformed themselves—but nevertheless remain distinguishable from both market and managed capitalism.

In developing this argument the chapter focuses on France, the UK, and Germany as representatives of the three varieties of capitalism. That is not to deny other member states their own capitalist identity but simply a means of managing material within the limited space of this chapter. It is also worth pointing out that, in the enlarged EU of twenty-five member states, it is possible that a new model may emerge from the central and eastern European states. However, given their transition from economies that were based on different principles during the Cold War era, and the associated transformation in their levels of development, it is difficult to accommodate those states in the argument about 'models' of political economy that follows. But like the other member states, with their longer experience of capitalism, the central and eastern European states have been experiencing the dual challenges of globalization and Europeanization, albeit in much more sharpened form and over a shorter time-frame.

---

[1] Although France epitomizes state capitalism, Italy can be seen as state capitalism '*manqué*,' in particular the 'first Italy' of northern industrial firms and nationalized industries in which the state had the power and ambition but not the capacity to lead firms or control industrial relations. By contrast, the 'third Italy' of regionally based economies in the north east and north west bears greater resemblance to managed capitalism.

Post-war varieties of capitalism

In the post-war period, the economic policies developed in a situation of 'embedded liberalism' (Ruggie 1982)—where countries benefited from the protective barriers of capital exchange controls, fixed but adjustable exchange rates, and optional barriers to trade—helped consolidate very different systems of economic management and development. While monetary policy was not a defining characteristic of any particular variety of capitalism, ranging as it did from 'hard' to 'soft' depending on national factors, government policies toward industry and labour were defining on the basis of whether government's role was liberal, enabling, or interventionist as were business practices on whether firms were competitive, cooperative, or state-led, and industrial relations, whether fragmented, coordinated, or state-controlled (see Table 16.1).

Monetary policies ran the gamut from 'hard money' policies focused on stability and the fight against inflation to 'soft money' policies, primarily neo-Keynesian, that 'primed the pump' in times of economic downturn, used inflation as a spur to growth, and devaluation as a way to cool down the economy while making exports more competitive. Although managed capitalist countries such as Sweden and the Netherlands engaged in 'soft money' policies, Germany was closest to the hard money end of the spectrum. It had an independent central bank, the Bundesbank, charged first and foremost to guard against inflation—a result of the German fear of a return to the 1920s,

Table 16.1 Characteristics of the post-war varieties of capitalism (1950s–1970s)

	Market capitalism (Britain)	Managed capitalism (Germany)	State capitalism (France)
Monetary policies	Softer	Harder	Softest
Government role	Liberal	Enabling	Interventionist
Policies toward industry	Arbitrator	Facilitator	Director
Policies toward labour	Bystander	Bystander	Organizer
Business relations	Competitive	Cooperative	State-led
Inter-firm relations	Contractual	Mutually reinforcing	State-mediated
	Individualistic	Network-based	
Investment sources	Capital markets	Banks	State
Time-horizons	Short-term view	Long-term view	Medium-term view
Goals	Profits	Firm value	National political-economic priorities
Industrial relations	Fragmented	Coordinated	State-organized
Management–labour Relations	Adversarial	Cooperative	Adversarial
Wage-bargaining	Market reliant	Coordinated	State imposed

when inflation had so spiralled out of control that it took a wheelbarrow full of money to buy a loaf of bread. It sought to ensure steady economic growth through price and monetary stability. Market capitalist Britain had much softer monetary policies. These were focused not so much on the stability of the currency as on its value in order to maintain the pound sterling as an international reserve currency—a matter not only of national pride given the history of Empire but also of economic interest given ties with the Commonwealth and the desire to maintain the international attractiveness of the City's financial markets. The focus on the value of the pound, however, together with governments' on-going commitment to full employment, engendered the 'stop-go' economic policies in which governments were constantly intervening either to curtail demand in efforts to ease balance of payments and sterling crises or to expand demand in response to economic slowdown and rising unemployment. Such policies left the British economy as a whole with shorter cycles of expansion than other European countries and British business in particular facing the disadvantages of the pound when the currency was strong and without the time needed to build up investment reserves when the pound was weak. By contrast, state capitalist France had arguably the softest monetary policies. The government's primary focus was less on the value or stability of the currency than on the health of business, which the government-controlled central bank sought to promote through the use of high rates of inflation that enabled companies to invest despite relatively high levels of indebtedness followed by periodic aggressive devaluations of the franc against the dollar, which in turn would give French firms a temporary competitive advantage in exports.

Industrial policy also differed widely among European countries in the postwar period, the product of governments which saw their role either as arbitrator, facilitator, or director of business activities. Market capitalist Britain's liberal or 'spectator' state generally had arms' length relations with business (Grant 1995). Thus, it sought to limit its role to arbitrating among economic actors while leaving the administration of the rules to self-governing bodies, although this did not stop it from providing aid to industry on an ad hoc basis and intermittently intervening through planning experiments, nationalized industries, or government sanctioned, privately regulated cartels. Managed capitalist Germany's 'enabling' state was instead focused on facilitating business activities through more targeted aid to industry by way of regionally provided subsidies and loans, support for research and development, as well as education, apprenticeship, and training programmes, while often leaving the rules to be jointly administered by economic actors (Katzenstein 1989). State capitalist France's *dirigiste* or interventionist state, by contrast, sought to direct economic activities through planning, industrial policy, and state-owned enterprises in addition to in all the ways the other states promoted business, while it administered the rules itself, as often as not through the derogation of the rules in favour of business (Hall 1986; Schmidt 1996).

Business practices in European countries were equally varied. Relations among firms were either individualistic, mutually reinforcing, or state mediated. Investment capital came from either the capital markets, the banks, or the state. And business time horizons and goals involved either a short-term focus on profits, a long-term emphasis on company value, or a medium-term concern with national political–economic priorities. In market capitalist Britain, relations among firms were generally competitive, contractual, and individualistic—even though competitive behaviour was sometimes moderated by 'gentlemanly' agreements, tacit understandings, and cartel-like arrangements among firms. The financial markets, as the main source of investment capital, put pressure on firms for steady profits on a quarterly basis or risk take-over (Coates 1994). In managed capitalist Germany, by contrast, inter-firm relations were cooperative, with mutually reinforcing networks of firms linked through supervisory boards, cross-shareholdings, and close connections with customers, suppliers, and the banks provided guidance in corporate strategy and 'patient capital' more concerned with market share and firm value over the long term than profits in the short-term (Soskice 1999). In state capitalist France, finally, business practices were state-led. The state mediated inter-firm relations, set medium-term corporate strategies through planning and industrial policy, and underwrote the investment of traditionally under-capitalized business, sometimes demanding no financial return at all if the state's medium-term goals were being fulfilled, such as maintaining employment or increasing production in strategic areas (Schmidt 1996).

Labour policy and industrial relations in European countries were similarly differentiated. Labour–management relations were either adversarial or cooperative. Wage-bargaining was either highly fragmented, centrally coordinated, or state-controlled. And the state was a bystander to, co-equal in, or an organizer of labour relations. In market capitalist Britain, labour–management relations were highly adversarial and wage bargaining among weakly organized employer associations and unions highly fragmented. This generally led to a high level of confrontation and inflationary pressure on wages. In consequence, although the liberal state saw its role as one of bystander to 'voluntarist' or free collective bargaining, this did not stop it from intermittently intervening through wage controls when the pound was under pressure or from attempting social concertation experiments and 'incomes policies' in failed attempts to coordinate wage restraint (Edwards 1995). In managed capitalist Germany, by contrast, labour–management relations were cooperative and wage-bargaining was centrally coordinated among strong, cohesive employer associations and unions. This reduced confrontation and promoted wage restraint. The 'enabling' state, moreover, remained largely a bystander to such relations not only because, unlike in Britain, it had little need to intervene, given wage restraint, but also because it lacked the legal right—which made it different not just from Britain but also from other managed capitalist countries such as the Netherlands or Sweden, where the state often sat at the table with management and labour as a co-equal (Thelen 2001; Soskice 1999). In state-capitalist France, finally, labour–management relations were as adversarial as in Britain and employer associations and unions even weaker and more fragmented, leading to much confrontation. But here, rather than acting as a bystander, the interventionist state organized wage-bargaining and even imposed wage settlements when business and labour were unable to reach agreement, thus moderating wage rises and managing confrontations more effectively than in Britain but not nearly as successfully as Germany (Howell 1992).

The pressures for change

All three post-war configurations of capitalism worked, for better or for worse, relatively unconstrained by major external pressures until the early 1970s. Of the three countries, Germany expanded most rapidly between 1950 and 1973, having started lowest in terms

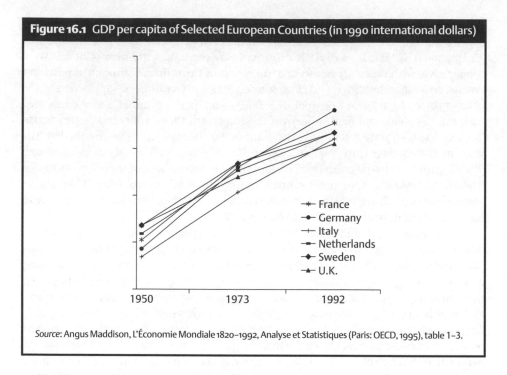

Figure 16.1 GDP per capita of Selected European Countries (in 1990 international dollars)

—*— France
—●— Germany
—+— Italy
—■— Netherlands
—◆— Sweden
—▲— U.K.

1950   1973   1992

Source: Angus Maddison, L'Économie Mondiale 1820–1992, Analyse et Statistiques (Paris: OECD, 1995), table 1–3.

of Gross Domestic Product (GDP) per capita and ended up highest. Britain started higher and grew more slowly by comparison not only with Germany but also with France as well as most other advanced industrialized European countries (see Figure 16.1).

German competitiveness benefited from monetary policies that created a stable and favorable economic environment for business; from industrial policies that underwrote product innovation and employee training; from business practices that promoted strategic cooperation among firms as well as investment in plants, machinery, technology, and human resources; and from industrial relations and labour policies that fostered high waged, high skilled workers with high rates of productivity. All of this together ensured steady profits over the long term from export-led growth fueled by high quality, high cost, but highly competitive goods (Streeck 1997). British competitiveness, by contrast, suffered from monetary policies that created an unstable and unfavorable economic environment for business; from industrial policies that did little for product innovation or training; from business practices that focused more on squeezing out profits than on investing in new plants, machinery, technology, or human resources; and from industrial relations and labour policies that fostered low waged, poorly trained labor and high production costs—all of which led to products that were low in quality and high in cost, especially when the pound was high (Coates 1994; Lane 1989). French competitiveness was somewhere between Germany and Britain. It benefited from monetary policies that created an unstable but favourable economic environment and from industrial policies that underwrote business investment and product innovation in strategic areas (especially in state-owned enterprise in public utilities and infrastructural services such as electricity and railroads). But it suffered from business practices that, absent state support or outside the state sector, failed to invest in new plants, machinery, technology, or human resources and from industrial relations and labour policies that fostered low waged, poorly trained labor and high production costs (Schmidt 1996; Hall 1986).

But whatever their economic management systems and whatever their relative competitiveness, between the 1950s and the 1970s they all experienced steady growth in national wealth, rising living standards for their populations, and more money in people's pockets to fuel the consumer society. All of this was to be severely challenged beginning in the early 1970s, however, first with the collapse of the Bretton Woods system of fixed exchange rates based on the dollar, which ushered in an era of floating exchange rates, and then by the first oil crisis in the mid-1970s, which brought the sudden fivefold rise in the price of crude oil, followed by the second oil crisis in the late 1970s, all of which together produced growing currency volatility, rising inflation, and declining competitiveness. The challenges of the 1970s, moreover, were followed in the 1980s and 1990s by two other sets of economic challenges, which can be summed up in two words: globalization and Europeanization.

As an economic challenge, globalization can be defined most succinctly as the competitive pressures stemming from the rising internationalization of national markets for goods, capital, and services. There is no room here, nor any need, to get into the on-going debates over the origins of globalization—whether seen as unique in history or as a continuation of processes of internationalization interrupted by the two world wars; its impact—as dramatic or minimal; and its intrinsic value—as a threat or an opportunity.[2] For whatever the differences in opinion on the origins, impact, or value of globalization, all agree that its manifestation is in the exponential growth of the financial markets and in the rapid expansion of international trade. For example, currency markets that traded in the 1970s at around $10 to $20 billion traded at $1.5 trillion by 1998. Securities markets such as the New York Stock Exchange went from a Dow Jones industrial average of 2000 in 1987 to over the 10,000 mark in 1999. World foreign direct investment (FDI) flows went from $60 billion in 1979 to over $1.2 trillion in 2000. And cross-border mergers and acquisitions in the 1990s alone went from $70 billion in 1992 to $1.1 trillion in 2000.

For EU member states, Europeanization represents an even greater economic challenge than globalization, since it involves integrating in a single market—and not simply opening to external competition—national markets for goods, capital, services, *and* labour in addition to eliminating national currencies in favour of a single currency, the euro. As a result, it has often intensified the competitive pressures from globalization as it has added its own specifically European pressures. For example, the phased elimination of capital controls beginning in the 1980s together with the deregulation of the rules limiting financial market access and tradable instruments has opened up EU member states to intra-European competition on top of the global in the capital markets. Moreover, the end to tariff barriers between European countries by 1969 made European countries even more susceptible to

[2] The globalization literature is vast. For an overview of the debates, see Marsh and Hay (2000). On the uniqueness of globalization, see Held *et al.* (1999), for its historical grounding, see Hirst and Thompson (1996); on its dramatic impact, see: Cerny (1994); Strange (1996); for its minimal impact, see: Garrett (1998); and for the most recent arguments, see Weiss (2003).

rising competition in European product markets than they would have been had they only been subject to the tariff reductions related to the GATT agreements. Subsequently, growing product market integration related to the reduction of non-tariff barriers through harmonization and mutual recognition in the Single Market programme only intensified competition, as did deregulation first in competitive industrial sectors and then, increasingly in the 1990s, in public utilities and infrastructural services such as telecommunications and electricity. Deregulation in the latter case not only opened up formerly closed sectors to global as well as European competition but also threatened deep-seated notions about public interest obligations in some member states (especially France). Finally, European Monetary Union (EMU), with the introduction of the euro, has only added to the competitive pressures, by providing greater transparency in prices while reducing the costs of cross-border transactions.

The greater economic significance of Europeanization than globalization can be seen in the trade figures alone: In 2000, EU member states were responsible for 67 per cent ($770 billion) of world FDI outflows and attracted 50 per cent ($617 billion) of world inflows. Intra-European investment was a major component of such flows, since 50 per cent of the outflows were to other member states and 80 per cent of the inflows were from other member-states. Moreover, EU financial markets and trade are more important for EU member states' economies than global markets per se, as evidenced by the EU's percentage of trade with the external world, which in 2000 was around 12 per cent, up only 3 points since 1990, when it was around 9 per cent, and the same as the US.

Europeanization has not just been a conduit for globalization—in the international financial markets by promoting further liberalization and in international trade by progressively eliminating tariff and non-tariff barriers. It has also served as a shield against it, by reducing European member states' exposure to the volatility of the international currency markets through European monetary integration, by improving EU member states' international competitiveness through the economies of scale afforded by the Single Market and the discipline of monetary integration, and by providing protection through the common agricultural policy (CAP), anti-dumping measures, and common industrial policies. Only in the labour arena have member states been left to cope largely on their own with social security deficits, unemployment, and/or poverty in a climate of budgetary austerity—which was itself intensified by the belt-tightening related to meeting the convergence criteria for European Monetary Union in the 1990s and continues as part of the Stability Pact since EMU. Moreover, it is primarily in this arena that member states also run the risks of regulatory competition. This is because the 'negative integration' represented by the 'market-creating' policies of liberalization and deregulation that follow from the treaties, in the absence of 'positive integration' from 'market-correcting' measures through agreement by member states on common policies, can lead to rising pressures for reductions in such things as payroll taxes and labour protections in order to increase countries' attractiveness to investors and national firms' competitiveness (Scharpf 2000a). Only recently have common efforts through the 'open method of coordination' following the Lisbon and Luxemburg Summits started to address these issues—although here, too, the focus is more on market creation—by finding ways to promote labour market flexibility—than on market correction—by arriving at common solutions, say, to the crisis of pensions systems.

Europeanization, in short, has exerted even greater pressures on EU member states than globalization, given that it adds institutional pressures for policy adjustment to the economic ones. Common European policies have only further restricted the range of policy choices in monetary, industrial, and labour policy arenas that governments have come to believe effective and feasible in the context of the globalization and Europeanization of national economies. But although governments may all have adopted similar policies within a narrower range, they still have exercised choice not only in the timing of reform but also in its content.

Changing government policies

Differences in the nature and timing of government policy responses to the economic challenges of the 1970s, 1980s, and 1990s have depended upon a variety of factors. These include countries' differing levels of vulnerability to global and European economic forces, the degree of fit (or misfit) of governments' policy initiatives with long-standing policies and preferences; the political interactions and institutional arrangements that affected governments' capacity to reform; and the legitimizing discourses that enhanced governments' reform capacity by persuading the public not just of the necessity of change in light of the failure of long-standing policies to solve the economic problems but also of its appropriateness in terms of national values. These factors together help explain the differences in how, why, and when countries altered their monetary policies through monetarism and European monetary integration, their industrial policies through business deregulation and privatization, and their labour policies through labour market deregulation and decentralization.

Policy change in the 1970s

Beginning in the mid-1970s, all countries found themselves highly economically vulnerable as a result of the collapse of the Bretton Woods system and the first oil crisis, which produced an economic environment of increasing currency volatility and of 'stagflation'—stagnation combined with inflation—as unemployment rose while inflation threatened. In terms of policy responses, countries faced a choice between 'hard' money policies focused on maintaining the real value of currencies by fighting inflation through higher interest rates and reduced government spending, even if this meant momentarily rising unemployment and diminishing business investment. Or they could follow 'soft' money policies which allowed inflation to rise in efforts to maintain employment and investment. In the case of hard money, the risks associated with rising unemployment were largely avoidable if, among other things (for example reduced government spending), the unions engaged in wage moderation. In the case of soft money policies, the risks associated with rising inflation were largely avoidable again if, in addition to other things (for example periodic devaluations), labour moderated its wage rises (see Scharpf 2000b). Germany chose the first route. The Bundesbank tightened monetary policy and essentially forced the unions to agree to wage restraint as the way to reduce escalating unemployment.

The turn to monetarism fitted with the Bundesbank's traditional preference for stability and its focus on the fight against inflation above all else. The non-accommodating monetary policy worked, however, only because of the capacity of the 'social partners'—business and labour—to deliver on wage moderation.

Britain and France, by contrast, took the second route. Both first chose Keynesian reflation in keeping with long-standing policies and preferences, and increased government spending in efforts to maintain employment and encourage investment. For France, neo-Keynesianism proved only a short-term fix, though. By 1976 the government had switched to a moderately hard money policy through restrictive monetary and fiscal policies to combat rising inflation. This in turn led to a concomitant rise in unemployment, although the government managed to avoid greater job losses by using the nationalized firms as buffers and by expanding early retirement programs. By contrast, neo-Keynesianism did not even prove to be a short-term solution for Britain. In a situation of rising inflation, the government did not have the capacity to impose wage moderation, nor could the unions ultimately ensure it. The result, after a short period of 'incomes policy' in the shadow of an International Monetary Fund bailout, was exploding wages, double-digit inflation, and major strikes, followed by Margaret Thatcher's victory in 1979 and Britain's turn to monetarism.

Policy change in the 1980s

Following the second oil crisis in the late 1970s, the turn to monetarism appeared almost inevitable in an environment of rising real interest rates and growing costs of public debt, with tighter monetary policies from the now monetarist US Federal Reserve Bank. Moreover, the creation of the European Monetary System (EMS) in 1979—the joint initiative of France and Germany to regain control in the face of increasing currency volatility—only added to that inevitability, given established bands of currency-value fluctuation for those European Community members who chose to join the Exchange Rate Mechanism (ERM) of the EMS—which included France and Germany but not Britain (McNamara 1998).

Since Germany was already monetarist, with a non-accommodating monetary policy and accommodating unions, it managed to weather the recession linked to the second oil crisis reasonably well. Its goods remained highly competitive internationally and its money was on the way to becoming an international reserve currency, even though initially unemployment rose moderately (Scharpf 2000b). As the lead European economy with the lead currency and as the leader of European monetary policy by way of the Bundesbank, Germany experienced little economic vulnerability during the 1980s. In consequence, it felt little challenge to its traditional policies and preferences, and so it did little to reform its industrial or labour policies, whether by deregulating and privatizing business or by deregulating and decentralizing labour markets, although it did tighten social expenditures.

By contrast with Germany, Thatcher in Britain, faced with tremendous economic crisis, successfully imposed radical neoliberal reforms across policy arenas. In this, she benefited from the institutional arrangements of the 'Westminster model' and political interactions that insulated her from electoral sanctions, given a divided opposition. Her capacity to reform was also enhanced by a legitimizing discourse that resonated with the British public because it invoked not just the necessity of neoliberal reform—that 'there is no alternative,' or 'TINA'—but also its appropriateness—that this was the way to encourage individual responsibility and entrepreneurship (see Schmidt 2000). But public acceptance as well as economic turn-around did take a while.

Despite the switch to monetarism and the coming on stream of North Sea oil, which ended the balance of payments crises that had bedeviled all previous post-war governments, economic vulnerability remained high. In the short term, Mrs Thatcher's extremely restrictive monetary policies, together with the elimination of most protectionist barriers to trade, caused great competitiveness problems for British industry. Hurt by the rise in the value of the pound in export markets and the rise of competition in domestic markets, much of British manufacturing either went bankrupt or was acquired by foreign firms (Coates 1994). Moreover, inflation stayed high and wages continued to escalate along with job losses until the mid-1980s. But after that came greater wage moderation and labour market flexibility, the result of mass unemployment, the defeat of the coal miners' strike, and deregulatory labour policies that reduced unions' organizing and strike powers while increasing employers' ability to hire and fire at will. These labour policies effectively brought about the radical decentralization of wage-bargaining, with individual employer–employee contracts replacing the fragmented collective bargaining of the past (Howell 1999; Edwards 1995; Brown 1994: 31–2).

The labour market reforms in turn contributed to an increase in business competitiveness, which was also promoted through the 'big bang' liberalization of the financial markets in 1986 and the privatization and deregulation of business. Privatization was extensive—by 1987, nineteen state industries or 40 per cent of the state-owned industrial sector had already been sold off; between 1984 and 1996, when the major sell-off programme ended, the government had netted around 50 billion pounds in revenue (at 2000 prices). Privatization was also highly laissez-faire, with companies freely floated on the stock market. And it was focused as much on monopolistic public service enterprises such as telephone, gas, water, electricity, air transport, and railroads as on firms in the competitive sector, such as steel and oil companies. Deregulation, moreover, served as an accompaniment to privatization. It replaced voluntary self-governing arrangements and informal government–industry relationships with independent regulatory agencies in the financial markets and public service enterprises such as telecommunications, gas, and later the railways.

Taken together, these policies ensured that Britain's 'liberal' state would become more liberal. It became truly arms' length in industrial relations through the decentralization of the labour markets. And it become truly hands-off with respect to business not only through the sell-off of public enterprise and the proliferation of regulatory agencies but also through cuts in ad hoc subsidies to industry. Subsidies declined from 2.7 per cent of GDP in 1975–9 to 2.3 per cent in 1980–4, and down to 1.7 per cent in 1985–8, at a time when subsidies on other European OECD countries rose from 2.5 per cent of GDP in the first period to 2.7 per cent throughout the rest of the 1980s (Johnson 1993: 186). With its policies toward industry in particular, moreover, Britain anticipated many of the deregulatory initiatives of the European Community. It went farther faster than any other European member state in dismantling state control of an economy that had in any case been less state regulated than those on the Continent. This helps explain Margaret Thatcher's embrace of the Single Market, which she saw as the extension of British-style liberalism throughout the Continent, and her rejection of the Social Chapter of the Maastricht Treaty, which she condemned as reintroducing Continental-style 'collectivism and corporatism', and out of which her successor, John Major, opted. But although Mrs Thatcher's policy programme set the stage for the dramatic economic turn-around of the country, the price was very high in the short term with respect to the rise of unemployment and poverty (Rhodes 2000).

France was faced like Britain with tremendous economic crisis and had a similar capacity to impose reform. But instead of turning to monetarism, following President Mitterrand's election in 1981 it chose neo-Keynesian reflation and renewed state *dirigisme* or interventionism in industrial policy through large-scale nationalization and extensive industrial restructuring. By 1983, however, confronted with double-digit inflation, runaway spending, and declining business competitiveness as well as faced with having to pull out of the European Monetary System, the Socialist government completely reversed itself, imposing the 'great U-turn' to monetarism. The radical reversal in monetary policy brought austerity budgets and the policy of 'competitive disinflation' focused on damping inflation and keeping the franc strong. It was quickly followed by the liberalization of the financial markets, which got its biggest boost with the 'little bang' of 1986, and the privatization of business, which was made possible by the turnaround of the nationalized enterprises which had benefited from massive infusions of state capital along with state-led restructuring and rationalizing of operations.

The privatization of industrial and banking enterprises began in 1986 and continued intermittently but increasingly through the 1990s until today, raising a total of 70 billion euros in public share offerings by 2002. Unlike in Britain, it focused primarily on public enterprises in the competitive sector, and was highly *dirigiste* in approach, as the government decided how the shares were to be distributed among a hard core of investors and others in order to provide privatized firms with stable leadership and protection against hostile takeovers and foreign acquirers (Schmidt 1996). Deregulation in a wide range of industrial sectors complemented privatization, and substituted more arms' length relationships by way of regulatory agency and incontrovertible law for the closer, more accommodating relationships between ministry and industry of the past. Deregulation of the labour markets, finally, which began in 1982 with laws that established more direct worker-management dialogue, followed in the mid and late 1980s by a string of measures that promoted flexibility in hiring and firing and greater variation in pay related to performance, culminated by the end of the decade in the government's abandonment of the entire system of state-organized wage-bargaining (Howell 1992). These policies made the labour markets more flexible while they virtually guaranteed the radical decentralization of wage-bargaining. This brought a decline in union membership—from around 25 per cent in the 1960s down to around 9 per cent by the mid-1990s—and the end to strikes and job actions in all but a small (but strategic) part of the public sector.

The reforms, all taken together, produced greater currency stability, decreasing inflation, increasing business competitiveness, and higher labour productivity, even though unemployment continued to climb and France's economic recovery had been delayed by the comparatively late turn to budgetary austerity, giving it less time to benefit from the world economic expansion beginning in the mid-1980s. Moreover, by the end of the 1980s, the reforms had transformed the role of the state by radically reducing its interventionist policy instruments at the same time that they contributed to business independence, by providing it with new sources of funding from the financial markets.

But although much less interventionist, the state did not entirely given up on seeking to influence business or labour where it saw fit. It used privatization strategically, to promote firm coordination through its choice of hardcore investors and/or firm consolidation through its choice of acquirers. Although it left the fate of most firms to the markets, it still bailed out the biggest of failing industries such as the Crédit Lyonnais—albeit under the increasingly watchful eye of the EU Commission. Even though the state had largely given up on national planning and industrial policy focused on large firms, it continued to support small and medium-sized enterprises through regional planning, subsidy and loan programmes, and expert advice. It also upgraded state education and training programmes in view of providing firms with better-skilled workers. And finally, the state was forever tinkering with the industrial relations system, as governments of the right sought to liberalize the labour markets with regard to hiring and firing, work conditions, and working hours while governments of the left sought to 'moralize' them. As a result, the state essentially went from a leadership role to an 'enhancing' role.

Policy change in the 1990s and early 2000s

By the 1990s, European countries faced new challenges. These included the intensification of global and European competitive pressures in the capital and product markets; the count-down to EMU, beginning with the signing of the Maastricht Treaty in the early 1990s and culminating with the introduction of the euro in 1999; the EU Commission's growing activism with regard to deregulation in public interest infrastructural sectors as well as competitive industrial sectors; and the crisis of the welfare state. For most countries, this crisis got worse and worse, as social security deficits rose while the ratio of workers to retirees declined, as unemployment remained stubbornly high in some countries while poverty became a problem in others, and as growing numbers of women entered the workforce, increasing demand for family and elderly services, for part-time and temporary work, and for more individualized pension arrangements (Daly 2000).

The very country that seemed to have got it right in the 1970s and 1980s, Germany, seemed to be getting it wrong in the 1990s. Only European monetary integration caused Germany few problems—despite the fact that the giving up of the Deutschemark at the end of the decade was not very popular with the electorate. By contrast, German monetary integration which following upon the unification of East and West Germany caused serious problems, since it was extremely costly as a result of the political decision to convert the East German mark on a one-to-one basis with the West's. This only added to the costs resulting from the collapse of the East German economy, which engendered an immense transfer of wealth from West to East—to the tune of approximately $100 billion a year—and the exponential rise in unemployment and social security deficits (Streeck 1997). In the face of these costs as well as the growing pressures of international competition, Germany seemed to have little choice but to deregulate and privatize business, deregulate and decentralize labour markets, and overhaul the structure and financing of the welfare state.

Although deregulation and privatization of business began quite late compared to Britain and France and proceeded quite slowly, it was remarkably successful.

In addition to the massive privatization programme in East Germany, major monopolistic public service providers in telecommunications and air and rail transport were privatized while highly regulated markets such as the stock markets, electricity, and road haulage were deregulated. Success was the result of the political institutional capacity of the Kohl government to negotiate reform cooperatively with business, labour, and the *Länder*. This led to the transformation of a wide range of policy sectors with little disruptive impact on the traditional patterns of cooperative economic governance. Moreover, even EU competition policies that had initially appeared to jeopardize the 'enabling' role of *Länder* governments with regard to the provision of subsidies to business (for example the Volkswagen case) as well as the role of the regionally based public sector banks in the social market economy were resolved in symbiosis with the EU (Smith 2001).

But while the country did go ahead with deregulation and privatization of business, it was largely stymied with regard to reforming the structure of work and welfare. There were two main problems: first, how to render the labour market more flexible and responsive to market forces by allowing more temporary and part-time work and more differentiated wages to reflect the differential competitiveness of industrial sectors; and secondly, how to reduce the generosity of publicly funded pensions that were viewed as property rights. But little happened because business and labour could not agree on reform (Thelen 2001). Moreover, the Kohl government did not have the institutional capacity to proceed on its own to impose reforms that went against post-war policies and preferences, while it largely lacked the persuasive powers to reframe the terms of the discourse (Schmidt 2002). The few attempts at reform backfired, such as the 1996 law reducing sick pay compensation to 80 per cent from 100 per cent of salary, which led to massive union protests. What is more, the Schröder government, elected on promises of reform in 1998, did not have much more capacity to reform or a much more persuasive discourse. Only in 2000 did the government manage to freeze pension increases and only in 2001 was it able to negotiate a very modest partial privatization of the pension system. The government did succeed, however, in passing a major reform that could be seen as 'welfare for business', which eliminated the 50 per cent capital gains tax on firms selling shares in other firms—with potentially significant consequences for German managed capitalism, as we shall see below. By 2004 the Schröder government was again pressing on with reform, almost regardless of the electoral consequences.

Unlike Germany, France had already moved ahead with deregulation and privatization of business and deregulation and decentralization of industrial relations in the 1980s. But it still confronted significant problems in the labour arena, given soaring unemployment—which hit a postwar high of 12.8 per cent in 1997—and mounting social security deficits. Moreover, it also felt significant EU-related pressures with regard to EMU and to deregulation in public utilities and infrastructural services.

EMU, first of all, imposed significant economic costs on France. The greatest was probably the worsening of recession in the early 1990s because France stuck to its hard money policies—despite the run on its currency in 1992 and 1993 which had led many other member-states to exit the ERM—while the Bundesbank's interest rates, set to control German inflation, remained unnecessarily high for France. With the advent of the euro by the end of the decade, however, France was assured greater currency stability in a Europe-wide market as well as an equal voice in European monetary policy through the European Central Bank, which replaced the Bundesbank as leader of European monetary policy. The run-up to EMU also increased pressures on the welfare state, which was already in financial difficulty, by forcing French governments to cut expenditures through belt-tightening in benefits and services and reform of the pension system in order to meet the convergence criteria of the Maastricht Treaty. None of this was popular, but while private sector pension reform passed largely in silence in 1993, attempts at similar reforms in the public sector in 1995 led to massive strikes which paralysed the capital for over three weeks. The Jospin government elected in 1997 had greater success mainly because it spoke to the appropriateness of policy change as much as to its necessity with a discourse about balancing equity with efficiency in policies that mixed progressive and neo-liberal elements (see Levy 2000; Schmidt 2000). The Jospin government, moreover, also sought to 'moralize' the labour markets with the passage of the 35-hour working week. This measure aimed to reduce the number of working hours in order to increase jobs, although it actually did more to increase labour flexibility by enabling companies to use the negotiations to revisit most company working-time rules.

The difficulties of labour and welfare state reform were only compounded by EU-led deregulation in the '*service public*' sectors—the public utilities and infrastructural services such as telecommunications, electricity, air transport, and the railroads—which for the French are part of the welfare obligations of the 'Republican state' to ensure 'social solidarity.' Here, the government resisted deregulatory reforms that went against national policies and preferences. Moroever, it lacked the discursive powers to convince the public of the appropriateness of reforms which it was itself contesting in Brussels, and which public sector unions were protesting in the streets (Schmidt 2000). Only in telecommunications did French governments accept wide-scale deregulatory reform (Thatcher 1999). They allowed only the minimum in electricity, air transport, and railroads, and complied as minimally as possible with the resulting EU directives—unlike Germany which in most cases deregulated way beyond what was called for.

Britain, finally, had much less of a problem in the 1990s than either France or Germany, having reformed substantially in the 1980s. It was little affected by EMU, given that it had obtained an opt-out from it. Moreover, its exit from the ERM of the EMS in 1992—having only entered in 1990—after having suffered the worst single loss in monetary history as a result of the run on its currency, was a kick-start to renewed growth at a time when the other two countries remained in recession. In addition, EU-led deregulation in the '*service public*' sectors was a boon, since deregulation and privatization in these sectors had already begun in the mid-1980s at the same time as the competitive industrial sectors, and was in some cases taken by the EU as the model to follow. What is more, by the mid-1990s Britain had largely solved its high unemployment problems—which had plummeted to around 7 per cent as of the mid-1990s—as well as having its social security deficits under control. Labour now had job availability in place of the job security of the past, although it also had lower wages.

But the country still suffered from poverty, which began to be addressed only in the late 1990s by Tony Blair's 'New Labour' government. The government's discourse trumpeted the ability of the 'third-way' to solve these problems by promoting greater social equality and opportunity through market-oriented methods such as welfare-to-work and youth employment programmes. Moreover, at the same time that Blair embraced neo-liberal approaches to unemployment, he did reintroduce some positive rights and job protections for workers, along with a minimum wage for the first time in British labour history and the acceptance of the EU Social Chapter (Rhodes 2000). But the problems of poverty persisted. British levels of poverty remain far higher than those of either Germany or France, and social transfers do less to make up the difference (see Figure 16.2). Finally, membership in EMU was still an open question as of

Figure 16.2 Poverty levels and the effects of social transfers in selected EU welfare states in 1997. (Poverty rates (%) before and after social transfers with the exception of pensions; poverty is defined as income less than 60 per cent of the median income in Europe.)

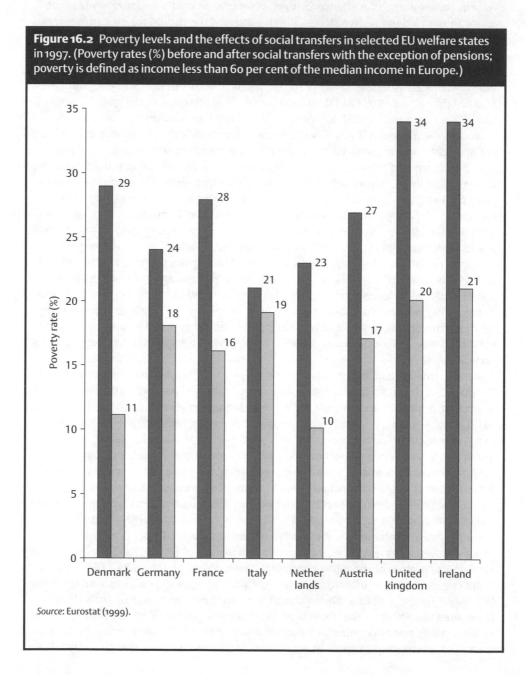

Source: Eurostat (1999).

2004, despite the promises of the Blair government beginning in 1997 to consider entry seriously 'as long as the economic conditions were right.' But Blair, although ostensibly in favour of entry, worried about the political costs, and had yet even to broach a legitimizing discourse that spoke to the necessity, let alone the appropriateness, of entry.

Our three countries, in short, altered their monetary, industrial, and labour policies at different times in different ways to differing effects in response to the pressures of globalization and Europeanization, following their own internal logics rather than some external logic related to the pressures of globalization or Europeanization. These internal logics also help explain the differential changes in business practices and industrial relations.

Changing business practices and industrial relations

The environment for business and labour throughout Europe changed dramatically with the hardening of monetary policy, the liberalization of the financial markets, the deregulation and privatization of business, the easing of labour market regulation, and EU-related market and monetary integration. Business practices and industrial relations changed in response. Financial markets became increasingly important sources of capital. Firms exposed to the capital markets became more concerned about profits, corporate governance demands for transparency and 'share-holder value', and takeover threats. Moreover, firms grew in size and scope through cross-border mergers, acquisitions, joint ventures, and alliances, while inter-firm relations became more competitive. At the same time, labour markets became more flexible, and wage-bargaining, more decentralized. However, although business practices across Europe became more market-driven and labour relations more market-reliant, significant differences nevertheless remained with regard to firms' interrelationships and exposure to the financial markets as well as to labor market organization and coordination.

Differential impact of financial markets on corporate governance

Although liberalization of the financial markets has ensured that firms across Europe have increasingly turned to equity financing to the detriment of other sources of financing such as the banks and the state, countries nevertheless continue to differ in levels of financial market capitalization, degree of takeover activity, and dispersion or concentration of share-ownership. These differences have made for continuing differences in business practices with regard to corporate governance and corporate control.

Although the large firms in all European countries have increased levels of financial market participation, British firms have consistently had much higher levels of market capitalization than either French or German ones. In 1997, British firms' market capitalization was over double that of French firms and over triple that of German firms (100.9 per cent of GDP vs. 40.6 per cent and 31.4 per cent respectively); by 1999, it had doubled while it remained double that of France (197 per cent of GDP vs. around 100 per cent). Moreover, Britain has also had the greatest merger and acquisition activity—in 1999, for instance, it was over double that of either Germany or France (25 per cent of GDP vs. around 12 per cent of GDP for each of the others). And it has had by far the highest foreign direct investment flows, whether in terms of foreign companies investing in Britain or British countries investing abroad. Inward investment flows in 1998 were over twice those of France and more than four times those of Germany (4.7 per cent of GDP vs. 2 per cent and 0.9 per cent respectively) while outward investment flows were over twice those of France and triple those of Germany (8.4 per cent of GDP vs. 4 per cent and 2.8 per cent respectively). In addition, share ownership is more widely distributed in Britain. British household equity holdings as a percentage of annual disposable income are around four times greater than that of either French or German households (82 per cent vs. 19 per cent and 22 per cent respectively), while Britain's pension funds are among the largest of all advanced industrialized countries and those of France and Germany are among the smallest (82 per cent vs. around 6 per cent in the mid-1990s). Only in the case of foreign equity holdings does France come out way ahead of both Britain and Germany (35 per cent of shares in the primary markets vs. under 10 per cent for the other two in 1997, with estimates of up to 50 per cent in 2001).

These figures, which serve to demonstrate British business' greater exposure to the international financial markets and international capital movements, help explain why British business is more financial market-driven than German or French business. Other factors also come into play, however, such as the fact that British firms depend more for corporate investment funds on the financial markets than do German and French firms, which tend to rely more on retained earnings for investment and turn to the primary markets mainly for the financing of firm restructuring and mergers and acquisitions. Also important is the share-ownership structure in Britain, which consists overwhelmingly of small shareholdings by portfolio investors and households (at 50 per cent and 30 per cent of all shares in the markets respectively), as opposed to the more concentrated share-ownership in both Germany, where a majority of shares are held by strategic investors rather than portfolio investors and households (57 per cent to 35 per cent) and France, with similar percentages (Vitols 2001). In Britain, the dispersion of share-ownership among small investors ensures the predominance of the interests of portfolio investors, who generally focused on a high return on their investment and on corporate governance concerns of transparency and maximizing 'shareholder value,' meaning profitability. In Germany or France, the interests of strategic investors hold greater sway, even if share-holder value has become of increasing importance as a result of firms' growing levels of market capitalization. Moreover, the more concentrated structure of shareholding, together with the lower levels of market capitalization, provide German and French businesses more insurance against hostile takeover than British business.

These differences in financial market exposure only add to the differences in corporate governance structures. In Britain, the emphasis on maximizing shareholder value is reinforced by governance structures in which CEOs tend to be held solely responsible for decisions for which they will be held accountable by the financial markets (Lane 1998; Vitols 2001). This is because British CEOs dominate the boards of directors while their firms have a relatively low degree of interconnectedness with other firms through interlocking directorships or cross-shareholdings, let alone network-based relationships, and their employees have little say except where they hold major shares in the company (generally limited to top management). Although this has long been the pattern of inter-firm and employee relations in Britain, the policy reforms beginning in the 1980s reinforced it. The liberalization of the capital markets intensified inter-firm competition and imposed greater pressures on firms for corporate performance in increasingly short time-horizons. Moreover, labor policies that crushed the unions, together with better human resources management practices (typically following the Japanese model), have virtually neutralized the employees. In consequence, British CEOs are largely autonomous, with the financial markets as the primary drivers of performance.

In Germany, CEOs are much less autonomous than their British counterparts and more driven by a wider range of concerns, of which the financial markets is only one. CEOs first of all lack autonomy at the top because they share decision-making responsibility with a supervisory board that is hard to dominate—since the two-tiered board system ordinarily gives them a seat only on the lower-level management board. Moreover, their autonomy is also limited by their interconnections with other firms through interlocking directorships, cross-shareholdings, and mutually reinforcing relations with suppliers, subcontractors, and customers. In addition, employees have much more say in the firm because they sit on the supervisory boards as a result of the system of co-determination, negotiate wages as members of unions in conjunction with management through the national wage-bargaining system, and set working conditions through firm-level works councils (Soskice 1999). All this together ensures that 'shareholder value,' or profitability, is only one among a number of 'stakeholder' interests, with firm value, strategic business interests, and employee concerns also significant. Although 'shareholder value' has been as much a part of German CEOs' discourse as it has that of British CEOs in recent years, it has been more directed at convincing employees and the public of the need to increase firm competitiveness in response to rising product market competition than at reassuring the financial markets of firm profitability (Vitols 2001).

This is not to suggest, however, that German corporate governance has remained unchanged. Much the contrary, since the traditional closeness of firms' networked-based relations has been loosening greatly in recent years in response to the demands of competition in the product markets and the pressures for corporate performance from the financial markets. Since the mid-1990s, inter-firm relations have become less cooperative and mutually reinforcing, as firms have been putting the squeeze on suppliers and subcontractors to cut costs while maintaining quality (in particular the car manufacturers Daimler-Benz and Volkswagen). Moreover, the close ties between business and banks have been unravelling (Lütz 2000). The largest firms, after a very late start compared to French or British firms, have been internationalizing their operations through mergers and acquisitions—for example the acquisition of Chrysler by Daimler-Benz—and listing their shares on the international financial markets at the same time that the big banks have been moving into international finance by buying British and US investment banks—for example Deutsche Bank's acquisitions of Morgan-Grenfell and Bankers' Trust. The 2002 elimination of the 50 per cent capital gains tax has only further contributed to a loosening of ties, as German banks seek to divest themselves of the holdings of poorly performing firms while managing the rest on the basis of 'shareholder value' principles. This turn to the financial markets means that German firms are like to become more susceptible to hostile takeovers of the kind that failed in 1997 when the German steel giant Krupp moved on Thyssen, and that succeeded in 1999, when British Vodafone acquired Mannesmann. But the takeover risks cannot and will not rise to the British level, given that the bulk of equity remains concentrated in the hands of banks as well as industrial enterprises—in 2001, corporations owned approximately 40 per cent of the German equity market while financial companies 25 per cent. What is more, the bedrock of the system, the regional banks and small and medium-sized firms, remains solid, despite challenges to the public status of the regional banks by EU competition policy as well as international competitive pressures.

In France, finally, CEOs are not only more autonomous than both British CEOs, since they are less subject to the dictates of the financial markets as a result of more concentrated share-ownership, and German CEOs, because they are less constrained by boards of directors, networked relationships, or the employees. They are also much more autonomous than they were themselves in the past in relation to the French state. Government privatization and deregulation of business has done away with state leadership of business, since it no longer underwrites investment, directs corporate strategy, or owns many businesses, while government deregulation and decentralization of the labour markets has neutralized labour. The state's new enhancing role, moreover, although sometimes not appreciated by firms even though exploited by them for their own benefit, as with the 35-hour working week, does little other than to enhance autonomy.

With the end of state interventionism in business, corporate governance in France has come to sit somewhere between that of Britain and Germany. Although the state had intended for privatization to reproduce the German managed capitalist pattern of corporate governance by selecting a set of hardcore industrial and financial investors to hold up to 20 per cent of the firm's equity, it produced only a very pale imitation which started breaking apart in the mid- to late 1990s, as hardcore investors sold and foreign institutional investors—mainly North American pension funds—bought. For some, this break-down in the hardcore shareholdings spelled the victory of market capitalism in France, given the high level of foreign share-ownership, CEOs' discourse of shareholder value claiming a new focus on profitability, new corporate governance rules, and an increase in takeover activity (Morin 2000). But in truth, these elements only add to France's distinctiveness. To begin with, French CEOs' discourse of shareholder value is designed not just to increase their own credibility and their firms' capitalizability on the financial markets but also to reinforce their autonomy vis-à-vis other stakeholders in the firm—whether labour, suppliers, subcontractors, or investors—as much as the state (Hancké 2001; O'Sullivan 2001). Moreover, French firms are still much less vulnerable to takeover than British firms. Hardcore share-ownership continues, after all, even though diminished. But French firms are still much more vulnerable than German firms, given the high level of foreign equity holdings in the French Bourse and the fact that French hardcore investors have none of the loyalty of German network-based investors—witness the hostile takeover by BNP of Paribas and Société Générale, which ultimately netted only Paribas. However, even if French businesses lack the deep network linkages of managed capitalist Germany, they are nonetheless more interconnected than the British. Interconnectedness comes both through the informal networks based on

CEOs' shared elite state education and career paths and through the vertically inte-grated relationship, or *partenariat*, of large firms with their suppliers (Schmidt 1996; Hancké 2001).

Differences in corporate production patterns and performance

The continuing differences in corporate governance patterns and the differential impact of the financial markets also affect corporate production patterns and perform-ance. And here, the differences continue to follow along the lines of development of the three countries' post-war varieties of capitalism.

Whereas Britain scores highest on financial market indicators, Germany does so on production-related indicators, with France, again, somewhere in between the two. For example, Germany ranks at the higher end of advanced industrialized countries in terms of the ratio of price to quality of domestic products by compari-son with foreign competitors, France at the lower end, and Britain at the level of many less developed countries—5th vs. 14th and 28th respectively in a World Competitiveness Yearbook (2000) survey. Germany has the highest levels of corpor-ate investment followed by France and then Britain—at 19.9 per cent of GDP in gross fixed capital formation in 1997 vs. 17.1 per cent and 15.6 per cent respectively. The same is true for state aid to manufacturing—at 37 per cent vs. 15 per cent and 5 per cent respectively among EU member states between 1995 and 1997. Germany also has the lowest relative unit labour costs in manufacturing, although France is close whereas Britain is far higher (88.8 per cent vs. 92.6 per cent and 141.5 per cent respectively in 1999, with 1995 as the baseline of 100). Only in overall productivity does France come in highest, ranked 6th in the world versus Germany's 8th (explainable by the fact that the East German numbers are added in with the West German) while Britain was way down at 21st. And only in red tape does Britain come out in better shape, with just four weeks to register a firm by contrast with eight in Germany and fifteen in France.

These differences in production profile are reinforced by countries' divergent industrial employment systems. Germany consistently scores at the top, France in the middle, and Britain at the bottom in terms of company or law-based employment protection, length of worker employment (11 years vs. 8 and 5 respectively), and provision of vocational training (34 per cent of a cohort vs. 28 per cent and 11 per cent respectively) (Estevez-Abe, Iversen, and Soskice 2001). Only in levels of unemployment does Britain do better than both Germany and France, the result of such factors as lower wages, greater availability of part-time jobs, more labor flexibility, meagre unemployment compensation, and a minimalist pension system that discourages 'welfare without work'.

Each of the three countries' varieties of capitalism, in short, has its comparative advantages and disadvantages. And as Europeanization proceeds, countries are likely to find their firms increasingly specializing in those areas of comparative advantage, while leaving the areas in which they have a comparative disadvantage to the firms of other countries, or acquiring those firms in order to regain the advantage. Over time, therefore, we may see increasing sectoral specialization along the lines of the three main varieties of capitalism. For example, firms in financial services, biotechnology, and the 'new economy' more generally are likely increasingly to operate along market capitalist lines; firms in high-precision engineering and high-end manufacturing are more likely to adopt the techniques of 'competitive' managed capitalism; and firms in sectors such as defence, which are influenced by the priorities set by national governments and the EU, or the railroads, which require heavy investments with low rates of return over long periods of time, are likely to follow the patterns of 'state-enhanced' capitalism.

Conclusion

All European countries were faced with major economic challenges, beginning in the 1970s with the end of the Bretton Woods System and the two oil crises that followed in the 1980s and 1990s with the growing competitive pressures in the capital and product markets from global and European forces, as well as with growing institutional pressures from the EU. And all adapted and adjusted their systems in a more market-oriented direction in response. But these responses remained nationally specific and path-dependent. Britain engaged in radical therapy beginning in 1979 that brought the system closer to the market capitalist ideal, with government policies even more arms' length and liberal, business practices even more competitive, and labour relations more market-reliant. Germany, instead, saw little deep-seated change in the country's managed capitalism before the mid-1990s, when the closeness of network-based business practices began to loosen and the cooperativeness of coordinated labour relations began to lessen, while government struggled to facilitate adjustment. France, finally, transformed itself beginning in the mid-1980s, with the move away from state-led capitalism to a more state-enhanced variety where business is more self-directive and labour more market-reliant but the state still has a role to play (see Table 16.2).

Figure 16.3 presents a rough sketch of how such changes might be plotted for the three countries for three different time periods: as of the 1970s, as of the early 2000s, and in the future, as a projection of current trends in the context of further European market and monetary integration (assuming that Britain joins the euro). Market capitalism naturally sits at the top of the triangle, given the pressures from globalization and European integration that tend to favour reforms in this direction. But as the sketch shows, although all three have moved up closer to market capitalism, there is no convergence at the top of the triangle. Rather, there is a somewhat smaller space toward the middle of the triangle within which differentiation continues to occur. First of all, Britain, which started out reasonably far from the market capitalist ideal in the 1970s but had moved up close to it by the 2000s, can be seen to move a bit back down, as European integration as well as internal forces lead to more state regulation and more labor market coordination. Germany, which began in the 1970s at the bottom left of the triangle as ideal-typically managed capitalist, moved not very significantly up from this by the 2000s. But we are likely to see a major jump in the future toward market capitalism, as firms become more market driven and wage-bargaining more decentralized—but nothing like a move to the market capitalist ideal. Finally, France, which found itself in the 1970s at the bottom right of the triangle as the ideal-typical

Table 16.2 Changes in models of capitalism by the end of the 1990s

	Market capitalism (Britain)	Managed capitalism (Germany)	State capitalism (France)
Monetary policies	Hard	Hard	Hard
Goverment role	More liberal	Still 'enabling'	Newly 'enhancing'
Policies toward business	More arms' length	Still facilitator	Much more liberal but still seeks to influence
Policies toward labour	More of a bystander	Still bystander	Newly bystander, 'moralizer' of labour markets
Business relations	More competitive	Still cooperative	Competitive
Interfirm relations	More contractual, individualistic	Loosening of networked relations	End of state mediation; autonomous
Investment sources	Capital Markets	Firm, capital markets, banks	Firm, capital markets
Times horizons	Shorter-term view	Less longer-term view	Less medium-term view
Goals	'Share-holder values'	'Stakeholder values'	Firm autonomy
Industrial relations	Market reliant	Still coordinated	Market reliant
Management–Labour	Neutral	Still cooperative	Neutral
Wage-bargaining	Radically decentralized	Still coordinated	Radically decentralized

Source: Adapted from Schmidt (2002).

state capitalist country, moved radically up toward the centre of the triangle as business was deregulated and privatized and wage-bargaining decentralized by the early 2000s. But although it is likely to go a little further in this direction, especially given the EU-related pressures for deregulation in the public utilities and infrastructural services, it, too, will not converge on any single market capitalist ideal. In sum, the emerging European political economy, with its single market and single currency, cannot do other than to allow for continuing diversity in national political economies. And this is a strength for Europe, not a weakness, given the comparative advantages of the differing national varieties of capitalism in different industrial sectors.

Europeanization, like globalization, has had a major impact on the three models of capitalism illustrated by the British, German, and French examples. There has undoubtedly been some convergence in practice, brought about by the single market rules and for EMU (albeit without the UK as a participant). However, as this chapter has revealed, the practice of capitalism remains distinct between the three states. The three models remain rooted in historical trajectories or pathways. Hence, whilst economic integration in the EU has promoted convergence, much like the picture for member state institutions (see Chapter 13), no single European model has supplanted distinct national practice.

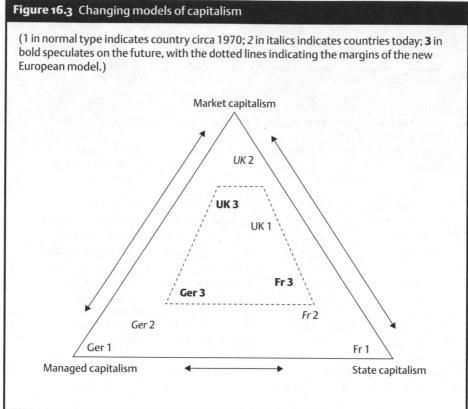

Figure 16.3 Changing models of capitalism

(1 in normal type indicates country circa 1970; *2* in italics indicates countries today; **3** in bold speculates on the future, with the dotted lines indicating the margins of the new European model.)

Further reading

The books listed below provide further detail on the material covered in this chapter. They lend insight into national responses to Europeanization as well as globalization in areas such as European monetary integration, government policies, business practices, and industrial relations. Thus the Hall and Soskice volume (2001) discusses varieties of capitalism as well as thematic issues. Schmidt (2002) and Kitschelt (1999) review developments in contemporary capitalism. Dyson is important for examining the impact of the Euro on the member states.

Dyson, Kenneth (ed.) (2002), *European States and the Euro* (Oxford: Oxford University Press).

Hall, Peter, and Soskice, David (eds) (2001), *Varieties of Capitalism: The Institutional Foundations of Comparative Advantage* (Oxford: Oxford University Press).

Kitschelt, Herbert et al. (eds) (1999), *Continuity and Change in Contemporary Capitalism* (New York: Cambridge University Press).

Schmidt, Vivien A. (2002), *The Futures of European Capitalism* (Oxford: Oxford University Press).

Weblinks

There is no immediately obvious website on the political economy of the EU and its member states. However, the European Central Bank is of central importance <**http:// www.ecb.int**>. Similarly, the EU's own portal is an important source for identifying the European policy developments that impinge on the member states <**http://www.europa. eu.int**>. For more analytical perspectives, see the <**http://eiop.or.at/erpa/**> portal of on-line papers, especially the series of the Max Planck Institute for the Study of Societies (MPIfG) Cologne.

References

Brown, William (1994), 'Incomes Policy in Britain: Lessons from Experience', in Ronald Dore, Robert Boyer, and Zoe Mars (eds), *Return to Incomes Policy* (London: Pinter).

Cerny, Philip (1994), 'The Dynamics of Financial Globalization', *Policy Sciences*, 27, 319–42.

Coates, David (2000), *Models of Capitalism: Growth and Stagnation in the Modern Era* (Cambridge: Polity Press).

Coates, David (1994), *The Question of UK Decline: The Economy, State and Society* (Hertfordshire: Harvester Wheatsheaf).

Culpepper, Pepper D. (2001), 'Employers, Public Policy, and the Politics of Decentralized Cooperation in Germany and France', in Peter A. Hall and David Soskice (eds), *Varieties of Capitalism: The Institutional Foundations of Comparative Advantage*. (Oxford: Oxford University Press).

Daly, Mary (2000), 'A Fine Balance: Women's Labour Market Participation in International Comparison', in Fritz W. Scharpf and Vivien A. Schmidt (eds), *Welfare and Work in the Open Economy. Vol. II. Diverse Responses to Common Challenges* (Oxford: Oxford University Press).

Edwards, Paul (ed.) (1995), *Industrial Relations: Theory and Practice in Britain*. (Oxford: Blackwell).

Estevez-Abe, Margarita, Iversen, Torben, and Soskice, David (2001), 'Social

Protection and the Formation of Skills: A Reinterpretation of the Welfare State', in Peter A. Hall and David Soskice (eds), *Varieties of Capitalism: The Institutional Foundations of Comparative Advantage*. (Oxford: Oxford University Press).

Garrett, Geoffrey (1998), *Partisan Politics in the Global Economy* (Cambridge: Cambridge University Press).

Grant, Wyn (1995), 'Great Britain: The Spectator State', in Jack Hayward (ed.), *Industrial Enterprise and European Integration: From National to International Champions in Western Europe* (Oxford: Oxford University Press).

Greider, William (1997), *One World, Ready or Not: The Manic Logic of Global Capitalism* (New York: Simon & Schuster).

Hall, Peter (1986), *Governing the Economy: The Politics of State Intervention in Britain and France* (New York: Oxford University Press).

Hall, Peter, and Soskice, David (2001), 'Introduction', in Hall and Soskice (eds), *Varieties of Capitalism*.

Hancké, Bob (2001), 'Revisiting the French Model: Coordination and Restructuring in French Industry', in Hall and Soskice (eds), *Varieties of Capitalism*.

Held, David, McGrew, Anthony, Goldblatt, David, and Perraton, Jonathan (1999), *Global Transformations: Politics, Economics and Culture*. (Stanford CA: Stanford University Press).

Hirst, Paul, and Thompson, Grahame (1996), *Globalization in Question: The International Economy and the Possibilities of Governance* (Cambridge: Polity Press).

Howell, Chris (1992), *Regulating Labor: The State and Industrial Relations Reform in Postwar France* (Princeton NJ: Princeton University Press).

Howell, Chris (1999), 'Unforgiven: British Trade Unionism in Crisis', in Andrew Martin and George Ross (eds), *The Brave New World of European Labor: European Trade Unions at the Milennium* (New York: Berghahn).

Johnson, Christopher (1993), *The Grand Experiment: Mrs Thatcher's Economy and How it Spread* (Boulder CO: Westview Press).

Katzenstein, Peter J (1989), 'Conclusion', in Peter Katzenstein (ed.), *Industry and Politics in West Germany: Toward the Third Republic* (Ithaca NY: Cornell University Press).

Lane, Christel (1989), *Management and Labour in Europe: The Industrial Enterprise in Germany, Britain and France* (Aldershot: Edward Elgar).

Levy, Jonah (2000), 'France: Directing Adjustment?', in Fritz W. Scharpf and Vivien A. Schmidt (eds), *Welfare and Work, Vol. II.*

Lütz, Susanne (2000), 'From Managed to Market Capitalism? German Finance in Transition'. *German Politics*, 9/2, 149–70.

McNamara, Kathleen (1998), *The Currency of Ideas: Monetary Politics in the European Union* (Ithaca NY: Cornell University Press).

Marsh, David, and Hay, Colin (eds) (2000), *Demystifying Globalization* (London: Macmillan).

Morin, François (2000), 'A Transformation in the French Model of Shareholding and Management', *Economy and Society*, 29/1, 36–53.

O'Sullivan, Mary (2001), 'Equity Markets and the Corporate Economy in France: Recent Developments and Their Implications for Corporate Governance'. Unpublished Manuscript.

Ohmae, Kenichi (1990), *The Borderless World: Power and Strategy in the Interlinked Economy* (New York: Harper Business).

Rhodes, Martin (2000), 'Restructuring the British Welfare State: Between Domestic Constraints and Global Imperatives', in Scharpf and Schmidt (eds), *Welfare and Work, Vol II.*

Ruggie, John (1982), 'International Regimes, Transactions, and Change: Embedded Liberalism in the Postwar Economic Order', *International Organization*, 36: 379–415.

Scharpf, Fritz W. (2000a). *Governing in Europe* (Oxford: Oxford University Press).

Scharpf, Fritz W. (2000b), 'Economic Changes, Vulnerabilities, and Institutional Capabilities', in Fritz W. Scharpf and Vivien A. Schmidt (eds), *Welfare and Work In the Open Economy. Vol. I: From Vulnerability to Competitiveness* (Oxford: Oxford University Press).

Schmidt, Vivien A. (1996), *From State to Market? The Transformation of French Business and Government* (New York and London: Cambridge University Press).

Schmidt, Vivien A. (2000), 'Values and Discourse in the Politics of Welfare State Adjustment', in Scharpf and. Schmidt (eds), *Welfare and Work: Vol I.*

Schmidt, Vivien A. (2002), *The Futures of European Capitalism* (Oxford: Oxford University Press).

Smith, Mitchell P. (2001), 'Europe and the German Model: Growing Tensions or Symbiosis?' *German Politics* 10/3, 119–140.

Soskice, David (1999), 'Divergent Production Regimes: Coordinated and Uncoordinated Market Economies in the 1980s and 1990s', in Herbert Kitschelt et al. (eds), *Continuity and Change in Contemporary Capitalism* (New York: Cambridge University Press).

Strange, Susan (1996), 'The Limits of Politics'. *Government and Opposition*, 30, 291–311.

Streeck, Wolfgang (1997), 'German Capitalism: Does It Exist? Can It Survive?', in Colin Crouch and Wolfgang Streeck (eds), *Political Economy of Modern Capitalism: Mapping Convergence and Diversity.* (London: Sage).

Thatcher, Mark (1999), *Politics of Telecommunications* (Oxford: Oxford University Press).

Thelen, Kathleen (2001), 'Varieties of Labor Politics in the Developed Democracies', in P. Hall and D. Soskice (eds), *Varieties of Capitalism*.

Vitol, Sigurt I. (2001), 'Varieties of Corporate Governance: Comparing Germany and the UK', in Peter A. Hall and David Soskice (eds), *Varieties of Capitalism: The Institutional Foundations of Comparative Advantage* (Oxford: Oxford University Press), 337–360.

Weiss, Linda (2003), *States in the Global Economy: Bringing Domestic Institutions Back In* (Cambridge: Cambridge University Press).

Conclusion

The European Union is once again in the midst of major transformation. First, the twenty-five Member States agreed in October 2004 upon a future European Constitution which has still to be ratified. The process of making this European Constitution effective is a major challenge (Weiler 1999). It will require positive referenda in several countries, including France and the United Kingdom. On the other hand, the enlargement process is far from being achieved. The EU is coming to grips with the reality of having twenty-five member states. Already it looks clear that some of the old foundations of integration may be affected, notably the centrality of the Franco-German relationship. New alliances, such as between the Nordic states and the Baltic states appear to be emerging, for example. We may need a few years before we see how relations between the twenty-five states 'shake down'. In addition, Rumania and Bulgaria are expected to become member states in the medium term, and Croatia will likely follow soon after. Most of the new member states, which joined the EU on 1 May 2004 or will join it later, are former communist countries with different historical experiences and different levels of economic and social development. These factors of heterogeneity have to be managed by the EU, and represent a bigger challenge than was the case with the Mediterranean countries in the 1980s. Inevitably the European Union is led to debates on introducing more flexibility and differentiation in its competences and policies.

The concepts of 'differential Europe' or 'flexible Europe' are not new (La Serre et Wallace 1997). The EU has always tolerated some margin of manoeuvre on the part of its Member States for the implementation of policies outside the Treaties. The exchange rate mechanism of the European Monetary System (1979) did not apply to all EC member states. The Schengen agreement (1985) on the free movement of people did not cover the UK and Ireland. In the 1990s the Maastricht Treaty gave more political attention to differentiation and organized it inside the Treaties. The notion of 'opting out' came onto the EU agenda with regard to the Economic and Monetary Union (euro), social policy and security and defence policy. The UK and Denmark were then allowed not to take part in certain of these policies unless their parliaments and public opinions gave support. The enlargements, first to the former EFTA countries in 1995, and then to the CEECs, Malta and Cyprus in 2004, made the debate on differentiation even more explicit. Becoming a new member state in 1995, Sweden has decided not to join the euro.

Differentiation has also been pushed forward by the 'founding' members of the EU—Germany and France, supported from time to time by the Benelux countries—because they feared a dilution of the EU and thus offered leadership through pursuing a 'pathfinder' role. From France and Germany emerged in the late 1990s a series of proposals on creating a 'core Europe' within the EU, an 'avant-garde', or a 'pioneer group' in which the Franco-German tandem would play the leading role. These proposals gave rise to anxious reactions from other countries where the Franco-German relationships has always been questioned: in the UK, small member states of the EU, and the new member states (Browne *et al.* 2004). The Franco-German proposal of institutionalizing more differentiation found a soft translation in the Treaty of Amsterdam (1997) and in the Treaty of Nice (2000). Under strict conditions, a limited number of member states may choose to develop a policy more closely while others do not. Defence, which could be a field of differentiation *par excellence*, was originally excluded from the scope of 'enhanced cooperation' (Philippart 2003). The European Constitution modifies this situation. It widens the mechanism to all areas of EU policy without exception. To start an area of 'enhanced cooperation', a minimum of two-thirds of member states is now required and the consent of all member states is needed. It makes use of the procedure easier, even if the new member states do not like it. They often get the feeling that 'enhanced cooperation' is a way to exclude them and to create a second-class membership.

Most of the new members of the EU—with the exception of Poland—are also 'small' member states. In the EU-25 thirteen member states are small states, if we define that as being with 10 millions inhabitants or less (Arter 2000; also see Table 1, Part 2). This situation becomes a source of tension when institutional questions are concerned. During the Convention and the IGC which drafted the European Constitution, the small/big state cleavage was at issue in the weighting of votes in the Council, the number of members of the Commission or the creation of a permanent seat for the presidency of the European Council. Nevertheless, the small/big cleavage has not to be overemphasized. It is one cleavage among several others in the EU. The Iraq war revealed that differences on what should be the Common Foreign and Security Policy goes beyond the question of 'smalls' and 'bigs'. The budgetary negotiations of 2006 will also show that net contributors/net recipients division will cut across the small/big cleavage.

National parliaments will be more involved in the future EU-25. Again, the issue is not new. When the President of the Commission, Jacques Delors declared in July 1988 that, in ten years time, 80 per cent of the national laws will be initiated by the EC, he created a lot of reactions in the national parliaments. The argument mostly stressed by national MPs since then has been that the EU reinforces essentially the powers of the governments. Thus, MPs argue that they should be more involved in the EU policy making to balance the powers of the executives because the European Parliament has not yet enough powers and legitimacy to do so. National parliaments also asked for more respect for the principle of subsidiarity, a principle which has its origin in Roman Catholic thought and exists in the constitutions of many federal states in the world. In its original sense the principle of subsidiarity holds that government should undertake only those initiatives which exceed the capacity of individuals or private groups acting independently (Wilke and Wallace 1990). It was introduced into the EU context with the Treaty of Maastricht in 1992. It specifies that in the areas which do not fall within its exclusive competences (which are explicitly defined in the Constitution), the European Community shall take action 'only if and in so far as the objectives of the proposed action cannot be sufficiently achieved by the member states and can therefore, by reason of the scale or effects of the proposed action, be better achieved by the Community'.

Regarding the practice of subsidiarity (Estella de Noriega 2002), the European Constitution has made a step forward. National parliaments are now entitled to scrutinize proposed EU laws and to object if they consider that a proposal oversteps the boundary of the EU's conferred competences. This new provision will increase the

European networking between the national parliaments, which already meet once under each Presidency in the framework of COSAC—the conference of specialized committees of EU parliaments. But it will also be a source of disagreement, because the vision of what policy should be European and what should remain national is not the same from one national parliament (and member state) to another.

As we hope this book has shown, as well as these emergent issues also demonstrate, EU–member state relations remain an important issue for research. To make further progress to understanding, scholars have to go beyond the question of the Europeanization of the national policy processes and of the adjustment of national institutions to the EU. Several questions seem to be relevant fields of investigation for future research.

Having experienced in recent years a burgeoning of studies on the impact of the EU upon the domestic level ('outside-in' studies), research has to learn more about the impact of the member states (and especially of the new member states) on the EU level ('inside-out' studies). The policy-oriented literature which has developed under the banner of new governance has clearly been an attempt to break away from intergovernmentalism and to give more importance to non-state actors involved in policy networks. In doing so, it has probably neglected the intergovernmental dimension of the EU policy-making, which remains relevant. More studies have to be undertaken on the role of the twenty-five national executives in the EU Council of ministers, on the different negotiating *modi operandi* which necessarily change with ten more member states, and more generally on the influence of the member states inside the Commission and the European Parliament. Enlargement is increasing the activities of member states at the EU level but is also making them more diffuse and heterogeneous. The domestic organization of the new member states and the institutional linkages between their capitals and Brussels have to be investigated on a comparative basis (Goetz 2000). To what extent are they distinct from what has been observed in the established member states?

Revisiting as a matter of priority the role of national institutions at the EU level does not mean that enough studies exist about the Europeanization of societal actors at the domestic level. Studies have still to be produced on the changes or stability of interest groups, associations, political parties (Mair 2000), public opinion (Rupnik 2004), especially in the new member states. We now have reasonable evidence about the foreign/European policies of the new member states' governments. Much less exists on the preferences of non-governmental groups or movements involved in EU level institutions. The mechanisms through which the EU influences the preferences of these societal groups and the impact which domestic institutional structures may have upon their adaptation must be identified more clearly. These questions plead for developing more micro sociological approaches of societal actors in the member states, with a strong comparative basis.

As we said above, the development of EU policy making gives the impression to the national Parliaments that their power is decreasing. But it is not obvious that their legitimacy is also decreasing in parallel. So, does a legitimacy/power gap exist? These questions of national political representation should be addressed, shifting the study of the EU from the problem of policy making to more normative questions on political representation or supranational democracy. Political philosophy has not to be forgotten when we study the EU–member state relations (Habermas 2000).

Finally, the impact of the EU-25 on the political economies of the member states is a further area which deserves greater attention. With the introduction of the euro, the Europeanization of the political economy of the euro-zone, the remaining utility of the Stability and Growth Pact, this terrain become ever more fruitful for research. How will the political economies of the new member states fit in with the developments outlined by Vivien Schmidt in Chapter 16? Economic pressures coming from the global context have given rise to different adaptations from one member state to another. Will integration encourage convergence on a single economic and social 'model' of all the member states, including the new ones who have rediscovered market economy for about fifteen years? Or will national characteristics resist these developments, and a central European model of political economy emerge?

We hope that most of the key issues in EU–member state relations are covered in this book. But we also hope we have opened, to students and scholars alike, new fields for further research and investigation.

References

Arter, David (2000), 'Small member states within the EU', *Journal of Common Market Studies*, 38/5, 677–97.

Browne, Matt and others (2004), *Le regard des autres. Le couple franco-allemand vu par ses partenaires* (Paris: Notre Europe, Etudes et Recherches n° 33).

Estella de Noriega, Antonio (2002), *The EU Principle of Subsidiarity and its Critique* (Oxford: Oxford University Press).

Goetz, Klaus (2000), 'European integration and national executives: a cause in search of an effect', *West European Politics*, 23/4, 211–31.

Habermas, Jurgen (2000), *Après l'Etat-nation. Une constellation politique* (Paris: Fayard).

La Serre, Françoise de, and Wallace, Helen (1997), *Flexibility and Enhanced Cooperation in the European Union: Placebo Rather than Panacea* (Paris: Notre Europe).

Mair, Peter (2000), 'The limited impact of Europe on national party systems', *West European Politics*, 23/4, 27–51.

Philippart, Eric (2003), *Un nouveau mécanisme de coopération renforcée pour l'Union européenne élargie* (Paris: Notre Europe).

Rupnik, Jacques (eds) (2004), *Les Européens face à l'élargissement. Perceptions, acteurs, enjeux* (Paris, Presses de Sciences Po).

Weiler, Joseph (1999), *The Constitution of Europe: Do the New Clothes have an Emperor?* (Cambridge: Cambridge University Press).

Wilke, Marc, and Wallace, Helen (1990), *Subsidiarity. Approaches to Power-Sharing in the European Community* (London: RIIA).

Index